A History of China in the 20th Century

Lü Peng

A History of China in the 20th Century

Volume I

palgrave
macmillan

Lü Peng
China Academy of Art
Hangzhou, China

Translated by
Bruce Doar
Sydney, Australia

ISBN 978-981-99-0733-5 ISBN 978-981-99-0734-2 (eBook)
https://doi.org/10.1007/978-981-99-0734-2

Cover illustration: Stefano Tronci/Getty images

This Palgrave Macmillan imprint is published by the registered company Springer Nature Singapore Pte Ltd.
The registered company address is: 152 Beach Road, #21-01/04 Gateway East, Singapore 189721, Singapore

This book is dedicated to my wife, Hu Jielan, and my daughter, Lü Jing.

Acknowledgments

There are so many names to write down of people who have helped me with my writing that I can only express my thanks here as follows:

For decades, my university classmates Tang Buyun and Sun Yujing have been discussants and helpers in my writing, especially in their opinions and views—on China's history and the changes of recent decades, which have always strengthened, changed, or consolidated my writing, and their support for my research endeavors has been both ideological and practical in nature and has constituted an enduring friendship. The photographer Wang Zheng was decisive in helping me to collect the historical images needed for this book, and he has given the images in my book their relative historical integrity.

And of course, crucially, I would like to express my sincere gratitude to Dr Bruce Gordon Doar, who has been engaged in art research and lived in China for many years. He translated my History of Chinese Art in the Twentieth Century and other works in a very professional style, and I appreciate his translation and knowledge of China's ancient and modern history. We have become friends who trust each other very much. The proofreading of the translation of this book by Dr. Sun Yue has been invaluable. Her English is the best among my many students, and I would like to extend my special thanks to her here!

Finally, I would like to thank Jacob Dreyer for his recommendation and persistence as editor of Palgrave Macmillan, which made it possible for this book to be published at this venerable publishing house.

Contents

About the Author

Lü Peng born in 1956, is an art historian, curator, and art critic. He is an Associate Professor in the Department of Art History and Theory at the China Academy of Art in Hangzhou; and a Distinguished Professor in the Faculty of Humanities and Arts at Macau University of Science and Technology. He is the Art Director of Chengdu Art Museum, and the Art Director of the Museum of Contemporary Art Yinchuan.

Major books published include: *A History of Art in Twentieth-Century China*; *History of China Modern Art: 1979–1989*; *History of China Contemporary Art: 1990–1999*; *Fragmented Reality: Contemporary Art in 21st-Century China; and Chinese Contemporary Art since 1989.*

List of Figures

Chapter Seven 1958–1978: From the Great Leap Forward to Great Cultural Revolution

Chapter Eight 1978–1989: Reform and its Politics

Chapter Nine 1990–2002: Marketization Trends and Involvement in Globalization

Chapter Ten 2003–2022: Towards a Structural Crisis

Volume I

Prologue

In everyday life, historians, especially those who reveal and expose problems that seem lost in the dust of time, are often unpopular, in part because they inevitably make people uneasy and shake their unquestioning faith in the legitimacy of the present order by attempting to change people's long-standing perceptions of the past. Moreover, this type of historian also constantly "dredges up" old matters, making people feel the historian wants to delay the good times that lie ahead and stymie the creation of a new history; for those people who do not want to hear about "history's old accounts", "optimistically looking forward" is their favored idiom. Indeed, people are more concerned with judgments or predictions about the future based on the usual dissatisfaction with reality and a desire for a better world. They feel this is positive and constructive—the pain of the past is over.

However, people are also concerned about the extent to which predictions about future possibilities can be verified or "cashed in". As with prophecies, they ask: what percentage of events or facts can be actually "predicted"? Unsurprisingly, no one can provide a satisfactory answer to this question. Back in the 1980s, Alvin Toffler's *Future Shock* imbued many young Chinese with hope for the future, and most Chinese born in the 1950s spent unforgettable years gleaning optimistic knowledge from this particular futurologist, until moving on to the forecasts of other futurologists, or eventually losing faith in such predictions. As a historian, I

L. Peng, *A History of China in the 20th Century*,
https://doi.org/10.1007/978-981-99-0734-2_1

have no intention of mocking the science of predicting the future. On the contrary, I do agree with Jorgen Randers's predictions based on his observation: "Without big changes, humanity would be in danger of growing beyond the physical limits of our planet". I even take seriously the conclusions of Randers and his colleagues: "Once the overshoot has occurred, there are only two ways to return to the fertile soil of sustainable growth: either a 'controlled decline' (managed decline)—by the orderly introduction of new solutions (fish from fish farms) or by 'collapse' (You have to stop eating fish because there are no fish—the fishermen's livelihoods don't exist, as was the case in Newfoundland after 1992). Overshoot is not sustainable".[1] However, according to the division of disciplines, these forecasts are not the work of historians unless we link these developed predictions to problems of the past we are studying, and the focus of our research is on historical issues. In this way, terms like "physical limits" and "collapse" are easily applied as they instantly evoke the China we see before us. Of course, we do not have a rigorous set of data to prove that China's "physical limits" will soon be reached, and so it is perhaps possible we will face either "managed decline" or "collapse", but we are reminded of the reports and scholarly warnings about China's environmental pollution, ecological destruction, and increasingly scarce resources that can be encountered almost daily in different media. For a humanist, even cursory observation reveals that the problem of "limits" extends far beyond the physical world and, in terms of morality, beliefs, and values, China already seems to be experiencing extreme levels of degradation, deficiency, and latent chaos that may well be all the more disturbing and anxiety-inducing.

In short, China's current problems are profound and, as a historian, I hope this book can serve as a timely reminder that today's problems and phenomena derive from historical factors. it is in political, economic, military, cultural, religious, and ideological traditions that we should search for the sources of these problems and phenomena and apply historical analysis to them. The landscape we see today is, in fact, just one part of a historical landscape. The basic tasks I set myself in writing this book are,

[1] Jorgen Randers, *2052: A Global Forecast for Next Forty Years*, White River Junction, Vermont: Chelsea Green Publishing, 2012. Chinese edition: Qin Xuezheng and Tan Jing trs., "Foreword", *2052 Welai Sishi Nian de Zhongguo yu Shijie* (2052 China and the world for the next forty years), Shanghai: Yilin Chubanshe, 2013, p. 005. Jorgen Randers was one of the co-authors of the Club of Rome's *The Limits of Growth* (1972).

firstly, to find and examine the causes of the identifiable problems that plague China today through research into the history of the twentieth century, and, secondly, through the description, analysis, interpretation, and judgments of history, to provide my readers a foundation for understanding history and facing the future. Indeed, people often analyze modern or contemporary Chinese history from the origins of Chinese history itself (variously estimated to go back to anything from three to five thousand years) and describe and explain the formation of Chinese history and its characteristics from its pre-Qin beginnings to clarify its ideological and cultural contexts. My approach at the beginning of this book will follow similar contours. In my "Introduction" (*Xuyan*) I provide a broad outline of pre-twentieth-century China, encompassing the sweep of Chinese history from the Qin-Han dynasties to the Reform Movement of 1898 to clarify the relevance of earlier events and phenomena for China's twentieth century in as succinct and brief a manner as possible, in order to remind readers that even today it is impossible to shrink from thinking about historical issues, such as the issue of the unique formation of the Qin-Han polity that took shape more than two thousand years ago and persisted through different periods and in different contexts and discourses.

The appearance of history provided by different historians often differs. This is not the point I am emphasizing but wish to focus instead on a particular question: when the history of a country and nation is limited to the information and single perspective provided by government authorities or political parties and is used over the long term in education and propaganda directed at an entire population, such history seems highly questionable. Like the implicit question that the historian, John King Fairbank, asked, when he returned to the Chinese mainland in 1972 after more than two decades away from the country, and saw the circumstances of his old friends: "In a country known for its etiquette and pursuit of education, China's 'egalitarians' vent their personal anger at these intellectuals, and where is Confucianism in all of this? This is a question that demands an answer". This question signified that the study of Confucian tradition alone was not enough to explain China after 1949. Fairbank, who traveled to China in the 1930s to study China–U.S. relations, later wrote: "If a person is not interested in China-U.S. relations, and is not surprised, annoyed, or alarmed by the subject, then his research on China will not long endure".[2] In fact, the expression, "surprised, annoyed, or alarmed", encapsulates a predetermined historical attitude. Studying issues and providing a critical analysis and judgment of them are basic qualities underlying historical research; otherwise, historical texts imposed by the authorities or the Party's ideology will infringe upon the spiritual civilization of mankind. Unlike critics or thinkers, the criticality of historians is not expressed as straightforward opinions and bold conclusions about events, but in their careful selection of information and documents, their arrangement and utilization of value positions, and their presentation of their own views and judgments in the process of describing, analyzing, and interpreting what are considered to be historical facts. Among historians in mainland China, there are few achievements in writing general histories covering the period from the nineteenth to the twentieth centuries, and research on this period by historians of the generation, or more, before me was clearly constrained by the influence of the political system and the ideology and culture in which they were located. It is not that different schools were subject to so many historical conditions of their own that we need to be careful with the contributions of earlier historians, but rather that the academic value of historical research had largely disappeared under the ideological pressure that historians need to avoid as much as possible.

This book, therefore, does have the purpose of trying, through its description and examination of a particular period of history, to remind readers to change or even abandon their long-standing attitudes and rethink the legitimacy of existing historical statements. Of course, my reiteration of matters past is intended to make people realize that impeding the creation of history will not delay the good times ahead of us; on the contrary, our creation of a new history needs a re-examination and analysis of the past that will enable us to adjust our plans and even strategies, as much as possible, in order to avoid "collapse" from occurring. This might disturb some people, but it is only by critically looking back and describing their views and positions in language based on historical facts that historical researchers can make a positive and constructive impact on the future. As someone born in the 1950s, I have been a witness to

[2] John King Fairbank, *Chinabound: A Fifty-Year Memoir*, New York and London: Harper Colophon, 1983; New York: HarperCollins, 1982. Chinese editions: Lu Huiqin and Zhang Kesheng tr., *Fei Zhengqing dui Hua Huiyi Lu*, Shanghai: Zhishi Chubanshe, 1991; *Fei Zhengqing Zhongguo Huiyi Lu*, Beijing: Zhongxin Chubanshe, 2013, p. 447.

almost half of the history in this book. My personal experience of this past makes it easy to "revisit" that history. However, we are also outsiders and the voracious reading of the 1980s enabled some of our generation to think freely and freed us, as much as possible, from the intellectual dogma created by ideological control and established intellectual habits enabling us to critically understand the past. As a historical researcher, I can make a fresh selection of facts from that past and determine what are general facts and what are historical facts based on the questions I pose and the concerns I have about historical issues, and to freshly describe, analyze, and judge those facts.

In China, from 1949 to the 1980s, free thinking in the field of history was very limited. Now, after almost four decades of reform, albeit largely confined to the economic sphere, there has been some influence from unavoidable Western ideas, but self-training and intergenerational education in history circles have not resulted in what might be called a shared body of historical knowledge in this country. Nor do we see a shared knowledge of theories, research ideas, and solutions, so thinking in the field of humanities is still limited by the political system and ideology, and the official monopoly on publishing has determined the scope and limits of what historians can achieve. It should be noted in particular that in the field of the study of modern Chinese history, the classification of approaches into what are called the revolutionary historical paradigm, the modernization paradigm, the West-centric paradigm, and the Sino-centric paradigm are only general formalistic conceptual groupings. Although the works of J. K. Fairbank, Jonathan Spence, Paul A. Cohen, and other Western historians of China have been translated into Chinese, this has not resulted in the emergence of unique "paradigms" in Chinese historical research. However, in mainland China, the emergence of the "revolutionary historical paradigm" was initially related to China's social reality, and some radical intellectuals took Marxism's theory on the basic contradictions of society as their starting point. Stimulated by Lenin's theories on how Western imperialism influenced Chinese history, they sponsored a narrative expressing the contradictions between imperialism and the Chinese nation, and between feudalism and the Chinese masses, seeing these as the two basic contradictions in Chinese society since the Opium War, and for a long time this "paradigm" constituted the mainstream of historical research in mainland China. The success of the "revolutionary historical paradigm" was related to the violent political turmoil that engulfed China after the 1920s and, especially after October 1949, the confrontation with the West and the designation of class struggle as the main domestic contradictions China faced made the "revolutionary historical paradigm" occupy a dominant position in Chinese historical circles. In the history after 1949, we constantly see how such a paradigm participated in specific political struggles and dictated the lexicon of academic terminology. Constituting the basic historical structure of this "paradigm", the "two processes" (the combination of imperialism and Chinese feudalism, which was a process that transformed China into a semi-colonial and colonial country, a process that also resulted in the Chinese people resisting imperialism and those serving it as "running dogs"), "three high points" (Taiping Heavenly Kingdom, 1898 Reform & Boxer Movement, and 1911 Revolution), and "Eight Major Events" (Opium War, Taiping Heavenly Kingdom, Foreign Affairs Movement, Sino-French War, Sino-Japanese War, 1898 Reform, Boxer Movement, 1911 Revolution) together dictated a dogmatic writing pattern, which lacked rational judgment on the complexities of history and the causes of events and betrayed a lack of analysis of the internal factors in society, the economy, and culture. At the same time, under the guidance of partisan political aims and ideology, the selection, description, analysis, and judgment of historical facts precluded historians from adopting an independent position, and historical writing was often merely the tool of a political movement (or factional struggle within the Party).

In mainland China, the so-called "modernization paradigm", for a long time after 1949, did not form the mainstream in the field of Chinese history, in which it could barely survive given the domination of the methodology of class analysis. Only when the specific political period needed the support of scientific and economic materials did the "modernization paradigm" acquire some legitimacy. This was why the "modernization paradigm" gradually emerged in China after 1979. Writers in history circles had been familiar with a methodology close to the "modernization paradigm" adopted by Jiang Tingfu in writing *Zhongguo Jindai Shi* (A Modern History of China) back in 1938, in the Republican period. Jiang had posed the following questions: "Can the Chinese modernize? Can they catch up with Westerners? Can they use science and machinery? Can they abolish the concept of family and hometown and organize a modern nation-state? If they can", he concluded, "then the future of our nation is bright; if they cannot then this ethnic group has no future. This is because all countries in the world which can accept modern culture will definitely become rich and strong, but those that cannot will be defeated, without exception, and the sooner this fact is accepted the better". Jiang was able to write in a way that reflected a global perspective back in 1938: "Modern history is the history of the Europeanization of the world, and the modern history of China is the history of the modernization of the Chinese nation, that is, the history of the Chinese nation's acceptance of modern European culture". ("General Theory", *A Modern History of China*) The response of historical circles in mainland China to this research orientation could only be seen after the 1980s. In fact, the "modernization paradigm" also provided historical facts that went beyond political objectives and ideological requirements in serving a narrative of history in line with the discipline of history.

The "modernization paradigm" could, of course, easily veer towards the "West-centric paradigm". The historical view of John King Fairbank and Teng Ssu-yü seen in their *China's Response to the West* (1954) was easy to understand, because the history of China, following its encounter with the West, seemed to provide many examples that conformed to Fairbank's impact-response model or to Joseph Levenson's tradition-modernity model, especially when Chinese intellectuals were anxiously proclaiming the slogan of "total westernization", which made such historical analysis more acceptable. We should also note that, compared with Fairbank, Levenson even stressed the absolute necessity of accepting Western transformation. As for the "Sino-centric paradigm" developed in the 1970s, it can be seen as a decisive correction to the "impact-reaction" paradigm or the "tradition-modernity" model in its emphasis on the internal causes of historical change, what Paul A. Cohen called "internal approach", a formulation which signaled that Chinese history should start with internal factors in Chinese society (a "Chinese perspective") rather than from external, so-called Western (or imperialist) factors, because China has a Chinese context. Cohen, of course, explained what he meant by a Sino-centric perspective: "As more and more scholars seek the 'story line' of Chinese history itself, they are wonderfully aware that this main line does exist, and in 1800 or 1840, the main line was completely uninterrupted, nor has it been preempted or replaced by the West, which remains one of the most important central clues throughout the 19th and even twentieth centuries". In emphasizing "differentiation", Cohen rejected the existence of a single "paradigm" (Western paradigm), saying that the concept of the "West" could be subdivided, as in the confrontation between the United States and Europe and in the fact that the United States could further divide, and that the result of such a view could easily lead to the neglect of a historical methodology of "integration". However, the basic historical fact that should be acknowledged is that the differences between Europe and the United States (political, economic, cultural, religious, customs, etc.) are much smaller than those between China and the United States, not to mention that conflict, competition, or stimulation often produces new commonalities. If we lose sight of integration and induction, and ignore some important historical facts, we will fall into the trap of amplifying the regional and the local and have no way of pursuing structured historical writing. In historical studies, the use of such dichotomous terminology as "Oriental"/"Western" or "Chinese"/"foreign" requires extreme caution. Moreover, since the seventeenth century, in historical research of any country or region the methodologies prompted by such terms as "trends", "connections", "differences", and "synthesis" are all important. No one's history is stable and pure, and no one's history does not owned its special structure. Premised by such disciplinary cautions, historians need to acknowledge that the dichotomies of "progress"/"stagnation" or "continuity"/"development" are merely the final narrative process in historical research: they are comprehensive judgments made in a particular historical context.

In discussing the methodology of historical research, I prefer to use the term "research orientation" rather than "paradigm", and we know that the "research orientation" used by different generations of historians always related to their knowledge background and value orientation, and that the complexity of history itself cannot be summed up by the particular "paradigm" of historians. So, we need to understand that the "impact and response" of Fairbank and others might have a mechanistic characteristic, but as long as we go deeper into the study of "response" to the traditions of a civilization, specific contexts, and personal experiences, we will not simplify "response". Based on this, the research orientation of this book is broadly limited to the strategic interaction of "political systems" and the "clash of civilizations". This is because it can be readily appreciated that the persistence of the Qin-Han polity was not only the perfection of a structure of its own civilization, but it also featured persistence yet vulnerability in later dealing with Western civilization from the late Ming to the late Qing dynasty. If the land-based connection between faraway China and Europe prior to Marco Polo occurred simultaneously with the formation and growth of the Chinese order, the connection between Chinese civilization and Europe after the Great Age of Exploration began to expose obvious institutional differences and even conflicts, and by the nineteenth century, Chinese civilization, together with its political system, was not only strongly shaken by Western civilization, but also almost completely collapsed in the course of the accelerating impact. Confucianism was of course the basis of the ideas and concepts of Chinese civilization, but the principles of the Legalists were actually the secret and unspoken core of Chinese rule, although the rulers also borrowed from Buddhist and Taoist thought through the work of scholars over generations in using such ideas to retouch Confucianism with metaphysical features, but in the end Confucian dogma was used to explicate the legitimacy of rule by the Qin-Han polity. When the Manchus entered China, they inherited the political system of the Ming dynasty and a complete Confucian culture. These served to make the Han people more adaptable to their rule, and the Manchus moreover did not have a complete and mature political system and ideological culture of their own. However, the Qing court appointed Manchus to almost all important positions in the bureaucracy, prohibited marriage between Manchu and Han, initiated a "literary inquisition" to destroy Han writings expressing dissatisfaction with the Qing dynasty, and forced Han males to wear pigtails to remind the Han people of Manchu ethnic rule, all of which fueled anti-Manchu sentiment and resistance up to the time of the final anti-dynastic revolution.

In my understanding of the discipline of history, I do not think that an abstract historical ontology exists. With the purpose of providing readers with a "brief history", I want to construct the basic skeleton of Chinese history in the twentieth century from the perspectives of the "political system" and the "clash of civilizations"; a "brief history" is after all general history, and it does not allow too much detail. Of course, in describing the history of this century, I will still have recourse to the study of cultural differences. Historical studies concerned with cultural differences have been questioned by some historians, who argue that such an approach can easily lead to "cultural essentialism", but it is an indisputable fact that cultural differences and even the resulting emotional differences have triggered a large number of historical events and affected historical trends. The "*Four Books* and *Five Classics*" and "Marxism" have served different historical functions in different historical periods, and I am aware of the need to be alert to the different characteristics of the same culture or its expression at different times. Fortunately, historians with Chinese experience at any time in the twentieth century, especially after 1949, have long known that basically there is no static culture or stable ideological system and, in their view, the study of the cultural differences in a particular context or the characteristics of the same kind of thought in different periods is what has determined the nature of Chinese historical research today.

In terms of historical periodization, the twentieth century is not simply a temporal concept. It initially might seem difficult to see 1900 as the beginning of the history of China in the twentieth century, just as some historians believe that the twentieth century of world history should begin with the First World War in 1914 or that the twentieth century should end with the collapse of the Soviet Union in 1989. The 1911–1912 Revolution might have served as a starting point for the history of China in the twentieth century, yet it would be difficult to answer a perplexed reader who wants to know about this history and reads an account that begins with the sound of gunfire coming from Wuhan, and asks: Why was history so precipitate? Why was the Qing government in Beijing so vulnerable? It might also seem appropriate to put the historical starting point of twentieth century China in 1840, because after the Opium War, China began to show signs of a complete collapse from politics to the economy, society, and culture and many of the factors that led to the 1911 Revolution can be found during this period. Historians who adopt a Marxist historical position are more inclined to use the Opium War as a historical node associated with modern times, which they maintain reveals how China's semi-colonial and semi-feudal society was formed.[3]

[3] See: Liu Danian, "Several issues in the study of modern Chinese history", *Historical Research*, 1959:10. Before the twentieth century, Chinese historical works were largely confined to traditional chronicles, and dynasties were the important basis for presenting history. The use of a different calendar also precluded Chinese contemporaries chronicling the history of the late Ming or late Qing from using the words "seventeenth century" or "nineteenth century", respectively. It was mainly in the second half of the nineteenth century, under the influence of Western history and with the emergence of Liang Qichao's New History that Chinese historians began to pay special attention to more recent historical issues. Before 1949, academic and political positions determined historians' periodization schemata, judgments, and characterization. Early in the twentieth century, Chinese scholars had sought to find terms corresponding to the English term "modern times", and their understanding of the English term determined the temporal range of their writing, many works using the vague coinage "*jinshi shi*" 近世史 for the idea of "recent [i.e., modern] history". What was meant by "*jinshi*" (recent/modern)? Chinese historians had two main designations of the demarcation point signaling the advent of "recent/modern" history: the late Ming and the Opium War. The earliest works that treated the Opium War as the beginning of "modern history" include Meng Shijie's *Zhongguo Zuijinshi Shi* (The recent history of China, Tianjin,

However, before 1793, didn't the Qianlong Emperor's attitude towards the British mission signal the imminent decline of the Qing dynasty? In

1926), Li Dingsheng's *Zhongguo Jindai Shi* (The modern history of China, Shanghai, 1933), Huagang's *Zhongguo Minzu Jiefang Yundong Shi* (The history of China's national liberation movement, 1940), Zhang Jianfu's *Zhongguo Jin Bainian Shi Jiaocheng* (Course on the history of China's last hundred years, Guilin, 1940), and Fan Wenlan's *Zhongguo Jindai Shi* (The modern history of China, 1947), First Section, Volume 1. The first histories that commenced modern Chinese history with the late Ming were Guo Tingyi's *Jindai Zhongguo Shi* (Modern Chinese history, Chongqing, 1941) and Zheng Hesheng's *Zhongguo Jinshi Shi* (The recent history of China, Chongqing, 1944). There seemed to be adequate reason for this division or periodization, as Zheng Hesheng explained: "Since the discovery of new maritime routes, world communications underwent great changes, and human life and international relations, when compared to ancient times, saw obvious differences, and this is why we demarcate medieval history from recent (modern) history. The changes in recent history comprise trends towards 'opening', and all its manifestations exemplify ancient achievements that are carried forward. The new emerges from the past, and in turn contains the seeds of future trends. Each nation's thought is the driving force behind its evolution. Therefore, the category of "recent history" encompasses nearly three or four hundred years of history, whether we consider the history of China or the West". Ref: Zheng Hesheng, "Introductory Points", *Zhongguo Jinshi Shi* (The recent history of China), Chongqing: Nanfang Yinshuguan, 1944. Here quoted from Zhang Haipeng, *Zhongguo Jindai Tongshi Diyi Juan: Jindai Zhongguo Lishi Jincheng Gaishuo* (Comprehensive modern history of China, volume 1: An overview of the processes of modern Chinese history), (Nanjing: Jiangsu Renmin Chubanshe, 2009, p. 11).

Zheng Hesheng's view looks quite similar to today's position of writing Chinese history from the perspective of global history. In the search for a more effective Chinese terminology, some writers began to use the now familiar words *jindai* and *xiandai* for "modern", so that there are titles such as Fan Wenlan's *Zhongguo Jindai Shi* (1947) and Cao Bohan's *Zhongguo Xiandai Shi* (Modern History of China, 1947), in which the historians do not seem to discriminate between *jinshi* (recent), *jindai*, and *xiandai*. If we understand the changing social environment and ideological motivations in the field of history at the turn of the century, we realize that this is obviously the result of the rapid changes in the world that required historians to find more effective methods for rewriting history, especially the writing of recent (or modern) history, so it was natural to emphasize their contemporary stance as historians. This is how Luo Jialun, for example, explained this development in his introductory remarks for Guo Tingyi's *Jindai Zhongguo Shi* (Modern Chinese history, Chongqing, 1941):

"To know the past history and evolution of the human race or nations, their present status and environment, and their future survival and development, all require the study of modern history. This is not to say that we should not study the distant past, or that such research is not important, but rather that the more recent should be studied more and is especially important. Therefore, to be a modern person, we must study modern history, and to be a modern Chinese, we must study the modern history of China". Ref: Luo Jialun, "Introductory remarks", Guo Tingyi, *Jindai Zhongguo Shi* (Modern Chinese history, Chongqing, 1941; Taipei: Shangwu Yinshuguan, 1963). Quoted here from Zhang Haipeng, *Zhongguo Jindai Tongshi Diyi Juan: Jindai Zhongguo Lishi Jincheng Gaishuo*

fact, the continuation of dynasties has revealed a state of exhaustion. In the "Introduction" I encapsulate the history from the Qin-Han dynasties to the dynastic reforms of 1898 to deduce a thread of development with the intention of providing readers with a basic historical background to twentieth-century Chinese history since 1900. I do not subscribe to the view that either the late Ming or the Opium War can serve as markers for twentieth-century Chinese history. It means that I stress that history changed over time, although the pace of change in the nineteenth century accelerated significantly.[4]

As a result of my research, I regard the Qing dynasty's efforts to devise a constitution as the beginning of Chinese history in the twentieth century, because the constitutional movement that began shortly after the signing of the *Boxer Protocol* in fact started a core enterprise in China throughout the twentieth century. The implementation of a

(Comprehensive modern history of China, volume 1: An overview of the processes of modern Chinese history), Nanjing: Jiangsu Renmin Chubanshe, 2009, p. 7.

Historians (such as Fan Wenlan and Hu Sheng) did a great deal of work on historical periodization and dating, but their historical views largely accepted official ideological positions, which made the narrative of modern history naturally and completely veer towards political history or revolutionary history, especially the political and revolutionary history of the Communist Party. The writing of modern history before 1949 had almost ignored the existence of the Communist Party, but after 1949 the KMT's image in history books produced on the mainland was, in turn, close to that of simplistic political caricature. Until the end of the 1970s, the history books produced in the PRC almost all used "class analysis" to examine the historical process, with the "semi-colonial and semi-feudal" concept used to characterize Chinese society, and "anti-imperialism and anti-feudalism" seen as basic historical tasks from the Opium War onwards. Such historical writing still continued until the publication of *Ershi Shiji Zhongguo Shigang* (Outline history of twentieth-century China) in 2009! Even though its author Jin Chongji presented a confused account of simple class analysis in this four-volume work, this did not change the fact that this book adhered to all the Communist Party's ideological norms for writing history. Until the 1980s, modern history writing in the PRC was largely limited to writing within the framework of the "two processes", "three high points", and "Eight Major Events". Indeed, there was nothing more harmful to the development of new history in China than such a framework.

[4] As far as research in Chinese history is concerned, the traditional historical phases and periodization schemes of the dynasties are certainly not the basis of my study. Although I emphasize the importance of the Opium War of 1842 in my "Introduction", it does not serve as a node in my periodization or treatment of time. Moreover, neither "late imperial" nor "early modern" are terms I care for and use.

constitution remained a goal, regardless of the initial motives for devising a constitution and the reasons for its original de facto failure. Driving political, economic, cultural, ideological, and social changes in China for more than a hundred years, constitutional government, as a great political undertaking of the Chinese people, has not been realized even today—in the twenty-first century. however, the constitutional ideology and early steps towards its implementation completely rescinded the legitimacy of the Qin-Han polity; it is the "constitutional" problems that have arisen at different times in the twentieth century in China that constitute the most basic historical problems of this century. Prior to the 1911 Revolution, the term "century" was not used in the chronicles of Chinese history, and if we use the variant Chinese words for "modern" (*jindai* or *xiandai*), it is difficult to relate them to the name of dynasties (*chaodai*) and their rise and fall. As the author of a brief history, I regard the richness of history as the result of a number of basic factors. Moreover, although traditional ideas and culture do always have an impact on history, and Chinese intellectuals have never stopped discussing Confucianism and its cultural traditions, among the extremely complex historical elements, historical events triggered by the conflict between the political system and civilization have shaped the basic historical contours of China for more than a hundred years. For example, to the present day, the Communist Party, which controls the regime ruling the Chinese mainland, remains hostile to the universal values of the West. The richness of history is certainly not an embellishment but a fact, yet any historical writing can only take into account a particular subject. We cannot describe how in 1839 Lin Zexu wrote to Queen Victoria to demand an end to the terrible opium trade while describing life on the streets of Guangzhou at this time to show the details of the continuity of history. Here I would like to reiterate that, in terms of historiography, this book is intended to focus mainly on historical materials related to the themes of the "political system" and "the clash of civilizations", which include ideological movements within the intellectual field and many historical "patterns" attached to the skeleton provided by these two themes. It is clear that the interweaving of these two themes began when the missionaries first came to China and continued until the late Ming and early Qing period gradually exposed the complex and deadly clash of civilizations.

Since December 1978, a large number of historical documents have come to light and been published, which have facilitated our re-consideration of history, especially the period since 1900, so that this book can avoid examination and argumentation of existing documents, and focus on the different issues and their relationship, as raised by the new documentation. The new documents allow us to reorganize this stretch of history in order to clarify its true face, or at least one that was once difficult to see. My aim is not to add a new account to the field of modern and contemporary Chinese history, but to alert people to the need to understand history anew and discover the problems that have always existed in the field of history in order to promote "timely decisions and changes", at least in the realm of thought. To be clear, this book will provide readers with a college education today with a twentieth-century Chinese history that has the contours I understand, and if readers develop a skeptical attitude and critically reflect on and gain a fresh understanding of the appearance of history, this book will have achieved its goal: for young readers, in particular.

When I wrote the first passage in this Prologue, it was when the Third Plenary Session of the 18th CPC National Congress released its *Decisions of the CPC Central Committee on a number of major issues in the comprehensive deepening of reform* (13 November 2013), and at the same time I read an interview with the economist Xu Xiaonian on WeChat: "Without the establishment of an independent reform department, reform will be difficult to implement" ("Interview" by Song Houliang, *Weibo News*, 12 November 2013). I found that there were problematic discrepancies between the two documents. Jorgen Landers would have described the first document as exemplifying "managed decline", while the latter conveyed a deep sense that the foundations have been destroyed, so that it is likely that "collapse" is coming. Xu Xiaonian pessimistically reminded people that "the golden age of reform and opening up is over". Therefore, can we afford to leave the validity of different views or opinions for time to address? Will we again limit ourselves only to "anxiously" reminding, suggesting, and expecting, and continue to reassure ourselves in the face of the future after the next possible tragedy occurs? Do we continue to agree that the old state apparatus has the power to shape history and that human history does not have a common basis in values at all? The revision of the Constitution in the "two sessions" of meetings organized by the Chinese Communist Party in the spring of 2018 presented two questions that historians need to ask: Is there really nothing that can be done to history that historians only need to heed the victory of the will of the authorities that leaves them no room to move? Let's look back at history and provide our own answers.

Lü Peng

Wednesday, 13 November 2013, on a flight from Chengdu to Hangzhou

Saturday, 4 February 2017, revised on a flight from Luang Prabang to Chengdu

Wednesday, 18 April 2018, revised on flight from Milan to Beijing

Introduction: China prior to the Twentieth Century

I

The history of China is said to begin with the "Three Emperors and Five Sovereigns", but different ancient books present different statements about these "three emperors and five sovereigns".[1] Roughly speaking, the period from 2070 to 256 BCE is said to be the time of the Three

[1] The "Three Emperors and Five Sovereigns" is a formulation reflecting only one interpretation of the ancient Chinese portmanteau term "*Sanhuang Wudi*", which can also be rendered into English as the Three Emperors and Five Progenitors. The term is variously defined and assigned, sometimes even within the one ancient Chinese text, e.g., as Tianhuang, Dihuang, and Taihuang [lit., the Emperors of Heaven, Earth, and the Ultimate] in "Annals of Qin Shihuang", *Shi Ji* (Records of the Historian); as Tianhuang, Dihuang and Renhuang [lit., the Emperors of Heaven, Earth, and Man] in "Supplementary Annals of the Three Emperors", also in *Shi Ji*; as Suiren, Fuxi, and Shennong in the "Da Chuan" of *Shang Shu* (The Book of History); as Fuxi, Nüwa, and Shennong in *Chunqiu Yundou Shu*; as Fuxi, Shennong, and Huangdi in *San Zi Jing* (The Three-Character Classic); and as Fuxi, Shennong, and Gonggong in *Tongjian Waiji*. The "Yellow Emperor" also appears in listings of the "Five Emperors" (the others being Chuanxu, Diku, Yao, and Shun), but once again there were also various alternate groupings. One thing is clear: The Three Emperors and Five Sovereigns were not rulers of states in the sense we now recognize but were chieftains of tribes or tribal alliances. Historians tend to refer to the age of the "Three Emperors and Five Sovereigns" as "the archaic era", "antiquity", or even "the mythical era".

L. Peng, *A History of China in the 20th Century*,
https://doi.org/10.1007/978-981-99-0734-2_2

Dynasties designated Xia, Shang, and Zhou, respectively,[2] but it is only from the beginning of the Shang dynasty that we have textual evidence from the time in the form of inscriptions on oracle bones and bronze objects. The collocation of ideographs that today denotes "China" and which is now read "Zhongguo" makes its earliest appearance in an inscription on a bronze vessel,[3] which has been dated to the early years of the Western Zhou dynasty.[4] Yet the "central realm" (*zhongguo*) indicated by that term does not refer to what is "China" in the modern Chinese language but to the district surrounding the capital city of the Western Zhou. This polity later evolved to form the region known as the "Central Plains" (Zhongyuan)[5] occupying a larger area around the middle and

[2] The Xia, Shang, and Zhou dynasties, collectively termed the Three Dynasties, were only loose alliances, utterly unlike the dynasties from Qin onwards.

[3] This bronze was unearthed at Jijiacun in Shaanxi in 1963. Its inscription reads: "After King Wu of Zhou conquered the capital of Shang, he held an awesome ritual at which he proclaimed to Heaven: 'I now hold this Central Kingdom, and I will personally rule its people'".

[4] The Western Zhou dynasty lasted from 1046 to 771 BCE, about 275 years. The dynasty had a total of 12 kings spanning 11 generations. In the fifth year of his reign, King Cheng of Zhou shifted his capital from the area southwest of present-day Xi'an in Shaanxi province to the east with the construction of a new capital at Luo Yi in the area of present-day Luoyang, Henan. As for the Xia and Shang dynasties prior to Zhou, we have no material or textual evidence of the Xia, but inscriptions on bronze and oracle bones attest to the existence of Shang. Zhou was initially controlled by Shang, but later the King of Zhou, Xibo, aided his son in destroying the Shang dynasty, although the specific date when this happened is disputed. After their deaths, Xibo and his son were given the posthumous titles "King Wen" and "King Wu", respectively, and by these titles (rather than by their lifetime titles) they are known to history.

[5] Until the Manchu people entered the Central Plains and established the Qing dynasty, the use of the term "Zhongguo" for "China" was largely limited to the Han people and was not applied to the concept of a multi-ethnic state. In the mid-nineteenth century, the Muslim unrest in Xinjiang and Yunnan was calmed, and the Qing regime once again took steps to consolidate its rule over the frontier. For example, Zuo Zongtang (1812–1885) moved a large number of Han Chinese to the west. Later, Taiwan also gained provincial status, and the north-eastern Manchu region was also administratively divided (later becoming the prototypical "Three [North-] Eastern Provinces"). In the late nineteenth century, the Qing government rescinded its ban on Han migration to Manchuria, because of famine and the threat of eastward expansion by the Russians. In order to bring the long-standing Ming dynasty to an end as soon as possible, the Qing rulers from the beginning also designated the area they occupied as "China" and did not exclusively refer to it as the "Greater Qing". Despite the antipathy this aroused among ethnic Han officials, they grew used to the multi-ethnic meaning of "China" as time went on and the Qing regime consolidated. This conceptual change was notable among those who

lower reaches of the Yellow River. The early inhabitants of these Central Plains called themselves in turn the "Huaxia" (both an ethnonym and toponym that is first seen in a terse record for the 26th year of the reign of Duke Xiang [roughly equivalent to 547 BCE] in the ancient *Zuo Zhuan*, which states "Chu lost Huaxia", specifically indicating the lands of the Huaxia people of the Central Plains).[6] In 221 BCE, the young Ying Zheng (259–210 BCE) led the army of the state of Qin to destroy six neighboring states (Qi, Yan, Han, Zhao, Wei, and Chu) over the course of a decade, ending the age of kingdoms headed by aristocrats, the last phase of which is traditionally termed the "Warring States", and establishing a unified monarchy. He regarded himself as the first emperor, as indicated by the title "Shi Huangdi". This "First Emperor" became known to history as Qin Shihuang. After unifying the Central Plains, he led his armies to subdue the Hundred Yue to the south and campaign against the Xiongnu (Huns) to the north.[7] In 214 BCE, the Qin armies brought the

began to ponder the national and ethnic crisis in the wake of repeated invasions by the Great Powers, and so the concept of "China" as a vast multi-ethnic country came to be reintroduced, and we see this usage in the writings of ethnic Han scholars like Wei Yuan (1794–1856). By the late Qing, the Qing emperors regarded their regime as the "Chinese government" when they negotiated sovereignty with Western countries and signed diplomatic documents.

[6] In terms of historical geography, the Central Plains refers to the middle and lower reaches of the Yellow River with its center extending from Luoyang to Kaifeng (more or less equivalent to today's Henan province). In a large number of literary and political narratives, the "Central Plains" often simply denotes "China" and is sometimes even synonymous with "China". Similarly, "Huaxia civilization" is also used to simply denote "Chinese civilization".

[7] The "Hundred Yue" of the Qin period referred to the peoples of the coastal area south of the Yangtze River, equivalent to today's Zhejiang, Fujian, Guangdong, and Guangxi. Historically, the Xiongnu was a nomadic people living north of the Central Plains at the close of the Qin dynasty and the beginning of the Han dynasty, who were said to be a branch of the descendants of the Xia dynasty. When Qin Shihuang ordered Meng Tian to attack the Xiongnu, the latter were forced to leave the Hetao region circled by the Yellow River and move north. When the Qin dynasty collapsed, its border garrisons fled back to the Central Plains, and the Xiongnu regained control over the Hetao region and became mortal enemies of the Han dynasty. *Shi Ji* records: "From Chunwei all the way to Touman is more than a thousand years, and the Xiongnu were at times significant and at others only minor players, but for most of that time they were scattered and divided. ... However, by the time of Modu the Xiongnu were at their most powerful and had completely subjugated the northern barbarians and were enemies of the China to their south". For the first two centuries years of the Han dynasty, the Xiongnu were at war with the Han. In 121 BCE, the Han dynasty accepted the surrender of King Hunye

whole Lingnan region, specifically the area south of the Nanling mountains roughly equivalent to today's Guangdong and Guangxi provinces, within the fold of the territory of the Qin dynasty, and in 214–213 BCE the Qin general, Meng Tian (?–210 BCE), led 300,000 troops in an assault on the Xiongnu, forcing them to move northwards and evacuate the Central Plains. At the same time, the Qin dynasty successively forced large numbers of the once wealthy people of the former Six States, as well as prisoners and commoners, to migrate to the area north of the Yellow River, to labor on land reclamation projects, to establish borderland farming colonies and defend the northern borders, while also opening up lands in the southwest inhabited by national minorities, thereby extending the reach of the borders of the Qin Empire. This expansion of territory increased the overall costs of defense and maintaining the army. In order to prevent Xiongnu harassment and incursions, the Qin dynasty, on the basis of existing protective walls in the previous states (such as those of Qin, Zhao, and Yan), embarked on a wall-building project, creating what would become known as the Great Wall. Qin Shihuang thus may have thought that he established the first borders of the Qin Empire (China).[8] The political governing mode implemented by the Qin dynasty entailed the abolition of the original decentralized feudal system (*fenfengzhi*), weakening the old aristocracy by strengthening Qin's autocratic monarchy, and using military merit as the determinant in promoting men to the new aristocracy. In this way, the Qin polity dissolved the original rules of clan law determined by blood relations, replaced the hereditary system of the aristocracy with a new bureaucracy, and established an

of the Xiongnu and Han opened up four prefectures of the western Hexi region (Jiuquan, Wuwei, Dunhuang, and Zhangye), facilitating communications with the Western Regions. From the time when Qin attacked the Xiongnu to the year 91 CE (4th year of the Yongyuan reign-period of Han Emperor He), when the Han army defeated the Xiongnu's ruler, the Northern Shanyu, at Jinweishan (in the present-day Altai Mountains) and the Xiongnu were destroyed, there were about centuries of complex conflict, reconciliation, and war with the Xiongnu.

[8] In discussing Meng Tian driving out the Xiongnu and regaining the area south of the Yellow River in his *History of China*, Lü Simian questions the assertion that the Qin general also dispatched troops to conquer the Southern Yue, suggesting that this was an assertion dictated by the times and such historical exaggeration was not unusual: "China's extent and borders were delineated by 'the Great Wall in the north and the Lingnan region in the south'. This became an established formula for denoting China and its Eighteen Provinces, largely later accepted as a given". Reference: Lü Simian, *History of China*, Beijing: New World Publishing House, 2017, p. 43.

administrative and bureaucratic system based on prefectures and counties (*jun-xian*) that extended from the central seat of power out to the local levels of the prefecture and county.[9] Such an institutional and administrative framework continues to the present day, even though technical modifications and supplementary adjustments to individual ruling systems were made by emperors of subsequent dynasties. Repeated reference by later generations of Chinese intellectuals to the "burning of books and burial of scholars", initially enacted by the Qin dynasty, should not serve as a historical metaphor for the destruction of progressive books and the persecution of intellectuals by authoritarian dictatorships in modern societies.[10] However, "The Annals of Qin Shihuang" in *Shi Ji* (Sima Qian's *Historical Records*) makes it clear that Qin Shihuang specifically targeted

[9] Accordingly, Qin Shihuang unified the currency and measures; his standardization of the written script had the effect of subjecting all aspects of civilization to a uniform ideology marked by identical symbolic habits of thought.

[10] During the Spring and Autumn and Warring States periods (771–221 BCE), because there were different centers of power, many rival doctrines emerged, resulting in the growth of many different philosophical schools, known by historians as the Hundred Schools of Thought. At the beginning of Qin Shihuang's unification of the country, he faced the question of whether to continue to break up the fiefs of the various princes of the former states. Swayed by Li Si's argument that these relatively independent proto-feudal fiefs of the Western Zhou engendered political turmoil, Qin Shihuang decided to establish a hierarchical administrative system centered on prefectures and counties throughout the country. However, some Confucians and other itinerant political advisers criticized current politics by citing the Confucian classics (for example, *Shang Shu* which recorded the ancient sage kings' philosophy of ruling, and *Shi Jing* [The Classic of Poetry] which also praised wise rulers of previous generations), which aroused the ire of Qin Shihuang. In 213 BCE, the 34th year of the reign of the First Emperor, the court again hosted arguments about whether to follow past policies in the present day, and some suggested returning to the system of proto-feudal, loosely independent fiefs (*fenfeng-zhi*), but this was regarded as spreading ideas and institutions from the past. Prime Minister Li Si suggested a "burning of the books" to Qin Shihuang: (1) With the exception of the *Qin Records* (Qin Ji), medical texts, works of prognostication, and classics of the Agriculturist school of philosophy, other writings by philosophers and historical books would be submitted to the government for destruction within a limited time. If books were not submitted within thirty days, those who failed to comply were to be punished by having their faces tattooed or sentenced to four years' hard labor. (2) Those who discuss the *Classic of Poetry* or *Book of History* will be executed, while those officials who blindly denigrate or deny present achievements in the light of [alleged] ancient precedents will face the same punishment. (3) Among those enthusiastic about and versed in these laws and orders, it is the minor [lower-level] officials who will serve as teachers. Qin Shihuang approved all these proposals by Li Si. Within less than 30 days, the classical documents from the years prior to the Qin dynasty were all reduced to ashes, leaving only a single collection of books in the Imperial Library. In the following year, necromancers who had

"those who recite Confucius". This was widely interpreted as referring to the intellectuals of the time, so that the event named the "burning of books and burial of scholars" was often regarded by later generations of various historical periods as a precedent for the persecution of intellectuals and the atrocities committed against them by subsequent tyrannical or authoritarian dictatorships. In 206 BCE, the Qin dynasty came to an end. Those once affiliated to the previously destroyed Six States and all those who contributed to the destruction of Qin attempted to take advantage of the new situation and restore the earlier system of independent feudal fiefs; among the victors, Xiang Yu (232–202 BCE) embarked on implementing this restoration. However, in the wake of the constant conflicts and slaughter triggered among the various contending forces, Xiang Yu was finally militarily defeated and subsequently committed suicide by cutting his own throat in Wujiang (today's Hexian county, Anhui) in 202 BCE. The "world" (*Tianxia*, in fact, another ancient and ambiguous term for "China") was subsequently unified as the Han dynasty. In the eyes

failed to fulfill their commitment to secure for Qin Shihuang an elixir conferring immortality began to accuse and slander Qin Shihuang for his obstinate and selfish nature, his greed for power, and his arbitrary and dictatorial actions. When Qin Shihuang learned that rumormongers were stirring up the people, he ordered they be hunted down, and he personally singled out ["circled"] the names of more than 460 people who were to be buried alive in the capital Xianyang. That is the event termed "the burial of the scholars".

The purpose behind "the burning of the books" was to unify ideology and, at this time, given the Confucian respect for antiquity, the nobility of the former Six States invoked the Confucian principle of "practicing restraint and restoring the [ancient Confucian] rites" in an attempt to restore the proto-feudal system of the Zhou dynasty, so they were obviously diametrically opposed to the concentration of power by the Qin dynasty and to Qin Shihuang's mission to unify China. The evidence for "the burial of the scholars" is attributed to a statement by Fu Su, the oldest son of Qin Shihuang, as quoted in the *Shi Ji*'s "Annals of Qin Shihuang": "When Tianxia [China] was first established, people from afar had not yet been brought together and all students recited Confucius, so the Emperor insisted that Law must bind the people together. But I fear the world is restive and the Emperor must investigate this". However, the Eastern Han scholar Wang Chong wrote in the "Yu Zeng Chapter" of his *Lun Heng* (Doctrines Evaluated): "The *Classic of Poetry* and *Book of History* were burned as a result of remonstration by Chunyu Yue; the burial of the scholars was occasioned by their rumor-mongering". The historian Lü Simian commented: "The burial of the scholars was occasioned by their slander of the emperor, but the intention was not to eliminate Confucian scholars, so it cannot be compared with the burning of the books". He further commented: "The scholar burial incident was precipitated by those who slandered the emperor; the intention was not to destroy Confucianism, and it cannot be discussed together with the burning of the books". Historically speaking, it would therefore seem preferable to discuss Qin's "burial of the scholars" and "the burning of the books" as a linked event.

of Liu Bang (247–195 BCE), who was born a commoner but rose to become the first Han emperor, Emperor Gaozu, "the world" enclosed by the borders Qin had demarcated was now his. However, he simply inherited the system as it had been set up by the Qin dynasty and perfected this centralized *imperium*. Through the bureaucratic division of duties described as "[administration by] the three leading court officials and nine chief officers (*sangong-jiuqing*)", Liu Bang ultimately concentrated all power in his own hands as the emperor. The system would prove effective and was constantly refined over time so that the governing institutions, which experienced long periods of stability and which we today call the "Qin-Han polity", essentially remained in place until the middle of the nineteenth century, after which China was plunged into irreversible crises.

In 138 BCE, a young man named Zhang Qian[11] headed an expedition to the Western Regions comprising more than one hundred men who set out from Longxi, today's Lintao In Gansu province.[12] The emperor entrusted Zhang with the task of convincing the Indo-European people

[11] Zhang Qian (164 114) was a native of Chenggu in Hanzhong (today's Chenggu county in Shaanxi province). When Emperor Wu assumed the Han throne, Zhang Qian served at his court. According to historical records, in 138 BCE Zhang Qian was recruited to act as an envoy to the Yuezhi people.

[12] The term "Western Regions" is used differently and from different perspectives at different times, but in terms of its original historical and geographical scope, the history books are relatively clear. The "Preface to the Account of the Western Regions" in *Han Shu* (History of the Han Dynasty) records: "The Western Regions, which began to be opened up in the time of Emperors Xiao and Wu, originally comprised thirty-six nations, which later divided into more than fifty. They are all located to the west of the Xiongnu and to the south of the Wusun. There are high mountains to the north and south. A river traverses the center of the Western Regions, which extend more than six thousand *li* from east to west, and a thousand *li* from north to south. In the east it borders Han, and this boundary is marked by the passes named Yumen and Yangguan; in the west it extends to the Pamirs". Simply put, the Western Regions is the general name for the region bounded by the Yumenguan and Yangguan passes in the east and by the Pamir Plateau on the west. Of the thirty-six states of the Western Regions, some were the polities of nomadic tribes while others were based on walled towns or oases. Around the turn of the millennium, when the Han dynasty suffered an abrupt political break known as the Wang Mang Interregnum, the original 36 states fractured into 55 states. Later, the term Western Regions was also used to include what is now Qinghai and Tibet. Moreover, down to the present day, the term "Western Regions" has sometimes even included Western countries and regions in Europe, especially when discussing the political and historical implications of the "Silk Road".

known as the Greater Yuezhi[13] to form an alliance with the Han dynasty to launch joint attacks against the Xiongnu to the north. Entering the Hexi Corridor, which was under the control of the Xiongnu, Zhang Qian and some of his men were captured by the Xiongnu army, detained, and placed in detention. Zhang Qian was forced to marry a Xiongnu woman, with whom he had a number of children, and he and several others remained in Xiongnu custody for ten years. In 129 BCE, Zhang left his wife and children, and escaped with his entourage, resuming his journey to the kingdom of the Greater Yuezhi. After traveling for many long weeks in grueling and dangerous conditions they reached the state of Dayuan.[14] The King of Dayuan was familiar with the Han dynasty,

[13] Yuezhi was the name of an ancient state and ethnic group of the Western Regions. From the fifth to the early second century BCE, the Yuezhi grazed their herds in the western part of the Hexi Corridor from Zhangye to Dunhuang. In the Qin-Han period, the Yuezhi were very powerful, and shortly before 177 BCE, the Yuezhi defeated the Wusun, a nomadic tribe located near Dunhuang; the latter fled to seek refuge with the Xiongnu. However, in 177–176 BCE, the Xiongnu defeated the Yuezhi, and again in 174, forcing the Yuezhi to move west towards the Ili River basin and the vicinity of Lake Issyk-kul. A remnant group of Yuezhi remained in the Hexi Corridor and mingled with Qiang people who lived in the Qilian Mountains; this group was called the Lesser Yuezhi while those who migrated westwards were called the Greater Yuezhi. In 139–129, the Wusun attacked the Greater Yuezhi in the west and seized the Ili River valley and another territory. The Greater Yuezhi then moved further west, settling on the northern side of the Amu Darya. In the early first century BCE, the Greater Yuezhi campaigned against Daxia (Bactria) located south of the Amu Darya. The Greater Yuezhi divided into the Five Xihou (Satrapies), known individually as the states of Xiumi, Shuangmi, Guishuang (Kushan), Xidun, and Dumi, who maintained their separate autonomy. In the first century CE, the Guishuang Xihou attacked the other four Xihou and established the Kingdom of Kushan, but China continued to call them the Greater Yuezhi.

[14] Dayuan, another of the polities of the ancient Western Regions, was an agricultural state located on the western slopes of the Pamir Plateau and in the Fergana Valley of what is today Uzbekistan on the middle and lower reaches of the Syr Darya. The original inhabitants were predominantly Saka people with Caucasian characteristics and their customs were similar to those of Daxia (Bactria) to the south. Zhang Qian's expedition to the Western Regions took him first to Dayuan, which was renowned for the "blood-sweating horses" its warriors rode into battle against the Han dynasty. In 329 BCE, Alexander the Great conquered the Fergana Basin in the western part of the Pamir Plateau, and the ancient Greeks adopted the name Dayuan for the place, which progressively prospered under the Hellenized Seleucid Empire and the subsequent Greater Bactrian period until 160 BCE, when as a result of the migration of the Greater Yuezhi, Dayuan was separated from the Greek world. [Around 250 BCE, the satrap of Bactria, Diodotus I, had declared his independence from the Seleucid Empire and established Greater Bactria (which was destroyed by the Greater Yuezhi in 125 BCE), and Dayuan came under the rule of Greater Bactria.] The wars and exchanges between the Han dynasty and Dayuan

so to show his good intentions, he provided Zhang Qian with guides and interpreters to travel to Kangju,[15] a state whose territory fell within what is today Uzbekistan and Kyrgyzstan. It was via Kangju that Zhang Qian reached Daxia (Bactria),[16] occupying an area roughly equivalent to today's valley of the Amu Darya. Subsequently, Daxia sent them on to the Greater Yuezhi. Zhang Qian and his party remained with the Greater

can be regarded as early contacts between Chinese and Indo-European civilizations, which were later continued because of the "Silk Road".

[15] Kangju was the name of an ancient state of the Western Regions. Located between Lake Balkash and the Aral Sea, it bordered Wusun on the east, Yancai on the west, Greater Yuezhi to the south, and Dayuan to the southeast. The central area occupied by Kangju extends from the lower reaches of the Syr Darya to the Kirghiz Steppe [Plain]. Before Zhang Qian traveled to the Western Regions, in, 133 BCE, Chinese scholars had already mentioned Kangju, making it one of the earliest states of the Western Regions with which the Han dynasty must have had contact.

[16] The inhabitants of Bactria, one of the ancient states Zhang Qian referred to when he returned from the Western Regions, may have been Indo-Europeans (also known as the Saka), who were referred to in ancient Greek literature as Tochari, the name (Tokhgra or Tochari) that was transliterated as Daxia. Balkh (20 km from present-day Mazar-i-Sharif in Afghanistan), the capital of Bactria, was rendered in Chinese as Lanshi Cheng (lit., "Blue Market"). From c. 139 to 129 BCE, the Greater Yuezhi who were resident in the valleys of the Ili and Chu rivers moved westwards and the Daxia became their subjects. When Zhang Qian encountered the Greater Yuezhi, they had subjugated Daxia. Ancient Chinese texts record that the Tochari were Greek migrants who established the kingdom of Bactria at the foot of the Hindu Kush (called Paropamisus in Greek) and on the upper reaches of the Amu Darya (Greek: Oxus). Bactria was in turn ruled by the ancient Persian Empire (550–330), by Alexander's empire, and by the Seleucid kingdom (312–64 BCE). In the mid-third century BCE, Bactria under the rule of its governor Diodotus became independent of the Seleucid kingdom, and after independence the rulers of Bactria were descendants of Greek immigrants, so history books also refer to the state as Graeco-Bactria. During the reign of Diodotus II, a satrap of the northern part of Bactria, Euthydemus seized power from Diodotus' family and proclaimed himself king. After his son Demetrius (190–167) succeeded to the throne, he incorporated into the territory of Bactria lands to the south (parts of what is today Afghanistan and Pakistan), and so the kingdom of Bactria attained its zenith. By moving the capital to Pataliputra (today's Patna) in ancient India, Demetrius balanced Greek culture with ancient Indian culture, arousing opposition among the Greeks of Bactria. Around 168 BCE, the Greek noble Eucratides occupied Bactria and became king. Thus Graeco-Bactria was divided into two: one part in Bactria itself and the other in India. In 128 BCE, when Zhang Qian traveled to the Greater Yuezhi on the Amu Darya, the Tocharians were settled in Bactria, and shortly after the Tocharians in Bactria broke away from Greek rule, they were conquered in turn by the second westward migration of the Greater Yuezhi. Bactrian was an Indo-European language of the Iranian language family which was originally written in the Aramaic alphabet but began to be written in the Greek alphabet under the rule of the Yuezhi.

Yuezhi for more than a year but they were unable to persuade their hosts to join a strike force with the Han dynasty targeting the Xiongnu. In 128 BCE, Zhang Qian prepared to return to the Han Empire, but on the road he and several other members of his party were again captured by the Xiongnu and kept as prisoners for more than a year. It was not until the beginning of 126 BCE (the 3rd year of Yuanshuo) that he took advantage of turmoil among the Xiongnu to escape and returned to Chang'an, the Han capital. It would seem that Zhang Qian failed to achieve the goal of his expedition to the Western Regions, but his long time in the Western Regions made him knowledgeable about the area's geography, resources, customs, and way of life. His report to Emperor Wu became the main source of the information provided in the "Account of the Western Regions" in *Han Shu*, the "official" history of the Han dynasty. In 119 BCE, Zhang Qian embarked on a second diplomatic mission to the Western Regions. By this time, Han was in control of the Hexi Corridor and Emperor Wu adopted Zhang Qian's proposal to invite the Wusun[17] to return east to the Dunhuang region and join Han in resisting the Xiongnu. At the same time, he intended to link up with other states of the area to subjugate the Xiongnu. When Zhang Qian returned from this second mission in 115 BCE, there were already Wusun envoys in Chang'an. The Han dynasty later sent envoys further afield—to Anxi (Persia), Shendu (India), Yancai (between the Caspian and Aral seas), Tiaozhi (a satrapy of Persia), and Lijian (said to be Alexandria in Egypt). Henceforth, communication routes between Han and the Western Regions were fully established, and the term "Western Regions" was gradually no longer limited to designating foreign states,

[17] In the early second century BCE, the Wusun were nomadic pastoralists inhabiting the Dunhuang-Qilian area and speaking a Turkic language. In the Tang dynasty Yan Shigu in an annotation on "The Account of the Western Regions" in *Han Shu* wrote: "Among all the barbarians of the Western Regions, the Wusun are the most unusual in appearance, and their blue eyes and crimson beards make them resemble macaques". In fact, they appear to have been a Caucasian ethnic group. Between 177 and 176, the Xiongnu defeated the Yuezhi and drove them to the Ili River basin, after which the Xiongnu and Wusun joined forces and attacked the Yuezhi driving them south into Bactria. As a result, the Wusun people completely abandoned their ancient home between Dunhuang and the Qilian Mountains and moved to the Ili River basin. When Zhang Qian returned from the Western Regions, he suggested that the Han dynasty make use of the Wusun and join with them in attacking the Xiongnu, and to this end the Han dynasty and Wusun entered into a number of royal marriages. In 410, the Wusun were wiped out by the Rouran, and today's Kazakhs are considered by some to be the descendants of the Wusun.

but also included lands within the purview of the Han dynasty, as Han rule expanded.[18] In fact, up to the time when Qin Shihuang built the Great Wall to protect the Central Plains, China's western boundary was only just outside Lintao and Yumen; prior to Zhang Qian's expedition, the countries to the west of the Congling (Pamirs), such as Dayuan, Wusun, Greater Yuezhi, Kangju, and Daxia, were not influenced by the Han dynasty. However, Zhang's expedition brought China into contact with states west of the Pamirs, and the country subsequently developed trading, cultural, and political contacts with Central Asia, Western Asia, and even southern Europe. Zhang Qian's route was subsequently traveled and supplemented by later generations, ultimately forming what was termed the "Silk Road" by the German geologist Ferdinand von Richthofen at the end of the nineteenth century. This Han dynasty route thus facilitated the earliest communications between the civilizations of China, India, and Greece,[19] being among the major routes along which

[18] In 60 BCE, Prince Rizhu, named Xianxianshan, of the Xiongnu surrendered with his men to Han, and Xiongnu control of the Western Regions was seriously weakened. The Han dynasty began to formally set up an administrative structure in the Western Regions, with the establishment of the Protector-General of the Western Regions near Luntai county (85 degrees east, 42 degrees north, at an altitude of 990 meters) in what is today the Bayin Gol Mongolian Autonomous Prefecture ("Bazhou"). At that time, the town was called Wulei City (but it had formerly been a small city state known as Luntai). The Protector-General served as the administrative body used by the Han dynasty to manage the political, economic, cultural, and military affairs of the 36 countries in the Western Regions, and the eighteen officials who successively filled the post were, according to *Han Shu*, all appointed by the emperor.

[19] Many inhabitants of the ancient Western Regions in the area west of the Pamirs were ethnically Caucasian, indicating that early armies of "European" people had invaded this territory, leaving military or related personnel resident there who intermarried and reproduced, which is why historical and cultural traces of ancient Graeco-Roman civilization can be found in these exotic lands. For example, in 329 BCE, after Alexander the Great conquered Fergana, he built the city of Alexandria Eschate (today's Khujand in Tajikistan) on the southern bank of the Syr Darya. Given that Alexander's teacher was Aristotle, he would have surely been determined to perpetuate Greek culture and, of course, such cities also displayed his power as emperor and were used to settle veterans and Greek mercenaries. They could be defended against attacks by nomadic tribes of the grasslands, similar to the way in which soldiers were retained to serve as border guards following the expansion of the Qin dynasty, in the hope of fixing the border and serving as a base for future expeditions. Most of these Caucasians did not cross to the eastern side of the Pamirs, though it has been hypothesized that the Wusun were Caucasians who did cross the Pamirs and traveled directly to the Dunhuang-Qilian region of Gansu. At the same time, the Aryans who were ancient migrants to northern India mixed with the Dravidians of southern India, to form the various Aryan Indian languages.

ancient religions, philosophies, and cultures entered China. For example, we know that Buddhism crossed the Pamir plateau into China, and this was a major factor leading to the flourishing of Buddhist art in China during the Northern Wei period (386–534).[20] By the Tang dynasty, when interaction and exchanges between China and the Western Regions in culture, art, religion, and material production reached their peak, the Tang capital city Chang'an seemed to have become the center of the world.

II

By means of warfare and military might, Qin unified China, and consequently Qin Shihuang was praised for "determining everything under Your sole authority".[21] Later, however, it was largely through ideology or philosophy that the Han dynasty (206 BCE–CE 220) consolidated this unity and expanded China's territory. At first, the Taoist idea of "ruling through inaction" informed the theory of governance of the first Han emperor, Liu Bang; its purpose was to satisfy the desire for peace, rest, and recuperation after many years of war. Liu Che, better known to history as Han Emperor Wu (140–87 BCE), implemented highly successful political centralization. Obviously realizing that the way to maintain centralized rule was to shape people's ideas, he chose Confucianism, and as a result "the hundred schools of philosophy were shelved, and the practice of Confucianism was given precedence". However, he did not personally shape the ideology; that task fell to Dong Zhongshu and others. Before turning to Dong Zhongshu, Han Emperor Wu had begun to take measures to avoid the dissemination of the ideas of schools other than Confucianism, and his government only invited Confucian scholars to serve as officials. At the same time, he installed "doctors in the Confucian *Five Classics*" who studied *The Classic of Poetry*, *The Book of History*, *The Book of Rites*, *The Book of Changes*, and *The Spring*

[20] The art of the Northern Wei dynasty was dominated by sculpture, concentrated in the grotto temples of the time, and influenced by ancient Indian art. The wide distribution of Buddhist grottoes is surprising: roughly from present-day Gansu in the west, to Liaoning in the east, the most famous being the Yungang Grottoes (Datong), Longmen Grottoes (Luoyang), Dunhuang Grottoes, Maijishan Caves (Tianshui), Binglingsi Caves (Yongjing), and the Tianlongshan Caves (Taiyuan).

[21] "Biography of Li Si" in *Shi Ji*: "Now Your Majesty controls all of China, determining everything under Your sole authority".

and Autumn Annals. Confucianism thus became the official intellectual study or system; such "doctors" became skilled in applying interpretation of Yin-Yang philosophy and Five Element theory into Confucian dogma, imbuing Confucianism with components of metaphysics. The role of these "components" was to legitimize the uniqueness of the emperor, because at that time people believed in the objectivity of the ultimate existence of "Heaven" and the "Way". This legitimization was based on the conviction that only the emperor could "implement the Way on behalf of Heaven", maintaining that only he had the natural legitimacy to exercise all power, an eternal reality that people should acknowledge from the outset. The main function of Confucianism was to provide a theoretical basis and methodology for the Qin-Han polity. This idea was articulated by the Western Han scholar Dai Sheng who wrote in his *Li Ji* (Book of Ritual): "Heaven cannot have two suns, the earth cannot have two kings, a family cannot have two masters, and there cannot be two things that are the most venerated". Such expressions were passed down and praised over generations, embedding themselves in the national psyche. Finally, regardless of what other doctrines continued to circulate freely, the Han dynasty was founded by commoners, rather than aristocrats, and so a hereditary system could not be implemented to promote officials. The establishment of an examination system instead for recruiting and promoting officials was placed on the agenda and the criteria to be examined were the only consideration. Since Confucianism was singled out as the philosophy to be venerated, the government set up a Supreme College (Taixue) for which the Confucian Classics naturally provided the main content of its examinations. Therefore, those embarking on a career as an official had to conform to the requirements of the Han Empire's philosophy,[22] the "Confucianism" that Dong Zhongshu and Gongsun Hong (200–121 BCE) helped to bring to completion. The key question was of course: Why Confucianism?

The time of the Spring and Autumn (770 E–476 BCE) and Warring States (475–221 BCE) periods is reminiscent of the age in ancient Greece that gave rise to Socrates, Plato, and Aristotle, the sources of Western

[22] The elevation of Confucianism by Han Emperor Wu (r. 140–87 BCE) served to establishment an ideological basis legitimizing his rule and, thereafter, emperors would invariably use Confucian ideology and Legalist principles to govern the country and would never solely implement Taoist government. Confucian scholars served as the defenders of the legitimacy of the ruler's governance.

thought, and it was characterized by rivalry between contending philosophical schools in what would seem to have been an ideologically liberal era. Sima Tan (?–110 BCE), father of the historian Sima Qian, was the first scholar to classify the various thinkers of the time into different schools, encompassing philosophies designated the Yin-Yang School, Confucian School, Mohist School, School of Names, Legalist School, and Taoist School. Each school of thought had its own particularity, for example, the Legalists' emphasis on law might suggest some Western thought based on rules and systems, while the essence of Legalism was the hope that through violence and centralization the rulers could implement their governance. However, it was ultimately Confucianism and Taoism that Chinese respected and applied over millennia, and the use of Legalist techniques and even of the philosophy of Legalism by the ruling class was confined as visceral and undeclared knowledge. Therefore, the basic characteristic of what came to be called the Qin-Han polity was an undeclared Legalist system wrapped in Confucianism, and the level of attainment of successive emperors was determined by how flexibly and effectively they could use Confucianism to implement what were ultimately Legalist measures. Confucianism was neither religious theology nor metaphysics, but merely political theory, which is why successive dynasties always reinterpreted Confucianism. Every emperor needed to provide legitimacy for his own words and deeds in inevitably different historical circumstances.

It is usual to say that Confucius (551–479 BCE) was the creator of Confucianism, but whatever criteria are applied to verify this statement, the results are uncertain. Moreover, what did Confucius have to do with the *Six Classics* of Confucianism[23]—*The Classic of Poetry*, *The Book of History*, *The Book of Changes*, *The Book of Rites*, *The Book of Music*, and

[23] For the earliest Confucians there were *Six Classics*: *The Classic of Poetry*, *The Book of History*, *Yi Li*, *The Book of Music*, *The Changes of Zhou* (*The Book of Changes*), and *The Spring and Autumn Annals*. Following Qin Shihuang's "burning of the books" and "burial of scholars", *The Book of Music* was lost; in the Eastern Han dynasty, *The Analects* and *The Classic of Filial Piety* were added, bringing the number of classics to seven. In the Tang dynasty, *Zhou Li*, *Li Ji*, *Chunqiu Gongyang Zhuan*, *Chunqiu Guliang Zhuan*, and *Erya* were added, bringing the number to twelve. In the Song dynasty, *The Book of Mencius* was added, bringing the number to thirteen. Later people began to speak of the "Four Books and Five Classics", the "Books" being *The Great Learning* (a chapter of *Li Ji*), *The Doctrine of the Mean* (another chapter from *Li Ji*), *The Analects*, and *The Book of Mencius*, while the Five Classics comprised *Zhou Yi* (*The Book of Changes*), *The Book of History*, *The Classic of Poetry*, *Li Ji*, and *Zuozhuan*. Until the end of the nineteenth century, these were the books that officials and scholars had at hand for constant reference.

The Spring and Autumn Annals? Did he write, compile, or annotate these works? Most people favor the view that these works were in existence before Confucius' time and that many people taught with them as classics; those who had this knowledge and taught these classics were simply called *Ru*, the word that has over time come to be simplistically understood and translated to mean a "Confucian scholar". Moreover, Confucius is recorded to have acknowledged that he "expounds but will not write", so perhaps he should be taken at his word. In any case, being a teacher, Confucius would be familiar with the knowledge in these classics and would certainly have his own explanations and interpretations of the texts. His students compiled the scattered remarks he made in the course of his lectures and edited them as *The Analects* (Lunyu) which became the anthology encapsulating Confucius' thought. Many of the thoughts in the *Six Classics* were digested in *The Analects* and became the de facto "work", as it is difficult for us to imagine or deduce what the original author (of the *Six Classics*) really meant. For example, in explaining *The Book of Poems*, Confucius said, "The three hundred *Poems* are, in a word, 'thought without heresy'" ("Wei Zheng"·*The Analects*). On the basis of this remark, his students understood the role of poetry to be moral guidance. Confucius' method or habit of terse comment was subsequently adopted by many thinkers, so that "annotation" became a Chinese academic approach and tradition, while these experts thus came to be roughly referred to as "Confucians" (*Rujia*), and "*jia*" is equivalent to what we would now call a "school of thought".

As a collection compiled by Confucius' students, *The Analects* has no systematic logic of presentation, and most issues touched on are teachings on governance, moral cultivation, human life, and personal codes of conduct. Confucius was venerated for his wisdom and refined language; he would often express an idea as a question, which is another notable characteristic of the presentation of his ideas. In the "Ba Yi" section of *The Analects* we encounter the following passage: "Confucius said, 'Zhou surveyed the previous two dynasties. What a wealth of culture! Let us emulate Zhou'". We do not have to enquire too deeply about the rites (ritual) of the Zhou court respected by Confucius, but we know that he believed that when it came to the hierarchy of society and the rules governing a nation's behavior, even the monarch cannot disrespect ritual (protocol). Therefore, in the same chapter, he is also quoted as saying: "A ruler employing his ministers should be guided by ritual, and a minister serving his ruler should be guided by loyalty". So important was ritual that we even read the following in the "Yan Yuan" section of *The Analects*: "Look at nothing that negates ritual, listen to nothing that negates ritual, say nothing that negates ritual, and make no move that negates ritual". In fact, whether or not the "ritual" of which Confucius spoke was limited to the ritual of Zhou, for thousands of years the ruling class enshrined "ritual" in their own established order, so that the resulting hierarchy would remain unchanged. Therefore, the core of "ritual" hinged on the injunction that "a ruler must behave as a ruler, a courtier must behave as a courtier, a father as a father, and a son as a son", according to the "Yan Yuan" section of *The Analects*. It was this system and structure that had sole legitimacy. In *The Analects*, the words "benevolence", "righteousness", "courtesy", "wisdom", and "faith" are often used, and Confucius is quoted as saying: "Only those who possess benevolence (or reciprocity) can be either fond of people or hate people in the right way" ("Liren", *The Analects*). He told his students that if they were determined to cultivate benevolence and virtue, it would be impossible for them to become evil people, and they would treat all people, whether rich or poor, noble or humble, correctly, because the true gentleman would not abandon benevolence and virtue because of exigency or circumstances. Confucius told his students: "Strength, boldness, simplicity, and cautiousness approximate benevolence". However, the benevolence he spoke of had other meanings.[24] The words and deeds of a noble and ethically superior man are, moreover, nothing more than respect for the rules of "righteousness", about which Confucius remarked: "The gentleman deals with the world without partiality or enmity, and this can be likened to righteousness" ("Liren", *The Analects*). Thus, the gentleman pays attention to "righteousness", while the morally inferior man only recognizes "personal advantage". Confucius also attached great importance to the level of writing of a man of ethical quality: "When substance prevails over ornamentation there is savagery, and when ornamentation prevails over substance there is pedantry. Only when substance and ornamentation are balanced does one have the true gentleman" ("Yong Ye", *The Analects*). Confucius' words are very much those of the true gentleman.

[24] For example, the student Zizhang asked Confucius: What is *ren* (benevolence, reciprocity)? Confucius said: "The ability in the world to implement courtesy, generosity, honesty, due diligence, and kindness (clemency)" ("Yang Huo", *The Analects*). People with these five virtues could thus be said to possess benevolence.

Here it should be clearly understood that the attainment of deep self-knowledge was extremely difficult for the Chinese literary intellectual and that, in the difficult task of achieving just the right degree of balance between substance (solidity) and ornamentation, he would rather preserve substance in order to express his true heart-felt meaning.[25] The importance of practice and action was of course emphasized by Confucius because benevolence (reciprocity) was not a matter of lip service but was embodied in action. When students asked Confucius how to be benevolent, he answered: "Benevolence (reciprocity) can only be attained after initial difficulties; that is what being benevolent entails" ("Yong Ye", *The Analects*). In fact, in the section of *The Analects* which treats "politics" ("Wei Zheng"), Confucius stated that to be a gentleman, a man should "first practice what he preaches, and only then preach what he practices". Confucius had personal insight into this observation; he was ambitious to contribute to the governance of the country, but had no opportunity to play a part, and so felt he might have failed to adhere to his own injunction. Thus, he admitted to himself that his learning may be similar to that of other teachers, but he had not yet attained the standards of a gentleman or superior man in his actions.[26] In ethical teaching, when students asked him whether, when the ancient sages Bo Yi and Shu Qi each declined the throne in favor of the other so that finally no one occupied the throne, they regretted their actions, Confucius replied: "They sought benevolence and attained benevolence. Why should they grieve?" ("Shu Er", *The Analects*) Here, noble moral qualities are regarded as most important for a noble person, and in Confucius' view, utilitarian purpose is insufficient.

[25] In his commentary on the *Four Books* titled *Sishu Zhangju Jizhu*, the Song dynasty Confucian thinker Zhu Xi discussed Confucius' distinction between "rusticity" and "pedantry" in the following passage: "By 'rusticity, Confucius meant that a man was untutored, and by 'pedantry' he meant that a man was so adept at handling documents that he was excessively informed and insufficiently sincere. When balanced things are detailed, extremes are held in check. When a scholar is either deficient or excessive, the balance must be restored; as for virtue, he cannot plan to be natural and then be spontaneously natural. Yang commented: 'Neither ornament nor substance can predominate. If substance predominates, there is a willingness to accept and be influenced. If ornament prevails then substance and what was original are eliminated. How does one apply ornament? Better as a scribe, than as a rustic'".

[26] "As far as trying goes, I think I do not compare unfavorably with others. But in fulfilling the duties of a gentleman in actual life, I have not had the opportunity to show what I can do" ("Shu Er", *The Analects*).

Confucius made many statements that would be recited constantly by future generations, but reality fell far short of his ideals, and even if we are talking about the literary intellectual community, his sayings cited below are in marked contrast to the Chinese history of the twentieth century we later examine:

> Be of unwavering faith and love learning. Be defensive and ready to die for the Way of virtue. Do not enter a country that foments danger, nor remain in one that is in turmoil. When the Way prevails in the land, then reveal oneself; when the Way is absent, then conceal oneself. When a country possesses the Way, then it is shameful to be poor and obscure; when a country does not possess the Way, then it is a disgrace to be wealthy and honored.[27] ("Tai Bo", *The Analects*)

> When the stables burned down, Confucius withdrew from court, and asked, "Was anyone hurt?" He did not ask about the horses. ("Xiang Dang", *The Analects*)

> Ji Lu asked whether one should serve ghosts and spirits. Confucius said, 'Until you can serve men, how can you serve ghosts?'
> 'Can I venture a question about death?'
> Confucius replied: 'Until you know about the living, how can you know about the dead?'" ("Xian Jin", *The Analects*)

> Yan Yuan asked about benevolence. Confucius said: "He who can restrain himself and restore ritual is benevolent. If one day [a ruler] restrains himself and restores ritual, the world (nation) will return to benevolence. Benevolence stems from the self, and not from others". ("Yan Yuan", *The Analects*)

> Zigong asked about government, and Confucius replied: "Sufficient food, sufficient weapons, and the confidence of the people".

[27] A similar idea is expressed in another passage in *The Analects*: "When a country is ruled in accordance with the Way, [the gentleman] accepts rewards; when the country is not ruled according to the Way, he is ashamed to receive rewards ("Xian Wen", *The Analects*). In another passage in the same chapter of *The Analects*, Confucius (as interpreted by Zhu Xi) said: "When the Way prevails in the nation, be bold in speech and action. When the Way does not prevail, be bold in action but conciliatory [or cautious] in speech". It is in the edition of *The Analects* edited by Zhu Xi and titled *Zhuzi Jizhu* that we read these interpretations.

> Zigong then asked: "If you had to dispense with one of these, which would you first forgo?" Confucius replied: "The weapons".
> Zigong further asked, "If you had to forego one of the remaining two, which would it be?" Confucius replied, "Food. Since ancient times, all men know mortality, but if the people have no confidence in their ruler, the state will collapse". ("Yan Yuan", *The Analects*)

> Qi Jinggong asked about government, and Confucius replied: "a ruler must behave as a ruler, a courtier must behave as a courtier, a father as a father, and a son as a son". ("Yan Yuan", *The Analects*)

> Ji Kangzi asked Confucius about governance, saying: "If I were to slay those who do not have the Way in order to benefit those who do have the Way, what would you say?" Confucius replied: "A ruler is there to rule, so what use is slaughter? If the ruler desires what is good, his people will be good as a result. The force of the gentleman is that of the wind; the force of the mean man is that of the weeds. When the wind passes over weeds, the weeds bend". ("Yan Yuan", *The Analects*)

> A gentleman, when things he does not understand are mentioned, should maintain a reserved attitude. If language is incorrect, then what is said does not conform to what was meant, and if what is said does not conform to what was meant then what should be done cannot be carried out; if what should be done cannot be carried out, then ritual and music will not flourish. If ritual and music do not flourish, then punishments and fines will be inappropriate, and if punishments are inappropriate then the people will have nowhere to turn. ("Zi Lu", *The Analects*)

Mencius (c. 372–289 BCE), who lived around 300 BCE during the Warring States era, was a student of Confucius' grandson, Zi Si, and he accepted all of Confucius' basic ideas benevolence, righteousness, courtesy, and wisdom.[28] Moreover, he left a much more substantial body of

[28] Mencius explained these virtues as follows: "The feeling of compassion is the manifestation of benevolence. The feeling of shame and dislike is the manifestation of righteousness. The feeling of modesty and compliance is the manifestation of propriety. The feeling of approval and disapproval is the manifestation of knowledge. People have these four manifestations (principles), just as they have four limbs" ("Gongsun Chou, I", *The Book of Mencius*). "The feeling of compassion is benevolence; the feeling of shame and dislike is righteousness; the feeling of reverence and respect is propriety; the feeling of approval and disapproval is wisdom" ("Gaozi, I", *The Book of Mencius*).

writing treating the application of these ideas to government and politics. It can be seen that, in Mencius' view, all these ideas simply served to establish and maintain a state loved by everyone, in which people could live and work in peace and harmony, and this constituted the highest realm of human life. However, it was of course very difficult to attain this level. Mencius lived in turbulent times, addressing which he also adhered to the principles of "benevolence and righteousness" in discussing questions of governance with the rulers of various states. Thus, when King Hui of Liang (400–319 BCE) asked him what gain his country could derive from Mencius having traveled so far to visit, Mencius retorted: "Why talk of gain? Benevolence and righteousness are enough" ("King Hui of Liang (A)", *The Book of Mencius*). With King Hui of Liang, Mencius discussed concrete measures for implementing benevolent government: "If Your Majesty implements benevolent government for your people, then be sparing in the use of punishments and fines, lighten taxes and levies, plough the fields deep and remove the weeds. Thus, the able-bodied will have days of leisure to cultivate their filial piety, fraternal respect, sincerity, and truthfulness, and people will serve their fathers and older brothers at home and go out to serve their elders and superiors. You will then have people who can serve by taking up wooden stakes to oppose the armor and powerful weapons of the states of Qin and Chu" ("King Hui of Liang (A)", *The Book of Mencius*). Here he expresses his belief that if other countries do not have benevolent government, depriving their people of a livelihood and breaking up families, then a country which implements benevolent rule will prevail over them without recourse to war. When asked who could rule the world, Mencius replied, "The one who does not kill can" ("King Hui of Liang" (A), *The Book of Mencius*). Mencius further illustrated the inevitability of this approach, saying: "Once it rains, the seedlings lying in the dry parched earth during the seventh and eighth months will be able to grow vigorously. No one can resist such growth, like water flowing to lower ground". Even if this example sheds further light on Mencius' original argument, it is hard to imagine that by solely relying on his good intentions (benevolence and righteousness) a man can achieve the worthy outcomes he desires. Mencius asserted that man was innately good and argued that if harmony prevailed between a king and his people or even if the relationship between two states was grounded in benevolence and love, then there were no conflicts or problems that could not be resolved. Mencius looked back on history by similarly stressing the importance of "benevolence": "The Three Dynasties gained 'the world'

(*Tianxia*) through benevolence and lost it when they were not benevolent. The decay and flourishing, preservation and perishing of nations depend on the same principle. If the ruler is not benevolent, he will not be able to protect all within the Four Seas; if the nobles are not benevolent, they will not be able to protect the state temple; if the officials are not benevolent, they will not be able to protect their ancestral temples; and if scholars and commoners are not benevolent, they will not be able to protect their lives" ("Li Lou" (A), *The Book of Mencius*). When the state of Qi defeated Yan and won vast territory, Mencius warned the King of Qi that other countries were preparing to fight Qi because Qi had not implemented benevolent government in a timely way. He advised that Qi allow the prisoners of war it had taken to return home, desist from plundering valuable goods from Yan, discuss with the people of Yan their selection of a new king to rule them, and withdraw its people from Yan. By doing this, other states would not form alliances to attack Qi. Mencius even distinguished between those rulers he designated "kings" and those he called "hegemons"; the former derived their strength from the morality of benevolence and righteousness, and the latter relied on force and power while merely paying lip service to ethical principles. Therefore, the king in ethical and moral aspects must serve as an exemplar for his people, so that "if the sovereign is benevolent, all will be benevolent, and if the sovereign is righteous, all will be righteous" ("Li Lou" (B), *The Book of Mencius*). In the governance of a country, Mencius provided many examples and hypothetical scenarios, but subsequent events did not evolve as Mencius predicted; the court of Qi did not listen to his advice and did not implement a policy of benevolence, but such a statement saying it finally fail for this reason was hardly convincing.

In Mencius' philosophy, his discussion of the concept of "Heaven" (*Tian*) and "the people" (*min*) is both important and interesting. Mencius posited an invisible cosmic power called "Heaven", which was the supreme commander arranging everything. Thus, in discussions regarding whether Yao passed his authority on to Shun by conferring the "Empire" (*Tianxia*) to him, Mencius reminded people that no such transfer could have taken place because no Son of Heaven (as the supreme ruler or emperor was styled) has the power and ability to confer the *Tianxia*, literally "that which is under Heaven", on anyone, because this is a decision that can only be made by "Heaven" itself. Mencius outlined how such a transfer of power should proceed: The Son of Heaven would select and recommend candidates to "Heaven", which would then silently exercise its power to accept candidates and let the people know who the new "manager" of "the world" (that which is under Heaven) would be. "Heaven" is invisible, untouchable, and silent but is made manifest through the specific words and administrative actions of the Son of Heaven, the feudal lords, and the leading officials. Explaining this process was difficult, but Mencius provided examples to clarify his thinking:

"Shun assisted Yao in government for twenty-eight years, a task beyond a mortal and being in fact the work of Heaven. After the death of Yao, when the three years' mourning was complete, Shun withdrew from the son of Yao and retired to the south of South River. The feudal lords of the nation who had attended court rallied not to the son of Yao but to Shun, litigants went not to the son of Yao but to Shun, and those who composed and sang folksongs eulogizing not the son of Yao but Shun; therefore, I say it was Heaven that gave Shun the throne. It was only after this that Shun went to the nation's seat of government and occupied the throne of the Son of Heaven. If before this time, he had taken up residence in the palace of Yao and applied pressure on the son of Yao, this would have constituted usurpation and would not have been the workings of Heaven". The Supreme Oath (*Tai Shi*) states: "Heaven sees as my people see, and Heaven hears as my people hear". Thus, it stated ("Wan Zhang" (A), *The Book of Mencius*).

From the monarch down to the common people, for thousands of years there was no objection to this proclamation of "Heaven" which underpinned the relationship between the fate of the nation and Heaven, the individual and Heaven, and inevitability and Heaven. If the monarch was brutal, he would ultimately die a violent death having lost Heaven's mandate, and he would have gained a bad reputation for all time.[29] This would of course be understood as a monarch violating "Heaven's will", as was the case for example of Emperor Yang (596–618) of the Sui dynasty, who was excessive in conscripting his subjects into forced labor, in launching military expeditions, and in spending money recklessly. He therefore came to be seen as a tyrant and was believed to have infringed excessively on the will of Heaven, namely by "lacking in benevolence" as

[29] "A ruler who oppresses his people in the extreme will be slain and his kingdom will perish. If a ruler's oppression is somewhat mitigated, his life will still be endangered, and his kingdom weakened. He will be styled the 'Dark' or the 'Cruel', and although he may have filial sons and affectionate grandsons, he will never shake off his nickname for a hundred generations" ("Li Lou" (A), *The Book of Mencius*).

the Confucians saw it, then Heaven could condemn him to be killed by his rebelling subjects in a mutiny. Matters of regret, especially if they were unintended or tragic outcomes, were also understood to be a failure of "Heaven" to respond. To this day, Chinese are fond of saying that "people act while Heaven watches", which not only expresses aversion and disgust for what is malevolent or evil, but also serves to clarify a personal moral position. Later emperors would use formulaic expressions like "upholding Heaven and destiny" that might also be generally explained as deriving from the ancient sages, but the right to interpret "Heaven" has varied from ancient times to the present according to circumstances, players, places, and times.

Many people have noted Mencius' emphasis on "man", and in addition to emphasizing that the king should be kind to the common people and govern with benevolence in order to establish a harmonious state without enemies, he went as far as saying: "Benevolence is man, and harmony between them is the Way" ("Jin Xin" (B), *The Book of Mencius*). This might suggest that Mencius upheld notions of democracy similar to those of today, but in fact the love and obedience extended by the common people to benevolent government mainly reflected a basic need for food, clothing, shelter as well as security, nothing more comprehensive, and in an age still deficient in its degree of civilization, this seems to have sufficed. In any case, Mencius' philosophy consistently exemplified ideas of love, benevolence, and compassion, as well as constant concern for others, and was not simply limited to personal considerations. This was why he was disgusted by the doctrines of Yang Zhu (395–335 BCE) and Mo Di (c. 468–376 BCE): Yang Zhu because of his overemphasis on the "self" and his disregard for the importance of the monarch; Mo Di because his doctrine of "universal love" lacked the hierarchical concerns of Mencius' benevolence and righteousness and dismissed the importance of the position of the father which, at least as Mencius saw it, was contrary to the basic teachings of Confucianism. Mencius, like Confucius, left to posterity many notable sayings which have become aphorisms covering various situations. These include:

> Those who labor with their minds govern others, while those who labor with their strength are governed by others. Those who are governed by others support them, while those who govern others are supported by them. This is a universal principle throughout the world. ("Teng Wen Gong" (A), *The Book of Mencius*)

> The definition of the great man is one not corrupted by wealth and honors, one not swayed if reduced to poverty and ignominy, and one who does not bow to power and military force. ("Teng Wen Gong" (B), *The Book of Mencius*)

> When the men of antiquity achieved their ambition, they conferred benefits on the people; when they did not achieve their ambition, they cultivated themselves and became illustrious. If poor, they attended to their own virtue in solitude; if successful in society, they extended their virtue throughout the land. ("Jin Xin" (A), *The Book of Mencius*)

> When the Way prevails throughout the empire, the Way must accompany one's person; when the Way does not prevail, one's body will perish with one's principles. ("Jin Xin" (A), *The Book of Mencius*)

Since Confucian philosophy always sought to defend the hierarchy of its Way, it was of course adopted by rulers of successive generations, although they regarded Confucianism as a moral creed to be followed mainly by their subjects, and they expected to present it in the most concise and clear way for their subjects to follow.[30]

Surveying imperial governance by successive emperors, we find that while Confucian dogma may have provided ethical admonition supporting "civilian or literary administration" (*wenzhi*), was every

[30] When the Kangxi Emperor (r. 1662–1722) was young, he composed a set of maxims titled the *Sacred Edict*, a code of conduct based on Confucian principles which people throughout the nation were called on to follow. For example: "It is decreed that filial piety forms the basis, and talent and abilities are of secondary importance"; "Knowledge of the vessel [of ethics] has priority over literature and arts"; "All study should be of orthodox writings, all who teach must be orthodox teachers; genuinely defend the true rites and righteousness, vigilantly maintain integrity and a sense of shame". ... "A renowned Confucian scholar who has a noble conscience outside the court will serve the nation as a worthy official". This *Edict* was then posted in each town and village and officials of all ranks throughout the country were required to regularly give lectures on the maxims to the general population. During the reign of his successor, the Yongzheng Emperor (r. 1723–1735), this *Sagely Edict* was greatly expanded and became known as *Amplified Instructions on the Sacred Edict*. During the Guangxu reign (1875–1908), the *Amplified Instructions on the Sacred Edict* became mandatory and could be enforced. As China embarked on diplomatic relations with other countries, the *Amplified Instructions on the Sacred Edict* were translated and published in several languages. Even Chinese studying abroad were required to attend lectures on the *Sacred Edict* conducted by the Overseas Study Management Bureau every seven days.

emperor consciously able to conform to it? As the thinker Han Fei (280–233 BCE) saw it, it was not possible to rely solely on "benevolence" in governing. At least Qin Shihuang realized from the beginning that Han Feizi's ideas were in line with his own views, and he agreed with Han Feizi's writings to the extent that he even said: "If I can meet this man and 'journey' with him, I will die without regrets!" ("Biographies of Laozi and Han Fei", *Records of the Historian*) Han Feizi is considered to be representative of the Legalists, but prior to him there were: Shen Dao (c. 390–c. 315 BCE), a contemporary of Mencius, had stressed "power" (*shi*), and was what we would today call authoritarian; Shen Buhai (c. 385–337 BCE) advocated "craft" (*shu*), which was essentially methods and strategy; while Shang Yang (c. 390 BCE–338 BCE) emphasized "law" (*fa*) which could be understood as laws and regulations. Yet Han Feizi synthesized the ideas of these three earlier Legalist thinkers, emphasizing the unity of "law", "craft", and "power", all of which he regarded as indispensable. Han Feizi agreed with the idea of Xun Kuang, better known as Xunzi (c. 313–c. 238 BCE), that "the nature of man is evil" and disagreed with Mencius' idea that "the nature of man is good", saying that everyone has "self-interest", which is almost what we today call selfishness. In this philosophy, the relationships between people are relationships of mutual use, a principle that even characterizes the relationships between a ruler and his courtiers and between father and son. For example, high rank, salary, and rewards are conferred by a ruler on his subjects as a reward for loyalty and, conversely, a subject is loyal only in order to gain fame and advantages. Therefore, Confucian benevolence, righteousness, ritual (decorum), wisdom, and faith were regarded as not providing solutions for any substantive problem unless drastic rewards and punishments were the measures used to implement action. In this way, the ruler must develop a legal system so that all people comply with its implementation, and as a result rewards and punishments are imposed, which is how "the Law is compiled and documented in the official offices and then proclaimed to the people" (*Difficulties III*); the appointment, removal, and execution of officials embody the implementation of "craft", which remains concealed as "tricks hidden in heart". The supreme ruler then has the authority to enact "law" and exemplify "craft", and these are the role and implication of what is called "power". Han Feizi told rulers that Shang Yang's policy of governing the state of Qin focused on "law" while lacking "craft", so that while Qin was able to acquire the power to develop the wealth and military might of the state, the ministers also increased their power and this threatened the state's supreme ruler. As for Shen Buhai's excessive emphasis on "craft", this did not help the monarch formulate consistent rules and, as a result, in different periods there were inconsistent standards within laws and this led to unceasing conflict, because each subject has his own legal basis. So, both these approaches made it difficult for the king to achieve his desired hegemony over the "empire" (*Tianxia*). Therefore, the monarch had to always cling to "power", by always exerting controlling power over the formulation of laws, the implementation of laws, and determining whether anyone was breaking laws; in other words, everything should be in the hands of the monarch, so as to attain and consolidate his rule. The Qin Emperor certainly endorsed and implemented this philosophy. Though some might suggest that it was surely a good thing to formulate laws and decrees, the key thing here is that the power to make laws and decrees was exclusively in the hands of the monarch, which determined that everything in the country could be changed in accordance with his will. Such laws were thus an individual's laws, and in the exercise of absolute power ("power"/*shi*) the laws were thus arbitrary, not to mention that the "craft" of ruling was secret, so no one knew the ideas and intentions of the king at any time, which is why successive ministers had no sense of security and would at the same time use their power to attack each other. The fate of common people could at any time be decided by officials at all levels. Seen in this way, Confucianism might in fact be decorative moral propaganda, but the craft of the Legalists was a tool in the hands of rulers that served to bring about real effects. Later rulers generally used the teachings of both these schools in accordance with their own ruling needs, which became the basic feature of the historical drama played out by the integrated "Qin-Han polity" until the Late Qing period.

Another school of thought which in contrast expressed a transcendental attitude was the school known as Taoism. The ideas of the philosophers labeled "Taoists" were the antithesis of Confucianism. According to the Taoist view, the Confucian notions that resulted in "losing one's life as a result of upholding the Way" or "martyring oneself in order to uphold the Way" were simply unnecessary and even misguided. Taoists maintained that the world, whether or not one changes it, does not depend on decisions one makes deliberately. The ritual and restraint venerated by the Confucians invariably limit people's natural feelings and desires and restrict their freedom. The relationship between the world and people is natural and spontaneous; society is also composed of people, so man's emotions and moods and attitudes to existence all determine the requirements and rationale of society, the state, and the system. In *Liezi*, Yang Zhu is quoted as saying: "If in ancient times a man could contribute a single hair to improve the world (nation), he would not do so; if you asked the whole world to support him, he would not accept it. If everyone refuses to contribute a single hair and makes no effort to improve the world, the world will be well governed of itself". In the same way in which Confucianism encompassed complexities, there were also differences between Taoist thinkers. People regarded Yang Zhu, who was a contemporary of Mencius, as a precursor of the early Taoists because Yang's concern for the "self" and disregard for the world seemed similar to that of Laozi and Zhuangzi. However, in terms of the basic tenets and clarity of the Taoists, Laozi (c. 570–c. 471 BCE) is still generally regarded as the founder of the Taoist school.

Since Confucius is thought to have asked Laozi about "the rites of Zhou", Laozi may have been an older contemporary of Confucius. Laozi was a "historian" at the Zhou court, responsible for managing the archives. Like Confucius, Laozi spent time in the state of Lu, but he eventually went to the state of Qin to live as a recluse. In compliance with requests from followers, Laozi wrote his classic *Lao Zi*, also known as the *Dao De Jing* (Classic of the Way and the Power).[31] Like *The Analects*, *Lao Zi* is a terse text with very short sentences, which is normally understood as different in expression from today's Chinese language. Moreover, the repeated interpretation and translation of these classics demonstrate the textual difficulty and ambiguity of their refined phraseology. The method of interpretation based on specific linguistic and historical contexts merely provides a relatively academic treatment of wording. To understand Taoist thought, people always begin with *Lao Zi*'s first chapter:

[31] Like *The Analects*, *Lao Zi* was originally simply a collection of comments, with no chapters, and was not designated as a "classic". It is also difficult to describe it as a coherent discourse (exposition), and it is not appropriate to use the words "system" or "complete" to describe such works by the ancients. Only in the Han dynasty was it edited and divided into chapters by Wang Bi, and this became the version that is commonly known today; punctuation was later added, but at every stage of editing an editor brings his own ideas to the text.

> The Way that can be articulated is not the constant Way; the name that can be named is not the constant name.
> Nothingness was the name of the beginning of Heaven and Earth; existence was the name of the mother of all beings.
> So be constantly in 'nothingness', if one desires to observe its secrets,
> Be constantly in existence, if one desires to observe its manifestations.
> These two are really the same, but diverge in name as they emerge; being the same, they are called mysteries,
> Mystery on mystery, the gateway of all secrets.

According to Laozi's philosophy, there is something called the Way, but even though it can be called the Way in words these do not encapsulate the constant Way. We can use the word "name" to express the form of the "Way", but Laozi at the same time also said that this "name" is not a constant "name" though it could be explained. It is very interesting that the philosopher used the word "nothingness" to describe the situation of the world in primordial disarray; he named "existence" as the origin of everything in the universe. He stressed that we should always observe and understand the mystery of the "Way" from the perspective of "nothingness", but we could usually only observe the manifestation of the Way from the perspective of "existence". "Nothingness" and "existence" have a shared source but are named differently. Yet both can be described as abstruse and remote. It is the ultimate path for understanding the mysteries of the cosmos, Heaven and Earth, and all things. He was telling people that an understanding of the extremely profound and mysterious "Way" requires a process of observation and consciousness that progresses from "nothingness" to "existence". In short, an exhaustive study of the several dozen characters quoted above could hardly be clearly understood even with a substantial volume. Chinese characters are essentially hieroglyphics, and so the character for "Way" presents an image of life as a head that is walking. We understand it to mean a "road", a "way", or a "path". However, Laozi's "road" is not a "road" in the general sense but refers to a nameless natural path, trajectory, or order ("inevitability" or an eternal "essential power", in modern terminology), but it is difficult in Western languages to use any one word to translate the concept. Reading Taoist thought does not entail a rush to understand every word in the text; in fact, if one has endless interpretations of each sentence within the text, one can find an entry point for understanding Chinese culture, and with the extensions, derivations, associations, and even repetition of individual phrases or sentences, one could connect all his knowledge already in mind. This is the charm of Laozi's writing. Indeed, to understand Taoism intellectually requires extreme caution, because unlike most Confucian writings in which the author's purpose is obvious, the language of Taoist thinkers is not easily accessible, any misunderstanding might lead to the partiality for metaphysics. Today's scholars are of course accustomed to looking for "laws" or "a consistent thread" running through classical works to enable them to classify or categorize what they read, but in reading Taoist thought it is actually better to allow sentences to empirically develop or move towards meaning. For example, the *Lao Zi* text is often also called the *Daode Jing*. While the two characters that make up the collocation "*daode*" have the modern meaning in Chinese of "morality" in fact they are two different concepts: *dao* (meaning the "Way") and *de* (meaning "power". Firstly, we read: "The Way is the vast ravine (abyss), ancestral to the ten thousand things [i.e., all things]" (*Laozi*, Chapter 4). Another example: "The Way begets a unity; that one divides in two, the two turn into three, and from that three come the ten thousand things" (*Laozi*, Chapter 42). In these two passages the "Way" is clearly the origin of the universe; could the "power" then simply be understood as the manifestation of intuitive feelings? According to Taoist tenets, if this "*de*" (power) is imbued with sociality, this does not measure up; yet if it is only the manifestation of "*dao*" and lacks social elements, how will a person be able to manifest himself or herself? There is no doubt that Taoist doctrine was not intended for "natural persons" ("persons living within nature"), but rather to teach a person how to respond appropriately within society. If the "Way" as a "source" is natural, then why do people need to pursue it? If the "Way" is the rationale of a person's life, then what is the meaning of life? These are all questions to be considered when reading *Lao Zi*.

Passages in *Laozi* often appear to present, or hint at, conflicting meanings, problems, and relationships, as in these consecutive passages from Chapter 2 of *Lao Zi*:

> All people in this world recognize beauty to be beauty, and so there is ugliness; all recognize virtue to be virtue, and so there is evil.
> Thus existence and nothingness generate each other, difficulty and facility cause each other to form, as the long and the short shape each other, as the

high and the low lean towards each other, as the sound and the resonance harmonize with each other, and as what is front and what is behind follow each other.

Ultimately, Taoist thought was always fully understood and applied in the contexts of arranging one's life when feeling lost, dealing with conflicts with society when feeling confused, or having life-changing experiences. When Confucians urged intellectuals to follow the injunction to "cultivate one's person, manage one's family, rule one's nation, and pacify the empire" by devoting themselves to the state and society, Taoists were teaching people to be well aware of the true life and society when encountering difficulties on the path of "cultivating one's person, managing one's family, ruling one's nation, and pacifying the empire" and do not care about gains and losses. In the end, according to the Taoists, a man must transcend secular society so as to allow himself to be completely free and liberated.

The Way of Heaven benefits and does not harm, The Way of Man is action without striving. (*Laozi*, Chapter 81)

Zhuangzi (c. 369–286 BCE) had a philosophy similar to that of Laozi, he lived two centuries later, and certainly their view of the universe seems almost identical:

> Now the Way is imbued with emotions and trustworthiness, non-action and formlessness; it can transmit but not receive; it can be attained but not seen; it is based in itself and rooted in itself, and when Heaven and Earth did not exist, it had unquestionably existed for all time; it gave the spirits and rulers their spiritual powers, and gave birth to Heaven and Earth; to Tao, the zenith is not high, nor the nadir low; no point in time is long ago, nor by the lapse of ages has it grown old. (*Zhuangzi, The Great Supreme*)

Thus, the "Way" remains the ultimate cause and the ultimate destination of the world. This Taoist description and analysis of the "Way" as being both inexhaustible and unending were not seen to be excessive. However, as with Laozi's interpretation of the "Way", Zhuangzi's view that "all things are equal and as one" simplified all Taoism's complex problems, so that the dualities of more and less, of existence and nothingness, and of sameness and difference, now depended on the relativist perspective from which they were viewed. So, what were the boundaries? This was ancient relativism; this ongoing debate would prove endless when characters and words cannot fully describe the particularities and relationships of each thing. This mode of thought would invariably lead to simple induction, and the meaning and transformation of characters and words in this narrative process left too much scope for accommodation and interpretation. For example, Zhuangzi wrote: "The admissible is admissible; the inadmissible is inadmissible" Surely here he is removing all restrictions making judgments? "A path is made by walking on it; things are so by their being named". Here, a path is made by people walking, what path is made by man's design? The names of things are of course conferred on them by people, so what is he saying here? "What is so? It is the so of being so". Things are the way they are, so why do we need to question this? "What is not so? It is the not so of being not so". If things are like this, then there is no thing that is incorrect; everything has its own rationale. By extension, the difference between everything in the world is the difference itself; everything always has its own rationale, which is pointless to fathom. In the end, the deconstruction of one thing is the completion of another; and the completion of one thing is the destruction of another. Therefore, the deconstruction, completion, and destruction of things are all connected, and merge in Chaos ("reconnect as one"). Zhuangzi thus came to a bold conclusion: his view that the universe never possessed all things is the highest and wisest understanding of all. This is the rationale presented in the *Zhuangzi*'s·*Argument on the Equality of Things*. People find it difficult to go on discussing such sentences that do not state a problem in the manner of a Western philosopher,[32] but

[32] For example, the early Greek philosopher Thales, who lived in the fifth century BCE in the Greek colony of Miletus, regarded "water" as the origin of the world, and he argued that "everything is water". It would appear that Thales' "water" and the Taoist "Way" are essentialist concepts, but Thales' analysis of water includes questions, arguments, answers, and intention. Thales observed that there are all types of things in the world, but his observations of natural phenomena led him to conclude that the originating principle of nature and the nature of matter are ultimately water, in that water can be a liquid or solid, and between the liquid and solid states there is a continuous cyclical process generating physical forms that can be observed, analyzed, and comprehended, thereby raising the question of change to the level of philosophical discussion. Thales leads us to think about what is constant and about the changes water undergoes as it transitions between different states and forms. Finally, even if his conclusion that "everything is water" is not consistent with observation and evidence, it alone proves that an understanding of the world can be achieved, because the conclusion provides a logical starting point for subsequent argumentation. What matters is not the water, but the analytical logic associated with why it may or may not be water. In this way, people cannot simply provide any unsubstantiated argument, because their conclusions must also depend on observation

they can lead to endless ideas and associations. In both the East and West at this time thinkers were searching for the origins of the world and humanity: What is the world? How did the world come about? How will the world change? Human beings were confronting the world as intuitive, perceptive, reflective, articulate, and linguistically expressive beings, and they expressed all such inquiries through the medium of language to similar questions.

In particular, in explaining the forces of nature or the universe, Zhuangzi emphasized the contrastive properties and roles of stillness and motion, opposition and transformation:

> Yin and Yang reflect each other, cover each other, and regulate each other. The four seasons succeed each other, give rise to each other, and slay each other. Likes and dislikes, avoiding this and moving towards that: this is how things then arose. Female and male are two halves that constantly exist. Security and danger interchange, as calamity and good fortune give rise to each other. Slowness and urgency are in constant friction, while gatherings and dispersals occur. (*Zhuang Zi · Ze Yang*)

Like Laozi, Zhuangzi was poor, but although he was a drifter and wore tattered clothes, he was extremely relaxed and humorous. When Zhuangzi wanted to borrow rice from the river superintendent, the official said he could lend him rice after the local taxes had all been paid, so Zhuangzi told him the following anecdote:

> Yesterday on the road I heard someone shouting and saw a catfish lying in a rut made by the wheels of a cart to one side of the road. I asked the fish: "What's wrong?" The fish replied: "I am a messenger of the Dragon King of the Eastern Sea. Sir, will you save me? A bucket of water would be enough, or a liter of water would be ok!" I replied, "No problem. But I'm now on my way to an audience with the King of Wuyue. The water level in these upper reaches of the Yangtze River will shortly be rising, so you will be okay when it reaches you?" The fish was very angry, "I have lost my water and have nowhere to live. I am not asking much, but a bucket or

and evidence—this is the starting point of early Western philosophy: ideas cannot depend on endless conceptual interpretation, and words must be quickly chosen to conform to the logic of the observation and analysis.

liter of water would save my life. But given that you have such important things to discuss, you'd better return via the local store where you'll find me dried out and on sale!" (*Zhuang Zi* · *Waiwu*)

Zhuangzi imparts a wealth of meaning through such vividly humorous anecdotes that convey the truths he seeks to impart.

The Confucian and Taoist classics require careful reading, because these two schools of thought provided far-fetched interpretations of each other's teachings throughout their development, but the basic differences were obvious. The Confucians engaged with the world in order to solve national and social political problems, but the Taoists advocated rejecting the world and emphasized observing, experiencing, and conforming to nature, while expounding the principle of "non-action as the way of handling all things", which meant that by not going against the will of nature, all would be safe and carefree. The Taoists saw this as the way to solve problems related to physical and mental health as well as personal problems. The Confucians were fully cognizant of the importance of social relations (maintained through the establishment of a hierarchical structure), while the Taoists argued that society needs to be governed by non-action, otherwise the world is disorderly: "Heaven does nothing and so finds serenity; the earth does nothing and so comes rest" ("Supreme Pleasure", *Zhuang Zi*). The Confucians acted knowing what could not be done, while the Taoists simply abandoned efforts on behalf of human beings in the social sense. It is particularly worth noting that the Confucians not only had no interest in physical labor but were disdainful to varying degrees of skills in actual production, while the Taoists who wanted to understand the movements of nature and investigate its mysterious origins could obliviously conduct experiments in alchemy, even though they had no possibility of deriving science from their magical arts. It would seem that the defenders of Confucianism were content to live in society and frequent ancestral temples, oblivious to the environment, and for the sake of establishing "righteousness" could even sacrifice themselves in order to attain Confucian "benevolence". By contrast, the advocates of Taoist ideas remained hidden in the mountains and forests, avoiding both the blessings and disasters perpetuated by man and leading pure lives of non-action roaming freely as their goal. Confucians called them "floating recluses". However, people are creatures of experience, and even if the desire to withdraw from the world is inborn, in real life it is difficult to fully accomplish, and so those who try to attain a quiet and peaceful life may ordinarily have some Taoist yearnings but in daily life may possibly only be able to indulge them a little, without demanding perfection. More often, when those who frequent the imperial court and work as officials in government offices encounter frustrations or even complete failure in their careers as officials, they also might adopt Taoist attitudes to life. They then often escape back to their hometowns where they work the fields or gardens and withdraw to mountain glades with friends to drink wine and chat, discussing the difficulties of life and the beauty of nature. For such men the vague formulation praising "the harmony of Heaven and Man" becomes their mantra.

In short, being close to nature and maintaining harmony with it have long been widely shared emotional sensibilities among Chinese people, who maintain great respect for and attachment to nature, which can be fully appreciated through the prominence of traditional landscape painting (*shanshui-hua*) among the classical Chinese arts. In such paintings, man is depicted as only a part of nature, so that the position of the figure in the landscape is insignificant, like an ordinary tree or stone maintaining harmony with nature. As in the words of "*Zhuangzi · Autumn Waters*": "I am situated between heaven and earth, like the small stones and trees in the mountains".[33] Therefore, the emergence

[33] The Chinese term "landscape [painting]" (*shanshui*) is different from the general Western word for a geographical vista or "landscape", which Chinese translate as "*fengjing*". The Chinese term for a landscape painting comprises the words "mountain" (*shan*) and "water" (*shui*) as the earliest pictographic expressions of physical phenomena in nature, indicating that in ancient times a section of mankind used these two words as imagery to correspond to their understanding of nature. This meaning of "landscape" in landscape painting may have begun without a sense of boundaries—the river winds into the distance and the hills roll on without end, while the Western word for a geographical "landscape" is made up of "land" and "-scape", which suggest a selected or defined scene within nature. From an etymological point of view, the earliest German term "Landschaft" did not express the natural landscape but indicated a geographical area defined by a political boundary. The usual Chinese sense of "landscape" indicates a post-observational delineation of part of the natural land, regardless of whether it is presented as an image on paper, silk, or canvas.

Malcolm Andrews writes in the chapter titled "Land into Landscape" in his book *Landscape and Western Art*: "'Landscape', cultivated or wild, is already artifice before it has become the subject of a work of art. Even when we simply *look*, we are already shaping and interpreting. A landscape may never achieve representation in a painting or photograph; none the less, something significant has happened when land can be perceived

and connotations of Chinese landscape painting are related to the painter's experience, background knowledge, and world view. In the year 353, a group of Chinese poets held a gathering at the Orchid Pavilion, in Shanyin (present-day Shaoxing, Zhejiang province), which was a significant turning point. The basic reason for the gathering derived from the custom of gathering to offer sacrifices beside natural waters twice annually, in the spring and autumn, in order to exorcise "demons and malign forces". This was originally a somber event, but, after the Han dynasty, this outdoor sacrifice evolved into a playful gathering, and the sacrifice to eliminate demons merely provided a pretext for the literati to enjoy a seasonal excursion to a natural setting where the real purpose was to drink wine and compose poetry in appreciation of the natural scenery, as well as to be invigorated by nature. Some of the poets in attendance described this event in verse:

> Today I have travelled here
> My spirit soars, my mind at peace
> ……
> This joyful gathering is a seasonal excursion
> Our hearts open up and our spirits soar
> (Wang Suzhi, *Orchid Pavilion Poems*)

> Relaxed among the hills and streams
> We easefully forget the reins that bind us
> (Wang Huizhi, *Orchid Pavilion Poems*)

as 'landscape'. We may well follow an impulse to sketch or photograph a particular tract of land in view and call the resulting picture 'a landscape', but it is not the formal making of an artistic record of the view that has constituted the land as landscape. Whether or not we are artists, we have been making this kind of mental conversion for centuries. The habit is part of the whole history of our relationship with the physical environment, and the visual tradition of landscape representation from the start has been one vital element in that relationship". Ref: Malcolm Andrews, *Landscape and Western Art*, Oxford University Press, 1999, p. 1. According to Malcolm Andrews' logical conclusion, the process might, therefore, be formulated as twofold: land into landscape; landscape into art. Malcolm Andrews adds to and revises the views of Kenneth Clark presented in *Landscape into Art*. Ref: Kenneth Clark, *Landscape into Art*, London, 1949.

An explanation via etymology can also be explained by reference to the second chapter of the book, "Subject or Setting?" In short, in the Western language world, landscape is associated with the meaning of the physical world's urban boundaries, suburbs, and background.

Again we turn to the mountains and waters
To dispel the gloom that binds us
(Sun Chuo, *Preface to Orchid Pavilion Poems Written on the Third Day of the Third Month*)

Such a state of mind is little different from the sentiments of people in any period undertaking a pleasure trip to a natural setting. However, in the closing years of the Western Jin dynasty, the unbridled spread of Taoist metaphysics led to a proliferation of abstruse poetry; the quest for immortality and the attainment of the Way became important reasons for people venturing into nature, so that the praise of nature became imbued with the idea of meditation or of undertaking a long mental journey.

To the present day, we have little surviving evidence about the situation of landscape painting in the Tang dynasty (618–907), although the paintings titled *Painting of Wangchuan* (Wangchuan tu) and *Riverside after Snow* (Jiang gan xue ji tu) attributed to the prominent Tang dynasty poet Wang Wei (701–761) are frequently cited (but given that today we can only study Wang Wei's landscape paintings via copies made by Guo Zhongshu [?–977] or Yan Wengui [967–1044], artists who lived much later, we have little reliable evidence of Wang Wei's work). For research purposes, the most likely elements of painting that we can extract from the concept of landscape painting in the Tang dynasty are to be found in the relatively quiet genre of bucolic poetry in which Wang Wei was important. Wang Wei's motivation in returning to the countryside at the age of 26 to live as a hermit seems not to have been a failure to realize his ambitions, but a traditional yearning to which he succumbed. In fact, when he was 27 years old Wang Wei served as an official in Qishang (in what is today northern Henan province) but took up residence there as a recluse in the following year. When he was 29 years old, he moved to the capital Chang'an where he lived in retirement, but when he was 34, he took up residence in Songshan mountain again as a recluse, and at 41 again retired from officialdom and lived as a recluse in the Zhongnan mountains outside the capital. From 742 to 756, he served as an official but at the same time he was operating the Bieye Garden in Wangchuan, leading a semi-reclusive life. After the chaos of the An Lushan Rebellion and subsequent unrest, he reluctantly served as an official, but still lived on a farm in a picturesque rural setting. His poems reveal the peaceful life face to face with nature. For example,

The empty hills look fresh after rain
The chill night air brings autumn
The bright moon shines among the pines
The clear spring flows across the rocks
Bamboo rustles, the washer woman returns
Lotuses move, the fishing boat launches
Let it go whether the spring comes or goes
As a recluse I could stay here for a long time
(*Autumn Dusk by My Mountain Home*)

Indeed, the later copies of Wang Wei's *Painting of Wangchuan* reflect a rural landscape of idealized tranquility. In his *Record of Renowned Paintings of the Tang Dynasty*, Zhu Jingxuan evaluated Wang Wei's paintings as characterized by "mountain valleys with winding glades, clouds scudding above flowing waters, thoughts transcending dusty travails, and wonders fashioned by his brush". The relationship between the work of art itself and such near-literary descriptive comments is perplexing; later, Jing Hao simply praised the work for its "simple use of brush and ink to create a rhythmic breath that is lofty and pure". In the words of these critics, we see the articulation of early internalized elements of what would be called "literati painting" (*wenren-hua*). It is owing to Su Shi (also known as Su Dongpo, 1037–1101) that Wang Wei's painting has come to be regarded as obviously exemplifying the concept that poetry and painting are one; the formulations that proclaim that "there is poetry in the painting" and "there is painting in the poetry" have become customary language in Chinese painting theory, obscuring the psychological difference between the perception of the image and of text.

Of course, the painter begins by respecting what the eyes see, which is the general experience of painting. For example, as a wine loving "hermit" fond of cultivating the Way, Fan Kuan was described in the following way in volume 1 of *Xuanhe Huapu*, a catalogue of paintings named for the Xuanhe reign-period (1119–1125) in which it was compiled: "After he followed a divination and took up residence as a recluse among the rocks and forests at the foot of Mount Taihua in the Zhongnan mountains, he had an indescribable vista in all weather. Here he could silently enter into a spiritual encounter and from the tip of his brush a myriad of rocks and valleys emerge or suddenly we find ourselves traveling with him along a secluded path through mountains, and even in summer heat we feel we must wrap up to keep warm".[34] How could the author of *Xuanhe Huapu* know how Fan Kuan felt after gazing at his "indescribable vista" and affirm his silent "spiritual encounter"? Before the thinking of the Song dynasty literati assumed its definitive form, Fan Kuan's paintings already exemplified the overriding concern for the absolute truth of nature among painters of the Five Dynasties and early Song dynasty period. As Michael Sullivan observed in *Symbols of Eternity*: "Fan Kuan's aim is to make us feel that we are not looking at a picture at all but actually standing on those rocks beneath that great cliff, until, as we gaze on it, the sounds of the world about us fade away, and we hear the wind in the trees, the thunder of the waterfall, the clatter of hooves on the stony path".[35] However, Su Shi commented: "In recent years, only Fan Kuan abbreviated ancient techniques, and the results were slightly vulgar".[36] This comment about the vulgarity of Fan Kuan's work seems in fact to be a reaction to or disdain for experience and facts, or what we might call realistic elements.

Indeed, from the Five Dynasties to the beginning of the Northern Song dynasty, there were significant differences in the brushwork techniques of northern and southern Chinese painters. For a long time after the painter Ju Ran (fl. tenth century), a court painter of the Southern Tang dynasty (937–975), the south produced very few other well-known painters, and while imperial patronage, with its concomitant economic support and authority, ensured that the northern painting style occupied a dominant position, painters in the north were limited by their dry brush "hemp fiber" (*pima cun*) painting method when painting landscapes. However, during the Southern Song dynasty (1127–1279), there was interaction between northern and southern painters in brushwork methodology, so that the four major painters of the period (Liu Songnian, Li Tang, Ma Yuan, and Xia Gui) all used three major brushstroke methods known as the hemp fiber, axe-cut, and curling cloud techniques. In the end, the differences between what came to be called the Northern and Southern schools were supplanted by the techniques promoted through the style of the Imperial Academy of Painting. Differences in brush and

[34] *Xuan He Hua Pu*, Vol. 11.

[35] Michael Sullivan, *Symbols of Eternity: The Art of Landscape Painting in China*, Oxford: Clarendon Press, 1979, p. 69.

[36] *Dongpo Ti Ba*.

ink style were discussed in excessively abstract terms by painters and critics in different periods, and only when we examine the works themselves can we discern the subtle changes in style that emerged from the more free-flowing use of brush and ink.

Ideas are usually presented through text, and the painters known as "literati painters"[37] were from the beginning associated with a class of

[37] What is usually called "literati painting" (*wenren-hua*) is not simply equivalent to what is called "literati brush-and-ink" (*wenren-bimo*). The uses of the term "literatus/literati" (*wenren-shidaifu*) can also be very different, so it is a superficial mistake to define "literati painting" as a painting style or genre. The literati of the Song dynasty emphasized technique, describing their own paintings as "ink play" (*moxi*), and they were contemptuous of "resemblance" (*xingsi*, literally "form and likeness", i.e., realism), and venerated the "intention" (*yi*) created in a work. So, the two words, *xie-yi* ("writing the idea") were a convenient portmanteau term to describe their painting. Perhaps the earliest description of "literati painting" was Su Shi's description of what he called "scholar painting" (*shiren-hua*). Su Shi also drew a distinction between "scholar paintings" (*shiren hua*) and "painters' paintings" (*huagong-hua*), believing that the former focused on "the spirit" (*yiqi*), and the latter only dealt with "the external appearance" (*pimao*). The "scholar painting" is based on the ability to capture the essential shared quality of an object or its "constant *raison d'être*" (*changli*), and this interpretation is related to "spirit" or "temperament" (*xingqing*). In his essay titled "Jingyin-yuan hua ji" (Notes on paintings of the Jingyin Academy), he proposed using the contrastive concepts of "constant *raison d'être*" and "constant form" (*changxing*) to distinguish between "scholar paintings" and "painters' paintings" (*gongren-hua*):

> When I once discussed painting, I took the view that people and animals, palaces and rooms, containers and utensils all have their constant forms, whereas mountains, rocks, bamboo, trees, water, waves, mist, and clouds all lack constant forms but have a constant *raison d'être*. If the constant form is missing, everyone knows; but when the constant *raison d'être* is not in place, even those who understand painting might not realize. Therefore, all those who set out to deceive the world in their quest for fame will necessarily make use of that which is without constant form. However, the loss of constant form ends with what is lost and cannot destroy the overall effect; if the constant *raison d'être* is not in place, everything is lost. When the form is not constant, then one must take care with its *raison d'être*. The artisans of this world may be able to create forms perfectly, but when it comes to the subject's *raison d'être*, unless one is a superior man or outstanding genius one will be unable to achieve it.

In the 1920s, Chen Shizeng pointed out that "literati paintings" was not a term for paintings executed by literati: "Paintings that contain the nature of literati within them and embody the artistic temperament of the literati". Ref: "*Wenren-hua zhi jiazhi*" (The value of literati painting", *Huihua Zazhi* (Painting Magazine), 1921, issue no. 2. However, without some explanation and categorization of just what is meant by "the nature" and "the artistic temperament" of literati, this explanation is problematic.

elite scholars, and it is very easy to think of Su Shi as an exemplar of such important court officials. In the Song period, the painters who lived among the common people never had any influence, and the legitimacy and lasting influence of literati paintings that seemed to be far removed from the style of the imperial court drew equal support from the legitimatizing Confucian ideology and from Taoist attitudes to life. The political views of Su Shi, the original advocate of literati painting, were based on the argument that since the scholar-bureaucrat class was a major component of the country's strength, why not improve its quality by applying a strict Confucian spirit and high-level culture, thus raising the "ethical quality" of the entirety of government institutions? However, Confucian philosophy, epitomized by certain classics, can be explained using various interpretations because of differences in the intellectual background and education, political status and aims, as well as the group interests and goals, of those with authority, so there were obvious differences in the interpretation of "ethical quality".

The actual and conceptual meanings of the early Chinese terms "scholar" (*shi*), "educated official" (*daifu*), and "literatus" (*wenren*), vis-à-vis the modern concept of "intellectual" (*zhishifenzi*) in different historical periods, are also of great importance. However, records left to us show that as long as we know that in the Song dynasty those who advocated ideas about paintings and brush-and-ink methods different from the style of the imperial court style were in fact responsible Confucian intellectuals of that era and that they maintained the position that the classics of Confucius were their personal destiny ("the scholar's ideal Is the Way") ("Liren", *The Analects*),[38] then we can appreciate the basic knowledge and educational background of these advocates of literati painting. The Confucian classic *The Great Learning* (Da Xue) states that if one wants to rule the country, one must first regulate one's family, and to regulate one's family one must first regulate oneself: "To regulate oneself, one must first rectify one's mind, and to rectify one's mind, one must first be sincere in one's ideas. To be sincere in one's ideas one must first have innate knowledge". The rectification of mind, sincerity, and innate knowledge were subjects of discussion over the many centuries from the time of the earliest Chinese philosophers until the interpretations of the Classics by the Song dynasty Neo-Confucian scholar Zhu Xi (1130–1200) were

[38] "Li Ren", *The Analects*.

legitimized and recognized as orthodox. The antipathy of Song Neo-Confucians to technology reached its zenith in the writings of Cheng Yi (1033–1107).[39]

As a writer and advocate of "literati painting", Su Shi has an outstanding reputation for the genius of his literature, poetry, and calligraphy. In the field of prose Su Shi is known as one of the "Eight Prose Masters of the Tang and Song", in *shi* poetry he is venerated together with Huang Tingjian (1045–1105) as "Su-Huang", in lyric poetry (*ci*) he and Xin Qiji (1140–1207) are celebrated as the "Su-Xin" and, in calligraphy, which is inextricably linked with painting, Su Shi together with Huang Tingjian, Mi Fu (1051–1107), and Cai Xiang (1012–1067) are called the "Four Song Masters". This underscores the importance of writing for literati painting. The text in Su Shi's widely quoted "Two poems written for the Chief Scribe, Wang of Yanling's painting *A Sprig of Blossom*". One of them has long puzzled many writers and researchers:

> If one talks of a painting as forms and likeness
> One sees things like a neighbor's child.
> If one writes of a poem in terms of itself
> One will fail for sure to know the poet.

[39] "Q: Can the writing of poetry be learned? A: If one tries to learn it, one must strive to conform to the personality of a poet. But if one has to expend such effort, this is a bad thing. An ancient poem reads: "Chanting these five words, He broke his heart". In other words: "It is tragic to break one's heart for just five words". This poem makes a good point".

"Q: Does writing prose harm the Way? A: It does. I think that if the text is not dedicated to an idea it will not work, and if it is dedicated to an idea then the intention will be limited to this, and so how can the writer be expansive like heaven and earth? *The Book of History* relates how 'toying with an object destroys the will" and writing is also a form of "toying with an object'".

The following anecdote introduces two prodigies of the High Tang period—Zhang Xu, the master of grass-stroke calligraphy, and Lady Gongsun, the renowned dancer of her time, extolled for her sword dance: "Q: Zhang Xu was practicing grass-script calligraphy, when he saw a porter arguing with a princess who was blocking his way, after which the "princess", Lady Gongsun began practicing her swordsmanship. Zhang was then enlightened in his brushstrokes. Is this not a case of mind moving along familiar paths of thought and then reaching a point of inspiration? A: Yes. Zhang Xu had a sudden inspiration, but if he had not first been absorbed in thinking, how would he have reached that point? Unfortunately, Zhang Xu remained absorbed in calligraphy, but if he had in that moment of inspiration shifted his mind to the Way, what would he not have achieved? "

(Ref: *Er Cheng Quanshu* (Complete Writings of the Brothers Cheng). The Brothers Cheng are Cheng Hao (1032–1085) and Cheng Yi (1033–1107).

Poetry and painting follow the same rule:
Inspired craft creates purity and freshness.[40]
(*Dongpo Shi Jizhu* [Anthology of Su Dongpo's *Shi* Poetry Annotated], fasc. 27)

Expressing "poetic sense" was in fact a tradition of Confucian education, and the meaning of poetry and painting following "the same rule" is the focus for understanding Su Shi's argument. However, what is that makes Su Shi supremely confident that poetry and painting follow "the same rule"? Su Shi in his poem titled "On a stone screen collected by my teacher Ouyang [Xiu]" wrote:

The most artful and clever thoughts cannot be expressed,
They turn to mist and are absorbed in stone.
Never have masters of painting been ordinary scholars,
Their depiction of objects is like that of poets.
(*Dongpo Shi Jizhu* [Anthology of Su Dongpo's *Shi* Poetry Annotated], fasc. 30)

Obviously, the technique of "metaphor" (*bixing*) in poetry entered the field of painting under the influence of Su Shi's statements.

The poems and paintings of the Tang and Song dynasties have been regarded by Chinese people of all times as exemplifying the period of Chinese culture's greatest achievements. Even during the most intense period of the Chinese modernist art movement in the mid-1980s, no avant-garde artist denied this. Like Italian art of the European Renaissance, Tang and Song literature and art were regarded as an inexhaustible resource for later generations: resplendent, extraordinary, refined, and subtle; in general, no compliment was regarded as excessive. In those works that variously present philosophical attitudes, we are always able to find the spiritual background of Confucianism and Taoism. However, even the landscape and pastoral poetry of the High Tang period, the term for a golden age of culture that lasted for approximately fifty years of the Kaiyuan and Tianbao eras (c. 713–755), were examples of classical literature created by writers who were recluses who became officials or officials

[40] *Dongpo Shi Ji Zhu*, Vol. 27.

who became recluses, but everything depended on the context in which the literary artist created his work and his corresponding philosophical state of mind. Most people recognize that poems which simultaneously present an individual's inner depths and a shared universal psychology, like the lyric poetry of Li Yu (937–978) of the Southern Tang, are always profound and enduring masterpieces that examine life's turning points and inner characteristics:

When do the spring flowers and autumn moon end
for one with so many memories?
Last night in my upstairs room the east wind blew
A painful reminder of the moon shining in my land, now lost!
The carved balustrades and marble steps must still be there
But the painted faces will have changed
If you ask how much my sorrow has grown,
I can only stare, as spring's swollen rivers surge east.
("To the tune *The Beauty, Lady Yu*")

The spirit and temperament exemplified by this poem continuously permeate Chinese spiritual civilization as it has evolved to the present day,[41] blending the Confucian way of life with the Taoist way of nature

[41] For example, the Southern Song general, Xin Qiji could also compose tragic and moving lyric poetry:

Below the gloomy terrace flow clear streams,
Between which many passers-by shed tears
To the capital now lost I gaze northwest,
But all I see are endless hills.

The green hills cannot hold back
the waters surging east.
At dusk the streams grow sadder,
I hear a partridge cry in a distant glade.
(To the tune *Pusa Man*)

III

At the beginning of the Yuan dynasty, the courtly life of the literati of the Song ended abruptly. Because of the war and carnage that accompanied the Mongol conquest of China, painters, poets, and scholars fled Hangzhou, the final capital of the Song dynasty after it retreated to the south, to live in nearby locales like Wuxi, Suzhou, and Yangzhou. Political repression and further loss of power under the Yuan dynasty, together with the brutal cultural habits and controls imposed by the Mongol court, pushed the surviving intellectuals of the late Song dynasty further towards introversion. Symbols and metaphors like those used earlier by Su Shi became very common in the Yuan dynasty. Images closely related to nature—the plum, orchid, bamboo, and chrysanthemum, came to be repeatedly used as visual images that expressed an author's political attitude and moral sentiment. The "archaizing" attitude in this period of history was less a pursuit of interest than a decisive evasion and escape. The literati had no concept of the future, but of a past about which they could be proud, and the only way to express this new zeitgeist was with the help of history, or the use of past brush and ink techniques and attitudes to express complex heart-felt feelings. Painters were convinced that the nature they painted was completely divorced from real nature, but they could use their ink and line-work to create interesting paintings; this habit of not questioning nature or society subsequently became the established practice of the later literati. However, at the same time as Chinese traditional civilization was entering a period of convoluted evolution, the power of another civilization was gradually emerging.

One thousand three hundred and ten years after Zhang Qian's expedition to the west of China (now Central Asia), a 17-year-old Italian youth named Marco Polo (c. 1254–1324) accompanied his father and uncle on a journey east along the Silk Road. They traveled across ancient Persia, crossed the treacherous Pamirs, and by the time they arrived in the Mongol capital Shangdu, the journey had taken them nearly five years. It would be twenty-four years before they arrived back in their hometown of

Venice, but one year after returning Marco Polo was imprisoned in Genoa because a maritime war had broken out between Venice and Genoa. With the help of his friend, the romance writer Rusticiano of Pisa, Marco Polo related an account of his long journey, especially in China, which was eventually translated into dozens of different languages in many versions and published in English as *The Travels of Marco Polo*. *The Travels* played a major role in acquainting Europeans with the Orient, especially China, fueling the imagination and curiosity of Europeans about the outside world and generating new knowledge about the world and their place in it. Many subsequent geographical discoveries[42] made by explorers were regarded to have been inspired by *The Travels*.[43] Yet Marco Polo told

[42] In 1492, Columbus (1451–1506) on his voyage to the New World took his personal copy of *The Travels of Marco Polo* with him, in anticipation of having an audience with the Great Khan after arriving at his putative destination. This Latin version of *The Travels of Marco Polo* with Columbus' notes and annotations is now in the Columbus Library attached to the main cathedral in Seville, Spain.

[43] In different translations, translators made cuts or additions to suit the perceived needs of their market. However, the original manuscript was lost, raising questions about the veracity of the later version and whether Marco Polo and the others ever made the journey. Chinese only began to learn in the second half of the nineteenth century that there was such a book about China by an early European traveler. For example, on 1 October 1853, the Hong Kong publication *Chinese Serial* (*Xia'er Guizhen*, lit. "Gems from Far and Near") in its third issue reported in an article titled "Details of Western Traders" (*Xiguo tongshang yuanwei*): "The first to arrive on Chinese soil was called Marco Polo, and in all Western countries he is praised for being the first traveler to complete the journey".

As proof of the veracity of Marco Polo's account, we can cite the introduction to Yangzhou city in chapter 145 of *The Travels*: "The people are subjects of the Great Khan, they use paper money, and are idolaters. ... There is much trade and craft, and military equipment is made here in vast quantities. A great many soldiers live in and around the city". The Chinese translator of *The Travels*, Feng Chengjun (1887–1946) made a note on this passage:

> "Roughly thirty-five years after Marco Polo left China, Friar Odoric of Pordenone passed through Yangzhou and variously recorded its name as 'Iamathay', 'Iansu', and "Ianzu'. He noted that in the city "our Minor Friars have a house. And here also are three churches of the Nestorians. This is a noble city, and hath a good forty-eight to fifty-eight *tumans* or fireplaces, every *tuman* being ten thousand. In this city are to be had in great abundance all kinds of things on which Christian people live. And the lord of this city hath from salt alone a revenue of five hundred *tumans* of *balis*; and a *balis* being worth a florin and a half, thus a *tuman* maketh fifteen thousand florins ... This city hath also a vast amount of shipping". Feng Chengjun tr., *The Travels of Marco Polo*, Shanghai: Shanghai Shiji Chuban Jituan, 2006, p. 316. Feng Chengjun cited the French translation of *The Travels*

a very detailed story about China—its politics, warfare, wealth, religion, daily life, and folk customs, all of which provided a mythical Orient for eager European audiences. However, the time required to complete a trading expedition from the Central Plains to Venice was very long, and the traveling merchant was subject to natural disasters, banditry, tribal wars, and regional plagues on the way. These factors meant that the cost of such a journey prohibitively increased. All the difficulties and obstacles of the overland route became fears that could never be dispelled about developing these communication lines. The overland "Silk Road" evoked wealth or conversions to merchants and missionaries, respectively, but it was also a road of slavery, warfare, and plague, and for those who wanted to exchange goods or spread their faith, the cost to live on was often too high. More than one thousand years after the Silk Road was first opened up, the Polo family members endured countless hardships and expended massive efforts to make the journey, which at times brought them perilously close to death, but they did succeed in returning home and this gave people incredible faith. We are sure that when humans choose ways and paths to survive and develop, they will always discover new possibilities by applying their intelligence, so the history of only taking the overland route to develop trade and disseminate religious faiths would be transformed.

On 12 October 1492, Christopher Columbus (Cristoforo Colombo), who had grown up reading *The Travels of Marco Polo*, inadvertently discovered the American continent. His yearning for adventure and wealth led Columbus to end up not in Asia but in the Americas, even though he initially thought he had reached the Oriental world of gold and spices. The discovery was, of course, decisive, but when news of the New World reached Europe, it triggered an acrimonious conflict between the Empire of Portugal and the Crown of Castile. In the end, the two European kingdoms of Portugal and Spain would sign the *Treaty of Tordesillas* on 7 June 1494, naively but ambitiously believing that the whole world

of Odoric of Pordenone. This translator has cited Sir Henry Yule tr., *Blessed Odoric of Pordenone: The Travels of Friar Odoric*, originally published in 1866 but in a recent edition: Grand Rapids, Michigan and Cambridge, UK: William B. Eerdmans Publishing Company, 2002, pp. 132–133.

could be divided by such a treaty.[44] In fact, as early as the second half of the fifteenth century, the Portuguese royal family had begun to recruit navigators or adventurers to explore the Orient, and John II (João II) of Portugal, known as the "Perfect Prince", spared no effort to extend Portugal's known coastline, even if many mariners died on dangerous and arduous voyages. It was not until 10 July 1499, when Vasco de Gama led the surviving one-third of his crew back to Europe from Calicut to dock at Cascais near Lisbon, that the world's landscape immediately changed in a radical way. Indeed, the *Treaty of Tordesillas* impelled the Portuguese royal family to plan a maritime expedition to India, and the competition to gain the advantage in maritime trade was a thrilling and frenzied fight for wealth between Portugal and the Spanish kingdom in the late fifteenth and early sixteenth centuries.[45] Conflicts and wars based on religious,

[44] A papal bull, *Romanus Pontifex*, issued on 8 January 1455 by Pope Nicholas V (1397–1455) agreed to give territory discovered on the African coast to the Portuguese, as well as endorsing Portugal's existing occupation of Cuerta. Spain was deeply dissatisfied with the hegemony of the emerging Portuguese empire, and in 1479, Spain (Castile and Aragon) and Portugal signed the *Treaty of Alcaçovas*, which limited the scope of Portugal to all islands on the Atlantic seaboard of Africa discovered to date, though giving to Portugal any other islands between the Canary Islands and Guinea that might be discovered or captured in the future. However, Columbus's impending discoveries would completely overturn all that, and the world's imagination. In Portugal's view, Columbus' discovery of the New World should be seen as a violation by Spain of Portugal's rights granted by the Pope. However, in order to spread the Catholic faith and expand the power of the Church, Pope Alexander VI (1431–1503) agreed to the Spanish occupation of all the land discovered by Columbus. In order to regulate the conflict between Portugal and Spain, in 1494 the two countries signed the *Treaty of Tordesillas*, and Pope Alexander VI, in arbitration, agreed to demarcate the border at 370 leagues west of Cape Verde, also known as the "Pope's Meridian". New "discoveries" to the east of the line would belong to Portugal, those to the west of the line to Spain, Spain and Portugal effectively dividing the whole world outside Europe between them. Although the maps used by the two kingdoms to divide the world into their respective spheres of influence are not preserved, the *Treaty of Tordesillas* would influence European colonial policy for centuries.

[45] Although Venice at the end of the fifteenth century was still regarded as the "gateway to the East", in a diary written in 1502, the Venetian merchant who also served for a time as Doge, Girolamo Priuli (1486–1567), as he turned from Venice to Lisbon, wrote in horror: "In this I clearly see the ruin of the city of Venice" (p. 189). Jerry Brotton also has a description of this moment of realization in his *A History of the World in Twelve Maps*:

> At its height in the mid-sixteenth century the Portuguese empire was dispatching more than fifteen ships a year to Asia, returning with an annual average of over 2,000 tons of cargo, rising to nearly double that towards the end of the sixteenth

economic, and cultural competition became more complex and acute after the voyages of Vasco da Gama, so much so that modern espionage geared to warfare began to obtain knowledge and information from the drafting, theft, and reproduction of maps.[46]

Just before Columbus was anxiously preparing to sail to the New World, the German geographer Martin Behaim completed his most famous work, the Nürnberg Terrestrial Globe which he dubbed the

> century. Nearly 90 per cent of Portugal's imports were made up of spices from the Indian subcontinent; pepper accounted for over 80 per cent of these spices. By 1520 the revenue of these imports represented nearly 40 per cent of the Portuguese crown's total revenue, although even that did not include the money collected from customs duties on trade moving in and out of Portugal's overseas possessions throughout the Indian Ocean. The wealth that flowed into Lisbon and the Portuguese crown's revenues enabled the kingdom to transform itself into one of Europe's richest empires. Portugal's wealth and power now lay not in the possession of territory, but in the strategic control of commercial networks that lay thousands of kilometers from the imperial centre. Unlike earlier empires built on the acquisition and control of land, this was a new kind of empire built of water.

Jerry Brotton, *A History of the World in Twelve Maps*, London: Penguin Books, 2012, p. 189.

[46] In response to the de facto rivalry between Portugal and Venice for control of Eastern trade, a letter written in August 1501 by Angelo Trevisan, secretary of the Venetian ambassador to Castile, to his friend Domenico Malipiero revealed how Venetians craved information on maps of the route to India and how difficult they were to obtain:

> We are daily expecting our doctor from Lisbon, who left our magnificent ambassador there; who at my request has written a short account of the [Portuguese] voyage from Calicut, of which I will make a copy for Your Magnificence. It is impossible to procure the map of that voyage because the king has placed a death penalty on anyone who gives it out.

Less than a month later, however, Trevisan wrote to Malipiero again, with a very different story:

> If we return to Venice alive, Your Magnificence will see maps both as far as Calicut and beyond there less than twice the distance from here to Flanders. I promise you that everything has come in good order; but this, Your Magnificence may not care to divulge. One thing is certain, that you will learn upon our arrival as many particulars as though you had been to Calicut and beyond.

Jerry Brotton, *A History of the World in Twelve Maps*, London: Penguin Books, 2012, pp. 189–190.

"Erdapfel" ("apple of the Earth").[47] This spherical construction inspired the ambitious Ferdinand Magellan to circumnavigate the Earth in what proved to be a successful voyage (22 September 1519–8 September 1522),[48] which changed the European view of the world forever. The world inhabited by man was transformed from a flat plane to a spherical planet, and a maritime competition to acquire global territory was now in full swing in both the eastern and western hemispheres.

However, 87 years prior to Columbus' discovery of the New World a series of major ocean voyages were undertaken by mariners visiting different countries. In 1405, a Chinese fleet set sail from Nanjing, comprising a number of vessels that were dozens of times larger than Magellan's ships and were manned by crews far more numerous, on what was in fact the first of seven expeditions to the South China Sea and the Indian Ocean staged over the subsequent three decades. The commander of these seven maritime expeditions was the great navigator Zheng He (1371–1433), who died at sea on the seventh expedition in 1433. The main aim of Zheng He's expeditions, unlike the purpose of the later European voyages of discovery, was not primarily to find riches, but rather to demonstrate China's awesome power by means of a fleet of enormous ships, to establish and consolidate the system of tribute, and to inform the world that China is a country with vast lands and enormous wealth and resources that does not require any outside help and is the undisputed center of the world. Indeed, Zheng He's flagship vessel was more than 40 meters long and had a displacement of nearly 10,000 tons. By the time of the fourth expedition (1413–1415), the Chinese fleet comprised

[47] As early as the third century BCE, Greek astronomers concluded that the earth is spherical. In 1492, the German navigator Martin Behaim teamed up with the painter George Glockendon to create the world's first globe, dubbed Erdapfel (German for "Earth apple"). The globe consisted of two hemispheres made of laminated linen, reinforced by wood, and covered with a map drawn by Glockendon. Although the globe does not include the Americas because Columbus has not returned to Spain, and there are also inaccuracies, such as the over-large area of Japan (Cipango) and its position considerably to the south of its actual location, the globe presents a familiar cartographic conception of the Earth, as we know it today. The globe was placed in the reception hall of the Nuremberg City Hall until the sixteenth century, when it was returned to the Behaim family. In 1907, the globe was transferred to the Germanic Museum in Nuremberg.

[48] Although Magellan was killed by local tribes when he landed on the island of Mactan in the Philippines in April 1521, most of the 237 crew members died on the voyage, and eventually only eighteen or nineteen survivors arrived in Seville in September 1522, after which they were received by the Spanish king, Carlos I.

more than 200 ships which were divided according to function, with more than 27,000 personnel on board the last expedition.[49] However, the Chinese fleet stocked with expensive goods such as porcelain and silk fabrics failed to attract foreign products of comparable value—even though the giraffes brought back to China were repeatedly admired and painted. Although Zheng He and the emperor he served, Zhu Di (1360–1424), better known by his reign title as the Yongle Emperor, may have had the intention of consolidating the tributary system, Zheng He not only intervened in the internal strife of Sumatra, but also provided military support for the King of Malacca at the fortress of the Straits of Malacca to get out of the control of Ayutthaya (a kingdom in present-day Thailand), in order to establish a major entrepot for Chinese trading vessels. However, as early as 1371, the first Ming Emperor Taizu, Zhu Yuanzhang (1328–1398) had made a ruling, which in his later years was issued as an injunction contained in his *Record of the Instructions of the Ancestor of Imperial Ming*:

> The barbarians of the four directions are all confined in places made inaccessible by mountains and seas; acquiring their lands provides little and acquiring their people is not useful for us. If they do not assess the situation and violate our borders, they are threatening; if they do not present a danger to China yet we attack them with our troops, this is also threatening, as I fear that my descendants would rely on China's wealth and power and, greedy for victory in war, would fight for no reason and inflict many casualties. We must not forget to never do this.

In 1371, Emperor Taizu also said: "The ancients had a saying: 'Having extensive lands is not a long-term security plan, as people's travails will be a source of chaos'" (*Veritable Record of Ming Emperor Taizu*, fasc. 68). Obviously, the expansion of Ming territory was not a basic intention behind politics, and the economy, of the dynastic rulers. At the same time, there is no information to show that Emperor Zhu Di and his expeditionary commander Zheng He were like the kings of Portugal and Spain and their adventurous navigators, who were eager to expand their territory and wealth as far as possible, sending astronomers, cartographers, and fearless sailors to explore continuously in uncharted territory.

[49] In the spring of 1518, King Carlos I of Spain provided Magellan with merely five vessels for his circumnavigation of the world, only one of which survived the voyage.

In summary, on the basis of its wealth and strength and given that excessive opening might bring instability to its internal order, China had no interest in seeking out possibilities through exploratory voyages into the unknown.

It is surprising that, although Marco Polo's *Travels* had been published in Europe over nearly two hundred years and versions of the book in different languages abounded, until 1508 the Portuguese who wanted to travel by sea to China almost knew nothing about China.[50] For example, in an instruction to an expedition leaving in April led by Diogo Lopes de Segueira to "find" Malacca, the king of Portugal Manuel I (1469–1521) said:

> The project is, You will ask of the Chinese [called "Chins" in original text], where and how far they come from, how often they go to Malacca, where they do business, what goods they are trading. You will try to know the design of their ships, if they go back in the same year they arrive, if they have administrators and houses in Malacca or elsewhere. You will try to find out whether they are rich merchants, strong or weak fighters, if they have weapons or artillery, how they dress, if they are big. You will ask whether they are Christian or pagan, if their country is vast, if they have more than one king, if Moors or any other believers other than they live among them. You will also find out what they believe in and worship, what their culture is and what their boundaries are.[51]

De Segueira arrived in Malacca on 11 September 1509, and encountered three Chinese ships, but he returned to Portugal in 1510 without obtaining more information about China. In 1511, Portugal occupied

[50] As early as 1425, the brother of the Portuguese navigator Infante D. Henrique (1394–1460), better known to English readers as Prince Henry the Navigator, visited Venice and, after learning about commercial activities and navigational facilities, brought back a copy of *The Travels of Marco Polo*. Two manuscript copies of *The Travels* were found in the library of King Duarte (1391–1438) of Portugal in the latter half of the fifteenth century, after the king's death. In 1502, the German printer Valentim Fernandes published a Portuguese text of *The Travels* in Lisbon, on the eve of Vasco da Gama's second trip to India. Yet the Portuguese king's advice to de Segueira would seem to indicate that no knowledge of China had been gleaned from *The Travels*.

[51] See: Donald William Ferguson ed., "Introduction", *Letters from Portuguese Captives in Canton, Written in 1534 and 1536: With an Introduction on Portuguese Intercourse with China in the First Half of the Sixteenth Century by Donald Ferguson*, Bombay: Education Society's Steam Press, Byculla, 1902. Reprinted from *The Indian Antiquary*, a journal published from 1872 to 1921.

Malacca, which would lead to the failure of the Portuguese envoy to arrange to visit China not long after, because the Portuguese were utterly unaware that this action directly undermined the interests and arrangements of the Ming dynasty's tributary system, even though the Chinese emperor had no idea that the trading networks in East Asia, as well as those of the Pacific and Indian oceans, were about to change dramatically. In 1517, a fleet under the command of Captain Fernão Pires de Andrade who had been appointed by the King of Portugal to escort the first Portuguese ambassador, Tomé Pires (1465—1524/1540) from Malacca to China.[52] On 15 August, Captain de Andrade, carrying a letter of peace and friendship from the King of Portugal, first arrived at Tuen Mun Island. The Portuguese informed the Chinese naval commander that it would require a Chinese naval captain ("Pio") to arrange for a pilot to guide the ship to Guangzhou. However, Captain de Andrade was told that he could not enter the city without the permission of the city's governor. A few days later, Captain de Andrade presented as ordered a gift to the Pio, but this had no effect. After many unsuccessful attempts to negotiate, the Portuguese captain decided to arrange unilaterally to proceed to Guangzhou, but his ships unexpectedly encountered a storm and were damaged. Captain de Andrade arranged to repair two ships and first sail to the port of Nantou, where he would meet the Pio and apply to enter Guangzhou. At the end of September, the Portuguese could proceed to Guangzhou. After a show of authority and imperial dignity by Guangzhou's top executives, de Andrade and Pires received permission from Guangzhou's officials to enter the port. This was the beginning of Portuguese diplomatic engagement with Chinese officialdom.[53]

[52] Tomé Pires (c. 1465–c. 1540) was an apothecary for King João II of Portugal. In 1511 he sailed to the Orient, going first to India and then to Malacca. He wrote his first book, *Suma Orientale* (fill title: *Suma Oriental que trata do Mar Roxo até aos Chins*, English: Summary of the East, from the Red Sea up to the Chinese), which introduced the Portuguese to Asia, with a special chapter treating China, although he had learned about China only indirectly. However, he notably introduced China's tribute system. This made Pires eligible for appointment as Portugal's first envoy to China.

[53] Before the formation of the tribute system of the Ming dynasty, foreign ships were not allowed to enter China at all. It was in the earliest years after the establishment of the Ming tribute system that China allowed Portuguese envoys to enter Guangzhou, "in the name of presenting tribute". The asymmetry of the rules governing this type of trade meant that the Portuguese mission to China was condemned to failure.

The differences between the Portuguese and Chinese in protocol and cultural background, however, coupled with the lack of requisite ethics and basic education on both sides, led the Chinese emperor either to disdain or doubt the genuine trading intentions of the Portuguese mission. In particular, from Malacca came continual reports of the Portuguese occupation, their destruction of the long-established pattern of tribute trade, and their disruption of people's livelihoods, together with demands that the Ming government punish them.[54] As a result, the Portuguese envoy's request to meet the Chinese emperor and establish trade relations with China failed and the mission was utterly unsuccessful. Tomé Pires was taken prisoner and eventually died in China.[55]

In the sixteenth century the Portuguese scholar and historian João de Barros published a work in many folios titled *Asia*,[56] and in a chapter

[54] It was in a letter to the Chinese Emperor that the King of Malacca described the deplorable local actions of the Portuguese, and his fury and disappointment with them:

> The Feringhi [the Chinese name for the Portuguese, which was a Euro-Arab loan-word, *editorial note*] are brazen bandits, who occupied and plundered land in Malacca, killing many people, looting, and imprisoning many locals. The remaining local inhabitants were ruled over by the Feringhi, which saddened and enraged the King who fled in fear to Bintan taking with him the seal presented to him by the Chinese emperor, and he remains there. My brothers and relatives fled elsewhere. The Portuguese envoy who is now on Chinese soil is an imposter, lacking all sincerity, who intends to deceive the Chinese monarch, imploring the emperor to show him pity. As the King of Malacca, I am deeply saddened to present these gifts and to request that You make troops available to aid and rescue us so that we might recover our lost land.

Source: Wan Ming, *Zhongguo Rongru Shijie de Bulü: Ming yu Qing Qianqi Haiwai Zhengce Bijiao Yanjiu* (China's Steps into the World: A Comparative Study of Foreign Policy in the Ming and Early-Qing), Beijing: Forbidden City Publishing House, 2014, pp. 189–190. Wan Ming takes this passage from: Rui Manuel Loureiro ed., *Cartas dos Cativos de Cantão: Cristovão Vieira e Vasco Calvo (1524)*, Macau: Instituto Culturel de Macau, 1992, pp. 35–36.

[55] It was in the years 1513–1519 that the navigator and geographer Francisco Rodrigues most likely published his *Livro da Geographia Oriental* (Book of Oriental Geography), which was clearly the result of a great deal of information gathering by the author in India and the Spice Islands, rather than relying on imagination as European writers had previously done. He also has the distinction of being the first geographer to use the name "China" on a map, specifically on the periplus documenting his voyage from Malacca to Guangzhou.

[56] João de Barros, *Décadas da Ásia* (Decades of Asia), in four volumes titled consecutively: *Primeira Década da Ásia, dos feitos que os Portugueses fizeram no descobrimento dos*

(specifically volume III, part I, Chapter VII) of that work with the lengthy title "Account of the land of China and its situation, being mainly an account of the city of Canton, the place discovered by Fernão Pires de Andrade"), he left the following description of the Great Wall of China:

> Now we will focus on discussing one of the wonders of the land of China, which is a wall that crosses it and at its greatest length we calculate it runs between the forty-third and forty-fifth latitudes, starting in the west at the walls and moat of a city called Ochioy [Jiayu], which lies between two very high mountain ranges, where the wall serves as a local pass and gateway, and extending eastwards until it is surrounded by another high mountain range and arrives at a headland on the eastern coast. Its length seems to be more than two hundred leagues. It is said that construction of the wall was ordered by the king of China to defend his land from the people we call Tartars or Tancas (another name for them), even though lands of these Tartars north of the wall had already been seized. The wall is depicted on a map of the country made by the Chinese, with the names of all mountains, rivers, cities, and towns marked on it in their script.[57]

Although the record here is not very precise or accurate, it is the first record of the Great Wall of China since the time of Marco Polo and the European writers of the Yuan dynasty, though Marco Polo in fact made no mention of it. This suggests that only when a new generation of adventurers arrived in China would it be possible to obtain a true picture of the country, and de Barros' account falls far short of touching on even the basic details of this country with such a long history and cultural richness.

mares e terras do Oriente, Lisbon: Germão Galherde, 1552; *Segunda Década da Ásia &c.* Lisbon: Germão Galherde, 1553; *Terceira Década da Ásia &c.*, Lisbon: João da Barreira, 1563; and *Quarta Década da Ásia &c.* (as edited and reworked by *cosmógrafo-mor* João Baptista Lavanha), Madrid: Imprensa Real, 1613.

[57] João de Barros' *Décadas da Ásia* has never been translated into English in its entirety. This translation is based on a passage from the third *Década* of Barros' massive work included in the Chinese selection: João de Barros (Portugal) and Bernardino de Escalante (Spain), He Gaoji tr., *Shiliu Shiji Putaoya Wenxue zhong de Zhongguo: Zhonghua Diguo Gaishu* (China in Sixteenth-Century Portuguese Literature: A General Description of the Chinese Empire), Beijing: Zhonghua Shuju, 2013, p. 27.

Early in the Qin and Han dynasties, China had developed a model of tributary relations based on a sense of its own absolute political and economic superiority.[58] In the view of successive Chinese emperors, foreign kings were nothing more than subjects and they were accorded subordinate positions within the tributary relationship. Chinese emperors always claimed to maintain peace and harmony throughout "the world" (*Tianxia*) by providing military protection and bestowing property, thus retaining the absolute authority of the dominant state. Because his power was absolute, the emperor would rather give more to a vassal state and not calculate the value of tribute exchanged in order to present an image of benevolence, kindness, generosity, and magnanimity. The Chinese emperor regarded himself as the head of the household of the world and, like a father giving gifts to his children, he did want to appear calculating, so that "the generosity of patronage" became the pride of the Chinese monarch and the embodiment of his grace. However, adhering to the principle of "gazing on everywhere the sun and moon shine, whether far

[58] The tribute system, which dates back to the third century BCE, was initially adopted by monarchs of the states of the Central Plains region to deal with forces from surrounding areas, who were presented with titles, credentials, and seals (*cefeng*) in the feudal manner also implemented through the inner kingdoms under the Zhou royal house which extended the notion of a central dominant power and was intended to maintain peace with outlying areas and states that were essentially foreign. The formulation that "all under Heaven is the land of the sovereign" was a concept of "the world" (*Tianxia*) that appeared in the Zhou dynasty, but it was in fact no more than a wishful formulation. However, as the Central Plains continued to expand, the scope of the concept behind the presentation of titles, credentials, and seals changed, and the process also extended to include the so-called "Hua-Yi" (literally, the "Chinese" people and the adjacent "barbarians" or non-Chinese, a distinction which did not recognize the fact that, according to Chinese histories of antiquity, many Hua groups had Yi origins). After the Han dynasty's Emperor Wu defeated the Xiongnu, the unequal nature of the relationship between the centrally located Han overlord and the outlying foreign vassal state, as defined by the tribute system, became markedly apparent. In "The Annals of Emperor Wu", fascicle VI of *Han Shu*, the annotation by Yan Shigu (581–645) reads: "All states denoted as vassal states retain the name of the state but belong to the Han dynasty, and so are called vassals". The administrative status of vassal states was what the Han dynasty attempted to implement throughout the Western Regions. However, as China's central regimes changed, this type of tribute relationship proved unstable, and from the year 291 to the Yuan dynasty, with the exception of the Tang dynasty and some periods of division, the tribute relationship was muted. In fact, a stable and systematically functioning tribute system was not reestablished until the Ming dynasty. In 1371, Zhu Yuanzhang who founded the Ming dynasty and ruled as Emperor Taizu listed fifteen countries as "barbarians that do not need to be subjugated". These included Korea, Japan, Greater Ryukyu, Lesser Ryukyu, Thailand, Sumatra, and Java.

or near, with benevolence" (*Veritable Records of the Ming Emperor Taizu*, fasc. 37) was of course only possible when based on the premise that the world was absolutely subject to the supreme authority of China; accrediting foreigners as vassals by awarding them seals and titles was also based on the foreigner's acceptance of a subordinate position in a hierarchical system, which was not possible for the Portuguese, even though they behaved with courtesy and patience as much as was possible. In fact, the Ming dynasty's system of tribute was effectively a state monopoly of overseas trade, which melded political diplomacy and trade exchanges into a unified authoritarian system. However, conducting trade in this manner by bestowing property and presenting tribute was not customary for, nor recognized by, the Portuguese. In the early Ming dynasty, the state strictly prohibited Chinese merchants from going to sea and foreign merchant vessels coming to trade, yet the Portuguese believed that trade should be conducted freely. This might explain why the Ming Emperor appeared to take no interest in the Portuguese demands, and why the Portuguese failed to analyze accurately China's lack of cooperation.[59] At this time, there was no possibility of compromise between the two trading systems, making friendly trade relations difficult to initiate.

The failure of the Portuguese embassy's visit to China led to the easing of bilateral relations more than thirty years later. However, the Chinese refusal to permit trade between Portugal and China led determined Portuguese merchants to go instead to the regions of Fujian (e.g., Zhangzhou) and Zhejiang (e.g., Ningbo) to engage in illegal commerce, and even become involved in the smuggling operations known as the "Japanese scourge".[60] This undoubtedly deepened the Ming dynasty's

[59] The Portuguese had some understanding of the tribute system, but in the early sixteenth century, due to the decline in the system coupled with the growth in private overseas trade and the relaxation of Chinese government controls over trade between private Chinese and overseas merchants, those Europeans who first arrived in China somewhat mistakenly believed that tribute vessels and private merchant ships were different in nature and so thought free trade was not problematic. Indeed, at this time Malacca which still had a tribute relationship with the Ming dynasty was in fact also beginning to trade freely with many other countries. When Zheng He's expeditions attempted to expand the scope of tribute trade into the Indian Ocean, the port of Malacca was already being visited by merchant ships bringing goods from Cairo, Mecca, Aden, Turkey, India, Central Asia, and Southeast Asian countries.

[60] Between 1401 and 1547 Japan sent only eighteen ships to China. In the meantime, in 1523, the trade representatives of two Japanese *daimyō* clans, the Ōuchi and Hosokawa, became involved in a brawl in Ningbo, and this prompted the Ming government to close

distrust of Portuguese and other European merchants, which in turn reinforced the "maritime trading ban" and even led to the Ming government ordering a prohibition of twin-masted vessels in August 1525. In December 1529, it was officially announced that any mariners in possession of concealed "foreign goods" or who had built large ships would be "harshly punished". As a result, strict prohibitions were imposed on building or leasing vessels, on inviting foreign merchant vessels, and even on cooperating with overseas official bodies.[61] This policy, which failed to reflect the growing maritime trade, fueled widespread discontent among civil society, and more and more Chinese people participated in the maritime smuggling trade, even joining the ranks of the "Japanese pirates".[62] Mixing with foreigners not only added new destabilizing

its Trading Department in Ningbo and stop the tribute trade with Japan. Thereafter, the "Japanese scourge" (*wohuan*), the Chinese pejorative term for illegal maritime privateer trading managed by Japanese, gradually emerged.

[61] It is generally believed that, unlike the Japanese pirates in the late Yuan and early Ming, the "Japanese pirates" during the Jiajing reign-period (1522–1566) of the Ming dynasty comprised Japanese pirates, Portuguese privateer traders, and Chinese pirates and maritime groups, who were all opposed to the Ming government's maritime ban policies and strived for free trade to prevail. This was contemporary with the beginning of the period of global maritime trade, and for those involved in the competition for maritime trade, there were huge risks resulting from maritime anarchy. Hence, the privateer phenomenon of "both trade and plunder" became very common, and the simultaneous rapid rise in maritime trade was a constant challenge to the irrational "legitimacy" of the Ming maritime ban.

[62] There is a great deal of documentary evidence of Chinese commoners joining the ranks of the "Japanese pirates" at that time, several examples of which appear below:

Example 1. "Sanzei dang" (Scattered bandit groups), fasc. 12, *Chouhai Tupian* (An Illustrated Discourse on Maritime Defense):

> Pirates do not necessarily first gather for a common purpose. Some are men with grievances that are difficult to resolve, and their anger prompts them to drift towards piracy. Some have the backing of a family or faction whose power will benefit pirates. Some have lost their livelihood and out of hardship do business with pirates. Some have lost their good reputation and throw in their lot with pirates out of pride. Some are indentured into piracy in order to eat as a result of poverty. Some have knowledge of *fengshui* (geomancy) that pirates wish to put to good use. Some have relatives who have been captured, and so they are willing to become involved with pirates. Some have been press-ganged into piracy because of their strength.

Example 2. "Huangming siyi kao", fasc. 67, in Zheng Xiao, *Wu Xue Pian*:

factors to coastal cities,[63] but also forced civilians to expand their power as much as possible under illegal circumstances, and Wang Zhi known as "king of the Japanese pirates" is a typical case. Wang was a merchant from Huizhou, and a murderous siege conducted by government troops forced him to flee to Japan to develop his own power base; he gradually became a major smuggler operating along the coasts of Zhejiang and Fujian, and even hired "real Japanese pirates", which demonstrated his extraordinary ability. In order to win legitimacy for maritime trade, he negotiated the "opening of trading ports" with the Ming authorities in order to reduce

> Poor commoners were compelled by the greedy to suffer as laborers to pay their taxes, and trapped by hunger and cold, they were forced to put to sea as pirates; such cases were thus not simply limited to the "crooked merchants" (smugglers) of Chaozhou, Huizhou, Zhangzhou, Quanzhou, Ningbo, Shaoxing, Huizhou, and Shexian.

Example 3. "Wobian shilüe", in *Jiajing Dongnan Ping Wo Tonglu* (Comprehensive Account of the Pacification of Pirates in the Southeast during the Jiajing Reign):

> Since maritime trade was halted in the first year [1522] of Jiajing, whenever foreign goods arrive, bribes must be paid to the smugglers. Over time, the smugglers became deceitful and overbearing. Unwilling to pay them, the foreigners berthed near offshore islands, and sent people to press their demands, but they were not successful. The foreigners lacked food, so they put to sea and resorted to piracy. Over time, more than a hundred ships were embroiled in piracy, and their daily raids meant that no one dared put to sea. Poor commoners itching for a skirmish began to go to sea and join up with the pirates. Thugs, prison escapees, dismissed officials, crafty Buddhist monks, unemployed scholars, unsuccessful students, and those lacking ambition, worked as agents and guides for the pirates. Thus, the followers of Wang Wufeng, Xu Bixi, and Mao Haifeng were all Chinese, and donning golden crowns and dragon robes these pirates proclaimed themselves the Kings of Pirate Island. They attacked cities and plundered villages, and no one dared to oppose them. Zhejiang was ruined.

[63] In 1556 Gaspar da Cruz, a Portuguese Dominican missionary, who had been in China for many years, wrote: "The Chinese who had been with the Portuguese and the Portuguese themselves had nothing to do all day, and so they began to commit robberies and they killed some commoners. These vile acts continually increased, and their victims were extremely vocal, not only appealing to provincial and local officials, but even appealing to the emperor".

Ref: Gaspar da Cruz's "treatise on things Chinese", the full title of which was *Tractado em que se comtam muito por estenso as cousas da China, con suas particularidades, e assi do reyno dormuz*, Ch. 23.

Japanese pirates and smuggling activity. The authorities promised to "tentatively allow private trading markets", so Wang Zhi turned himself over to the authorities and returned home. However, in 1559, he was nevertheless executed by the authorities and his head was paraded in public in Hangzhou, but this only exacerbated the growing pirate problem.

Of course, the official debate on whether or not to continue the maritime ban persisted, hinging on the question of whether to close off the country and stop tribute trade or whether to open up to private overseas trade. Finally, in 1567, the reality of the inability to ban maritime trade prompted the Ming government to announce the opening of a bureau for the management of customs clearance at Yuegang port in Zhangzhou, Fujian for Chinese merchants engaging in maritime trade. Prior to this, there had been years of attacks and sieges, and though after 1549 Portuguese merchants were able to travel between Fujian, Zhejiang, and Guangzhou, they were still subject to attacks by Chinese officials for being illegal. However, in 1553, the Portuguese captain Leonel de Sousa negotiated with local officials and obtained agreement that the Portuguese could use Macao as a base for doing business with China. In 1557, the Portuguese began "building accommodation" in Macao[64]; in 1582, the Liangguang Governor-General Chen Rui agreed that the Portuguese could officially reside in Macao under the "jurisdiction of

[64] Anders Ljungstedt (1759–1835), who worked for the Swedish East India Company and lived in Macao, has left an account in which he reports that in 1557 the Portuguese first gathered in Macao and were allowed by the local Chinese official to live there: "...the Strangers obtained liberty to erect on the desert island of Ama some sheds for drying goods, introduced under the appellation of tribute, ... By liberally feeding the nearest inspecting authorities the Foreigners were, by degrees, permitted to build substantial houses. This epocha [*sic.*] dates by the Peregrination of F. M. Pinto from the year 1557, though there is good reason from Dr. Morrison's 'View of China', to believe that Europeans came as early as 1535 to Macao and had in 1537 temporary shelters on the Island". It should be noted though Macao was in fact a peninsula, it was only by convention that it was described as an island. As Ljungstedt points out, the name Macao was derived from the local name Ama for the venerated Goddess of the Sea, Mazu. Ref: Anders Ljungstedt, *Contribution to an Historical Sketch of the Portuguese Settlements in China, Principally of Macao, of the Portuguese Envoys and Ambassadors to China, of the Roman Catholic Mission in China, and of the Papal Legates to China*, Macao, 1832, pp. 6–7. For an account of the settlement of Macao, see also: Louis J. Gallagher tr., *China in the Sixteenth Century: The Journals of Matthew Ricci: 1583–1610*, Book 2, Chapter 2, "The Chinese Expedition Is Again Attempted by the Jesuits", New York: Random House, 1953, pp. 127–135.

Chinese officials"[65]; and in 1583 a diocese was established in Macao, chaired by Bishop Melchior Carneiro, and this series of changes quickly

[65] In his *Diaries*, Matteo Ricci relates in compelling detail how a visiting Liangguang Governor, "Cinsui" [i.e., Chen Rui], who was "decidedly avaricious", "took advantage of the settlement of Macao" (p. 136), although the upshot was that he allowed Portuguese merchants and missionaries to reside there:

> As a good-will offering to the Viceroy, for fear he might interrupt the trading, the City presented him with a gift from the people, made up of a collection of things which they knew were specially prized by the Chinese. There was cloth of pure silk, which the Chinese did not know how to make at the time, pleated garments, crystal mirrors and other such novelties, valued in all at more than a thousand gold pieces. The representatives were received by the Viceroy with a grandiose display intended to frighten them rather than to do them honor, but when he saw the gifts, which were intended for such an emergency, his supercilious mien immediately disappeared. Then he informed them with a smile that everything might continue at the settlement as formerly, subject of course, to the rules of the Chinese governors. This was only a customary formal announcement because the Portuguese at Macao were governed by Portuguese laws, and other nationalities there lived as they pleased. Even the Chinese, when they became Christians, put aside their Chinese clothes and dressed as Europeans. The other Chinese were subject to the officials appointed there by the Canton Government.
>
> To return to the Viceroy or Governor, he insisted that he could take nothing for which he did not pay and questioning the interpreter as to the price of each article, he ordered the total amount to be weighed out in silver in the presence of his attendants. This he did because in this province it was forbidden under severe penalty for any government official to receive such a gift. Later on, he secretly sent a messenger to his visitors to tell them that the silver he had given them was for the purchase of another allotment of their novelties, which were to be delivered to him in person and privately. …

Ref: Louis J. Gallagher tr., *China in the Sixteenth Century: The Journals of Matthew Ricci: 1583–1610*, Book 2, Chapter 3, "Three Times in 1582 the Missionaries Are Admitted to China, but Fail to Establish a Residence", New York: Random House, 1953, pp. 136–137.

The above passage makes it clear that the permission the Portuguese missionaries received had not been issued through regular channels and that everything might change if the Viceroy were to lose his position. Ricci elaborates:

> Besides various other matters relating to the general good of the Province, the following, which concerns us very intimately, is to be noted with reference to those residing at Macao. Serious complaints have been made that various crimes and abuses of the law have been perpetrated at Macao, which are attributed to the Chinese interpreters employed by the foreigners. These interpreters are soliciting the strangers and teaching them the ways of our people. Most serious of all, we are all well informed that they have persuaded certain priests from abroad to learn the Chinese language and study Chinese letters, and that now these priests are

made Macao an important stronghold for global trade from the second half of the sixteenth to the first half of the seventeenth century.

In 1575, the Spanish arrived in China, hoping to secure a port like Portuguese-occupied Macao for trade and missionary work. In August 1598, the Spanish Governor of the Philippines sent a representative to China to request formally the right to trade, and before they won Chinese consent, the Spanish planned to amalgamate several houses to settle down at Hutiaomen port, but in the end they did not succeed. In 1602, the Netherlands formed the "Vereenigde Oostindische Compagnie" (Dutch East India Company) and in the following year sent representatives to China to secure the right to trade, but they also failed. In 1622, the Dutch joined with Great Britain in an attempt to force China to trade with them, but the Dutch were defeated by a Chinese garrison with the participation of the Portuguese. After this defeat, the Netherlands occupied Penghu, also known as the Pescadores, but in 1624 the Dutch were driven out by a Chinese force from Fujian and so they occupied Taiwan instead.

IV

Although the *Treaty of Tordesillas* codified an attempt by Portugal and Spain to divide the world between them, Pope Leo X further clarified this division in a papal bull *Dum fidei constantiam* issued on 3 November 1515, granting Portugal concessions to discover and occupy the lands "from the Cape of Bojador to the Indies, wherever situated, or even though in our day unknown". It stipulated that anyone who wanted to trade, fish, or even sail within this domain must have the permission of the King of Portugal. It could be imagined that, in return for this concession, the King of Portugal would finance the development of the Catholic Church in new lands, build churches, and send missionaries. With the age of great discoveries, it is not surprising that trade and faith irresistibly marched together into the Far East. George H. Dunne reminded readers

> demanding a residence at the Capital, in order to build a church and a private house. This we declare to be injurious to the realm, to which no benefit can accrue by admitting foreigners. The said interpreters will be put to a cruel death if they do not immediately desist from the practices mentioned.

Ref: Louis J. Gallagher tr., *China in the Sixteenth Century: The Journals of Matthew Ricci: 1583–1610*, Book 2, Chapter 3, New York: Random House, 1953, p. 143.

in his *Generation of Giants: The Story of the Jesuits in the Last Decades of the Ming Dynasty* that:

> It is impossible to doubt the genuine religious zeal of many Spanish and Portuguese rulers of the Age of Discovery. They were men of strong and ardent faith with a high conception of their obligation to extend the Kingdom of God. It was the realization of this fact which prompted the Holy See to give its support to the enterprise.[66]

Portuguese and other Europeans trying to reach the New World were surprisingly ignorant of what constituted "India", "China", the "Far East", and "Asia". After the Catholic Church was spreading with the support of Rome, and the Benedictine order had completed its basic ordering of European civilization, they initially thought they had completed full coverage for their faith and that their religion blended with culture seemed invincible. They were shocked and excited by the great discoveries being made, and since humans had space far beyond what they knew in the past, a new missionary phase was initiated.

Catholic missionaries initially followed merchants to these newly discovered lands with the rival "Europeanist" attitudes they had established, but they soon found themselves powerless to open China's doors. In 1563, for example, there were more than 900 Portuguese in Macao, where eight Jesuit missionaries had already begun their work. However, when in 1565 the head of the Jesuits there applied for permission from Guangdong officials to undertake a mission to mainland China, he was politely refused. Three years later, Juan Bautista Ribeira, a Spanish Jesuit who had unsuccessfully tried to enter China to preach, brusquely told the head of mission: "There is no hope of converting [the Chinese], unless one has recourse to force and unless they give way before the soldiers". He was not the only person to make such a suggestion, and a preacher named Alfaro even remarked: "With or without soldiers to wish to enter China is to attempt to reach the moon".[67] A new mission strategy was not developed until the Italian Jesuit, Alessandro Valignano

[66] Ref: George H. Dunne, *Generation of Giants: The Story of the Jesuits in the Last Decades of the Ming Dynasty*, Notre Dame, Indiana: University of Notre Dame Press, 1962, p. 8. The subsequent quotation from Juan Bautista Ribeira is from George H. Dunne, op. cit., p. 16.

[67] George H. Dunne, *Generation of Giants: The Story of the Jesuits in the Last Decades of the Ming Dynasty*, Notre Dame, Indiana: University of Notre Dame Press, 1962, p. 17.

(1538–1606), was stationed in Macao from October 1577 to July 1578. Valignano wrote to the general of the Society of Jesus: "The only possible way to penetration [of China] will be utterly different from that which has been adopted up to now in all the other missions in these countries".[68] Valignano arrived in Macao in July 1579 and, in November of the following year, went to Guangzhou, where the Italian Jesuit Michele Ruggieri (1543–1607) had accepted his advice and was learning Chinese. When Chinese officials later met with Portuguese merchants, they always invited Ruggieri to attend meetings, because he was beginning to understand and respect Chinese etiquette and culture. In 1583, Ruggieri and the newly arrived missionary Matteo Ricci were given permission to begin building the first Catholic building in Zhaoqing which they planned to use tacitly for their mission, but they must have had mixed feelings when they thought of the Spanish Jesuit Francis Xavier (1506–1552) who had arrived in China thirty-one years previously on a Portuguese merchant vessel but failed to secure entry into China from Shangchuan Island near Taishan in Guangdong where he died.[69] However, "zeal for the glory of God and the salvation of souls does not lie dormant; rather it inflames and energizes the hearts it captivates", and Xavier's successors knew that "chains and slavery and even a violent death were not worth considering, when there was question of liberating souls from the danger of eternal death in everlasting servitude", Ricci explained.[70] Now, we can say that the factors that really began to influence and change the course of Chinese history may be discovered in the work of the missionaries from another civilization.

The Italian Matteo Ricci (1552–1610) was a missionary who not only spread the gospel but also made a significant contribution to Chinese

Quoting A. Van den Wyngaert ed., *Sinica Franciscana, Relationes et Epistolas Fratrum Minorum*, II, p. 180.

68 Idem.

See: S. J. Henri Bernard, *Aux portes de la Chine* (At the Gates of China), Tianjin: Ēcole des Hautes Ētudes, 1933, p. 141.

69 Francis Xavier first arrived in Goa from Japan, leaving Goa in April 1552 to reach Malacca, where he was severely hampered by the Governor. In July, Xavier left Malacca for China. On 2 December, Xavier died of illness on the island of Shangchuan, where Portugal was trading with the Chinese.

70 Louis J. Gallagher tr., *China in the Sixteenth Century: The Journals of Matthew Ricci: 1583–1610*, New York: Random House, 1953. From Book Two, Chapter 1, "Blessed Francis Xavier Undertakes to Enter China, but Fails", pp. 121–123.

culture. He joined the Jesuits in 1571 and, at the age of twenty-five, went to Portugal where he waited to travel to India. In Portugal, he was taught Chinese by Valignano.

It is difficult to understand and believe that when the missionary cause was constantly running up against obstacles, Matteo Ricci received an invitation from the local magistrate he described as the Governor of Zhaoqing (Ricci's "Sciauquin"), Wang Pan (Ricci's "Guam-puon") and, with the approval of the Viceroy, it seemed to come as no surprise that "a piece of property [was] granted by the State for the erection of a church and a house". Despite the difficulties and troubles that plagued the construction of the church and the beginning of the mission, Ricci and other missionaries continued to advance the cause. When an official (supposedly Wang Pan) saw a map of the world ("a cosmographical chart of the universe") in Latin script ("done with European lettering") hanging on the wall of the Mission House's reception room, an idea of the immensity of the world dawned upon Ricci's visitors. Wang Pan wanted Ricci to prepare a copy of the map and translate it into Chinese, which Ricci did. However, he fully understood that Chinese had never changed their view that China was the center of the world, and so he drew the new map with China at the center; he did not violate the science, but also satisfied the Chinese who "firmly believe that their empire is right in the middle". However, those literati with skeptical spirit and knowledge who visited Ricci thus began to change their view of the world, and such a change may have played a decisive role.[71]

[71] Ricci wrote: "Because of their ignorance of the size of the earth and the exaggerated opinion they have of themselves, the Chinese are of the opinion that only China among the nations is deserving of admiration. Relative to grandeur of empire, of public administration and of reputation for learning, they look upon all other people not only as barbarous but as unreasoning animals. To them there is no other place on earth that can boast of a king, of a dynasty, or of a culture. The more their pride is inflated by this ignorance, the more humiliated they become when the truth is revealed. When they first saw our delineation of the universe, some of the uneducated laughed at it and made fun of it, but it was different with the better instructed, especially when they studied the placement of the parallels and meridians and of the equator, relative to the tropics of Cancer and of Capricorn. Again, when they learned of the symmetry of the five zones, and after reading of the customs of so many different people and seeing the names of many places in perfect accord with those given by their own ancient writers, they admitted that the chart really did represent the size and figure of the world. From that time on, they had a much higher opinion of the European system of education. This, however, was not the only result. There was another, and of no less importance. When they saw on the map what an almost unlimited stretch of land and sea lay between Europe and the Kingdom of China,

The initial encounters between Western civilization spread in the form of Catholic teachings and Chinese culture with its totally independent history of development were bound to entail serious conflicts. The Roman Empire's eventual acceptance of Christianity was in part the result of Greek cultural influence and, in contrast with Chinese cultural tradition, these were only elements within a single system of civilization. For those missionaries, even given their selfless spirit of sacrifice, were working in a completely unfamiliar cultural context and they helplessly courted the obvious danger of relying on strategies and methods that put them at risk of "betraying the Christian faith". In his years in China, Ricci gradually realized that in order for Chinese to convert to Christianity, he had to accept their knowledge and habits, such as familiarity with Confucianism, and bring Catholic teachings as close as possible to those of Confucianism, so that the Chinese were receptive to Catholic philosophy. However, Confucianism itself had undergone changes, and in the Song dynasty Zhu Xi established a type of Confucianism that could not be connected with Catholic teachings. Ricci found that ancient Confucianism was closer to the path of interpretation he could arrange, and so he attempted to spread his religious thought by looking for similarities between Catholic teachings and early Confucianism. Such an approach would prove effective. In this, Ricci's efforts confirmed that cultures, philosophies, and religions from civilizations with different backgrounds could find points of accommodation on the basis of mutual understanding rather than indoctrination. Of course, providing such an explanation of Christian doctrine required not only a profound and thorough understanding of the Chinese language and its attendant philosophies, but also an accommodating linguistic strategy and a calm and charming personality, all of which were qualities that Ricci possessed. In 1592, Ricci had a decisive

that realization seemed to diminish the fear our presence had occasioned". Ref: Louis J. Gallagher tr., *China in the Sixteenth Century: The Journals of Matthew Ricci: 1583–1610*, New York: Random House, 1953. From Book Two, Chapter 1, "Blessed Francis Xavier Undertakes to Enter China, but Fails", pp. 165, 167.

discussion with Valignano, before adopting a new mode of attire.[72] Previously, the strategy of Ruggieri and other Jesuit missionaries had been to wear the attire of Buddhist monks when approaching Chinese people, but this stratagem had little effect. Since the literati and officialdom were the most highly educated and potentially the most likely group in Chinese society to join the Catholic Church, Ricci simply adopted the attire of a Chinese literatus. Ricci realized that orthodox symbolism, like the forms, customs, and language developed by the Catholic Church, were very important, and this mode signified acknowledgment of a highly symbolic identity. He explained: "For us it is necessary, when visiting local officials or when other important persons come to visit us in their formal attire, to wear a silk gown and matching headgear".[73] By wearing attire that Chinese scholars and officials found familiar and natural Ricci developed cordial relations with these men, and In the course of interacting

[72] The letter giving official approval from Rome to adopt Ricci's suggestion that Jesuit missionaries in China adopt the costume of the Chinese educated class was given to Ricci in July 1594 by Lazzaro Cattaneo (1560–1640), who came to China to work with Ricci. "In order to promote the Christian cause", Cattaneo then "followed the example of Ricci". Ref: Louis J. Gallagher tr., *China in the Sixteenth Century: The Journals of Matthew Ricci: 1583–1610*, New York: Random House, 1953, p. 287.

[73] When Ricci left Nanjing for Nanchang, he was used to wearing a silk scholar's gown, and in Nanchang, he had smooth exchanges and communication with local officials and intellectuals. More than two hundred years later (in the 1870s), missionaries from the West still faced such problems, as the English missionary frequently acknowledges in his *Reminiscences*. In the following passage he outlines a stratagem he devised and a Chinese response to it:

> Pondering the question of costume, I wondered if I would have more visitors of the better class if I wore Chinese dress. So, one day I put on the native dress, shaved my head, and wore an artificial queue. ... As I walked down the street, it seemed as if a telephone message had been sent to every house, for men, women, and children all came out to stare at the spectacle. I overheard one man say to another, "Ah! He looks like a man now". That very afternoon I was invited into a house to drink tea. I understood now that there had been a sound reason for not asking me before. Being in foreign dress, the sight would have been so strange that if I were inside a house all sorts of onlookers would have come to the paper windows....when the foreigner put on Chinese dress, he was like an ordinary Chinaman and not worth looking at.

Ref: Timothy Richard, *Forty-five Years in China: Reminiscences*, London: T Fisher Unwin, 1916, p. 80.

Ricci began to convey aspects of European civilization such as knowledge of mathematics, geometry, astronomy, and cartography, as well as humanist ideas. The teachings of the Catholic Church were subtly spread in the course of daily interaction and the dissemination of scientific knowledge, and this missionary work yielded gratifying results.[74] In fact, in order to spread Catholic teachings effectively, Ricci also took full advantage of the understanding of many intellectuals of that time, such as members of the Donglin Academy, to ascertain their ability to understand Catholic doctrine by discussing Confucianism with them, and then encouraging these scholars to convert to Catholicism to influence more Chinese. Ricci's strategy and efforts were reflected and exemplified by the work of a number of renowned intellectuals including Xu Guangqi (1562–1633), Li Zhizao (1565–1630), and Yang Tingyun (1557–1627). Ricci's strategy suited the Chinese context of the time and because the legitimacy of the mission itself was so precarious, he and other missionaries were often intimidated and even driven out of some places. So, even if he was able to find security in one city, he was careful to remain low-key, given his experience preaching in Nanchang which he described in a letter (12 October 1596) to friends in Rome:

> I do not think that we shall establish a church, but instead a room for discussion and we will say Mass privately in another chapel, or perhaps use the reception hall as a chapel; because one preaches more effectively and with greater fruit here through conversations than through formal sermons.[75]

After arriving in Beijing in 1601 and gaining the tacit approval of the Chinese emperor to continue his mission, Ricci further refined his strategy. He would realize his mission through cultural immersion and the exchange of ideas, so he discussed books and scholarship with officials and intellectuals, which proved a natural and subtly effective approach.

[74] In a letter to Girolamo Costa of October 28, 1595, Ricci described the many visits from Chinese he enjoyed in Nanchang: "I don't have time to eat until at least one o'clock in the afternoon. Two or three times a week I am invited [to dinner] and some times [*sic.*] to two places on one day, and I have to go to both of them ...".

Ref: George H. Dunne, *Generation of Giants: The Story of the Jesuits in the Last Decades of the Ming Dynasty*, Notre Dame, Indiana: University of Notre Dame Press, 1962, p. 41.

[75] Ibid., p. 46.

Although this strategy and attitude were sometimes also adopted by foreigners in China in later periods, this approach would at different times elicit quite different responses.

Even though missionaries later discovered from the Nestorian Tablet that they had Christian predecessors who had entered China many centuries earlier to preach,[76] the large-scale missionary advance on Asia which began in the sixteenth century was based on improved communications and the rapid opening up of horizons ushered in by the Age of Discovery. The times demanded that a country, especially one with a glorious history, adapt to the changes in the world landscape and quickly discard its inertia and ineptitude. However, by this time China and its Ming government were already in a state of decline: the emperor was incapable, and eunuchs controlled the entire court; those officials who wanted to help the emperor and contribute to the nation were invariably embroiled in conflict and struggle with the "eunuch party". In Beijing, Ricci was unable to persuade the Wanli Emperor, a timorous and disengaged monarch who heeded the advice of treacherous officials, to give him authorization to spread the gospel legally. Later, he abandoned his efforts to persuade the emperor to provide him with a clear mandate to spread the gospel, and through translation, publishing, and constant, passionate conversations, that is, through the dissemination of ideas and warm conversations, he gradually reached out to China's literati and officialdom.

Indeed, this thorough approach to mission work and the actual dissemination of knowledge (ethics, philosophy, science, and technology) entailed the transformation of doctrine and Confucian rhetoric. This was a difficult problem, because although phrases replete with ideas could

[76] The early introduction of Nestorian Christianity to China, where it was called "Jingjiao", is documented by an inscribed stone tablet, called "Monument to the Spread to China of the Jingjiao of Da Qin', known simply as the "Nestorian Tablet", among the earliest evidence of the spread of Christianity to China. The text on the plaque comprises a preamble, which describes how the religion and its teachings came to China in the 146th year of the Tang dynasty, and a hymn which is translated from Persian and appears on the plaque in Chinese and Syriac. During the crackdown on Buddhism under Tang Emperor Wu, the Tablet was buried. It remained buried for more than 1100 years and was unearthed in 1625. In the Ming dynasty, the Nestorian Tablet was first seen by the French Jesuit Nicolas Trigault (1577–1628), the man who translated Ricci's diaries into Latin. The Portuguese missionary Alvaro de Semedo (1585–1658) subsequently translated the inscriptions on the Tablet into Portuguese and European scholars thus learned of it.

express the connotation of them, within a particular civilization the traditional use of language of itself forms a structured discourse that is not as easy to decode and reassemble as Ricci imagined. The Chinese language "tiao shi" means "adjustment", that is, to change the form or structure of a specific object, but although Ricci could even appreciate the obvious differences between Song and Ming dynasty Neo-Confucianism and ancient Confucianism, the fact that the two systematic civilizations had developed completely independently meant that simply translating doctrine from Italian, Portuguese, Latin, or other European languages into Chinese was extremely difficult. Chinese has its own history of references or connotations, and so translating a Latin text into Chinese entails many choices regarding what wording to select. Expressing Christian or specifically Catholic ideas in Chinese or borrowing Chinese words and giving them new meanings can easily lead to ambiguity, and a Chinese person will of course easily revert to a familiar meaning rather than accept a newly assigned meaning for seemingly familiar linguistic elements; it can be almost impossible for him to appreciate the meaning of the newly translated text in the way intended by the translator (let alone access the original meaning in the translator's mother tongue). In this way, reinterpretations or variations in meaning were inevitable, and it was difficult for Chinese readers to easily access or retain the logic of the original ideas. In explaining the Christian concept of "God", Matteo Ricci used Confucian teachings encapsulated in Confucianism's hierarchical definitions of obligatory social relationships termed the "Five Human Relationships" (*Wulun*) and "Three Bonds" (*Sangang*) to explain Western monotheism, or when discussing the immortality of the soul, he drew on the Confucian emphasis on moral perfection. Since he adopted the methodology of giving new meanings to existing words, there were linguistic ambiguities and blind spots for those attempting to understand his intended meanings. For example, he encountered the dilemma of deciding whether to express the meaning of "God" using the word "Shangdi" (the emperor or ruler of Heaven) or the word "Tianzhu" (the lord, master, or controller of Heaven), but were they precise? For missionaries, it would take a long time to establish the legitimacy of the doctrine they were disseminating, given the need to explain collocations of terms repeatedly and determine which translations of individual terms were acceptable. Of course, Ricci and his colleagues invariably solved translation problems through constant interpretation and textual rewrites, while at the same time avoiding words with which Chinese people were unfamiliar. For example, they avoided the interpretation of "suffering", "original sin", or "redemption" as much as possible, though these were at the core of Christian doctrine, in order to spare their Chinese audiences potential discomfort or prevent visceral resistance when listening to these teachings. This was why Ricci's mission was also regarded as deviating from the Vatican's teachings. However, the reality was that as Chinese gradually understood the nature of these concepts in the course of accepting the doctrine, they naturally moved away from Confucianism and Buddhism, not to mention Taoism. In any case, Ricci's work could be seen as the earliest major effort by European civilization to adapt and he achieved remarkable success after entering China, although the strategy of his mission was often seen as adapting Catholicism to Confucianism. This effort was strong proof, as Matteo Ricci wrote in a letter to his brothers in late 1608, that he could happily report that his nearly three decades of joint efforts with other missionaries had proven successful, because in China there were already "two thousand Christians, among them many scholars".[77] Two years later, Ricci died and the Chinese emperor issued a proclamation, granting Ricci a burial plot in Beijing: this meant that the mission was recognized and it would provide a basis for the work of the missionaries that followed. Thus, even in death Ricci made a final contribution to the Catholic Church. Most importantly, those in the later ranks of missionaries who followed Ricci's strategy of accommodation were always able to achieve results, while uncompromising "Europeans" often faced serious setbacks and defeat.

Among Chinese scholars, Ricci's friend, Xu Guangqi exemplifies an open-minded intellectual who enthusiastically developed an understanding of Western civilization. Like Ricci, he encountered the problem of how the two cultures could fuse. Xu Guangqi discovered that Western intellectual principles could solve specific problems and that Confucianism, especially Song and Ming dynasty Lixue (Neo-Confucianism), was too esoteric and vague. He told those self-righteous Confucians about his experiences of association with Ricci: "As I travelled with Master Ricci, we would discuss the Tao and at times we would touch on logic and mathematics. His statements about Tao and logic were thoroughly presented and there was never anything spurious or illusory in his

[77] Ref: Dunne, op. cit., pp. 104–105.

arguments".[78] However, in the end, Xu Guangqi's aim was to "supplement Confucianism and change Buddhism". He was dissatisfied with the contemporary state of Confucianism, but more disgusted by the present-day teachings of Buddhism, so for this Chinese scholar the entirety of Western culture enlisted in Christianity became an intellectual tool. In an age of crisis, Xu Guangqi's knowledge and abilities certainly presented an opportunity, the looming threat of the Manchus to Ming territory compelled the emperor to order Xu Guangqi and Li Zhizao to train the army along European lines. In the end, however, ideas were no match for the system, and Portuguese troops on their way to Beijing from Macao were stopped in Nanchang by imperial decree and ordered to return to Macao, ensuring that advanced weapons were not used at that time.[79] Nevertheless, in the dissemination of knowledge from the West, Xu Guangqi spared no effort, and in the last days of his life he was still concerned with rectifying the calendar. The emperor ultimately accorded Xu Guangqi a solemn funeral using treasury money, demonstrating that the Catholic mission initiated by Ricci had found some solid ground in China.[80]

[78] Ref: Wang Zhongmin ed. and annot., *Xu Guangqi Ji* (Anthology of Xu Guangqi), I, p. 66.

[79] The fears of Portuguese influence among the local merchants of Guangzhou spread as a result of this troop deployment to the mainland, and they tried to bribe officials in the capital to persuade the emperor that the Manchus could be pushed back without the assistance of these foreigners. The Guangzhou merchants then relied on this intervention to prevent the Portuguese from expanding their business in Guangzhou.

[80] In fact, despite the high tide of missionary work after Ricci's death, the mission in China remained very difficult. At court the missionaries faced opposition from those sympathetic towards the "eunuch party". For example, Shen Que (1558–1634), a teacher at the palace school of eunuchs who later served as vice-minister of the Board of Rites in Nanjing, minister of the Board of Rites in Beijing, and Scholar of the Eastern Hall, a school for princes, issued three memorials attacking Christian missionaries in 1616 and 1617, the last of which (issued in August 1617) dealt a huge blow to missionaries everywhere, but despite this, by 1622, the number of Jesuits in China had increased. There was also a rift in missionary ranks regarding the most effective stratagem that the mission should adopt in China. The successful mission was often seen as the result of the adaptive methods espoused by Ricci, but a questioning emerged in some quarters about the validity of missionaries teaching sciences such as mathematics, philosophy, astronomy, and geography. Valentim de Carvalho, the Jesuit Provincial (i.e., head) in Japan, when evacuating the headquarters of the Jesuits from Japan to Macao, promulgated an edict in 1615 proscribing the methods developed by Ricci. Having returned to Rome from China in 1613, Nicolas Trigault (1577–1628), the editor and translator of Ricci's diaries, urged the Holy See to look favorably on the concessions related to an adaptive mission

V

Politics in the late Ming years was plagued by acute crisis. The bureaucrats who assisted the emperor and the leading scholars of the land who defended the institutional orthodoxy were constantly attacked, ostracized, and tossed aside, and only in the advent of the emperor inevitably facing yet another crisis was it ever possible for capable officials to resume their original positions. Exemplifying this were events surrounding the fate of the Donglin (Eastern Forest) Academy. This organization traced its origins back to 1604, when Gu Xiancheng was dismissed from government service for many years. With the help of friends and scholars including Gao Panlong, Gu Xiancheng worked to restore a memorial shrine for the Song dynasty Confucian scholar Yang Shi in what had become known as the Donglin Academy, where they established a college for writing and publishing lectures discussing Confucian teachings. They set out to rescue Confucianism and its Classics from what they regarded as the by then debased emptiness of Wang Yangming's Neo-Confucian School of Mind, and to provide an accurate understanding of the essence of the teachings of Confucius and Mencius, in order to prevent Confucian scholars of their day from being led astray by misreading the Classics and then disseminating or applying erroneous teachings. The Academy adhered to the following basic principle: "Henceforth, except for discussing the Classics and expounding

first introduced by Ricci. Eventually a decree was issued, and Pope Paul V promulgated it in the brief titled *Romanae Ecclesiae Antistes* issued on 27 June 1615, which ruled in compliance with practices established by Ricci that: permission to adopt the headpiece modeled on the ceremonial hat worn by Chinese scholars was granted to all missionaries in China even when conducting Mass; Mass could be conducted in Chinese; the Bible could be translated into Chinese; and so on. However, these rulings were ineffectual because Trigault failed to send copies of the documents back to China in time, and the logic of Valentim de Carvalho's "Europeanism" continued to block Ricci's "adaptive" approach. In fact, however, efforts to get Chinese not only to accept religious creeds, but also to obey all the laws and regulations of the Church and the customs of Europe or other colonies were never successful. We also know that when Trigault returned to China from Europe in 1621, the persecution of Catholics by the Ming government was at its height. A great deal of historical evidence suggests that the so-called "intransigent" authoritarian or purist positions and attitudes of missionaries always attracted Chinese antipathy, or exacerbated conflict leading to more serious persecution, arrests, and deaths.

the Way, all political matters and issues ranging from those of the imperial court down to the local level of prefectures and towns will never be addressed" ("Mister Wu Qinhua's Proposed 'Donglin Agreement'", *Donglin Shuyuan Zhi*). However, the Academy's intellectual and theoretical commitment to "revitalizing ethics" had both a direct and indirect impact on the political status and domineering behavior of the sycophantic followers at court of the corrupt and powerful eunuchs". In addition, some activists of the Donglin Academy entered the political arena in the first few years of the 1620s and they were drawn into more direct conflict and contention with malevolent forces at court. As political differences became increasingly acute, Wei Zhongxian (1568–1627), who was unequivocally embraced by an array of incompetent officials as their exulted leader, instructed his cronies to compile a *Listing of Members of the Donglin Clique*.[81] This named a total of 309 people, so that the Donglin "Clique" came to be regarded throughout the country as a "gang" that posed a serious political threat to the court. Eventually, because the eunuchs exerted unchallenged power and the emperor was both incompetent and impotent, those men of conscience who wanted to safeguard the national interest and assist the court were, one by one, tried and executed, clearly demonstrating that merely upholding the so-called Confucian orthodoxy was ineffectual for maintaining justice and eliminating iniquity.

The expansion of the Manchus certainly exacerbated the crisis of the Ming dynasty,[82] but even if the competent officials at court had the

[81] Although "Donglin Dang", the label given to the Donglin Academy and its members by their political enemies, is sometimes translated as "Donglin (Eastern Forest) Party", the ancient pejorative term "*dang*" is more correctly translated as "clique" or "faction". Prior to the founding of the Zhong Xing Hui in 1894, China had no history of "political parties" ([*zheng*] *dang*) in the modern sense and the word *dang* had only appeared historically in such contexts as "the disaster of faction[alism]" (*dang-gu zhi huo*) in the Eastern Han, "the struggle between the Niu and Li factions" (*Niu Li dang zheng*) in the Late Tang, "new faction" and "old faction" (*xin dang*, *jiu dang*) in the Northern Song, and "false teachings and oppositional factions" (*weixue nidang*) in the Southern Song. At the same time as the *Listing of Members of the Donglin Clique* (Donglin-dang ren bang) was issued, other documents—*Roll Call of Donglin Generals* (Donglin dianjiang lu), *List of the Donglin Comrades* (Donglin tongzhi lu), *The Donglin Register* (Donglin jiguan lu), and *The Donglin Bandit Clique* (Daobing Donglin huo)—appeared consecutively, all intended to identify the Academy's members for eventual arrest and execution.

[82] Historians see today's north-eastern region of China as the original home of the Manchus. Their origins are thought to date back more than two thousand years to the

opportunity to petition for reform, they were soon defeated in the game of palace politics. The weakened Ming dynasty was first badly damaged by

ancient Sushen and later the Yilou, Wuji, Mohe, and Nüzhen (Jurchen). The ancient chronicle *Zuozhuan* records that "Sushen, Yan, and Bo" were "the northern lands" of the Zhou dynasty. By the Tang dynasty these gradually formed several tribes. In 725, the Tang court established Heishui prefecture in the territory of the Heishui Mohe and conferred the titles of governor and censor on the tribal chieftains, and appointed an administrator to supervise them, additionally conferring the surname Li (also the surname of the Tang imperial family) on them. In the Five Dynasties period, the Heishui Mohe changed their name to "Nüzhen (Jurchen)", which was used until the end of the Ming dynasty. In the Liao dynasty, the Nüzhen (and specifically the Wanyan tribe within the Nüzhen), under the leadership of their chieftain Wanyan Aguda, staged an uprising against the Liao and established the Jin dynasty. After their joint destruction of the Liao, they were locked in battle with the Northern Song dynasty, which they overthrew and then confronted the Southern Song dynasty. After the Jin dynasty occupied the Central Plains region, they moved their capital to Yanjing (within the area of what is today Beijing) in 1153, and the Nüzhen who settled in the Central Plains further integrated with the Han. After the Mongols destroyed the Jin dynasty, they were classified as equivalent to the "Han" in racial status, and thus the Manchus had a shared rank with the Han people in the Mongol "apartheid" system. In the Yuan dynasty, the Nüzhen and Han people lived together, further integrating. In the Ming dynasty, the Nüzhen switched from a hunting economy to agriculture, supplemented by hunting and gathering. For geographical reasons, the Ming dynasty's rule of the Northeast relied on Manchu hereditary tribal leaders to strengthen their control through the use of titles and fiefs, as well as through a policy of "dividing and ruling" their tribes. From 1583 onwards, Nurhachi unified the Nüzhen of Jianzhou, and in the next 30 years, Nurhachi united the Nüzhen scattered over different regions of the Northeast. During this period, the Eight-Banner system was established and in the process of centralization, the Manchus' system and culture became subject to differing degrees of Sinicization. In 1616, Nurhachi founded the Greater Jin State, also known as the Later Jin, in order to evoke memories of the historical Jin Empire. In 1626, the Qing Emperor Taizong, Taiji assumed the Manchu throne, and changed the reign title to "Tiancong". In 1635, the ninth year of Tiancong, the second leader of the Qing, Emperor Taiji changed the name of the tribe to Manzhou (Manchu), following the advice provided by an ethnic Han official, in order to remove any trace that they had previously been vassals of the Ming dynasty. The term Manzhou/Manchu was later used both as an ethnonym and a geographical concept, referring to the territory in the northeast, which is why the Manchus were so called before the 1911 Revolution, but this does not mean that the ethnic groups in the northeast were limited to the Manchus, given that the northeast's population in the Ming was ethnically diverse. As the Manchus broke with tribalism, they began to transform into a political organization challenging the Ming. In 1636, Emperor Taiji changed the national and dynastic name to "Da Qing" (Great Qing). In 1644, the Qing army entered China Proper, gradually unified the country, began the rule of the Manchu nobles in the political system roughly described as "the Qing dynastic system", but further strengthened the emperor's control of government affairs, while the personnel system implemented the Manchus' policy of ethnic discrimination. The Manchu script is thought to have been created at the end of the sixteenth century, but the original

Li Zicheng's rebel army and brought to the verge of collapse, after which the Manchus defeated Li Zicheng (1606–1645) with the support of the Ming general Wu Sangui (1612–1678) and a number of officials. When the Qing army of the Manchus entered Beijing, the Jesuit Johann Adam Schall von Bell (1592–1666), who had served the last Ming emperor, did not leave; his knowledge of astronomy, as well as science and technology in general, led to his appointment by Dorgon, the Manchu Imperial Regent, to the position of head of the Imperial Board of Astronomy. He later became a friend of the Manchu emperor Shunzhi and revised the national calendar for the court. In fact, Adam Schall von Bell who had been awarded an honorary plaque in 1638 by the last Ming emperor that read "Studies of the Heavens with Imperial Commendation" (*Qinbao Tianxue*), in recognition of his contribution to astronomy, soon gained the trust of the incoming Qing government; von Bell's status and prestige also served to protect other missionaries.[83] This also showed that rational knowledge was from the outset a tool that could be put to use by

Nüzhen script, developed from Chinese characters as a syllabary, ceased to be transmitted. At the end of the sixteenth century, Nurhachi and Emperor Taiji, respectively, initiated the linguistic reforms dubbed "Old Manchu" and "New Manchu". After the middle of the Qing dynasty, the Manchus basically used the Northern Chinese dialect, and Manchu was limited to use only on certain occasions by Bannermen and Banner officials until it gradually disappeared.

[83] In 1650, the Portuguese Jesuit Vice-Provincial Manoel Dias the Younger (1574–1659) wrote of Adam Schall von Bell: "Would that we had a hundred Adams, for despite the distance he is so real a help to us that we need only to say that we are his companions and brothers, and no one dares venture a word against us". Dunne, *Generation of Giants*, p. 325, citing Alfons Väth, *Johann Adam Schall von Bell, S. J.*, Köln: J. P. Boehm, 1933, p. 159, n. 13. Despite this, palace politics were so cruel and volatile that towards the end of his life, after the death of the Shunzhi Emperor in 1661, Adam Schall von Bell lost his imperial patron and was persecuted by Yang Guangxian and Oboi, a Manchu who served as one of the Regents overseeing the government while Shunzhi's infant son had not yet attained his majority. These two men were extremely hostile to the Catholic church, and Schall von Bell was sentenced to an excruciating death (but fortunately he was saved by the mother of the Shunzhi Emperor and others).

"All the missionaries acknowledged the influence of Schall; his favor with Shun Chih counted for much in obtaining Manchurian toleration. 'We all preach the Gospel under the shadow of his name', wrote Father Smogulecki in 1652. When Canton was taken by the Manchurians, Semedo, taken prisoner and threatened with the worst treatment, was set free when his jailers learned that he was a fellow religious of T'ang Jo-wan. [Tang Ruowang, the Chinese name of Adam Schall von Bell._tr.] Several missionaries, Diestel, Grueber, Verbiest, were summoned to the court, thanks to Father Adam, travelled about at the Emperor's expense and were received everywhere with great honor".

any emperor. Such an association with science and technology provided the foreign civilization with an opportunity for survival. As the eighteenth century approached, references to foreign influences proliferate in Chinese literature and art, and the phenomenon seems to have not been at all disconcerting. For example, in the drama *Peach Blossom Fan* by Kong Shangren (1648–1718), there were many references to those subtle changes:

> The Western glass is clear
> Bought in Hong Kong Bay
> Made into lenses, round like coins
> I gaze at *Autumn Waters* through two apertures
> Covering the eyes, yet clarifying sight,
> One can see the fine detail.
> By the dark window I now read the fine print
> Which I could only have done when young.

It can be said that earlier dynasties seem to be mirrors of those that come later, and the millennia of Chinese history can be seen as an endless history of cycling changes of dynasty. Within such a pattern, the establishment of the Qing dynasty is the most recent example of such a change prior to the Revolution in 1911.[84] In 1662 the last prince of the Ming royal family was executed by Wu Sangui using a lethal arrow, but Qing rule in China Proper began as early as 1644 with the Manchu occupation of Beijing, this dynastic change being a cataclysmic event in Chinese history. Yet, based on the goals and efficacy of governance, the Qing dynasty soon restored the political system of the Ming dynasty and reintroduced the imperial examination system,[85] thereby demonstrating the perpetuation of Confucianism and its implicit cultural traditions. As a

Ref: Boston College, Jesuit Online Library, *Woodstock Letters*, Volume LXVI, Number 1, 1 February 1937, J. de la Servière, "Father Adam Schall" (originally published in *Revue d'Histoire des Missions*), p. 27.

[84] Some historians of Qing history argue that this dynasty was unique and unlike previous Chinese dynasties. However, its continuity can clearly be seen in the system (the Qin-Han polity) and the culture (the domination of Confucianism), so although the borders might enclose territory twice the size of that of the Ming, its population heading towards five hundred million, and its ethnicity more pluralistic, these aspects of the Qing are insufficient for describing the Qing as fundamentally different from earlier dynasties.

[85] As the nation's path and method for selecting bureaucratic talent, the examination system began with the testing of government recruits in the Sui dynasty, and assumed

result, in its subsequent three centuries of rule, the Qing dynasty effectively defended and consolidated the established Chinese civilization. Dorgon's successor, the Shunzhi Emperor, was an aficionado of vernacular Chinese fiction and plays, and the Kangxi Emperor (1654–1722), selected by Shunzhi as his successor, might have listened to the views of Adam Schall von Bell, but he was a loyal student of the Confucian "Four Books and Five Classics". In order to convince the ethnic Han population to willingly serve the new dynasty, Kangxi studied the Confucian classics with great diligence and respect. Kangxi, as emperor, tried to convince Han intellectuals and high officials that he was also a guardian of the Chinese cultural tradition and was maintaining an orthodox moral order, although the Qing government also made constant efforts to preserve Manchu culture and religion.[86]

prototypical form in the Tang dynasty, with the division into both regular and occasional examinations, and by the Song dynasty the system had further developed. By the Ming dynasty, a three-tier examination system had been set up: provincial examinations, metropolitan examinations, and palace examinations. The system provided opportunities for ordinary people to enter all levels of government because, regardless of birth and status, all test scores were used to grade the results attained at different levels. Because the content of the examinations was limited to the quotation and repetition of the Confucian Classics, the candidates were said to "study what could not be put to use and put to use what they had not studied". In the Song dynasty, Wang Anshi wrote: "Today when men have the strength of youth, they immerse themselves in expounding the principles of the world and behind closed doors they study how to compose poetry and prose. On becoming officials, they must deal with worldly matters for which their studies have not prepared them. This examination system [to its highest level] is corrupt, and so talents do not excel as they did in ancient times". At the beginning of the Ming dynasty, a type of prose writing called the "eight-legged essay" was required for the composition of examination essays, and this format seriously regulated and restricted a candidate's ideas. The Ming loyalist, Gu Yanwu (1613–1682), wrote: "The eight-legged essay is as harmful as burning books". And: "As long as this requirement remains unchanged, talent will be wasted, and scholarship impoverished with each passing day. The world that has come down from the Five Sovereigns and the Three Kings will have a sorry end". By the late Qing, such repeated condemnation, coupled with the impact of the entry of Western civilization on traditional culture, exposed the ineffectiveness of the system for training talented men who could meet the needs of the state and society, and so the traditional examination system would be finally abolished in 1905.

[86] During the Yongzheng reign (1723–1735), the *Treaty of Kiakhta* (1727), a supplement to the *Treaty of Nerchinsk* (1689) with Russia, was signed; it even specifically included a clause calling for the encouragement of Russians living in Beijing to learn Chinese.

Under the orders of the Qianlong Emperor (r. 1736–1795) the most ambitious bibliographic and publishing project in Chinese history was undertaken. Titled *Siku Quanshu*,

No single important event can thoroughly change the force of history. After the Qing army occupied Beijing, a large number of intellectuals demonstrated their ongoing commitment to legitimism by resisting the newcomers and refusing to cooperate; some expressed this loyalism by staging hunger strikes or even by committing suicide. A small number of philosophers wrote histories and presented theories that sought to find a way to change reality or even rewrite history: Wang Fuzhi (1619–1692) wrote a critique opposing the "Study of Mind" of Wang Yangming (1472–1529), in order to address the ethical crisis he perceived; Huang Zongxi (1610–1695) analyzed the redistribution of imperial power and emphasized the importance of moral power; and, Gu Yanwu hoped that people would acquire a fresh understanding of China's ancient intellectual heritage in order to find real solutions to real problems. Excluding the academic challenges it faced, Wang Yangming's philosophy "combining knowledge and action" was widely praised and had many followers, but the scope of his definitions of "knowledge" and "action" did not fundamentally break free from Confucian restraints, and so his "new philosophy might have activated intellectual circles", as the early twentieth-century educator and humanist, Cai Yuanpei, pointed out, "but it was not a subversive theory that could change the social system".[87]

the "Four Treasuries" (a reference to "its four main components of classics, histories, philosophy and miscellaneous literary works") "ended up comprising 3,450 complete works and commentaries on 6,750 others, filled 36,000 manuscript volumes and took ten years to complete". [Ref: Jonathan Spence, *The Search for Modern China*, New York and London: W. W. Norton and Company, 1999, p. 100.].

[87] Wang Yangming (1472–1529) was a thinker who remained influential from the sixteenth century onwards. Originally, he reinterpreted the Confucian Classics under the influence of the Song dynasty Neo-Confucian School of *Li* (a concept roughly equivalent to "rational principles"), hoping to revise again people's understanding of the Classics: he argued that Mind (literally, "heart-mind") and Nature are one, emphasizing the inspiration of Mind; in other words, only through inner understanding can Reason be apprehended, or as he said: "The Mind is Reason. The world has things beyond Mind, but can Reason be found outside Mind?" This approach meant that the words of the ancient sages did not need to be followed rigidly. Unlike the Neo-Confucian teachings on Reason of the Cheng Brothers and Zhu Xi which were influenced by Buddhism and neglected action, Wang Yangming emphasized the unity of knowledge and practice. Translating Wang Yangming's teachings on Mind today, it is clear that his understanding of "the knowledge of Mind" encompassed experience and action, otherwise it is incomplete. Thus, wanting to eat is "intention" (the Mind desirous of eating), which must be followed by the action of eating. "Mind" itself thus has the capacities of self-determination, self-improvement, and of not seeking external help. Such a view places a clear emphasis on action. Ancient

People were repeatedly reminded that if the power of the individual could not change society, then the individual should find a solution to the problem within himself, and the adjustment of the "inner mind" became of paramount importance. Changes in social structure were limited by political changes at court, and in those endless political struggles intellectuals who supported the emperor were always either driven into exile or had to hide away as recluses. It is true that for several centuries innumerable volumes of reiterated interpretations and annotations had sought to explain the *Four Books* and *Five Classics* of Confucius and Mencius, but China's basic civilizational and political structure had not changed significantly. Conscience and morality had become the central themes of Confucian theory, but the interpretation of conscience and morality was always amended with a change of power. While there were seemingly endless explanations of how to accommodate conscience or to realize morality, it was not until the spirit of evidential analysis (***kaozheng***) prevailed in the Qianlong period, causing scholars to re-examine the classical texts of the Han dynasty, believing that new truths could be discovered through the philological analysis of classical writings, in order to assist the emperor who was ruling the country.

The period from the Kangxi to Qianlong reign is regarded as a flourishing age by Chinese people, From the eighth year of his reign in 1669, the Kangxi Emperor was most proud of his suppression of the rebellion

intellectuals always discussed the question of becoming a sage, but compared to Zhu Xi and others, Wang Yangming to some extent paid more attention to the importance of practice in the process of becoming a sage. However, after a careful study of Wang Yangming's writings, we find that what he calls "knowledge" is not the information we obtain, but wisdom regarding the "Way", in other words truth, and this view of course facilitates a return to endless idealistic discussion. Knowledge is a universal thing while practice is specific, and so his formulation that "knowledge and practice are one" still needs to be re-interpreted through the subjective Mind. Therefore, Wang Yangming's theories, like those of Cheng-Zhu and others, still largely lie within the Confucian tradition, and do not represent a departure from that tradition. Culturally speaking, this is why Confucian traditional thought could not address the new problems that arose after the seventeenth century. The internal elements within a political system are related to cultural traditions, and when a political system cannot solve the problems arising from social change, it can only be influenced by new cultural forces that come along. As far as China is concerned, because the new foreign culture did not match the traditional culture, and the political system maintained by the traditional culture lacked the mechanism to reconcile and redistribute resources, the personal interests and abilities of the emperor and the officials in power not being part of institutional arrangements, this naturally would result in conflict.

of the Three Feudatories (San Fan) between 1673 and 1681, the recapture of Taiwan with the assistance of fleets led by commander Shi Lang following Zheng Zhilong's surrender to the Qing in 1683, including Taiwan within the map of Qing dynasty, and the signing of the *Treaty of Nerchinsk* with the Russians after twice attacking their armies at Yaksa, which subsequently maintained the border between Russia and China. As a result of the stability brought by the *Treaty of Nerchinsk*'s demarcation of borders and agreement with Russia, Kangxi had the energy and confidence to defeat the Junggar Rebellion led by Galdan (1696), which stabilized the areas at its far west. Decades later, the Qianlong Emperor arranged for the army to eliminate the remnants of the Junggar tribes (1759), setting up an administrative agency there, which enforced the administration of the northwest area. Most of Qianlong's later political actions entailed the conduct of foreign wars (Burma, Vietnam, Nepal) and the suppression of anti-Qing rebellions (Wang Lun, Muslim Rebellion, and the White Lotus uprising).[88] Yet by the time of Qianlong's "abdication" in 1796, his rule and reputation were largely destroyed by the corruption of his favorite courtier Heshen (1750–1799) and the bureaucrats who served the latter. It should be noted that, until the outbreak of the Opium War, subsequent Qing rulers did not devote energy and concern to dealing with maritime threats; they lacked sufficient awareness of the dramatic changes in the world pattern that had been revealed in the Ming dynasty. Indeed, up to the Qianlong period, the Qing government did not have a special diplomatic department to manage contacts with the outside world. Although relations with neighboring Asian countries were handled by the Board of Rites, the continuously arriving missionaries were simply received under arrangements determined by the emperor's family retainers. The concept that "everything under Heaven is the king's territory" had always existed in the minds of Chinese emperors, and it seems

[88] In 1744, a rebellion erupted in Shandong which was led by a medical doctor called Wang Lun. Most of the rebels were commoners, including farmers, boatmen, road transport laborers, fishmongers, oil vendors, bean-curd sellers, monks, entertainers, and unemployed itinerants. The composition of these participants indicated the spread of discontent and the general crisis in social life. The two Muslim uprisings which broke out in Gansu in the 1780s do not seem to have been precipitated by any obvious ethnic antagonism. The White Lotus uprising that broke out in the 1790s was directly related to government corruption and incompetence, wanton malfeasance by officials, silting up of the canal system, empty grain silos, social disorder, and problems of people's livelihood.

that the countries peripheral to China were of no concern and not worth thinking about.

By the Qing dynasty, trade between China and European countries was still hampered by an extremely complex historical process, and basically speaking, the Qing government, like the Ming, had little interest in overseas trade, and maintained its lack of interest in any foreign culture. When the constant requests to engage in foreign trade were presented, the Qing government maintained its entrenched attitude of "extending hospitality to people from afar and nurturing barbarians" (*Veritable Records of Qing Emperor Gaozong*, fasc. 143) which was not positive, let alone even-handed. Previously, if Portugal and Spain did not accept the status of vassal states within the tributary system it would not have been possible to establish trade relations with China, and if the Dutch had not helped the Kangxi Emperor suppress Zheng Chenggong's power on the east coast in the mid-seventeenth century then Holland would not have been granted the opportunity to trade. Later, British merchants also came to China wanting to trade. In 1680, the Qing government abolished its maritime ban and China's trade with Western countries gradually expanded with the emergence in the 1720s of the grouping of merchants known by its Cantonese name as *Co-hong* (Mandarin: *gonghang*) to control China's interests in the event of price adjustments.[89] Merchants operating under the *Co-hong* even accepted government directives to guarantee that foreign traders paid taxes in the course of conducting trade. Once there was an opening, trade would of

[89] After the opening of Guangzhou to trade, a place of residence for foreigners was established outside the city's western gate, and these quarters were called "factories" in English, the traders being "factors", and "*yiguan*" (literally, "barbarian buildings") in Chinese. Rooms in the adjacent buildings were rented out separately to individual "foreign traders" (*yishang*, literally "barbarian merchants"), whose activities were largely confined to the buildings and the immediate vicinity. The only Chinese specifically approved by the central government's Ministry of Households (Hu Bu) to trade with "barbarian merchants" were called "*hong* merchants", and between them they were organized into a trade association known as the "*Co-hong*" (Cantonese for *Gonghang*, literally, "public businesses"), to protect their interests and play the role of go-between in transactions between local governments and foreigners in China. It is important to note that "*hong* merchants" most probably first appeared during the Wanli reign (1573–1619) of the Ming dynasty, when 36 such merchants were engaged in trading activities with some "fourteen countries", but by the end of the Ming the number of "*hong* merchants" had dropped to only thirteen. Based on commercial interests, "*hong* merchants" usually worked well with foreign merchants and the two sometimes helped each other, intent on maintaining a reputation for fair trading.

course only grow. The British East India Company established in 1600 was granted a British government-sanctioned monopoly over trade out of East India and no ordinary merchant could compete for the scope and scale of its trade. The British merchants were far from satisfied with the Qing government's various restrictions on trade, not to mention the fact that in the process of dealing with China, they were never able to enjoy the rules governing international trade which they took for granted. They frequently encountered bribery, conflicts, and complaints, and the emergence of a trade deficit led British merchants to start bringing in opium to trade with China, which sowed the seeds for the deadly conflict that eventually ensued. In any case, the British decided to break up the Guangzhou trading system, a monopoly exemplified by only a single port with trading activities subject to restrictions and corruption. Great Britain attempted to establish a trading relationship with the Chinese government in line with the new international trading order. The mission led by George Macartney (1737–1806), which set off from London in September 1792, represented Great Britain in its attempt to negotiate as a world power with China on the occasion of offering presents to the Qianlong Emperor at his birthday celebrations, with the aim, of course, of securing British business interests and expanding trade with China. To be sure, until this time, the Qing government still had little interest in trade between the two countries, and the British trading overtures were received with only formally perfunctory expressions of politeness. This is vividly recorded in *An Authentic Account of an Embassy from the King of Great Britain to the Emperor of China* written by the secretary of the mission, Sir George Staunton (1737–1801), on his return to England in 1797.[90]

[90] Staunton in the following passage describes the Chinese government's attitudes as reflected by those of the court official (called by Staunton the "Colao") responsible for hosting tributary delegations such as those from Tibet, attending to Macartney's party in Rehe (Jehol):

> His Excellency found it necessary to use great tenderness, and many qualified expressions, in conveying any idea that a connection between Great Britain and China could be of any importance to the latter, either by the introduction of European commodities, of which taken in barter, the necessity was not felt; or by the supply of cotton or rice from India, which some of the Chinese provinces were equally fit to cultivate; or of bullion, of which the increase had sometimes the inconvenience of unequally increasing the prices of the useful or necessary articles of life; or, lastly, of the assistance of a naval force to destroy the pirates on the coast, against whose mischief the sure resource existed of an internal communication by

Staunton, in his account, described how Britain sent envoys, "naturally for commercial purposes" (Chapter I). Previously, European trade in China had been largely limited to Portuguese, Dutch, and Spanish merchants. To guard their interests, the merchants from these countries also attempted to hamper British trade with China; at the same time, China knew very little about Britain, which is one of the basic reasons why the Chinese government initially required British envoys to conform to the protocol of kneeling three times and performing the kowtow nine times.[91]

Anyhow, the Qianlong Emperor treated the British arrivals with arrogance and might, and he was willfully unimpressed by the scientific and technical level exemplified by the British warship with its 64 large cannons that could safely reach the Chinese coast from the sea. The Qing government's arrogance and short-sightedness would endure down to the end of the nineteenth century and a passage from Qianlong's letter to George III hinted at the crisis facing China at this time:

rivers and canals. Such were the avowed or affected notions entertained by the Chinese government, of the superiority or independence of the empire, that no transaction with foreigners was admissible by it on the ground of reciprocal benefit, but as a grace or condescension from the former to the latter.

The Embassador [*sic.*] was not unwilling to negociate [*sic.*] even on those terms: and the Colao obligingly said, that they should have frequent opportunities of meeting during the continuance of his Excellency's visit at the Chinese court".

Sir George Staunton, *An Authentic Account of an Embassy from the King of Great Britain to the Emperor of China*, London: G. Nicol, 1797, 2 v., v. 2, ch. 4, pp. 221–222.

[91] Staunton wrote: "The whole of this relation [referring to reception and subsequent conflict of an expedition of English merchants in Guangzhou in 1634] marks the moderation of the Chinese towards strangers, or, perhaps, the weak and unsteady administration of a declining dynasty; but shews [sic.], at the same time, under what adverse auspices, the English were first introduced in China: these rash adventurers appearing as if not belonging to any nation, or avowed by any power, and misrepresented by those [referring to the Portuguese] on whom they had placed dependence; nor had they been preceded by any English traveler, actuated by motives of piety or curiosity, who might announce, at least, the name of his country to some advantage. It continued to be so little known, even after the English had begun to traffic at Canton, that they were long distinguished, only, by the contemptuous appellation of *Hoong-mow-zhin*, which, as nearly as can be translated, may answer to that of *carotty-pated race*".

Sir George Staunton, *An Authentic Account of an Embassy from the King of Great Britain to the Emperor of China*, London: G. Nicol, 1797, 2 v., v. 1, ch. 1, pp. 11–12.

> We have never valued ingenious articles, nor do we have the slightest need of your country's manufactures. Therefore, O king, as regards your request to send someone to remain at the capital, while it is not in harmony with the regulations of the Celestial Empire we also feel very much that it is of no advantage to your country.[92]

The mission did not achieve its purpose in coming to China, angering Macartney who wrote in his journal: "The Empire of China is an old, crazy, first rate man-of-war, which a fortunate succession of able and vigilant officers has contrived to keep afloat for these one hundred and fifty years past, and to overawe their neighbors merely by her bulk and appearance" (quoted by Spence, p. 123).

VI

The Qianlong reign nevertheless registered many impressive achievements: the uprising of Hui Muslims in Xinjiang and the turmoil in Taiwan were suppressed, and the administration of Tibet was enforced; following a year of poor harvests, farmers throughout the country were exempted from paying taxes for a year.[93] Moreover, at vast cost to the national budget, the 80,000-volume *Siku Quanshu* (Four Treasuries Library) was

[92] Jonathan D. Spence, *The Search for Modern China*, 1999, pp. 122–123, quoting J. L. Cranmer-Byng ed., *An Embassy to China: Lord Macartney's Journal, 1793–1794*, London, 1962, p. 340.

However, this debate about "protocol" did not need to be seen from the perspective of who was "advanced" or who was "backward". The major reason for the failure to achieve a mutual understanding that could lead to conflict or disagreement was that neither side would make the necessary concessions on this issue. In fact, one of the reasons there was clarity and stability regarding borders in the Kangxi period was that China did not treat Russia as a vassal, and their respective emissaries accorded each other's sovereigns politely at the request of the other side.

[93] The population of China during the Qianlong reign reached 300 million, but the increase in arable land was gradually falling behind the growth in population, which determined that per capita arable land was decreasing, while the price of grain was increasing. Documents show that in the nineteenth-century grain prices were five times higher than they were in the seventeenth century, which led to famine, disease, and unrest, and imposed overall pressure on society. The increase in incidents of social unrest led to an increase in military spending (e.g., to confront the rebellious White Lotus, the Qing government spent 220 million silver taels) and a decline in national strength, and eventually the Qing government was unable to cope with the general outbreak of social unrest with the emergence of the Taiping Heavenly Kingdom.

compiled and published.[94] This was a monumental bibliographical legacy that later generations revered. However, when Qianlong died in 1799, 800 million taels of silver were seized from the home of his adored courtier, the Manchu Heshen, at a time when the government's annual income was only 70 million and even if the seized hoard had only been one-tenth of this amount, it would have been sufficient to reveal the extent of the government's corruption, incompetence, and advancing chronic decline.

By the nineteenth century, even ordinary British households began to demand tea, once a precious herbal commodity, but it could only be purchased from China with silver, as the Qing government had implemented a silver standard. In fact, in previous years, the trade balance between Europe and China always favored the latter, because of China's lack of obvious interest in foreign goods, while Europe's demand for Chinese goods increased constantly to the extent that foreign traders, like the British East India Company, needed to amass silver from everywhere, including central Europe, Japan, and South America, to balance their books while replenishing stocks of Chinese tea, porcelain, spices, silk, jade, and other luxury goods. As a result, there was a huge trade deficit in favor of Chinese parties. When the opium trade began, the situation fundamentally reversed and large quantities of silver began to flow

[94] In fact, since the beginning of the Qing dynasty, the government had stopped allowing scholars to gather and form associations (*jiqun zuodang*, "cluster in large groups to form cliques"), and publication was limited to books related to the imperial examinations, so the space for relatively free discussion among scholars was further narrowed. The teaching materials in schools were the stipulated Song dynasty Confucian works and the interpretation of the Confucian Classics was limited to that of Zhu Xi. Prose writing tended towards the formulaic genre of the eight-legged essay, and individuality was lacking. A scholar expressing himself freely ran the risk of committing the serious crime of lèse-majesté, described as "slandering the politics of the court in one's belly and insulting one's sovereign". The Kangxi Emperor initiated a "Literary Inquisition" which is remembered by Chinese writers to the present day. (Guilt was defined by the discovery of a text or ideological statement in a book or essay that was alleged to defame the court or the monarch, and the offender was convicted as a result. However, most cases were the result of far-fetched and arbitrary interpretations or even of deliberate lying by the accuser.) The *Siku Quanshu* project was in fact conducted in conjunction with the Literary Inquisition of the Qianlong reign. The project stipulated which works were off-limits to readers, and these works were confiscated and destroyed. According to the literature, between 1774 and 1782, there were 24 incidents of book bans (book burnings), in which 13.862 works were destroyed and more than 60 persons imprisoned. At the same time, these works were not included in the *Siku Quanshu*, and in many cases even descriptions of the content of these banned works were destroyed.

out of China.[95] However, in the long-term opium trade, Britain played a role behind the scenes role directing and manipulating the trade, so that it appeared that only the despised dealers selling opium at sea or on street corners were engaged in dealing this particular commodity.[96]

As early as 1729, the Qing government had issued a ban on opium trafficking. However, the later constant prohibitions and adopted measures seemed ineffective and, as a result, extensive smuggling appeared and opium usage proliferated, so that by 1838 no less than 40,000 cases were being imported annually. The history of the opium trade and the "Opium Wars" is difficult to recount briefly, but suffice it to say that William Napier, appointed as Britain's first Chief Superintendent of Trade at Canton signifying the ending of the British East India Company's

[95] The Ming naturalist and pharmacologist Li Shizhen (1518–1593) in his *Bencao Gangmu* (Outline Herbal Pharmacopeia) recorded: "Opium (*yapian*) in earlier dynasties was rarely heard of, but recently there are those who consume it". The word "opium" comes from Arabic, and it can be understood as a traded product of the Western Regions. The Chinese popular name for it was "pod poppy" (*yingsu*) and in poetry it was termed "*xiangsi-cao*" (literally, "the herb of longing"), a name that indicates its psychological impact. Tariff statistics for 1589 reveal that two *jin* (pounds) of opium worth two silver bars were taxed at an import excise rate of two silver "cash" (*qian*, 1 *qian* = 3.73 grams) for every ten pounds of opium. Prior to the Qing dynasty, opium was a class of medicinal herb used for its analgesic, calmative, and relaxing properties. People who consumed it easily became addicted. It is true that the dopamine released by opium consumption can make people excited and happy, but long-term consumption can also result in physical and mental decline, leading in turn to general social problems. At the same time, its consumption led to an outflow of silver, which would eventually empty the state's coffers. According to historians, between 1752 and 1800, 105 million silver dollars (about 26.25 million English pounds) flowed into China, while between 1808 and 1856, 384 million silver dollars flowed in the opposite direction to Britain. Lin Zexu said: "If [the trade] continues at this rate, after several decades, the Central Plains will be unable to defend itself against enemy soldiers, and there will be no silver. When we realize this, we cannot buy opium!"

[96] The entire process of opium production and trading was as follows: The British East India Company commissioned the growing of opium poppies in India and oversaw the production of opium, followed by the supervision of packing and transporting it to Kolkata for auction. Then, opium smugglers shipped the opium to the Chinese coast (mainly to Lintin Island at the mouth of the Pearl River), where Chinese wholesalers bought permits from opium dealers in Guangzhou and exchanged them for opium, which was later distributed. Throughout this process, of course, the traders could encounter government inspection boats, were subject to bribery or to attacks from pirates. By the 1830s, opium cultivation was also already widespread in inland China (mainly in Yunnan and Xinjiang), and by the time of the Opium War, there was already a nationwide opium trade.

monopoly on British trade with China, failed in his mission to communicate with the Chinese government and establish a legitimate and equal trading relationship. Although the Macartney mission had long since reported the Chinese rejection of British trade, until Napier's time the British monarch was simply unwilling to accept that China was not interested in trading with any country, unless that country's merchants came to pay tribute or accepted the Chinese emperor's avowed graciousness. In fact, as soon as Napier arrived in Guangzhou, he did not follow Chinese regulations. His insistence on submitting documents to the Liangguang Governor Lu Kun (1772–1835) as an equal infuriated the governor,[97] with the result that Qing troops surrounded the British "factory", preventing them from conducting any further trade. Therefore, the self-righteous protests by Napier were ignored and, in the eyes of the Qing government, his demands lacked even basic legitimacy:

> ...... Britain was willing to send state officials to replace the East India Company, and they are free to do so. Yet our country adheres to the old system, limiting contacts with the barbarians to those through the Co-hong, which we are also free to do. Apart from ceremonial visits and tributary missions, there has never been a direct relationship between our country and a foreign country. The British Government appointed Mr. Napier without any prior notice, and he himself did not bring any letters of appointment with him, and regarding this completely new issue he did not give the Governor time to receive a letter of instruction from Beijing. They eventually broke the laws of the Qing state by bringing troops and

[97] As the Ming dynasty's efforts to improve the tributary system affecting trade not only remained in force, a psychological inertia within the Confucian cultural tradition simultaneously took shape, whereby "the Heavenly dynasty as the supreme nation" could not enter into trading relations or trade as equals with "the various states outside the [Chinese civilizing] transformation" (*huawai ge bang*, a formula which designated Western countries in the main). In the eyes of officials at all levels of the Qing government, the moral duty of a benevolent China as "the Heavenly dynasty" and "supreme nation" was to implement a policy of "extending kindness to strangers from afar". Yet for Napier and other British this attitude and strategy was seen as arrogance and pomposity, and they sought to establish "free" and "equal" trade with China. In 1838, Charles Elliot went to Guangzhou to deliver his letter to the Chinese government, but because the title of the Chinese text of the document did not include the word "*bing*" 禀 ("report", specifically indicating a report sent from an inferior to a superior"), the Liangguang Governor Deng Tingzhen felt compelled to "discard and return the letter with its original seal unopened" because of Elliot's presumption in asserting equal status.

weapons into the factories, shelling the forts, and forcing their way upriver [to Guangzhou]…….[98]

The answer of the Governor-General in Guangzhou largely remained unchanged. Under pressure from the Qing government, Napier was forced to retreat from Guangzhou and trade was restored. However, Governor-General Lu's harsh language in the document of response to the British and Napier's failure and death left an excuse for the later conflict because it meant that those British merchants who wanted to protect the opium trade were further vindicated by what they regarded as China's arrogant and foolish views upholding isolation. There was a debate within the Qing government over whether to allow opium or to ban it, even though the Sino-British trade had stalled in March 1839, but the outcome was that the emperor decided to send Lin Zexu to Guangzhou as his plenipotentiary, with the title Imperial Commissioner, to ban opium.

From the 3rd to the 25th of June 1839, Lin Zexu directed the destruction of opium at Humen, the Bogue, in Guangzhou, degrading the opium with brine and lime and then incinerating it. He destroyed all the opium confiscated from the foreign merchants based in the "factories". In the process of banning opium in Guangzhou, Lin Zexu studied all information he had collected from the Co-hong, the comprador go-betweens, and members of the public, which included translated documents and background material. He attempted to make sense of foreign information, to fully ensure that he reduced errors to a minimum in his implementation of the ban. After Lin was scapegoated and eventually dismissed from his post. He later managed to pass on some of the "suspect" maps and documents to a junior colleague, Wei Yuan, well known for coining the expression "mastering barbarian technology to bring barbarians under control", in the express hope that Wei's thorough research might reveal more about the "barbarians".[99] Nevertheless, in his ignorance of the

[98] [FN18] Chen Shunchen, *Yapian Zhanzheng* (The Opium War), Chongqing: Chongqing Chubanshe, 2008, p. 70.

[99] As a result, Wei Yuan completed his renowned *Haiguo Tuzhi* (Illustrated Treatise on the Maritime Kingdoms) in 1843. This work clearly negated the earlier Chinese view that foreigners are barbarians, stating: "Among these guests from afar are those who have clear views of propriety, behave righteously, examine the heavens, survey the geography of the earth, and show even-handedness and equanimity in their dealings. Throughout history they have excelled as warriors on sea and land and within their domain they are excellent

world, especially of the laws of Great Britain and its new world order, Lin Zexu left himself open to criticism in the process of implementing his ban on opium. For example, in locking up a government official such as Capt. Charles Elliot in the merchants' factories together with opium dealers, revealed a lack of understanding of modern notions of diplomacy. Most seriously, by accepting the opium Elliot handed over on behalf of the opium merchants, Lin Zexu effectively transformed what had been a domestic opium ban into state intervention, providing a sufficient basis for Elliot to demand that the British government engage in war.

Indeed, as the German missionary Karl Gützlaff (1803–1851), comparing the British and Chinese navies, wrote in his report included in *British Parliamentary Papers* (v. 39, pp. 133–141): "All of China's thousand war-junks cannot withstand one small frigate". From the Battle of Chuenpi (Mandarin: Chuanbi)[100] to the final forced signing by the Qing government of the treaty terminating the conflict, the British warships and troops swept all before them, and China's ships, forts, and troops fell without delivering effective retaliation. The unexpected Tsim Sha Tsui Incident,[101] coupled with the hegemonic objectives established by

companions" Therefore, he hoped that China's attitude should be: "The sages regarded the world (*Tianxia*) as one family and all men within the Four Seas as brothers, and so showing kindness to strangers from afar and politely receiving foreign envoys showed the great magnanimity of the king: toleration of others' customs and having a sweeping knowledge of the world constitute the broad knowledge of the intelligent scholar". The book ignited a passion among Chinese intellectuals and aspiring bureaucrats to understand the world, and "Chinese thought" began to be questioned among those who wanted to save the dynasty from collapse.

[100] The English and Chinese versions of this battle differ. According to Lin Zexu's memorial, on 3 November 1839, following negotiations with Chinese merchants at Humen, also known as Bocca Tigris or the Bogue, the British merchant vessel *The Royal Saxon* had signed the Chinese bond and was preparing to sail to Guangzhou when prevented by the Chinese. A military engagement between the British and Chinese broke out at sea outside Chuenpi (Chuanbi). In January 1841, the *Chuenpi Convention* was signed by both parties.

[101] In July 1839, Lin Weixi, a villager of Tsim Sha Tsui on the Kowloon Peninsula, was beaten to death by a drunken Briton. The Qing authorities demanded that Charles Elliot, who had moved from Canton to temporary living quarters on Macao, hand over the perpetrators. Elliot invoked English law as the grounds for not cooperating. Based on his research into international law, including British law, Lin Zexu stated that Elliot should follow Chinese law and hand over the guilty party or parties, but Elliot pleaded that it was not clear who the specific perpetrators were. Under pressure from the Chinese side, the Portuguese Governor of Macao informed Elliot that it was difficult to guarantee his safety in Macao. As a result, the British men, women, and children who had returned

the British government, eventually led to the full outbreak of fighting between China and Britain in June 1840. The serious threat presented by the British army from its first attack at Dinghai on Zhoushan island until it reached Tianjin in the vicinity of Beijing forced the emperor to remove Lin Zexu from his post and replace him with Qishan (c. 1790–1854) to negotiate with the British. In the course of negotiations, the British army brought constant pressure to bear on the Qing court by increasing its demands, and its attack on the Jingyuan Fort at Humen led to Qishan adopting a concessionary strategy in the negotiations, which meant that Qishan also had to be dismissed. The various Qing armies in Guangzhou were not strong enough to fight, and at the same time as they disregarded the enemy and plundered local people, they even fought to the death among themselves. The British army's expeditionary force, after reoccupying Zhoushan, and taking Xiamen, Dinghai, Zhenhai, and Ningbo, continued to attack Zhapu in Zhejiang and took the Wusong fort near Shanghai. Finally, the British army attacked Zhenjiang and was poised to attack Nanjing. At this juncture, the court surrendered to the British, and on 29 August 1842, the *Treaty of Nanjing* was signed on board the British warship *HMS Cornwallis*. The treaty was historically symbolic, because the missionaries who had once sacrificed their lives in the unfinished mission of enabling Western civilization to take root in China, could finally resume their work in the wake of opium and guns.

The explanations for the events of the 1840s and 1850s are many and various: (1) the political and economic vitality brought about by the Industrial Revolution in England stimulated the expansion of territory and the extraction of resources by the British Empire; (2) China was at this time the hapless victim of its emperor's incompetence, the court's stubborn conservatism, an economy in collapse and decay, and the general deterioration of morality, and so was ripe for defeat; (3) advanced theories and weaponry provided strong support for the expansion of Christian civilization; (4) the nature of the conflict was the new rules of international free trade resulting from maritime exploration pitted against a tribute system characterized by arrogance, stupidity, and backwardness;

from Guangzhou to Macao all boarded a ship to take refuge. Because the supply of food to the ship was cut off, on November 3rd Elliot resisted by simultaneously arranging for British warships and armed merchant ships to fire on Chinese naval vessels while protesting, effectively starting the Opium War. In February 1840, the British government formally decided to send troops to China.

and so on. Indeed, until 23 October 1838, the Daoguang Emperor was still prevaricating about whether or not to "relax" the ban on opium and he asked his chief officials in the Grand Council (Junjichu) to present their views on the subject, but two days later an imperial prince and a prominent noble were reported to have been found smoking opium in the Forbidden City. In the following month, it was learned that in Tianjin, which was near Beijing, 130,000 taels worth of opium from Guangdong had also been found, just when it was time to make a final decision on banning opium. However, the main reasons why war broke out between China and Britain, leading to China's utter defeat, were the entire court's persistent disdain for "aggressive barbarians", its ignorance of Britain's fundamental aims and military strength, its failure to ever regard "prohibiting opium" as a foreign relations matter, and its total unpreparedness on the ideological, political, and military fronts.[102]

Captain Charles Elliot, the Abolitionist who promoted the Opium War, began to show a distaste for opium smuggling when he acted as the British Foreign Secretary's representative in China, as revealed by a statement he made in 1836: "It cannot be good that the conduct of a great trade should be so dependent upon the steady continuance of a vast prohibited traffic in an article of vicious luxury, high in price, and liable to frequent and prodigious fluctuation".[103] He even reminded Lord Palmerston, the Foreign Secretary, that "no man entertains a deeper detestation of disgrace and sin of this forced traffic on the coast of China than the humble individual who signs this dispatch".[104] However, such an opinion did not affect his view that the opium trade was financially beneficial for the British. When he learned that Lin Zexu had issued an order to arrest

[102] From May 1839, when there was an assault on the forts at Humen, the Bogue, until 24 March 1840 when the British frigate *H.M.S. Druid* arrived in the waters off Guangdong, Lin Zexu regarded the many reports of British warships coming to China as "rumors" or "falsehoods". By mid-June, when four British warships had already arrived off the Guangdong coast, Lin Zexu insisted on writing in a memorial to the throne: "Having investigated the recent arrival of British barbarian ships, they appear to be well armed but are all in fact ships continuing to carry opium". However, by the time the memorial reached the Emperor (17 July), the British had already occupied Zhoushan for twelve days.

[103] Julia Lovell, op. cit., p. 63, Quoting *Correspondence Relating to China (1840)*, p. 190.

[104] Julia Lovell, op. cit., p. 63, Quoting *Additional Papers Relating to China (1840)*, p. 5.

the British opium dealer, Lancelot Dent, he did not hesitate to place the latter under his protection, stating that this was his "duty" on the grounds that foreigners and their property should be protected from harm. Later, when Lin Zexu ordered the cessation of all trade and sealed off the "factories" on 24 March 1839, Elliot finally elevated the incident into a conflict between the two countries and made his position clear:

> I feel assured that the single mode of saving the coasts of the empire from a shocking character of warfare, both foreign and domestic, will be the very prompt and powerful intervention of Her Majesty's government for the just vindication of all wrongs, and the effectual prevention of crime and wretchedness by permanent settlement. Comprehensively considered, this measure has become of high obligation towards the Chinese government, as well as in the public interests and character of the British nation.[105]

In Britain, Elliot's behavior in China clearly had many defenders, and the garrulous Thomas Macaulay described in the British Parliament, in a rousing and unforgiving tone, what had happened to the British in Guangzhou:

> The moment at which he [i.e., Elliot] landed he was surrounded by his countrymen in an agony of despair at their situation, but the first step which he took was to order the flag of Great Britain to be taken from the boat and to be planted in the balcony. This was an act which revived the drooping hopes of those who looked to him for protection. It was natural that they should look with confidence on the victorious flag which was hoisted over them, which reminded them that they belonged to a country unaccustomed to defeat, to submission, or to shame—it reminded them that they belonged to a country which had made the farthest ends of the earth ring with the fame of her exploits in redressing the wrongs of her children; that made the Bey [Hansard text gives this as Dey_tr.] of Algiers humble himself to her insulted consul; that revenged the horrors of the black hole on the fields of Plessey; that had not degenerated since her great Protector vowed that he would make the name of Englishman as respected as ever had been the name of Roman citizen. They felt that although far from their native country, and then in danger in a part of the world remote from that to which they must look for protection, yet

[105] Julia Lovell, op. cit., p. 68, Quoting *Correspondence Relating to China (1840)*, p. 387.

that they belonged to a state which would not suffer a hair of one of its members to be harmed with impunity.[106]

Such inflammatory speeches were nothing more than a search for compensation for the opium confiscated by China and a demand to establish a legitimate basis for the subsequent opium trade. As much as he disagreed with this arrogant argument, William Gladstone, in a very gentlemanly tone, stated his opposition "because I never knew, and never read in a book, of such an unjust war, which would forever become a war of dishonor. A gentleman who had just disagreed with me spoke of flying the glorious British flag in Guangdong. However, the flag was flying to protect the infamous smuggling of goods. If such a flag were to be raised off the coast of China now, we could not but feel terror and shudder at the sight of it".[107]

The Co-hong clearly monopolized trade between foreigners and the Qing government and was in fact manipulated by local officials, but foreigners had engaged in trade under this system for many years. How to change the system in order to facilitate better and freer Sino-foreign trade did not, until this time, seem to be a problem the Qing government wanted to solve. At the time of Lin Zexu's prohibition of opium In Guangzhou, the well-known American physician and missionary, Peter Parker, translated for Lin the Swiss legist, Emmerich de Vattel's (1714–1767) *Law of Nations*, and gave the selected part the title *Geguolüli*). From it, Lin Zexu learned that it was established international practice that if a person committed crimes in a foreign country he should be dealt with by the law of that country. This was also why Lin Zexu boldly insisted on extradition, presenting a letter to Elliot demanding that he accord with the needs of the Chinese side and cooperate in surrendering the British seaman responsible for the drunken brawl in Kowloon that precipitated what came to be called the Tsim Sha Tsui Incident.

The general situation was that, after 1793, China's veil had been completely lifted, and China was gradually beginning to be described in less flattering terms, as "a belligerent nation with a hollow reputation", "a shamefully stagnant country", "a mummy that had been embalmed",

[106] Quoted from *the Opium War* by Chen Shunchen, translated by Bian Liqiang, p. 157.

[107] Ibid.

and the like. In short, with the advent of the maritime age, when Europeans discovered that the rules governing international trade that they had invented had not taken effect in China, their wish to defy the decrees of the "Celestial Kingdom" and knock down the gates of China became the main reason for their engaging in war. The immediate cause of the defeat of the Qing government in the Opium War was, of course, the obvious disparity in military strength, as well as in military technology and tactics. When the missionary Ferdinand Verbiest (1623–1688) had produced more than 500 cannons for the Qing government, the latter had been aware of the important role played by new weaponry. However, now during the Daoguang reign, the Qing army's cannons faced British warships and weapons far more advanced than their own, but in the end it was the backwardness, arrogance, and stupidity of the "Celestial Empire" in the political, military, ideological, and cultural fields that led to the utter defeat of the country. This ignorance was so total, that after Guan Tianpei and other generals were martyred defending their country at Humen, the Daoguang Emperor did not convene his leading ministers at court to review the lessons of the defeat and analyze the problem, but instead shifted the responsibility to Qishan: "To console the souls of those loyal men, you must take full responsibility for what happened".[108] This was already a worn-out state system that would be inevitably toppled by "frigates and powerful cannons".[109] Indeed, the period from the British

[108] Mao Haijian, *Tianchao de Bengkui: Yapian Zhanzheng Zai-Yanjiu* (Collapse of the Celestial Dynasty: A Re-examination of the Opium War), Beijing: Sanlian Shudian, 2005, p. 233, quoting *Chouban Yiwu Shimo* (The Management of Barbarian Affairs from Beginning to End), Daoguang Reign, v. 2, p. 86.

[109] On 21 March 1842, the military governor for Zhejiang, Liu Yunke submitted a memorial to the throne in which he outlined "ten concerns". In a question–answer format, he addressed the previous Chinese defeats in the War. He made the following points: One: In Zhejiang the Qing army has suffered two major defeats that have debilitated our troops and made it difficult to recover. Two: We continue to mobilize strong troops from the northwest, but they are far away from Zhejiang province and will not arrive in time to save the situation. Three: British weapons are abnormally lethal and cannot be resisted. Four: The British army is highly skilled in warfare on land. Five: Even if the Qing army has a fortuitous victory on land, the British troops will board their boats and flee, while the Qing army can only "look on and sigh". Six: The British army bestows small favors to win people's hearts and provide mutual security, whereas [China's] vast numbers of people "are anxious that large armies will decimate them, which is why the common folk rarely expend hatred on the common enemy". Seven: "When a large army is repeatedly defeated, the enemy is emboldened but we are discouraged, which makes it difficult for us not only to launch an attack, but even to stage a defense". Eight:

attack in the autumn of 1840 to the failure of the Qing army's counter-offensive in eastern Zhejiang in March 1842 was punctuated by the lies, ignorance, and incompetence of the Chinese officials, in addition to which the heroic sacrifice of so many Qing soldiers, meant that the metaphor of "petals falling onto flowing water" well describes the failures of the Qing armies in the Opium War.

The most arresting provisions of the *Treaty of Nanjing* were the cession of territory, the large indemnity to be paid, and the opening to Western trade of Guangzhou, Xiamen, Fuzhou, Ningbo, and Shanghai. However, the opening of these five ports to trade, the abolition of the *Co-hong* system, and the newly formulated customs excise system could be seen as a British push to adapt China to the world trading system, in fact forcefully bringing about a change in China's relationship with the world. During the War, on 10 September 1841, an article in *The Times* included this harangue:

> Something approaching to absolute terror must be inflicted before arrogancy so great, and self-confidence so deeply rooted, can be expected to give way ... There is now, unhappily, but slight apparent chance of terminating this affair without the infliction of some fearful specimen of the horrors of war.[110]

When the shipments of grain from Zhejiang are not completed, and "less than half of the harvest is done", "the atmosphere that neither will be completed prevails". Nine: Zhejiang last year suffered disastrous snowfalls, which led to an outbreak of widespread banditry in Hangzhou, Huzhou, and Shaoxing, where the situation was extremely tense". Ten: The defense budgets of seven provinces are already enormous, so "how will the troops ever be paid?" Ref: Mao Haijian, *Tianchao de Bengkui: Yapian Zhanzheng Za-Yanjiu* (Collapse of the Celestial Dynasty: A Re-examination of the Opium War), Beijing: Sanlian Shudian, 2005, pp. 414–422, citing *Yapian Zhanzheng Dang'an Shiliao* (Archives and Historical Documents of the Opium War), v. 5, pp. 88–92. All of these ten concerns relate to the corruption of the Qing armies: the unusually slow deployment of troops in the provinces, the lack of understanding of the military technology of the British army, the lack of understanding of the British army's land combat capabilities, the lack of advanced weaponry, the conflict between officials, the army and the people affecting the concentration of resistance against the British army, lack of confidence in the future of the war, the lack of government food, fear of civil resistance to the Qing government, and a lack of funds to conduct a war. These ten deeply felt anxieties were something no one at any level at court could solve, and in fact, the "ten concerns" revealed how the Opium War was accelerating the collapse of the "Heavenly dynasty".

[110] Quoted by Julia Lovell, *The Opium War*, London: Picador, 2011, p. 176.

However, after the signing of the *Treaty of Nanjing* in 1842, Elliot's view after several years' of experience in China was as follows:

> The least that is necessary for your purposes in China is best, and those purposes, or that purpose, is the security of your trade. A safe seat for your commerce is all you require in China, and all you can have without damage to yourselves. ... Avoid political combinations as much as possible, and endeavour rather to link yourselves to the people and system of China (wonderfully pliant) than force them into your Pall Mall fashions and usage.[111]

In 1851, Britain held the world's first exposition, the Great Exhibition in London's Hyde Park. Charles Dickens, viewing the Chinese products on display, took the opportunity to sneeringly comment:

> Consider the materials employed at the great Teacup Works of Kiang-tiht-Chin (or Tight-Chin) ... the laboriously carved ivory balls of the flowery Empire, ball within ball and circle within circle, which have made no advance and been of no earthly use for thousands of years.[112]

The British were increasingly dissatisfied with what they gained from the 1842 *Treaty of Nanjing* that concluded the Opium War. In 1854, citing the vague provisions of the *Wangxia Treaty* concluded between the United States and China in 1844, the British demanded the Qing government comprehensively amend the *Treaty of Nanjing*, but China rejected their demands. In 1856, when the twelve-year period covered by the *Wangxia Treaty* concluded, the United States, Britain, and France reached a tacit understanding that they would once again request to amend the *Treaty*, but this still proved unsuccessful. As a result, occasioned by events termed the *Arrow* Incident and the Margary affair, respectively, the Second Opium War broke out.[113] In June 1858, the

[111] Susanna Hoe and Derek Roebuck, *The Taking of Hong Kong: Charles and Clara Elliot in China Waters*, Richmond: Curzon, 1999, p. 206. As quoted by Julia Lovell, *The Opium War*, London: Picador, 2011, p. 172.

[112] Julia Lovell, *The Opium War*, London: Picador, 2011, p. 242.

[113] The Arrow Incident and the Father Margary Incident were referred to by the British as the "Arrow War", which together with the "Anglo-French expedition to China" or the "Second Anglo-Chinese War" were collectively known as the Second Opium War because of the connection of these events with the first Opium War. In the autumn of 1856,

Qing government separately signed the *Treaty of Tianjin* with Russia, Britain, France, and the United States, respectively, following the loss of the Taku (Dagu) Forts outside Tianjin, and in the same year, Russia forced the Manchu General Yishan (1790–1878) of Heilongjiang to sign the *Treaty of Aigun*. In August 1860, the Qing dynasty's regrets regarding the *Treaty of Tianjin* led to the renewal of warfare and the second loss of the Taku forts, after which the Qing government's attempts to negotiate peace failed, the British negotiator Sir Harry Smith Parkes, accompanied by a group of soldiers, the 39 people were stranded on September 18 at Zhangjiawan (south of Tongzhou outside Beijing), where the negotiations had taken place. In response, the Anglo-French coalition's offensive forced the Xianfeng Emperor and his entourage to flee to the imperial summer resort in Rehe (Jehol), and on October 13th the coalition forces entered Beijing, and discovered that the Qing forces had tortured the British and French envoys to death. A vengeful operation was launched: the Yuanming Yuan (Summer Palace) and the Jingyi Garden were looted and burned by the coalition forces on 18th October and more than 300 eunuchs and palace women died in the conflagration. Finally, Yixin (1833–1898), representing the Qing government, signed the *Treaty of Peking* with the representatives of the Allied armies.[114] The Second Opium War, which lasted more than four years

the Qing government seized a Chinese ship with a British flag (at that time, for a fee, the Hong Kong administration would allow anyone to fly a British flag) and imprisoned its crew as pirates. Sir Harry Smith Parkes (1828–1885), the British consul, protested, claiming that the ship should be handed over to Hong Kong because it was registered in the British colony. Ye Mingchen, the governor-general of Liangguang, only returned the captives, but did not meet the British demand for the British flag to be raised back to the top of the ship's mast, leading the British side to refuse to accept the captives. The upshot was that the captives were ordered to be beheaded, leading to the escalation of the conflict. At the same time, Britain invited France to join in a declaration of war against China, and Emperor Napoleon III used the murder of the French missionary Auguste Chapdelaine (1814–1856) in Xilin, Guangxi, as a pretext to form a coalition with the British in a war against China. In December 1857, the coalition army took Guangzhou, where Ye Mingchen was captured and taken to Calcutta, where he died.

[114] In the game between the Qing dynasty and the Western powers on the commitment to honor the *Treaty of Tianjin*, on 8 March 1860 the British and French envoys sent a letter to the Qing court making four demands, to which the Qing court did not agree and the fighting against the British and French coalition forces was resumed. The Qing forces were defeated and withdrew. The British sent Sir Harry Smith Parkes to negotiate with Senggelinqin who had "retreated" to Tongzhou. When Parkes proposed to enter Beijing to present a letter from the coalition nations to the Xianfeng Emperor, the request was

from October 1856 to November 1860, ended in China's defeat. As a result, China lost more than 1.5 million square kilometers of territory in the northeast and northwest. Subsequently, foreign embassies in Beijing strengthened their influence over and links with the Qing government, and the tentacles of foreign capital began to penetrate the country from the south-eastern coast. Over the next few years, the Qing government would have to rely on assistance from the Great Powers to surround and eliminate the Taiping Heavenly Kingdom. On 26 April 1863, *The New York Times* reported that British opium traffickers tried to thwart the Chinese government's opium ban.[115]

VII

In the period of more than a decade after Dickens described the concentric ivory spheres from China in the pages of *The Times* until *The New York Times* reported that Britain had not reduced its opium exports to China with the signing of the *Treaty of Nanjing* but had shamelessly expanded the trade, China's politics, economy, and society continued to weaken and deteriorate, and an increasing number of problems began to emerge, accumulate, and interconnect.

refused and only after the Qing court later backed down was Parkes allowed to see the emperor. However, it was stipulated that he had to perform the kotow, so Parkes refused. As a result, the Qing court detained 39 members of his mission. Ref: "The Annals of Emperor Wenzong" in *Draft History of the Qing* (fasc. 20) recorded: "On the *guihai* day of the eighth month, when foreign soldiers arrived in Tongzhou, the sixth Prince Yi, Zaiyuan [who had the confidence of the Xianfeng Emperor] bribed officers to arrest the English envoy Parkes and transport him to Beijing". (In fact, as early as 14 September, before the negotiations, the Xianfeng Emperor had already issued an edict, ordering that Parkes and the others "be detained in Tongzhou, not allowed to return, and be prevented from conspiring". Only after the conclusion of peace negotiations, after the war, would they be released.) Subsequently, the allies attacked, and the emperor fled. When the Qing dynasty returned the hostages, only nineteen of them were still alive and the rest had been tortured and died. Finally, the British retaliated by burning the Summer Palace to the ground. The British commander Lord Elgin pointed out to Harry Parkes in early October that burning the palace would be punishment for the Xianfeng Emperor alone, rather than his people as would an attack on the capital. Ref: Frederick Wakeman, *The Fall of Imperial China*, New York: Simon and Schuster, 1975, p. 158.

115 Zheng Xiyuan ed., *Diguo de Huiyi: "Niuyue Shibao" Wan-Qing Guancha Ji* (Reminiscence of the Empire: Notes on The New York Times' Reports on Late Qing China), Beijing: Sanlian Shudian, 2001, pp. 24–25.

In January 1851, the same year that Britain hosted the Great Exhibition, Hong Xiuquan (1814–1864) announced the establishment of his "Taiping Heavenly Kingdom", proclaiming himself the "Heavenly King" of this "new dynasty". The Heavenly Kingdom's followers were mainly the poor of the Lingnan region. Because of his early introduction to *The Holy Bible* in Chinese translation by Protestant missionaries, Hong Xiuquan, who had suffered a number of early academic failures and had no career prospects, decided to "reform" Christian teachings, justifying his actions and claim that he was the younger brother of Jesus Christ. This distinguished the Taiping Heavenly Kingdom from most previous Chinese popular uprisings. The Taiping Heavenly Kingdom issued a manifesto attacking the corruption and incompetence of the Qing court and calling on Chinese people to overthrow this dynasty and its Manchu rulers, effectively marking the resistance of believers. Based on the support of more disgruntled people against the Qing government, the self-proclaimed Taiping Heavenly Kingdom lasted fourteen years (1851–1864) and their sacking of cities posed a direct threat to the dynasty, but its guiding ideology ostensibly based on Christianity was in fact far removed from Christian doctrine. It is easy to regard the words and deeds of the leaders of the Taiping Heavenly Kingdom as those of a cult: their regulations called for the implementation of abstinence, the separation of men and women, and the elimination of prostitution, yet the leaders dressed as deities and demons and were utterly promiscuous in their lifestyle.[116] The Taiping Rebellion led to the deaths of more than 20 million people, and the resulting disasters saw the outbreak of plague and the further breakdown of society. In fact, the Taiping leaders had no shared determination to achieve victory and remained locked in sanguinary internal power struggles. Moreover, the Western powers

[116] W. A. P. Martin (1827–1916), the Amer[can missionary who had lived for a long time in China and had originally planned to aid the Taiping Heavenly Kingdom, has provided this assessment: "While it is true that nothing but the active aid of foreigners saved the Manchu government at more than one critical moment in the course of this long conflict, it is equally certain that the ignorance of the rebel chief is primarily responsible for his disastrous failure" (p. 133). And of Hong Xiuquan, Martin provided the following description: "He sanctioned robbery and violence, and himself set the example of polygamy, an example eagerly followed by his subordinates, who had no scruple in filling their harems with the wives and daughters of their enemies". Ref: W. A. P. Martin, *A Cycle of Cathay, or China, South and North, with Personal Reminiscences*, Edinburgh and London: Oliphant Anderson and Ferrier, 1897, p. 135.

were self-interested and did not lend them support simply because the teachings of the Taiping Heavenly Kingdom were ostensibly related to Christianity. Instead, they decided to uphold and consolidate the implementation of the treaties previously signed with the Qing government by helping the latter annihilate the Taiping Heavenly Kingdom. It seems that there was also no cooperation between the Taiping Heavenly Kingdom and other contemporary anti-Qing peasant rebellions, including the Nian Army in the north and the Red Turbans in the south, so these various independent forces all ultimately failed.

The Qing armies engaged in besieging the Taiping Heavenly Kingdom and Nian Army were mainly led by Zeng Guofan, Li Hongzhang, and Zuo Zongtang. Although these prominent officials were ethnic Han, the Manchus lacked any ability to address the court's problematic external relations so, even if the Qing dynasty discriminated against the ethnic Han in their unspoken rules, the chaos into which the nation had been plunged forced the court to turn to these ethnic Han officials. It would seem that a significant reason why Zeng Guofan and other ethnic Han officials sought to repress the Taiping Heavenly Kingdom was to defend Confucian orthodoxy forcefully in the face of the Taiping Heavenly Kingdom's so-called Christian teachings, so that the nationalist anti-Manchu slogans of the Taiping Heavenly Kingdom were naturally also temporarily suppressed. Thus, the Manchu-ruled state and the Confucian orthodoxy continued to support each other. In the suppression of the Taiping Heavenly Kingdom the Manchu reliance on ethnic Han officials enhanced the local power of the latter, and this development culminated in the "Southeast Mutual Protection Agreement" of 1900 that sought to avoid the chaos in the north resulting from the warfare triggered by the Boxer Rebellion. Throughout this period, ethnic Han officials were beginning to occupy important positions in the power structure within the Qing government.

After the Taiping and Nian rebels were defeated, the Qing court could relax a little, as though it still had hope, and some people began to use the term "*Zhongxing*" (mid-term revival or restoration) to characterize the Qing government's new lease of life. Although this new climate had its origins during the reign of the Xianfeng Emperor (r. 1851–1861), because many achievements of the new policy appeared in the subsequent reign of the Tongzhi Emperor (1861–1874), historians more commonly speak of the "Tongzhi Restoration".[117] In 1860, the peace negotiated by the Qing government with the Anglo-French coalition temporarily eased the tension with the Great Powers, and the annihilation of the Taiping Heavenly Kingdom (1864) relieved the dynasty of the threat of imminent overthrow. Clear-sighted Chinese officials, pondering their country's military defeat in the two Opium Wars, had a keen understanding of the importance in warfare of being equipped with advanced ships and weaponry, as Qian Mu pointed out in his *Guoshi Dagang* (Outline History of China): "In his diary entry for the 7th day of the 5th month of the 1st year of the Tongzhi reign-period [3 June 1862], Zeng Guofan discussed the meaning of the concept of *yangwu* (usually translated as 'the Foreign Affairs [movement]'): 'The way to effect Self-Strengthening and to improve policy is to seek out virtuous and talented persons for urgent tasks, such as studying the manufacture of explosives and cannons, shipbuilding, vehicle construction, and other practical skills'". [Hsü, p. 345; Teng and Fairbank, *China's Response*, p. 62] The improved policies which Zeng Guofan envisaged would preoccupy the subsequent period of nearly four decades of difficult and productive change, and the enterprises developed and the issues involved in the changes effected during those years are so difficult to demarcate that historians tend to characterize the developments in this period using vague portmanteau terms such as the "Foreign Affairs Movement" (*yangwu yundong*), "Self-Strengthening Movement" (*ziqiang yundong*), and "new administration of the Tong-Guang reigns" (*Tong-Guang xinzheng*).

In the decades of the "Foreign Affairs movement", people again felt that Western missionaries played a role. Even though the cult practices of the Taiping Heavenly Kingdom in the name of Christianity fueled suspicions about Christianity, the threats and psychological changes brought about by two Opium Wars led the missionaries to once again play a

117 This term was first used by Qing scholars in 1869.

role and command attention.[118] In 1843, W. H. Medhurst (1796–1857), an English missionary, set up the London Missionary Society Press (known in Chinese as the Mohai Library) in Shanghai and, through its translations, became a modern publisher of many books treating Western technology and culture. Wang Tao (1828–1897), who worked at the Library, had at one point corresponded with the Taiping Heavenly Kingdom and as a consequence became a fugitive hunted by the Qing government. However, he went on to become the editor-in-chief of *Global Daily* (Xunhuan Ribao) in Hong Kong which enthusiastically promoted the ideas of self-strengthening and reform and as a result was accepted by the Qing dynasty's *yangwu* (Foreign Affairs) modernizers. At the same time, when the poor were invariably welcomed by missionary-run schools though the rich and powerful despised such schools, it was easier for lower-class young people from unprejudiced families to accept the influence of foreign teachers. Such schools trained students like Yung Wing (1828–1912) and Zheng Guanying (1842–1922) who would later play significant roles as reformers.[119] With exchanges and communication

[118] In 1724, the Yongzheng Emperor declared Christianity to be a pernicious cult and, as a result, the work of Western missionaries was further hampered. However, the mission did not completely end because of these difficulties, as W. A. P. Martin made clear:

> In 1724 the missionaries were banished, and their converts sent into exile. The little communities scattered throughout the vast interior owed their preservation then, as they may again, to a want of concert among mandarins in enforcing the prohibitory laws. In China, as in the Roman empire, persecution raged in one province, while Christians were unmolested in another. For a century and a quarter, the supreme power showed no disposition to revoke its prohibitory enactments, and from time to time they were put into spasmodic execution. At the close of the opium war a good many of the faithful were still in exile.
>
> During all this time a few missionaries were able to conceal themselves in Christian villages, whither they penetrated at the risk of life, that they might comfort and sustain their persecuted brethren.

Ref: W. A. P. Martin, *A Cycle of Cathay, or China, South and North, with Personal Reminiscences*, Edinburgh and London: Oliphant Anderson and Ferrier, 1897, p. 440.

This situation continued until 1844, when the Sino-French treaty led to the express lifting of the ban on foreign missionaries.

[119] Yung Wing started out as a student at a preparatory school linked to Robert Morrison's school and later moved directly from Macao to Hong Kong, where he attended Robert Morrison's school. Zheng Guanying studied at the Anglo-Chinese School, run by the British missionary John Fryer in Shanghai, where he attended night classes in English, as well as learning about Western politics and economics.

with foreigners becoming more frequent, knowledge of foreign languages became an important tool. In 1862 (the 1st year of the Tongzhi Reign), the Qing government opened the Tongwen Guan (College of Foreign Languages), a school teaching foreign languages in which the teachers were all foreigners.[120] Subsequently, in 1863, the military governor of Jiangsu, Li Hongzhang issued a memorial requesting to be allowed to set up a Tongwen Guan in Shanghai, which would later be renamed the Guangfang Yanguan (College of Foreign Languages, lit., College of Languages of Far-flung Places), and in 1864, Guangzhou also set up a Tongwen Guan. Through the efforts of prescient officials, the original Tongwen Guan set up an additional science division in 1865, known as the Kexue Guan (Science College). These initiatives were all part of the Self-Strengthening Movement. A memorial submitted to the emperor by Prince Gong, Yixin had this to say:

> It is apparent that the foreign manufacture of machinery, artillery, and other objects, as well as of ships and military vehicles, all derives from a knowledge of astronomy and mathematics. Now Shanghai, as well as Zhejiang and other places, are requesting various types of steamships, and this will entail real efforts grappling with fundamentals, because if we only concern ourselves with external aspects this will be of no practical benefit. I and several others discussed how we should proceed, so now we propose to add another college [to the Tongwen Guan] and recruit Manchu and Han graduates (*juren*) of the metropolitan examinations, as well as the five other kinds of 'tribute students' (*gongshi*), if their written Chinese is fluent and they are more than twenty years of age. ······ They will all study the principles of mathematics and science, the technology for designing machinery, and the keys to surveying and measurement and, if this is all done precisely, pragmatically, and thoroughly, this will be China's path of Self-Strengthening.

120 Originally the Hanlin College compiler (*bianxiu*) Guo Songtao issued a memorial calling for the provision of studies of Western languages. The subsequently established imperial language college called the Tongwen Guan had as its founding English-language teacher the British missionary John Shaw Burdon. In 1863, the Tongwen Guan also established French and Russian language departments. Among later teachers at the school were John Fryer, and subsequently the American missionary W. A. P. Martin. The school's first intake of students comprised eight Manchu Banner students, but given a limited pool of Manchu students to draw on, the intake was later open to ethnic Han students.

The measures adopted for learning from the West were resisted and opposed by conservative officials. For example, Zhang Shengzao (1819–1896), the Censor overseeing the Shandong Circuit, was firmly opposed to the College accepting Manchu and Han graduates of the metropolitan examinations, saying that such students should be limited to studying the teachings of Confucius and Mencius, to prevent them from losing the purity of Confucian ethics and rites through the study of technical skills. Grand Secretary Woren argued bluntly that barbarians could not be used as teachers, otherwise the Chinese nation would perish. However, none of this resistance stopped the development of education employing missionaries and foreigners to impart Western knowledge, and in the forty-year history of the Tongwen College it is clear that the work of the American Presbyterian missionary W. A. P. Martin and the Irish missionary C. H. Oliver was extremely influential. In 1863, Feng Guifen (1809–1874]) first proposed inviting foreigners to serve as teachers and Li Hongzhang memorialized that the court approve the establishment of the Shanghai Guangfang Yanguan. In 1868, the Jiangnan Arsenal's Translation Hall was established and in the following year it was integrated with the Shanghai Guangfang Yanguan. In this new enterprise the British John Fryer,[121] as well the American missionary Young John Allen[122] made remarkable contributions through their teaching and translation work.

[121] John Fryer (1839–1928) came to China in 1861 and taught successively in Hong Kong, Beijing, and Shanghai. In 1868, he was hired as a translator by the Jiangnan Arsenal, and also served as a teacher at the Guangfang Yanguan (College of Foreign Languages) in Shanghai, as a director of the Shanghai Polytechnic (Gezhi Shuyuan) and was editor-in-chief of the *Chinese Scientific Magazine* (Gezhi Huibian). He translated some 77 titles in the military, engineering, and social science fields, and his work provided the basis for establishing norms for translation in China.

[122] Young John Allen (1836–1907) came to China in 1860 as a missionary. He entered the Guangfang Yanguan (College of Foreign Languages) in 1869 and resigned in 1881 to work as a translator at the Anglo-Chinese College and as a missionary. He was responsible for translating more than 250 works. John Fryer recalled: "Allen worked assiduously at that time, day and night and in all weather. Every morning he taught at the College of Foreign Languages, and in the afternoon he rushed to the Manufactory to translate books, and in the evening he edited *Review of the Times* [Wanguo Gongbao]; on Sunday he worked day and night preaching and handling church affairs. We were colleagues for ten years, and I never saw him take a break, even though I urged him to rest a little from his labors, to safeguard his health; it can be said there was not a single lazy bone in his body". Quoted From Zhao Rui, *Ziqiang Xinzheng* (The New Self-Strengthening Administration), Shanghai: Shanghai Shudian, 2002, p. 74.

Liang Qichao (1873–1929) made the following assessment of the careers of these men and their Chinese colleagues:

> [After the Opium War,] alarmed by the Westerners' powerful ships and armaments, the Arsenal in Shanghai was established and to it was attached the College of Foreign Languages (Guangfang Yanguan). Like the Tongwen Guan established in Beijing, it sent students to study in the United States, the purpose being to train a pool of specialist translators. The students' aspirations did not go beyond this. Therefore, for several decades, there was no change in the realm of ideas, but the Arsenal did succeed in translating some thirty scientific books, variously produced by Li Shanlan, Hua Hengfang, and Zhao Zhonghan. These men were all intellectually solid and their translation work was conscientious and committed, so their achievements were as impressive as those of Xu Guangqi and Li Zhizao in the Ming dynasty.[123]

In 1887, Protestant missionaries, diplomats, and businessmen from the United States and Great Britain founded the Christian Literature Society for China in Shanghai. The main members were Alexander Williamson (the founder, 1829–1890), Timothy Richards (who served successive terms as the Society's director), William Muirhead (1822–1900), Young John Allen, Joseph Edkins, William A.P. Martin, Gilbert Reid (1857–1927), and other missionaries. In fact, the Society was primarily a publishing institution, compiling and publishing more than 2000 works not limited to theology and technology; it also produced books treating history, politics, law, business, literature, and other subjects. When the Guangxu Emperor was preparing to implement his reform program in the late 1890s, he purchased more than a hundred books treating new Western studies, 89 of which were published by the Society. Kang Youwei (1858–1927), who was behind the push for reforms in 1898, acknowledged that his ideas for change came mainly from the writings of Timothy Richards and Young John Allen.

In view of the fact that the two Opium Wars highlighted the inability of the Qing government's two original bodies for handling foreign relations—the Li Bu (Board of Rites) and Lifan Yuan (Court of Colonial Affairs), to deal with China's diplomatic imbroglio, largely because

[123] Quoted in Zhao Rui, op. cit., p. 75.

foreigners refused to accede to China's protocols treating foreign countries as tributary states or vassals, the Qing court in 1860 set up a diplomatic agency called the Fuyi Ju (Barbarian Pacification Bureau). However, Westerners already regarded the word "*yi*" ("barbarian") as a slur on them, and in the text of the *Treaty of Tianjin* explicitly requested that the Qing government discontinue the use of the term. On 11 January 1861, Prince Gong (Yixin) met with Gui Liang and Wenxiang and together they compiled the "Six Draft Articles Proposing General Preparations for the Establishment of the Barbarian Affairs Office", which can be regarded as the beginning of the *Yangwu* (Foreign Affairs) Movement. In accordance with the requirements of the reform, the name of Fuyi Ju (Barbarian Pacification Bureau) was changed to Zongli Geguo Shiwu Yamen (Office for General Management of the Various Nations' Affairs), more simply known as the Zongli Yamen (Office for General Management). Thus, a national body for handling foreign relations was created, a far cry from the previous situation when the Xianfeng Emperor merely conferred on his Plenipotentiary Minister in Guangzhou the authority to deal with "barbarian matters" (*yiwu*). In November 1861, Prince Gong (Yixin) and the Empress Dowager Cixi entered into an agreement and staged a coup, placing real power in the hands of Cixi. Subsequently, the Zongli Yamen was gradually transformed from an office temporarily handling foreign affairs into a military cabinet proposing reform initiatives. Having previously won the palace's support for his political victory in successful negotiations with Britain and with the support of the Great Powers, Yixin[124] made the following observation: "When we drew up the six-point proposal, our major concern was investigating the enemy and enhancing our defense, in order to prevent future disasters. However, this constituted only the trunk of the tree, and we failed to explore the root problem. A policy of exploring the root problem hinges on Self-Strengthening, and the art of Self-Strengthening lies in the training of soldiers". In the process of besieging the Taiping Heavenly Kingdom, the

[124] The British ambassador, Sir Frederick Bruce, expressed his support for the coup at court in a report to the British Foreign Office: "Over the past twelve months, we have been successful in cultivating a faction that favours and believes in the possibility of friendly engagement and effectively helped that faction take power. We have established a satisfactory relationship in Beijing and have, to some extent, become advisers to the government, whereas eighteen months ago we were at war with that government". Quoted in Xu Zhongyue, *Zhongguo Jindai Shi* (Modern Chinese History), vol. 1, Hong Kong: Chinese University Press, 2006, p. 264.

Qing government, at the same time as purchasing foreign ships, artillery, and military weapons, hired Westerners to train its revamped armies. In view of the seriousness of the situation, the Qing court needed increasingly effective support, and so ethnic Han armies, Zeng Guofan's Hunan Army and Li Hongzhang's Huai Army, also benefited from modern weapons outfitting and training. Zeng Guofan was so eager to build military ships and expected to win the decisive victory in the war that he began setting up an armaments factory after the capture of Anqing in 1861, which became the Anqing Arsenal. In 1866, China's domestically built warship, the *Huanghu*, was successfully launched, marking the birth of China's modern military industry. Below is a list of the major industrial achievements pioneered by those supporting the Foreign Affairs or Self-Strengthening movement:

1861: Zongli Geguo Shiwu Yamen (Foreign Office) was established, and Zeng Guofan set up the Anqing Arsenal.
1862: Tongwen Guan was established in Beijing; Xu Shou[125] succeeded in the manufacture of China's first practical steam engine; Li Hongzhang founded the Shanghai Maritime Artillery Bureau and hired German officers to train Chinese military personnel in the use of rifles.
1863: Li Hongzhang opened a foreign languages school in Shanghai (Guangfang Yanguan), and Prince Gong organized the purchase of eight British steamships.
1864: Li Hongzhang set up the Foreign Artillery Bureau in Suzhou; Tongwen Guan set up in Guangzhou
1865: Li Hongzhang set up Jinling Machine Factory; Zeng Guofan and Li Hongzhang set up the Jiangnan Arsenal in Shanghai.
1866: Zuo Zongtang set up the Fuzhou Dockyard at Mawei outside Fuzhou; Chonghou set up the Tianjin Machine Factory.
1867: Li Hongzhang set up the Jinling Machine Factory.
1869: Fuzhou Machine Factory set up.
1872: Zuo Zongtang set up the Lanzhou Machine Factory; Li Hongzhang supported the inauguration of the China Merchants'

[125] Xu Shou (1818–1884) was born in Wuxi, Jiangsu Province. He is an erudite who has studied western natural science and engineering technology. He once made a compass and quadrant. In Anqing Inner Ordnance Institute, he participated in the manufacture of China's first practical steam engine.

Steam Navigation Company (Zhaoshang Ju); Zeng Guofan and Li Hongzhang issued a proposal to send thirty boys to the United States to study.
1875: Ding Baozhen proposed the establishment of the Shandong Machine Factory.
1878: Kaiping Coal Mines Bureau was established.
1879: Sheng Xuanhuai (1844–1916) set up Jingmen Coal Mine in Hubei; Zuo Zongtang founded Lanzhou Cotton Mill; the telegraph line between Dagu (Taku) and Tianjin was inaugurated.
1880: Li Hongzhang set up a telegraph office and naval academy in Tianjin.
1881: Li Hongzhang and others oversaw the opening of the Pingquan Copper Mine in Chengde; completion of the telegraph line between Shanghai and Tianjin.
1885: The Qing government inaugurated the Board of the Admiralty in Beijing.
1886: Zhang Zhidong (1837–1909) established a textile mill in Guangzhou.
1888: Establishment of the Beiyang Fleet.
1889: Zhang Zhidong prepared to construct an iron mill at Hanyang in Hubei.
1890: Zhang Zhidong established the Daye iron mines, the Hanyang iron mill, and the Pingxiang coal mine.
1891: Li Hongzhang established a paper mill in Shanghai.
1893: Li Hongzhang established a comprehensive mechanized cotton textile mill.
1894: Hubei Match Company established; Hubei Textile Company established as a "joint government-merchant undertaking".
1898: China's first modern bank, Imperial Bank of China (Zhongguo Tongshang Yinhang), opened.

Shortly after the conclusion of the *Treaty of Beijing* between the British, French, and Qing governments, Li Hongzhang was well aware of China's inherent problems. His letter to Prince Gong and Wenxiang in 1864 is an extremely important historical document, quite unlike statements by most court officials. At this point, Li stressed the importance of accepting Western scientific knowledge, the need for the country to reform, and the simultaneous importance of training talented men in this new knowledge:

> I, Hongzhang believe that for everything in the world, when all means are exhausted, changes have been necessary; once changes have been made, a solution emerges.. China's scholar-officials are immersed in the accumulated conventions of classical rhetoric and epigraphy, and while our military officers and soldiers are brave and uncomplaining, they are also ignorant and far from meticulous, and as a result must apply what they have not studied and have studied what has no application. When there is no threat, they can only denounce foreign weaponry as strange and devilish trickery that there is no need to study; when there is a threat, they fear foreign weaponry as strange and devilish trickery that they are incapable of studying. They fail to realize that foreigners have committed themselves to the study of weaponry for hundreds of years. Once this fact is realized and the requisite creative forces are mustered, then there will be a true overall direction and what is wanted can be quickly achieved. ...To begin with Britain and France regarded Japan as a foreign dependency and made outlandish demands of the country. Japanese officials were enraged and resolute, selected the most talented of the sons of their aristocrats and officials and send them to factories in the West to study various disciplines, and also purchased machines which could be studied and mastered in Japan. They are now able to navigate steamships and manufacture heavy ordnance. ······ If China wishes to strengthen itself, then it is a priority to study foreign weaponry. To learn what makes foreign countries "special" there is nothing better than studying the machines that make machines, mastering their methods without having to use their people. If one wants to acquire such machines and the persons who produce them, then we should specially select a group of scholars who are rewarded for their commitment, so that the industry can take shape and be refined, and talented persons will also be attracted to it.[126]

Based on deeply rooted Confucian traditions and a self-sustaining network at the Qing court, the Foreign Affairs Movement was, after all, a national movement enforced by events and the participating Confucian elites clearly hoped, through their own efforts, to help the Qing government survive, prosper, and grow strong. The Foreign Affairs Movement first took on the task of construction related to national military technology and strength as a result of witnessing the effective annihilation

[126] Teng and Fairbank, *China's Response to the West: A Documentary Survey*, Cambridge: Harvard University Press, 1954.

of the Taiping Heavenly Kingdom by Western military forces and their new weapons. At the same time, in order to reduce the heavy-handed bullying of the Great Powers and to do their utmost to maintain the dignity of the "Chinese world", the reformers also needed new weapons, and they reasoned that by relying on their own production they could guarantee achieving the goals they set themselves. This was a movement copying only one aspect of Western civilization and was far removed from industrialization's historical logic and processes, but now a minority elite group, whose members with the exception Manchu Prince Gong, were all ethnic Han, was making the utmost effort to save the imperiled Qing dynasty. A number of factories and mills suddenly appeared in China, and the nation's landscape began to change. However, even though government officials in many localities promoted and supported the movement, this did not mean it was a broad-based private industrial movement, as major factories and manufacturing bureaus were largely in the hands of government officials, with whom businessmen worked but accepted their leadership. Such businesses were called ***guandu-shangban*** enterprises, meaning those "supervised by officials and run by businessmen". In terms of capital investment specifically, enterprises built as part of the Foreign Affairs Movement were financed mainly by local officials and, as the head of the central government, the emperor's involvement was by and large limited to simply granting permission. However, capital was always limited, so that the comprador with private capital became the element facilitating the introduction of industrialization. In view of the fact that the Foreign Affairs Movement meant government officials decided on industrial policies and were responsible for regulating them, as well as providing legitimacy for the approval and planning of projects, and that agents of private capital were the actual managers of enterprises, this was the earliest example of bureaucratic capitalism using government resources and mobilizing private forces to achieve governmental or national goals. Given that foreign capital was determinedly prevented from entering China,[127] this system was temporarily more powerful in

[127] Based on the 1858 *Treaty of Tianjin*, which allowed the Chinese and British parties to revise the provisions of the treaty after ten years, the two sides took the opportunity to complete a new revised text, which did contain provisions for further reform encouraging cooperation. However, since the signed revised version did not contain terms that British merchants and entrepreneurs hoped for, such as provisions for investing in China so that China would not simply be regarded as a future market for commodities other than opium but also as a source and production base for industrial raw materials, the revised

promoting enterprises than purely private industry. However, the movement's intended purpose was obviously to directly serve the state and the regime, and it was not part of any movement to develop its economy in line with the logic of Western industry. Even though the "Foreign Affairs" (*yangwu*) policy was seriously criticized within the Qing government and many stubborn and conservative officials believed that it was contrary to traditional Confucian views, those critics discovered that the technocratic officials were growing increasingly powerful. However, no member of the "Foreign Affairs" group believed that the development of the private economy was justified and worthy of encouragement, unless it served to make the country prosperous and strong. The slogan of the Foreign Affairs Movement in its early stages was "self-strengthening", and later "enriching the nation". It is therefore easy to understand how the Foreign Affairs movement which lasted more than three decades was expressed as "state capitalism".

As a member of the elite ranks of the Foreign Affairs Movement, Feng Guifen, who was a *jinshi* graduate of the palace examinations of the Daoguang reign (1821–1850) and entered the service of Li Hongzhang after the latter's Huai Army arrived in Shanghai, provided intellectual nourishment for the new Self-Strengthening order. Feng in his collection of works titled *Essays of Protest from Xiaobin Studio* (Xiaobinlu Kangyi) wrote: "For China, the Confucian teachings are the source, which can be supplemented by technology to make the country rich and strong". Feng regarded the traditional Confucian classics as China's core teachings, and as long as China was equipped with Western technology, they could continue to ensure the rule of the Chinese Empire. Feng even made suggestions directed at avoiding excessive centralization and bureaucracy in the organizational structure of government administration, and his views which emphasized both military and diplomatic issues strongly influenced Li Hongzhang. Previously, Wei Yuan had insisted on using Western technology to resist Westerners, expressed as "a mastery of barbarian technical skills to resist barbarians"; now, it was being more clearly argued that the use of Western technology could in fact serve

document was not approved by the British Parliament. The positions of Prince Gong and Li Hongzhang, who advocated further cooperation with the British, were thus also significantly weakened at court. Later, under provisions of the *Treaty of Shimonoseki*, Japan was permitted to open factories on Chinese territory.

China's philosophical orthodoxy. Sheng Xuanhuai and other leading officials active in the Foreign Affairs Movement summarized this new view with the formulation "Chinese fundamentals and Western applications" (*Zhong ti - Xi yong*), meaning that the fundamentals or corpus (*ti*) of Confucian orthodoxy did not need to be changed. However, what could be changed were the specific techniques or technologies and applications (*yong*) for maintaining the fundamentals. At this time, many people hoped that the nation could be salvaged from its plight using this reformist dichotomy between fundamentals and applications. Philosophically, these people argued that neither the teachings of the ancient sages and the ancient methods of the archaic period (Feng Guifen's formulation) nor the teachings of Yao, Shun, Yu, Tang, Kings Wen and Wu, and the Duke of Zhou (Xue Fucheng's formulation) should be changed, and the use of Western technology would serve fortuitously to maintain the ways of the ancestors. Even so, the Foreign Affairs group found it difficult to implement their enterprise, as for example with construction of railways. The Foreign Affairs reformers argued that there was a pressing need to construct railways but, as foreign journalists noted at the time, the Qing dynasty recoiled from the new foreign technologies, and the government maintained that the construction of railways would result in the unemployment of coolies, cart drivers, and boatmen, and rouse opposition to the government. At the same time, it argued that, as a result of the introduction of new technologies, the power of foreigners would increase so that "interaction with foreigners would become viciously complicated", in addition to which the Qing populace by dint of their feudal superstitions would see the construction of railways as destroying the *fengshui* of their land and adversely affecting their lives and agriculture.[128] By 1876, the British firm of Jardine Matheson in Shanghai had, without the permission of the Qing government, built a railway running 15 kilometers from Wusong to Shanghai, but after more than a year of operations, the Qing government simply resumed it for 282,000 taels of silver and dismantled it. In August 1878, in North China the Kaiping Mining Bureau presided over by "Foreign Affairs" reformers officially opened, and in order to transport coal from the mining area to the docks for loading, Li Hongzhang presented a memorial at court requesting that a railway be built. Li hired the Kaiping Mining Bureau's engineer, the

[128] *The New York Times*, 3 June 1867.

Englishman Claude William Kinder, to take charge of construction, and on 9 June 1881, construction finally began on China's first railway, the Tang-Xu Railway.[129] In 1886, pushed by the Foreign Affairs group, the Kaiping Railway Company was established to operate the railway business independently. After that, the railway continued to expand, to Tianjin (1888), and further afield in different directions. China's railway history was underway.

An important element transforming Chinese history at this juncture was the movement to study abroad, which was actively promoted by Yung Wing, who had studied as a youth in the United States and eventually graduated from Yale University. In fact, those leading figures in the Foreign Affairs group had from the beginning noted the extreme importance of acquiring Western technology and the corresponding talent to enable the nation to "self-strengthen". Li Hongzhang perspicaciously told a group of recruits inducted into the school newly established at the Jiangnan Arsenal: "In setting up this manufacturing bureau and opening the college for teaching, you are providing the basis for an uplifting plan. By going abroad to study in this field and exchanging wide-ranging ideas, your work will be of benefit for a long time to come". At the same time as Zeng Guofan commissioned Yung Wing to buy machinery in the United States, his efforts to send Chinese directly to the West to study were about to be realized. Even though the earlier employment of Westerners as language teachers at Tongwen Guan had met with opposition from traditional Confucian scholars, this did not prevent Zeng Guofan and Li Hongzhang from signing a charter in 1871 to select children to go the United States to study, and in 1872 Yung Wing and Chen Lanbin led the first group of thirty youngsters to study in the United States in what came to be known as the Chinese Educational Mission (1872–1881), under whose auspices 120 young Chinese boys went to the New England area to

[129] When the Kaiping Railway was still in the planning stage, the court again called off construction, so that the only recourse of the Kaiping Mining Bureau was to excavate a canal to transport coal. However, the canal had to be dug through high and steep terrain at Xiugezhuang village, and the river could not be led uphill. The Mining Bureau again requested to be allowed to construct a railway, and the court approved the request on condition that only a small section between Xiugezhuang village and Tangshan be constructed. However, in consideration of not angering the spirits of the Qing emperors interred at the Qing Eastern Mausolea (Dongling), the Qing court prohibited the use of locomotives to pull the carriages and only permitted that they be dragged along by horses, which became known in Chinese history as the "iron horse railway".

pursue studies at American schools, colleges, and universities. It seemed that the Mission eventually met with failure when in 1881 the Zongli Yamen submitted a memorial calling on the emperor "to recall all the students who had gone overseas", and on 21 August an American pastor organized a farewell party for the first of three batches of Chinese students about to leave the United States to return to China. Indeed, it would seem that the opponents to Western learning in the Qing government had won out, and the students who had studied telegraphy or railway construction and now had liberal beliefs were ignored and not even given a second glance on their return to their homeland:

> What a sea of faces surround us, yet there is no friendly recognition, no kindly smile greeted our forlorn band. Instead, crowds of coolies, wheelbarrows and jinrickshaw men were shouting, gesticulating, and quarreling for business.
> Only one person came to pick up us, who was Mr. Lu, the one took care of our letters and he was so stupid that even common Chinese people would be better than him. We were taken to the harbormaster's office not in sedan chairs nor even in rickshaws but on large, uncomfortable, open-air wooden wheelbarrows customarily used by the lower classes. We went so slowly on such a thing and were again exposed to those people with surprise and ridicule.[130]

Above Huang describes part of "the shabby and mean treatment we received at the hands of our paternal government". Although Li Hongzhang inducted seventy of the returning students into his Beiyang Naval Academy, but given the political decline of the Qing government, those among them with Western technical knowledge who later became intelligent and courageous officers would never be able to reverse the damage caused by China's defeat in the Sino-Japanese War. Yet the Chinese students sent to the United States a decade previously would

[130] Huang Kaijia (1860–1906) in a letter of 28 January 1882 to his host parent in the United States, Mrs. Fannie P. Bartlett. The above passage is excerpted from: Edward J. M. Rhoads, *Stepping Forth into the World: The Chinese Educational Mission to the United States, 1872–81*, Aberdeen, HK: Hong Kong University Press, 2011, pp. 184–185.

in fact greatly contribute to changing China through their mastery of Western ideas and their responsible careers.[131]

The Foreign Affairs Movement had long been underway when Zhang Zhidong published his *Quan Xue Pian* (Exhortation to Learning) in 1898. This work was intended to serve as general reading material summarizing issues of popular concern regarding the Self-Strengthening reforms. It demarcated the boundaries between "new" and "old" knowledge for people at this time and expressed the author's understanding of the stance Chinese people should adopt regarding the cultural duality of "fundamentals" and "applications":

> The *Four Books*, *Five Classics*, China's histories, works on statecraft, and ancient maps are all "old studies"; Western politics, Western arts, and Western history constitute "new studies". The old studies form the fundamentals of tradition, but the new studies represent practical applications that cannot be neglected. ("Establishing Learning", *Exhortation to Learning*)

He also indicated the correspondence between Chinese learning and Western learning, with old studies and new studies, respectively:

> Chinese learning is directed inwards while Western learning is directed outwards; Chinese learning is for cultivation of the mind, while Western learning is used to tackle world affairs. One should not be confined by the Classics, nor obstinately follow the meaning of the Classics. If one has the mind of a sage and acts like a sage, upholds a morality based on filial concern and loyalty to the truth, and maintains a political attitude which

[131] The Qing government officially sent a total of 120 students in four batches to study in the United States, the last batch leaving in 1875. After returning home, many of these students worked as experts in telegraphy (Fang Boliang, Tang Yuanzhan, Zhou Wanpeng, etc.), railway engineering (such as Zhan Tianyou), and medicine (such as Lin Lianhui), as well as politicians (Rong Xingqiao), and diplomats (Liang Cheng, Liu Yulin), After the 1911 Revolution, the first Prime Minister of the Republic of China, Tang Shaoyi was also a former student in the United States. In fact, as early as immediately after the Boxer Rebellion, Yuan Shikai began to make a point of employing students who had studied in the United States. In June 1896, the Qing government again sent students to study abroad. The subsequent wave of students sent to study in Japan and Europe had a great influence on and changed the history of China in the twentieth century.

respects one's master and protects the people, then even in the morning one may drive a car and, in the evening, take a train, none of which will tarnish one's sagely behavior. ("Thorough Understanding", *Exhortation to Learning*)

Such thinking clearly demonstrated that Chinese scholarly traditions had begun to explicitly embrace Western technology that had once been disdained; it also meant that Western knowledge and Confucian traditions could each run along their separate tracks as appropriate to social life and to inner needs, without contradiction. Such an attitude provided an opening for the introduction of Western science and technology and even related knowledge. Zhang Zhidong was so anxious about China's current situation and future that in 1903 he sent his son to study in the United States at his own expense.[132]

Like Confucian civilization, Western civilization naturally had its own internal logical structure. For example, a missionary might provide knowledge from European civilization, but what formulation of fundamentals and applications could this knowledge play out in another system of civilization undergoing a complex evolutionary process? History so often records how a chance misunderstanding between different civilizations might only require a specific incident or event to evolve into full-scale

[132] Even in China in 1903, there were still doubts about studying abroad. *The New York Times* reported on 14 April 1903, in a story treating the Empress Dowager Cixi inviting Zhang Zhidong to the capital to discuss the political situation, that Zhang paid for his own son to go to the United States to study, an act which became the focus of intense public opinion and greatly shocked local high-powered officials.

confrontation and rejection.[133] From the intransigence of absolute rejection of Western studies to the window-dressing epitomized by the formula

[133] The Western missionary enterprise in China always faced conflict arising from differences in civilization. At the same time, daily contradictions in secular society were complicated by the stance of belief and religious attitudes. Given the forceful measures taken by the Great Powers to subjugate China, the Chinese people always harbored a hatred of foreigners to varying degrees. This also made those dissatisfied with Western missionaries or "foreigners" to look for opportunities to stir up trouble, for example, by spreading rumors that would damage the reputations of preachers or foreigners. In 1869, more than a decade after the Anglo-French occupation of Tianjin in 1858, the French church Notre Dame des Victoires built a "nursery" on the foundations of a Buddhist temple demolished in the previous year and, in good faith, the person in charge paid a premium to encourage people to send babies to the nursery for care and support, resulting in vicious incidents in which rogue "child brokers" would even kidnap babies. At this time, it was rumored that the nursery was conducting satanic rituals on the babies, mutilating them, and making medicine from their body parts. The prevalence of rumors led the local superintendent of trade, Chonghou to call for a mandatory search of the nursery, which uncovered nothing untoward. The French consul in Tianjin was humiliated and angered by the large crowd that gathered at the orphanage when the search was conducted, and the outcome was that a servant of the local magistrate attempting to disperse the crowd was shot and killed, sparking anger among locals. Not only were the consul and his companion killed on the spot, but the church and nursery were also razed. In all, seventeen foreigners, including ten nuns were killed, and four other British and American churches were destroyed. The Governor-General of Zhili, Zeng Guofan, was appointed by the court to investigate the case, and he concluded that there had been no wrongdoing in the nursery and ordered that fifteen people be executed for their part in the massacre. Zeng's handling of the case was rejected by the court, and Li Hongzhang was ordered to take over the case from Zeng Guofan. He reduced the number of people to be executed, paid compensation for the losses incurred, and sent a delegation to Paris to apologize, with the two countries reaching a settlement. However, the incident damaged relations between China and France, and there was heightened xenophobia once again at the Chinese court and in society at large.

The missionary W. A. P. Martin later concluded: "Since that date there have been twenty or more anti-foreign – not altogether anti-mission – riots of sufficient magnitude to be visible across the seas; culminating this year in the expulsion of missionaries from the capital of Szechuan, and the massacre at Kucheng, near Fuchau. Most of these have conformed to the original type in every particular – beginning with tracts and placards as their exciting cause, followed by studied negligence on the part of mandarins (who always contrived to come too late when their aid was invoked), and finishing with an inquiry how many heads and how much money would satisfy the resulting claims". Ref: W. A. P. Martin, *A Cycle of Cathay, or China, South and North, with Personal Reminiscences*, Edinburgh and London: Oliphant Anderson and Ferrier, 1897, p. 445.

However, the Tianjin Massacre also led the Qing government to pay more attention to diplomatic communications, and many officials realized that there was an urgent need to appreciate, understand, and emulate the West. This led to the approval in the following year of Zeng Guofan and Li Hongzhang's memorial to the court endorsing a sixteen-year of "Western studies and Chinese origins" (Xixue-Zhongyuan), a formula favored by the Kangxi Emperor, and then on to adopt "new learning for applications", there was a transformation taking place in the intellectual atmosphere of the nation, at the same time as there were material changes in political, economic, military, and social life. Such a change in the spirit of the times was not only the result of social change, but also the cause of social change, which is why, when the Qing government and the Western powers continued to be involved in conflict there were often quite different responses in Chinese society. Zhang Zhidong expressed his response to this condition in the following passage:

> Those who seek to remedy the present situation talk of new learning; those who fear that it will impede the Way hold fast to the teachings of the ancients. Both groups are unable to reach agreement. The conservatives resemble those who give up eating because they have difficulty in swallowing, while the progressives are like a flock of sheep that has arrived at the crossroads and does not know where to turn. The former group does not know how to adapt; the latter are ignorant of what is fundamental. Not knowing how to adapt, the conservatives have no way to confront the enemy and deal with the crisis; not knowing what is fundamental, the innovators regard the teachings of the sages with contempt. Thus, those who cling to the old order increasingly despise the innovators who in turn violently detest the conservatives. As the two groups are engaged in mutual recriminations, imposters and adventurers do not hesitate to resort to falsification and distortion and spread their theories to confuse the people. Students consequently doubt which course to pursue, while perverse opinions spread throughout the country. When the enemy comes, we are not capable to fight him; yet when the enemy does not come, we are not able to communicate peacefully with him. I fear that China's crisis does not come from abroad but is fomented right here inside China. ("Preface", *Exhortation to Learning*)

program promoted by Yung Wing, the first Chinese to have studied in the United States, to send students to study abroad.

Zhang Zhidong's point of view was the stance of some scholars who were attempting to find an intellectual position appropriate to the radical changes that had occurred after the Sino-Japanese War, and so the formulation, "Chinese learning for fundamentals, Western learning for practical applications", became a radical catch cry.[134] At that time, people readily accepted the proposal that Chinese culture should serve as the main body, the fundamentals, and learning from the West was supplementary. Thus, in the later period of the 1898 Reforms, two million copies of Zhang Zhidong's *Exhortation to Learning* were printed, far more than the introductions to modern thought authored by Kang Youwei and Liang Qichao.

Most people judged situations in terms of their preconceived knowledge and personal experiences, not to mention what they would personally gain and lose from changes. Only those with a sense of social responsibility and courage were willing to subsume their personal gains and losses beneath those of the nation. The *Treaty of Tianjin* of 1858 and the *Treaty of Beijing* of 1860 called for the reciprocal exchange of diplomats, so foreign relations were no longer only a matter of international ritual, but also a system to facilitate exchanges between countries. However, for the Xianfeng Emperor, this was undoubtedly an all-round loss of face. In his view, the clause stipulating the exchange of permanent envoys was more serious in its implications than the exemption from customs duties among other items and at the conclusion of the Second Opium War, the exchange of envoys was from the outset largely non-negotiable.[135] By 1876, China's first diplomat to be posted abroad, Guo Songtao, who had been a roommate of Zeng Guofan at the Yuelu

[134] Advocacy of the formulation, "Chinese learning for the fundamentals, Western learning for practical applications", was not limited to Zhang Zhidong, and it also appears in the writings of Feng Guifen, Wang Tao, Zheng Guanying, and Chen Zhi, but only Zhang Zhidong provided a clear explanation of the concept. Liang Qichao wrote in his *General Discussion of Qing Dynasty Scholarship*: "China's military defeat in the Sino-Japanese War of 1895 rocked the entire nation, and young and prominent scholars began to talk with great concern about the urgent need for reform, and such prominent elder statesmen as Li Hongzhang and Zhang Zhidong were, to a certain extent, in agreement. The popular formulation, 'Chinese learning for the fundamentals, Western learning for practical applications of the people', was fondly discussed by Zhang Zhidong, and the whole country believed this formulation to be most apt".

[135] In the negotiations, the two sides appeared to be completely unable to communicate when discussing this issue. Acting as a stand-in for the official translator, Dr. Williams, who was not familiar with the northern dialect, the missionary W. A. P. Martin (p. 158)

Academy in Changsha, had gone to London to serve as "Imperial Envoy to Great Britain". This was 16 and 14 years respectively after James Bruce (1811–1863) and Anson Burlingame (1820–1870) took up posts in China representing Great Britain and the United States of America.[136] Nevertheless, this signaled that, following the Margary Affair, China was finally entering a new age of protocol and regulations governing international engagement.[137] Indeed, the reason for Guo Songtao's mission

recorded the following dialogue Dr. Williams had with a Chinese delegate who is identified as a "provincial treasurer" (*fantai*):

Dr. W:	Your sovereign receives embassies from neighboring states, such as Siam, Corea, etc.; why not open the gates of his capital to the envoys of the great nations of the West?
Fantai:	It is solely from fear of giving offense that he hesitates to do so. A certain rite is required of them, with which *you* would be unwilling to comply. They are vassals, and perform the koto; you are brethren, and would require to be treated on a footing of equality.
Dr. W:	Brethren did you say? Is it treating us like brethren to keep us standing outside of the door?
Fantai:	When brethren have once divided their interests and set up separate establishments, good feeling is best maintained by remaining apart. There is danger, too, that some foreigners, if admitted to the capital, might abuse the privilege for the accomplishment of sinister ends.
Dr. W:	The residence of a British minister at the capital would have prevented any such misunderstanding as the present.
Fantai:	It is useless to insist on that point. We may as well drop the subject. It has been tabooed by the high commissioners.

Ref: W. A. P. Martin, *A Cycle of Cathay, or China, South and North, with Personal Reminiscences*, Edinburgh and London: Oliphant Anderson and Ferrier, 1897, p. 158.

136 Previously, on 21 November 1867, the Qing court formally appointed the retired ambassador of the United States, Anson Burlingame to act as "Authorized Foreign Relations Envoy to Various Countries", effectively a position as a roving ambassador for the Chinese government. During his tenure, Burlingame signed the *Burlingame Seward Treaty* (1868) on behalf of China with the United States. It contained the provisions of the Qing government to send students abroad, which was the legal basis for the subsequent approval of the memorial of Zeng Guofan and Li Hongzhang calling for the dispatch of Chinese students overseas.

137 W. A. P. Martin (p. 165) recorded a conversation between Chinese officials and the British during the negotiations on the 1858 Treaty of Tianjin between China and the United States, when the British negotiator, Captain Dupont suggested that to the Chinese Viceroy that China ought to send consuls to look after her people in the United States:

Viceroy: It is not our custom to send officials beyond our borders.

was to apologize on behalf of the Qing government for the murder of Augustus Raymond Margary,[138] but, for this China's new diplomat, who had been the first scholar of the Hanlin Academy to submit a memorial to the Xianfeng Emperor requesting that the court open a foreign language school, understanding the world was already an urgent priority, and it was perhaps out of a sense of helpless awareness, that the Qing court appointed him the Qing dynasty's resident minister in London. Guo has left a diary of his 50-day journey from Shanghai to London to take up his post. Edited and titled *Chronicle of the Mission to the West* (Shi Xi Jicheng), it was based on the account he wrote and he copied this for the Zongli Yamen, wanting to share what he saw and heard with his government colleagues and superiors, in order to promote the new policy of Self-Strengthening and to ensure the survival of the nation. Guo Songtao's account roused a torrent of abuse, and he was roundly scolded for statements like, "[Great Britain's] law is strict yet enlightened, and imbued with benevolence and righteousness, while its desire for wealth and power has made the nation embrace the [world's] lands and seas". The historian and *jinshi* graduate of the Guangxu reign, Li Ciming (1830–1894) was especially vociferous in his condemnation of Guo's views. In fact, this was an age in which the rejection and hatred of foreign things was widespread, and before Guo Songtao embarked on his mission, Liu Kunyi (1830–1902) asked accusatorily: "If you travel so far across

Dupont: But your people on the far shore of the Pacific are very numerous, numbering several tens of thousands.
Viceroy: When the emperor rules over so many millions, what does he care for the few waifs that have drifted away to a foreign land?
Dupont: Those people are, many of them, rich, having gathered gold in our mines. They might be worth looking after on that account.
Viceroy: The emperor's wealth is beyond computation; why should he care for those of his subjects who have left their home, or for the sands they have scraped together?

Ref: W. A. P. Martin, *A Cycle of Cathay, or China, South and North, with Personal Reminiscences*, Edinburgh and London: Oliphant Anderson and Ferrier, 1897, p. 165.

[138] In 1875, the British Embassy translator Margary traveled up the Yangtze River and then southwest to the Myanmar border, in an attempt to explore the trade route between China and India. At the border, he was killed by local militiamen. China and Britain finally resolved what came to be called the "Margary Affair" with the signing of the Sino-British *Chefoo Convention*, known in China as the *Treaty of Yantai* (13 September 1876): the British side demanded compensation of 200,000 silver taels from the Qing government and asked for a delegation to apologize to the United Kingdom.

oceans to consort with foreigners, how will you ever be able to again face your fellow townsmen and account for yourself to your descendants in China?" Students from Hunan participating in the provincial-level examinations even met to discuss whether they should destroy Guo's family home. As a tool of the conservative forces, Liu Xihong, sent to Great Britain with Guo ostensibly to serve as his deputy but in fact charged with the task of monitoring and restraining Guo, submitted a report charging Guo Songtao with ten breaches of rules of conduct, including the following: he omitted to use the word "*qinchai*" ("Imperial envoy") in his memorials to the Emperor, injecting a fundamental lack of respect for the Emperor into diplomatic correspondence; when visiting a British fortress he broke protocol by wearing Western attire; he mimicked foreigners by carrying a parasol rather than a traditional fan; and he permitted women in his retinue to study foreign languages and attend the theater, among other breaches of conduct. Because of his praise for the West and his rejection of the traditional injunction to "distinguish between Chinese and foreigners", Guo Songtao was attacked from all directions at court.[139]

In 1884, Guo Songtao presented his "Proposals related to current affairs occasioned by French matters [i.e., Sino-French War]" (*Yin Fashi tiaochen shizheng shu*), which showed that the worldview of some scholars at that time was extremely disdainful of the West:

> Examining Western communications with China, we find these began in the Western Han dynasty, while maritime trade originated in the Sui-Tang period and continued for more than a millennium. By the Daoguang reign, opium smoking had become prevalent in China. When banning opium was first proposed, there were disagreements about how this should be implemented, and these became a source of open conflict. Subsequently there were battles at Dinghai and Ningbo, and then at Zhenjiang, Guangzhou,

[139] Although Guo Songtao became officer of foreign affairs when he was only 22 years old, however, Guo Songtao was not convinced that by simply studying foreign technology, the Chinese could counter foreigners. In 1875, he served as Fujian's judicial commissioner, and in a memorial to the throne titled "Article on Maritime Defence Matters", he emphasized political governance, i.e., "rectifying the court entails rectifying all officials"; at the same time, he also stressed supporting private "businessmen" to develop industry and commerce, opposed the idea of government officials running enterprises, and criticized the *guandu-shangban* model of state capitalism that entailed "supervision by officials and management by businessmen".

> and Tianjin. These episodes of armed conflict, which entailed extreme military force and an enormous waste of expenditure, eventually resulted in an increase in the number of trading ports and in the payment of indemnities for military losses, and this pattern seems to have been fixed for the subsequent fifty years. During the more than eighteen hundred years that Western countries have adhered to the principle of trade and been engaged in trading with this country, their military strength has greatly increased, their manufactures have become more refined, and their pressure to increase the number of ports where they can trade has accordingly grown. While foreign countries rise and fall, grow weak or strong, and experience major changes over decades or centuries, only those of the West remain consistent in their emphasis on trading and throughout history this has remained unchanged. They have occupied territory and traveled many tens of thousands of miles, all in the name of trade, and while, at the outset, they might not intend to use troops, their constant exchanges to achieve their ends invariably result in quarrels that lead to war; while they might also not wish to acquire territory, their constant battles and incursions amount to the use of force to occupy land. Their invasion and occupation of all the islands of Southeast Asia have resulted from this, therefore, to negotiate Western trade matters can in principle be acceded to and not fought against; we can be honest with them and should not be hypocritically pompous; we can rely on their strengths and attempt to self-strengthen, and we should never be jealous of their strengths and try to beat them.[140]

There are various reasons why the Foreign Affairs Movement was doomed. At the outset, the central government had no unified plan or integrated resources. Moreover, this was an age of decline characterized by general poverty and a lack of resources. Constant humiliating defeats at the hands of the Great Powers had increasingly depleted the nation's treasury. Overall knowledge about the West was lacking, and there was no systematic understanding of Western civilization. The social atmosphere was shaped by the ignorance and insensitivity of the vast majority of the population. These were the most salient reasons, among many, for failure. This was a country and nation that Hegel and other Western thinkers considered had no history and, like Dickens, they cited examples of how Chinese life and thought were characterized by repetition and a lack of creativity, given that Confucianism was so closed

[140] Guo Songtao, *Shi Xi Jicheng*, Shenyang: Liaoning Renmin Chubanshe, 1994, pp. 97–98.

and illogical. Indeed, in this period, people in China mocked those who had dealings with foreigners and acquired Western knowledge. They despised "compradors who [function as] foreign slaves" (*yangnu maiban*) on whom Chinese who communicated and traded with foreign countries needed to rely.[141] They tore up railway lines and facilities built by foreigners, destroyed churches, and killed missionaries and nuns who were considered to be demons. In a country in which minds were completely closed and modern civilization was lacking, it was difficult to expect any non-traditional endeavor to develop smoothly and rapidly. Eventually, however, people came to appreciate the various shortcomings of the Foreign Affairs movement, and China's modern industry, enterprises, and commerce did develop, albeit at vastly different rates. Then sensitive and dedicated Chinese began to exert themselves to change the country's political system.

VIII

When the intransigent conviction of most Chinese that they were located at the center of the world and the lands outside China were inhabited by barbarians was repeatedly invalidated or rebuked in conflicts with the Western "barbarians", intense shock and anger could easily erupt. In the Sino-Japanese War, which began in July 1894 and ended in the April of the following year, Japan, once a tributary vassal, decisively defeated the Chinese navy at sea. Although the War seemingly only involved the

[141] As a consequence of the Opium War as well as of the needs of those involved in the Foreign Affairs Movement, the "comprador" (*maiban*) class was initially considered to be a group lacking ethical legitimacy. The term "comprador" was originally applied to a Chinese representative employed by a "foreign company" (*yanghang*). Even though the comprador was disparaged as a middleman, he played a vital role in coordinating business between foreigners and Chinese, facilitating communications and resolving conflicts. However, because of shared interests, he basically represented the company employing or commissioning him. Given the real-world complexity of the "comprador" role, the "comprador" was not limited to the economy but was invariably associated with culture and politics. However, in the development of national industry and national capital, the comprador class played a de facto role in promoting and participating in the development of Chinese capitalism in the earliest stage. Many compradors were also stakeholders in enterprises of the Foreign Affairs Movement, like Zheng Guanying who was an investor in the Shanghai Telegraph General Administration. It should be remembered that there were differences in the political positions, ideological tendencies, and cultural upbringing of compradors, due to their intellectual, familial, and experiential backgrounds.

participation of China's Northern Fleet and the fleets in Guangdong and Fujian were kept safely out of the war, the Northern Fleet was completely wiped out, and the forts at Dalian and Lüshun were lost to Japanese occupation.[142] Most historians see the Treaty of Shimonoseki (1895), which was the outcome of the Sino-Japanese War, as signaling the failure of the Foreign Affairs Movement or the new policy of Self-Strengthening. In fact, China's previous defeat in the negotiations concluding the war with France (1883–1885) over territorial control of China's former vassal Annam (northern Vietnam), and her loss of suzerain status in 1885 over Burma, which had been encouraged by the British to break with its status as a vassal of China, had fully demonstrated that historically accrued institutional weaknesses had not been rectified by the Foreign Affairs Movement. Indeed, those who had expended decades of hard effort in the contestation and war with the Great Powers had not won, and in the eyes of many observers, the Qing government was not salvageable, as Robert Hart,[143] Inspector General of China's Imperial Maritime Customs Service, commented to W. A. P. Martin several months prior to the Sino-Japanese War: "I am afraid we are tinkering a cracked kettle".[144] Li Hongzhang went to Japan to negotiate peace in February 1895, and in April signed the *Treaty of Shimonoseki* which compelled China to recognize the independence of Korea, to "compensate" Japan by paying an indemnity of 200 million silver taels, to "cede territory" (Taiwan and

[142] The Qing government began to establish a Navy in 1875 and on 12 October 1885 it established its Office of the Admiralty. The North Sea Fleet had a total of 22 military vessels, but in the process of building up its navy, enormous sums allocated for the purpose were, in fact, misappropriated by the Empress Dowager Cixi for her new Summer Palace (Yihe Yuan) construction project.

[143] Sir Robert Hart was an Irishman who in 1863 was appointed Inspector-General of the Imperial Maritime Customs Service of the Qing government, a position he occupied until 1908. Before the Foreign Affairs Movement, the customs service of the Qing dynasty was utterly corrupt, but after Hart assumed office the excise regulations were overhauled, European and American staff members were employed, and strict management was instituted. During Hart's tenure, excise revenues increased annually by 20 million silver taels. This sum served to pay off the indemnities owed by treaty to the British and French, to provide loans to Shanghai, Guangzhou, and Fujian, and to meet the costs of the western expedition of Zuo Zongtang suppressing Muslim rebels. The financial contribution of the Imperial Maritime Customs Service played an important role in the period of the Foreign Affairs Movement.

[144] W. A. P. Martin, *A Cycle of Cathay, or China, South and North, with Personal Reminiscences*, Edinburgh and London: Oliphant Anderson and Ferrier, 1897, p. 411.

its affiliated islands, Liaodong Peninsula), to open the Chinese cities of Chongqing, Suzhou, and Hangzhou to foreign trade, and to allow the Japanese to set up factories in China. The widespread shock, coupled with the grief and shame that had been imposed by repeated defeats,[145] eventually led 603 provincial student candidates to petition the Guangxu Emperor in a *Ten-Thousand Word Memorial* (Wanyan Shu) calling on the government to "reject the peace treaty", "move the capital and resume the war", and "initiate institutional reforms", a set of events that has become known as "the petition of the candidates" (*gongche shangshu*).[146]

The young man whose signature had prime position on the petition was Kang Youwei, a man of 37 years who was confident that he could change history by virtue of his intelligence and passion. From being an insignificant student with no status he quickly rose to acquire access to the Guangxu Emperor in the course of presenting eight such petitions (the first of which he drafted when he was 30) and eventually gained the full confidence of the Guangxu Emperor, although it must be quickly pointed out that the latter had in fact no real power. Even though Kang Youwei, through his writings (*A New Study Examining Forged Classics* and *Research on Confucius as a Reformer*) and lectures (delivered at the Wanmu Studio he established in Guangzhou), had acquired great influence and many followers (the most notable being Liang Qichao and Tan Sitong (1865–1898), who would both become involved in the Reform of 1898 he helped initiate), he was amazingly

[145] Wu Yuzhang recalled: "I remember how when the news of our defeat in the Sino-Japanese War reached my hometown, my second oldest brother (Wu Yongkun) and I cried for ages ... no words can express the depths of our grief". Ref: Wu Yuzhang, *Xinhai Geming* (The 1911 Revolution), Beijing: Renmin Chubanshe, 1974, pp. 32–33.

[146] *Gongche shangshu*: "the petition of the candidates". This term first appeared in the Han dynasty in a passage in "Biography of Dongfang Shuo" in *Shi Ji* describing how when Dongfang Shuo went to the capital Chang'an, he sent three thousand petitions to the throne using the "public vehicle" (*gongche*), the name for the Han-dynasty official (a type of ombudsman) who received petitions from people outside the court, and the term was later used to refer to provincial graduates who entered the capital to sit for the metropolitan examinations. In the spring of 1895, following China's ignominious defeat in the Sino-Japanese War, the year's batch of provincial graduates in Beijing for the metropolitan examinations were anxiously awaiting their results when news of the Treaty of Shimonoseki broke and roused the anger of the students. On 22 April, Kang Youwei on their behalf drafted a 1800-character-long petition addressed to "the present emperor", which 603 graduates from all over China signed on 2 May, and thousands of citizens gathered at the gates of the Censorate when the petition was delivered.

ignorant of the political manipulation in and around the imperial court. He knew that the Empress Dowager Cixi rather than the young emperor held the real power in the dynasty, but his words and deeds revealed that he paid insufficient attention to how the reforms he hoped to see enacted could ever be achieved. He formulated what he thought were concrete measures to initiate political reforms, but he had no strategy or experience for promoting their implementation; he arranged for his students and peers to enter important government bodies, but he knew next to nothing about the operation of large, centuries-old government institutions. He could appreciate that there was widespread enthusiasm for change as well as appreciating the changes that had taken place since the Opium War (witness the Self-Strengthening Movement within the government), but he seriously ignored how people's concepts are influenced by their position and the need for a gradual change in perceptions. All in all, this young man convinced of his greatness and destiny was well aware that China was immersed in a profound and unprecedented crisis, but he would ultimately fail politically because his idealism could not accommodate reality.

In his youth Kang Youwei's teachers had been his paternal grandfather Kang Zanxiu (1806–1877) and Zhu Ciqi (c. 1807–1881), followers of the Song and Ming dynasty Neo-Confucian School of Reason, so he had no interest in the somewhat fragmented work of the philological evidential exegetists and wished to have independent and innovative insights. He subsequently also rejected the School of Reason that "only discusses the study of Confucius relevant to self-cultivation and fails to appreciate the teachings of Confucius that offer social salvation", highlighting how at the core of Kang Youwei's own ideas was the desire for social reform. It is said that after Kang Youwei had read the ancient classics, he was one day seated in quiet contemplation when he suddenly realized he had to turn his attention to the study of "practical statecraft" (*jingshi zhiyong*). Yet existing works of "practical statecraft" by Chinese thinkers, such as Gu Yanwu's *Balance-Sheet of the Nation's Administration* (Tianxia junguo libing shu) and Gu Zuyu's (1631–1692) *Essentials of Historical Geography* (Du shi fangyu jiyao), he found far from satisfactory, and so he began to read Western writings. In 1882, Kang Youwei traveled to Beijing in order to compete in the metropolitan examinations and during his return home to Guangdong, he traveled through Shanghai where he was impressed by the influence and pervasiveness of Western culture. Inspired by his impressions, his subsequent reading provided him with some understanding of the capitalist system, and he became convinced of the need for thorough social and economic reform.

Kang Youwei's scholarship was strategic, and while his two major works, *A New Study Examining Forged Classics* and *Research on Confucius as a Reformer*, were ostensibly based on the ideas of Confucius, this was a feint to ensure that the alleged source of his readily comprehensive ideas and arguments had a veneer of ideological legitimacy. However, his *New Study Examining Forged Classics* proclaimed that the Confucian Classics, in which people had long maintained unquestioning faith, were in fact forgeries, and *Research on Confucius as a Reformer* recast the steadfast and conservative Confucius as a reforming activist; Kang injected ideas of democracy and the concept of equality into Confucius' teachings, which was considered shocking at that time. Those who knew Kang Youwei realized that this was his theoretical preparation for sweeping reforms. Kang Youwei presented petitions to the emperor on a number of occasions before he was finally summoned to an audience with the Guangxu Emperor on 16 June 1898 in the Hall of Diligent Administration (Qinzheng Dian) at the Yihe Yuan (New Summer Palace). Guangxu appointed Kang as a Secretary (*zhangjing*) in the Zongli Yamen, so that he could undertake preparatory work for an eventual reform program. Kang put forward reform proposals in the political, economic, military, cultural, and educational fields, including the formulation of a constitution, the establishment of a "Bureau of Government Reorganization" (Zhidu Ju), the prohibition of foot binding for women, the abolition of redundant officials, the placement of officers with no duties, the abolition of the Yellow River and Grand Canal regulatory bureaus, the rescinding of the *likin* tax, the abolition of the Green Battalion divisions of the government armies, the disbandment of the Qing Banner armies, the abolition of the eight-legged prose format for composition in the imperial examinations, the reform of the Imperial Academy (Shuyuan), the destruction of the local temples to heterodox deities, the protection of industry and commerce, the retraining of the navy and army, the abolition of the imperial examination system, the establishment of new intellectual disciplines and schools, and so on. Over more than one hundred days, dozens of laws and regulations related to reforms were issued nationwide, but officials at all levels did not implement or enforce the new regulations, knowing that Guangxu was emperor in name only. At the outset, the Empress Dowager Cixi agreed to the reforms, thinking that simply putting these measures in place would minimize the humiliations and defeats that had preceded them, provided there were no changes to the Confucian orthodoxy and the system under her control. However, she found that the enacted decrees far exceeded her wildest imaginings. Once she became aware that the reforms would see her power stripped away from her, which was indeed part of Kang's plan, the reform initiatives quickly transformed into a power struggle within the court. The Guangxu Emperor and Kang Youwei had not won the support of Yuan Shikai, who had in fact secretly informed Ronglu, the key official of Cixi's military cabinet, the Grand Council, that he would conduct a military operation leading to arrests and executions that would end the reforms. The resulting coup saw the Guangxu Emperor placed under palace detention, while Kang Youwei and Liang Qichao fled to Japan. The four Reformist members of the Grand Council (Tan Sitong, Lin Xu [1875–1898], Yang Rui [1857–1898], and Liu Guangdi [1859–1898]), together with the Supervisory Censor Yang Shenxiu (1849–1989), and Kang's younger brother, Kang Guangren (1867–1989), were all executed. Collectively, they were known as the "Six Gentlemen Martyrs", and with their deaths the Qing dynasty inside and outside the court was again shrouded in a murderous atmosphere of terror.

The court became more cautious after the coup and dealt with various external and internal problems and threats in a perfunctory manner. The positions of the reform-oriented Han officials in the government were now occupied by Manchus loyal to the Empress Dowager, and the demands made by the Great Powers were not calmly thought through but simply rebuffed in the absence of any strategic policy.[147] Social problems that emerged were simply allowed to fester. The influx of foreign goods and the effect of unequal tariffs significantly diminished the market

[147] In February 1899, in response to Italy's request to cede Sanmen Bay in Zhejiang, the Empress Dowager Cixi ordered that the Italians be repelled without hesitation. The success of her action led Cixi to believe that such an approach was sufficient to lift China out of its passive situation, so on the 21st of the following month, she simply instructed all provincial authorities not to reach any accommodation with foreign powers.

for similar products made domestically.[148] As a new means of transport, the railways not only led to an increase in unemployment and the size of the floating population but aggravated unrest in the streets, as well as triggering a decline in the economic prosperity along the canals where boat traffic commensurately shrank. Of course, the tone of officials' pronouncements, the compradors who were in fact often working in the capacity of go-betweens for foreign merchants, and the perception that commoners were becoming nominal Christians simply in order to win a livelihood fueled widespread discontent with foreigners and Western missionaries, and this situation provided an opportunity for pre-existing discontented and restive social elements. Following China's defeats in war and subsequent punitive indemnities, xenophobic hatred of Westerners grew, peaking in the last two years of the nineteenth century. As a result, missionaries arriving in China on trading companies' merchant vessels and even on warships were seen as the accomplices of invaders, while more rational voices found it hard to find a receptive audience. The xenophobia became all pervasive and these forces of blind ignorance were susceptible to exploitation, so they gradually developed into a powerful destructive force. In short, the economic downturn, encompassing the decline of canal transportation and the impact of natural disasters on agriculture, led to the outbreak of incidents perpetrated by the Yihetuan, known in English as the Boxers, in Shandong and Hebei in northern China. The Yihetuan, first known as the Yihequan (Righteous Harmony Fists) but later given the quasi-legitimizing name Yihetuan (Righteous Harmony Militia), was originally a popular secret society in Shandong and Hebei at the end of the eighteenth century. Unlike the Taiping Heavenly Kingdom, the Righteous Harmony Fists were originally widespread, but diverse, popular martial arts groups that went by a number of other names including Plum Blossom Fists, Divine Fists, or Big Sword Society. These groups lacked any clear program or agenda, and in certain places set up altars to various popular deities where they held secret gatherings, distributed pictorial charms painted on paper, and summoned deities. A

[148] Statistics for Tianjin, Yantai, and Jiaozhou reveal that in 1894 more than 180,000 *dan* (=50 kg) of yarn were imported, and by 1898 this had increased to 500,000, an increase of 264% over four years, a situation that would have a serious impact on the home handicraft industry in the rural areas of northern China. Ref: Peng Zeyi, *Zhongguo Jindai Shougongye Shi Ziliao* (Documents on the modern history of China's handicraft industry), v. 2, Beijing: Sanlian Shudian, 1957, p. 198.

large number of participants focused on training in arts conferring invulnerability to sword and bullet. The Righteous Harmony Fists were at their outset opposed to Manchu rule and rallied beneath the slogan, "Oppose the Qing and Restore the Ming". As a result, they were suppressed by the Qing government. However, in June 1898, the Shandong military governor Zhang Rumei proposed in a memorial to the throne that the Righteous Harmony Fists be formally given the new title, Righteous Harmony Militia (Yihetuan).[149] In 1899, when Yuxian was about to take up his new post as the replacement military governor of Shandong, he proposed that "these people can be used and the Militia can be pacified, and bandits must be exterminated". The Righteous Harmony Militia became the object of the government's lenient pacification policies and the Yihetuan's leaders took advantage of the general dissatisfaction with foreigners to change the Militia's slogan from "Oppose the Qing and Restore the Ming" to "Aid the Qing and Destroy the Foreigners". Henceforth, rather than banning this socially disruptive organization, the Qing government decided to give it covert support. On 12 January 1900, the Qing government issued a decree stating that those among the civilian population who had taken up arms for self-defense and the protection of their villages should not be regarded as bandits, thereby legitimizing them. The Qing government was so convinced by the Boxers' braggadocio about their invulnerability to weapons that a large number of government troops took up this martial arts routine similar to witchcraft, hoping that the mastery of these supernatural arts would enable them to vanquish the Great Powers. Soon, the Yihetuan went on an unchecked rampage of destruction, tearing up railway tracks and toppling power lines, revealing their indescribable antipathy towards modern civilization. In March, the Boxers also appeared to reengage in violent conflict with the Qing army, and the latter were unable to resist. As a result, the leader of the Boxers was guided to enter Tianjin, which was then plastered with posters welcoming the Boxers and expressing hatred for foreigners. In early June, the Boxers entered Beijing. Brandishing swords and knives,

[149] The Yihetuan was a loose organization, whose members had complex backgrounds comprising farmers, craftsmen, the urban poor, small traders, and transport workers, as well as lower-class people including prostitutes, in addition to some military officers, wealthy gentry, and even aristocrats. Later joining the organization were local rogues and criminal elements. The fact that its membership ranged from the highest to the lowest levels of society meant that the organization of the Boxers was representative of society in general.

they roamed the city, burning churches and related facilities. So bitter was their hatred of the missionaries as they believed that these "foreign ghosts" had altered the souls of their Chinese converts, enslaving them spiritually, in order to make it easier for Westerners to oppress them economically and politically. As a result, churches, together with the hospitals and schools associated with them, were prime targets of the Boxers. They even disinterred the graves of missionaries, including those of Matteo Ricci, Adam Schall von Bell, and Ferdinand Verbiest. Between the 13th and 15th June alone, thirteen churches, seven schools, seven hospitals, and 33 houses associated with foreigners were destroyed. Encouraged by the Qing government, the behavior of these "invulnerable" warriors was completely out of control. Previously, when the foreign diplomatic missions discovered that the heart of the current government at court had been taken over by xenophobic officials, they were no longer optimistic about the protection promised by the Qing government, and by the end of May, nearly forty foreign warships had assembled at the Taku (Dagu) Forts outside Tianjin that guarded the waterways leading to Beijing. On 10 June, British, American, Russian, French, Italian, Japanese, German, and Austrian soldiers, known as the Eight-Nation Allied Expeditionary Forces, advanced towards Beijing under the command of the British Admiral Seymour (1840–1929), and by the 17th the Dagu Forts had fallen to the coalition. In mid-June, the Qing government convened a meeting to discuss a course of action. At this meeting the Empress Dowager Cixi cut short the cautious advice proffered by her Director of the Court of Sacrificial Worship, Yuan Chang that the Boxers' alleged invulnerability to weapons was patently untrue, pontificating instead that the Boxers should continue to be inducted into the Qing armies, and that the foreign envoys be simply informed that they should desist from fighting and return instead to their own countries. On the 21st, the Qing government formally declared war on the Great Powers. In the midst of this chaotic crisis, two factors contributed to the rapid end of "the Boxer Incident". Firstly, local governors in the southeast, including Li Hongzhang, Liu Kunyi, Zhang Zhidong, and Yuan Shikai, did not carry out the orders of the court, and blocked instructions to organize Boxers to conduct the war, preventing further spread of the conflict. Secondly, the fighting power of the Western Allies' warships, weaponry, and armies proved unstoppable, and finally, on 14 August, when the coalition invaded Beijing and the besieged embassy staff members were rescued, the previously hardline officials Yulu (c.

1844–1900) and Li Bingheng (1830–1900) committed suicide, and the Empress Dowager forced the Guangxu Emperor to flee Beijing with her; after several months of overland travel, they reached Xi'an. The Boxer turmoil ended. In the course of these events, 231 foreigners and thousands of Chinese Christians were killed. Given that the *Treaty of Tianjin*, which China had signed 42 years previously, stipulated that people who practiced Christian teachings, whether foreign or Chinese, should not be subjected to hardship or persecution because of their faith,[150] the anger and bloody reprisals provoked by the Boxer rebels' brutal killings can be imagined. As a result, the destruction, looting, burning, and massacres perpetrated by the Allied forces after they entered Beijing were equally shocking, as a Russian journalist recorded:

> Half of the mighty Imperial capital is destroyed and burned, and it has been ravaged to the point as though everything has died. On either side of the Legation Quarter are ubiquitous piles of rubble, stones, ash, rubbish, and filth. Chinese bodies, heaped on each other, litter the roads, and everywhere there is debris of every type.
>
> The French soldiers have burned down the houses and shops around the Northern Cathedral. Charred bodies lie exposed amid the debris, rubble, and ash. The Chinese who were shot and stabbed to death lie as piles of

[150] According to W. A. P. Martin, the main reason why the Qing government agreed in 1858 to protect religion was not because it recognized the legitimacy of religious freedom, but because it feared the besieged armies of the Taiping Heavenly Kingdom which ostensibly claimed to be Christian. The Qing court feared that if it did not agree to the demands of the Great Powers for religious protection, they might turn to the Taiping Heavenly Kingdom for assistance:

> That the Chinese commissioners so readily accepted the principle of religious toleration was a matter of surprise, as their experience with a fanatical horde of semi-Christian insurgents was not adapted to allay apprehension. The explanation,, is not far to seek. They feared that if they should reject our demands on that head the foreign powers might still turn to the rebels, who were in great force in the central provinces. Their acceptance of this article is not therefore to be compared with the spontaneous insertion in the Japanese constitution of a clause securing complete freedom of conscience. It was not the result of growing light, but of fear. (p. 183)

Ref: W. A. P. Martin, *A Cycle of Cathay, or China, South and North, with Personal Reminiscences*, Edinburgh and London: Oliphant Anderson and Ferrier, 1897, p. 183.

corpses on the streets. Not only have Chinese soldiers been killed, but all perpetrators reported to the Allies by Chinese converts.[151]

Empress Dowager Cixi now recalled Li Hongzhang, who had been dismissed after his defeat in the Sino-Japanese War, and at this critical juncture he was re-appointed Governor-General of Zhili (roughly equivalent to today's Hebei province) and Beiyang Commerce Minister, to negotiate with the foreigners. After more than a year of negotiations with the Great Powers and related transactions between the latter, on 17 September 1901 on behalf of the Qing court, Li signed the *Treaty of 1901*, better known as the *Boxer Protocol*, comprising 12 articles and 19 annexes. The treaty stipulated the execution of a group of Qing officials, including local officials, an enormous indemnity to be paid to the allied nations over a 39-year period,[152] an apology to Germany and Japan for their diplomats murdered by Boxers, a ban on Chinese arms imports, permission for foreign countries to station permanent embassy guards in Beijing, and so on, all of which impinged on China's sovereignty. The Allied troops withdrew from Beijing on the same day the treaty was signed.

As the diplomat representing the Qing government, Li Hongzhang signed and assumed direct responsibility for the *Treaty of 1901*, on behalf of a defeated state shamed by its provisions. Coupled with the *Treaty of Shimonoseki* he had previously signed, Li Hongzhang was branded a "traitor who sold out of his nation", a badge of infamy he wears to the present day. However, two months after Li Hongzhang's death, Liang Qichao dispassionately reminded people:

[151] Dmitri Polyanskii„ Xu Chongxin tr., Chinese edition title: *Baguo-lianjun muji ji*, Fuzhou: Fujian Renmin Chubanshe, 1983, pp. 335–338.

[152] The indemnity to be paid by the Qing government to the allies as stipulated by the treaty was 452 million silver taels, equivalent to $US330 million at the time, plus 4% annual interest for 39 years, coming to a total of 982,238,150 silver taels. Since payment was demanded in foreign currency rather than silver, there was an additional cost in order to exchange Chinese silver to foreign currency each year. However, in subsequent implementation, the United States returned US$10,785,286 million to China in 1908, and in 1924 waived the outstanding payments. The refunds were used to fund Chinese students' education in the United States. Other countries successively also waived repayments: Britain, 1922; Russia, 1924; France, 1925; Italy, 1925 and 1933; Belgium, 1928; and the Netherlands, 1933.

If we are to evaluate Li Hongzhang as a person, we must have a deep understanding of the country in which Li Hongzhang found himself and the times in which he lived.

First, the country Li Hongzhang was dealing with was a millennia-old imperial dictatorship, and he happened to come onto the scene in an era when the regime was fully matured, and its degree of despotism had reached its zenith.

Second, Li Hongzhang found himself in an ethnic Han nation under Manchu rule, at a time when the Manchu and Han peoples had only been coexisting for several years and Han rights were just beginning to slowly recover.[153]

Later generations often attributed China's failure to the "sale of the country" by Qing ministers such as Li Hongzhang. However, dispassionate historians discussed the reasons why a country that was once sovereign (China) was defeated by her former vassal (Japan). Like China, nineteenth-century Japan had similarly faced the question of how to deal with Western expansion. On the eve of China's Second Opium War, in 1853, the arrival of U.S. Naval Commodore Matthew Calbraith Perry (1794–1858) in Japan portended that the threat from the West was imminent. To which, Japan's reaction was clear and quick, perhaps China's failure in the First Opium War provided a lesson for the Japanese. The "Meiji Restoration" that toppled the Tokugawa Shogunate in 1868 is widely regarded by historians as an epochal event for Japan, because as a result the Japanese positively and decisively accelerated their emulation of the West by introducing technology, developing industry, and building a modern army. While retaining their own traditions, the Japanese learned as much as possible about Western culture and art, even drawing on the humanities and history.[154] In learning from the West, Japan indulged in

[153] Liang Qichao: *Biography of Li Hongzhang*, translated by Wu Man Ban Jiang, Hunan People's Publishing House, 2018, p. 11.

[154] In my *A History of Art in 20th-Century China* when discussing the situation of traditional Chinese calligraphy and painting at the beginning of the twentieth century, I wrote:"In this way, when looking at the transformation of history and civilization, the new historical attitude itself constitutes a re-interpretation of cultural and artistic issues. The Japanese translated and re-translated historical works, such as François Mignet's *Histoire de la Révolution Française*, François Guizot's *General History of European Civilization*, and Edmund Burke's *The Abridgement of the History of England*. By the time the Japanese government appointed officials to visit Europe and bring back books ..., Japanese history circles had embarked on a comprehensive historical revolution. Naturally, Japanese students

none of the hesitation or curtailments (such as the *ti-yong* dichotomy) that characterized China's approach. More importantly, in 1889, the Meiji government adopted a constitution, and the Japanese people's overall self-identification decisively supported the national strength and spirit. All this, in practice, drove the development of Japan, and through the *Sino-Japanese Friendship and Trade Treaty* of September 1871 Japan established its status as a sovereign state, and began to assume its position as an equal of China. At a time when scholar-officials at the Qing government were still anxious about whether learning from the West might result in the loss of China's ancestral heritage, Japan rapidly developed its power, as for example in 1879, when Japan extended its rule over the Ryukyu Islands, which the Qing government deemed to be rightfully its vassal state, incorporating them as "Okinawa Prefecture". This rapid move led directly to Japan's relationship with Korea, as Japan became increasingly daring in engaging in conflicts and disputes with China over Korea's internal problems, until a direct confrontation with China finally resulted in warfare in 1894. In fact, in the ensuing Battle of Pyongyang and in naval warfare, China's military forces were utterly defeated by the Japanese in this cruel and bloody war and China was compelled to sign the *Treaty of Shimonoseki*.

Prior to the Sino-Japanese War, the Western powers, although they had various interests in China, had not yet made a final judgment on China's political and military power, and they were at that time busy dividing up Africa. However, the signing of the *Treaty of Shimonoseki* showed them the extent of China's weakness and impotence, and the "carving up of the Chinese melon" (*guafen*), as the division of China into foreign spheres of influence and control came to be referred to in Chinese, began to proceed with impunity. For example, Russia, Germany, and France,

in this period were already familiar with the history of French civilization, German positivism, and the sociology of Condorcet in France. Therefore, the appearance of a work like *The History of Chinese Painting* by Nakamura Fusetsu and Kojika Sei'un in 1913 was not surprising. Unlike Japanese scholarship, it would be quite some time before any scholar in China would be able to use Western ideas and concepts to provide an objective and systematic interpretation of China's art history, in contrast to the revisions necessitated by the concept of 'national essence' in the field of literature".

Ref: Lü Peng, *Ershi Shiji Zhongguo Yishu Shi* (A history of art in twentieth-century China), Beijing: Peking University Press, 2006, p. 107.

using the pretext of ensuring the independence of Korea,[155] demanded that Japan return the Liaodong Peninsula to China, hoping to realize their own respective interests by taking advantage of China's hatred of Japan. In order to resist possible further Japanese attacks on China and Korea, Li Hongzhang hoped to enlist Russia's help, so on 3 June 1896, he signed a compact with Russia regarding privileges associated with the construction of the China Eastern Railway, the section of the Trans-Siberian Railway that passed through Chinese territory to Vladivostok, so that Russia gained control of the entire northeast of China by secretly pledging a joint alliance with China against Japan. Subsequently, as a result of the 1897 Caozhou Incident (also called the Juye Incident) in Shandong, in which two German missionaries were killed, Germany sent troops to occupy Qingdao, and forced the Qing government to lease to them Jiaozhou Bay and Qingdao, as well as to grant them the right to build railways and develop mines in Shandong. Russia then sought to maintain the balance of power in North China by leasing Lüshun and Dalian. This was followed by the British demanding to lease Weihaiwei, Kowloon, and the entire Yangtze River basin, while France obtained the right to lease Guangzhou-wan (Kwangchow Wan), as well as obtaining rights in Guangdong, Guangxi, and Yunnan. The unbridled "division" of China by the Great Powers was slowed by the second declaration of an "Open Door" policy by the United States on 3 July 1900, by which the United States reminded countries to protect the integrity of China's territory and sovereignty. When this fierce contest to divide up China was taking place and the Qing government was already hopelessly corrupt, Li Hongzhang's effectiveness can be appreciated. Liang Qichao cautioned those lacking historical understanding to think again about Li's position: "In February and March 1895, and again in August and September

[155] In the transition from the Ming to the Qing dynasty, Korea was an important tributary vassal of China. On 24 February 1876, Japan and Korea signed the *Treaty of Kanghwa*, whereby Japan recognized Korea as an independent state enjoying the right to equality with Japan. China did not protest against this, with the result that China lost its former suzerain status in the tributary relationship, and Japan began to increasingly exert influence on Korea. On 18 April 1885, China signed the *Convention of Tianjin*, which included a clause in which Korea was awarded the right to protection from both China and Japan, whereby China lost its sole suzerain status. Later, the *Treaty of Shimonoseki* stipulated that the Qing government recognized the independence of Korea and the tributary relationship was formally ended, signaling that China had completely lost control over Korea.

1900, if his critics were placed in Li Hongzhang's position, would their behavior, decisions, and methods of handling the negotiations be really any better than those of Li Hongzhang?"

In a dialogue between Li Hongzhang and Ito Hirobumi(1841–1909), recorded in English in 1895, one can feel the helplessness of this capable statesman at that time:

> Li said: "China and Japan are the closest neighbours and moreover have the same writing system. How can we be enemies? ... We ought to establish perpetual peace and harmony between us, so that our Asiatic yellow race will not be encroached upon by the white race of Europe".
>
> Itō said: 'Ten years ago I talked with you about reform. Why is it that up to now not a single thing has been changed or reformed?"
>
> Li could only reply, "Affairs in my country have been so confined by tradition that I could not accomplish what I desire... I am ashamed of having excessive wishes and lacking the power to fulfil them".[156]

The historian Qian Mu (1895–1990) made the following observation regarding the political system of the Qing dynasty:

> All [the Qing's] institutions were based on those of the Ming dynasty, onto which [the Manchus] grafted many of their own private interests. These private interests can be described as a self-serving 'tribal regime'. Everything emanated from this self-serving heart of the Manchu tribe, so that they effectively relied only on rules and stratagems, rather than on any system as such.
>
> ...
>
> For example, when the Mongols and Manchus entered China, no emperor of either the Yuan or Qing dynasty, respectively, could personally exercise control over the entirety of the regime's power. In these two dynasties, the polities were backed up respectively by all the tribes of the Mongols and Manchus who supported these regimes. The Mongols and Manchus therefore constituted a special class or special elements within the regimes. Such regimes we can call tribal regimes. Both the Mongols and Manchus wanted to control the government and exert political power as an ethnic group or tribe. This kind of polity was, of course, self-serving, so that all measures adopted by such regimes cannot be regarded as those of

[156] Quoted from J. K. Fairbank, *The Great Chinese Revolution, 1800–1985*, New York: Harper and Row, 1986, p. 119.

a political system, but only as rules and stratagems that served as a means of controlling the regime.[157]

Such a polity, formed by privileged, self-interested groups, relegated ethnic Han officials to being mere instruments that the Manchus could change at any time that suited them. Any change or reform, even if it could even be implemented, was based on the premise of maintaining and consolidating Manchu rule and safeguarding Manchu tribal interests, so the conflict between the Manchu and ethnic Han intensified with the decline of the nation, which meant that China at this time lacked the type of nationalism forged by shared ideals that existed between the government and people of Japan after the Meiji Restoration. Of course, the stubborn conservatism of the thinking of China's rulers, the backwardness and decline of politics, the collapse and stagnation of the economy, and the corruption of the bureaucracy were all factors that doomed the Qing in its final days.

According to the early twentieth-century historian Jiang Tingfu, writing in 1936, "If the reform of the Tongzhi and Guangxu years had occurred in the Daoguang and Xianfeng years, China's modernization would have taken place twenty years earlier than that of Japan. The modern history of the Far East would have probably been utterly different. Unfortunately, people in the Daoguang and Xianfeng years did not heed the lessons of military defeat and acted in exactly the same insensitive and arrogant manner both before and after the [Opium] War. By 1861, the last year of the Xianfeng reign, the British and French allies invaded Beijing, yet only a minority of people had realized that it was imperative to learn from the West".[158] However, due to the closed nature of the ideology allowed by the system, the Qing court not only utterly failed to rationally assess the political and ideological basis of the problems facing the country, but even the essence of the Confucian Classics had been completely lost in endlessly voluminous trivial commentaries.

In any nation there are persons who are alert to the problems in daily life, who can perceive the crises in different events, who can discern the

[157] Qian Mu, *Zhongguo Lidai Zhengzhi Deshi* (An Assessment of Politics in China's Successive Dynasties), Beijing: Sanlian, 2016, pp. 144, 146.

[158] Tsiang (Jiang) Tingfu, *Zhongguo Jindai Shi Dagang* (Outline Modern History of China), Chongqing: Qiangnian Shudian, 1939, reprinted: Beijing: Dongfang Chubanshe, 1996, p. 16.

dangers that imperil peoples or nations in conflict, and who are then compelled to call for change and try to change history with their knowledge, ideals, and wisdom. Of course, when evaluating historical figures those who come later invariably have a different perspective to underline the wisdom of their own conclusions. In fact, history has little to do with the moral character and personal flaws of historical figures, or even to do with their degree of personal greed. Li Hongzhang, for example, was believed to have received a private bribe of 6 million rubles in grants after the *Sino-Russian Treaty of Alliance* was concluded in 1896. In fact, only problems, as well as people, events, and their consequences constitute the historical narrative, however imprecise or clear. People assess the deeds and personalities of these historical players from Lin Zexu, Qishan, the generals and the many other martyrs and participants in the Opium War, to Zeng Guofan, Li Hongzhang, and Zuo Zongtang of the Foreign Affairs Movement, including the Manchu officials active in the latter group, either over drinks or in serious seminars, including their assessment of these historical personalities' narrowness and the limitations or their virtues that left them thwarted and thus ineffectual.

A moth emerges from a silkworm's cocoon, but the change is absolute as it confronts a new environment. For example, even though Xu Jianyin (1845–1901) worked like his father Xu Shou at the Anqing Arsenal and was involved in the production of nitric acid, after being sent to Europe to purchase warships (having ironically been the man who helped build the warships *Zhenyuan* and *Dingyuan*), he visited the Houses of Parliament at Westminster, and observed British politics at first hand. On returning to China, Xu Jiayin became an advocate of political change, no longer confined to knowledge about technology and military hardware. Li Hongzhang's assistant, Xue Fucheng (1838–1894) can certainly be regarded as a member of the Foreign Affairs Movement, but after visiting Europe in 1890, his interest in "adopting Western engineering and mathematics" to serve the Confucian orthodoxy began to shift towards an interest in "democratic governments such as those of present-day Britain and Italy in which power is shared". This thinking clearly transcended that of his master he served who sought to "avenge the national shame and respect for the nation's fundamentals". Changes were certain but seemed to come too slowly to cope with the brutal aggression China endured. This slowness may have been an intrinsic mode of play in traditional Chinese culture. When someone unfamiliar with Chinese culture and tradition looks at landscape paintings of the Song, Yuan, Ming, and

Qing dynasties, it may be difficult to see the differences, and while there may be a preponderance of black and white and variations in the space these occupy, with only occasional subdued color, over a millennium and different dynasties landscape paintings still seem largely similar. This view and conclusion may possibly be the result of differences between civilizations and related perspectives, but another way of looking at the problem might lead to the conclusion that the Chinese people are themselves familiar with the changes and differences, and even have complex and refined tastes. However, in the end such change did not go beyond the familiar nest of traditional civilization, which can perhaps be described as "the Chinese order".

On 4 May 1901, within the embassy district of Beijing, the French colonel Marchand organized a celebration for the Allied command, inviting allied officers and Qing government officials to attend. A writer who served as a commandant with the French navy participating in the coalition, Pierre Loti (1850–1923), documented that night's activities in his *Les Derniers Jours de Pékin*, published as dispatches in *Figaro* in 1901 and published in the English translation of Myrta L. Jones in 1902 (Boston: Little, Brown and Company) in a scenario (pp. 285–287) which fully captures the complexity of that *fin-de-siècle* gathering and the onslaught of the new century:

> Eight o'clock in the evening. The long May twilight is almost over, and the curious lanterns, some of glass with long strings of pearls, others of rice-paper in the form of birds or of lotus blossoms, are everywhere lighted among the old cedar branches on the esplanade of the Rotunda Palace, which I had known plunged in such a melancholy abyss of sadness and silence. To-night all is movement, life, gay light. Already uniformed officers of all the nations of Europe, and Chinese, in long silken robes, with official head-dresses from which depend peacock feathers, are going and coming amid the wonderful decorations. A table for seventy is set under a tent, and we are awaiting our incongruous assembly of guests.
>
> Followed by small suites, they arrive from all quarters of Pekin, some on horseback, others in carriages, in chairs, or in sumptuous palanquins. As soon as any person of distinction appears at the lower door of the inclined plane, one of our military band, who is on the lookout, orders the playing of the national air of his country. The Russian Hymn follows the German, or the Japanese the march of the Bersaglieri. Even the Chinese air is heard, for someone pompously enters with a large red paper, which proves to be

the visiting-card of Li-Hung-Chang, who is below, but who, in accordance with the etiquette of his country, is announced before he makes his appearance. Preceded by similar cards, the Chief-Justice of Pekin and the Representative Extraordinary of the Empress are the next to arrive. These Chinese princes, who are to assist at our fête, come in gala palanquins, with a cavalry escort, and they make their entrance with the most inscrutable expressions on their faces, followed by a band of servants dressed in silk. It was hard to have them! But Colonel Marchand, with the general's permission, made it a point of honour to invite them. Mixed in with our Western uniforms, mandarins' robes and pointed hats with the coral button are numerous. Their presence at this barbarian feast right in the heart of the Imperial City, which we have profaned, will remain one of the most singular inconsistencies of our time.

Such a length of table as there is,—its legs resting on an imperial carpet which seems to be made of thick yellow velvet! Bunches of flowers are arranged in priceless, gigantic old cloisonné vases that have been taken out of the reserves of the Empress for a single night. Marshal von Waldersee,[159] with the wife of the French minister at his side, occupies the seat of honour; then two bishops in violet robes, the generals and officers of the seven allied nations, five or six women in evening dress, and, lastly, the three great princes of China, so enigmatical in their embroidered silks, their eyes partly concealed by their ceremonial hats and falling plumes.

At the close of this strange dinner, when the roses in the big, precious vases are beginning to hang their heads, our general, toward the close of his toast, turns to the Yellow Princes: "Your presence here among us," he says, "is a sufficient proof that we did not come here to make war against China, but only against an abominable sect," etc.

......

Then the Empress's representative takes up the ball with a suppleness characteristic of the far East, and, without turning a hair, replies (he was secretly a furious Boxer): "In the name of Her Imperial Chinese Majesty, I thank the generous nations of Europe for having extended a helping hand to our government in one of the gravest crises it has ever passed through".

A stupefied silence follows, and then glasses are emptied. ......

......

Loti goes on to conclude:

[159] Alfred Ludwig Heinrich Karl Graf von Waldersee (1832–1904) was a German field marshal who commanded the eight-nation international relief force sent to rescue the international diplomatic community in Beijing besieged by the Boxers.

It seemed to us that this evening had commemorated in a way the irremediable downfall of Pekin, or rather the downfall of a people. Whatever happens now, even though the remarkable Asiatic court[160] comes back here, which seems improbable, Pekin is over, its prestige gone, its mysteries are open to the light of day. (p. 296)...[161]

Loti's concluding passage can be seen as a reiteration of a remark by Macartney more than a hundred years previously: "She [the Chinese Empire's ship of state] may drift like a wreck for a while before hitting the shore and being smashed up, but she can never be rebuilt on the old foundation".

160 The old Summer Palace (Yuanming Yuan).

161 The Chinese translator of Pierre Loti's novel, first published in 1902, identifies "ce palais de la Rotonde" in the original text with the Tuancheng (Rotunda Fort), not far from the old Summer Palace in Beijing's northwest. See: Pierre Loti, *Les derniers jours de Pékin*, Chinese translation: *Beijing de Xianluo*, Jinan: Shandong Youyi Chubanshe, 2005, pp. 176–180. The translation here is based on the following French edition: Pierre Loti, *Les derniers jours de Pékin*, Paris: Julliard, 1991, pp. 305–306, 312.

Chapter One
1900–1912: The Era of Transformation

> China, for thousands of years, permanently adopted an unchanging stance, neither advancing nor yielding, never knowing the nature of change. However, buffeted by the billows of the oceans and driven by the wild sandstorms of the 19th century, this ancient and ancestral entrenched base has been gradually eroded and destroyed, and so the people of this nation, subject to this tragedy and suffering, embark increasingly on the road to change. Therefore, the situation in China today is like being on a boat that has long since left the shore and entered the current, but neither shore can now be seen.
>
> Liang Qichao, "On the Transitional Age", 1901

The Post-1898 Context

A month after the celebration organized by the French generals on behalf of the Allied high command to which the Qing officials were to be invited, *The New York Times* reported on 26 June 1901 with the theme "Lights will Lighten Beijing" that a German company had recently signed a contract with the Chinese government to provide electric lighting in the capital, Beijing.

The capital had fallen, but social life in Qing China went on as before, even though change was inevitable. Cities, especially open trading ports like Shanghai, were experiencing accelerating change, with foreign-style buildings, rickshaws, motor vehicles, factories, and modern steamships at

L. Peng, *A History of China in the 20th Century*,
https://doi.org/10.1007/978-981-99-0734-2_3

the docks, while cityscapes were altered with new environmental features like public parks and lawns. The image and identity of China were both beginning to change, as modern businesses transformed society. For several dynasties, including the Qing, Chinese society was said to mainly comprise four main classes—(officials) scholars, farmers, artisans (workers), and merchants—in addition to the impoverished. However, now social roles and identities in China were becoming more complex; often wearing modern Western-style dress, students, journalists, workers, capitalists, entrepreneurs, businessmen, and military officers as well as those Chinese with complex identities mingled with foreign pedestrians on the streets of China. Indeed, the modes of circulation peculiar to capitalism had begun to enter China back when the Foreign Affairs Movement was beginning around 1860. For example, when the outbreak of the American Civil War in 1861 cut off the supply of American cotton to the London market, leading to higher cotton prices, cotton produced in China and India became a sought-after commodity, and foreign merchants and factories in China became frantically involved in cotton speculation. Four years later, after the American Civil War ended, cotton prices plummeted, and the foreign factories of Shanghai involved in the cotton trade all found themselves in trouble. Foreign banks in Shanghai also became collectively involved in currency exchange speculation; the foreign factories in need of vast amounts of cash and trade through bill transaction, the daily turnover on Shanghai's foreign financial markets was pushed into millions of *yuan*, with market interest rates ranging from 18 to 36%. This eventually led to the first financial boom in Shanghai's history, such economic events signaled a new era was coming. In summary, in the last phase of the nineteenth century, important coastal cities in China underwent constant economic growth as a result of the involvement of Western commerce and markets, and the content and nature of their enterprises could be increasingly described as "modern".

Before the Reform Movement of the 1890s, China's industrialization had begun with the Foreign Affairs Movement, but the change to "learning from the West" was limited to the introduction and reproduction of machinery, technologies, and tools, but other humanistic knowledge as opposed to science was resisted or underestimated as much as possible. The conservative Preceptor (*daxueshi*) Woren [1804–1871] commented: "I had always heard that the way to establish a nation was to venerate the Confucian rites, not power and intrigue; this basic ambition depends on men's hearts, not on technology". He rebutted the idea of studying Western technology espoused by Prince Gong (Yixin, 1833–1898) and others, and remained convinced that the teachings of Confucius and Mencius were sufficient to support the establishment of the nation. However after the Boxer Rebellion, increasing numbers of people realized that it was not enough to limit oneself to "studying the technologies in which the barbarians excelled", to use the phraseology first coined by Wei Yuan, and questions related to Western thought and political systems began to receive attention.[1] Although the Reform Movement of Kang Youwei and Liang Qichao transcended the ideas of the Foreign Affairs Movement, the coup d'état of 1898 demonstrated that political change was in fact very difficult, yet the idea of changing Chinese politics continued to spread.

In the swift development of events, the signing of the *1901 Boxer Protocol* (Xinchou Tiaoyue) once again boosted the hopes of the missionaries and foreigners who acted as intermediaries of Western civilization. They seized the opportunity to remind the Chinese not to continue to indulge in restricted thinking, as the missionary Timothy Richards [1845–1919] wrote in the "Introduction" of his *Forty-Five Years in China: Reminiscences*, published in 1916:

> The problem before the missionary in China, as I found it forty-five years ago, was not only how to save the souls of a fourth of the human race, but also how to save their bodies from perishing at the rate of four millions per annum, and to free their minds, more crippled than the feet of their women, from a philosophy and custom which had lasted for many centuries and left them at the mercy of any nation which might attack their country. But, if the nation were liberated from the bonds of ignorance and harmful custom and were to receive the light of education – scientific, industrial, religious – it might become one of the most powerful nations on earth.[2]

The "philosophy and custom which had lasted for many centuries", as described by Timothy Richards, was enshrined in the Confucian Classics. The knowledge many of those missionaries wanted to spread was

[1] Although some sensitive people noticed such problems as early as the 1850s, Xu Jiyu and others' admiration for Western institutions such as the US Congress and the presidential system led them to prompt the court to send Chinese students to the United States.

[2] Timothy Richard, *Forty-Five Years In China: Reminiscences*, London: T Fisher Unwin, 1916, p. 1.

modern scientific knowledge and the corresponding enlightened thought and culture that the Chinese literati lacked. Indeed, the missionaries had once again acquired the space to expand their mission, and they even began to found universities. For example, when negotiating compensation for the massacre of missionaries in Shanxi by the Boxers, Timothy Richard proposed the establishment of a Western-style university in Taiyuan in 1901, "to remove the ignorance and superstition that had been the main cause of the massacre of the foreigners".[3] The agreement with the Shanxi government to build this university was signed in the following year and construction began soon afterwards. This was the predecessor of today's Shanxi University, and its curriculum at that time included mechanical engineering, painting, chemistry, physics, medicine, mathematics, law, and literature, with plans to construct an auditorium, library, gymnasium, and museum. The work of the missionaries was so effective that in 1916, when recalling the work of the Christian Literature Society (SDK or Guangxue Hui) he served from 1891 onwards, Timothy Richard relates how Zeng Guofan's daughter and son-in-law, as well as their son, became Christians, and such results were more far-reaching than simple missionary fieldwork.

In fact, the anxiety and even panic caused by China's repeated military defeats prompted more and more Chinese to undertake a thorough re-examination of everything, and with the introduction of Western civilization, the emerging new media began influencing the public. With the appearance of China's first truly modern newspaper *Shenbao* (masthead: *Shun Pao, Shanghai News*) in 1872, periodical media set up by missionaries or foreign businessmen began to influence society. This newspaper, founded in Shanghai by Ernest Major [1841–1908], a British tea and cotton tycoon, attained a distribution of 6000 copies a day by 1876 and aimed to "make world events known all over the world".[4] At first, *Shenbao* did not discuss political topics or state affairs per se, but it did report events and activities, and its discussion of these influenced the ideas and

[3] Ibid., p. 299.

[4] It was in 1872 that the businessman Major re-directed foreign bank investment towards media after the banks suffered a business setback in manipulating China's financial markets, and his is an excellent early example of the growing diversity of people's roles and the complexity of social life that would often be seen in China in the early twentieth century.

opinions of its readers throughout the country, thus providing a platform and channel for the dissemination of Western politics and ideas. On 9 April 1887, its editorial titled "A Discussion on Assessing the Popular Mood" (*Lun Yitong Minqing*) was a clear exposition of Western ideas on civil rights:

> In the West [there is democracy, in which] the people rule, as well as which there is rule shared between a monarch and his people. ... In the Western system a parliament is set up with houses in the national and provincial capitals. Rural townships are permitted to promote deputies, who then go to the county seat; the county seats in turn promote their deputies, who then go the prefectural centres. Such deputies must be worthy men of high moral standing and impeccable words and actions, and be familiar with current and foreign affairs (*yangwu*). In accord with the principle of the majority speaking as one, in Western parliaments the individual must follow the ruling of the majority, which is then enacted as legislation. All major affairs of state are discussed and heard in the upper and lower houses of parliament.[5]

In 1905, *Shenbao* introduced a twelve-item reform of the newspaper, which included the creation of "journalists"—a novel identity and profession in China. In the course of its history, the newspaper, which continued until 1949, recorded news and information throughout various distinctive periods, from the Tongzhi period of Qing dynasty until the Communist victory in the Civil War, and urged its elite readership to think deeply about national and political issues, its "Free Talk" column becoming an important platform for writers and thinkers in the twentieth century. *Shenbao* can be seen as creating a climate for change in late Qing politics. Similar early newspapers were *Xunhuan Ribao* (founded in 1874 in Hong Kong) and *Xinwen Bao* (founded in Shanghai in 1883). In the 1880s, a popular periodical that utilized and transformed the function of images was even published. Known as the *Dianshi-zhai Huabao* (Touchstone Studio Illustrated) and published in 1884, also by Ernest Major, this was an illustrated current affairs newspaper that featured lively scenes and events as depicted by the Chinese painter Wu Youru [*c.* 1840–1893]. Throughout its 14-year publishing history, regular issues of *Dianshi-zhai Huabao* presented Wu Youru's documentary sketches of events and

[5] Quoted from Zhang Yufa, *Qingji de Lixian Tuanti* (Constitutional Groups of the Qing Period), Beijing: Peking University Press, 2011, p. 57.

personalities gleaned from everyday life, occasionally branching out to cover international events. Its content drew on the chaotic coverage presented in most popular newspapers, but Wu Youru's accessible large-scale images comprehensibly informed Chinese readers about current affairs, urban life, popular culture, and foreign marvels. Wu Youru's blend of striking illustrations and informative anecdotal captions made this readable paper resemble a popular pictorial album, without the elegant and interesting trees and birds, not to mention the vivid brush and ink style, of elegant Chinese pictorial art. Through their years of social decline, the traditional literati and aristocrats might not regard the art presented in such a pictorial as being of consequence, but they too relied on such news and print materials to understand the outside world. In fact, it was the emerging media such as *Dianshi-zhai Huabao* that introduced new knowledge and informed readers about events in Shanghai, the rest of China, and abroad, changing people's interpretation and understanding of the world on a daily basis. To be sure, this illustrated reportage was well received as people grew more willing to accept news images that reflected the content of everyday life, at the same time as the realism of the illustrations provided access to the language of Western realistic painting which would soon be brought back to China from Japan and Europe by students who had studied abroad.[6] In 1889, the newspaper *Wanguo Gongbao*, its English masthead reading "The Globe Magazine", which had been discontinued for the five previous years, resumed publication under the auspices of the Christian Literature Society for China

[6] Wu Youru (?–*c.* 1893) was a native of Wu County near Shanghai. In his early years he studied traditional Chinese book illustration and became familiar with the use of fine linework in such printed works. Although he initially emulated the figural illustrations of Gai Qi (1773–1828) and Ren Xiong (1823–1857), the more obvious influence seems to have come from English newspapers such as *The Illustrated London News*, first published in 1842, or church materials like the books published by the Tou-Se-We (Tushanwan) Craft School in Shanghai. Wu Youru readily adapted to perspective and related illustrative methods used in these publications, although he often retained the use of parallel lines in the Chinese tradition of "architectural painting" that was independent of Western notions of perspective. Chinese traditional methods of assessing painting could not be used to evaluate these illustrations, because the painting methods and purposes were obviously far removed from the interests of the traditional literati, and at that time people were more interested in the news stories than the art. Zheng Zhenduo (1898–1958) in his essay titled "The Development of Chinese Painting over the Last Hundred Years" wrote: "The early history of China's semi-feudal semi-colonial society over the past century can be seen clearly in his illustrated news stories".

(Guangxue Hui), with Walter Medhurst continuing to serve as the chief editor. *Wanguo Gongbao* facilitated an understanding of Western thought and values for those bent on national salvation, while nurturing the concept among China's new-style intellectuals of using newspapers and magazines to pursue the cause of freedom. Basically, the failings of the Qing government naturally further undermined the credibility of the Qing court, and the rapid and large-scale emergence of Western-style media revealed increasing demands for the free and unchecked expression of opinion. After 1895, there was a rapid increase in the number of newspapers and magazines.[7] The publication of translated books was also widely popularized, and those gentry who accepted Western knowledge to varying degrees and readers who had gradually broken away from depending on tradition were eager to spread new knowledge and express their ideas through their own writing and publication. Liang Qichao in section 29 of his *General Discussion of Qing Dynasty Scholarship* (Qingdai Xueshu Gailun) has described the panic state of seeking knowledge in that chaotic period:

> The coup d'état of 1898, followed by the Boxer Rebellion of 1900, fully exposed the decline of the Qing imperial household. Young students were clamoring to study abroad and as Japan was close, most went there. From 1902 to 1903, translation work flourished and there were more than a dozen published magazines. Whenever a new book was published in Japan, several translators were ready to start work on it. The introduction of new ideas was in full swing. However, all the ideas and publications said to be in the 'Liang Qichao-style' followed no organization, no choice, no clear origins, and belonged to no known faction, yet all were expensive, and society welcomed them. It was like people who had spent a long time in a disaster zone and had been forced to eat roots, bark, frozen sparrows, and rotting mice, and so are happy to devour anything they can get their hands on, and do not question whether or not they can digest it or it will make them sick, which does not bode well for the health of this generation.[8]

[7] According to statistics and data prepared by the historian Zhang Hao, there were 64 new newspapers and magazines in the period 1895–1898, by 1913 there were 487, and by 1917 there were 2000, and more than 400 newspapers appeared in 1919 alone. (See Zhang Hao, "*Zhongguo Jindai Sixiang Shi de Zhuanxing Shidai*" (The Transitional Era in the History of China's Modern Thought), *Ershiyi Shiji* (21st Century), April 1999 issue.)

[8] Xiong Yuezhi, in his *Xixue Dongjian yu Wan-Qing Shehui* (Western Learning Travels East and Late Qing Society), provides detailed statistics on Western studies in China

In the wave of introducing Western thought, even though one can think of the early efforts of Guo Songtao and his contemporary Kang Youwei, Yan Fu (1854–1921) played the pivotal role in translating

between 1900 and 1911, and discusses five phenomena that characterize the dissemination of Western learning in this period:

1. *Altered transmission routes*. Prior to this period, China introduced and absorbed Western studies mainly through translations from English, French, German, and other Western languages. After 1900, the number of Western academic works imported via Japan increased sharply, with Japan becoming the main source for the import of Western studies. From 1902 to 1904, for example, there were 533 translations of Western scholarly works over three years, of which 89 were from English, accounting for 16% of the total number of translations in the country, 24 from German (4%), 17 from French (3%), and 321 from Japanese, accounting for 60% of the total.
2. *Unprecedented quantities*. From 1900 to 1911, China translated at least 1599 Western books from Japanese, English, and French, accounting for 69.8% of the total number of translations made in the last century of the late Qing dynasty, more than twice the total number of Chinese translations in the previous 90 years. Of these, 899 were translated from 1900 to 1904, more than in the previous 90 years.
3. *Increase in the proportion of social science works*. In the three years from 1902 to 1904, for example, there were 327 translated social science books in literature, history, philosophy, economics, and law, accounting for 61% of the total number of translated titles. During the same period, 112 natural science books and 56 applied science books were translated, accounting for 21% and 11% of the total, respectively. The proportion of translations of social sciences to natural sciences and to applied sciences was the reverse of that in previous decades. This demonstrates a shift in China's imported Western studies from material culture including technology and artifacts to spiritual cultural concerns such as philosophy and scholarship.
4. *Deeper impact*. The influx of Western studies, especially new textbooks of various levels, spread throughout urban and rural areas, and into thousands of households, so that the influence of Western studies had never been greater. Dazzling new disciplines and dazzling new terminology made the academic and publishing worlds look completely new. Many of the basic concepts and terms used today, such as society, political parties, government, nation, class, doctrine, thought, concept, truth, knowledge, materialism, idealism, subject, object, subjectivity, objectivity, object, concrete, abstract, etc., were all neologisms established at that time by Japanese scholars using Chinese characters as "roots" and subsequently adopted into Chinese.
5. *The emergence of China's first generation of prominent translators*. Before the late Qing period, the usual pattern adopted for the translation of Western books into Chinese, was that translators such as Li Shanlan, Xu Shou, and Hua Hengfang, would work with collaborators who were versed in the foreign language and these translators would be responsible for refining this raw material into elegant Chinese even though they did not understand the original foreign language. However, beginning with Yan Fu (1854–1921) and Ma Junwu (1881–1940), modern China acquired its own first generation of hands-on translators initiating this transitional period in the history of Western studies transmission.

and commenting on Western thought. From the beginning, Yan Fu's words sounded an alarm. In contrast with Zheng Guanying's 1893 work *Shengshi Weiyan* 盛世危言 (Words of Warning for a Prosperous Age), a title which tempered its "words of warning" with a reassurance that Zheng was writing for an optimistic "age of rising prosperity", Yan Fu unequivocally told readers in 1895 that China's problem was that it was about to "perish". In his view, China's very survival was at stake, as was made clear by China's defeat in the Sino-Japanese War, an event that impelled him to quickly write five articles on China's political situation.[9] He clearly supported the reforms proposed by Kang Youwei and his colleagues, construing his articles as an important aspect of their ideological push for reforms; Yan simply asserted: "If we do not reform, we will perish". He asserted, "If we use Western technology, we can attain wealth and power". The "Western technology" he cites here was no longer limited to familiarity with machinery or the knowledge of military, shipbuilding, and other technologies; Yan Fu had begun to focus attention on the significance of Western political thought for China, something his friend Guo Songtao had signaled when they were both in London. To be sure, Yan Fu's conclusions were also based on the fact that he kept abreast of the latest intellectual developments after he went to England in 1877. Although Yan Fu initially studied advanced mathematics, chemistry, physics, naval tactics, and naval warfare at the Royal Naval College in Greenwich, he quickly turned his attention to politics, socioeconomics, and law, at a time when the Social Darwinian ideas of Thomas Henry Huxley (1825–1895) and Herbert Spencer (1820–1903) were at the fore of British thought. During his time studying abroad, Yan Fu acquired an understanding of Darwin's theory of evolution expounded in his 1859 publication *The Origin of Species*. After returning home, Yan was hired to teach at the Fujian Arsenal Academy in the port of Fuzhou and at the Beiyang (North Sea) Naval Officers School where he introduced Western ideas. When he learned of the fall of Weihaiwei and the defeat of the Beiyang Navy by the Japanese, he immediately published an article introducing Darwin's theory of evolution titled "On Strength" (*Yuan Qiang*) in the newspaper *Zhibao*, in which he discussed

[9] Yan Fu's articles "On the Speed of World Change", "On Strength", "A Refutation of Han Yu", "On Strength, Sequel", and "On Our Salvation" were all written in 1895.

the concepts of "the survival of the fittest" and "natural selection", in order to warn his compatriots: if the nation-state does not strive for self-strengthening it will perish in the competitive struggle for survival, stressing the significance of Darwin's basic ideas. "When *The Origin of Species* first appeared", he wrote, "almost every home in Europe and the United States had its own copy of the book, and scholarship and politics in the West all underwent change. Intellectual discussions were utterly transformed, ideas changed, and even the validity of Newtonian science and astronomy was called into question". When in 1898 Yan Fu published his translation of T. H. Huxley's *Evolution and Ethics* under the Chinese title *Tianyan Lun* meaning "The Theory of Heaven's Unfolding", Yan Fu again introduced Darwin's theory.[10] Although Huxley had no interest in Darwin's gradualism, Yan Fu clearly took advantage of Huxley's defense of Darwin's theory of evolution and application of the theory to human society, and argued that man as a social animal, like other animals, was necessarily driven by the logical imperative that there are "winners and losers, but only the fittest survive". Yan Fu believed that this kind of social Darwinism was the philosophy most needed in China at that time. He was afraid his readers would lack understanding of the original work, so he provided annotation and even explanatory notes in the translation, which also served to explain Yan Fu's ideas prior to embarking on his translation of T. H. Huxley's work. As far as the professionalism of a translation is concerned, people expect that a translator strictly follow the original author's ideas and meaning and that a translator's personal views and opinions not intrude on the original. However, Yan Fu had his own concept of translation. While he felt that the translator must truly and accurately convey the author's ideas, those ideas above all must also be conveyed through the translation, not to mention the "disciplinary" concern that it was difficult to find terminological correspondences between the two languages. Later translators were hard-pressed to find fault with Yan Fu's translation, because Yan Fu had a very high level of understanding of Chinese, especially of the full sweep of meanings opened up by ancient Chinese and English, and he believed in the ability of traditionally educated Chinese scholars to comprehend his text, which is why he couched his translation in the ancient Chinese style

[10] Yan Fu began translating this work in 1895.

of writing with which they were familiar.[11] However, those who compare Yan Fu's translation with Huxley's original text and at the same time understand Darwin's and Spencer's ideas inevitably point out that Yan Fu's translation was organized, arranged, and modified to suit the translator's own purposes. Precisely because Yan Fu fully understood the core ideas of these thinkers, was he able to organize organically the sentences of the original Western writing in the elegant language of his readers. This intervention with the original text was motivated by the urgency of his need to alert readers to the profound crisis confronting China. As a matter of course, he deliberately ignored some of the ideas in the original work—for example, he disagreed with Huxley's view that social and ethical progress must be a struggle waged against the cosmic process, and he only wanted to highlight and emphasize as much as possible that a struggle for survival existed within human societies as in the biological world. In his translation, he turned the debate between Huxley and Spencer about whether a nation could play a positive or negative role in generating universal happiness into the theme of whether a nation could generate national prosperity and strength. In fact, Yan Fu only wanted to emphasize that in the social realm, there was necessarily also ethnic competition; China, because of its defeat or at least serious losses in the struggle for survival, was unbearably weakened. In short, he stressed that in a society, as in the natural world, there was a struggle that could "protect the nation" and lead a country to "wealth and strength". This was the key to introducing Social Darwinism and Yan Fu achieved that goal. He

[11] In the preface outlining the principles he followed in translating T. H. Huxley's work, Yan Fu succinctly categorized these as "*xin* (faithfulness), *da* (expressiveness), and *ya* (elegance)", principles to which most translators to the present day also subscribe, except that the translation of texts in the humanities and social sciences must follow standards far removed from those adhered to in translating a technical or scientific text. Therefore, there is a gulf between different languages in translation; as Yan Fu stated in the preface of his translation, titled in Chinese *Tianyan Lun*: "The famous British intellectual John Stuart Mill stated that if one wishes to examine the language of a country, and to see its logic, this is impossible if one does not understand the languages of several countries. I was originally skeptical about this statement, but now I am deeply convinced of its veracity and sigh that his arguments are unalterable". (*Yan Fu Sixiang Zhitan* [An Investigation of the Principles of Yan Fu's Philosophy], Dadong Tushu Gongsi, 1980). However, although Yan Fu considered the effectiveness of the dissemination of ideas, his text also still has the obstacles to reading. Liang Qichao commented that Yan Fu's "prose is too elegant, deliberately imitating the pre-Qin style, and for those not well versed in ancient books, it is difficult to understand". (*Xinmin Congbao* [New People's Miscellany], No. 1, 1 January 1903.)

used the eight Chinese characters "物竞天择优胜劣败" to translate the twin concepts of "the struggle for existence" and "survival of the fittest". Hu Shi later recalled:

> Within a few years after the publication of *Tianyan Lun*, the work had become popular throughout the country, and it was reading material for middle school students. ... In the wake of China's repeated defeats and the humiliations occasioned by the Boxer Rebellion and subsequent *Boxer Protocol*, "let's drink to the survival of the fittest" even became a popular toast.[12]

Although Yan Fu also mentions that there are similarities between Western thought and ancient Chinese philosophers, his recommended Western writings were clearly different from the Confucian tradition, and even fundamentally different from the work of scholars who wished to transform Confucianism from the inside. Confucianism had undergone its own restoration and development: *Kaojuxue*, translating roughly to evidential textual studies or empirical exegesis, can be regarded as a transformation beginning in the Ming dynasty towards a general empiricism, but the factuality demanded by those scholars did not stem from reality, but from texts, and so its requirements were utterly different from the Western doctrine of empiricism that went back to Francis Bacon (1561–1626). Therefore, even if the scholars engaged in empirical exegesis were able to level a critique against the hollow arguments produced by the Song and Ming dynasty Neo-Confucian School of *Li* ("reason"), their efforts to find answers in the classical writings were unsuccessful in generating "practical policies" (*jingshi*), and Kang Youwei's practice can be regarded as the latest proof of the failure of text-bound empiricism. Thus, as Yan Fu saw it, it was necessary to adopt "Western techniques" (*Xiyang zhi shu*), which was completely different in nature from the previous advocacy by the Foreign Affairs group of "Chinese learning for fundamentals and Western learning for applications", because it envisaged a comprehensive borrowing of Western political, economic, and cultural ideas. Of course, this raised the question of the role played by Confucian values in the nation's rise and decline, and the relationship between "protecting the [Confucian] teachings" and "protecting the nation", which Kang Youwei saw as one and the same. In Kang's view, the nation and Confucianism

[12] Hu Shi, *Sishi Zishu* (Autobiography at Forty), 1930.

were both in crisis as a result of Western expansionism, and so his program of reform measures had at its core the inseparability of "protecting the [Confucian] teachings" and "protecting the nation". At this time, many people had realized to varying degrees that an insistence on "Chinese learning for the fundamentals" might entail the loss of the nation, and such a sense of reality clearly led to the emergence of a new position, namely ethnic nationalism (*minzu-zhuyi*). This nationalism's uniqueness rested on the premise that providing this "[ethnos] nation-state" could be preserved, what had in the past been regarded as national (ethnic) traditional culture and ideological traditions could be put aside for the time being, not to mention the fact that most activists thought it was extremely difficult, or at least too late, to find something useful in the vastness of traditional culture. Were there not readily available tools and methods at present, they asked, that could ensure that the nation become rich and powerful?[13] Given that there were, these should be put to immediate use! This was what motivated Yan Fu to go on to translate Adam Smith's *The Wealth of Nations*, John Stuart Mill's *On Liberty*, Montesquieu's *Esprit des Lois*, Edward Jenks' *A History of Politics*, and John Stuart Mill's *A System of Logic*. He did his utmost to introduce Western economics, political science, law, and logic to China, so that those who wanted to save China from perishing could put them to use as soon as possible, his motivation being to change Chinese thinking and psychology by translating Western works. Thus, using the term "total westernization" to describe the scope of his translations in the humanities does not seem to be an excessive description of his attitude, but people discovered that the ideological peaks Yan Fu established in his early years were in sharp contrast to the political positions and attitudes towards life he adopted in his later years.[14]

[13] Even though Zhang Zhidong did not agree with Kang's views, he regarded it as important to "protect the country" (of course, by "country" Zhang Zhidong meant the Qing court), Yan Fu obviously also held out no hope for Kang's New Text Confucian classics that provided the theoretical basis for Kang's 1898 reform initiative. In a letter to Liang Qichao in 1897, Yan Fu wrote: "The [Confucian] faith cannot be preserved, and if one asserts that we should advance even while preserving the faith, it is not the original faith that is being preserved".

Benjamin Schwartz, *In Search of Wealth and Power: Yen Fu and the West*, Cambridge, Massachusetts: Harvard University Press, 1964, p. 48.

[14] This may be a valuable subject for those studying Yan Fu to examine. Yan Fu certainly lent his support to Yuan Shikai's restoration of the imperial system, and this seems to

Unlike Yan Fu, who mainly disseminated Western ideas through his translations, Liang Qichao (1873–1929), who was a follower and colleague of the reformist Kang Youwei, chose political action, writing,

have been the result of complex factors including changes in ideological strategy and a reassessment of China's reality. Aside from this, Yan Fu in 1913 endorsed the Kongjiao Hui which proposed that Confucianism be declared a state religion and he was indeed an active participant in this movement, which shows that he not only revised his previous disregard for Confucianism, but it also led people to feel that this "sage of Western learning" had now completely turned his back on any idea of "total Westernization". However, given his knowledge of the Chinese classics in his early years, Yan Fu had throughout his intellectual career often linked Western thought to the ideas of ancient Chinese philosophers. But in the face of the unprecedented shock of the human suffering in the First World War, we probably need to understand why Yan Fu would rethink and reevaluate his earlier assessments of civilizations and their history. Therefore, assessing the development of thinkers whose career spans half a century or more needs to be cautiously undertaken and fully cognizant of history:

> I have grown old and, having personally witnessed the historically unprecedented bloody warfare that our Republic has been subjected to for seven years and Europe has endured for four years, I have come to feel that the West's progress during these three hundred years has only led to selfishness, slaughter, corruption, and shamelessness. When I look back at the Way of Confucius and Mencius, and undertake a genuine assessment of the world, I must favour my native land. This is not simply a comfortable linguistic preference, but a choice that many Western intellectuals are also making.

Ref: "Letters to Xiong Chunru", in Wang Shi ed., *Yan Fu Ji* (Anthology of Yan Fu), v. 3, Beijing: Zhonghua Shuju, 1986, p. 642. Benjamin Schwartz, *In Search of Wealth and Power: Yen Fu and the West*, Cambridge, Massachusetts: Harvard University Press, 1964, p. 235, quoting letter no. 59 (June 1923).

Yan Fu was clearly very familiar with Laozi and Zhuangzi, which enables us to understand this statement in a letter written after returning to his village in 1921, the year of his death:

> Idling in my little pavilion, I watch the clouds and listen to the rain, and when I feel buoyant, I sit by the pond and bask in the sun. In the past I was interested in books on philosophy and history, but now I cannot read them and take no interest in current affairs. The trees are dying, but I have not died, but to long remain breathing in the world of man serves no purpose! I prefer to concentrate my mind, follow my heart, and acquiesce in change.

Benjamin Schwartz, *In Search of Wealth and Power: Yen Fu and the West*, Cambridge, Massachusetts: Harvard University Press, 1964, p. 236, quoting letter no. 74 (August 1923).

Such a mood is typical of elderly Chinese intellectuals throughout history who have been frustrated by seeing their ideals not realized.

journalism, and newspaper editing as his vehicles for popularizing Western thought. In 1896, Liang Qichao, together with Huang Zunxian and Wang Kangnian, set up the newspaper *Shiwu Bao* (*The Times*, masthead: *Chinese Progress*) in Shanghai; this was the same year in which the Commercial Press was founded and Liang Qichao published "A General Discussion of Reforms" (Bianfa Tongyi) and many other articles related to the issue of national salvation. After the failed coup in 1898, Liang Qichao fled to Japan where in December he founded the periodical *Qingyi Bao* (*Pure Discussion*, masthead: *The China Discussion*, Yokohama, 1898) which marked a turning point in his ideas and methods, signaling his rejection of Kang Youwei's reliance on "Old Studies" and a new recognition of the need to inform people and promote their understanding of the importance of new knowledge. Liang stressed paying attention to Western warnings regarding "the survival of the fittest". This journal, which was published every 10 days and ran to 40 pages per issue, had sections specifically devoted to promoting civil rights, explaining philosophical principles, shedding light on developments at the imperial court, and documenting the intensifying national shame; it regularly carried articles on the theory of evolution, natural human rights, bourgeois revolution, and theories of the nation. However, *Qingyi Bao* was partisan in continuing to argue for "protecting the Emperor", while regularly featuring content attacking the Empress Dowager Cixi, Ronglu, and Yuan Shikai. In 1902, Liang Qichao founded *Xinmin Congbao* (New People's Miscellany), which focused on the importance of constitutionalism; this semi monthly periodical featured columns covering major topics such as theory, doctrine, current affairs, politics, history, geography, education, religion, scholarship, agriculture, industry, commerce, military affairs, finance, and law. Liang Qichao wrote copy for *Xinmin Congbao* as often as he could, and the timeliness and relevance of his articles ensured that *Xinmin Congbao* was far more influential and played a much larger role than the earlier *Shiwu Bao* and *Qingyi Bao*. During this period, Liang Qichao's activist attitudes were politically inflammatory:

> Arise, arise, arise! Compatriots! Arise, arise, arise, youth of our New China! Our generation cannot survive under this despotic regime, our generation cannot live under this despotic regime! This despotic regime is the

Ref: "Letters to Xiong Chunru", in Wang Shi ed., *Yan Fu Ji* (Anthology of Yan Fu), v. 3, Beijing: Zhonghua Shuju, 1986, p. 714.

common enemy of our generation and is the thing we loathe. It is either the autocracy or us. I am not willing to stand with it, I would rather die fighting it! What has putrefied our history for millennia? This despotic regime. What has transformed our land into a terrain where terror lies in wait? This despotic regime. What has reduced our hundreds of millions of people to living in hell? This despotic regime. This autocracy today harms us in a hundred ways but provides not a single benefit! If our generation remains respectful and stands together with this regime, then we will bring disgrace to our ancestors, be unable to live with ourselves, and bring no honor to our children and grandchildren. Our generation must now organize a mighty army, sacrifice our lives, and vow to destroy this regime; only then can we eat for another day. With our strength we have nothing to fear; our troops will accrue renown as we proclaim [this regime's] crimes to the whole world, and all will hear us and come to know them.[15]

Unlike Yan Fu who emphasized elegant prose, Liang Qichao tried to use new words and styles in the process of spreading new ideas, and he founded the journal *New Fiction* to emphasize the need to change the thought and content of popular literature, as well as to devote efforts to literary style. As early as the spring of 1892, most people learned that the 20-year-old Guangxu Emperor had begun to learn English, and for Chinese this signified that the time had come to understand the civilizations and ideas of the rest of the world in order to deal with the country's overall crisis, and that learning a new language was the beginning of new ideas.[16] In fact, even the Chinese written language

[15] Liang Qichao, "Nitao Zhuanzhi Zhengti Xi" (Call to Arms against the Despotic Regime), *Liang Qichao Xuan Ji* (Selected Works of Liang Qichao), p. 380.

[16] Isaac Taylor Headland records how In 1894 the Christian women of China decided to present a New Testament to the Empress Dowager on her sixtieth birthday which occurred in the following year, and a lavish edition was prepared, which was duly taken by the English and American ministers to the Chinese Foreign Office to be sent to her majesty. On the following day the Emperor sent to the American Bible Society for copies of the Old and New Testament, as were being sold to his people, but hastens to add that "It must not be inferred from this that the emperor was becoming a Christian. Very far from it, though the interest he took in the Christian doctrine set the people to studying about it, not only in Peking, but throughout many of the provinces, as was indicated at the time by the number of Christian books sold". Ref: Isaac Taylor Headland, *Court Life in China: The Capital, Its Officials and People*, New York and Chicago: F. H. Revell Co., 1909, pp. 37–38.

needed to be relearned at a time when the country was in danger. The Japanese language employed a large number of Chinese characters which were the result of borrowings during the Three Kingdoms period, and more especially during the Tang dynasty, and now the Chinese were borrowing neologisms expressed in Chinese characters back from the Japanese. Indeed, if the Japanese had not begun to translate Western (English, German, French, etc.) writings into Japanese from the beginning of the Meiji period, there would have been no new compound Chinese words to express new concepts, and if there had been no Chinese students studying in Japan to introduce and draw on this Japanese-generated Chinese-character lexicon used to express the new knowledge, Chinese who wanted to understand, translate, and use material in foreign languages expressing new ideas would probably have ended up using the same method of linguistic recombination or recycling which the Japanese had earlier adopted. The reality was that Chinese people, mainly young students, simply brought back the new Chinese words which the Japanese had redefined or reassembled in the process of translation, and it was via this new terminology that people quickly assimilated new knowledge. This did of course also entail the transformation of language and text, and even though Yan Fu's translated works had indeed played a role in the dissemination of new knowledge, a clear gap nevertheless remained between his writing and the general reading public. Without new terminology it was also difficult to more fully express foreign ideas in all their richness—or to

Isaac Taylor Headland goes on to describe the Emperor's subsequent interest in learning English: "It was about this time he began the study of English. He ordered that two teachers be appointed, and contrary to all former customs he allowed them to sit rather than kneel while they taught him. At the time they were selected I was exchanging lessons in English for Chinese with the grandson of one of these teachers and learned a good deal about the progress the young man was making. He was in such a hurry to begin that he could not wait to send to England or America for books, and so the officials visited the various schools and missions in search of proper primers for a beginner. When they visited us, we made a thorough search and finally Dr. Marcus L. Taft discovered an attractively illustrated primer which he had taken to China with him for his little daughter Frances, and this was sent to Kuang Hsu. One day a eunuch called on me saying that the Emperor had learned that the various institutions of learning, educational associations, tract, and other societies had published a number of books in Chinese which they had translated from the European languages. I was at that time the custodian of two or three of these societies and had a great variety of Chinese books in my possession. I therefore sent him copies of our astronomy, geology, zoology, physiology and various other scientific books which I was at that time teaching in the university". Isaac Taylor Headland, *Court Life in China: The Capital, Its Officials and People*, p. 39.

rebut them. As a corollary, the use of new terminology naturally led to a change in the style of language. Once the classical-style text (*wenyan-wen*) had acquired "transitional" characteristics and lost the clipped quality and succinctness characteristic of classical Chinese prose, it could no longer support the use of new and longer terms. By way of contrast, the new prose style could effectively resolve problems of translating new ideas because in the new prose style sentence structure and rhythm were very free. In the process of writing, authors could now be more relaxed and not limited to traditional collocations, not to mention the obligation to use classical allusions, and to balance out long and short sentences, and the many other corollary demands placed on the writing of classical Chinese. Such new prose could disseminate new ideas with facility and break with the habits of thinking associated with classical Chinese. As a result, the new style gradually changed the linguistic logic and habits that had long determined people's speech, argumentation, and thinking. This change was subtle, but distinctly disruptive. Since no words to express new ideas could be found in the traditional lexicon, the new terminology brought back from Japan began to be used with increasing frequency. Indeed, these characters and words drawn from classical literature had meanings different from their usages at this time, as well as differing syntactic adhesion, and could even have meanings quite opposite from their original denotation or connotation.[17] As a result, people began to turn to new books to understand the meanings of terms borrowed from ancient texts, and the recombination and changes in meaning ushered in by the new terminology eventually led to unfamiliarity with, and estrangement from, traditional texts, as the new language was accepted. At this time, the form or style of prose was no insignificant matter, as it affected the efficacy and influence of the dissemination of ideas. Liang Qichao's far-reaching influence in this period was directly related to his new prose style. In short, intellectuals who advocated reform venerated the new prose style and the later "vernacular" (*baihua*) prose. In terms of practical writing, the new style Liang Qichao pioneered conformed to the logic of foreign grammar, and his plain and smooth simplified classical Chinese was a direct challenge to the predominant style of classical Chinese termed the

[17] Although the Japanese neologism for the concept of a "constitution" was 憲法 (read in Japanese: *kempō*, Chinese: *xianfa*) was adopted from a passage that occurs in the "Jin Yu" section of *Guoyu*, the word's original meaning was "the overriding law of a state", its connotation included no hint of "democracy". Indeed, it connoted the opposite.

Tongcheng School. Unlike Yan Fu's use of ancient terms, Liang Qichao's articles changed from basically using traditional Chinese terms to Japanese terminology between 1898 and 1901, providing the basis for modern "vernacular" (*baihua*) expression. Hu Shi made the following evaluation of Liang Qichao's work at this time: "Mr. Liang's prose has clarity and lucidity imbued with rich enthusiasm, so that the reader irresistibly follows him and his ideas".[18]

During the Reform Movement, Liang Qichao was invited to participate in Hunan's relatively relaxed political activities and, with the support of many local gentry and officials, he participated in the new-style education of the Shiwu Xuetang (Current Affairs College) in Changsha that provided a Western understanding of Confucianism, as well as in the

[18] Hu Shi, *Autobiography at Forty*. Wu Qichang (1904–1944) has also described his memories of Liang Qichao's work on cultural and intellectual history and Song dynasty history:

In those years there was a group of young writing prodigies who were part of the reform movement developing their own distinctive writing styles. ... Tan Sitong's prose emulated the prose of Gong Zizhen which was bold and showy, but hardly amenable to popularization. Xia Zengyou's prose featured an admixture of elements drawn from Zhuangzi and Buddhist writing, and this was even less likely to catch on. Zhang Binglin's writing style emulated the archaisms and elegance of Wang Chong's *Lun Heng*, and it too was unlikely to become popular. Yan Fu's writing style drew on the philosophers of the Han-Wei period, but its metaphysical purity did not recommend it for bold writing. Lin Shu's prose had its source in Liuzhou [i.e., Liu Zongyuan], but despite its ease and fluidity it was only suitable for epigrammatic essays. The prose of Chen Sanli and Ma Qixu was like the Tongcheng style of Yao Xie, but its scope was restricted. Zhang Shizhao's prose could later become lively, but it would also suddenly get stuck in the Tongcheng style and tangle itself up in knots. As for prose that could roar like thunder, evoke powerful emotions, chronicle dramatic events, and terrify the reader, as it could in turn arouse through sorrow, mournfully evoke lamentation, be lyrically sensitive, or rousing, and imbued with full emotional force, at the same time as it could flow fluidly and sustain a narrative for ten thousand words, yet balance elegance and vulgarity, and which could be read without tiring, could stir the reader to rage or sorrow, it is not idle flattery to say that only the prose of Liang Qichao could achieve all this! Liang Qichao's prose not only dominated the period from before the 1898 Reforms through to the eve of the 1911 Revolution, in other words from around 1896 to 1912, but Master Liang also dominated public opinion throughout those sixteen years and was the period's leading writer. As the tide of revolutionary thought rose, Liang's political views took up the slack as the ideas of Kang Youwei declined into enervation, and Liang's rousing spirit seemed to hasten Kang's decline. The preparation for the subsequent reform movement championing vernacular prose was initiated and readied by Liang Qichao throughout those sixteen years, as he firmly established his new prose genre with its distinctive style.

Ref: Li Xisuo and Yuan Qing, *Liang Qichao Zhuan* (Biography of Liang Qichao), Beijing: Renmin Chubanshe, 1994, p. 151.

school's political agitation. This was of course in the special period just before 1898, when there was a vibrant new ideological trend widely supported by diverse social players ranging from Qing officials to members of the local gentry. The threat of partition by the Western powers that loomed over China for several decades had led to the demand for "reform" (*bianfa*), but people were divided regarding what forces "reform" could rely on, what resources (including ideological resources) "reform" could draw on, how "reform" should be interpreted, and the extent and scope of "reform". In fact, when the call for "reform" threatened the Qing dynasty and those local officials and gentry squires who could protect themselves by relying on the sweep of the entire authoritarian system, many parts of the "reformist" political spectrum began to gravitate towards the red end of the spectrum, expressing opposition to "reform" or even adopting the dynastic position by imposing measures that ranged from suppression to expulsion of the radicals.[19]

[19] For example, in July 1895, Kang Youwei began organizing the Qiang Xue Hui (Society for the Enhancement of Learning), in which not only reformers but number of government officials also participated, including Zhang Zhidong, Liu Kunyi, Weng Tonghe, Sun Jianai, Li Hongzao, Yuan Shikai, and many others; some even provided financial support. However, there were clear differences of opinion among members in understanding how to move forward with reform. Zhang Zhidong adhered to his position of having "Chinese learning as the corpus", but when Kang Youwei advocated abandoning the use in newspapers of Qing dynastic regnal dates in favor of dating that commenced with the year of the birth of Confucius, this move met with great dissatisfaction. At the same time, diehard conservatives from time to time accused some members of the Society of using it as a forum for "inappropriate" political activity or even as a prohibited private association that endangered the security of the court, so the Society was banned a few months later (22 January 1896). In 1896, Kang Youwei and Liang Qichao promoted the reform movement in Hunan, where because of the writing of, and the foundations laid by, Wu Dazheng, Chen Baozhen, Huang Zunxian, Jiang Biao, and others, an atmosphere conducive to the Reform Movement had been created. Liang Qichao's ideas encouraged more young people in Hunan to join the reform movement. However, with the more radical attitudes and initiatives of Liang Qichao and some others, such as when he suggested to Chen Baozhen that Hunan break away from the central government in response to the German occupation of Jiaozhou in 1897, a number of participants distanced themselves from the Society, even though Liang Qichao's views on realizing nationalistic autonomy and ethnic self-determination seemed to be oblivious of the Qing government's high degree of centralization and control. Then, in 1897, Liang Qichao and a number of local enlightened officials and gentry founded the more politically radical Southern Study Society (Nan Xue Hui), and stimulated the emergence of more societies of this nature. At this time, Liang Qichao constantly promoted his own ideas, so that the Southern Study Society became a local council of sorts, and through the publication of newspapers such as *Xiangbao* (Hunan News) and the establishment of schools

After the coup that defeated the 1898 Reforms, the division in stance became so obvious that two political camps comprising diverse groups of constitutionalists and revolutionaries gradually formed and, as the situation changed, the two factions were drawn into increasing conflict and direct opposition regarding the terms, means, and even the purposes of reform.

The difficulties China faced between 1901 and 1904 continued to deepen and, after the *Boxer Protocol* was signed, the threat posed by Japan was temporarily eliminated. In helping the Qing government suppress the Boxers, Russia had occupied China's three north-eastern provinces, and in July 1900 the Qing government required that Russia withdraw as required. However, Russia brazenly took advantage of China's weakness and instead demanded new privileges. On 16 February 1901, Russia even proposed a new treaty demanding monetary compensation for its occupation and the losses of its railway company, and further insisted that the China Eastern Railway be extended to Beijing. In 1902, the Qing government and Russia signed the *Agreement between Russia and China with Regard to Manchuria*, which stipulated that Russian troops would withdraw from China in three phases. However, Russia did not withdraw its troops. Instead in Lüshun (later called Port Arthur and located near Dalian, which the Russians called Dalniy) it set up the office of Viceroy (*Namestnik*) of the Russian Far East (1900–1905) and reoccupied Fengtian (Shenyang). At the same time, Japan, Britain, Germany, Italy, and other countries, because of their own interests, warned China not to sign an exclusive agreement with Russia. Chinese public opinion in turn demanded that China enter into an alliance with Japan and Great Britain to oppose Russia. The Qing government, with Li Hongzhang as its representative, was caught between the foreign powers and plagued by internal divisions within the court. In November 1903, the British army invaded Tibet. In 1902–1903, Great Britain, the United States, and Japan consecutively signed Treaties of Commerce and Navigation with

and libraries, a practical political structure was created. Rapid radicalization eventually led to deep misgivings among those who had supported reform to varying degrees, and eventually led to a coalition of conservative forces attacking reform. Liang Qichao and others' ideas and statements had developed into a direct challenge to the Qing government's authoritarian system. At the same time the boundaries of Confucianism had been significantly broken, which aroused the fears of Zhang Zhidong, who in 1898 ordered Hubei officials to cease subscribing to newspapers publicizing reform. Chen Baozhen memorialized the Qing court urging that Kang Youwei's *Kongzi Gaizhi Kao* be burned.

China which stipulated that Chinese businessmen who set up factories in the treaty ports must pay an ad valorem tariff to China Imperial Maritime Customs, in the same way as did foreign merchants who set up factories in trading ports. In August 1904 a German warship sailed upriver to Jiangxi. In 1905, at the same time as it was engaged in war with Japan, Russia entered Kashgar and Ili in Xinjiang. The Great Powers involved in the plundering of territory, railways, mines, and other resources all forced China to adopt a more appropriate response to these developments, and as a result the Zongli Yamen was revamped as the Waiwu Bu (Ministry of Foreign Affairs) and the Shang Bu (Ministry of Commerce) was set up, all in response to the changing situation. However, these isolated measures seemed to come too late to rectify the slow and inevitable mistakes resulting from institutional flaws, and the crisis-ridden reality inflamed those who emphasized the need for political innovation. Enlightened by the 1898 Reform, people now regarded reform of the political system as top priority, and the reform movement gradually entered the stage described as the constitutional movement.

On 7 June 1901, Liang Qichao published a proposal for a "Constitution" in the pages of *Qingyi Bao*, and provided a clear introduction to the constitutional political system:

> There are two kinds of politics in the world: politics with a constitution (also known as constitutional politics) and politics without a constitution (also called autocracies). The adoption of a particular type of politics to govern a nation is what people call a polity. There are three types of polity in the world: the monarchical authoritarian polity, the monarchical constitutional polity, and the democratic constitutional polity.
>
> ……
>
> What is a constitution? When a constitution intended to endure for a long time is implemented, all people of that nation, whether the monarch, the officials, or the people, must work together to defend it. It is the source of all the laws of the nation, and all subsequent regulations and alterations to any law must never depart from [the Constitution's] original intention.
>
> ……
>
> The constitutional polity is also known as the regime of limited powers, while the authoritarian polity (autocracy) is called the regime of unlimited

powers. "Limited powers" means that: the ruler has the powers of the ruler, but those powers are limited; the official has the powers of the official, but those powers are limited; the people have the rights of the people, but their rights are limited. Therefore, the constitutions of all countries first address the sovereign's right to rule and the succession to the throne, clarifying the limits on the powers of the sovereign; they next define the divisions between the government and local politics; and then they define the positions in the parliament and the freedoms of the people, clarifying the limits of their rights.

Today's world is the age in which real autocracy is being replaced by constitutional polities as the new replaces the old. As a universal principle, when two disproportionate forces contest for supremacy, the old will lose and the new will win. Therefore, all countries on earth will eventually acquire a constitution, in conformity with the inevitable logic of reason.[20]

Espousing constitutional politics, Liang Qichao distinguished himself clearly from previous elite figures of the Self-Strengthening Movement, such as Zhang Zhidong, who advocated limited reforms based on Confucianism, and this also clearly set him apart from Kang Youwei. In Liang Qichao's view, social reform could not be realized if it was dependent on the authoritarian system, and Zhang Zhidong's only purpose in advocating "self-strengthening" was to maintain stability of the centralized authoritarian Qing government (Zhang's concept of the nation). As for Kang Youwei, he relished his status as teacher of the emperor, hoping to realize the goals of reform by manipulating the emperor's resources to change the power structure within the court, by allowing those with reformist ideas to assume power. Liang Qichao's political thinking went much further. The Qing government's crackdown on the Reformers saw bounties placed on the heads of the survivors, forcing them to flee to Japan, and this clearly accelerated the pace of change advocated by Liang Qichao and other activists.

In Japan, Liang Qichao discussed cooperation with the revolutionary Sun Yat-sen, although they differed in their views on politics and the path to China's salvation. However, from the beginning, Liang Qichao understood the motives and purposes of the revolution and he agreed with the

[20] Liang Qichao, *Yinbing-shi Heji: Wenji V*, v. 1. Cited in *Liang Qichao Zishu* (Liang Qichao's Autobiographical Writings), Beijing: Renmin Ribao Chubanshe, 2011, pp. 340–341.

idea of a republic, but based on China's need to develop the wisdom of its population, from the perspective of China's national condition, he advocated maintaining an orderly political strategy. So, from the beginning, Liang Qichao promoted the process of developing constitutionalism on the basis of Japan's experience:

> The first step is to request the emperor to issue an enlightened decree addressing all his subjects, announcing that China will become a constitutional monarchy in perpetuity.
>
> Two. Three prominent officials should be sent to European countries, as well as to the United States and Japan, to examine the advantages and deficiencies of each country's constitution and determine what is appropriate for a Chinese constitution, as well as what should be added and what should be abandoned.
>
> Three. When these representatives return, the government should establish a legislative bureau to draft a constitution which will be available for *examination* by the emperor.
>
> Four. The original texts of other countries' constitutions and works interpreting them should be translated and issued to the public by the legislative bureau, so that the population is aware of these original constitutions and is fully informed and able to contribute to the final version.
>
> Five. Once the draft constitution is completed, it will not be immediately finalized, but will first be sent to the government gazette office, so that the educated population and commoners of the country can examine and discuss it, either by writing books, by publishing news articles, by making speeches, or by writing to the legislative bureau, so that every item of the constitution is examined in detail, and after five or as many as ten years, the final version of the constitution can be determined. It can then not only be promulgated, but any future changes to the constitution cannot be made without the vote of approval of the whole people.
>
> Six. From the date when the political system [defined by the constitution] is established, a period of twenty years should be allowed for the implementation of the constitution.[21]

[21] Liang Qichao, *Yinbing-shi Heji: Wenji V*, v. 1. Cited in *Liang Qichao Zishu* (Liang Qichao's Autobiographical Writings), Renmin Ribao Chubanshe, 2011, pp. 340–341.

In the following year, Liang Qichao wrote *On Legislative Powers* (Lun Lifa Quan), in which he explained the separation of powers between the "legislature", "executive", and "judiciary", and introduced the theories of law and politics of Montesquieu and Bentham as "new knowledge". Liang was less interested in the wide-ranging intellect of Montesquieu (Charles-Louis de Secondat, Baron de La Brède et de Montesquieu, 1689–1755), than in the ideas on the division of powers in constitutional politics outlined in the French Enlightenment thinker's *Esprit des Lois* (The Spirit of Laws, 1748).[22] In fact, the European historical and ideological context supported Montesquieu's ideological logic, such as the idea that law "originates in the inevitable relationship that flows from the essence of things", and that law exists in nature and human society, which explains the relationship between God's creation and the law of human society, given that the Enlightenment period set out to solve the legal problems of human society itself. However, Liang Qichao ignored the ideological and historical background of these European societies. He was concerned with the interpretation of the separation of Montesquieu's legislature from the executive, and he knew that in the history of Chinese thought there was no explanation of how the determination of the power of the monarch could be shifted from the uncertainty of Heaven's will to actual legitimacy. The Confucians, who defined the logic of the state as dependent on the relationships between a sovereign and his officials and a father and his sons, had no bearing on the establishment of constitutional rule with a separation of powers. Even though some ancient Chinese classics had a democratic tinge, such as Mencius' argument that "the people are noble, the community comes next in importance, and the gentleman is unimportant", the ancient classics including such ideas never touched on any institutional arrangements and were simply limited to moral admonition. In *On Legislative Powers* (Lun Lifa Quan, 1902), Liang Qichao set out to provide an explanation for Chinese readers including of course officials at the imperial court:

[22] Another focus of Montesquieu's *L'esprit des lois* was a discussion of the impact of climate on customs, morality, and government forms, but it seems that Liang Qichao was not interested in such an analysis of the subject. At this time Liang Qichao was eagerly looking for ways and means to change Chinese political ideas, and It seems that he felt it was too late to think about the impact of China's climate and geography on the country's history and political system.

> It goes without saying that in Europe, America, and Japan the powers of the legislature, executive, and judiciary are separate, and this separation of powers is understood in Europe, the United States and Japan even by women and children. However, the Chinese state has been established for several millennia, yet this principle of political science is yet to be invented.[23]

Liang Qichao compared European history from ancient Greece and Rome to the eighteenth century regarding the independence of legislative power from the monarchy with the history of the absence of legislation in ancient China, in order to point out that China's lack of legislation needed to be rectified to reflect the changes that had occurred over time. "Qin was more than two thousand years ago but the law remains the same", resulting in "officials remaining out of touch and fearful to improve things, replicating their impoverished views and unable to plan with foresight; the ordinary people have not assumed their [rightful] place, and none dare to find alternatives. Like the constant re-plastering of a surface that is as inevitable as one day being followed by the next, this is a truly unique Chinese phenomenon, as well as being the root source of corruption". Here Liang Qichao is describing the fundamental characteristics of the "Qin-Han polity" that continued to his time. Liang wanted to emphasize that ancient Chinese monarchs were typical autocrats, being both legislators and enforcers, and even judges of the right and wrong of law enforcement. The monarch could choose to be unrestricted by any law and could at any time enact a law or abrogate a law, so running the country depended solely on the monarch's intentions and whims. The result was that the ethics and character requirements determined by the ancient sages were individually arbitrated only by the monarch or by those enforcing the will of the monarch. Thus, when a monarch was of a relatively sound mind, had essential historical knowledge, and an acceptable human nature, coupled with a reverence for traditional ethics, his words and deeds would help the running of the country, but if there was any deviation, it was necessary to see what chance factors could be corrected and compensated for. However, reliance on chance was extremely unreliable, not to mention that the monarch could

[23] Cited in *Liang Qichao Zishu* (Liang Qichao's Autobiographical Writings), Beijing: Renmin Ribao Chubanshe, 2011, p. 342.

be prompted by private desires to incline towards his own personal interpretation of what constituted "Heaven's will", given that "Heaven's will" was the standard formula providing legitimacy for all the emperors who had preceded him. In Montesquieu's view, authoritarian government had little legitimacy from the outset, because the will and behavior of the monarch did not follow any stable legal rules; dictatorships were prone to coups and instability, so Montesquieu was concerned that power be implemented in the correct manner. Liang Qichao drew on the logic of Montesquieu's reasoning: If a person or a department has both legislative and executive power, it is beyond the reach of anyone if that entity both enacts and exercises a harsh law, as for example by enacting a law to seize another's property and then exercising the power to confiscate the other's property. Thus, dictatorships lack virtue, honor, and courage, and only possess obedience, intrigue, and fear; everyone can only act by complying with the will of the monarch or in accordance with the will of the monarch (even if that is presented as an order or mandate from Heaven and is described as "acting on behalf of Heaven"). Montesquieu discussed the republican and constitutional monarchical systems. In the former a minority or majority rules in accordance with the laws, and in the latter just one man rules in accordance with the laws; since in both cases this is rule in accordance with the laws, comprising the constitution, legal statutes, and other rules based on the constitution, both systems provide stability, either by guaranteeing the status of the monarch or by having legitimacy endorsed by public opinion. Yet who is the legislator? To answer this, Liang Qichao borrowed from the ideas of Jeremy Bentham (1748–1832) when he answered, "the majority of citizens". Bentham was a utilitarian who firmly believed that the greatest happiness of the greatest number is the measure of right and wrong. Liang Qichao suggested that obedience to the will of the monarch of an authoritarian government cannot achieve this, because the will of the state is actually the will of the monarch, and the individual is not likely to ensure the happiness of others or of the majority of people; only when the majority of candidates out of the representatives act out of concern for the will of more people can the legal system thus formulated produce the happiness of the greater number of people. Such a theory had never previously been considered in China. For example, in political practice, how could the existence of the happiness of others produced by the individual be appreciated?! In any case, Liang Qichao's focus was on denying the assumption that the nation was the private property of the monarch, and on asserting that it was "the public property of the nation", in which case, the arrangement of public property must of course be determined by the will of the majority of the people and, as a result, an individual monarch does not have the power to become the main legislator, otherwise the country "will not be fit for survival in the world". Here, Liang Qichao includes Yan Fu's admonition within a political arrangement that will enable progress and development within a competitive environment. At the same time, Bentham's argument that an idea could be justified in the Utilitarian manner (using what Bentham called the "hedonic calculus" or the "felicific calculus") quietly replaced the vague Confucian ethical arguments (moralism) that often served as a pretext for authoritarianism. Thus, no promise or moral statement by a monarch could provide a legitimizing basis because such a commitment or statement cannot be measured. In other words, people cannot know whether legislation or decision-making determined by the will of the monarch as an individual will result in more happiness that suffering, or whether the cost of the results will be less than the benefits. Democratic politics was promoted by utilitarianism, happiness being the aim and democracy the means to make the country rich and strong and the people happy, which bring glory and gain to the monarch (if we assess things in Benthamite terms). Liang Qichao thus attempted to theoretically overthrow the monarchical system, while advocating constitutional politics.

Newspapers began to treat the subject of constitutional politics more intensely from 1902 onwards, and the media discovered that "men of the world" were discussing constitutional issues morning and evening. In 1903, *Da Gong Bao* (masthead: *L'impartial*, founded in Tianjin, 1902) began publishing articles on constitutional politics, such as "On the Principles of a Chinese Constitution", and in that year Liu Yazi, stylizing himself "the Asian Rousseau" (Yalu), published "The Question of China Establishing a Constitution" in the sixth issue of *Jiangsu* (founded in Tokyo, 1903). Liu's article was an impassioned appeal to his compatriots: "All enlightened scholars among our 400 million people at home and abroad stride forward breathlessly, calling out for establishing a constitution".[24] At this time, calls for a constitution far outnumbered calls for revolution.

[24] Quoted from Gao Fang et al., *Qingmo Lixian Shi* (History of Late-Qing Constitutionalism), Beijing: Huawen Chubanshe, 2012, p. 78.

Long before Liang Qichao, many Chinese had discussed Western politics: Liang Tingnan (1796–1861) had provided an introduction to American politics, Xu Jiyu (1795–1875) to the British Parliament and judicial system, and Zheng Guanying (1842–1922) to Western parliaments. Later, the constitutionalists began to discuss party politics in their own journal, *Shiwu Bao*, while *Guowen Bao* (masthead: *National News*, Tianjin, 1897) and *Xiang Xuebao* (*Hunan Journal*, Changsha, 1897) were also important media introducing Western political parties and the concept of parliamentary discussion. In the third issue of *Shiwu Bao*, an article introduced readers to the two major political parties of the United States (at that time the Federalist and Republican parties), pointing out that "everyone wanted their own party representatives to hold seats in government". In the 49th issue of *Shiwu Bao*, there was an article explaining the relationship between political parties and constitutional politics simply titled "A Discussion of Political Parties" (Zhengdang Lun) which had been translated from the Japanese periodical *Dai Nihon Zasshi*:

> The political parties are connected to constitutional government like a bird to its wings. When there is no constitution, political parties do not flourish; if there are constitutional politics but no political parties, this is like a bird without wings.[25]

As early as June 1897, Yan Fu explained, in an article in *Guowen Bao* titled "Party Divisions for China" (Lun Zhongguo Fen Dang), how Western political parties were completely different from the "sectarian societies" (*pengdang huishe*) of Chinese history:

> China's so-called "political parties" (*dang*) have their beginnings in personal sectional interests, which become matters of vengeance, and ultimately conclude with the defeat of the gentleman and the victory of the petty man, while the country falls in with these developments. These parties all develop with the momentum of events, eschew the development of knowledge, and cannot survive their ultimate defeat. Western political parties have their own thinking which informs their views. Given they are informed, they are comfortable and stay their hand when issues do not present themselves, and by maintaining their views, they have room to

[25] Zhang Yufa, *Qingji de Lixian Tuanti* (Constitutional Groups of the Qing Period), Beijing: Peking University Press, 2011, p. 30.

debate with those who hold different views. Maintaining different positions, two parties can emerge who do not seek to simply annihilate the other.[26]

Later, Liang Qichao and his colleagues published articles on party politics in *Xinmin Congbao* (masthead: *The New People*, Yokohama, 1902), and although Liang Qichao remained very cautious about whether his own organizations, such as the Zhengwen She (variously known in English as the Political News Society *or* Political Intelligence Society), were political parties in the strict sense of the term, efforts to promote constitutional politics and the establishment of political parties embodied the goals of constitutionalists.[27] Revolutionaries benefited from the dissemination of information about Western representative politics and party theory, but they had a different understanding of these from the constitutionalists. As a result of the propaganda and work of the constitutionalists, for a long time the Chinese community was paying more attention to what the constitutionalists were saying, whether at home or abroad, and as a result, the word "constitutionalist" (*lixian-pai*) came to eclipse the term "reformer" (*weixin-pai*).

After the signing of the Treaty of Shimonoseki, the basic consensus view was that the Chinese "melon" was being even more rapidly carved up by the Great Powers and, in response, what was called "nationalism" (*minzu-zhuyi*) was proliferating in different forms. Kang Youwei and Sun

[26] This article was originally published in the June 13 and June 14 issues of *Guowen Bao*. Quoted in Zhang Yufa, *Qingji de Lixian Tuanti* (Constitutional Groups of the Qing Period), Beijing: Peking University Press, 2011, pp. 33–34.

[27] In his *Manifesto of the Zhengwen She* (Zhengwen She Xuanyan Shu, 1907), Liang Qichao provided the following discreet explanation: "We have been asked whether the Zhengwen She is a political party calling for a constitutional state to now be established. The answer is that while this remains a firm hope, for the time being we do not articulate this ideal. The establishment of all political parties requires not only that they must bring together like-minded worthy men from throughout the nation, but that there must be a framework in place, if the party is to be able to function practically, otherwise an organization cannot be called a political party. For now, the Zhengwen She comprises small groups that are only beginning to merge into a larger organization; in the country, the most talented need to first achieve an accord, so that the worthy can later come forward, and until those filled with political ardor and those rich in political knowledge and ability have more of a hearing, we are not entitled to describe this coming together as a political party".

Cited in *Liang Qichao Zishu* (Liang Qichao's Autobiographical Writings), Beijing: Renmin Ribao Chubanshe, 2011, p. 359.

Yat-sen both tried to use the Boxers in their political causes. Sun Yat-sen praised members of the Boxers for being willing to sacrifice their lives, saying "they fight the coalition forces with swords and bare flesh, and although the coalition troops have killed tens of thousands of them and there are piles of their corpses, other fighters step into the shoes of their fallen comrades; their courage is irrepressible, and one can only look on them with amazed admiration". Therefore, after that bloodbath, foreigners realized that China has a national consciousness and that an ethnic group like this cannot be annihilated.[28] However, the Boxers' blind hatred of missionaries and foreigners and the Qing government's ignorant sacrifices had nothing whatsoever to do with nationalism that demanded sovereignty, justice, and independence, and the slogans posted by the Boxers at their altars or on street corners could also only be seen as a manifestation of ignorance.[29]

In this particular historical period, even the "nationalism" vaunted by intellectuals did not necessarily relate to sovereignty, equality, or freedom, and in many cases was nothing more than an anti-Manchu racist position. Even though the Manchu people and the Manchu government were two different entities, the fact that China was ruled by an alien ethnic group was widely reflected in the nationalist position of the slogans, and the rising anti-Manchu sentiment consolidated the support of increasing numbers of Han Chinese for opposition to the Qing government.[30] From the writings and slogans of the early revolutionaries, we

[28] Ref: *Sun Zhongshan Xuanji* (Selected Works of Sun Yat-sen), Beijing: Renmin Chubanshe, 1981, pp. 758–759.

[29]

> The men are immoral, the women are sluts
> As parents they give birth to monsters
> The sky doesn't rain, and the land is all parched
> The churches have paralyzed Heaven
> When the foreign devils are all driven out,
> Mighty Qing can unite the nation.

For more than a hundred years, the ignorance and sacrifice of the Boxers was often used as a historical example of nationalism, endorsing political parties or governments, especially in inciting propaganda against foreign countries.

[30] For example, people at that time said: "After 1900, the mighty ideal of driving out the Manchus was gradually understood, and all educated people spoke mostly of ethnic nationalism (*minzu zhuyi*)". See: Zhang Yufa, *Qingji de Lixian Tuanti* (Constitutional

can clearly see that the main targets of their opposition were imperialism and the Manchus. This was exemplified by the sloganeering in *Warning Bell* (Jingshi Zhong), a work of 1903 by Chen Tianhua (1875–1905), a student who drowned himself in Tokyo Bay to protest the Japanese government's restrictions on the political activities of Chinese students: "Kill! Kill! Kill! … If the masses of people advance, to kill the foreign devils, they must first kill the traitors who surrendered to the foreigners. If the Manchus help the foreigners kill us, then we must first kill all these thieving officials. Kill! Advance and kill! Advance and kill! Kill! Kill! Kill!".

In the same year, Zou Rong (1885–1907) published a pamphlet titled *Revolutionary Army* (Geming Jun), which hammered home the position of "Han ethnocentrism", asserting that although the Han people were "the most prominent race in the history of the Orient", they are now "the loyal servants of the Manchus". The focus of these young student activists was rage directed at the Manchu government, and so, in their view, anyone who worked for the Qing dynasty, even if they were ethnic Han members of the government, like Zeng Guofan, Zuo Zongtang, and Li Hongzhang, was a traitor to the entire Han ethnic group. Of course,

Groups of the Qing Period), Beijing: Peking University Press, 2011, p. 229, n. 1. Liang Qichao first used the concept of "nationalism" (*minzu zhuyi*) in his "An Alternate Argument Regarding a Change in the Concept of the Nation" in 1901, using a Western concept borrowed via Japanese. However, particular care should be taken in addressing how the term "nationalism" was used by constitutionalists and by revolutionary parties, even if the understanding of the term among revolutionists was often inconsistent. For example, Sun Yat-sen said in a speech carried in the inaugural issue of *Minbao* published in Tokyo: "The original cause of the national revolution is an unwillingness to allow the Manchus to destroy our country, and dominating our politics is a determination to destroy that government and re-create our nation's state. Seen in this way, we do not hate the Manchus, we hate the Manchus of the Han people [i.e., of China]. When we conduct our revolution, the Manchus of Manchuria will not come to harm us and will never seek revenge". This passage is quoted from: Zhu Yuhe, Ouyang Junxi, and Shu Wen, *Xinhai Geming Shi* (History of the 1911 Revolution), Beijing: Renmin Chubanshe, 2001, pp. 222–223. Yet Wang Jingwei wrote in an article in *Minbao* in 1907: "The nationalism my generation advocated sought to achieve ethnic unity, in a single nation. We never rejected the non-Han nor refused to allow them to survive in China but sought to create Chinese people who were ethnically assimilated with the Han". This passage is quoted from ibid., p. 224. If one examines nationalist movements and ideas from different periods in China throughout the twentieth century, nationalism is also almost always a tactic of authoritarian dictatorships to rule the country. It is quite different from the many nationalist movements in Europe in the nineteenth century, such as the Greek independence movement of 1810 or the nationalist movement for freedom and democracy in Hungary in 1848.

as a student in Japan, Zou Rong was familiar with the ideas in Rousseau's *Social Contract*, as he made clear: "The inalienable rights of the individual are granted by Heaven. Life, freedom, and all interests are rights bestowed by Heaven. There can be no infringement on man's freedoms of speech, thought, and publication ...".

Indeed, the historical origins of the Manchu dynasty have always been a problem for Chinese historians, who have always tended to believe that, although the history of the Manchus can be traced back to the Tang dynasty and the even more distant past, the ethnic and racial demarcations that separated the Manchu from the Han are not considered to be as distinct as those that separate the Han from other ethnic groups.[31] The cultural assimilation of the Manchus after they crossed the Great Wall and entered China Proper seems to have greatly eliminated the distinctions between the Manchu and Han communities, as revealed by the outline history of the Manchu population presented earlier in this book. Thus, at this time, the integrity of the Manchus and their traditions was emphasized, perhaps more out of the need to overthrow the political idea behind the Manchu dictatorship. For example, after the conquest of Xinjiang by the Qing dynasty in 1759, it was the Manchu officials stationed in Xinjiang who bullied the Muslim Uighurs (manifested in the imposition of heavy taxes, the enforced collection of tribute, etc.), and it was the pride and luxury of the Manchus that led to Muslim rebellion. During the Opium War, the Han people's distrust of the Manchus fed by the Manchu distrust of the Han people had led to a sense of obvious repugnance. For example, the defending Manchu generals stationed in Zhenjiang sought

[31] The historian William T. Rowe, even pointed out that in 1688, Tong Guogang, an ethnic Han official belonging to the Plain Blue Banner, memorialized the Kangxi Emperor, requesting that his registered ethnicity be changed from "Han [military]" to "Man[churia]". However, his uncle and father had served the Ming dynasty. Based on his family's eventual service to the Qing dynasty and his marriage into the royal family, the Kangxi Emperor agreed to Tong's request to classify his family as Manchu [Manzhou], but his distant relatives were not allowed to change their "ethnic citizenship". This fact shows that the identification of race according to biological or genetic factors was relative, and the definition of "race" could be negotiated according to historical conditions and needs; the Mongols' attitudes to the Han in the Yuan Dynasty could also be similarly conditional. However, some Chinese historians and Han elites are more inclined to believe that Han culture and the corresponding way of governing and management were necessary for foreigners to rule China, otherwise foreigners would not have been able to rule China, which seems like an attempt to explain, through cultural traditions, that China has always been "an integrated whole".

to consolidate their local dominance by means of martial law, arrests, ill-treatment, and even the execution of local Han Chinese and, as a result, in the resistance to a British attack, the more than 400 soldiers killed in the fighting were Manchus, while the Han troops simply stood by. Later, the incompetence and successive defeats of the Manchu government led to Han people growing more inclined to think that to save China from danger, the Manchu government must be overthrown, at which point this nationalistic position seemed to provide an effective path for revolutionaries to exploit. In his historical judgment of Manchu rule of China, Liang Qichao said at an early date that even if Manchu assimilation by Han culture signified that the Manchus had been "subjugated" by the Chinese and had long lost their credentials as a nation (ethnic group), "the very fact that they [i.e., Han Chinese] were only nominally said to be dominated by a different ethnic group could not have been tolerated".[32] Liang's hatred of Manchu Qing rule was so total that he even shifted all the blame for China's defeat in the Sino-Japanese War onto the heads of the Manchus and categorically did not present it as a defeat of the Chinese.

Multi-ethnicity was a legacy to China of the Qing dynasty, although the dynasty, in dealing with conflicts and troubles in border areas and ethnic minority areas, suffered psychologically and expended a great deal of money. In the 1870s, for example, the suppression of the Muslim regime of Yakub Beg (1820–1877) in north-western Xinjiang, and the related dealings with the United Kingdom and Russia, consumed one-sixth of the annual expenditure of the treasury (40 million silver taels). Moreover, during this period, Li Hongzhang also anxiously waited for treasury funds to develop the navy, in response to the disputes between China and Japan over the territory of Taiwan and other coastal areas, and Li Hongzhang was in turn locked in endless disputes with Zuo Zongtang over issues of maritime defense and border security. However, it was the Qing dynasty who signed the *Treaty of St. Petersburg* with Russia in 1881 and, in 1884, accepted the suggestion of the Imperial Commissioner charged with supervising military affairs in the Xinjiang region, Liu Jintang, that Xinjiang be incorporated as a province, not only reclaiming

[32] Cited in Liang Qichao, "The Significance of the 1911 Revolution and the Fortuitousness of Double Ten: Speech at the Celebration of Double Ten by Tianjin Academic Circles", *Liang Qichao Zishu* (Liang Qichao's Autobiographical Writings), Renmin Ribao Chubanshe, 2011, p. 398.

land occupied by the Russians, but also limiting their presence in North and Northeast China, thereby also transforming what had only vaguely been Chinese territory from ancient times into de facto national territory. Indeed, multi-ethnicity and changes in territory are to this day complex problems, and during the decline of the Manchu Qing dynasty, "Manchu rule" did at least serve to foster Han ethno-nationalism. Overthrowing the Qing government was not only a political goal, but also encompassed a response to the Qing conquest of the ethnic Han Ming dynasty more than 300 years previously, and the Revolutionary Party especially invoked resentment of this historical defeat.

In 1903, Liang Qichao went to the United States on a study tour, and his views underwent an obvious change. He went from holding radical "destructive" views and cherishing the concept of an "anti-Manchu revolution" to a more strategic and moderate stance. In the United States, he studied the political arrangements of the republican system, visiting Congress and the House of Representatives. But he concluded that the British constitutional monarchy was superior to the American republican system. Prior to this, he made it clear that China was in a transitional period, as he explained in "Essay on an Age of Transition" published in 1901 in *Qingyi Bao*: "Today's China is a China in an age of transition". Yet that "age of transition" was a joyous era, filled with hope, because only now could those who care about China's future, constitutionalists and revolutionaries alike, address the question of how to achieve their goals and the path they should adopt. Perhaps the fact that the Qing government began to prepare for a constitution in 1905 gave the constitutionalists solid political hope, and Liang Qichao finally decided that an enlightened autocracy could set China on the path to solving her problems, as he explained in an article titled "Enlightened Autocracy" (Kaiming Zhuanzhi Lun) published in 1906 in *Xinmin Congbao*. Liang Qichao believed that any political change should consider the specific national conditions, in light of the particular state of three elements—"the people", "the land", and "the times". In the case of China, the implementation of enlightened autocracy during the historical transitional period would be conducive to the ultimate realization of a constitutional system. In outlining his reasons for this assertion, he cited the lack of enlightenment of the Chinese people as an important factor and, to address this, a period of "tutelary government" (*xunzheng*) would be needed. For the time being, this need could only be provided by the existing authoritarian system, but this authoritarianism required "enlightenment". Even though Liang was only envisaging a political strategy, his advice was the basis for an attack on his ideas by the revolutionists. Yet it was Kang Youwei who first drew the ire of the advocates of revolution on account of two short articles he published: "A Letter to Chinese in America Discussing Why a Constitutional Monarchy and Not a Revolution Is Feasible" and "A Letter to Fellow Students on the View of Liang Qichao and Others that the Fall of India Was Because Its Provinces Became Independent". In June 1903 in the pages of *Subao* (*Jiangsu News* or *Revival News*, Shanghai, 1898), Zhang Binglin published "A Letter Refuting Kang Youwei" which satirized the Guangxu Emperor and advocated revolution, directly precipitating what would be called the "*Subao* Incident", which saw Zhang Binglin thrown into jail.[33] Emboldened by events, Zhang Binglin commented: "My refutation of Kang Youwei might have been ineffectual, but the Qing government even sent lawyers as their representatives to confront our party, which rocked the entire nation and greatly enhanced the reputation of our revolutionary party".[34]

In 1905 a revolutionary group called the Tongmeng Hui, short for Zhongguo Tongmeng Hui and generally translated as the Revolutionary Alliance, was founded, and the differences of opinion between the constitutionalists and the revolutionaries became more public. In 1905, the League changed the name of its journal *Ershi Shiji zhi Zhina* (Twentieth Century China), founded in the previous year by Huang Xing, Song Jiaoren. and Chen Tianhua, to *Minbao* (People's Paper, Tokyo, 1905), which would serve as a revolutionary publicity organ in direct opposition to Liang Qichao's *Xinmin Congbao.* Liang Qichao adhered to his constitutional views, based on his understanding of China's political reality as it related to revolution, and he asserted that China was better off

[33] In 1903, in response to the increasingly fiery revolutionary rhetoric coming from Zhang Taiyan (Zhang Binglin), Cai Yuanpei, and others writing in *Subao*, a newspaper published in Shanghai and edited by Zhang Shizhao, the Qing government arrested Zhang Taiyan, after which the revolutionist Zou Rong turned himself in to the police. *Subao* was raided and shut down, and Zhang and Zou were given three- and two-year sentences, respectively. Zou Rong died in prison. The upshot of the "*Subao* Incident" was that "the single issue of driving out the Manchus became ingrained in the minds of [China's] four hundred million people", according to an article in the fourth issue of *Jiangsu.*

[34] Zhang Binglin, *Ziding Nianpu* (Autobiographical Chronology), p. 10. Cited in Li Yunhan, *Zhongguo Jindai Shi* (Modern History of China), Beijing: Sanlian Chubanshe, 2018, p. 162.

pursuing a constitutional monarchy than a republic, and that a constitutional monarch was better than an enlightened despot. At the very least, it would prevent as much as possible the bloodshed that a revolution would entail, because a revolution would come with huge political and collateral costs. The idea behind this political arrangement was the same as that of the Emperor Protection Society first mooted by Kang Youwei in 1899 and later also supported by Liang Qichao: the aim was not conservatism, but to protect the emperor so that he could implement the reform movement, and push forward reforms from the top down in order to minimize conflict during this fundamental historical transformation. It was because of these considerations and in order to avoid misunderstandings and clarify political objectives that, after the Qing dynasty announced it was preparing a constitution, the name of the Emperor Protection Society was effectively changed to the Chinese Empire (or Imperial) Constitutional Association, by dissolving the former in 1907 and replacing it with the latter.[35] In short, as Liang Qichao saw it, this is nothing more than a politically operational strategy. Liang Qichao published a number of articles explaining his ideas: political revolution was necessary, but the key was to have an "orderly revolution", otherwise "spontaneous riots" might erupt and the results would be social chaos and division, leading

[35] The Bao Huang Hui (Emperor Protection Society), the full Chinese name being "Baojiu Daqing Guangxu Huangdi Hui" and its later English name being the "Chinese Empire [or Imperial] Reform Association", was set up by Kang Youwei, allegedly acting in accordance with a secret edict given to him by the Guangxu Emperor, the gist of which was that, "in view of the fact that the reform measures were unable to save China, given that the Empress Dowager did not agree to them, I am now unable to protect myself, and so I entrust my hope of salvation in you". However, the veracity of the secret edict has never been determined. However, on the strength of it, Kang set up the Emperor Protection Society in Canada on the thirteenth day of the sixth month of the twenty-fifth year of Guangxu's reign [i.e., 20 July 1899]. The organization grew in China, as well as overseas, with branches in the Americas, Southeast Asia, Honolulu, Australia, Hong Kong, Macao, Shanghai, and Ningbo. In the ninth lunar month of the following year (October 1901), Kang Youwei, in his *Letter to the Emperor*, wrote, "Millions of people have joined, and meetings are held in dozens of port cities". Zhang Yufa wrote: "In the six or seven years following the establishment of the Emperor Protection Society, it greatly expanded to comprise more than 160 organizations at home and abroad, laying the foundations for the future 'Zhengwen She' and 'Diguo Xianzheng Hui' (Imperial Constitutionalist Society)". The Emperor Protection Society's activities included schools, bookstores, newspapers, and businesses. On 13 February 1907, the Emperor Protection Society was renamed the Chinese Empire [or Imperial] Constitutional Reform Association. See: Zhang Yufa, *Qingji de Lixian Tuanti* (Constitutional Groups of the Qing Period), Beijing: Peking University Press, 2011.

to intervention and partition by the imperialist powers. Articles published in *Minbao* by the revolutionists denied Liang's arguments that the Great Powers might interfere in China's internal affairs. However, the tone of the revolutionists' arguments seemed to suggest, and they also explicitly stated, that even if imperialist interference was aroused, this would in turn stir the people to seek vengeance, so without a strong government how would it be possible to truly resist the foreign powers? Based on strategic considerations, Liang Qichao did not agree with giving priority to the ethnic differences between the Manchus and Han people and in debate Liang also spoke of "homogeneity" and "lack of division" between the two races; he questioned the insistence of the revolutionists on "expelling the Tartars". Liang regarded the revolutionists' calls for attacking or even exterminating the Manchus as "ethnic revenge" (*minzu fuchou-zhuyi*), and he stressed that the purpose of the revolution was not to eliminate the Manchus, but merely to replace the system of tyranny they perpetuated. The revolutionists countered by arguing that driving out the Manchus was a priority for achieving the goals of the revolution, because the Manchu Qing government could not be expected to institute constitutional government. Addressing the revolutionists' slogans including those that called for "equal land rights" and "nationalizing land ownership", Liang Qichao regarded the outcomes they expressed as revealing that the revolutionists envisaged a total social revolution and he told those advocates of revolution that it was the private ownership of property that stimulated people's enthusiasm for production, and only after capitalism had achieved a high degree of development would it be possible to implement socialism. Of course, the revolutionaries ignored Liang's statements and firmly believed that state ownership of land could effectively mobilize people's enthusiasm and promote productivity. On the questions of the qualifications of a citizen or the level of enlightenment of the people, the revolutionists maintained that divinely conferred human rights were irrefutable and that once a democratic government was established, the people would naturally exercise their ability to participate in democratic politics. In fact, some members of revolutionary parties had no trust in, or theoretical understanding of, constitutional politics. As Zhang Binglin put it: "Instituting representative government will only be feudalism in disguise".[36] Of course, even if the revolutionists had agreed to a constitution, they would have found it impossible to embrace the idea of its introduction by a Manchu monarch, because in the eyes of the ethnic Han revolutionary parties, there could be no accommodation with Manchus. Xu Xilin, an important member of another revolutionary party, the Guangfu Hui (Restoration Society) that had been founded in 1904, made the following impassioned statement: "When all the Manchus have been killed, the Han Chinese will of course be strong, and only then will it be timely to implement a constitution".[37] To a great extent, the ethnic nationalism of the revolutionists overwhelmed their thinking on political theories related to constitutionality and revolution. In other words, the ethno-nationalistic revolution was not the same thing as a political revolution that encompassed multi-ethnicity and other aspects, and this directly exacerbated the revolutionists' negation of the activities of the constitutionalists. They did not have the patience to remind the constitutionalists whom they opposed that China's fundamental problem was not an ethnic problem but that of an authoritarian regime, and they remained ideologically dependent on violent revolution.

The debate between the constitutionalists and revolutionaries, which was particularly intense among expatriates outside China, lasted for several years, and by the end of 1906, Liang Qichao discovered that the revolutionary forces had won over more than half of the Chinese students in Japan, and the theories of the revolutionary parties opposing those of the constitutionalists had been widely disseminated, to the point where "everyone all the way down to shopkeepers and underlings was talking about revolution". In August 1907, Liang Qichao decided to suspend the publication of *Xinmin Congbao*, and in its stead set up *Zhenglun* (Political Discussion), which was distributed from the offices of the Zhengwen She (known in English as the Political News Society *or* Political Intelligence Society) in Shanghai. Although *Minbao* continued to refute Liang's

[36] Quoted in Hou Yijie, *Ershi Shiji Chu Zhongguo Zhengzhi Gaige Fengchao* (Political Reform Trends in Early Twentieth Century China), Beijing: Renmin Chubanshe, 1993, p. 166.

[37] Quoted in Hou Yijie, *Ershi Shiji Chu Zhongguo Zhengzhi Gaige Fengchao* (Political Reform Trends in Early Twentieth Century China), Renmin Chubanshe, 1993, p. 169.

views, Liang and his constitutional colleagues were now fully engaged in the practical push for constitutionalism.

From New Administration to Constitutional Preparations[38]

On 29 January 1901, while on the road evading the conflict between the Allied Expeditionary Force and the Boxers in Beijing, the Empress Dowager Cixi issued an edict, in the name of the Guangxu Emperor, the central idea of which was the announcement of a decision to initiate political reform which, of course, she would lead.

The previous Reforms of 1898 may have been the prelude for what was called *Gengzi Xinzheng*, meaning the New Administration of *Gengzi*, the 26th year of the reign of the Guangxu Emperor that ran from 31 January 1900 to 9 February 1901, because the reforms now announced by the Qing government were exactly those which Kang Youwei and his group had wanted to implement only a couple of years previously. In fact, even though a general arrest warrant for the activists of 1898 was still in place, the Qing government had never completely stopped the implementation of the new reforms in business, schools, and the military. However, the Empress Dowager Cixi had a self-serving explanation for her volte-face, albeit allegedly voiced by the Emperor: "It is well known that the new laws propounded by the Kang rebels were less reform laws (*bianfa*) than lawlessness (*luanfa*). These rebels took advantage of the court's weakened condition to plot sedition. It was only by an appeal to the Empress Dowager to resume the reins of power that the court was saved from immediate peril and the evil rooted out in a single day". After taking into account the legitimacy and coherence of all reforms up to the preparatory

[38] Xinzheng, the term that came to be used for the "late Qing reforms" and variously translated as the New Regime, New Administration, or even New Deal, is a vague term that first emerged in the 1880s and was used by Chinese officials who visited Japan to outline the reforms of the Meiji era. Researchers have mainly used it for the different stages in political reform adopted by the Qing government from the 1898 reform period to the preparation of the Constitution in the first decade of the twentieth century. Although the reform program addressing the political system began in 1898 and the reforms in the New Administration era announced in the edict of 29 January 1901 were in fact the continuation of the reforms of the previous period, the term "New Administration" is used to refer mainly to the continuum of structural reforms of the political system.

constitution that were decided on, and having pointed out the one-sided nature of the previous Foreign Affairs Movement's emphasis on "Western politics as the fundamental source" and having redrawn the scope of the reform, it may be useful to quote parts of the above-mentioned edict:

> We should give our knowledge and express our views within two months. Then I will report it to the Master to consider perfection and implement it effectively.The root of China's weakness lies in harmful habits too firmly entrenched, in rules and regulations too minutely drawn, in the over-abundance of inept and mediocre officials and in the paucity of truly outstanding ones, in petty bureaucrats who hide behind the written word and in clerks and *yamen* runners who use the written word as talismans to acquire personal fortunes, in the mountains of correspondence between government offices that have no relationship to reality, and in the seniority system and associated practices that block the way of men of real talent. The curse and the ruin of our nation are contained in two simple words - "selfish" and "profits". Those who have studied Western methods up to now have confined themselves to the spoken and written languages and to weapons and machinery. These are but surface elements of the West and have nothing to do with the essentials of Western learning. Our Chinese counterparts to the fundamental principles upon which Western wealth and power are based are the following precepts, handed down by our ancestors: "to hold high office and show generosity to others", "to exercise liberal forbearance over subordinates", "to speak with sincerity", and "to carry out one's purpose with diligence". But China has neglected such deeper dimensions of the West and contents itself with learning a word here and a phrase there, a skill here and a craft there, meanwhile hanging on to old corrupt practices of currying favour to benefit oneself. If China disregards the essentials of Western learning and merely confines its studies to surface elements that themselves are not even mastered, how can it possibly achieve wealth and power? To sum up, administrative methods and regulations must be revised, and abuses eradicated. If regeneration is truly desired, there must be quite and reasoned deliberation.
>
> We therefore call upon the members of the Grand Council, the Grand Secretaries, the Six Boards and Nine Ministries, our ministers abroad, and the governor-general and governors of the provinces to reflect carefully on our present sad state of affairs and to scrutinise Chinese and Western governmental systems with regard to all dynastic regulations, state administration, and official affairs, matters related to people's livelihood, modern

schools, systems of examination, military organisation, and financial administration. Duly weigh what should be kept and what abolished, what new methods should be adopted and what old ones retained. By every available means of knowledge and observation, seek out how to renew our national strength, how to produce men of real talent, how to expand state revenues and how to revitalise the military. …

The first essential, even more important than devising new systems of governance, is to secure men who govern well. Without new systems, the corrupted old system cannot be salvaged; without men of ability, even good systems cannot be made to succeed. … Once the appropriate reforms are introduced to clear away abuses, it will be more than ever necessary to select upright and capable men to discharge the functions of the office. Everyone, high and low – take heed! The Empress Dowager and We have long pondered these matters. Now things are at a crisis point where change must occur, to transform weakness into strength. Everything depends on how the change is effected".

Within the Qing court, the concept of "reform" was once again a fashionable term, and few officials again invoked "ancestral laws". On 21 April 1901, the Qing government requested the establishment of a Bureau of Government Affairs (Zhengwu Chu) that would serve as an office of supervision and administration, reviewing the rules, promoting the New Administration, and assessing its performance. Yikuang (Prince Qing), Li Hongzhang, Ronglu, Kungang, Wang Wenshao, and Lu Chuanlin were supervisory administrators, and Liu Kunyi and Zhang Zhidong, fresh from suppressing an uprising in Hankou in 1900 staged by Tang Caichang's Independence Army—and instigated ironically by the "reformer" Kang Youwei, were appointed as advisors.[39] Later the Bureau of Government Affairs became the actual planning department for reforms. Generally speaking, from 1901 to 1904, as the Qing government

[39] In the autumn and winter of 1899, Tang Caichang (1867–1900), an important Hunanese member of the Emperor Protection Society, discussed armed uprisings with Liang Qichao and others in Japan and returned to Shanghai to form the Zili Jun (Self-Reliance Army). In 1900, when the Boxer Movement broke out, Kang Youwei urged that the opportunity be seized to "save the emperor, restore him to the throne, and return to the reform administration (Xinzheng)" (*Notice on Rescuing the Monarch*). In August, the Self-Reliance Army was preparing to stage an uprising, but the attempt failed. Zhang Zhidong hunted down and executed 20 people involved in the failed uprising including Tang Caichang.

continued to push for the implementation of the New Administration, the Zongli Yamen effectively became the Ministry of Foreign Affairs and the Ministry of Commerce was fully established. When the Ministry of Commerce asked the provinces to set up local chambers of commerce, this meant that the emerging bourgeoisie had acquired its own legitimate government organizations, and these bodies in fact constituted an important force in promoting the national economy and supporting constitutional and revolutionary causes during this period.

After the coup unseating the reformers in 1898, Japan provided a safe haven and resource for China's reformers and revolutionaries alike. Japan provided this support because China's repeated defeats since 1860 alerted the Japanese to the dangers their own reforms faced, given that China had in the past provided the Japanese with a model from which to learn. Japan's elite identified problems and found solutions in China's experiences in defeat, and while Chinese ports, such as Shanghai, were filled with foreign ships, and Europeans could tread with confidence and often arrogance on Chinese soil, sensitive Japanese were aware that they potentially faced a dilemma similar to that of the Chinese. As a result of the situation in China, Japan decided to go all out to catch up with the West, and in Japan calls to move away from Asia and towards the West were often heard in the media, in stark contrast to the high level of complacency and conceit at the Qing court where most officials maintained a high degree of self-satisfaction and conceit about their culture. A minority within the Qing court, such as Li Hongzhang, after seeing the speed of change in Japan which had a late start, was oblivious to China's historical inertia when discussing with the somewhat racist Japanese prime minister Ito Hirobumi how China and Japan could work together to deal with the white race from Europe and America. The Meiji reforms and Japan's later developments were certainly a model for China's reformers, which is why Kang Youwei introduced Japan's reforms and achievements in submitting his own reform package. Indeed, the 1895 Sino-Japanese War convincingly confirmed Japan's rise, which sent shock waves through the Qing court and Chinese society. It was clearly time for China to learn from the Japanese, which prompted the Qing government to start sending young people to study in Japan. It is hardly surprising that Zhang Zhidong greatly encouraged overseas study, writing: "Going abroad for a year is better than studying Western books for five years, … and one year in a foreign school is better than three years in a Chinese school" (*Exhortation to Study*).[40] Such a way of thinking eventually led to the abolition of the imperial examination system. Unsurprisingly, a large number of Chinese went to Japan, absorbing new ideas in the course of their studies and constant observation. Later the Qing government realized that many students after returning from abroad were not only stirring up trouble for the Qing court but were even digging its grave.

The Qing government nevertheless believed that reforming the education system was the best way to adapt to change, and in 1901, the Qing government abolished the eight-legged essay and discussed whether the Classics could be used to introduce Western political questions. The first lesson officials learned from their dealings with Westerners was that the Chinese must understand Western languages and the West, and as the government needed talent in this area, students trained abroad were naturally needed. However, this was hardly enough to address China's crisis, and so the questions of reforming education and training new talent were brought back for consideration after the Reform Movement was re-ignited.[41] In 1904, Zhang Zhidong, together with Zhang

[40] In 1897, the Japanese officer Kamio Mitsuomi was invited to visit Zhang Zhidong in Wuhan, and he told Zhang that he hoped that China and Japan would join forces "to protect themselves from Russia and Germany". The concerns of China and Japan prompted a quick resumption of dialogue and cooperation between the two countries. Zhang Zhidong subsequently sent Yao Xiguang of the Ministry of Personnel to head an investigative mission to Japan, and after returning to China on 22 April 1898 Yao submitted the report on his trip titled "Overview of Japanese Schools", which provided information on various types of schools in Japan, including military and art academies, after which Zhang Zhidong completed his *Exhortation to Learning* (Quan Xue Pian).

[41] On 11 June 1898, the Guangxu Emperor issued an edict: "The establishment of Capital University will be given priority, leading the initiative to establish a university in each province ... Those who want to study at the university will all be recruited to study for professions, with the view to producing a generation of talented graduates who can lend assistance in these difficult times". On 10 July, a further imperial edict stated: "The provinces have as a general rule not yet set up elementary and secondary schools. The overall plan is that every provincial capital, prefecture, and county will set up a college, which can be supervised and cared for by local officials who will set up respective academic offices which will be provided with funds limited to two months for them to provide detailed reports from an examination of requirements... the size of existing provincial, prefectural and county colleges will be enlarged to accommodate schools providing Western learning". On 4 August, it was ordered that a preparatory school be set up in Beijing, which could send students to Capital University. On 29 August 1901, one of Cixi's initiatives to promote the New Administration was to "abolish the use of the eight-legged essay (*shiwen*) in the imperial examinations and replace it with

Baixi and Rongqing, formulated a set of regulations for a new education system titled "Memorialized Suggestions for a Schools' Charter" (Zouding Xuetang Zhangcheng), which established a three-tier school system encompassing primary, secondary, and higher education, and suggested also recruiting non-government funded students who had returned from Japan, since the new schools' system was derived from the Japanese model. In the same year, the Qing government introduced a policy of establishing new schools and encouraging study abroad. In 1905, the Qing government established a Department of Education (Xue Bu) responsible for managing education throughout China. On 2 September of that year, the government announced that the imperial examination system would be completely abolished in 1906, and at the same time the establishment of new-style schools, which was already underway, was further accelerated.[42] Previously, people had hesitated about having to choose between schools run by traditional graduates and

essays on current affairs, Western law or political economy as a basis for selecting officials". On 12 September 1901, Cixi promulgated a letter ordering all traditional academies in all provinces be converted to universities in provincial capitals, and that all districts, counties and centrally administered jurisdictions [specifically Zhili and Nanjing] set up local secondary schools and all prefectures and counties set up primary schools". On 17 September 1901, it was further ordered that "given the excellence of the earlier decisions of Jiangnan, Hubei, Sichuan, and other provinces to send students to study abroad, all provincial governors will now follow this example. All specialized professions and practical learning will be emphasized so that students can return to China with useful qualifications". Of course, we can see from the examination questions posed in 1901 and 1902 that these reform measures were enthusiastically followed. Examples of those questions are: "Chinese and Western laws are very different, and if the West does not accept our jurisdiction and wants to infringe on our right to autonomy, what plan should we propose? What is the reason for the economic prosperity of all Western countries? According to international law, can any country interfere in the domestic affairs of a foreign country?" These examination questions reveal that a nation that had been exercising authoritarianism since the First Emperor of Qin destroyed the remaining six warring states and ideology was subsequently brought to a standstill had now begun to change significantly.

42 Soon, even remote cities began to set up new-style schools. In 1904, the Governor of Yunnan-Guizhou sent 40 students to Japan to train as teachers, and in 1906, 30 students returned to China and were sent to set up schools throughout Yunnan. (Ref: "Jingwai Xuewu Baogao" (Report on Educational Matters outside the Capital), *Xuebu Guanbao* (Department of Education Official Reports), 1906, no. 1). In 1904, Guizhou sent 151 students to study in Japan, 29 trainee teachers returned home and were sent to set up schools throughout the province, and one student named Zhou Gong founded 10 primary schools and one middle school alone. Ref: See He Jingwu, "Xinhai Geming qianhou de Guiyang Jiaoyu" (Guiyang Education before and after the 1911 Revolution), *Guiyang Wenshi Ziliao Xuanji* (Anthology of Guiyang Cultural History Information)

the new-style schools, not knowing whether to embark on the rigorous study required to compete in the imperial examinations or to give themselves a greater flexibility of choice regarding future careers by pursuing the "new studies". Once the imperial examination system was ended, this dilemma was resolved. Since people entering new schools to acquire new knowledge were qualified to fill vacant positions as government officials, this in fact opened up government departments to students versed in the new learning. As a result, not only did the transmission of knowledge of the Confucian classics face a crisis but, more importantly, this meant that the Confucian dogma that supported the original political power structure was deeply shaken by the abolition of the imperial examinations. Despite the discontent and resistance of the traditional gentry, Confucianism remained a subject of study in the new-style schools, and the emperor's examination for merit still bore remnants of the old system for some time, but young people who felt that history was changing rapidly were well aware that the realization of their ideals must be based on knowledge from the West or Japan. Jiang Menglin (1886–1964), the later chancellor of Peking University, recalled in Kunming during the later Anti-Japanese War: "In lieu of the imperial examination system there was a new educational system copied from Japan, and Japan's educational system was modeled on the West, so in terms of its origins, China's new educational system was ultimately derived from the West. China was now unequivocally on the road to Westernization".[43] The abolition of the imperial examinations ended the possibility of Chinese students acquiring the status or image of the scholar-official or would-be literatus, which meant they no longer clung to their hometown, because they could no longer enter the imperial examination system at the local level, so people discovered that as long as they had an education in the new knowledge they could become needed members of society. The many years of publishing efforts by missionaries and the large number of materials printed by government and private publishers meant that print media

Series 2, Guiyang Municipal Committee for the Study of Cultural History, 1981, pp. 127–141. See: Shang Xiaoming, *Liu Ri Xuesheng yu Qingmo Xinzheng* (Chinese Students Studying in Japan and the New Administration of the Late-Qing), Nanchang: Jiangxi Jiaoyu Chubanshe, 2002.

[43] Jiang Menglin, *Xichao yu Xinchao*, Beijing: Tuanjie Chubanshe (Unity Press), 2004, pp. 86–87. This book was first published in the United States in English (1945) as: Chiang Monlin, *Tides from the West: A Chinese Autobiography*, New Haven, Yale University Press. It was later published in Taiwan in 1957.

became a major platform for readers, as newspapers and magazines with a modern outlook flooded into community associations and schools, where they were circulated, discussed, and assessed; this lively intellectual environment generated new ideas and groups engaged in constant discussion, that often resulted in further political action.

In the past, China's prototypical political parties (*pengdang*) emerged within the bureaucracy, but after the failure of the 1898 Reforms forced Kang Youwei to flee via Shanghai on a British ship to Japan, intellectuals who accepted Western ideas began to form new political groups and organizations outside the center of power. For Chinese students in Japan in particular, the relatively relaxed learning environment helped them quickly open up to new ideas. The officials sent by the Qing government to supervise and control these students' ideas were not only ineffective, but instead inflamed students' dissatisfaction with the Chinese government's authoritarianism. In particular, from 1905 onwards the Qing court set up a system of awards, designed to recruit graduating students who had studied abroad and present them with degrees and government positions on the basis of their results. At least 1000 graduates from the overseas student cohort entered government institutions at all levels, which subtly altered the ideological persuasion and consciousness of officialdom throughout the government. At the same time, there were nearly 8000 Chinese students abroad in 1905 alone. In fact, in the decade or so from 1895 on, Japan was also competing with the West for China's resources for its own purposes, which when, of course, mixed with a "pan Asian" opposition to white people lent great support to the endeavor of having Chinese study in Japan.[44]

[44] In 1906, Timothy Richard perceptively discovered that the influence of Western missionaries on China seemed to have given way to that of Japan:

However Peking may regard Tokyo [note the suggestion here of friction at the official level], it is plain that throughout the eighteen provinces Japanese influence had made enormous strides. Japanese travellers, commercial agents, teachers and drill-sargeants are to be found in the remotest parts of the empire. The sons of the Chinese nobility and ruling classes are being educated in Japan by the thousands and return home fired by her example and emulous to repeat it. The best of the native Chinese papers are in Japanese control, and the amazing growth of this native press is in itself one of the most significant of all the phenomena of revolution.... We expect nothing startling from the spread of Japanese influence believing that Japan's true policy is not to force China into a sham similitude of western civilization or ideals, but *to use the accessories if the Occident for the preservation of the fundamentals of Oriental life and polity.* Ref: Douglas R. Reynolds, *China, 1898–1912: The Xinzheng Revolution and Japan*, published by the

The implementation of the New Administration was particularly prominent in the training of the New Army. Previously, the regular Qing army comprised the Eight Banner forces and the Green Battalions.[45] However, China's series of military defeats impressed upon the Qing court that it would be difficult to save the Qing Empire from collapse without constructing a brand new modern army. On 29 August 1901, the traditional military examination system was suspended, and the Qing government called on all regions to reorganize the army and set up military schools. In 1902, students who had returned home from studying in Japanese military schools became the main force in the formation of the New Army, which initiated the Qing government's establishment of universal national armed forces. In 1903, on the initiative of Yuan Shikai, the Qing government set up an office called the Lianbing Chu (officially translated as the Commission for Army Reorganization) in Beijing to control the recruitment and training in the provinces of military personnel, who would eventually take control of the army. Those troops trained according to foreign, especially German and Japanese, military doctrines and standards were commonly all referred to as "the New

COUNCIL ON EAST ASIAN STUDIES, HAVARD UNIVERSITY, 1993), pp. 8–9. Ito Hirobumi's speech of 14 February 1899 can be seen as a document analyzing the ability in this period to move from the hatred between China and Japan occasioned by the Sino-Japanese War to the resumption of friendly cooperation between the two countries: "I believe", he declared, "that extending assistance to [Korea and China] to the fullest extent of our power is truly essential not only in terms of preserving our own national interests but also in terms of the whole Far Eastern situation". Ref: Douglas R. Reynolds, *China, 1898–1912: The Xinzheng Revolution and Japan*, p. 37.

[45] The Eight Banner Army and the Green Battalion Army were the old-style armies of the Qing dynasty: the former was based on the traditional Manchu Eight-Banner system, a social organization of military-civilian unity, serving the functions of administration, production, and conducting military expeditions. After the Qing dynasty unified China, an ethnic Han Eight-Banner Army and an ethnic Mongol Eight-Banner Army were also established. Based on the superior status of the Manchus and their early military experience, the Eight-Banner Army was superior to the Green Battalions in terms of ability and their treatment. After the Eight-Banner Army was set up in China, corruption led to a decline in combat ability, and during the Qianlong years the Eight-Banner Army gradually became weaker than the Green Battalion Army. During the Taiping Heavenly Kingdom period, the Green Battalion Army also underwent a marked decline and gradually lost its function as a standing army, and the Qing government began to rely on the Xiang (Hunan) Army and the Huai Army. In the early years of the Republic of China, the Green Battalion Army was reduced to serving as localized security guards.

Army".[46] In 1904, the New Army was planned as a standing army of 36 divisions (*zhen*, an earlier term for garrison [towns]), each comprising 12,500 officers and soldiers, all under the control of the Training Service. The New Army's officers were former Chinese students who had been trained at Japanese cadet schools. The government not only promulgated "New Military Academy Measures" but also instituted a comprehensive military education program from army primary schools to army universities, and the emerging system of officers was also supplemented by recruiting those students who had completed military studies abroad. In 1906, the Commission for Army Reorganization was merged with the Ministry of the Army, which commanded all armies throughout the empire. The army was commanded by a Manchu official named Tieliang, and in 1909 a proclamation declared that the country's army was under the command of the emperor. Even Yuan Shikai's Beiyang Army was eventually merged into the Central Army in 1910. In China in the past, being a soldier had been a transitory calling, with only unemployed vagrants and bankrupt farmers enlisting to earn a livelihood. However, the funding for military construction was centrally concentrated in the hands of the Commission for Army Reorganization although it was not adequately supported by regional military governors. With the government's support for the construction of the New Army, the requirements demanded that a military education for students abroad was more in line with modern standards and the status of officers was raised to levels equivalent to those of civilian officials, not to mention the fact that the image of a soldier belonging to an army in which the emperor was the supreme commander and boasting healthy physical and military skills as well as a modern education was beginning to be established. People came to see the New Army in a positive light, and even members of the gentry were now willing to join the New Army as officers. At the beginning of July 1909, the General Staff Office (Junzi Fu) was established and this organization was the military planning center under the command of the Emperor.

[46] As early as 1895 and 1896, respectively, the Jiangnan Army College and the Hubei Military Preparatory School were established. Zhang Zhidong adopted the German military system, and the two schools hired no less than 40 German military officers. In addition to the conflict between German instructors and Chinese students, the German occupation of Jiaozhou in Shandong in November 1897 also raised concerns among Chinese officials about continuing to hire German instructors. Japan's initiative resulted in China changing its decisions on sourcing instructors.

The officials first sensitive to the need to change the status of the military were, unsurprisingly, Zhang Zhidong and Li Hongzhang, who were both ethnic Han officials. In 1898 Zhang Zhidong initially sent four military cadets from the Zhejiang Military Academy to study in Japan, followed by 24 from Hubei and Hunan, and then 20 were sent separately by the Beiyang (Northern Naval) Military Commander and the Nanyang (Southern Naval) Military Commander.[47] Subsequently, individual provinces sent students to Japan to undertake military studies. Documents provide the following statistics: In 1902–1903, the Seijō School in Japan had almost 200 students from China enrolled in classes of different levels. From 1903, when the military preparatory school called the Shinbu Gakkō was established in Tokyo, until 1914, a total of 1000 Chinese students were educated and trained at this establishment. Between 1900 and 1911, 690 Chinese graduates of the Seijō and Shinbu schools enrolled in officer training colleges, and after returning to China most became senior officers, chiefs of staff, or instructors in the Chinese army. Of course, invitations to hire Japanese military experts to come to China to conduct training projects were also frequent and effective, and a large number of Japanese military experts went to China to offer military instruction or fill related positions. Between December 1901 and August 1902, Yuan Shikai even hired a Japanese officer, Tachibana Koichirō (1861–1929), and two captains who had performed excellently in fighting the Boxers. In November 1902, when Yuan established the Beiyang Military Medical College in Tianjin, he hired Hiraga Seijirō (1866–1916) as the head of general teaching, along with ten Japanese who would work in China for ten years and were honored by the emperors of both Japan and China. In the course of such a military reform, China gradually accepted the German and Japanese military systems and doctrines, and military terminology all came from Japan. Interestingly, it was after the Russo-Japanese War that China was quite sanguine about learning from Japan, despite the conflicts and wariness that existed between the two countries:

> There were also specific advantages in using Japanese advisers. The employment of Japanese reduced the language problem, for they were more willing than most foreigners to learn to speak Chinese. Japanese officers

[47] In the following year Zhang Zhidong also sent his eldest grandson, Zhang Houkun, to Japan to study. Subsequently, other Qing court officials sent their children to study in Japan.

> were less expensive to employ; they would accept poorer treatment than Occidental officers; and they more readily adapted themselves to Chinese realities. The Japanese had modeled their army on that of Germany; so the transition from German to Japanese instructors did not necessitate a major change in training methods or techniques. Also, the Japanese sought with considerable success to persuade China that Japan had adopted the best points of all the European armies and that their military system was the one most suitable to the Asiatic peoples. Finally, the shift to Japanese advisers was indicative of growing belief that Orientals could match the prowess of the West. This conviction was to be immeasurably strengthened by the defeats which the Japanese delivered to the Russians in 1904–1905. The overall result was a tendency to increase Japanese influence in the internal affairs of China.[48]

In fact, there were many talented graduates among the Chinese students who undertook military studies in Japan, some of whom, like Cai E, Sun Chuanfang, Yu Xishan, Li Liejun, and Chiang Kai-shek, became influential figures in China's subsequent military and political history.

Even though the Preparatory Constitution was promulgated in 1906, in 1901 the Qing government and the United Kingdom had concluded a Sino-British treaty on trade and navigation, and both sides determined that the British abandon the concept of extraterritoriality, which constituted the actual beginning of the reform of this legal anomaly. In 1901 and 1902, Liu Kunyi and Zhang Zhidong co-signed that memorial and Yuan Shikai's memorials clearly related to the reform of the legal system. On 15 May 1904, the Committee for Revising and Compiling the Civil and Criminal Codes (Xiuding Falü Guan) opened for business under the Ministry of Criminal Justice, which was renamed the Ministry of Justice in 1906. From its opening to 1910, the Committee organized the translation of 69 laws from thirteen countries, as well as a number of other works on law and jurisprudence. These foreign legal texts became an important reference for the compilation between 1907 and 1911 of *The Executive Criminal Code of the Great Qing Dynasty*, *The New Criminal Code of the Great Qing Dynasty*, *The Draft Civil Law of the Great Qing Dynasty*, *The Draft Commercial Law of the Great Qing Dynasty*, and other legal documents. Japanese legal experts and Chinese students who had studied in Japan were the main participants in the entire legal codification project.

[48] Writing in 1955 By Ralph Powell. Ref: Douglas R. Reynolds, *CHINA, 1898–1912: The Xinzheng Revolution and Japan*, Harvard University, p. 158.

The principles of nationalism or Western values embodied in the new legal texts posed a serious challenge to traditional Chinese teachings on the family: the hierarchical principles embodied in the Confucian "bonds" of subservience were no longer regarded as fundamental, and identity as a free citizen was now regarded as something that a rich and powerful nation really required. The conflict of ideas in the process of codification should be regarded as a clash of civilizations that had to be handled effectively, but as soon as the new laws were written down, the new concepts they embodied immediately signified change.

Reforms were continually rolled out by the Qing court's New Administration, but people felt that the pace of change in the years following Empress Dowager Cixi's return to Beijing in early 1902 was too slow, and the slowness of the government initiatives frustrated those who were in a hurry to complete the historic transition overnight. The tardiness of change was attributed to the authoritarian system of the Qing government, so the desire for political reform was becoming increasingly urgent. In 1903, the idea of constitutional monarchy began to take hold among the Chinese community concerned about China's fate at home and abroad, and the members of the gentry who ran business enterprises already clearly felt the need to change the political system, so although constitutional politics was a cause promoted by intellectuals, it clearly affected the capitalist class. Zhang Jian (1853–1926), for example, was a complex constitutional advocate and promoter, who had an excellent reputation in the fields of business and education, at the same time as he had good relations with court officials such as Weng Tonghe, Yuan Shikai, and Zhang Zhidong, as well as with reformers like Kang Youwei. *A Discussion of Reform* (Bianfa Pingyi), which Zhang completed following discussions with Tang Shouqian and Shen Zengzhi in the wake of the Boxer Rebellion, is regarded as an important document of the early constitutional movement, after which Zhang devoted more time to the specific promotion of constitutional politics, for example helping Zhang Zhidong draft the *Proposed Constitutional Amendments* and translating *The Constitution of Japan* into Chinese with Zhao Fengchang, both in 1904. In fact, throughout the subsequent constitutional movement the influence of Zhang Jian and many other representatives of the national bourgeoisie can be clearly discerned.

As early as the summer of 1901, there were officials within the Qing court. such as Li Shengduo (1859–1934), who had participated in study tours to examine Western political institutions and clearly advocated implementing a constitutional monarchy: "Having examined legislative reform programs in various countries, we found that all began with a constitutional framework as the foundation on which the nation would be established. As for the structure of the nation, political systems can be divided into monarchies and democracies, but whatever changes are made will in every case depend on the constitution as the foundation of the nation". The Qing court responded to Li Shengduo's advice to "learn from the nearby lesson provided by Japan's prosperity and keep at a distance the warning provided by Russia's chaos. Remain determined to adhere to the intention to first promulgate the constitution and only then clarify the nature of the state".[49] The changes within the bureaucracy were obvious. The Chinese ambassador in France, Sun Baoqi (1867–1931) wrote to the Bureau of Government Affairs in 1904, proposing that a constitutional monarchy be implemented. He pointed out that the Constitution which Japan issued and implemented 22 years after the Meiji Restoration had influenced "society from top to bottom, resulting in social consolidation and stability". Although government officials put forward different views because of their respective backgrounds and positions, the constitutionalists progressively won the support of Tieliang, Duanfang, Zaizhen, and Xu Shichang, and soon afterwards, the Yunnan-Guizhou Governor Ding Zhenduo, the Liangguang Governor Cen Chunxuan, the Hu-Guang Governor Zhang Zhidong, the Liangjiang Governor Zhou Fu, and the Guizhou Military Governor Lin Shaonian all presented memorials, requesting that a constitution be promulgated. There were of course many who resisted the idea of a constitution, but their influence faded as China's situation grew increasingly fraught.

The urgency of the situation put pressure on the government to reform the status quo. Public opinion, which began in the summer of 1904 to demand that the United States abolish a treaty restricting Chinese workers, reached its climax in 1905. It is well known that Chinese laborers played a role in the history of developing the American West, but in the 1870s the United States sought to deal with a domestic economic crisis by adopting a policy of excluding Chinese laborers to alleviate the social conflicts and crises caused by the unemployment facing American workers.

[49] "Zhuilu Li Muzhai Xinshi Tiaochen Bianfa Zhe" (Envoy Li Muzhai's Memorialized Proposals on Reform), *Shibao*, 28 November 1905. This article is quoted in: *Wan-Qing Zhengzhi Xinlun* (New Arguments regarding Late-Qing Politics), Beijing: Commercial Press, 2018, p. 206.

Ten years later, in 1882, the US government enacted the Chinese Exclusion Act, which Chinese felt to be discriminatory, but the US Congress felt this legislation would make the standing policy effective. The Chinese however believed that such an Act must be repealed. [The act followed the Angell Treaty of 1880, a set of revisions to the US–China Burlingame Treaty of 1868 that allowed the United States to suspend Chinese immigration. The Act was initially intended to last for 10 years but was renewed in 1892 with the Geary Act and made permanent in 1902.] At the end of 1904, more than 100,000 overseas Chinese petitioned the Qing government demanding that the Treaty be revoked, and the Chinese Exclusion Act be repealed. The US and Chinese governments did not reach an agreement on the issue, and in May 1905, the Shanghai Chamber of Commerce decided to launch a boycott of American goods. Not only did dozens of groups and industries in Shanghai take part in the boycott, but cities such as Guangzhou, Suzhou, Changsha, Beijing, Tianjin, and Zhengzhou also rallied to take part; the participants were not limited to the business community, but also included intellectuals, workers, and people from all walks of life. The boycott was ultimately not a success, but it was agreed that it was not so much imperialism, as the incompetence and corruption of the Manchu government, that was the key to the problem. The atmosphere of social unrest was heightened and trust in the Manchu government was further diminishing, a situation of which the Qing court should have been aware.

An important reminder came with the war between Japan and Russia fought over Chinese territory. When Japan and Russia went to war in north-eastern China in February 1904, the constitutional movement was also coming to a climax. People wondered whether Russia as a large country would defeat a small country like Japan, or whether the final victory would depend on the differences between races and political systems. During the war, the constitutionalists judged and calculated the ultimate fate of a small Japanese country that was better than Russia in its political system. There was a bitter political row between the constitutionalists and the conservatives, and the constitutionalists were hoping to prove that, if a constitutional state was instituted, even the yellow race could defeat white people. Public opinion maintained that "a country's strengths and weaknesses do not derive from race but from its political system".[50] When the Russian fleet was sunk in the Straits of Tsushima in May 1905, it was said that the Qing government had no reason to hold back on conferring civil rights on its subjects. "The war between Japan and Russia was not regarded by most people as a military contest, but as a political contest. The final victory of Japan and defeat of Russia was a contest in which a dictatorship clearly lost to a constitution".[51] So, it was the Japanese–Russian war that removed the final reticence in the Empress Dowager's thinking, prompting her to finally decide to fully accept the constitutional politics that had long been publicized among her people.

In 1905, Empress Dowager Cixi asked Duanfang, which of the reform measures remain to be implemented? Duanfang told her: "You still haven't implemented a constitution". Duanfang also told her: "The constitution will make the throne hereditary". This was a major point of concern for Cixi; for her the reforms were designed to consolidate the Manchu-Qing regime, and remaining the supreme ruler who always held the highest power of the state became the basic idea for all central power holders facing reform at different times in the entire twentieth century that was to follow. The Empress Dowager's consent aroused the enthusiasm of many officials who looked at the speech and observed her demeanor, and the palace began to reverberate with discussions about instituting a constitution. Yuan Shikai, who had previously been offended by the covert actions of the Guangxu Emperor and the Kang-Liang reformers and effectively became a "whistleblower", now saw the opportunity to turn his position and image around, and in May he issued a memorial, jointly with Zhou Fu and Zhang Zhidong, calling for the implementation of a constitutional political arrangement.

On 16 July 1905, the Qing government issued *Imperial Edict to Investigate Constitutional Politics*, ordering a group of senior government officials to travel abroad to study Western politics in preparation for introducing a constitution:

[50] "Lun Ri-E zhi Zhan zhi Yi" (On the Benefits of the War between Japan and Russia), *Zhongwai Ribao Yaowen* (Highlights of the Chinese and Foreign Daily News), 28th day of the 12th month of the 29th year of Guangxu (=13 February 1904).

[51] Shen Qichang, *Yiyuan Yaolan* (Parliamentarians' Handbook), Yubei Lixian Gonghui Yin (Printery of the Preparatory Constitutional Association), 1910, p. 61.

> Edict to the Cabinet: The situation at present is difficult and a myriad of things remain to be done. The court has repeatedly issued edicts and has strived to carry out reforms. Outside, opinions abound. Over the past few years, although matters are taking shape, the results remain unclear. Those outside the court undertaking activities lack attention to fine points, nor are they able to grasp the full picture. Just going along like this, how will we overcome our weakness and save the situation? Now, we have especially selected Zaize, Dai Hongci, Xu Shichang, Duanfang, and members of their retinues to go in groups to Japan and various Western countries to investigate all different political systems, so that in time we might choose, and follow what is best. ... Allocations for the expenditures of mission members will be from the funds of the Foreign Ministry and the Ministry of Finance.[52]

In the summer and autumn, the preparation of constitutional affairs began. From the end of 1905 to the beginning of 1906, the five ministers of the Qing government finally left the country to examine foreign political institutions. The delay in the departure dates of the five ministers going abroad was dramatic. At first the group comprised Zaize, Xu Shichang, Shao Ying, Dai Hongci and Duanfang, but later Xu Shichang and Shao Ying were replaced by Shang Qiheng and Li Shengduo. On 24 October 1905, when the special train carrying the five ministers was about to depart, its departure was prevented by a bomb thrown by a well-known revolutionist, Wu Yue. The incident indicated that although the government had indeed embarked on reforms, the revolutionary parties had completely lost patience.[53] The incident elicited differing responses, was widely discussed in the news media, and even led Sheng Xuanhuai and Yuan Shikai at one stage to issue statements balking at the idea of proceeding with the introduction of the constitution. Due to the large number of people advocating a constitution in the face of the immediate

[52] Ref: *Daqing Dezong Jing Huangdi Shilu*, fasc. 546, cited in Gao Fang et al., *Qingmo Lixian Shi* (Late-Qing Constitutional History), Beijing: Huawen Chubanshe, 2012, p. 89.

[53] Wu Yue was a member of a revolutionary party. On 24 October 1905, Wu availed himself of the opportunity provided when five ministers—Zaize, Duanfang, Dai Hongci, Xu Shichang, and Shaoying, were preparing to embark on their overseas trip at the Zhengyang Gate, to detonate a bomb in an assassination attempt. He inadvertently killed himself, and Zaize and Shaoying were slightly injured. On 26 October, Cixi replaced the two injured members of the team and instructed the delegation to continue its journey. Duanfang and Dai Hongci left Beijing on 2 December, and Zaize and the two replacements, Shang Qiheng and Li Shengduo, left Beijing on 11 December.

national crisis, the expedition by the ministers proved unstoppable. On 19 December 1905, Dai Hongci and Duanfang left via Shanghai, to focus on Japan, the United States, Germany, Austria, Russia, and Italy; they also intended visiting the Scandinavian countries of Denmark, Sweden, and Norway, as well as the Netherlands and Switzerland. Zaize, Shang Qiheng, and Li Shengduo separately left Shanghai on 14 January 1906, at the head of delegations of officials and gentry from Hubei, Fengtian, Guangdong, Hunan, and Jiangxi provinces to visit Japan, the United States, Britain, France, and Belgium. Six months later, they returned home and were united in advocating the implementation of a constitutional system. On 1 September 1906, they and all court officials knew that work on the constitution itself was finally about to begin.

There is no evidence that the Qing court's arrangement of five ministers going abroad was simply a perfunctory gesture. In fact, the arrangements regarding accompanying personnel were intended as far as possible to include "open-minded knowledgeable" people, and the ministers were accompanied along the way by invited students with experience abroad, and the minsters even visited the residences of students who were studying abroad and invited them to participate. As a result, in addition to selecting central and some local officials, students abroad also participated. Based on the professional requirements of the entourage, members of revolutionary parties even infiltrated the groups and made use of their officers, such as Yang Dusheng, who participated in the assassination attempt on the five ministers, together with Sun Yue, who was also a member of the entourage accompanying Zaize. Impressively, at Xiong Xiling's suggestion, Duanfang, when in Japan. invited Yang Du (1875–1931) and Liang Qichao to draft constitutional study and research documents, and Yang submitted his "Draft Outline of a Chinese Constitution Drawing on the Outstanding Features of Other Countries" and Liang submitted a report titled "The Implementation of Constitutional Procedures". The two major constitutional documents submitted after the return to China of the investigative teams were Zaize's "Secret Memorial Requesting the Proclamation of a Constitution" and Duanfang's "Memorial Requesting Which National Situation Will Determine the Large Plan". Duanfang wrote:

> China today is at the center of international rivalry; the extent of her territory, her large population, and the richness of her natural resources are the envy of other nations, who view her as a battleground for commercial and military rivalry. If her government is not improved, her autocratic system not reformed, and a constitutional political system not introduced, then the flow-on effects of wealth and power will not be realized. … From this I argue that if China wants national wealth and military power, then the only means of achieving this is through the adoption of a complete constitutional system.[54]

However, based on China's institutional practice, Duanfang's proposed China follow the constitutional steps and precautions of Japan's Meiji restoration by first declaring and making public a constitution so that the whole country could be prepared. He proposed taking 15–20 years to prepare for the implementation of the constitution. Zaize was more familiar with the psychology of the Empress Dowager Cixi, so he prepared a list of 17 items in his document advocating a constitution to show that a constitutional monarchy guaranteed the monarch would still hold power. He stressed that if a constitution was promulgated, a permanent monarchy would ease serious external problems and the potential of civil unrest. The reformist attitude was urgent and concrete, and on 25 August 1906, Dai Hongci and Duanfang again memorialized to change the bureaucratic system. On the basis of the itemized memorial prepared by Zaize and others, from 25 to 28 August, the Empress Dowager organized a series of meetings of princes and chief ministers, attended by Prince Chun (Zaifeng) and the Beiyang Minister Yuan Shikai, to discuss constitutional issues. Given each individual's position and stance, the views of the participants were also different: Sun Jianai, Rongqing, Tieliang, and others advocated slowing the pace; Yuan Shikai, Yikuang, Xu Shichang, and Zhang Baixi hoped to start immediately; and Zaifeng and Qu Hongji emphasized further preparations. Regardless of these proposals, on 29 August, three days after Yikuang "personally presented his memorial to the throne, urging the implementation of a constitution", that is, on 1 September 1906, the Qing court issued a proclamation announcing "the preparatory trial constitution be implemented", which was the official

[54] Gao Fang et al., *Qingmo Lixian Shi* (Late-Qing Constitutional History), Beijing: Huawen Chubanshe, 2012, p. 112.

declaration that the Qing government was now ready to promote constitutional government.[55] The imperial edict did not announce a specific time for implementing the constitution but stressed the need to start with reform of the bureaucracy, which was also the opinion of the majority of the participants in the meeting. On 4 September, Banshi Jigou Bianzhi Guan (Bureau of Constitutional Arrangement), an office for the reform of the bureaucracy, was established and it put forward five basic principles, the first being "the adoption of a constitutional monarchy". The principles temporarily precluded consideration of establishing a parliament but did clarify the principle of a tripartite separation of powers, proceeding from the executive to judicial decisions. The reform of the official system involved the repositioning of almost all officials, from the central down to the local level, and assessing the possibility of their continuing to serve in the government in the future, so this was a complex political maneuver which impacted vested interests and redistributed power from the central to the local levels, which naturally aroused anxieties and fears throughout officialdom. However, the complex contest was not simply limited to competition between the constitutionalists and their opponents. The reforms raised a hue and cry among the princes and the aristocracy, to which were added the lamentations of the eunuchs. The Empress Dowager felt so hard pressed she thought "the best thing might be to drown herself in the palace lake".[56] There were even more differences of opinion within the ranks of the constitutionalists themselves, many of whom thought that Yuan Shikai's manipulation of the reform of the bureaucracy paid scant regard to the standard requirements of constitutionalism.[57] This top-down institutional reform ended

[55] Yikuang is believed to have been in the pay of Yuan Shikai. Yuan's enthusiasm for Yikuang's proposed constitutional monarchy with a Cabinet after the Qing court decided to prepare a constitution generally believed to have been motivated by a desire to protect himself, given that he had earlier betrayed the Guangxu Emperor in the 1898 reform period, Yuan was not a member of the royal family, and that he had to forestall any subsequent redress of history by the Guangxu Emperor, and a Cabinet position would provide Yuan with enhanced capital for any future political ambitions.

[56] Tao Xiang, *Dong Qi Yeyu* (Anecdotal History of Eastern Shandong), quoted in *Xinhai Geming Qianhou* (Before and after the 1911 Revolution), p. 29. Cited in Hou Yijie, *Ershi Shiji Chu Zhongguo Zhengzhi Gaige Fengchao* (Political Reform Trends in Early Twentieth Century China), Beijing: Renmin Chubanshe, 1993, p. 79.

[57] Yuan Shikai expressed a more positive interest in quickly organizing a Cabinet, and he actually directed those reorganizing the bureaucracy to help arrange the necessary

with the appointment of Yuan Shikai and Zhang Zhidong as ministers in the Junji Chu (lit., "Military Cabinet") on 4 September 1907, though on the face of it, the two men, especially Yuan Shikai, lost control of the army. However, in addition to indicating the complexity of constitutional reform at this time, the various voices of opposition within the court could not find effective measures to block the moves to prepare for the implementation of a constitution, and the reform measures all had the characteristics of an overall transition to a constitution. For example, by limiting the number of ministers in the Junji Chu, there was greater decentralization of power in favor of the Shangshu (made up of heads of the ministries); there was no longer a rule that there had to be a balance between Manchu and Han officials throughout the bureaucracy; the administration and the judiciary began to be separated; and preparations were underway to establish a National Assembly (Zizheng Yuan), an Audit Department (Shenji Yuan), and an Admiralty or Ministry of the Navy (Haijun Bu).

Statistics can shed light on the speed of development of the nation's industry and commerce between 1900 and 1911, but the establishment of the Shanghai Chamber of Commerce on 22 February 1902 and the issuance by the Qing government of *Concise Charter for Chambers of Commerce* in January 1904 suffice to illustrate developments. According to this *Charter*, the establishment throughout the country of chambers of commerce and branches, with offices even in villages and towns,

documentation so that Yikuang could become prime minister, and he himself could serve as deputy prime minister, thereby being able to use the Cabinet to control administrative and personnel matters, or at least avoid as much as possible retaliation if the current reforms were reversed and light were shed on his earlier betrayal of the Guangxu Emperor in 1898. However, many reformists opposed the immediate establishment of a responsible cabinet because it ran counter to the legitimate constitutional procedure of establishing a parliament which could implement legislation and itself establish a cabinet. At that time the Censor Zhao Binglin (1876–1927) wrote the following assessment of Yuan Shikai: "Since the coup of 1898, there has been a rift between Yuan Shikai and the Emperor, and Yuan fears that if the Empress Dowager should die, disaster will befall him, and so in the name of wanting a constitutional monarchy, he is desperate to first establish a cabinet which can covertly abrogate monarchical power. By securing a seat in the cabinet, he would not be superfluous and could surreptitiously avoid disaster, and secretly work to transfer imperial power to himself".

Ref: Zhao Binglin, *Jianyuan Zou Shilu* (Account of the Memorial Calling for Establishing the Cabinet), fasc. 1, p. 18. Hou Yijie, *Ershi Shiji Chu Zhongguo Zhengzhi Gaige Fengchao* (Political Reform Trends in Early Twentieth Century China), Beijing: Renmin Chubanshe, 1993, p. 84.

could provide investors and business operators with business litigation and surveys, as well as facilities for establishing companies, registering patent applications, and handling bankruptcy and other business matters. By 1911, the vast majority of provinces in the country had set up chambers of commerce (56 general chambers of commerce, 669 branches, and a large number of business offices for which statistics are not available). This entirely new economic structure and mode of operation was naturally conducive to people entering the fields of business consultation, discussion, mutual assistance, and participation in cooperative or co-investment arrangements. The democratic approach of capitalism rapidly began to permeate industry and commerce throughout China. For example, for Shanghai businessmen and entrepreneurs, the Shanghai Municipal General Engineering Bureau established in 1905, had the aim of realizing common goals, protecting industrial autonomy, and resisting local government interference. The Bureau could even set up its own policing force, implement utility management, and share local taxation powers, which were measures which all necessitated institutional accommodation. The eight-month campaign boycotting American goods launched by the Shanghai General Chamber of Commerce in 1904 had a strong impact, and the subsequent changes in all domestic economic matters, such as the movements to reclaim railway and mining rights, had the full participation of local businessmen, especially the chambers of commerce they organized, showing that this new social element had begun to show its strength, and that there was an increasingly clear economic and political narrative of demands. After the proclamation announcing that a "prepara tory trial constitution would be implemented", the pro-constitutional governor, Cen Chunxuan used the industrial and commercial forces to urge the entrepreneur Zhang Jian to organize constitutionalist groups to promote the constitution. On 16 December 1906, a group of gentry businessmen in Shanghai established the "Preparatory Constitutional Association", whose membership elected 15 directors, with Zheng Xiaoxu voted president and Zhang Jian and Tang Shouqian, vice presidents. By 1910, the Association's membership had grown to 374, from more than 10 provinces as well as participants from Hong Kong, Macao, and South East Asia. The Association established the *Preparatory Constitutional Association News* (Yubei Lixian Gonghui Bao) on 29 February 1908 (in 1910 the periodical's name was changed to *Constitution Journal* [Xianzhi] published every ten days, and then to *Constitution Journal*

Daily [Xianzhi Rikan] or *Constitution Daily* [Xianbao]). This publication provided information on all aspects of constitutionalism, including such topics as the Qing Constitution, National Assembly, civil administration, self-rule, and political parties. When the Government lacked professional manpower and needed help, the Preparatory Constitutional Association even assisted with the establishment of local governments and the establishment of the National Assembly, as well as in the preparation of commercial laws. Other influential early constitutional groups included the Shanghai Constitutional Research Association founded in December 1906 with Ma Xiangbo as Director-General.[58] There was also the Jilin Self-Government Society, Yang Du's Constitutional Association (Xianzheng Gonghui), and the Guangdong Business Autonomy Association with gentry businessmen from Guangdong making up the main body of the group.[59]

[58] Ma Xiangbo (1840–1939), originally known as Ma Zhide and whose Christian name was Joseph, was a native of Jiangsu who made outstanding contributions and wrote extensively in the early days of New Education. He founded Aurora University, Fudan University, and Fudan Middle School, of which he was also the founding chancellor. Cai Yuanpei, Yu Youren, and Shao Lizi were his followers.

[59] During the constitutional movement, Yang Du stressed that drawing up the constitution, establishing a responsible cabinet, and convening a parliament were important elements of a program of political revolution, and that early convocation of a parliament was a prerequisite step. He called on people to "concentrate on trying to convene the parliament as soon as possible. If there is no parliament, there can be no constitution, but once there is a parliament, there will be a higher type of constitution". The role of parliament is to "serve as a weapon to form responsible government". As a revolutionist desperately competing to wrest the power to change history, Yang Du in his eagerness even described parliament as "the only way to save the country".

See: Yang Du, "Jintie-zhuyi Shuo" (My Theory of Iron Philosophy), *Zhongguo Xinbao* (China New Journal), issues 1–6, quoted in Hou Yijie, *Ershi Shiji Chu Zhongguo Zhengzhi Gaige Fengchao* (Political Reform Trends in Early Twentieth Century China), Beijing: Renmin Chubanshe, 1993, p. 179.

Under Yang Du's call and guidance, a large number of articles calling for the convening of parliament as soon as possible appeared, and by the spring of 1908, in the national press and media "the daily calls for establishing a parliament were deafening".

See: "Lun Jinnian Guomin Quanli Wei Guohui Qingyuan Yishi" (On This Year's Popular Calls for Establishing a Parliament), *Shibao*, 26–27 February 1908, cited in Hou Yijie, *Ershi Shiji Chu Zhongguo Zhengzhi Gaige Fengchao* (Political Reform Trends in Early Twentieth Century China), Beijing: Renmin Chubanshe, 1993, p. 189.

Yang also used his Constitutional Discussion Group (Xianzheng Jiangxihui) to reach out to constitutionalists, political groups, and students around the country to sign a document calling for the convocation of a parliament, which provided a precedent for the subsequent peaceful petition.

After 13 February 1907, when the Emperor Protection Society was renamed the Imperial Constitutional Society, Kang Youwei and Liang Qichao designated their purpose as establishing a "constitutional monarchy" and, to enable them to return to China to campaign for and promote constitutional work, they urged the Qing government to openly ban Manchus from participation in political parties. In October, Liang Qichao, together with Jiang Zhiyou,[60] and Xu Fusu,[61]: set up the Zhengwen She (Political News Society) in Japan and changed the name of *Xinmin Congbao* (New People's Miscellany) to *Zhenglun* (Political Discussion). The platform announced by the Political News Society was as follows:

> Firstly, implement a national parliamentary system and set up responsible government; secondly, formulate laws and ensure the independence of the judiciary; third, confirm local self-government and a separation of powers between the central and local governments; and fourth, carefully emphasize foreign relations and maintain reciprocal powers.

The Political News Society has three general aims:

> (1) Establish constitutional government and ensure that all citizens can participate in national politics; (2) Clarify and act on all advantages and pitfalls in domestic politics and foreign relations, in order that citizens fulfill their responsibilities to the nation; (3) Rouse the political enthusiasm of the nation's people and nurture their political intelligence and ethics.[62]

[60] Jiang Zhiyou (1865–1929), a Zhejiang native, studied in Japan in his early years and was a member of the Restoration Society. He was the editor-in-chief of *Zhenglun* (Political Discussion). His basic position was support for a constitutional monarchy.

[61] Xu Fosu (1879–1943), a native of Hunan, was involved in the 1898 Reforms in his early years. After the failure of 1898, he studied in Japan. In 1903, together with Huang Xing and others he organized the Huaxing Hui in Changsha. He was later a writer for *Xinmin Congbao* (New People's Miscellany), advocating a constitutional monarchy and opposing the democratic revolution. With Liang Qichao, Jiang Zhiyou, and others in Tokyo, he set up the Zhengwen She (Political News Society). In 1910, when constitutionalists founded *Guomin Gongbao* (Citizens Gazette), he became its editor-in-chief. After the failure of the third petition, he was quoted as saying: "My colleagues all returned to their home provinces, informing the Consultative Council of their political despair regarding Qing politics, and we decided to secretly plan a revolution".

[62] Liang Qichao, "Zhengwen She Xuanyan Shu" (Manifesto of the Political News Society), *Liang Qichao Zishu: 1898–1929*, Renmin Ribao Chubanshe, 2011.

At this time, various constitutional organizations working on the preparation of the constitution in fact played a role in explaining theoretical principles, activating public opinion, and arousing more people across the country to urge the Qing government to speed up the constitutional preparatory work.

Pressure urging the Qing court to promote the constitution as soon as possible came from various political and violent activities by the revolutionary parties, especially in the context of the increasing intensity of the revolutionary movement after 1900. Even the colleagues of Kang Youwei and Liang Qichao agreed with the revolutionists on this issue. On 6 July 1907, when Xu Xilin of the Restoration Society was in Anqing organizing students at a Police Training School, the Military Governor Enming was shot and killed. This violent act was first reported in the pages of *Shenbao* (20 July). As the first news report was accompanied with a photograph of the incident, the event made a huge social impact. This incident increased fear within the Qing court, and so it was hoped that seizing the opportunity to institute a constitution as soon as possible might avoid revolution. Jiang Zhiyou in the Political News Society's paper *Zhenglun* provided this analysis:

> Following the assassination of the Military Governor of Anhui and the decree of the 28th day of the 5th month in the 33rd year of Guangxu [=8 July 1907] announcing preparations for implementing a constitution, we firmly promise to lend support to the constitution and to eliminate the scourges of assassination and revolution. The Constitution itself will suffice to eliminate assassination and revolution. Assassination and revolution would only eliminate the possibility of a constitution, so there is no better law and those who are truly knowledgeable also agree this is the case.[63]

On 8 July 1907, the Qing court issued a decree which stated: "Anyone familiar with the preface of the preparatory implementation of the constitution must prepare to voice their opinion on each item". The decree called on officials at all levels of government across the country with different aims and purposes to submit memorials discussing the

[63] From the first issue of *Zhenglun*. Quoted in Zhang Yufa, *Qingji de Lixian Tuanti* (Constitutional Groups of the Qing Period), Beijing: Peking University Press, 2011, p. 228.

[proposed] constitutional politics. Even though the texts of the memorials revealed the complex views of officials of different status and ideas, and some people (e.g., the Secretary of the Grand Secretariat Huang Yunfan) even wrote, "Please stop all discussion of the constitution", this did not affect Yuan Shikai who, on 28 July 1907, submitted a memorial aptly titled "Please Expedite the Implementation of the Preparatory Constitution". This memorial presented ten proposals: (1) proclaim the constitution; (2) elevate men of talent; (3) invigorate the nation; (4) reconcile Manchu and Han; (5) implement rewards and penalties; (6) clarify party groupings; (7) establish the constitutional political system; (8) Set up the national assembly; (9) Ensure the autonomy of local governments; and (10) Introduce universal education. No one could deny the legitimacy of these ten proposals, regardless of Yuan Shikai's personal motivation. At the same time as the memorial was presented, an attachment proposed: "Please send ministers to Germany and Japan to examine their Constitutions". And: "Send princes close to the imperial line to the United Kingdom and Germany to study their political and military arrangements". The idea behind these attachments was that government officials should be given a better understanding of the history and current situation of constitutionalism in various countries, and that more officials should have knowledge of the preparatory constitution if they were to carry out work on the constitution. As a result, on 9 September, the Qing court sent Wang Daxie, Dashou, and the conservative official Yu Shimei to visit Great Britain, Japan, and Germany. The released schedule suggested that the work of promoting constitutionalism was an urgent task and, not long after Yuan Shikai's memorial was submitted, a memorial from Prince Qing, Yikuang, and others, which requested that the Kaocha Zhengzhi Guan [official English title: Committee for the Investigation of the Principles of Modern Politics and Government] become the Xianzheng Biancha Guan [official English title: Committee for Drawing up Regulations for Constitutional Government],[64] was approved. On 13 August 1907, the Qing court

64 The Kaocha Zhengzhi Guan or the Committee for the Investigation of the Principles of Modern Politics and Government was established on 25 November 1905, to work in conjunction with the five ministers who went abroad to study foreign constitutional political systems. Its responsibilities were to "draw widely on talented persons, undertake careful research, and choose from the political and legal institutions of various countries what is appropriate for Chinese governance, consider their pros and cons, write up these materials, present them in a timely fashion, and await decisions". See: "Sheli

promulgated the establishment of the latter Committee, which meant that a body for specifically reforming legislative processes and implementing them was formally established. As most of the staff of the Committee for Drawing up Regulations for Constitutional Government had received professional training and studied abroad, ten days later the Committee submitted to the throne its 16-item Constitution, which was approved on the same day.[65] It is clear that the Committee for Drawing up Regulations for Constitutional Government was quite different from the previous Committee, which had merely been a preparatory body for collecting and collating related literature, because it provided leadership in constitutional reform: formulating legal provisions, submitting them for deliberation, and implementing subsequent decisions. The charter of the Committee for Drawing up Regulations for Constitutional Government stipulated that it set up a Revising Bureau, a Statistical Bureau, and other relevant sections and departments. The terms of reference were very specific:

> (1) The purpose of the review is to: Examine the memorials on constitutional government and to submit to the Junji Chu an investigation into the matter; (2) Investigate the constitutions of other countries and to draw up a draft constitution; (3) Investigate the draft codes of the Committee (codes refer to the civil law, commercial law, criminal law,

Kaocha Zhengzhi Guan Canzhuo Geguo Zhengfa Cuanding Chengshu Chengjin Yu" (Proclamation Establishing Committee for the Investigation of the Principles of Modern Politics and Government, to Review the Political and Legal Codes of Various Countries, Write up this Material and Present it to the Throne), *Qingmo Choubei Lixian Dang'an* (Archives on the Constitutional Preparations of the Late-Qing Dynasty), vol. 1, Beijing: Zhonghua Shuju, 1979, p. 43. This book is quoted in Shang Xiaoming, *Liu Ri Xuesheng yu Qingmo Xinzheng* (Chinese Students Studying in Japan and the New Administration of the Late-Qing), Nanchang: Jiangxi Jiaoyu Chubanshe, 2002, p. 6.

The legislative drafting members were Wang Rongbao, a graduate of Waseda University, Cao Rulin, a graduate of Tokyo Law School, and Zhang Zongxiang, a graduate of the Imperial University of Tokyo. Their work was initially under the direction of the Zhengwu Chu (Bureau of Government Affairs), but in November 1906 the Bureau changed its name to the Huiyi Zhengwu Chu (Committee of Ministers), and later the work of the Committee was incorporated into the Committee for the Investigation of the Principles of Modern Politics and Government.

65 The archives for 1907 show that the Committee for the Investigation of the Principles of Modern Politics and Government employed 47 young people who had returned from studying abroad (41 of whom had studied in Japan). In the core body of the Committee, the Revising Bureau (Bianzhi Ju), there were 21 young persons who had studied abroad, 17 of them in Japan.

criminal procedure law, civil procedure law, etc.), the various specific regulations of ministries and departments (these specific regulations or "single-purpose laws" refer to statutes rather than law codes), and administrative regulations (e.g., the statutes regulating appointments, etc.); (4) Survey the statistics of various nations, issue formats, and bring together national statistical tables and statistical tables comparing China and foreign countries.[66]

On 19 October 1907, the Qing court ordered the provincial governors to set up consultative bureaus in the provincial capitals as soon as possible and prepare councils at the prefectural and county levels. On 22 October, Yikuang and others submitted a memorial requesting the establishment of related bureaus of investigation in each province and of statistical offices in every government ministry to complement the work of the Committee for Drawing up Regulations for Constitutional Government.

Preparing a constitution and confirming its regulations was not a purely domestic political matter. In October 1907, Yuan Shikai, in accordance with the British and Qing government's loan agreement to build the Shanghai-Hangzhou-Ningbo Railway, urged the imperial court to issue a decree conferring this railway's rights to the United Kingdom, while Chinese investors could only participate in the stock. This gave the constitutionalists an opportunity to raise the issue from being one of railroad rights into a constitutional demand for civil rights. Although the Qing government signed the draft agreement in 1898, public opinion said that such a loan would not have gone ahead if a parliament had been in place to supervise the government. As a result, speeding up the opening of parliament became a slogan addressing this. Dealing with such historical issues was not easy. When students in Jiangsu and Zhejiang, and even Beijing, also became involved in moves to reject railway loans, the Qing court took disciplinary measures to prohibit teachers and students from "interfering in national politics". Article 35 of the *Law on Association and Assembly*, which was drafted by the Committee for Drawing up Regulations for Constitutional Government on 11 March 1908, was far removed from the regulations on freedom of association and speech in the subsequently promulgated *Constitutional Outline*, as it did not, for example, confer rights of association and assembly on teachers, students, women,

[66] Quoted from Gao Fang et al., *Qingmo Lixian Shi* (History of Late-Qing Constitutionalism), Beijing: Huawen Chubanshe, 2012, p. 206.

and illiterate persons. Despite this, political association, rallies, and open public lectures were allowed. Even so, the restrictive provisions of the *Law on Association and Assembly* were widely censured and criticized in the press. For example, an article in *Shenbao* (27 December 1907) described how this document of the Qing government was ostensibly constitutional, but authoritarian in reality, and the following opinion was published in response to the *Law*: "What is the law regarding journalism? While it simply talks about tidying up the press, it gags the newspapers and prevents them from speaking out, and that is the true spirit of this Law".[67] The pressure on the Qing court from demands in petitions from the provinces was increasing, and the complex tripartite game between the constitutionalists, the Qing government, and the revolutionary parties was becoming increasingly intense. However, the general political situation can be characterized as a general consensus regarding the need for a constitution, the parties merely disagreeing about aspects of its timing, methods, and strategy. Gradually, advocates of the constitution within the government were winning decisive support from Empress Dowager Cixi in the internal contest with opponents of the constitution. Yikuang told Cixi that delaying the introduction of the constitution threatened the country's survival. He pointed out that the implementation of the constitution would benefit the monarch and the people, but would be to the detriment of bureaucrats, so in order to avoid obstruction by "disadvantaged officials", the constitution should be enacted as soon as possible so the monarch would not lose support among the people.

On 27 August 1908, the Committee for Drawing up Regulations for Constitutional Government and the National Assembly prepared a series of memorials—*Outline of the Constitution*, together with *The Essentials of the Parliamentary Law*, *The Essentials of the Electoral Law*, and *The List of Annual Preparations for Drawing up the Constitution*. As the *Outline of the Constitution* had 14 articles on "the powers of the monarchy" but only nine articles on the rights and obligations of the subjects, many anxious constitutionalists considered this to be perfunctory obstruction by the Qing court. However, under the limited constitutional provisions,

[67] "Tan Bao Lü" (Lamenting Newspaper Regulations), *Zhengzong Aiguo Bao* (Orthodox Patriotic News), 26 March 1908. Quoted in Hou Yijie, *Ershi Shiji Chu Zhongguo Zhengzhi Gaige Fengchao* (Political Reform Trends in Early Twentieth Century China), Renmin Chubanshe, 1993, p. 188.

the envisaged constitutional monarchy differed in nature from an authoritarian regime in which the monarch could decide everything. At the same time, despite the limited qualifications of subjects, such provisions as rights of expression, writing, publication, and assembly, the freedom of association, and the protection of private property and rights of residence existed within the scope of the envisaged laws, which provided people with a glimpse into the actual content of the preparatory work on the constitution. Quite clearly, the *Outline Constitution* promulgated by the Qing government copied the first chapter [or preamble] of the Japanese Constitution as closely as possible, and it was also based on the Japanese experience (in Japan the time from the issuance of the decree to the convening of the National Assembly was also nine years). In the *Outline Constitution* the statement concerning "the sacred dignity and inviolability of the monarchy" was of course a definition of the power of the monarch included by the Qing government after the constitution was first announced, and the full preservation of the monarchy in the Japanese Constitution was indeed in line with what the Qing government wanted. Prior to this, in 1906, the Qing court had been very satisfied with the introduction to the Japanese Constitution provided by Ito Hirobumi whom it had invited to China: "Your country has been a sovereign state for thousands of years, and your sovereignty is vested in the monarch, not in the people, as in Japan".[68] However, the text did include constitutional constraints on the monarch, and the outline preamble read: "From the imperial court down to the subject masses, all must abide by the Constitution, with a view to always following the laws, with no transgression".[69] Yang Du, who drafted the *Outline*, and those who debated the document should have been clear about the intentions of Cixi, but they were also focusing on the wording that surreptitiously included a separation of the three important powers (legislative, executive, and judicial) and constraints on the exercise of power by the monarch, these being the important core content of the constitution:

[68] Zaize, *Kaocha Zhengzhi Riji* (Diary of the Investigative Trip Examining Political Systems), p. 12. Quoted in Hou Yijie, *Ershi Shiji Chu Zhongguo Zhengzhi Gaige Fengchao* (Political Reform Trends in Early Twentieth Century China), Renmin Chubanshe, 1993, p. 209.

[69] *Qingmo Choubei Lixian Dang'an Shiliao* (Late-Qing Preparatory Constitution Archives and Documents), v. 1, p. 57, quoted in Hou Yijie, *Ershi Shiji Chu Zhongguo Zhengzhi Gaige Fengchao* (Political Reform Trends in Early Twentieth Century China), Beijing: Renmin Chubanshe, 1993, p. 209.

> The monarch implements the constitution, which confers on the government the major power to rule the country, and all legislation, administration, and justice are held aside, so that the parliament approves legislation, the government supplements and executes the legislation, and the judiciary respects the legislation.[70]

Basically, this meant that the monarch's rulings were premised first and foremost on the decisions of the parliament, the government, and the courts. In any case, this was a decisive start, regardless of what opinions or even contempt for the provisions in the *Outline* people had at this time. A constitutional system had been legitimized in China. The *Constitution Outline* was very reminiscent of the prototype of the Prussian Constitution, which fulfilled the hopes of Friedrich Engels when it was announced half a century previously.[71]

People who wanted the parliament to have decision-making powers and not just the power to advise were also unhappy with *The Essentials of the Parliamentary Law*, but it did include a series of provisions relating to such matters as the state budget and the impeachment of ministers. Moreover, when the parliament discussed matters, it was only after the two houses of parliament had reached agreement that decisions could be put into effect, and so this marked the beginning of placing limitations on the unimpeded flow of the monarch's will.

There was great concern about *The List of Annual Preparations for Drawing up the Constitution*, which was a timetable for effectively

[70] *Qingmo Choubei Lixian Dang'an Shiliao* (Late-Qing Preparatory Constitution Archives and Documents), v. 1, p. 57, quoted in Hou Yijie, *Ershi Shiji Chu Zhongguo Zhengzhi Gaige Fengchao* (Political Reform Trends in Early Twentieth Century China), Beijing: Renmin Chubanshe, 1993, p. 210.

[71] Prior to the introduction of the Prussian constitution in 1850, Friedrich Engels wrote of Prussia's need for a constitution in 1847, when Prussia was an autocracy in crisis and its "national assembly" was limited to approving new taxes and loans, and discussions were restricted by the limited scope of the law and petitions needed to be submitted to the King. In *The Prussian Constitution*, Engels wrote: "Thus, the Prussian constitution, insignificant in itself, is, for all that, the beginning of a new epoch for that country, and for all Germany. It marks the downfall of absolutism and nobility, and the ascendancy of the middle classes; it marks the beginning of a movement which will very soon lead to a representative constitution for the middle classes, a free press, independent judges and trial by jury, and which will end God knows where". This article was first published in the British newspaper, *The Northern Star*, no. 489, 6 March 1847.

assessing whether progress was being made in actually preparing the constitution and was not limited to empty talk.

The *List* first outlined several basic administrative steps. Preparations for Provincial Assemblies (Ziyi Ju) would be made in 1908, and in 1909 elections for all these assemblies would be held. In that same year, the regulations for the National Assembly (Zizheng Yuan) would be issued and selections made for posts in the temporary National Assembly, with a general election of representatives to be held for the opening of the National Assembly in 1910. Regulations for local autonomy, at the city-, town-, and village-levels, were announced in 1908, with a preparatory charter for local self-government of towns and townships promulgated and a Self-Government Instruction Office (Zizhi Yanjiusuo) set up in 1909. Self-government would then be introduced progressively down to the village-level, a process to be completed to the township-level by 1913 and to the village-level by 1914.

The *List* also envisaged a system of eventually registering voters by moving from the survey and registration on the traditional basis of households (*hukou*) to a more modern census (*renkou*) system, though still cognizant of households, rather than individuals. Rules governing household registration were promulgated in 1908, with the total number of households surveyed in 1909. The total population of the provinces was to be surveyed in 1911, a new household registration law to be promulgated in 1912, and a *Household Registration Law* (Huji Fa) enacted in 1913. Addressing government finances, the *List* stipulated that: in 1908, a fiscal charter would be promulgated; in 1909, an investigation undertaken of the total amount of revenues and expenditures of the provinces; in 1910, provisional national accounts would be drawn up, and an *Accounting Law* promulgated; in 1915, a budget and funds for the imperial household and an Auditing Office (Shenji Yuan) would be established, while the *Accounting Law* would be implemented. In 1916, a final budget for the year would be released, as well as the estimates for the following year's budget.

The *List* also noted that the barriers between the Manchu and Han ethnic groups would be dissolved: in 1908, a modified Banner system would be established, and in 1915 the modifications would be completed, eliminating these ethno-institutional barriers.

The *List* envisaged universal education: in 1908, simple literacy textbooks and essential textbooks for "citizens" (*guomin*) were to be edited, and then to be issued in 1909; from 1910 to 1912, literacy schools were to be promoted at local levels, so that by 1914, 1% of the general population (*renmin*) would be literate, by 1915 2%, and by 1916 5%.

The laws were a major item on the *List*: In 1908, the criminal law would be amended, and a new criminal law drawn up, as well as a civil law and commercial law, and criminal and civil procedural laws; in 1910, the new criminal law would be proclaimed; in 1913, the new criminal law would be enacted, and the civil law, commercial law, and criminal and civil procedural laws would be promulgated. In 1915, civil law, commercial law, and criminal and civil procedural laws would be enacted.

Addressing the bureaucracy and the rules governing officials, the *List* announced: in 1909, the central bureaucracy would be determined, as would the system of local officials in 1910; in 1911, the government would introduce civil service examinations, as well as new statutes governing appointments and official salaries; in 1912, the new central and local bureaucracy systems would be promulgated, to be introduced on a trial basis in 1914, and fully implemented in 1916.

Addressing the judiciary, the *List* set out the following envisaged milestones: in 1909, the *Law Establishing the Judiciary* (Fayuan Bianzhi Fa) would be promulgated, and courts at all levels in provincial capitals and commercial centers would be organized; in 1910, these judicial establishments (*shenpan ting*) would be set up in all provincial capitals and commercial centers, and then, from 1913 to 1915, in all localities. In addition, in 1909–1910, all police stations at local levels were to abolish torture, and from 1911 onwards, police patrols were to be organized, to be in place before 1915.

Finally, the Constitution was to be proclaimed in 1916, and an imperial ceremony enacting it would be held. In the same year, the Parliament (Yihui) would proclaim the *Law of the Houses of Parliament* (Yiyuan Fa) and the *Electoral Law* (Xuanju Fa), and the election of members of Parliament would be held. In that year, the Privy Council (Bide Yuan) would also appoint its members (*guwen-dachen*).[72]

Reactions to these documents issued by the Qing court widely differed across China's provinces, prefectures, and counties. Apart from those who

[72] These measures are outlined in full in *Qingmo Choubei Lixian Dang'an Shiliao* (Late-Qing Preparatory Constitution Archives and Documents), v. 1, pp. 61–67, and are summarized in Hou Yijie, *Ershi Shiji Chu Zhongguo Zhengzhi Gaige Fengchao* (Political Reform Trends in Early Twentieth Century China), Renmin Chubanshe, 1993, pp. 207–208.

insisted on amendments to the content and provisions of these documents, the National Assembly petitioners from the three north-eastern provinces stressed the long-term "salivating" effect of the measures on the Great Powers and so hoped that the National Assembly would be convened as soon as possible to provide a constitutional system which would guarantee China's sovereignty, pointing out that the introduction of a constitution at the end of a nine-year preparatory period might be too late. Some calmer people, such as the petitioner representatives from Zhejiang, believed that, since the establishment of the Provincial Assemblies (Ziyi Ju) and the National Assembly (Zizheng Yuan) were following the timetable for introducing legislation and setting up offices, constitutional work would be carried out in a planned and orderly fashion, otherwise it would always be caught up a pointless debate which would prevent concrete action.

The excitement surrounding the preparation of the constitution was growing and the actual pace did not let up. Even the successive deaths of the Guangxu Emperor and the Empress Dowager Cixi on 14 and 15 November 1908, respectively, did not affect the advancing work on the constitution. The Regent Zaifeng had been previously appointed by Cixi and he continued his work in compliance with the last will and testament of the Guangxu Emperor which stated: "Break with the accumulation of bad habits, and adhere to the previously issued proclamations and edicts, dealing effectively with matters in compliance with the annual preparatory timetable, so that in just nine years the constitution can be proclaimed". Zaifeng had no intention of changing the pace. Zaifeng was young and inexperienced, but he was committed to putting his best efforts into the constitutional cause. He said in response to the provincial congress petition campaign: "The provincial petition representatives will come to Beijing to attend the National Assembly, and if we do not set an early deadline, I fear that this will disappoint the aspirations of the nation and alienate the citizens from their rulers. At present, it is an urgent matter that we set the rules so that we can announce the deadline for the next meeting of the National Assembly as early as possible. We must on all accounts stick to our word, otherwise nothing can be implemented".[73] On the day after the new emperor, the Xuantong Emperor, ascended the throne, Zaifeng demanded that "it would be disrespectful not to continue the tasks which the previous monarch set out to complete". On 8 December, the Qing court requested that all authorities strictly implement the preparatory constitutional schedule that had been established.

The power shift led to political strife within the court and, in response to Yuan Shikai's power and the potential threat he posed, Zaifeng and the constitutionalists sought to strip Yuan of his power and came to a decision to let Yuan return home temporarily in January 1909 to recuperate from an illness. Yuan Shikai had no alternative but to "return home to farm", in the company of his son Yuan Keding. 受 The impact of Yuan's retirement was that the court now lacked someone with sufficient political experience and military resources; after Yuan retired as commander of the main Qing army, it was controlled by his former ministry, leaving the possibility open for Yuan Shikai to re-enter the political center. These complex political and personnel conflicts did not, however, halt the preparation of the constitution. On 17 February, on the basis of *Charter of the Provincial Assemblies* and *Charter for the Selection of Delegates to the Provincial Assemblies*[74] issued on 22 July in the previous year in the name of the Committee for Drawing up Regulations for Constitutional Government (Xianzheng Biancha Guan) and the National Assembly (Zizheng Yuan), the Qing court ordered that every province had to establish a Provincial Assembly within the current year. In fact, from March onwards, a number of provinces began to report on the progress of their work towards the preparation of the constitution, and the Committee for Drawing up Regulations for Constitutional Government and local authorities initiated a working dialogue. Information on the provincial preparatory work was then compiled and reported by the Committee, and each provincial governor's office was then urged to set up a Constitutional Preparatory Office to promote this work within each

[73] In *Shengjing Shibao*, 21 July 1908, quoted in Hou Yijie, *Ershi Shiji Chu Zhongguo Zhengzhi Gaige Fengchao* (Political Reform Trends in Early Twentieth Century China), Renmin Chubanshe, 1993, pp. 217–218.

[74] These two documents were prepared by former students in Japan who worked in the Committee for Drawing up Regulations for Constitutional Government, as the National Assembly had not in fact yet been established.

province. Beginning in January 1909, the Committee also sent out telegrams urging slow-moving provinces to speed up this work. Young people who had studied abroad, especially those who were graduates in law and politics, played an important role in the preparation of the Provincial Assemblies, as no less than 149 members of this cohort became delegates of the Provincial Assemblies, and this would have made it easier to reach agreement in subsequent consultative meetings and provincial liaison.

On 14 October 1909, the Provincial Assemblies of all provinces (with the exception of Xinjiang which came later) opened, and their responsibilities were very specific, ranging from determining final financial accounts, tax laws, and public debt to the election of members of the National Assembly, as well as responding to matters for consultation between the National Assembly and the provincial governor, and even giving the authority to examine violations by the provincial governor to the Provincial Assembly in the event of his violation of the law. In addition, the Provincial Assemblies had the power to petition the National Assembly, and all these responsibilities showed the beginnings of the exercise of constitutional power. Despite the many problems in the charter governing the Provincial Assemblies, decentralization and increased participation in politics were so new that local gentry and chambers of commerce were actively involved, at least in setting up organizations, like the Jiangsu Assembly Consultative Council Research Association (Jiangsu Ziyi Ju Yanjiu Hui), to participate in the preparation of the Council. The criteria for voters and potentially elected members were very broad for that time; voters had to be men with more than 5000 yuan in business capital or real estate, and to have lived in the province for ten years or more, while potential candidates had to be men with more than 10,000 yuan in business capital or real estate in the province, and also to have lived in the province for more than 10 years. College students, primary school teachers, and illiterate charity workers did not have the right to vote or to be elected; low-level officials, soldiers, and policemen were also ineligible. The speaker of the house and other positions in the Provincial Assembly were all democratically elected within the Assembly. In fact, the identities of the first members of the provincial parliament and the speaker of the house were not surprising: there were many people with traditional honorary titles, but many other active members of the Provincial Assembly had studied abroad, received Western-style educations, or were knowledgeable about the West. Activists in the constitutional movement, including Zhang Jian, Tan Yankai, and Pu Dianjun, began to use the Provincial Assemblies to conduct the earliest experiments in defending constitutional politics. The establishment of the Provincial Assemblies and the launch of local self-government movements led to the emergence of more constitutionalist groups, and a large number of civil society political organizations rapidly began providing wide-ranging grassroots political resources for the wave of parliamentary petitions soon to be directed at the Provincial Assemblies.

On 18 January 1909, the Qing court promulgated the *Charter of Towns and Local Self-Government* and the *Charter of Towns and Local Elections*, and even though in the eyes of some intellectuals the Chinese people were not sufficiently open intellectually to these developments, the majority of the rural gentry at the grassroots level became a great force for political reform. In fact, the promulgation of reform documents led almost directly to widespread change. Problems were indeed widespread, with abuses by local officials, chicanery by ethically questionable members of the gentry, a lack of public understanding, and the occasional conflict and even riot in the reform of local self-government, all of which little dented the enthusiasm and effectiveness of constitutional reform sprees throughout the country by constitutionalists (government officials, intellectuals, and the gentry).

Once key institutional reforms were promoted and agreement was reached on their implementation, more radical criticism and action by constitutional advocates who previously lacked a legitimate basis now had legitimacy. The previous petitions regarding the opening of the National Congress were spontaneous acts of civil organization, and now radical constitutionalists were using the Provincial Assembles as a legitimate platform for a more concerted constitutional push. As head of the Jiangsu Provincial Assembly, Zhang Jian, in the name of that body, initiated the petition calling for convening the National Congress in conjunction with the Provincial Assemblies of the other provinces, and a petitioners' group composed of representatives or listed representatives from 19 provinces submitted the petition to the Censorate (Ducha Yuan) on 16 January 1910. The stated reasons for convening the National Congress were: (1) only with a National Congress could the people truly participate in politics and then supervise the government; (2) only with the establishment as soon as possible of the National Congress could the government's failures in foreign affairs and decision-making be reduced; and (3) with a National Congress, the people could entrust specific responsibility to the cabinet, rather than to the emperor. In a proclamation issued on 30

January, Zaifeng responded to the petitioners, stating it was the established policy to continue to advance the constitution, but at a measured pace in the nine-year period of preparation which, coupled with a program of introducing universal national education, would not be a problem. The petition group has not yet completed its tasks, before it could set up a National Congress Support Group to mobilize individuals and groups in the provinces. So, on 27 June, Zaifeng once again rejected these requests of the petitioners' group. The delegation continued to draw lessons from the petition and proceeded to expand its ranks, increasing membership of the delegation to include members of the Provincial Assemblies and establish branches of the National Congress Support Group. On 4 July 1907, the second *Russo-Japanese Agreement* was signed wresting special interests from China in its three north-eastern provinces, and on 22 August Japan signed a treaty with Korea, signifying that Japan had in fact annexed Korea. For most people, this was a sign that China's demise was imminent, and the political atmosphere surrounding the petition to fast-track the National Congress had become so intense that the majority of provincial governors were calling for the convening of the National Congress and a responsible cabinet. Prominent among the reasons cited in *Provincial Governors' Draft Memorial Calling for Setting up the Cabinet and National Congress* for why 19 provincial governors were calling for the establishment as soon as possible of a responsible cabinet and National Congress was the following: "With the conclusion of the Russo-Japanese Agreement and the attendant demise of Korea, the changing balance of power between the Major Powers require da change of policy, the current danger far exceeding that when Emperor Dezong (the Guangxu Emperor) was in office. There was no longer any possibility of delay. The Cabinet and National Congress must be immediately established, in a joint effort by all levels, and we are afraid that if there is any delay, and we wait several years in accordance with the timetable it will be too late to do anything!"[75] At this time, in the face of incessant calls to speed up the convocation of parliament emanating from the center down to the local level, Zaifeng heeded the advice of Zaize and decided to advance the convocation of the National Congress to 1913, but asked for the dissolution of the petitioners' delegation. Although some constitutionalists expressed their approval of this outcome, with Zhang Jian for

[75] Quoted in Hou Yijie, *Ershi Shiji Chu Zhongguo Zhengzhi Gaige Fengchao* (Political Reform Trends in Early Twentieth Century China), Renmin Chubanshe, 1993, p. 315.

example arranging for the Jiangsu Provincial Assembly to telegraph the National Assembly "expressing thanks", a greater number of people were very dissatisfied and when the petition groups telegraphed the provincial assemblies asking whether the petition groups should be discontinued at this time, there was widespread opposition. Several Provincial Assemblies sent back messages warning the petition group in Beijing not to disband, but to continue efforts to urge the Congress to be convened as soon as possible. The upshot of the repeated deliberations was that the petition groups decided to dissolve, but the Parliamentary Support Group would begin to participate in the work of constitutional amendment and the formation of political parties.

The government's preparatory work did not stop, and after the announcement in November of an early session of Parliament in 1913, the Qing court ordered the Constitutional Review Office (Bian Cha Guan) on 6 December to revise its preparatory planning in accordance with the new schedule to accommodate the changes brought about by the shortened timeframe. Nevertheless, the constitutionalists of the three northeastern provinces and Zhili continued to encourage society to put pressure on the Qing government to try to achieve the goal of convening a parliament immediately. However, the appeals, the petition with hundreds of thousands of signatures, and the efforts of various constitutional organizations publicized constitutional politics at street rallies, through publications, appeals for signatures, and newspaper articles, all effectively contributed to the popularization of constitutional ideas throughout China at the beginning of the twentieth century. However, the predictable result was that the tide of petitions did not achieve the immediate purpose of Parliament being convened, which greatly fueled discontent among those who had initially been less convinced of the promises of the Qing government and wanted to achieve constitutionalism as soon as possible. However, the number of people involved in the constitutional movement and the preparation of the Constitution became more visible, though there was a gradual increase in the number of constitutionalists who turned towards the Republican revolution.

The parties involved in preparing and implementing the constitution did not stop working because of the resistance and problems they encountered. On 3 October 1910, when the second session of the Provincial Assemblies was taking place, the first meeting of the National Assembly was held in Beijing. Documentation reveals that the members began to exercise their powers earnestly and seriously at the second session of the

Provincial Assemblies, and on most questions differences of opinion and power struggles between the Governors and the Provincial Assemblies were highlighted. Specific bills varied from province to province, but conflicts between Provincial Assemblies and Governors mostly focused on budget matters, such as the submission of projected budgets and arrangements of revenue and expenditure.[76] A historical overview shows that these new steps towards the constitution were more like experiments or trial and error, but the results could not be overlooked. For example, if we suspect all parties, especially those governors who headed lazy or corrupt administrations, we touch on the fact that national budget forecasts at this time were very complex. The taxes of the central Ministry of Finance (Duzhi Bu) and those of local authorities were not differentiated, which resulted in a very rough annual budget for the country, which could only serve as a general reference for the Provincial Assemblies, so it is understandable how difficult it was for a provincial governor to present a detailed budget of projected income and expenditure in a timely manner. The circumstances and criteria faced by the Assembly representatives and governors of different provinces were of course different, so much so that the budgets finally adopted after heated debates never seemed to satisfy all parties, and conflicts between the Assemblies and governors seemed inevitable.

At the time of the drafting of the "charters" governing the Provincial Assemblies, the Preparatory Office of the National Assembly was already involved in the work. On 10 July 1909, *Charter of the National Assembly* was nearly finalized, but in light of problems related to *Charter of the Provincial Assemblies*, special care was taken in drawing it up. For example, in view of Yu Shimei's belief that the National Assembly had too much power, "in future the state could use civil rights to oppose the government and use the National Assembly to standardize public opinion". So the final text of the *Charter of the National Assembly* was

[76] For example, Guangxi was considering the implementation of the bill to ban opium, which had been discussed and approved at the previous session; Zhejiang was protesting the Ministry of Posts and Communications' orders that were held to deprive civil rights by ordering changes in laws; Hunan was concerned with the problem of issuing public debt; Guangdong was placing time limits on gambling; and Yunnan was discussing the increase in salt prices ... all these conflicts between the Provincial Assemblies and the Governors hinged on the Assemblies' defending their own powers and the Governors infringing on those powers and laws given that they were still accustomed to exercising power arbitrarily.

amended to read "Provincial Assemblies and Governors must exercise caution in matters of disagreement, as in disagreements between the Provincial Assemblies of different provinces, and such matters must be referred to the National Assembly for arbitration and after a decision is reached, the President (Zongcai) and Vice-President (Fu-Zongcai) of the National Assembly must submit the decision to the throne, requesting the issue of an edict announcing the decision". This was a far cry from the "power to make decisions" provided for in the previous *Charter of the Provincial Assemblies*, and clearly there would be many similar revisions. In any case, on 23 August 1909, the *Charter of the National Assembly* presented to the throne by the Provincial Assemblies and the Junji Chu was approved and compliance from the central to local levels commenced. On 26 October, the electoral charter of the National Assembly was also in the process of approval by the throne. Because the transition to convening the Parliament had not yet taken place, the establishment of the National Assembly was of an interim nature in preparation for the formal Parliament and the establishment of a responsible cabinet. This was of course flawed politically since the constitution needed to be formulated and amended by the Parliament and then approved by the monarch. At this time, the legislative power of the National Assembly was incomplete, and its responsibilities were not balanced with those of the Junji Chu. If there was disagreement between a bill of the National Assembly and the views of the Junji Chu, then the matter had to be submitted to the monarch for "Imperial arbitration", the result being that the monarch remained responsible for the bill. In the eyes of the constitutionalists, there were different degrees of compromise between the charters governing the Assemblies and their electoral provisions, and a real constitutional system was still a long way off. For example, some of the Assembly members were "selected by the monarch", as was the President (Zongcai). In the subsequent process of amendment, the Charter came to have a ratio of equal numbers of members "selected by the monarch" and those who were elected (100 each). In the view of activist constitutionalists, this seriously affected the full participation of the people in politics, so in debates on this issue in the National Assembly, there was an invisible divide between members belonging to the "government party" and those belonging to the "democratic party". However, as a legislative body had been created, the institutional framework of constitutionalism was being set up. The National Assembly had the power to decide on the state budget, final accounts, tax law and public debt; the right to draw up new legal statutes outside the Constitution and its revised powers had devolved to the National Assembly. The constitutional preparatory work in fact showed a marked advance. Constitutionalists who wanted to participate in politics had a legitimate power platform to assert civil rights, push for convening the Parliament and improving the constitutional system, and constitutionalists hoped to refine the framework of the constitution and strived to meet constitutional standards in their subsequent work. It was an important fact that there were twelve outstanding graduates who had studied abroad among the "selected" members of the National Assembly. These included Wang Rongbao and Wang Jingfang, who graduated from Waseda University, and Lu Zongyu, who graduated from Tokyo's Hōsei University. They worked together and even combined roles as elected members in the National Assembly with their constitutional work. On 23 September 1910, at the official opening ceremony of the National Assembly, the speaker of the house, Pulun (1874–1927), announced that the opening was "a grand occasion that has never been held for millennia in our country". At the beginning of the following month, the National Assembly began to perform its deliberative duties. The wrangling and heated arguments during the assembly's first three months (4 October 1910 to 11 January 1911) cannot be regarded as a happy constitutional transition for members. Decisions on "speeding up opening of the Parliament", "the impeachment of the Minister of the Junji Chu", and "amnesties for state crimes" were all pre-constitutional efforts to promote and exercise the power of those elected, and members were always fighting to hold their ground in difficult disputes with those forces in the Qing court who were essentially conservative and opposed to the constitution per se. For example, the "impeachment of the Minister of the Junji Chu" developed from opposition to a minister's infringement of the law to direct dissatisfaction with the monarch's decisions, the core issue being to make full use of legitimate power to provide the most effective resistance to the authoritarian system. During the first sessions, the members did not secure the passage of all bills, but people could still see the effective practice of constitutional politics. *Empire Daily* (Diguo Ribao), on 14 January 1911, reported that the bills discussed "are the most important matters in the early constitutional legislative period of our country, but all those passed were without defects, which is not to say that these sessions were not also colorful".[77] If we look through the documents from those sessions, we see that the bills debated in the house were valuable precedents for constitutional politics in the early twentieth century.

The constitutional preparations were the last dangerous political operation that the Manchu nobles had to pull off to save their rule. Although that rule had lasted for nearly three hundred years (and the Qin-Han polity itself had lasted for two thousand years), the rulers now seemed impotent in handling any of the state's affairs: on 27 March 1911, the Qing government accepted six amendments by Russia to the *Treaty of Nerchinsk*; and on 27 April the Revolutionary Alliance led by Huang Xing staged an uprising at Huanghuagang in Guangzhou, which was evidence of the discontent and resistance of society as a whole. Although the provisional charter regarding cabinet appointments and offices was in place on 8 May, the final outcome was that nine of the 13 cabinet members were appointed outright by the court, with the imperial family accounting for seven of the appointments, a result that was totally contrary to constitutional principles. The cabinet was made up of members of the imperial family and was not to be accountable to Parliament, not to mention that it was established without a meeting of parliament, and so was only accountable to the monarch. The imperial cabinet on 9 May countersigned the imperial decree implementing the policy whereby the main railways in China were state-owned, on 17 May refused the request of the National Assembly to convene an interim meeting, and then requested that Sheng Xuanhuai act on behalf of the Qing government, When on 20 May Sheng met with the British, French, German, and American four-nation banking group to sign the Huguang Railway loan contract, people's expectations of the Qing government-led reforms had almost totally evaporated.[78] In

[77] Quoted in Hou Yijie, *Ershi Shiji Chu Zhongguo Zhengzhi Gaige Fengchao* (Political Reform Trends in Early Twentieth Century China), Renmin Chubanshe, 1993, p. 378.

[78] In 1905, the Yue-Han (Guangdong-Hankou) railway was redeemed from an American who had acquired the rights. The Guangxu Emperor issued a decree that this railway would be built with private stock of developers from three provinces, without foreign capital. In 1908, Zhang Zhidong was put in charge of the Yue-Han and Chuan-Han railway projects, and he approached the British to secure a loan to construct these railways. In 1909, the Qing government proposed to banks from Britain, France, and Germany that it would sign a railway loan contract, after which banks from the United States were inserted into the proposal. In October, Zhang Zhidong died, and the loan negotiations were handed over to the Ministry of Posts and Communications. In August

a letter from a foreign tax officer at Changsha Customs to his superior General Tax Department in the middle of this month (16 May), it was clear to foreign bystanders what they thought of the crisis situation at the time:

> China's future seems bleak. I think a revolution is inevitable soon. Revolution is now being openly advocated and has received general sympathy, and the Government has not taken any preventive measures, but has been playing around with all its trickery.[79]

Members of the Provincial Assemblies were displeased by the establishment of the imperial cabinet and the unconstitutionality of its governance; on 12 May, a total of 41 representatives of the Provincial Assemblies of 19 provinces (which increased to 62 in the course of the meeting) arrived in Beijing to convene the second meeting of the Federation of Provincial Assemblies.[80] Although twelve bills had been submitted and discussed by delegates, the central issue had shifted to how to bring

1909, the Hubei Constitutional Preparatory Committee held a dissenting meeting. In October, after the establishment of the Provincial Assembly, a motion was put forward to refuse to borrow foreign debt to build roads, and the Hubei Commercial Railway Association was established. A series of subsequent initiatives led to the Ministry of Posts and Communications agreeing in March 1910 to set up a commercial railway company in Hubei, and to issue shares to finance setting it up. At the same time, Hunan also under the leadership of its Provincial Assembly strove to obtain approval from the Ministry of Posts and Communications to build the railway themselves. In January 1911, Sheng Xuanhuai became Minister of Posts and Communications, and on 20 May, on behalf of the Qing government, Sheng Xuanhuai signed the Huguang Railway loan contract with the four-nation banking group, triggering the Huguang and Sichuan railroad protection movement.

[79] *Diguozhuyi yu Zhongguo Haiguan* (Imperialism and China's Maritime Customs), v. 13, Beijing: Zhonghua Shuju, 1964, p. 88. This reference is quoted in Jin Chongji, *Ershi Shiji Zhongguo Dagang* (Outline of Chinese History in the Twentieth Century), Beijing: Shehui Kexue Wenxian Chubanshe, 2009, p. 47.

[80] In February 1910, the petitioners from the Provincial Assemblies calling for convening the National Assembly were gathered in Beijing, and they proposed organizing a meeting of a Federation of Provincial Assemblies. The purpose of the meeting was to study political issues common to the different provinces and to coordinate the work of the Provincial Assemblies, while at the same time interpreting and looking at revising the limits on the rights of the Provincial Assemblies included in *Charter of the Provincial Assemblies* drawn up by the Committee for Drawing up Regulations for Constitutional Government (Xianzheng Biancha Guan). On 12 August, 50 delegates from the Provincial Assemblies of 20 provinces took part in the first meeting of the Federation of Provincial

down the imperial cabinet and establish a truly constitutional responsible cabinet. In order to achieve this goal, the parliamentarians even overlooked errors in political procedure; their overall objective in opposing the inclusion of members of the imperial family in the cabinet was reduced to simply opposing the imperial family filling the prime minister's (*zongli dachen*) position and retaining the imperially appointed minister of state (*guowu dachen*). This outcome meant that the legitimacy of the imperial cabinet had the de facto recognition of the delegates. The imperial cabinet then became more brazen, telling Assembly members that the Federation's claims were "contrary to the constitutional monarchy and preclude consent". This led to a stronger resolve to overthrow the imperial cabinet, followed by a document signed by the leader and 42 members of the Provincial Assemblies, *Further Submission to the Censorate Calling for a Proclamation Reorganizing the Cabinet*, and *Report to the Federation of Provincial Assemblies of the Zhili Provincial Assembly*, which both more clearly announced that the Imperial Cabinet was seriously not in keeping with the principles of the constitutional monarchy. The wording of the document was unequivocal in its attitude to the Qing government, and the language in the *Report*, sent to the provinces and published in the press, had the tone of a political ultimatum:

> …… If we want to save the country from extinction, we must have a policy of national salvation. If we want to determine such a policy, we must have a completely representative cabinet, and if we want that, we must first break with the imperial family as a political class. …[81]

The two documents indicated that the Federation of Provincial Assemblies was issuing a larger challenge to the Qing government. When the cabinet decisively responded ("Subjects should all comply with the imperially determined constitutional outline and not present disorderly requests, in order to conform to the principle of constitutional monarchy"), the Federation issued its *Further Petition on the Cabinet Issue for the Information of All Provincial Groups*, which simply pointed out: "All pernicious

Assemblies, passing the *Charter* and the rules governing Assembly meetings. The chair of the meeting was Tang Hualong, and the deputy-chair was Pu Dianjun.

[81] Quoted in Hou Yijie, *Ershi Shiji Chu Zhongguo Zhengzhi Gaige Fengchao* (Political Reform Trends in Early Twentieth Century China), Renmin Chubanshe, 1993, pp. 422–423.

aspects of politics today have been created by our government".[82] Thereafter, the Assembly members in the Federation shifted away from their earlier focus on patient compromise and accommodation with government forces to oppose foreign aggression, thereby abandoning the Qing government itself. During the Federation's meetings, the media echoed this political position and began to call on the people to defeat the government. On 6 June, the newspaper *Shibao* suggested that present problems were "no longer simply the question of a loan or whether a railway was state-owned, but of fundamental corruption that seemed insoluble".[83]

At the same time as the Provincial Assemblies launched the Federation meetings on 12 May, Hunan and Hubei had begun their struggle for railroad rights. After the Federation sessions closed on the 25th and had issued the *Report to the Federation of Provincial Assemblies of the Zhili Provincial Assembly*, on 6 June the Guangdong Railroad Company (Yuelu Gongsi) held a general meeting of shareholders and adopted a resolution to defend railroad rights. Yet it was the railroad rights protection campaign that broke out in Sichuan in mid-June that rocked the Qing government's already shaky foundations. When news of the Huguang Railway loan contract arrived in Chengdu, and constitutionalists and local gentry learned of the loss of railroad rights, the President and Vice-President of the Provincial Assembly, Pu Tianjun and Luo Lun, decided to mobilize citizens to fight for their rights and interests through the Railway Protection Support Association which they established, and which won wide support. Over the course of twenty days, more than 100,000 people from all walks of life and political parties joined the Railway Protection Support Association, which put pressure on the Qing government by protesting locally and sending people to deliver a petition in Beijing. The Qing government's misjudgment and high-handed response triggered a more general revolt, and on 24 August Chengdu College went on strike and there was a general market strike through the city. The Sichuan Governor Zhao Erfeng carried out a military crackdown, not only placing Pu Dianjun and others under house arrest, but ordered a massacre in which dozens were killed and injured. On 8 September Support Associations from many different places gathered in Chengdu, sparking a wider

[82] Ibid., p. 423.

[83] Ibid., p. 426.

political storm. In fact, the news that Duanfang had been ordered to lead the Qing army from Wuhan to Sichuan to suppress the demonstrators led the New Army to stage a preemptive uprising, and the constitutionalist-led railway protection movement became the trigger for the subsequent Wuchang Uprising. Duanfang himself was also killed in Zizhou on 27 November.

The essence of the railroad protection movement originated with the determined support for the constitutional system and the rights of the citizens among the bourgeois representatives who began to hold seats in the Provincial Assemblies and the National Assembly. As Zhang Lan and Luo Lun pointed out to Governor Zhao Erfeng: "If the loan contract is not debated in the parliament and cabinet, then those with rights in the provinces cannot debate the issue in the Provincial Assemblies, which actually violates commercial law, deprives businesses of their right to act, and violates the law and everything associated with the law. Such a constitution is deceitful chicanery".[84]

The government's preparatory constitutional work was still underway. On 3 July 1911, Pulun, Zaize, Chen Bangrui, Li Jiaju (1871–1938), and Wang Rongbao (1878–1933) began to discuss drafting the Constitution. Prior to that, on 5 November 1910, the Qing court had appointed Pulun and Zaize to be responsible for drafting the Constitution, but such a procedure was totally unconstitutional, and the constitutionalists declared that the constitution had to be written by "representatives of the people" and then submitted to the monarch to decide on and approve. That was the legal process. Since the convening of the Parliament had been delayed, at least the people who drafted the constitution should not have been appointed by the monarch. Pulun did in fact also consult with the Junji Chu, but the text of the Constitution "after future revisions

[84] Peng Fen, "Xinhai Xun Qing Zhengbian Fayuan Ji" (Origins of the Anti-Qing Coup of 1911), *Xinhai Geming* (The 1911 Revolution), v. 4, p. 366, quoted in Hou Yijie, *Ershi Shiji Chu Zhongguo Zhengzhi Gaige Fengchao* (Political Reform Trends in Early Twentieth Century China), Beijing: Renmin Chubanshe, 1993, p. 209.

Zhao Erfeng on 30 August sent a telegram to the government cabinet stating the Ministry of Posts and Communications "abandoned the Constitution, in a spirit of authoritarianism that the people find difficult to accept. All disputes about treaties, railways, and loans must be resolved on the basis of the Constitution and not by suppressing the railroad movement". Ref: *Sichuan Baolu Yundong Shiliao* (Materials of the Sichuan Railroad Protection Movement), quoted in Hou Yijie, *Ershi Shiji Chu Zhongguo Zhengzhi Gaige Fengchao* (Political Reform Trends in Early Twentieth Century China), Beijing: Renmin Chubanshe, 1993, p. 457.

would be submitted to the National Assembly to be fully debated, and then resubmitted to the throne with a request to promulgate it", but that final proposal was denied. There was widespread anger and abhorrence at the unconstitutionality of this procedure, and the newspapers constantly reiterated this sentiment: "Having the authority of the monarch approve the Constitution is unwise because it can easily be despotism in disguise, with dire consequences!"[85] "Our people want to be constitutional citizens and not need to struggle for their basic survival, because that will solve nothing and will remove all hope!"[86] "Naturally, people also wonder whether there is anywhere in the twentieth century where an authoritarian regime has not been set up? Our people do not have full power today yet do not obviously appear to at loggerheads with the government. However, everyone is cynical about the government, complaining about its toxic aspects, and eventually there will be an explosion. In the past, because we hoped for peace, we could bow down and endure things for a time. Yet when the situation changed and people were forced into an intolerable position, there has been a rethink and there can be no thinking about the consequences!"[87] Li Jiaju and Wang Rongbao were writing the draft constitution, Chen Bangrui was responsible for the revisions, the changes were reviewed by Pulun and Zaize, and it was to be signed off by Zaifeng. By 20 September, the draft constitution was completed, and Wang Rongbao's diary records that "the draft comprises 86 articles with 116 clauses". On 10 October, the Wuchang Uprising took place, and even though in the two months around this time the constitution was still being amended, history had moved on and it was no longer the era of preparatory constitutional work. People soon forgot the laws that had been revised in the preparatory period, and the draft constitution had not yet been made public.[88] During the drafting of the Constitution, Li Jiaju

[85] *Da Gong Bao*, 30 November 1912, quoted in Hou Yijie, *Ershi Shiji Chu Zhongguo Zhengzhi Gaige Fengchao* (Political Reform Trends in Early Twentieth Century China), Beijing: Renmin Chubanshe, 1993, p. 402.

[86] *Shen Bao*, 1 July 1911, quoted in Hou Yijie, *Ershi Shiji Chu Zhongguo Zhengzhi Gaige Fengchao* (Political Reform Trends in Early Twentieth Century China), Beijing: Renmin Chubanshe, 1993, p. 402.

[87] *Shengjing Shibao*, 16 July 1911, quoted in Hou Yijie, *Ershi Shiji Chu Zhongguo Zhengzhi Gaige Fengchao* (Political Reform Trends in Early Twentieth Century China), Beijing: Renmin Chubanshe, 1993, p. 403.

[88] These include: 1908, the *Newspaper Code* [OR *Newspaper Law*] (Bao lü), *Code of Association and Assembly* (Jieshe jihui lü) and *Code of Police Contravention* (Weijing

and Wang Rongbao were excited to be finally able to participate in this work, and when Li Jiaju finished the writing he made a trip to Taishan and wrote a poem set to the rhymes of a poem written by Wang Rongbao at the Ming Tombs when they starting the work:

> The vast land subject to so many storms is today transformed
> As we leave the Central Plain's cultural relics abandoned
> This journey is not driven by a passion for nature
> But by the need to inscribe a new foundational monolith.[89]

Despite the back-and-forth between the imperial cabinet and the National Assembly over the division of responsibilities and power, after 10 October, cabinet members struggled to accommodate the revisions of the constitution and other proposals coming from members of the National Assembly, all responding to attacks from all directions by the Revolutionary Army. However, while this did not affect the second session of the National Assembly held on 22 October, the outbreak of revolution in various places resulted in many local elected members not being able to attend the meetings, so decisions were reached by the majority of those who could attend—mostly unelected, imperially appointed members. However, the elected lawmakers still submitted scathing bills, such as those attacking the Minister of Posts and Communications, Sheng Xuanhuai, and the Governor of Sichuan, Zhao Erfeng, and others. The core issues were seen to be organizing a cabinet with full responsibilities, convening the next year's Parliament, and submitting the Constitution to the National Assembly for approval. In the course of the meetings, dramatic developments were occurring throughout the country. On the 27th, local military commanders collectively telegrammed: "Change the constitution, in conformity to the constitution

Lü); 1910, *Draft Commercial Law of the Great Qing Dynasty* (Daqing Shanglü Cao'an), drafted by the Ministry of Agriculture, Industry and Commerce; 7 February 1910, the promulgation of *Law on the Establishment of Courts* (Fayuan Bianzhi Fa) and *Provisional Statutes of the Division of Judicial Areas* (Sifa Quyu Fenhua Chanxing Zhangcheng); and 1911, the promulgation of the *New Criminal Law* (Xin Xing Lü). The *Civil Code* (Minfa) was amended in September 1911 but was not promulgated.

[89] Quoted in Hou Yijie, *Ershi Shiji Chu Zhongguo Zhengzhi Gaige Fengchao* (Political Reform Trends in Early Twentieth Century China), Renmin Chubanshe, 1993, p. 405.

of the British monarchy".[90] On the 29th, the New Army in Shanxi staged an uprising and set up a military government, and on the 30th Yunnan proclaimed its independence. On that day, Zaifeng issued four proclamations in response to memorials from the National Assembly, the main content of which was implementing the constitution, lifting the ban on political parties, submitting the text of the Constitution to the National Assembly for consideration, and organizing a full cabinet. On 2 November, the power to formulate constitutional provisions was transferred to the National Assembly, whose members studied the provisions of the Constitution and the corresponding drafts, and on 3 November the National Assembly issued and promulgated *The Nineteen Important Constitutional Articles*[91]:

> Article One. The Qing Dynasty shall reign forever.
> Article Two. The Emperor shall be heavenly and inviolable.
> Article Three. The power of the Emperor shall be limited by the Constitution.
> Article Four. The order of succession to the throne shall be prescribed by the Constitution.
> Article Five. The Constitution shall be drafted by the National Assembly and promulgated by the Emperor.
> Article Six. The power of amending the Constitution shall belong to the Parliament.
> Article Seven. The members of the Upper House shall be elected by citizens from among those particularly eligible for the position.
> Article Eight. The Parliament shall elect, and the Emperor shall appoint the Prime Minister. The Prime Minister shall recommend,

[90] The 20th Division commander-general (*tongzhi*) Zhang Shaozeng, together with the commanders (*tongling*) Wu Xiangzhen, Pan Juying, Lu Yongxiang, and Lan Tianwei, sent a joint telegram, to which they appended a 12-item political platform. These military officers warned: "When the situation is precarious, and the masses turn their back [on a military career], we are really at risk; 'mid-way recruitment' means that soldiers are not committed, and the overall situation cannot be salvaged". On 1 November, Zhang Shaozeng and the others also took aim at the omission of the army's demands in the imperial proclamation; they demanded that the constitutional outline be removed and that a "constitutional army" be organized.

[91] Discussion of The *Nineteen Important Constitutional Articles* was led by Yi Zongkui, a graduate of Japan's Hōsei (Law and Politics) University who had drawn up the document.

and the Emperor shall appoint the other members of the Cabinet. The Imperial Princes shall never be eligible to be appointed as the Prime Minister, Cabinet Ministers, or Executive Leaders of any province.

Article Nine. If the Prime Minister, on being impeached by the Parliament, does not dissolve the Parliament, he must resign, but a Cabinet shall not be allowed to dissolve the Parliament more than once.

Article Ten. The Emperor shall assume direct control of the army and navy, but when the power is used with regard to internal affairs, he must abide by the special conditions to be decided by the Parliament; otherwise, the Emperor is prohibited from exercising such power.

Article Eleven. Imperial decrees cannot be made to replace the law, except in the event of immediate necessity, in which case decrees having the nature of a law may be issued in accordance with special conditions, but only when they relate to the execution of a law or what has by law been delegated.

Article Twelve. International treaties shall not be concluded without the consent of the Parliament, but the conclusion of peace or the declaration of war may be made by the Emperor; if the Parliament is not sitting, the approval of the Parliament is to be obtained afterwards.

Article Thirteen. Ordinances in connection with the Administration shall be settled by acts of the Parliament.

Article Fourteen. In case the Budget fails to receive the approval of the Parliament, the Government cannot act upon the previous year's Budget nor may items of expenditure not provided for in the Budget be appended to it. Further, the Government shall not be allowed to adopt extraordinary financial measures outside the Budget.

Article Fifteen. The Parliament shall fix the expenses of the Royal Household, and any increase or decrease therein.

Article Sixteen. Regulations in connection with the Royal Family must not conflict with the Constitution.

Article Seventeen. The two houses of Parliament shall establish the machinery of an administrative court.

Article Eighteen. The Emperor shall promulgate the decisions of the Parliament.

Article Nineteen. The Provisional Assembly shall act upon Articles 8, 9, 10, 12, 13, 14, 15, and 18, until the convening of the Parliament.

For the Chinese of the early twentieth century, there was nothing more exciting and comforting than such a constitutional achievement: the basic principles of the Constitution laid down in the *Nineteen Articles* far exceeded being an imitation of the Japanese Constitution and were closer to the constitutional arrangements of the United Kingdom. Immediately after the *Nineteen Articles* were issued, the National Assembly continued to meet to promote the constitutional work as quickly as possible. On 8 November, the National Assembly elected Yuan Shikai as Prime Minister of the Cabinet; on the 13th the National Assembly proposed convening a provisional citizens' conference; and, on the 16th Yuan Shikai became the responsible person for establishing the Cabinet.[92] On 20 November, the revised Charter of the National Assembly was approved, and the National Assembly convened its twelfth meeting and debated and passed two items that were historically significant: the law calling for the removal of the queue and the switch to using the solar calendar. However, from 4 November onwards, Guizhou, Jiangsu, Zhejiang, Guangxi, Fujian, and Guangdong had all declared their independence, and it was clear that the Qing dynasty did not have much time. In mid-January 1912, as prime minister of the cabinet, Yuan Shikai called for the implementation of the Republic, and so all the constitutional amendments and resolutions prepared by the constitutional reform group lapsed. Many members resigned and returned home or turned to the revolutionary camp. In early February 2012, in view of the fact that the cause of the constitutional monarchy could no longer possibly continue, Xu Dinglin, who succeeded Li Jiaju as speaker of the National Assembly, asked to dissolve the house. Later he joined the Kuomintang.[93]

[92] Previously, on 1 November 1911, Zaifeng had awarded the Prime Minister's position to Yuan Shikai in preparation for the organization of the Full Cabinet. In view of the constitutionalists' view that the appointment was not in compliance with constitutional principles, with which Yuan Shikai was fully acquainted, the fact that he still wanted the Qing dynasty to take back its mandate was put through the voting process. This provided him with legal conditions for his subsequent political activities, negotiations, and chicanery with the revolutionary parties.

[93] Xu Dinglin (1857–1915) graduated as a *juren* in 1882, and in 1890 was appointed as a *zhongshu* (secretary) in the Cabinet and so prepared documents in that office. In 1893 he was appointed as the Chinese consul to Peru, then from 1896 to 1903 he served in Anhui as a salt transportation official, then as head of Luzhou prefecture, serving by proxy as head of Fengyang prefecture, then as the Datong tax supervisor, circuit intendant of Anhui, and as a representative for the Wuhu Circuit Office. In 1903 he was transferred to Zhejiang province to serve as the General Supervisor of the Bureau of Foreign Affairs. In

On 12 February 1912, the Qing Emperor abdicated. The literature on the preparation of the constitution, the achievements of some of the political reforms that had begun, the widely disseminated constitutional ideas, and the political objectives of achieving constitutionality were bequeathed to post-Revolutionary China.

The Revolution of 1911

When Tang Caichang decided to return from Japan to promote the emperor's cause, Liang Qichao and Sun Yat-sen followed Tang's example. Tang Caichang's Self-Reliance Army had both royalists from the Emperor Protection Society and revolutionists from The Xingzhong Hui as members, showing that at that time reformists and revolutionists had the intention and desire to cooperate, but after the failure of the uprising of the Self-Reliance Army, there would be divisions between these two groups. In 1900, Sun Yat-sen's uprising in Huizhou failed, and he explained that his uprising was utterly unlike the Boxer Rebellion, as his was an insurrection staged by a political party. Later, the influence of the revolutionary cause gradually expanded in Tokyo, Shanghai, Hubei, and Hunan. In 1901, *Guomin Bao* (Citizen's News) began to explicitly advocate a national revolution. In April 1902, Zhang Binglin staged an anti-Manchu event mysteriously referencing the year 1660 as "the loss of the nation", titled the "242-year-old commemorative meeting of the demise of China". In October of that year, Cai Yuanpei helped students

1911 he was first appointed to supervise the Benxi Lake Coal and Iron Company, then became supervisor of the Salt Administration, and Fengtian negotiator. It was in 1906 that he was appointed head of the organization department of the Preparatory Constitution Association, and in September 1909 he was appointed head of the organization office of the Provincial Assembly of Jiangsu, and in 1910 was appointed as a member of the National Assembly in Beijing. In 1911 he served as President (Zongcai) of the National Assembly for several days. In 1905, Xu Dinglin and Zhang Jian had founded the Yaoxu Glass Company, and together with Yan Xinhou and others they founded the Haifeng Flour Company in Haizhou. In 1910, Xu Dinglin founded the Ganfeng Machine Oil-cake Factory, and in addition, with Zhang Jian and Yan Xinhou as partners, he ran Zhenjiang Kaicheng Pencil-case Factory, Ganyu Haigan Reclamation Pasture Company, Shanghai Tongli Machine Textile Sacking Company, Shanghai Dada River Shipping Company, and invested in Beijing Boli Leather Factory, Jingdezhen Jiangxi Porcelain Company, and other enterprises. With Zhang Jian and Shen Yunpei, he was one of the "three celebrities of northern Jiangsu" active in "national salvation through industry". He joined the Kuomintang in early 1913 and became a member of the Jiangsu Provincial Parliament.

from the Nanyang Public School students set up a "Patriotic Study Society" and began to advocate revolution among Shanghai's community of teachers and students. In 1903, in Hunan, Hubei, and Jiangsu provinces, a number of periodicals presenting propaganda advocating revolution made their appearance, including *Hunan Travelling Student Translations*, *Hubei Student Circle*, *Jiangsu*, and *Zhejiang Tide*. The rhetoric of the revolution was growing shriller by the day, and *The Revolutionary Army*, completed in May 1903 by Zou Rong (1885–1905), could almost be regarded as a manifesto for the revolutionary parties:

> As they return to life, ghosts emerge from the eighteen layers of hell and ascend to the thirty-third heaven, energetic and exuberant, recklessly scaling the heights, peerlessly proclaiming their supreme moral purpose, "revolution". Glorious is the revolution. Magnificent, the revolution.
> I follow the Great Wall, ascend the Kunlun Mountains, and swim up and down the Yangtze. I trace the Yellow River to its source, raise the flag of independence, strike the bell of freedom, call out to Heaven and earth, and shout myself hoarse, summoning my compatriots: Hear ye! Our China today must stage a revolution.[94]

The antagonism between the revolutionary parties and the constitutionalists developed to the point where the revolutionists tried to undermine the constitutionalists' activities and disrupt their meetings.[95] During the discussions in the National Assembly on the bill regarding

[94] Ref: *Zou Rong Wenji* (Works of Zou Rong), p. 38.

[95] After 1903, the Kang-Liang Group (or later the constitutionalists) and the revolutionaries were diametrically opposed. Sun Yat-sen regarded Kang Youwei and Liang Qichao as "slaves of the Manchus" and "Chinese traitors". In 1905, when the constitutionalists and the revolutionaries were fully engaged in debate, Sun Yat-sen even announced a policy of "first clearing out the traitors within and then expelling the foreign race" (Speech to the Public on Revising the New Articles of Our Charter). In 1906, Xu Qin, a member of the Emperor Protection Society was giving an address explaining the constitution at the Guangdong Guild in Manila, when Yang Hao and Ouyang Hongjun created a scuffle and Xu Qin was injured by Ouyang. In 1907, when the constitutionalist Ma Xiangbo arrived in Yokohama, the revolutionaries distributed leaflets calling for a market strike and workers strike calling for the overthrow of the Qing government: "Kill the Qing officials and kill the constitutionalist party". In 1908, in Singapore the Imperial Constitutional Society and the Qing Consul held a memorial service for the Guangxu Emperor and the Empress Dowager, which was totally disrupted by the revolutionists. When the Political News Society (Zhengwen She) established a local branch in Tokyo, the meeting was broken up by revolutionaries. Harassment and attacks of this nature against the constitutionalists were

"amnesties for state crimes", when the petitioning Parliamentary Support Group requested pardons for Kang Youwei and Liang Qichao, the revolutionists hurled vitriol at those arguing this position: "Who do Kang and Liang think they are? People have rejected the belief in gods, and there is no place in the world for them." The Support Group is crazy and would do the bidding of any vicious thug. Have they any sense of shame? Indeed, they don't. … They wield knives and will only desist when they have killed all their enemies. Now, Kang, Liang, and the Support Group are not only the enemies of the imperial court, but the common enemy of all our compatriots".[96]

At odds with the revolutionary party's radical attitude, after the defeat of the Revolutionary Party's Guangzhou uprising on 27 April 1911, Liang Qichao still calmly expressed his feelings about the revolution, well aware that a bloodless political revolution relying on the Qing government was over:

> Revolutionary uprisings are something our party does not even approve of. In the general sweep of history, revolution is an unfortunate event. The strength of any country, in the wake of a large-scale revolution, cannot be restored within a decade or even decades. Today's China is close to death, like a withering desiccated tree that cannot withstand buffeting storms, frost, and snow. …
> However, the Revolutionary Party is also saying: "Today, the life of our five-thousand-year-old nation and the lives of our four hundred million people are in the hands of the present government, but what hope does the present government have?! With each passing day, we lose more of our original strength. Whether we die by withering or by poison, we are still dying. But there is a choice! Although poisonous medicine can kill, it can sometimes also cure a disease, so the die is cast, and in the midst of a thousand deaths, we still seek life.

frequently instigated by the revolutionary parties. In 1910, when the second parliamentary petition organized by the domestic constitutionalists failed, the revolutionary parties in Tokyo even organized a group to stage celebrations.

[96] "Chouzai, Tongzhi Hui" (Ugly Indeed Are the Constitutional Associations), *Minli Bao*, issue of 28 November 1910, quoted in Hou Yijie, *Ershi Shiji Chu Zhongguo Zhengzhi Gaige Fengchao* (Political Reform Trends in Early Twentieth Century China), Beijing: Renmin Chubanshe, 1993, p. 376.

> Such a position is difficult for non-revolutionaries, and non-revolutionaries cannot respond. ... In essence, it might not be possible in China today to bring revolutionary theories to fruition but opposing revolutionary theories in today's China is even more pointless.[97]

In short, after the Coup of 1898, and especially after the signing of the *Boxer Protocol*, while moderate reformist forces flourished, radical revolutionary elements also grew rapidly.

As early as 1894, Sun Yat-sen (1866–1925), after failing to secure a meeting with Li Hongzhang, set up the Xingzhong Society in Hawaii and the group made revolution rather than reform its goal. Nearly half of its members were middle class overseas Chinese. In February of the following year, the Hong Kong Xingzhong Society was established. The Society's slogan was "Drive out the Tartars, Restore China, and Create a United Government", so Manchus were clearly regarded as targets of the revolution to be eliminated before a republic could be realized. Soon, Sun Yat-sen nimbly took advantage of the domestic chaos caused by the Sino-Japanese War, to organize a military uprising, but it was defeated. The organization of the Xingzhong Society continued apace, but Sun Yat-sen devoted most energy to raising funds and developing theories supporting revolution. In October 1896, Sun was lured into the Chinese embassy in London and effectively kidnapped by the Qing government, but under pressure from the British Foreign Office, he was released. During his nine months of observation in England, Sun developed ideas related to his Three Principles of the People. He recalled how in London he examined European political practices and, by "making friends with worthy and noble people in politics and society at large", gained political confidence:

> I first realized that our country needed to be rich and strong and develop civil rights like those powerful European countries, though her people did not yet enjoy these delights. However, European idealists nevertheless have social revolutionary movements. I made the decision once and for all to

[97] Ref: Liang Qichao, "Yue Luan Ganyan" (An Emotional Statement about the Turmoil in Guangdong), *Yinbing-shi Heji* (Anthology of the Ice Drinker's Studio), *Wenji* 27 (Prose volume 27), pp. 66–67.

> simultaneously accept the importance of a people's livelihood, as well as solving the problems of ethnic and civil rights. This was the origin of the three people's principles that I came to advocate.[98]

Initially, Sun did consider drawing on the power of the constitutionalists, and he hoped to work with the reformists, especially Liang Qichao. Prior to 1893, Sun Yat-sen practiced as a doctor in a missionary bookstore in Guangzhou, where he went to buy books and hoped to meet Kang Youwei, but this was also the time when Sun was setting up the Xingzhong Society and trying to make personal contacts. In 1895, Sun Yat-sen noticed in Japan that the word "revolution" was not limited to its simple meaning of violent insurrection, and he became more inclined to revolution. At the beginning of the 1898 Reforms, Kang attempted to avoid Sun as much as possible because of the latter's association with revolutionary parties. After the defeat of the 1898 Reforms, Liang Qichao and Sun Yat-sen had several discussions about cooperating in Japan. Moreover, Liang Qichao and thirteen reformists (referred to as the thirteen rebels against Teacher Kang) even co-wrote a letter to Kang Youwei, advocating participation in "reforming the republic". The discussions between Liang Qichao and the revolutionaries came so close to achieving a consensus that in the autumn of the 25th year of Guangxu (1899), Liang Qichao went to Hong Kong to discuss the merger of the two parties with Chen Shaobai. This roused Kang Youwei's ire and opposition, after which there was no longer any discussion and cooperation between the reformists and the revolutionaries.[99] After 1905 a verbal war began between the two parties to win popular support and political resources, and Sun Yat-sen regarded the battle with the Kang-Liang group as more important than the anti-Manchu struggle.

In 1903, Russia's refusal to commit to withdraw troops from China's Northeast and her attempts to continue to exercise control there caused an uproar among Chinese students in Japan, and in the wave of protests and even voluntary participation in an army against Russia, students formed the Military National Education Association (initially called the

[98] Quoted from Li Yunhan, *Zhongguo Jindai Shi* (Modern History of China), Taipei: Sanmin Shuju, 2018, p. 137.

[99] Chen Shaobai (1869–1934) was an important member of the Xingzhong Hui and a leading associate of Sun Yat-sen, who in 1900 set up the first anti-Qing revolutionary newspaper *Zhongguo Ribao*.

Volunteer Army or the Student Army). "In resisting Russia", according to the *Military National Education Accord* (Jun Guomin Jiaoyu Gongyue) issued by the Association and describing its main objectives, "the responsibility of the organization's members is preserving the integrity of the nation's territory and fostering the people's power". At this time, increasing numbers of people were convinced that the endless acquisitions of Chinese territory by Russia and the Great Powers were the result of the incompetence of the Qing government, so only the overthrow of the Qing government could really save the country. Many members of the Military National Education Association left Japan to return home to promote the anti-Russian and anti-Manchu movement. Geography determined the emergence of different revolutionary organizations; in Hunan, Huang Xing and others organized the Huaxing Society, and in Zhejiang, Gong Baoquan and others began to organize assassination squads which later led to the founding of the Restoration Society.

The emergence of the Huaxing Society benefited, of course, from the ideological enlightenment provided by Liang Qichao and other leaders of the earlier 1898 Reform Movement. The leading revolutionary figure Huang Xing had also studied at Zhang Zhidong's Lianghu Academy, and then went on to study as a government-funded student at the Hirobumi Academy in Japan. It was after returning to Hunan that he was radicalized and advocated revolution. Paralleling the Zhongxing Society, whose members were mainly Cantonese and overseas Chinese, the Huaxing Society mostly comprised Hunanese members, but unlike the Zhongxing Society whose leading members were mostly businessmen, most of the Huaxing Society's leaders were intellectuals. In order to expand its membership and acquire resources, Huang Xing contacted other revolutionary parties or underworld organizations. In fact, from the beginning of the Qing dynasty, there were always anti-Manchu secret societies, and an anti-Christian and anti-foreign xenophobic movement also continued throughout the late Qing period, as social contradictions and conflicts were intertwined. After 1900, the blind rejection of foreigners was gradually replaced by the idea of national salvation, and a nationalistic mood began to permeate elements of modern thought. The complex evolution of society saw the structures defined by the traditional four main social classes (scholars, farmers, artisans, and merchants) irrevocably changing. Popular organizations were also moving away from their traditional aims as they developed and participated in social change, while intellectuals with new ideas used the power of party organizations to participate in revolutionary activities. Sun Yat-sen noticed these obvious changes, and in discussing his strategy for founding a new nation, he talked about the history of the Heaven and Earth Society (Hongmen) and the possibility of borrowing from it:

> The Hongmen was founded by Ming loyalists after the demise of that dynasty and it rose [to prominence] in the time of the Kangxi Emperor. Prior to the Kangxi period, martyrs and those loyal to the Ming dynasty's cause had wanted to exert their efforts to restoring that dynasty. They swore oaths to not serve the Qing and to sacrifice their lives, if necessary, in uprisings that were struggles to the death with the Tartars. However, they never succeeded in resuscitating the Ming. With the reign of the Kangxi Emperor, the Qing began to flourish, and the Ming loyalists mostly perished. A handful of surviving loyalists, seeing that the opportunity had passed and that there was no hope of reviving the Ming, wanted to transmit the seeds of ethnic nationalism to the generations coming after them. Having as a general aim opposition to the Qing and the restoration of the Ming, they formed an organization waiting for a later opportunity to rise and advance the national cause.[100]

Indeed, in organizing the Zhongxing Society in Honolulu Sun Yat-sen had been helped by the Triad Society (Sanhe Hui), and later he even joined the Hongmen as a member called a "red truncheon" (1904), in an effort to transform the popular organization, and incorporate his revolutionary ideas into the Hongmen's charter. His strategy was highly pragmatic, because by bringing a revolutionary mass base to the developing situation he could gain ground, closing the gap he would have faced by only turning to the Qing government's constitutionalists. In November 1904, the Huaxing Society had not yet completed preparations for staging an uprising and faced extinction, with Huang Xing, Song Jiaoren, and Chen Tianhua having fled for their lives to Japan. Until July of the following year, Huang Xing and Sun Yat-sen held a number of meetings in Japan to discuss merging their two organizations.

The Restoration Society (Guangfu Hui) had its origins in the memorial meeting organized in Tokyo in April 1902 by Zhang Binglin and Qin Dingyi to mourn the 240th anniversary of "the loss of the nation" to

[100] Zhongguo Guomindang Dangshi Hui ed., *Guofu Quanji* (Complete Works of the Father of the Nation), v. 2, p. 12, quoted in Zhang Yufa, *Qingji de Lixian Tuanti* (Constitutional Groups of the Qing Period), Beijing: Peking University Press, 2011, p. 44.

the Manchus in 1644 and it eventually integrated with members of the Military National Education Association, including Gong Baoquan, Xu Shoushang, and Cai Yuanpei. It is generally believed that the Restoration Society was formally established in November 1904, and in January 1905 and 1906, Xu Xilin and Qiu Jin, respectively, joined the Society. The members of the Restoration Society pledged to "Restore the Han people, regain China's lands, sacrifice one's self for the nation, and die if necessary". This reveals that the overthrow of the Manchu government was the main task of the organization. Similarly, the leaders of the Restoration Society were intellectuals, its main members were scattered through other revolutionary parties and the New Army, and it drew on assistance from secret societies such as the Elder Brother Society (Gelao Hui) to spread its ideas and grow its ranks. Its main sphere of influence was Zhejiang, but it also had contact with the Huaxing Society in Hunan. One of the founders of the Restoration Society was Zhang Binglin (1869–1936), even though he was still serving his prison sentence because of the "*Subao* Incident" at the time the Restoration Society was being formally set up; his ideas as well as his activities after his release from prison greatly influenced the Society. Zhang had originally been a [military] adviser to Zhang Zhidong, and when he was later suspected of being a member of the "New Party" at the time of the 1898 Coup, he went into hiding in Taiwan. In 1899, in response to an invitation from Liang Qichao, he traveled to Japan, where he also contacted Sun Yat-sen and other revolutionary party members. As someone committed to an anti-Manchu revolution, Zhang found intellectual sustenance in the firmly racist ideas of Huang Zongxi, Gu Yanwu, and Wang Fuzhi. In 1903, Zhang wrote the Preface for Zou Rong's *Revolutionary Army*, describing it as "the leading textbook for educating today's citizens", but he emphasized the difference between the concepts of "restoration" and "revolution":

> When people replace a dynasty of the same race, it is called revolution; when people seize power from a different race, it is called genocide. When people replace a political system of people of the same race it is called a revolution, when people drive out those of a different race who were ruling them, it is called restoration. Today's China was earlier destroyed by

> retrograde barbarians, and so planning to regain ethnic self-determination is restoration, not revolution.[101]

He was unequivocal in his comments made in an article in *Minbao*:

> The revolution I am discussing is not a revolution but a restoration – a restoration of the Chinese race, a restoration of China's lands, and a restoration of China's political power.[102]

Zhang Binglin would eventually question the legitimacy of the representative system of government, and his ideological tendencies determined that he was at odds with the ideas of the Revolutionary Alliance, and especially of Sun Yat-sen. When he learned that Sun's goal was to set up a republic, he was quite shocked, clearly revealing the Confucian ideas that he had thoroughly imbued. Some said that in September 1908, Zhang Binglin wrote a letter to Duanfang declaring that he was personally "opposed to revolution", and given that at that time he planned to travel to India and become a monk as soon as he had sufficient funds, this declaration seems plausible. One of the leading members of the Restoration Society was Qiu Jin, who in 1907 wanted to set up a Restoration Army, for which the organization and formation of the team were quite spectacular. Qiu Qin's ideas were very close to those of Zhang Binglin, and in her *Proclamation Announcing the Restoration Army's Military System* she expressed very clear racist views:

> Today's situation bears down on us and we have truly been left with no space for ourselves. As a result, there will be a massive uprising to restore our situation, which will begin by avenging my two hundred million female compatriots who have for two hundred years been shamefully reduced to the position of slaves by the Manchus and then we can restore our vast

[101] *Zhonghua Minguo Kaiguo qian Geming Shi* (Revolutionary History of the Period before the Founding of the Republic of China), v. 1, p. 133, quoted in Zhang Yufa, *Qingji de Lixian Tuanti* (Constitutional Groups of the Qing Period), Beijing: Peking University Press, 2011, p. 332.

[102] *Minbao*, issue no. 8, p. 13, quoted in Zhang Yufa, *Qingji de Lixian Tuanti* (Constitutional Groups of the Qing Period), Beijing: Peking University Press, 2011, p. 332.

new empire for ourselves. ... Fortunately, the spirit of our ancestor, the Yellow Emperor, will enable us to restore the old things, and create a new beginning for our people, which is the common feeling motivating all our Han people.[103]

Qiu Qin joined the Restoration Society following her introduction by Xu Xilin. In common with other racist positions of the Restoration Society, Qiu Qin was concerned with the restoration of ancestral lands for the benefit of the Han people. As a woman, Qiu Jin advocated female liberation, and in her *Announcement to My Two Hundred Million Female Compatriots* she warned: "You all know that the country is going to perish and the males cannot protect it, so do we still want to rely on them? If we ourselves do not make the effort, then when the country perishes, it will be too late". Qiu Jin's mode of dress, speech, and action were all quite radical, so she stood out in a conformist society and her appeals made a deep impact. The unique positions of Tao Chengzhang and Xu Xilin, leading members of the Restoration Society, and the visibly separatist rhetoric and deeds of the revolutionaries drew criticism from the Revolutionary Alliance even before the Revolution.

Given that the power of the revolutionary parties was scattered and their many attempted uprisings all met with failure, Sun Yat-sen began to develop the revolution in 1905 by contacting Chinese who had studied in Europe (Belgium, Britain, Germany, France), a path that led him to extend the influence of the revolution and develop contacts with forward-thinking intellectuals and the New Army. In July of that year, Sun Yat-sen arrived in Japan, where he tried to persuade the members of different revolutionary organizations or factions to pool their strength:

China now does not have to fear being divided up by other nations but should worry about our own internal fighting. This province wants to start something, as does another province, but they do not contact each other, and listen only to themselves. Eventually China will become more than twenty separate countries. At the end of the Yuan dynasty, there was chaos with separate forces led by Zhu (Yuanzhang), Chen (Youliang), Zhang

[103] This book is quoted in Zhang Yufa, *Qingji de Lixian Tuanti* (Constitutional Groups of the Qing Period), Beijing: Peking University Press, 2011, pp. 369–370.

(Shicheng), and Ming (Yuzhen). At that time if no one had intervened, China would undoubtedly have perished! With our different ideologies today, it is important that we all remain in contact.[104]

On 20 August 1905, members of the Xingzhong Society, the Huaxing Society, and the Military National Education Association established the China Revolutionary Alliance in Tokyo.[105] Sun Yat-sen prepared a succinct sixteen-character long credo for the new alliance: "Drive out the Tartars, restore China, set up a republic, and distribute equal land rights".[106] Sun Yat-sen's Three Principles of the People based on this credo would provide a program for setting up the republic. By placing the expulsion of the Manchus at the head of his credo, he was using the overthrow of Qing dynasty rule as his current political strategy, which conformed to the wishes of Han people of all different levels of education. Alliance members spanned different provinces, with membership covering 17 provinces, and these provided new resources for the expansion of Sun Yat-sen's power and influence. At the same time, branches and affiliates were developing rapidly, expanding into southern China, central China, northern China, Southeast Asia, the Americas, and Europe. Clearly, the Revolutionary Alliance was a revolutionary group with a complex composition of different classes including students, overseas Chinese, businessmen, peasants, workers, military personnel, bureaucrats, and young intellectuals, and so it encompassed a complexity of views. Even though the Revolutionary Alliance established three departments—in charge of the discussion of ideas, executive work, and judicial matters, the original members of different parties maintained close relationships through the Revolutionary Alliance, which meant that concealed and

[104] This book is quoted in Zhang Yufa, *Qingji de Geming Tuanti* (Revolutionary Groups of the Qing Period), Beijing: Peking University Press, 2011, p. 221.

[105] The Restoration Society did not take part in the founding of the Revolutionary Alliance, and very few members of the Society were members of the Alliance. After the founding of the Revolutionary Alliance, the Restoration Society kept its own name. However, in some revolutionary activities, the two organizations were indistinguishable through their cooperation and joint action.

[106] In fact, when the Xingzhong Society was founded in Hanoi in 1902, its revolutionary pledge had already been altered to this sixteen-character credo.

dangerous contradictions and conflicts sometimes emerged within the revolutionaries' ranks.

From 1905, when Wu Yue and others planned to assassinate the five envoys being sent abroad by the Qing court, to 1910, when the Huanghuagang Uprising was staged in Guangzhou, the Revolutionary Alliance organized and participated in dozens of assassinations or armed incidents, the most effective role of these acts of violence serving to force the Qing dynasty to reform as quickly as possible and speed up the introduction of the constitution. As the Qing court saw it, the introduction of the constitution might prevent the outbreak of full-scale revolution. Duanfang, for example, believed that most people wanted a constitution, even though this might "stir up a few who wanted the chaos of an anti-Manchu revolution".[107] However, the propaganda of the revolutionists and their debate with the constitutionalists did play a role in promoting revolutionary ideas. The first issue of *Minbao* on 26 November 1905 launched Sun Yat-sen's promotion of his Three Principles of the People:

> I maintain that the progress of Europe and the United States depended on three major doctrines: nationalism, civil rights, and people's livelihood. The demise of Rome saw the rise of nationalism and the independence of European nations. Ever since absolute monarchs exercised autocratic rule in their nations, the lower classes have not been able to endure the suffering, and this gave rise to civil rights. At the end of the eighteenth and beginning of the nineteenth century, the servants of despots established constitutional politics. With the opening of the world and the increase in wisdom, material comforts vastly improved more in the last century than in the previous thousand years. Economic problems followed in the wake of political problems, and now that the doctrine emphasizing the people's livelihood is taking off by leaps and bounds, the 20th century will be the age when people's livelihood is uplifted.[108]

[107] "Liangjiang Zongdu Duanfang Zouding Xianfa Fa Dianfan Fu Wei Yong Qing Bianding Fenbu Zhe" (Memorial of the Liangjiang Governor Duanfang Requesting Formulation of the Blueprint Constitution and its Promulgation), quoted in Zhang Yufa, *Qingji de Geming Tuanti* (Revolutionary Groups of the Qing Period), Beijing: Peking University Press, 2011, p. 311.

[108] *Minbao*, no. 1, quoted in Zhang Yufa, *Qingji de Geming Tuanti* (Revolutionary Groups of the Qing Period), Beijing: Peking University Press, 2011, p. 221.

From the beginning, *Minbao* carried criticism opposing the constitutionalists, and the revolutionary party always believed that the reforms of the Qing court were spurious and needed to be countered, since all the work of preparing the constitution was ultimately only intended to uphold Manchu rule, so in their eyes the constitutionalist's position lacked legitimacy from the beginning. In the summer of 1911, the preparation of constitutional work advanced to the full establishment of the National Congress and the division of powers, but the establishment of the imperial cabinet obviously revealed the intention of the Manchu powers at the Qing court to deny the Han people power, which naturally provided a basis for the revolutionary party's observations. In *Minbao*, Song Jiaoren published an article titled "The Dashing of the Constitutionalists' Hopes":

> The constitutionalists have by no means benefited from the present government. The avowed constitutionality of the present government is false and is only a pretense to perpetuate authoritarian rule. Therefore the National Assembly and cabinet that have been set up are not the legislature of a constitutional state nor a feature of responsible government. Thus the powers of the National Assembly are curtailed and the organization of the cabinet does not comply with the articles of the constitution. The articles of the constitution are a façade intended to deceive people, and for those who rely on the truth none of this can be believed.[109]

The debate between the revolutionaries and constitutionalists was difficult to distinguish in theory, but the idea of the Three Principles of the People and revolutionary thought were widely disseminated, and laid the ideological, and even emotional, foundation for the general response of the provinces after the Wuchang Uprising and the actions of the members of the Revolutionary Alliance. To a large extent, the historical role of the Revolutionary League was to concentrate the revolutionary will, mobilize social forces, enlighten people's thinking, and directly bring about the full outbreak of armed revolution. The successful parties were the Gongjin Hui (Society for Common Progress) and the central general department of the Revolutionary Alliance, as well as the armed forces under the control of the Restoration Society.

[109] *Minli Bao*, 1911.6.14, quoted in Zhang Yufa, *Qingji de Geming Tuanti* (Revolutionary Groups of the Qing Period), Beijing: Peking University Press, 2011, p. 295.

The Gongjin Hui (Society for Common Progress) was founded, against the background of the repeated failures of revolutionary armed uprisings, as a separate and restructured revolutionary organization by members of the Revolutionary Alliance, whose leader Sun Yat-sen was often out of China and so neglected the coordination of revolutionary forces and strategies, as well as by members of other revolutionary parties. As a result, members of the Revolutionary Alliance from Hubei, Hunan, Sichuan, and Jiangxi formed the Society for Common Progress in Tokyo in April 1907, with the aim of "combining the factions on the road to revolution, overthrowing the Manchu regime, and restoring the old [ethnic Han independence]"; it targeted the various revolutionary parties and the military for its future development. Unlike the "equal land rights" platform of the Revolutionary Alliance, the Society for Common Progress's oath addressed "equality and human rights", because important members of the Society were born as landlords with property rights, while they also believed that revolutionaries as members of the League should all have equal status and none should not be regarded as socially inferior, as had been the case in the past. In 1908, Sun Wu and Jiao Dafeng, who were leading members of the Society for Common Progress in Japan, returned to China to organize the revolution, the main participants being troops in the New Army. Since the beginning of the Foreign Affairs Movement, the social atmosphere in Hunan and Hubei had been open, and construction in industry, education, and the New Army had been significant. In June 1904, prior to the founding of the Society for Common Progress, a number of soldiers in the Hubei Army had set up the "Science Coaching Center", the real purpose being to organize the revolution and the restoration of the ethnic Han. In November 1905, Liu Daxiong, a member of the Science Coaching Center, contacted like-minded comrades to set up the Rizhi Hui (Everyday Knowledge Society) which sought to attract members through public lectures and educational activities. This Society was formally set up in February 1906, and a report by Liu Daxiong reveals the revolutionary atmosphere of that time:

> A few days ago Comrade Cao Yabo came from Hunan to Hubei, and with Hu Lanting and a brother, the three discussed expanding the Everyday Knowledge Society. Cao had been involved in related activities in Japan, so with the establishment of the newly reconstituted Everyday Knowledge Society, the charter and manifesto of the Society was prepared, and an Executive Department was accordingly set up. This Department would

> comprise comrades from the military and educational fields, who would assume full responsibility for informing people about national salvation and forming a new China. The descendants of the Yellow Emperor will no longer be slaves in a defeated nation. How can it not be fortuitous for our comrades, if it also fortuitous for our four hundred million Chinese compatriots?![110]

The Everyday Knowledge Society had some ten thousand members in the armed forces and educational circles. After March 1908, some of the members of the Everyday Knowledge Society reorganized the Revolutionary Alliance within the Hubei army, and later made the strategic move of changing names and organizing the Qunzhi Xue She (November 1908), Zhenwu Xue She (August 1910), and Wenxue She (30 January 1911), the latter being a powerful group within the New Army. In fact, as the revolutionary atmosphere intensified, more small revolutionary groups emerged in Hunan and Hubei, providing a growing revolutionary resource for the imminent uprising.

Due to the weakness of the core leadership of the Revolutionary Alliance, members of its central group began to regroup their guidance teams and strengthen the revolutionary executive force. On 31 July 1911, the Central China Bureau of the Revolutionary Alliance was established in Shanghai in a strategic move by members previously working in the core group of the Alliance after the failure of uprisings in Guangzhou. Huang Xing was so discouraged by these failures that he urged Tan Renfeng, Chen Qimei (1877–1916), Song Jiaoren, and others to revamp the Alliance's revolutionary work, convinced that the Alliance "had a common purpose, but no common plan; practical and talented members but an impractical organization". Such an assessment sketched out the limited organizational capacity and resources of the previous Alliance, and the difficulties presented by internal conflicts. The Constitution of the Central China Bureau revealed obvious differences with the aims of the Revolutionary Alliance, such as the abandonment of the idea of "equal land rights", and indicated the intention of reorganizing the independent political command body: "All members of the China Revolutionary Alliance will join under this law to become members of the new group" (per the *Constitution*). Because the programs of the Central China Bureau

[110] Quoted in Zhang Yufa, *Qingji de Geming Tuanti* (Revolutionary Groups of the Qing Period), Beijing: Peking University Press, 2011, p. 394.

and the Society for Common Progress were close, there was regional consistency, personnel exchange, and a concentration of power, which were all important reasons why the forces who hastily staged the Wuchang Uprising had the power and endurance to deal with the Qing army who subsequently laid siege to Wuchang, and also why Song Jiaoren, who was the responsible person of the Central China Bureau, could become an important revolutionary leader with a power base.

In any case, the outbreak of the 1911 Revolution in Wuhan was the result of the work by different revolutionary groups working with a leading revolutionary party. With the grimness of the situation and the changed timing, the Society for Common Progress and the Wenxue She could no longer rely on the guidance and instructions of the southern Revolutionary Alliance and so decided to stage the uprising in Central China using their own forces. At this time, the crisis caused by the Railroad Protection Movement in Sichuan had forced the Qing government to send the Hubei army under the control of Duanfang to stage a crackdown there, so the revolutionary forces in the New Army were thus weakened. On 14 September, the Wenxue She and the Society for Common Progress met to decide on whether to launch a revolutionary war, and on 24 September, the two organizations met again to discuss the mobilization plan. They promoted Jiang Bokui to serve as their military commander-in-chief, appointed Liu Gong as prime minister, and made Sun Wu and others members of the Permanent Political Preparatory Committee.

The 1911 Revolution broke out in unprepared haste because of the accidental explosion of bombs caused by the negligence of Sun Wu and Deng Yulin. On the morning of 9 October, the sounds of explosions came from Number 14 Baoshan Lane in the Russian Concession of Wuhan and a local patrol immediately rushed to the site of the explosion to arrest the two revolutionaries and two other accomplices who were still at the scene. There, revolutionary flags, a list of members, and leaflets calling for an uprising were seized. Initially, the incident went unnoticed, and this mishap by the revolutionary parties was treated as only an insignificant event in the newspapers the following day: "Last night, the area around the site of the accident was calm. Except for the Russian patrol, no one was to be seen. There is enthusiastic jubilation concerning the patrol's discovery and effective control of the situation".[111] However, the list of revolutionaries' names prompted the Qing court to undertake a more diligent search for the listed persons and three revolutionary party members (Liu Fuji, Yang Hongsheng, and Peng Chufan) were arrested on the same day and shot. Sun Wu's comrades revered Sun Yat-sen. Liu Gong, who was also a member of the Revolutionary Alliance, said, "If we do not act immediately, it will all be over". Among the four persons arrested were Liu Gong's younger brother and wife. Liu, who had previously studied law and military courses in Japan, revealed that the revolutionists had been planning to launch a revolution in eight provinces simultaneously in December, with the uprisings to be led by Jiang Yuwu of the Wenxue She and Sun Wu as chief of staff, but the unexpected explosion meant that the revolution had to commence early. At seven o'clock on the evening of the 10th, the revolutionaries in the 8th Battalion of Engineers opened fire, and Xiong Bingkun led a team to the Ordnance Bureau at Chuwangtai, which they took over and thus acquired weapons. With the agreement with Wu Zhaolin, an officer of the guard and a member of the Rizhi Society, Chuwangtai came under the control of the Revolutionary Army. Under the command of Wu Zhaolin, in the early morning of the 11th, the Revolutionary Army occupied the Governor's Office. Soon afterwards, New Army forces in Hanyang and Hankou responded to Wuchang, and by the evening, the three connected cities of Wuchang, Hanyang, and Hankou were under the control of the Revolutionary Army. In fact, most of the officers and soldiers in the New Army were if not revolutionaries then sympathizers, which meant that the Qing government had lost control of the revolution before it even broke out.[112]

On the morning of the 11th, when the Revolutionary Army occupied Wuchang, the commander of the 21st Provisional Forces of the New Army, Li Yuanhong, was elected by the soldiers to be Governor. Li Yuanhong was initially unwilling to take up the post. He was regarded as a

[111] Edwin J. Dingle, *1911–1912 Qinli Zhongguo Geming* (1911–1912: China's Revolution), Hangzhou: Zhejiang Daxue Chubanshe, 2011, pp. 21–22.

[112] Liu Gong said: "There are military officers who are friendly with representatives of the revolutionary parties all over China, and so they do not need to spare any effort to contact the soldiers. If the officers are not offering to help, because they have good relations with the representatives, then they cannot be mobilised. So, the arrest of revolutionaries by the governor or military governor will not be successful". Edwin J. Dingle, *1911–1912 Qinli Zhongguo Geming* (1911–1912: China's Revolution), Hangzhou: Zhejiang University Press, 2011, p. 23.

commander who "understood" and "loved" his men, but he was not a member of a revolutionary party. He dithered between standing on the side of the Qing court or the revolutionary parties. He even had several of the revolutionaries shot on the evening of the 9th, but Wu Zhaolin believe that Li Yuanhong might sway more soldiers to join the revolutionary forces, and he would rally other provinces to the revolution, and so he showed Li Yuanhong respect in order to win him over to the revolution. It was not until 17 October that Li Yuanhong, presiding over an official ceremony, publicly announced the revolutionary position that a republic was to be established. The constitutionalist Tang Hualong (1874–1918) was promoted to head civil affairs, demonstrating that there was a de facto recognition of the legitimacy of the already existing Provincial Assemblies. Previously, Tang Hualong had been one of the leaders of the group petitioning to convene the national parliament and now, in the name of the Provincial Assembly, he sent telegrams to Provincial Assemblies of all provinces calling on them to "raise the flag". When the US Consul in Hankou asked what type of political regime the revolution intended to set up, Tang replied: "A republic". At this time, the political and military situation in the other provinces was still unknown but, as a former constitutionalist, Tang Hualong had completely changed his position - from relying on the moderate political evolution of the Manchu government to participating in violent revolution. When people were still unclear about the future of the revolution and feared defeat, Tang Hualong said: "Success is our common goal, and defeat is death. We Han people have finally made a statement, and we have endured ten thousand failures, so everything depends on this uprising".[113] Although the constitutionalists played a role in stabilizing the situation, the revolutionists and Tang Hualong and other constitutionalists were locked in a contest regarding the formation of the Hubei military government, but finally the revolutionary party took control, forcing Tang and others to flee Wuhan.

Until 28 October, the Revolutionary Army was in a standoff with the Qing army. Huang Xing and Song Jiaoren arrived in Wuchang to drum up morale, but the revolutionary army's military strength could not yet compare to that of the Qing Army. On the 27th, the Qing court

[113] Jiannong, "Wuhan Geming Shimo Ji" (Full Account of the Wuhan Revolution), *Xinhai Geming* (1911 Revolution), v. 5, p. 176, quoted in Hou Yijie, *Ershi Shiji Chu Zhongguo Zhengzhi Gaige Fengchao* (Political Reform Trends in Early Twentieth Century China), Beijing: Renmin Chubanshe, 1993, p. 507.

appointed Yuan Shikai as Plenipotentiary Minister. Yuan Shikai not only restored military power, but also seized the power over finances. On 1 November, Yuan Shikai was appointed Prime Minister of the Cabinet, and two days later, the *Nineteen-Article Constitution* was promulgated, and Yuan was now the most powerful political figure in China. Under attack by the Qing Army, Hankou fell, and Huang Xing even resorted to a strategy of suing for peace. He wrote to Yuan Shikai in Wuchang on 9 November, urging Yuan "to rely on the credentials of Napoleon and Washington, and achieve what Napoleon and Washington had been able to achieve. Attack the enemy's headquarters and destroy the enemy as quickly as possible. Then not only will the people of Hunan and Hubei extol you as their Napoleon and Washington, but in every province of north and south China there will be no one who does not bow to your orders".[114] At this time, Yuan Shikai was still acting in accordance with constitutional principles in arranging for representatives to negotiate with Li Yuanhong, but to no avail, and the Qing Army continued to attack. The battle that followed saw the failure of Huang Xing to plan a counter-offensive against Hankou, which led to the revolutionary army's defense of Hanyang being more difficult. By the 27th, Hanyang was lost, and the revolutionary army retreated to Wuchang. By this time, the revolutionary army had killed and wounded thousands of people. However, Li Yuanhong told a foreign interviewer on 20 November: "Now we have the support of thirteen of the 18 provinces, and our Republican Party is very strong".[115] When Huang Xing left Wuchang on the 28th, Li Yuanhong sent telegrams to the governors of all provinces where there had been uprisings, asking them to send troops to support Wuchang as soon as possible.

As early as 10 November, basing himself on political strategy and a policy of strengthening the revolutionary forces but not retreating, Li Yuanhong sent telegrams to the independent provincial governors asking them to send representatives as soon as possible to discuss setting up an

[114] "Min Erchang Jiucun Youguan Wuchang Qiyi de Handian" (Min Erchang's Archive of Surviving Telegrams Related to the Wuchang Uprising), *Jindai Shi Ziliao* (Modern History Materials), 1954:1, quoted in Hou Yijie, *Ershi Shiji Chu Zhongguo Zhengzhi Gaige Fengchao* (Political Reform Trends in Early Twentieth Century China), Beijing: Renmin Chubanshe, 1993, p. 523.

[115] Edwin J. Dingle, *1911–1912 Qinli Zhongguo Geming* (*1911–1912: China's Revolution*), Hangzhou: Zhejiang University Press, 2011, pp. 5–6.

interim central government. Forming such a government raised the question of which city would house it and how the president would be chosen. Among the revolutionaries, a delicate power play was also taking place around the discussion of these questions. On the 15th, representatives of Jiangsu, Fujian, and Shanghai held a preliminary meeting in Shanghai taking Wuchang's views into account, and on the 30th, the various provincial representatives met in the British Concession of Hankou to discuss related issues against the background sound of constant cannon fire. On 2 December, at the suggestion of Zhang Jian, the Jiangsu representative Lei Fen proposed that this meeting even decide whether "Yuan Shikai should be selected as interim president". This suggests that the constitutionalists had adopted a political strategy to give themselves power, but the situation developed so that the focus was no longer on constitutional or republican issues, but on who would be president. On 4 December, following Huang Xing's suggestion, the delegates in Shanghai and Wuchang separately agreed that Nanjing should be the location of the provisional capital. On 12 December, the first sessions of the interim central government were held in Nanjing. On the 17th, representatives of the provinces decided to confer on Li Yuanhong the power of commander-in-chief to organize the interim government. However, there was no consensus among the various forces on who would be the president of the new government. Until 9 December, Huang Xing insisted that Yuan Shikai was more suitable to become president, telling Wang Jingwei: "Xiangcheng [i.e., Yuan Shikai] is a talented genius who fulfills the expectations of the nation. He is able to assess the overall situation and act in concert with the people and the army to quickly overturn the Manchu Qing government and stabilize the nation at an early date. He has been long known to foreigners and would be welcomed by the entire population of this country".[116] The representatives in Hankou took all these factors into account and decided to delay appointing an interim president, but if Yuan Shikai agreed to a republic, it would promote Yuan as the most realistic political choice to fill the position of president.

In this three-way dispute between the Qing court, the constitutionalists, and the revolutionary parties, Yuan Shikai was easily able to balance out these forces, and in such dramas, he was an astute player who

[116] Mao Zhuqing ed., *Huang Xing Nianpu Changpian* (Full Chronology of Huang Xing), p. 245, quoted in Zhu Yuhe, Ouyang Junxi, and Shu Wen, *Xinhai Geming Shi* (History of the 1911 Revolution), Beijing: Renmin Chubanshe, 2001, p. 398.

constantly revised his tactics. Yuan arranged for people to go to Wuchang on 11 November to negotiate a truce with Li Yuanhong and Huang Xing. Representing Yuan Shikai, Cai Tinggan explained the reasons why a republic was not suitable for China and stressed the importance of a constitutional monarchy like that of Great Britain. However, Yuan Shikai's proposal was not endorsed by the Revolutionary Army. Yuan decided to force the other side to change their attitude by launching a military strike. When the Qing army captured Hanyang on the 27th, Yuan carefully asked the British to mediate and, in a spirit of compromise, Li Yuanhong immediately announced that he was "ready to accept the constitutional government".[117] Yuan Shikai went on to express conciliatory views in favor of constitutionalism. Public opinion seemed to be divided between support for the republic in the south and for constitutionalism in the north. Liang Qichao, then in Japan, believed that China's current revolution and uprisings were not pre-arranged and had occurred suddenly without preparation, so perhaps this was the opportunity to introduce a constitution speedily. In Kobe, in an interview with the Associated Press, Liang continued to emphasize his claim that "republicanism is not in line with China's national conditions nor with the cultural identity of the people. Given the current unrest, I urge the creation of a civilized and progressive constitutional monarchy".[118]

Sun Yat-sen had no idea what had happened in Wuhan, and two days after the Wuchang Uprising, he learned of the news from the press. Sun clearly realized the importance and necessity of returning home to lead the revolution. He tried unsuccessfully to win support for and approval of the Revolution from Western countries before returning home, even though he had received a conditional commitment to the revolutionary government from Britain that it would stop loan negotiations between the four-nation banking group and the Qing government. In fact, the Great Powers were observing China's changing situation and were anticipating that Yuan Shikai's would be China's destiny. Western observers believed

[117] *Yingguo Lanpi Shu Youguan Xinhai Geming Ziliao Xuanze* (Selection of Materials Related to the 1911 Revolution from the British *Blue Books*), v. 1, Beijing: Zhonghua Shuju, 1984, p. 94, quoted in Zhu Yuhe, Ouyang Junxi, and Shu Wen, *Xinhai Geming Shi* (History of the 1911 Revolution), Beijing: Renmin Chubanshe, 2001, p. 422.

[118] Zheng Xiyuan ed., *Gonghe Shinian: Niuyue Shibao Minchu Guancha Ji* (Ten Years of the Republic: *New York Times* Reports of the First Ten Years of the Republic of China), Beijing: Dangdai Zhongguo Chubanshe, 2018, p. 20.

that if "a leader like Sun Yat-sen or Li Yuanhong was appointed president of the Republic, recognition by the Great Powers could not be expected at an early date. Sun Yat-sen knows nothing about Chinese conditions, and Li Yuanhong has no position outside his own province".[119] Sun learned from the British government that the Great Powers pinned their hopes on Yuan Shikai as the future head of government of China and he decided that, in view of the overall situation of the revolution, he was ready to let Yuan Shikai be president of the future government of the Republic of China. Sun Yat-sen said in a telephone call to the military junta of the Republic of China on 16 November: "The President that has been elected is Mr. Li. But I hear that Li has requested that Yuan be promoted, and he would be the suitable candidate. In short, it is appropriate to go with this recommendation as that would stabilize the nation".[120] On 18 December, Yuan Shikai's representative, Tang Shaoyi, and Wu Tingfang, appointed by the Revolutionary Army, formally held North–South peace talks, but the two sides made no concessions on the issue of the constitution and the nature of the future state. Yuan Shikai and the revolutionists were trying to win the support of the Great Powers, and at the same time, the financial crisis caused by the interim government's political instability and the differences of opinion within the revolutionary parties led to the further weakening of power.[121] The

[119] Lo Hui-min ed., *Qingmo Minchu Zhengqing Neimu* (Internal Politics in the Late Qing and Early Republic), v. 1, p. 818, quoted in Zhu Yuhe, Ouyang Junxi, and Shu Wen, *Xinhai Geming Shi* (History of the 1911 Revolution), Beijing: Renmin Chubanshe, 2001, p. 398.

[120] *Sun Zhongshan Quanji* (Collected Works of Sun Yat-sen), v. 1, p. 547, quoted in Hou Yijie, *Ershi Shiji Chu Zhongguo Zhengzhi Gaige Fengchao* (Political Reform Trends in Early Twentieth Century China), Beijing: Renmin Chubanshe, 1993, p. 523.

[121] Nanjing's interim government faced financial difficulties from its inception. Burdened with enormous military and government expenditures, Sun Yat-sen had asked the interim government-controlled provinces to make payments to Nanjing, but the provincial governors could hardly pay their own expenses. Customs revenues were controlled by the Powers who still had serious doubts about the interim government, did not recognize it, and therefore would lend it no money. Even Zhang Jian, then minister of the Lianghuai Salt Administration, warned Sun Yat-sen: "No matter how desperate the military budget is, there should be no move on the salt merchants", because the salt tax was used to offset "foreign debt", which would cause diplomatic difficulties if there was a breach of trust. The interim government also sought funding through internal and external debt, however, even if Sheng Xuanhuai suggested that the interim government borrow from the Japanese by agreeing to the Sino-Japanese Hanyeping Company, and even a draft agreement was signed, it has not been realized because of opposition from

revolutionists continued to support Yuan and as long as Yuan favored the republic, Huang Xing insisted "he must be the president". On 25 December, Sun Yat-sen returned to China, and on the 29th, Sun Yat-sen, in Nanjing as the symbol of the revolution and a returning idol, at the same time as the revolutionists were pursuing a strategy of applying pressure on Yuan Shikai as a northerner, Sun was elected interim president. His legitimacy derived from the Provincial Assemblies of sixteen provinces set up in the constitutional preparatory period, with a seventeenth delegate position given to Huang Xing. However at this time, Sun Yat-sen was well aware that the new government faced a financial crisis and his own military strength was far less than that of Yuan Shikai. At the same time, because the foreign powers placed a higher value on Yuan Shikai and did not recognize the newly formed interim government in Nanjing, the republican revolution was in crisis. At this juncture, the general trend was still moving in the direction of a republic, and Yuan Shikai was bent on becoming its president. When he learned that Sun Yat-sen had become interim president, he worried about not being able to achieve his goals and began to blame Sun. Sun Yat-sen told Yuan not to misinterpret the situation, and through Wu Tingfang informed Tang Shaoyi: "If the Qing Emperor abdicates, proclaim the republic. Then the interim government will not have to eat its words, Sun Wen [i.e., Sun Yat-sen] can formally announce his resignation and take the initiative of first recommending Yuan".[122] Sun Yat-sen's main purpose at this time was to overthrow the Manchu government and preserve the revolutionary forces to ensure that the racial revolution was a success. The repeated commitments of the revolutionary party led Yuan Shikai to focus on forcing the Qing court to abdicate. When Yuan saw that the Chinese Minister in Russia, Lu Zhengxiang, and others also urged the Qing Emperor to abdicate on 3 January, he finally made the decision to change his stance, and had Duan Qirui and Feng Guofeng take coercive measures on his behalf.[123] On 3 February,

all directions, because such cooperation would give priority to the Japanese in rights of China's mines, railways, power, and other sectors and would represent such a loss of sovereignty as a precondition that the suggestion attracted strong opposition from Zhang Taiyan, Zhang Jian, and others, and was eventually abandoned.

122 This book is quoted in Zhu Yuhe, Ouyang Junxi, and Shu Wen, *Xinhai Geming Shi* (History of the 1911 Revolution), Beijing: Renmin Chubanshe, 2001, p. 429.

123 In an effort to urge the Qing royal house to agree to abdicate as soon as possible, Duan Qirui said he could bring troops to Beijing to discuss the matter with the Manchu

the Empress Dowager Longyu told Yuan Shikai that there was no longer any point in her opening the Parliament, and that she would announce her abdication. North and South had different issues with the abdication arrangements, but finally Sun Yat-sen agreed to a humane settlement for the abdicating imperial household.

Although the true republican revolutionists were deeply dissatisfied with Yuan Shikai's appointment as president, the latter's success was by no means a fluke. By the time the Qing household began to implement the New Administration, the foreign powers had begun to take notice of this man who had never gone abroad and acquired a Western-style education but was sensitive to new things and had an understanding of Western civilization. When a Western journalist interviewed Yuan in 1905 when he was overseeing an autumn military exercise in Baoding as the commander-in-chief of the New Army, the reporter asked Yuan why he had not cut off his queue, Yuan replied, "Yes, I will, when the time comes". It was almost seven years later that the interim national government issued a decree to cut off the queue, so Yuan was clearly a politician with ambition in reserve. During the frenzy of the Boxer Rebellion, Yuan negotiated conducting an experiment with a Boxer leader to see if a bullet from a Martini-Henry rifle could pierce a Boxer's chest. The Boxers swore oaths that would make them impervious to bullets and blades. Yuan had the dead Boxer buried with full honors and his grave guarded by monks for a hundred days. When the Qing court needed Yuan Shikai to return to Beijing as soon as possible in its final crisis, Yuan prevaricated on health grounds until the Qing government promised to make him prime minister. By always acting at a measured and strategic pace, Yuan retained the hopes placed on him by both the monarchists and the revolutionists. It cannot be said at this time that Yuan Shikai was either really opposed to the republic or satisfied with the constitutional monarchy, but for Yuan Shikai, personal power was always more important than the form of government that was in place. Yuan Shikai's shrewdness was very much in evidence during his construction of the New Army. He used the Qing court's implementation of the New Administration to build his own Northern Navy (1904–1905) which of course meant that for him the introduction of the New Administration by the

and Mongolian princes, and Feng Guofeng also publicly declared his support for deploying troops in support of the Republic. The attitude of these officers helped urge the royal family to make a final decision.

court was the preparation for building up a powerful army loyal to him alone in the future. In this he was clearly very successful, and even during his three years of furlough at home, his old army remained loyal to him, and at the time of the demise of the Qing dynasty, his effective rivalry with the Revolutionary Army would reduce casualties as much as possible on both sides through negotiations, leaving room and strength for the possible political changes that would follow.

Whatever the complaints, worries, and grievances he elicited, Yuan Shikai was seen as a reform-driven and politically experienced man who, as a powerful military leader and highly qualified politician, was now president with universally accepted legitimacy, and the Nanjing Interim Senate even congratulated Yuan on being "the first Washington of the Republic of China". Indeed, although the emperor agreed to abdicate, the Qing imperial household preferred to leave the country in the hands of the familiar Yuan Shikai, rather than Sun Yat-sen, who was keen on violent revolution and had only just returned to the country. Even though members of the imperial family knew Yuan was a cunning opportunist, the Qing government explicitly authorized Yuan Shikai to form an interim republican government, although it is believed that the sentence authorizing him to do so was inserted by Yuan Shikai himself. On the 11th, Yuan Shikai who had earlier believed in constitutional monarchy sent the following telegram to the Nanjing government:

> A republic is the best political system for a country, as is world recognized. Today, by virtue of the emperor's political leap and subsequent follow-up, we have the public realization of many years of hard work, a republic of unlimited happiness. The Qing Emperor has already announced his abdication, a deed sanctioned and signed by [Yuan] Shikai, and the date of the announcement marks the end of imperial government, and the commencement of the Republic of China. Henceforth, we will strive to achieve a satisfactory status and ensure that a monarchy never again emerges in China.[124]

After Sun Yat-sen received Yuan Shikai's telegram, on 13 February, the day after the emperor's abdication, he issued the following statement to Parliament:

[124] This book is quoted in Zhu Yuhe, Ouyang Junxi, and Shu Wen, *Xinhai Geming Shi* (History of the 1911 Revolution), Beijing: Renmin Chubanshe, 2001, p. 433.

> This President believes that the will of our nation's people has seen the building of a republic, the toppling of autocracy, and the staging of a righteous military uprising that had the support of the entire nation. Seeing this overall situation, the Qing Emperor realized that the preservation of the monarchy would inevitably fail and so he argued for his abdication. Today, he has announced his abdication and acknowledged the Republic of China, and henceforth there will never be a monarchy in China, and the aim of a Republic has been achieved. With the founding of the Republic of China, the President was elected as a public servant and declared and promised that when autocracy has been overthrown and the Republic takes its place in the world and is recognized by the Major Powers, then the President would resign. Now the Qing Emperor has abdicated, autocracy has ended, north and south are of the one mind, there is no further turmoil, the Republic has been recognized by the various nations, and the time has now come when this President will fulfill his promise and resign his post.[125]

On the question of whether the interim government should be located in Beijing or Nanjing, Yuan Shikai and southern delegates from Sun Yat-sen held discussions that were deadlocked. In the end, under the pressure of time and strategic considerations, Cai Yuanpei suggested that the South agree to Yuan's appointment in Beijing. On 10 March, Yuan Shikai was sworn in as interim president. On 1 April, Sun Yat-sen formally resigned as interim president, and on 5 April, the interim Senate decided to relocate the interim government to Beijing. The United States and other countries successively recognized the newly created Republic of China. Many people thought this was a defeat for the southern revolutionary parties, but Sun Yat-sen's view was that the *Provisional Covenant of the Republic of China* promulgated on 11 March in Nanjing should act as a constraint on Yuan Shikai's future words and actions, and some members of the revolutionary parties shared this view, their confidence stemming from the adoption of the cabinet system in the *Covenant*.

From the accidental explosion in Wuchang to the abdication of the Qing emperor, these events collectively known as the Revolution of 1911, that being the year when the violent revolution took place, did not seem to have a unified leader, a unified organization, let alone a unified command, and throughout the course of the armed revolution, one cannot find a center of events. Wuhan, for example, was the city where the

125 Ibid., p. 433.

original accidental explosions occurred and where the process of revolution was jointly manipulated by the Society for Common Progress and the Wenxue She, but although the Wuchang uprising undoubtedly involved members of an alliance, this does not mean that the two organizations were subject to the unified command of the League. When the guns of the uprising rang out over Wuhan, the insurgents were busy looking for influential figures like Li Yuanhong or Tang Hualong to lead them. The leaders of the revolution in other localities also relied on the local forces of different revolutionary organizations. For example, in Zhejiang (which effectively extended from Shanghai to Hangzhou and Ningbo, as well as the rest of Zhejiang province) the revolution was realized through the efforts of the New Army controlled by the Restoration Society, although there was cooperation with the Revolutionary Alliance when the Restoration Society was in Shanghai. In any case, as during traditional Chinese New Year when adults and children celebrate by letting off firecrackers, the Qing government's desperate but uncoordinated efforts to set off fireworks around the country completely failed, and in the first few months, it was the interim government which issued laws and regulations—such as introducing the official use of the solar calendar, cutting off the queue, and prohibiting foot binding—which ushered in a new spring throughout Chinese society.

This was an era of disparate, conflicted, and urgent calls for help and hasty changes in response, and the different views concerning the purposes and political tasks of the revolution between the different political organizations are salient: the main aim of the Restoration Society was overthrowing the Manchu government; the Society for Common Progress never touched on the issue of people's livelihood; and, the Revolutionary Alliance had no way of realizing its political agenda of "equal land rights". So, when the Qing government was overthrown, the political forces confronting it dispersed and chaotic approaches to issues needed to be restructured. The Restoration Society even teamed up with members of the old bureaucracy in order to compete with the Revolutionary Alliance in the post-revolutionary struggle for control. Due to the lack of administrative organizers and managers in the revolutionary parties, the establishment and management of the regime after the victory of the revolution was naturally taken over by the experienced and capable constitutionalists and even more conservative forces. However, the idea of establishing a "republic" had been almost universally accepted, and any ideological tendencies limited to individuals and special organizations did not influence the national order imposed in the name of the Republic, so that after the abdication of the Qing Emperor, the country largely maintained unity rather than division.

As a representative figure of the constitutionalists, Liang Qichao described the 1911 Revolution, when celebrating its tenth anniversary, as a revolution with a triple significance in Chinese history. Firstly, he pointed out, the Chinese consciously realized that other people do not have the right to run China, and secondly, the Chinese consciously realized that they themselves do have the right to run their own country.[126] He enthusiastically said, "Looking back today on our country over the last ten years, we can now see the achievements of the past and contemplate our hopes for the future, and this gives me a delirious joy. I want to join with all you in shouting out three cheers for the Republic of China!" By this time, Liang Qichao and everyone could clearly see that, based on the opening provided by the 1898 Reforms, the subsequent dissemination and construction of the constitutional movement based on Western political theory and ideas, and the later assistance and cooperation provided by those who promoted constitutional politics in various parts of China to the revolutionary parties, the armed uprising of 1911 ensured the survival of the ideological and institutional reforms of 1898 and the Constitutional Movement, and so history did change: after more than two thousand years of the Qin-Han polity was transformed into a political form that made it difficult to restore the imperial system and was

[126] "I believe there are only three significant revolutions in Chinese history. The first was the revolution of the Zhou dynasty, which ended the tribal politics that had held sway since the time of Emperors Yao and Shun. The second was the revolution of the Han dynasty, which ended the aristocratic politics that had dominated politics since the time of the Three Dynasties. The third is the 1911 Revolution that we commemorate today". Ref: Liang Qichao, "Xinhai Geming zhi Yiyi yu Shinian Shuangshi-jie zhi Leguan: Shuangshi-jie Tianjin Xuejie Quanti Qingzhu Hui Jiangyan, 1921" (The Meaning of the 1911 Revolution and Optimism on its Tenth Anniversary: Speech at the Celebration of the Double Ten-Festival Organized by Tianjin Educational Circles, 1921), *Liang Qichao Zishu* (Liang Qichao in his Own Writings), Beijing: Renmin Ribao Chubanshe, 2011, p. 396.

called "republican" (a mixed political form based on Chinese tradition but melded with Japanese and Western elements).

It is also true that, despite the fact that the revolutionary parties precluded all hope for the constitutional movement of the first decade of the new century and the New Administration as well as the constitutional reforms carried out by the Qing government under their impetus, it was the fruits of the New Administration and the constitutional period—the New Army, the Chambers of Commerce and the Provincial Assemblies—that underpinned the final victory of the Wuchang Uprising. The various Provincial Assemblies (even though some adopted different names) served as the political institutions of the Republic of China for decades after the Revolution. Finally, it should be noted that the term "China" (Zhongguo) finally became the official name for the country after the Revolution. The Republic of China, founded in 1912, and the People's Republic of China, founded in 1949, are both referred to as "China" (Figs. 1, 2, 3, 4, 5, 6, 7, 8, 9, 10, 11, and 12).

Fig. 1 Nursery set up exclusively to raise abandoned children and homeless orphans inside a church in Yantai, Shandong province, early twentieth century

Fig. 2 Negotiations in 1900 between the representatives of China and the Eight Powers, led by Li Hongzhang and Edward Seymour (second from the right)

Fig. 3 1903, Dowager Empress Cixi enjoying the snowy scenery at the Summer Palace

Fig. 4 Plenipotentiary of the Great Qing Empire, Zaize (middle of front row), visiting the London Metropolitan Locomotive Workshop, 1906

Fig. 5 Several prominent constitutionalists at the time of the promulgation of the late Qing Constitution (Wang Rongbao is second from the left)

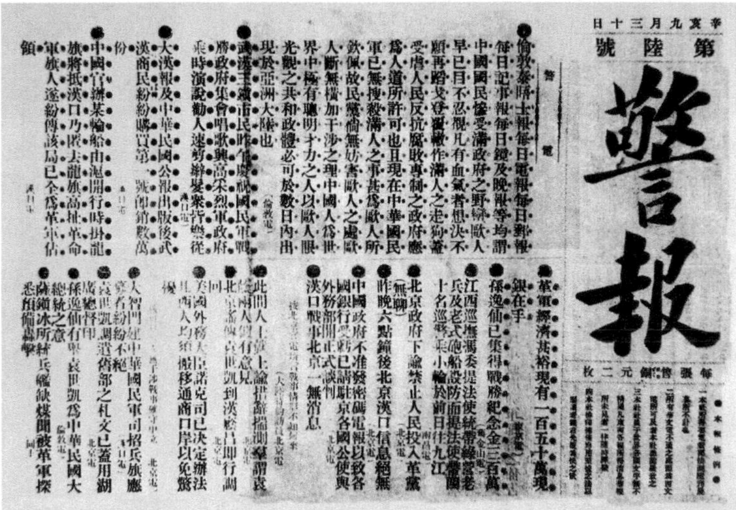

辛亥九月三十日

第陸號

警報

每張售銅元二枚

警電

倫敦泰晤士報每日電報每日郵報每日記事報每日鏡及晚報等均謂中國國民慘受滿政府之野蠻歐人早已目不忍覩凡有血氣者想決不願再蹈戈登覆轍作滿人之走狗羞受虐人民反抗腐敗專制之政府應爲人道所許可也且現在中華國民軍已無擾殺滿人之事甚爲歐人所欽佩故民黨尚無妨害歐人之處歐人斷無橫加干涉之理中國人爲世界中極有聰明才力之人以歐人眼光觀之共和政體必可於數日內出現於亞洲大陸也

Fig. 6 Late Qing Shanghai newspapers

Fig. 7 Liang Qichao

Fig. 8 Li Yuanhong

Fig. 9 Revolutionary Forces who staged the Wuchang Uprising, 1911

Fig. 10 Well-wishers from various walks of life in Shanghai farewelling Dr. Sun Yat-sen leaving to take up his post as President in Nanjing, 1911

Fig. 11 Photograph depicting Yuan Shikai receiving foreign envoys after formally taking up his post as President of the Republic of China, 1913

Fig. 12 Wedding photograph of Sun Yat-sen and Song Qingling in Tokyo, 1915

Chapter Two
1912–1927: Disarrangements of Power and New Intellectual Trends

They attack us at *New Youth* for being guilty of many crimes: destroying Confucian teachings, destroying the regulations of the Confucian rites, destroying the "national quintessence", destroying Confucian injunctions on chastity, destroying the old ethics (loyalty and filial piety), destroying the old arts (Chinese opera), destroying the old religion (belief in demons and ghosts), destroying the old literature, and destroying the old politics (rule by the privileged).

Of course, we at *New Youth* do not deny our actions, but do not acknowledge them to be crimes. It is only because we support Mr. Democracy and Mr. Science that we have committed these heinous crimes. To support Mr. Democracy, we have to oppose Confucian teachings, the system of Confucian rites, Confucian rules on chastity, the old ethics, and the old politics. To support Mr. Science, we have to oppose the old arts and the old religion. To embrace Mr. Democracy and to embrace Mr. Science, we have to oppose "the national quintessence" and the old literature. To consider these matters carefully, in addition to supporting both Mr. Democracy and Mr. Science, what other crimes must we commit? If there are none, then could you please not single out *New Youth* and have the ability and courage to oppose Mr. Democracy and Mr. Science and, then you could be regarded as good men, who appreciate what lies at the basis of our actions.

Chen Duxiu, "In Reply to Accusations Levelled against *New Youth*"

L. Peng, *A History of China in the 20th Century*,
https://doi.org/10.1007/978-981-99-0734-2_4

Restoration of the Monarchy and the Disarrangements of Power

Until he became President, Yuan Shikai was seen by people from all walks of life as a progressive, steady, promising, and powerful figure. In the early years of the Republic, Ding Wenjiang (1887–1936), a scientist who dismissed the adoption of the policy of treating "Chinese studies as the corpus and Western studies as application" and who had a sound understanding of Western political systems, pinned his hopes on Yuan Shikai, a position adopted by many others: "Everyone in this country who thinks hard certainly recognizes the extremely serious financial difficulties we are in, but generally hopes that now that we have a real leader, so we are going to get through them".[1] In fact, even those who had been radicalized and devoted their lives to the revolution, such as Zhang Taiyan (1868–1936) and Sun Wu (1879–1939), also became members of Yuan Shikai's forces, and the constitutionalist and entrepreneur Zhang Qian (1853–1926) wrote to Huang Xing (1874–1916) suggesting he disband the Revolutionary League. Moreover, Sun Yat-sen warned his comrades to stop confronting and attacking the government, openly declaring: "The racial revolution and the political revolution have been successful, and now is the time to begin constructing industries as part of the social revolution". In discussions with Yuan Shikai, Sun Yat-sen expressed his hope of completing the construction of 200,000 km of railways within 10 years, while Huang Xing stepped down from his post in the Nanjing Provisional Government in favor of Yuan Shikai on 14 June 1912, urging his colleagues, "Do not question my move. We are all working for the same cause". He also planned to devote his energy and attention to agriculture, forestry, and mining.

In November 1912, Kang Youwei instructed his student Chen Huanzhang to set up the Confucian Teachings Society (Kongjiao Hui) in Shanghai. In Kang's view, the fall of the Qing dynasty removed the authority that could have inherited Confucianism, and the Ministry of Education of the Nanjing Interim Government furthermore ordered schools not to study the Confucian Classics and not perform ritual sacrifices for Confucius. Kang Youwei commented that such a situation rendered China's population of 400,000,000 people "hesitant about

[1] This statement is quoted in Zhu Yuhe, Ouyang Junxi, and Shu Wen, *Xinhai Geming Shi* (History of the 1911 Revolution), Beijing: Renmin Chubanshe, 2001, pp. 442–443.

believing in anything", the spirit of the country ceased to exist, and the country and the nation were plunged into confusion. In China at this time, there was still a great deal of prevarication about the political form the state should assume; Yuan Shikai was more inclined towards Kang's idea of a Japanese model rather than Sun Yat-sen's idea of a Euro-American system. J.O.P. Bland (1863–1945), journalist, diplomat, and long-term resident of China, argued, in December 1912, that the Chinese government would largely learn from the Japanese model of establishing a constitutional monarchy but, most importantly, the entire government structure would be based on the Confucian system. Bland argues that this was the policy that Kang Youwei and the "Six Gentlemen of 1898" tried strenuously to implement and was the idea motivating the constitutionalists under the leadership of Liang Qichao, who were moderate reformers; with the Emperor Protection Society as their organization, these constitutionalists' numbers expanded daily. Yuan Shikai elaborated this fall on the idea that after years of political turmoil and even division, he believes only such a model of government can survive in this country.[2]

The atmosphere calling for the restoration of the *ancient regime* was described in the memoirs of Emperor Puyi: "With its second New Year's Day, the atmosphere in the Republic of China began to change", because on this year's lunar New Year's Day, "the Republic send a representative to the emperor to extend to him New Year's greetings, conveyed to the emperor by the Republic's president".[3] By this time, Yuan Shikai had gained the trust of Sun Yat-sen, who several months previously, on 5 October 1912, had said at a reception in Shanghai for the Nationalist Party (KMT), "I met with President Yuan in Beijing and we discussed state policy, and it was very satisfactory. Therefore, I believe that Yuan is a man who shoulders responsibilities and has a clear mind; he can see everything in the world clearly and his ideas are innovative. However, in his actions, he is somewhat old-fashioned.... to rule the Republic of China, it is not possible without new ideas together with old experiences and old methods, but President Yuan seems capable of doing so. Therefore, I recommend that Xiangcheng [i.e., Yuan Shikai, editor's note] will be

[2] From: Zheng Xiyuan, *Gonghe Shinian: Niuyue Shibao Guancha Ji, 1911–1921* (The Decade of the Republic: *The New York Times*, 1911–1921), Beijing (CASS): Dangdai Zhongguo Chubanshe, 2018, p. 71.

[3] Aisin-Gioro Puyi, *Wode Qianbansheng* (Autobiography: The First Half of My Life), Beijing: Qunzhong Chubanshe (Masses Press), 1980, p. 86.

the right man for the job".[4] Nevertheless, Yuan Shikai had his own plans prior to the convening of parliament, and he was determined to restore the political order with which he and many old bureaucrats were familiar. His view of the post-revolutionary situation was completely different from that of the revolutionary parties and radical youth. He believed that the demand for power by the provinces and local areas could precipitate a crisis for the central government and threaten its very existence, which would be detrimental for himself and the empire.

Among the leading members of the Revolutionary Alliance only Song Jiaoren was wary of Yuan Shikai politically, and he tried to organize a responsible cabinet through the political channels of the Party in order to limit Yuan's power. On 25 August, under the auspices of Song, the Revolutionary Alliance merged with the United Republican Party (Tongyi Gonghe Dang), Citizens Common Party (Guomin Gongdang), Citizens Progressive Society (Guomin Gongjin Hui), and Republican Progress Society (Gonghe Shijin Hui) to form the Kuomintang (Guomindang, hereafter KMT). Although Sun Yat-sen was chairman of the KMT, the execution and management of party affairs were in the hands of Song Jiaoren. As soon as the 1911 Revolution ended, due to differences in political opinions and complicated interpersonal relationships, a number of political parties appeared, and several smaller parties, represented by the United Party (Tongyi Dang) and People's Society (Min She), formed a Republican Party (Gonghe Dang) coalition opposed to the KMT. The constitutionalists, represented by Tang Hualong, also formed a Democratic Party (Minzhu Dang), at the end of August 1912, with Liang Qichao as their leader. Although the Republican Party and the Democratic Party merged to become the Progressive Party (Jinbu Dang) on 29 May 1913, in the first parliamentary elections at the end of 1912 the KMT had won most votes, becoming the majority party in parliament. Based on the differences between the Progressive Party's belief in the doctrine of the state's rights based on cooperation with the government and the KMT's proposition of a doctrine emphasizing civil rights, it seemed natural that the forces of two parties, one supporting Yuan and one opposing Yuan, would take shape.

[4] From: Hu Sheng, *Cong Yapian Zhanzheng dao Wusi Yundong* (From the Opium War to the May Fourth Movement), *xia* volume, Beijing: Renmin Chubanshe, 1984, p. 911.

The Cabinet system of concern to Song Jiaoren underwent a disturbingly dramatic sequence of events in 1912; over four months of the interim government in Nanjing, the revolutionary parties led by Sun Yat-sen formulated a basic framework for the future political system. This institutional framework, known as the *Provisional Covenant of the Republic of China*, was however not adopted by the subsequent Yuan Shikai government. Before Yuan Shikai gained the trust of the leaders of the interim government in Nanjing, he did not express any public objection to the provisions defining the cabinet system in the *Provisional Covenant*. However, as soon as the first Cabinet organized by Tang Shaoyi (1862–1938) became a reality, Yuan began to adjust the power structure in his customary way, often clashing with Tang Shaoyi and other members of the Revolutionary Alliance. The focus of these conflicts was basically the question of demarcating the boundaries of power and legality. Soon after, when the Provincial Council of Zhili asked Interim President Yuan Shikai to appoint Wang Zhixiang, who was closer to the Revolutionary Alliance, to be governor of Zhili, Yuan instead appointed Wang Zhixiang to Nanjing without the administrative advice of Tang, his deputy, even though Tang was a member of Yuan's camp and was valued by Yuan.[5] However, as a progressive student who had studied in the United States and at a Western-style college (Queen's College in Hong Kong), Tang Shaoyi knew that the newly promulgated political rules could not be treated casually. Moreover, violation of the items in the *Provisional Covenant* outlining to whom the Cabinet was responsible not only adversely affected the political objectives of the Revolutionary Alliance members, but was also obviously tantamount to depriving Tang of his power. Tang Shaoyi became the first Prime Minister of the Cabinet on 13 March, but resigned angrily on 15 June, because he was a victim of Yuan's manipulation of the Cabinet responsibility system, having no power over his own ministers. Cai Yuanpei, Wang Chonghui, Song Jiaoren, and Wang Zhengting then tendered their resignations in turn. Lu Zhengxiang became the second Prime Minister of the Republic, but Lu was mediocre andYuan Shikai removed him on 22 September and appoint Zhao Bingjun as acting Prime Minister. It seemed that the Cabinet system had survived, but the real power of the National Council was in the hands of Yuan Shikai—which is why Song put all his energy into

[5] However, by this time, Tang Shaoyi had joined the Revolutionary Alliance.

the parliamentary election campaign and then strongly advocated Cabinet accountability. In his *Main Political Opinions* (Da Zheng Jian), Song gave a full explanation of the significance of the Cabinet system:

> The essence of the system of Cabinet responsibility is that the Cabinet rather than the President is responsible to parliament and the Cabinet acts for the President. Today, the system in our country features a system of Cabinet responsibility, but the Cabinet only has responsibility in name, not in reality, so politics are stymied. Our Party advocates that the future constitution will adopt the system of Cabinet accountability and that formal government will be enacted responsibly through the Cabinet organized by the political parties. All orders of the President should not only be approved by the Cabinet but also be drafted by the Cabinet, and the President should be in the position of responsibility and make sure he is secure.[6]

At the end of the year, Song Jiaoren did succeed in the election, with the KMT winning 269 of the 596 votes in the House of Representatives and 123 of the 274 votes in the Senate. This meant the KMT had the power to elect the President and formulate the constitution. However, Song Jiaoren, sensing a new crisis, warned that despite the smooth election campaign, Yuan Shikai would try to undermine the result. In fact, Yuan feared that, in the next round of elections for the Presidency, he would lose power, so he arranged that Song be assassinated on 20 March 1913. Before he died after being shot, Song did not realize that the instructions for the assassination attempt came from Yuan. He even asked Huang Xing to call Yuan before he died, telling him: "I respectfully acknowledge that Mr. President is open-minded and fair, and strives to protect civil rights". However, documents and evidence obtained by the investigation into the assassination suggested that Yuan Shikai had masterminded it, and this became the fuse that unleashed the armed conflict of the ensuing "Second Revolution". Before General Li Liejun (1882–1946) set up the General Command of the Anti-Yuan Army in Jiangxi on 12 July, Yuan Shikai had signed on April 26 a loan

[6] *Song Jiaoren Xiansheng Wenji* (Anthology of Mr. Song Jiaoren's Writings), *xia* volume, p. 189. Quoted in Li Yunhan, *Zhongguo Jindai Shi* (Modern History of China), Taipei: Sanmin Shuju, 2018, p. 235.

contract of 25 million pounds with banks representing five countries—Great Britain, Germany, France, Russia, and Japan, without the matter even being debated by Parliament. This "ravaging of the legislature", as Zhang Ji and Wang Zhengting described it, caused widespread anger among KMT members. However, opinion within the Kuomintang was not unified; but weighing up the possibility of successfully resolving the situation by force with the legitimacy of anti-Yuan action, the idea of legally resolving the problem came to prevail within the KMT. However, after Yuan Shikai in June successively removed three KMT members from governorships—of Jiangxi (Li Liejun), Guangdong (Hu Hanmin, 1879–1936), and Anhui (Bai Wenwei, 1876–1947), the "Second Revolution" directed against Yuan Shikai finally broke out. Regardless of the extent to which the revolutionists revealed how Yuan Shikai had historically been the main betrayer of the 1898 Reformers and had now implemented a dictatorship, the failure of the "Second Revolution" won little sympathy, and even in Hubei, where the 1911 Revolution began, the KMT was banned by Li Yuanhong.[7] People had just been given a respite from warfare, and any action that might lead to further fighting and turmoil was unwelcome. At this time there was a general tendency to accept Yuan Shikai as the legitimate representative of the Republic of China, and those revolutionists who wanted to use force to overthrow him were epitomized as power-hungry "thugs" or "rioters". The constitutionalists clearly did not support a violent "Second Revolution", and the Western powers for the most part adopted a stance close to that of Yuan Shikai. *The Times* of London (29 July 1913) even described the "Second Revolution" as a "riot of suspicious and greedy politicians", and in Shanghai, foreign

[7] *Shibao* (The Times) reported on 14 November 1913: "The KMT's Hubei branch and sub-branches were dissolved by order of the President. ... All plaques, seals, party membership cards, badges and other items were burned. Even the register of party members and the governors' residences were immediately impounded and sealed up". Ref: *Xinhai Geming zai Hubei Shiliao Xuanji* (Selected Documents of the 1911 Revolution in Hubei), Wuhan: Hubei People's Publishing House, 1981, pp. 711–712. Li Yuanhong stayed together with Yuan Shikai at the beginning of the Second Revolution and began to shut down Kuomintang offices throughout Hubei province. The provincial assembly also initiated the expulsion of KMT MPs. In August, Yuan Shikai, because "Vice-President Li was excessively pained and troubled by the North–South chaos and war preparations" (*Shibao*, 29 August 1913), specifically presented Li Yuanhong with a plaque inscribed "Pillar of the Republic".

missions prevented Sun Yat-sen and Huang Xing from renting property in the foreign concessions of that city.

The failure of the "Second Revolution" also once again prompted important revolutionary leaders to flee overseas; Sun Yat-sen believed that the main reason for the failure was the dispersal of the revolutionary ranks and the lack of a firm and clear guiding ideology. He began to reorganize the revolutionary parties as the Chinese Revolutionary Party (Zhonghua Geming Dang), in Tokyo, and he hoped that the new revolutionary party would achieve victory in the anti-imperialist revolution. On 23 June 1914, Sun Yat-sen was elected Prime Minister, and on 8 July, he promulgated *General Charter of the Chinese Revolutionary Party*, which stated that its "general policy is implementing civil rights and the people's livelihood", with the aim of "sweeping away autocracy" and achieving its aims through three periods characterized in turn by "military government", "tutelary government", and then "constitutional government".

The "Second Revolution" did not prevent Yuan Shikai from moving to achieve what he wanted, as is clear from a speech he delivered at a political conference in December 1913, which echoed past conflicts between liberal or democratic movements and conservative political views:

> Today everyone talks about "equality", but equality is only equality before the law, and does not mean that the distinctions of hierarchy should be abolished, with everyone able to deny the law and impose their independent standards ... "Freedom" is another beautiful modern term, but it is confined by the law, but within that context man is free. However, unrestricted freedom is something that does not exist. Those who advocate equality and freedom without asking whether sanctions should be imposed on those who disregard the law clearly know these things do not exist. They use grandiose slogans to promote rebellion for their own advantage ... Furthermore, the word "republic" might also sound elegant, but foreigners only understand the term to confer general freedom of speech domestically and not as license for the whole population to interfere with the government's actions. What can result from such interference, apart from social chaos? As for the term "civil rights", in addition to extending

the highest privilege of electing a president, it also includes representative power and the right to vote; it must not be understood to include executive administration.[8]

Yuan Shikai subsequently took these as the basic ideas for his centralization measures, which in fact coincided with his hope of resuming the throne in the Forbidden City. Emperor Puyi had this comment to make: "Shortly after the New Year, on my birthday, on the 14th day of the lunar calendar, President Yuan Shikai sent a protocol officer to congratulate me formally on the occasion. With this continuous encouragement coming from Yuan Shikai, the princes and imperial ministers who remained silent and had disappeared from the palace during the first year of the Republic again began wearing imperial robes and full costume, official hats with red buttons and decorative feathers, and even began again riding decorated horses on the street accompanied by guards of honor. The activity outside Shenwu Gate and inside the Forbidden City was again bustling. ...In the first year of the Republic, most of these people came to the Forbidden City in plain clothes, and only changed into court robes once they entered the Forbidden City, but starting in the second year of the Republic, they dared to wear all of their court dress out on the streets of the capital".[9] On 19 October in this second year, Yuan Shikai, after he was elected president in the General Election, by way of a gift to Emperor Puyi wrote him a very humble report, in which apart from stating that he had been legitimately elected as President he also expressed a strong affection for the Qing royal house, which led the Forbidden City to suspect that Yuan Shikai was planning a "restoration". Puyi recorded: "By the third year of the Republic, some people were beginning to say that this

[8] Taken from J. K. Fairbank, *Cambridge History of the Republic of China*, vol. 1, Chinese edition, Beijing: Chinese Social Sciences Press, p. 271. In Zhang Zhidong, Zhang Baixi and Rong Qing eds., *Zou Ding Xuetang Zhangcheng* (Proposed Charter for Setting up Colleges), 1904, chapter titled "Xuewu gangyao" (Outline of Education) contains the following statements: "Foreign countries are rich and powerful because in all things they have politics and law. In China today those who plagiarize Western scholarship express it as 'civil rights', 'freedom', and other words"; "They do not realize that the words 'civil rights' and 'freedom' make up half of foreign politics and law"; "What foreigners call 'civil rights', is an obligatory term. What is called 'freedom' is a legal term. A subject is legally obliged to do his duty; power and freedom are the happiness he enjoys. Without legal obligation, how can there be rights and freedoms?".

[9] Aisin-Gioro Puyi, *Wode Qianban Sheng* (The First Half of My Life), Beijing: Qunzong Chubanshe, 1980, p. 86.

would be the year of the restoration of the monarchy. Excitement began growing among my isolated and incorrigible subjects: Yuan Shikai made offerings to Confucius and adopted the official titles accorded the highest officers of the imperial court, as well as setting up an office to undertake the compilation of the orthodox history of the Qing dynasty and employing many of the old courtiers who formerly served the Qing".[10]

In the preparatory run-up to the constitution, it was already clear that the constitutional arrangement stipulated that there would be a parliament to formulate a constitution and then finally an election of the president would take place. According to the *Provisional Covenant*, the National Assembly would be established after ten months on 8 April 1913, and the ensuing task was the drafting of the Constitution by the Constitutional Drafting Committee, which was also known to the majority of members of Parliament. Yuan Shikai reversed this procedure, asking the governors of 14 provinces to send telegrams to the National Assembly calling for the election of a president as soon as possible. This most basic political mistake did not meet much resistance, and the Progressive Party of the constitutionalists gave him their support. On 5 September, after the "Second Revolution", the KMT's power was significantly reduced, and on 5 October, the National Assembly passed its *Law on the Election of the President*. As a result, the members of the National Assembly were coerced into voting three times, because Yuan did not get enough votes in the first two ballots and only with the third ballot did Yuan attain his goal. In his declaration on taking office on 10 October, Yuan Shikai made a point of condemning the "Second Revolution". Some members of the National Assembly did not concede defeat, and three weeks later, a draft constitution was issued, in the hope that the Cabinet system would restrain the President. On 4 November, Yuan Shikai retaliated by exercising his presidential powers and revoking the KMT's membership of the National Assembly under the pretext of the Party's involvement in the "Second Revolution", resulting in the loss of a quorum for the House and Senate, and in January of the following year, the National Assembly effectively collapsed. At the same time, Yuan Shikai organized a political conference under his own control on 26 November 1913, and then asked the political conference to hold a meeting on the revision of the *Covenant* on 24 January 1914. On 14 March, Yuan Shikai

[10] Aisin-Gioro Puyi, *Wode Qianban Sheng* (The First Half of My Life), Beijing: Qunzong Chubanshe, 1980, pp. 89–90.

announced his 57 members and felt free to clarify his request regarding how the *Covenant* would be modified. Yuan proposed seven amendments on March 18th. The *Law on the Covenant of the Republic of China*, published on 1 May, further strengthened Yuan Shikai's grasp on political, military, and financial power, effectively changing the responsible cabinet system to a presidential system, although the amended document had nominally been passed by the conference. However, as Liang Qichao noted, "every word reveals the hand of Yuan". Yuan directly arranged that the presidential term would be ten years, after which he could be re-elected, and the president's successor was to be recommended by the incumbent president. In January 1915, when Yuan Shikai's oldest son, Yuan Keding (1878–1955), was being introduced at a banquet hosted by Yang Du (1875–1931), and he solicited Liang Qichao's views on the nature of the political state, it was clear that Yuan Shikai was making the final preparations for establishing an imperial system. Of course, Yuan Shikai wanted Japan's support and, after much thought, on May 9th he finally accepted Japan's *Twenty-one Demands* with only its fifth section deleted, even though he knew that all the other *Demands* seriously abused China's sovereignty and that the consequences could be unimaginable.[11]

[11] The *Twenty-one Demands* was the name given to a proposed new treaty governing Sino-Japanese relations presented to China by the Japanese ambassador on 18 January. The *Demands* comprised 5 sections and 21 articles. The core demands were that China recognize Japan's interests in Qingdao and Shandong; Japanese people could freely immigrate to southern Manchuria and eastern Mongolia; Japan would control the Hanyeping Iron and Coal Company ostensibly as a Sino-Japanese company; and China could not lease out any coastal harbors or islands to countries other than Japan.

The fifth section comprised a total of seven paragraphs, which included demands that the Chinese government employ Japanese as political, financial, and military advisers, and that the police hire Japanese; Japanese hospitals, churches, and schools in the interior of China shall be granted the right to own land; China could only purchase Japanese ordnance, and China would also co-organize military factories with Japan. Moreover, China would procure Japanese raw materials, and grant the rights to construct several railways in the Yangtze River basin (connecting Wuchang with Jiujiang and Nanchang, another line between Nanchang and Hankou, and another between Nanchang and Chaozhou) to Japan. The *Twenty-one Demands* made government very difficult for Yuan Shikai. The United States and Great Britain, because of their own interests, did not provide China with any assistance by interfering. Japan continued to pressure the Chinese government and, unable to continue delaying negotiations, the Chinese government signed the *Demands* with only the fifth section removed. This seriously undermined the legitimacy of Yuan Shikai's government. The subsequent boycott of Japanese goods and the May 4th movement stemmed from the signing of the *Twenty-one Demands*, which were not officially repealed until March 1923.

Yuan interpreted Japan's vague political analysis of China as support for his transition from a republic to an imperial monarchy, so he even issued an order on 18 June "suppressing the boycott of Japanese goods and activities instigated by the revolutionary parties". In August, Yuan Shikai's adviser, the constitutional expert Frank J. Goodnow published an article titled simply "Monarchy or Republic?", which came to be called the *Goodnow Memo*, in which Goodnow argued that the adoption of a constitutional monarchy, rather than a republic, was the more appropriate course for China. Goodnow's Memo was translated into semi-classical, semi-modern Chinese prose. Although it was suspected to have been written at Yuan Shikai's request, the two opening sentences seem to have been justified by later history:

> A country must have a certain form of government, and usually the particular form of government of a particular country is not the result of the choice of the people of that country. There is not any possibility even for the most intellectual to exercise any mental influence over the question. Whether it be a monarchy or republic, it cannot be the creation of human power, except when it is suitable to the historical, habitual, social, and financial conditions of that country. If an unsuitable form of government is decided upon, it may remain for a short while, but eventually a system better suited will take its place.
>
> ……In short, the form of government of a country is usually the natural and only result of its circumstances.[12]

This was the month (August) in which Yang Du published his pamphlet titled "A Constitutional Monarchy Will Save the Nation" (*Junxian jiuguo lun*), translated by Putnam Weale as "A Defence of the Monarchical Movement", defending Yuan Shikai's desire to replace the republic with a constitutional monarchy, and launched the Peace-Planning Society (Chou'an Hui) at Yuan's urging. The Society's aim was to study whether a monarchy or a democracy was better suited to China, in order to "plan for the peace and security of the nation". The public knew full well this was an attempt to prepare public opinion for the reintroduction of the empire. Members of the Peace-Planning Society, such as Yan Fu,

[12] Putnam Weale, *The Fight for the Republic in China*, London: Hurst and Blackett, 1918, Chinese edition title: *Luanshi Yuan Shikai*, Beijing: Shangwu Yinshuguan, 2016, pp. 134–135.

Liu Shipei, Sun Yujun, Li Xiehe, and Hu Ying, all had different reasons for joining the Society. Yan Fu, for example, was listed as a member without giving his permission, even though he did disagree with the view that China could achieve genuine democracy at that time. However, the Society's *Manifesto* also revealed that members did have varying degrees of anxiety about the future of the country at this particular time: What kind of national political body could ensure China's stability and development? This was also a period when Chinese intellectuals paid great attention to German constitutionalism and nationalism; Yuan Shikai had earlier hired German officers to train his Beiyang (North Sea) Army, and at this time, he also wanted "Germany to be the teacher" in settling up the political system. Born in Ningbo, but educated in Switzerland, Bertram Lenox Simpson (1877–1930), who knew China well and wrote extensively about the country under the penname Putnam Weale, was hired by Li Yuanhong as an adviser to the Presidential Palace in 1916. In 1918, he had this to say about Yuan Shikai's ambition to become emperor: "The man who instructed Goodnow to write that famous 'Memorandum' is now openly betraying the trust that the whole country has placed in him, ready to wade through blood to satisfy his foolish ambitions".[13] As a result of the efforts of the Peace-Planning Society, petitions urging the replacement of the republic with an imperial system were sent from all over the country to the House of Representatives, and on 20 November, the National Assembly voted to approve the monarchy by a vote of 1,993 votes in favor of the move. On 11 December, the provincial representatives went through a charade of recommending Yuan for the post of Emperor of the Chinese Empire and he feigned to reject the proposal, but a day after the feigned rejection, Yuan accepted the position of Emperor, and on 12 December announced that he would replace the Republic of China with the Chinese Empire, designating 1916 the "Hongxian New Year" (Year of the Magnificent Constitution), to signal the beginning of the new dynasty.

Although the KMT's domestic power was greatly weakened after the Second Revolution, Yuan Shikai on this occasion had completely misread the political situation in the country. On 12 December, the third day after Yuan Shikai's public announcement of the monarchy, Japan, Britain,

[13] Putnam Weale, *The Fight for the Republic in China*, London: Hurst and Blackett, 1918, Chinese edition title: *Luanshi Yuan Shikai*, Beijing: Shangwu Yinshuguan, 2016, p. 134.

Russia, Italy, and France issued a joint warning that they would monitor the political situation in case of unrest in China. For Yuan Shikai, the more threatening force opposing his assumption of the title of emperor was Liang Qichao and his Progressive Party. Yuan Shikai had not realized that Liang Qichao's support for him was based on an attempt to establish a true constitutional system through Yuan's political resources. Yuan's intimidation did not make Liang Qichao retreat because he was a committed scholar, and Liang also had the strong support of his student, the revolutionary military figure and Yunnan warlord Cai E (1882–1916). In order to defend the republic, it was time to regroup the forces of the various parties. Cai E jointly set up a National Defense Government and National Defense Army together with Li Liejun of the Chinese Revolutionary Party and the governor of Yunnan, Tang Jiyao (1883–1927), and on 25 December they electrified the nation by declaring independence and sending troops to crush Yuan. Governor Tang, Cai, and Li jointly made a vow in the hope of arousing a sympathetic response from all political parties and, pointedly echoing Yuan's claims to support, from the people of all ethnic groups across the country:

> To overthrow Yuan and save the country, we are of one mind, and we call on you to help us, in view of the situation, by joining us as comrades, mindful that all former party differences are now a matter of the past.
>
> China's five ethnic groups are one with the Republic. By destroying the Republic, Yuan has become the sworn enemy of China's five ethnic groups, who are united as one in the commitment to no more racial boundaries.
>
> ……

When Guizhou (27 January 1916) and Guangxi (15 March) also declared independence, Yuan Shikai asked for Japan's support, but was refused. Yuan felt that the problem was serious, and planned to return to the Republic to resume the presidency. On 21 March, Yuan Shikai signed a decree announcing the abolition of the imperial system, publicly acknowledging his mistakes, in which he said:

> [As my sincerity has not been such as to win the hearts of the people and my judgment has not been sound enough to appraise every man, I have myself alone to blame for lack of virtue. Why then should I blame others? The people have been thrown into misery and my soldiers have

been made to bear hardships; and further the people have been cast into panic and commerce has rapidly declined. When I search my own heart a measure of sorrow fills it. I shall, therefore, not be unwilling to suppress myself in order to yield to others.]

[I am still of the opinion that the "designation petitions" submitted through the acting Li Fa Yuan are unsuited to the demands of the time; and the official acceptance of the Imperial Throne made on the 11th day of the 12th month of last year (11 December 1915) is hereby cancelled. "The designation petitions" of the Provinces and of the Special Administrative Areas are hereby all returned through the State Department to the Tsan Cheng Yuan, *i.e.*, the acting Li Fa Yuan (Parliament), to be forwarded to the petitioners for destruction; and all the preparations connected therewith are to cease at once.]

[In this wise I hope to imitate the sincerity of the Ancients by taking on myself all the blame so that my action may fall in line with the spirit of humanity which is the expression of the will of Heaven. I now cleanse my heart and wash my thoughts to the end that trouble may be averted, and the people may have peace. ... In brief I now confess that all the faults of the country are the result of my own faults.][14]

The National Defense Army (Huguo Jun) ignored Yuan's strategy and continued to push to overthrow him. Yuan relied on his last forces, led by Xu Shichang, Duan Qirui, and Li Yuanhong, to try to defuse the crisis. On April 6th and 12th, Guangdong and Zhejiang declared heir independence, and even Kang Youwei, Zhang Jian, Tang Hualong, Wu Tingfang, Tang Shaoyi, and others called on Yuan Shikai to step down. Firstly Xu Shichang and then Duan Qirui asked to be allowed to resign while maintaining their distance from Yuan; Feng Guozhang had the opportunity to indulge his wish and replace Yuan as President, and so proposed to contact, on behalf of Yuan, the representatives of the provinces meeting in Nanjing to negotiate whether Yuan remain in his post, taking this opportunity to use the power of the provinces which had not yet declared independence to balance or at least dilute the strength of the National

[14] Putnam Weale, *The Fight for the Republic in China*, London: Hurst and Blackett, 1918, pp. 191–194. Putnam Weale gives the date of the *Decree Cancelling the Empire* as 22 March.

Defense Army, to create new political opportunities. However, the deliberations of the representatives did not proceed in accordance with the expectations of Feng and Yuan, and the majority of delegates agreed that Yuan should resign from the National Assembly. After Yuan discovered that Sichuan's governor Chen Yi (1870–1939) and Hunan's governor Tang Xiangming (1885–1975), whom he regarded as his most reliable supporters, had also declared independence, on 22 and 29 May, respectively, he took to his bed and died on 6 June. On the following day, the Republic of China was restored, and Li Yuanhong succeeded Yuan as President.

It was not until Yuan Shikai announced the abolition of the imperial system that people once again dared to speak out. On 21 May, Tang Shaoyi, who had studied in the United States as a child, was Yuan's associate in his youth, and served as the Prime Minister of the Republic of China, made this assessment of Yuan Shikai:

> Yuan's strategy is to pit one party against the other to form checks and balances. Sometimes he would send the same people to spy on each other and report to him each other's thinking about a particular plan. Fearing bombs and assassination, Yuan Shikai thus locked himself up behind high walls. For a leader elected by the people, it is extremely strange to be so afraid to face the public. During his four years in office, he only ventured out from his mansion on less than six occasions. He should have sat in an open-top car and showed his people the trust he had placed in them, or that he was not afraid of them.[15]

Liang Qichao, who had always politically adhered to support for a constitutional monarchy, later made the following comment on Yuan Shikai's restoration of the imperial system:

> He knew that the whole nation was opposed to him becoming emperor, but he thought they would be unable to resist as they had insufficient strength and he regarded the nation as hopeless. He believed that the main strength was guns and cannons and, with hundreds of thousands of soldiers under him, he was afraid of no-one. His second strength was finances, some as foreign loans and some he minted, so he was not concerned that

[15] From Zheng Xiyuan, *Gonghe Shinian: Niuyue Shibao Minchu Guanchaji* 1911–1921 (The Decade of the Republic: *The New York Times* 1911–1921), Beijing: Dangdai Zhongguo Chubanshe, 2018, p. 115.

people might not follow his direction. However, the upshot was that those hundreds of thousands of soldiers and tens of millions of dollars made almost no impact, and he would never become emperor. From this we can see that he did not have a clue and could never understand the power of the national will.[16]

In any case, Yuan Shikai's failure to restore the throne meant that the "imperial system" (the millennia-old Qin-Han polity) and the formal legitimacy of the Confucian political system had come to an end in China. However, as an acknowledged consensus, "constitutionality" was only a form of discourse, which in the context of inherited and still powerful Confucian ideology was simply a cheque that had not been honored; the politicians emerging in the wake of Yuan Shikai's demise, in order to make their governance appeared legitimate and the regime stable, would always strategically prepare new modes of discourse in order to protect and maintain the political arrangements that they designed and regarded as legitimate.

On 7 June 1916, the hesitant Republican, Li Yuanhong (1864–1928), took over as President. People discussed whether Yuanhong's "appointment" or accession to office was based on the *Provisional Covenant*, the constitution of 1912, or he was acting for the deceased President Yuan Shikai on the basis of the *Constitution* of 1914. Although Li Yuanhong had agreed to the Nanjing government's *Provisional Covenant* of the first year of the Republic (*Minyuan Yuefa*), Duan Qirui insisted that the appointment be based on the *Provisional Constitution* of 1914 (*Minsan Yuefa*) proclaimed by Yuan Shikai and introduced for the "tutelary" period after Sun Yat-sen resigned. These different interpretations led to a legal dispute, in which Sun Yat-sen and Liang Qichao warned Duan Qirui not to break the law, to avoid triggering a new political crisis. On 25 June, Li Dingxin (1862–1930), the naval commander based in Shanghai, and Lin Baoyi (1863–1930), commander of the First Fleet, announced their independence from the Beijing government and support for the South, and Feng Guozhang, who had built up a power base in Shanghai, also exerted pressure on Beijing to restore the 1912 constitution. The outcome of this wrangling was a victory for the revolutionists.

[16] Liang Qichao, "Cai Songpo and Yuan Shikai" (1926), *Liang Qichao Zishu: 1873–1929* (Liang Qichao's Self-selected Writings: 1873–1929), Beijing: Renmin Ribao Chubanshe, 2011, pp. 180–181.

Li Yuanhong announced he would comply with the *Provisional Covenant* of 1912 made public on 11 March, and on 1 August, the National Assembly, which had previously been dissolved by Yuan Shikai, reconvened, and Cai E was awarded the highest state honor by Li Yuanhong. However, addressing the need to balance power and meet the exigencies of the overall situation, the revolutionists' Military Commission was dissolved and Duan Qirui was appointed Prime Minister by Li Yuanhong. The legal problems created by Yuan Shikai's restoration of imperial rule were finally brought to an end.

Political stability had not however returned. After Li Yuanhong took over the presidency, he was in constant conflict with Prime Minister Duan Qirui; as a result, fundamental contradictions and wrangling between the Presidential Palace and the National Council led to constant changes of personnel within the government. The basic logic underlying political circles was by and large a persistence of the earlier division between constitutional and revolutionary factions. In the National Assembly, this rift manifested as a division between the KMT group's "Constitutional Consultation Society" (Xianzheng Shangque Hui) and the Progressive Party's "Constitutional Research Society" (Xianfa Yanjiu Hui). The main figures in the former group were Zhang Ji (1882–1947), Sun Hongyi (1872–1936), Lin Sen (1868–1943), and Wu Jinglian (1873–1944), who stressed that the constitution provide for the provincial constitutional outline, and that provincial governors be elected; in the latter group Liang Qichao, Tang Hualong, and Lin Changmin (1876–1925) were prominent figures who advocated centralization and the appointment by the central government of provincial governors. At meetings in the House and Senate, physical fights even broke out over constitutional issues. On 3 February 1917, the United States of America cut diplomatic ties with Germany, because Germany announced it was imposing a naval blockade using submarines in the North Atlantic and invited China to cooperate. Duan Qirui and Liang Qichao, as well as members of the Research Society in the National Congress, advocated entering into an agreement with the United States, breaking off diplomatic relations with Germany, and joining the Allies.[17] Liang Qichao and the others believed that participation in the War would enable China to recover concessions ceded to Germany and Austria and allow an extension of the period for repaying the Boxer Indemnity. However, when the case for entering the War was submitted to the National Assembly, the Kuomintang faction opposed the war, the important opponent being Sun Yat-sen, but Tang Shaoyi and Zhang Binglin also advocated neutrality. Unsurprisingly, in addition to Germany wanting to prevent China from entering the War, both Japan and the United States made a concerted effect to have China enter the War; Japan hoped to gain economic benefits and control over the Beijing government through China's participation in the war, and the United States wanted to strengthen the Allies and end the War as soon as possible. In order to achieve his own aims, Duan Qirui called a meeting of the provincial military governors and formed a group to issue a telegram announcing that China was declaring war on Germany. On 10 May, Duan also mobilized a "citizen's petition group" composed of people drawn from business, government, and military circles to surround the House of Representatives and force members to agree to the bill declaring war. These measures led to widespread resentment and anger over the illegality of his action, and even the foreign, judicial, agricultural, commercial, and naval ministers resigned. Finally, the House of Representatives decided to suspend the declaration of war on the grounds that members of the Cabinet had resigned. As a result, Duan Qirui's group of provincial military commanders clashed with some members of the National Assembly; the former demanded that Li Yuanhong dissolve the parliament, and the latter demanded that Duan reshuffle the cabinet and then resign. Li Yuanhong decided to remove Duan Qirui from the post of Prime Minister, but on this occasion, Li Yuanhong was prevented from doing so by Duan Qirui, because Li was relying on his order with a countersignature by Foreign Minister Wu Tingfang to announce the removal of Duan, but Duan instead issued a telegram, announcing that the dismissal

[17] The "Research Department" (Yanjiu Xi) can be regarded as a political faction led by Liang Qichao in the early years of the Republic of China. It took its name from the "Constitutional Research Society" established in Beijing in 1916. Because of its moderate attitude and manner, it was at odds with the Marxists of that period and the Kuomintang. On 1 September 1917, the KMT hired assassins to shoot Tang Hualong, an important figure in the Research Department, and in November 1925, a prominent functionary in the KMT, Zhu Jiahua (1893–1963), led a group of young students who burned down the offices of *Chenbao* (Morning News) published by the Research Department.

order without his personal countersignature was null and void. This triggered the declaration of independence from Li Yuanhong's government by several provincial governors and military governors. When Li Yuanhong could not find anyone appropriate to help mediate the situation, he summoned the military governor of Anhui, Zhang Xun (1854–1923), to come to Beijing. The first thing Zhang Xun did after leading 5,000 soldiers into Beijing was to demand that Li Yuanhong dissolve parliament. Not long after Li Yuanhong, as previously agreed, announced on 13 June the "dissolution of the House and Senate on the same day", and, using the same illegal abuse of power, Zhang Xun on 1 July simply pushed the Qing heir-apparent back onto the throne, as Emperor Puyi. Zhang Xun, who had planned this "Restoration" from the depths of his fondness for the Qing dynasty for whom he was a loyalist, knelt before the former emperor, Puyi, on entering the Forbidden City. However, before embarking on this new restoration attempt, Zhang Xun had sought agreement to his operation from Kang Youwei and from Feng Guozhang and Duan Qirui who had once been Beiyang allies. This also showed that, even though China was already in the sixth year of the Republic, many people still had warm feelings for the former Qing dynasty. Zhang Xun served as prime minister of the cabinet and succeeded Cao Kun (1862–1938) as governor of Zhili, but he did not give Duan an official post. Twelve days later, Zhang Xun was driven into the Dutch Embassy by Duan Qirui's army and, ironically, Zhang Xun felt that he was the one who had been betrayed.

After the failure of Zhang Xun's restoration, the remaining denizens and former officials of the Forbidden City turned their hopes of restoration to the new powers-that-be. As Puyi described in his *Autobiography*: "After Feng and Duan acquired power, the isolated court officials and eunuchs focused their hopes on these two new powerful incumbents".[18] This was because the "hopefuls" remaining in the Palace knew that these republican leaders had earlier been allies of Zhang Xun. They had not seen their own rejection of the new political rules as being of consequence, the only issue being in whose hands power rested and how could they expand their own spheres of influence. It would seem that after Yuan Shikai's death, the Beiyang clique began to split. The conflict between Interim President Feng Guozhang and Premier Duan Qirui led to the emergence

[18] Aisin-Gioro Puyi, *Wode Qianban Sheng* (The First Half of My Life), Beijing: Qunzong Chubanshe, 1980, p. 111.

of a Zhili clique (Feng) and an Anhui clique (Duan). From 1916 to 1927, the power of the Beijing government was almost entirely in the hands of warlords, so people generally refer to this as "the period of rule by the Beiyang warlords", during which war broke out between the Zhili and Anhui factions (1920), and the Zhili and Fengtian factions (1922, 1924), and finally in 1925 in a general melee between warlords (notably, Sun Chuanfang, Wu Peifu, and Feng Yuxiang). These wars for spheres of influence and power were unjust. The respective political banners and reasons to which these warlords appealed in their conflicts with their enemies lacked the political ideals and social aspirations of the modern state; the warlords were only interested in their own areas of influence and changing interests.[19] This meant that the wars between them would lead to the lack of credit in this country,[20] political disorder, economic decline, and social chaos.[21] This was why the Kuomintang, led by Sun Yat-sen, wanted to

[19] In 1916, there were about half a million people in the Chinese army; in 1918 there were more than 1 million; in 1924 there were more than 1.5 million; and by 1928 there were more than 2 million. The military spending of the Beiyang government in Beijing was more than 150 million yuan in 1916 and 600 million yuan in 1925. (See: Qi Xisheng, *Zhongguo de Junfa Zhengzhi: 1916–1928* [China's Warlord Politics: 1916–1928], Beijing: Zhongguo Renmin Daxue Chubanshe, 1991, p. 71).

[20] On 5 November 1924, Feng Yuxiang was encouraged by the Soviet Union to send all the staff of the Qing palaces to leave the Forbidden City within three hours. 470 eunuchs and more than 100 palace women were evicted from the palace. Feng allowed the eunuchs and palace women find their own way out, so that some of them who lacked any means of livelihood jumped into the 4-meter-deep moat. However, under the watchful eye of the international community, Empress Dowager Longyu signed a letter of abdication for Puyi, which handed over all Qing territory to the new Republic of China. The Republic of China, as a republic comprising five ethnic groups (Manchu, Mongol, Hui, Tibetan, and Han), adopted *Articles of Favorable Treatment for the Qing Royal Household*, which was a contractual commitment supporting members of the imperial household. On the following day, Duan Qirui called Feng Yuxiang to complain, but Feng Yuxiang did not think about tearing up the contract and replied: "This time we moved troops to Beijing, but I can say that nothing was done. Only Puyi was expelled, which is what the people wanted, and we can declare to the world that nothing shameful occurred". In fact, under the slogans of "revolution" and "people", all Chinese regimes had rarely troubled themselves over such concerns. Examining the reasons for this, it would seem China's spiritual cultural traditions lacked a contractual spirit, and the change of dynasties and the confirmation of legitimacy were brought mostly through force.

[21] The warlord factions of this period were very complex. In addition to the Zhili and Anhui factions, there was the Fengtian system of which Zhang Zuolin was commander-in-chief, as well as warlord factions in Shanxi led by Yan Xishan, the northwest led by Feng Yuxiang, Yunnan led by Tang Jiyao, Guangxi led by Lu Rongting, Hunan led by Zhao Huan, and in Sichuan led by Liu Cunhou (1885–1960) and Liu Wenhui (1895–1976).

launch a Northern Expedition, a campaign to overthrow the warlords of the north in order to achieve a true "Republic".

At the beginning, in response to Duan Qirui's "policy of declaring war on Germany" and his use of military governors, Sun Yat-sen launched the Constitution Protection Movement (Hufa yundong), his aim being to protect the original Constitution of 1912, otherwise China's reality would be no different from that of the recent imperial restorations. He wrote in a telegram to the authorities in Guangdong, Guangxi, Guizhou, Hunan, Yunnan, and Sichuan provinces: "Parliament is the center of the Republic and the Constitution is the basis of the founding of the nation. The patriotic public which supports the central government should make it their main task to protect the National Congress and the Constitution. Today, the law might have lost the power of sanction but we must not use military force to mete out punishment; killing large numbers of people will not eliminate the source of social chaos and stabilize the overall situation".[22] However, the soldiers and politicians who had cooperated with Sun Yat-sen under different conditions and circumstances now acted out of their respective interests and political objectives, leading to a series of defeats for Sun Yat-sen's "Constitutional Protection" battle. During the period of confrontation between the northern and southern governments, Sun Yat-sen tried to keep the concept of the "Republic" from being tarnished, and again and again raised the question of the legitimization of the Beijing government based on whether the parliament should be restored. However, the men Sun relied on, Lu Rongting and Tang Jiyao, were only interested in their own spheres of influence, and they had their own reasons for supporting Sun. Although they were among the forces opposed to Zhang Xun's imperial restoration, after Duan Qirui regained power from Zhang Xun, Lu, and Tang not only did not share in the spoils of this victory but were threatened by Duan Qirui's turn to eliminate them and so they hoped to gain far-reaching support from Sun Yat-sen to turn this situation around. In fact, the outcome of Sun Yat-sen's cooperation with the warlords was roughly similar to that of

[22] *Guofu Quanji* (Collected Works of Sun Yat-sen), vol. 3, p. 451. This work is quoted in Li Yunhan, *Zhongguo Jindai Shi* (Modern History of China), Taipei: Sanmin Shuju, 2018, p. 261.

Liang Qichao.[23]。Sun found himself trapped on a warship as a result of the opposition of the Commander-in-Chief of the Guangdong Army, Chen Jiongming (1878–1933), until Chiang Kai-shek arrived in Guangzhou on 29 June 1923 to help Sun, who was eventually freed and arrived back in Shanghai on 14 August. In January 1924, Chen Jiongming was driven out by the Yunnan-Guangxi Allied Forces and the Guangdong Army under Sun Yat-sen's command, and Sun returned to Guangzhou. Sun Yat-sen has this assessment of his own leadership of the Constitution Protection Movement:

> The battle to protect the constitution lasted for a total of six years; state losses were significant, people sacrificed a lot, and military action continued for a long time, so supporting the troops has been a heavy local burden. So, now as I announce the end of the Constitution Protection Movement, I must redeploy soldiers as builders to show my dedication to remedying what has been lost. If this proposition is implemented, it will benefit the nation and the people's prosperity; otherwise, the results achieved by the battle to protect the constitution will be that the concept of the constitution will have remained indestructible in people's minds, and the achievements of 1916 will be equal to those of 1911.[24]

As early as October 1917, following the campaign to overthrow Zhang Xun's restoration of the monarchy, the Anhui clique's Duan Qirui used his power in the National Assembly to get Xu Shichang, who had originally been an official (*Taifu*, Grand Mentor) at the Qing court, selected as official president—though the real power would remain in Duan's hands.

[23] In "Random notions on the current situation" (*Shiju zagan*), published in *New Youth* in 1917 (vol. 3, no. 4), Chen Duxiu made an interesting comparison between the Progressive Party, represented by Liang Qichao, and the Kuomintang, headed by Sun Yat-sen: "The Progressive Party has no shortage of virtuous and respectable people. Yet I would have to remark that the Progressive Party are also eager to win a name for themselves and attach themselves to the powerful; their fear of fundamental reform is their shortcoming. For this reason, Progressive Party members are happy to make use of the powerful who in turn make use of them. They were somewhat tainted by Yuan Shikai, and now they seem to be deceived by the warlords. The honorable behavior of the KMT is constantly defeated, while the ignominious and shameful of the Progressive Party always wins the day". (*Chen Duxiu Zhuzuo Xuan* [A Selection of Chen Duxiu's Writings], Shanghai: Shanghai Renmin Chubanshe, 1993, p. 317).

[24] *Guofu Quanji* (Collected Works of Sun Yat-sen), vol. 2, p. 191. This work is quoted in Li Yunhan, *Zhongguo Jindai Shi* (Modern History of China), Taipei: Sanmin Shuju, 2018, p. 265.

Xu had been the mastermind behind Zhang Xun's restoration plan.[25] On Xu becoming president, Puyi was again hopeful of becoming emperor; he not only followed relevant developments in the news,[FN026][26] but also paid special attention to Xu's political plans. What nostalgic Puyi observed and experienced revealed that the "Republican" period from Yuan Shikai's time to the May Fourth Movement was an age of political instability. Referring to this phenomenon in a speech to the Shanghai Youth Association on 8 October 1919 titled "The First Step in Transforming China", Sun Yat-sen emphasized that what was preventing national construction on the "exhausted graveyard" of China were the bureaucrats, warlords, and politicians. In the editorial policy statement for his magazine *Da*

[25] In describing the background of the "1917 restoration", Puyi had this to say about Xu Shichang:

"The germination of the second restoration attempt went back to the failure of the first attempt by the self-proclaimed Hongxian Emperor, Yuan Shikai. At that time, Yuan Shikai's Beiyang military system was embattled, and Xu Shichang, who had been dismissed for opposing Yuan Shikai's "overstepping" by seeking to be emperor, discussed the possibility of a second restoration in a secret telegram with Zhang Xun and the Beiyang general Ni Sichong (1868–1924), saying that "the Democratic Party has been forced to acknowledge it is best to return the Qing royal house and that Yuan Shikai remain in the post of Prime Minister and control the military". The proposal was agreed to by Zhang and Ni, but because they did not receive the support of the ministers of various countries they did not dare to act. After Yuan's death, they continued their activities, holding a series of meetings with officers of the Beiyang Army in Xuzhou and Nanjing. When public opinion moved in support of Yuan, the leaders and warlords of the Beiyang clique came to pay their respects they took the opportunity, under the auspices of Xu Shichang, to reach a unanimous decision to restore the empire". Ref: Aisin-Gioro Puyi, *Wode Qianbansheng* (Autobiography: The First Half of My Life), Beijing: Qunzhong Chubanshe (Masses Press), 1980, p. 108.

Later, Duan Qirui took advantage of Zhang Xun's eagerness to stage a restoration, and he succeeded in regaining power lost to Li Yuanhong. As Puyi saw it: The result of Zhang Xun's restoration "was completed by Duan Qirui and Feng Guozhang, one became prime minister again and the other became president, but Zhang Xun was the main culprit". Ref: Aisin-Gioro Puyi, *Wode Qianbansheng* (Autobiography: The First Half of My Life), Beijing: Qunzhong Chubanshe (Masses Press), 1980, p. 110.

[26] Puyi wrote: "Immediately after the failure of the restoration, *Shanghai Xinwen Bao* ran an opinion piece, in which one passage most moved people in the Forbidden City: 'Xu Donghai [Xu Shichang] did not behave at all recklessly, because this restoration was not the work of Zhang Xun but of the Beiyang generals who had already bowed down to the courtiers....' Not only was I moved for a few days by the popular enthusiasm that I become emperor again, but inside and outside the Forbidden City supporters of the ancien regime also widely cherished this idea, at least in the early days after Xu Shichang assumed his post". Ref: Aisin-Gioro Puyi, *Wode Qianbansheng* (Autobiography: The First Half of My Life), Beijing: Qunzhong Chubanshe (Masses Press), 1980, pp. 111–112.

Zhonghua (Greater China) in 1915, Liang Qichao wrote: "The dreams that my compatriots nurtured for so many years are now empty, and nothing remains. ...during the past twenty more years, at every level of society people advocated the New Learning and the reforms of the New Administration, but the upshot is that we have now reached the stage where these are things that all of society is exhausted by and loathes: talk of wholesome military training has been replaced by increasingly troubling brigandage and social order is increasingly disturbed; talk of financial management has increasingly given way to empty coffers and forced bankruptcies; talk of education has been replaced by a taming of the nation so that the people are no longer literate; talk of industrial enterprise has given way to the taming of the nation so that people can no longer even get the food they need. In a hundred other instances, it is the same story".[27] Such a status quo would naturally cast an indelible shadow and distress all those who had held out hope for the "Republic". To them, it now seemed that the post-revolutionary situation was not substantially different from the pre-revolutionary situation, so what reason was there for hope?

New Culture Movement and "May Fourth" Movement

The establishment of the Republic of China was a victory for anti-Manchu nationalism, but Yuan Shikai's restoration of the empire, the melee between warlords, and the corruption of powerful politicians, as well as the recklessness of the imperialist powers, shifted the focus of nationalism to anti-imperialism and a new awareness of ideas. Yuan Shikai's approval for implementing Japan's *Twenty-one Demands* was the trigger for a new round of anti-imperialism, with no one agreed that Japan appoint advisers or officers to serve in China's politics, finances, military, and police, as it would represent a complete loss of sovereignty. At the same time, more intellectuals had come to believe that only by bringing about a thorough awareness in the nation's thinking could ethical issues be tackled; only then could the nation adapt to the changing times and acquire a new lease of life. The emergence of a new generation of intellectuals initiated a new

[27] Liang Qichao, *Yinbing-shi Wenji* (The Anthology of Prose from the Drinker's Studio), vol. 33, p. 80.

movement in ideology and culture; the new phenomena in thought and culture during the period following the failure of Yuan Shikai's restoration to the Northern Expedition are generally described as the "New Culture Movement". Meanwhile, the May Fourth Movement, which broke out in 1919, is generally considered to be the climax of the New Culture Movement and the momentum of the New Culture Movement was launched in a political direction shaped by social practice. Indeed, throughout the twentieth century, only the New Culture Movement exerted a profound influence on subsequent historical periods, and it is often compared to the period of intellectual contention launched by the Hundred Schools in the Warring States period and so is sometimes called "China's Renaissance".

Given Cai Yuanpei's early involvement in the anti-Manchu revolution and the conditions he provided for young intellectuals after he became President of Peking University, Cai was regarded as the mentor of the New Culture Movement.[28]

In 1898, Cai Yuanpei renounced the option of assuming a position as an official at the Qing court by virtue of his success in the imperial examinations and returned to his hometown to serve instead as principal of the Shaoxing Chinese and Western School. He believed that the main reason for the failure of the 1898 reform movement was a lack of educated talent: "If we do not first train innovative talent but simply want to rely on a minority to seize power and reject conservatism, then we are completely deluded".[29] In 1901, Cai went to Nanyang Public School in Shanghai as the general teacher of its special class. One of his students, Huang Yanpei (1878–1965) later recalled how Cai Yuanpei encouraged his students to learn public speaking, to give them powers of social persuasion so they could enlighten people more effectively in the cause of national salvation. Unlike many revolutionary party members, Cai Yuanpei believed in the importance of public awareness, and so always insisted on training talented individuals through education. Cai Yuanpei explained the purpose of the China Education Association, which he

[28] Before taking over as president of Peking University in January 1917, Cai spent most of his time in politics. Although Cai Yuanpei was 36 years old and was involved in assassination organizations organized by Yang Dusheng, He Haiqiao, Zhang Shizhao and others, his outstanding contribution to Peking University left him with an image of moderation and scholarly refinement in the minds of later intellectuals.

[29] *Cai Zimin Xiansheng Yanxing Lu* (Record of Cai Yuanpei's Words and Deeds, vol. 1, p. 5).

founded with Ye Han, Jiang Guanyun, and others in April 1902, as realizing the republican ideal. Jiang Weiqiao, a former head of the Patriotic Girls' School, wrote in an article titled "Memories of the China Education Association" in *Dongfang Zazhi* (Eastern Miscellany, Volume 33, no. 1), published on 1 January 1936, that education should "on the surface conform to the principles of education but covertly advocate revolution". Cai Yuanpei himself, when talking about the Education Association and the Patriotic Girls School he later set up, admitted that when the school was "first founded" during the Manchu Qing dynasty, it was revolutionary in nature:

> At that time, most idealists, in view of the political ills of the Manchu Qing and the increasingly unwell state of the country which seemed like a seriously ill man not responding to medicine, would rise as a group and plan revolution to cure the county. Revolution was thus the prescribed treatment. The revolutionary group in Shanghai was called the China Education Association. Wherever the revolutionary spirit is to be found, in males or females, it should be promoted with education as its basis. Therefore, among girls' schools there is the Patriotic Girls' Schools, and among boys' schools there is the Patriotic Learning Association.[30]

In fact, the immediate reason for the founding of the Patriotic Education Association was the wave of school withdrawals in November after students at the Nanyang Public School clashed with the school because of their concerns about infringements on their freedom of thought and speech. Students at the Nanyang Public School believed that a teacher, Guo Zhenying was "blatantly treating students as slaves", and that the General Administration of the school had grossly "suppressed the freedom of speech of students", so those students who could not tolerate the situation decided to drop out of school. The school believed that the liberal thinking among the students was related to Cai Yuanpei's educational content and the revolutionary ideas he instilled in students, so they accused Cai of being responsible for the trend in the school. The upshot was that teacher withdrew from the school together with the students. The China Education Association founded the Patriotic Education Association soon after receiving a letter of support signed by the

[30] Cai Yuanpei, "Speech at the Patriotic Girls' School" (Zai Aiguo Nü Xuexiao zhi Yanshuo), 15 January 1917, *Dongfang Zazhi*, vol. 14, no. 1.

more than 200 students who had withdrawn. Three months later, Cai Yuanpei hired Zhang Taiyan, the first prominent scholar to cut off his queue in protest against the Manchu dynasty, to lecture at the Patriotic Education Society. It is entirely conceivable that this intellectual who regarded Zou Rong's *Revolutionary Army* as "the foremost textbook for today's national education" was primarily instigating participation in the revolution during his lectures at the Patriotic Society, as Zhang Taiyan personally acknowledged: "We were focused on issues related to the rise and collapse of the Ming and Qing dynasties, and were not concerned with study".[31] The model of instigation provided by Cai Yuanpei and other lecturers, especially their constant calls for free speech in the "Academic Trend" column of the newspaper *Subao*, inspired many events in the student movement of the day.[32] To a certain extent, the Patriotic Society readily recalls the Current Affairs College (Shiwu Xuetang) and Southern Studies Association (Nan Xuehui) presided over by Liang Qichao and Tan Sitong more than a decade previously in Changsha. The similarities encompass their intentional and unintentional transformation of a school into a relatively independent political planning organization, with students becoming members of political organizations and teachers naturally becoming leaders and organizers. On the other hand, just as Hunan's *Xiangbao* and *Xiang Xuebao* served as specialized newspapers for reformist organizations, *Subao*, after signing a contract with the Education Association, became the de facto political organ of the Education Association as a political group and related revolutionary party. It was not until June 1907, when Cai Yuanpei traveled to Germany with China's ambassador, Sun Baoqi, to take up study there, that Cai Yuanpei's political activities came to a temporary end.

In 1913, Cai Yuanpei, rebuking those who accused him of resigning together with Tang Shaoyi and thus influenced the upcoming National Interim Educational Conference, said that nothing could be achieved without the protection of the republican political system. As he had done

[31] "Taiyan Xiansheng Ziding Nianpu" (Mr. Zhang Taiyan's Autobiographical Annales), *Jindai Shi Ziaoliao* (Modern History Documents), no. 1, 1957.

[32] Cai Yuanpei and Wu Zhihui expressed their support in a telegram of April 1903 for Zhang Shizhao, Lin Yijun and the others of the 31 students who withdrew from Nanjing's Jiangnan Lushi Xuetang and helped them join the Patriotic Society. Soon after, Cai and Wu expressed support in the "Letter to Zhejiang Comrades" in *Subao* newspaper for the more than 80 students from the college Zhejiang Qiushi Daxuetang in Hangzhou, which suggested that the students set up their own school and promised them financial support.

a few years previously, in light of the political situation, he removed himself far from trouble, this time going to Leipzig to study. During the period of the "Second Revolution", Cai Yuanpei returned to China at the request of Sun Yat-sen to help conduct the revolution against Yuan Shikai, but Cai was not in favor of using force to solve problems. Before Yuan Shikai took the initiative and attacked the Kuomintang in the South, Cai Yuanpei issued a statement regarding what position he thought the Kuomintang should adopt:

> Our Party's revolution, which seeks happiness for the majority of the people must continue to assess the feelings of the majority of people. Most people now do not take the initiative in moving forward but are goaded and trampled; most of my compatriots share this common grievance. Our Party must simply keep up a steady pace and persevere, committing our lives to creating a true republic; only then will the majority of people sympathize with us, and our Party will one day be assured of victory. Comrades, in this time of peril and danger, only with careful and deliberate thinking can we build up our strength and draw on public opinion in order to uphold our greater task, and the prosperity of the Republic will be assured.[33]

Yuan Shikai's death and the subsequent change of power undoubtedly provided another opportunity for many responsible intellectuals to enter politics. After receiving a telegram from Fan Yuanlian (1876–1927), Minister of Education of Li Yuanhong's Government, Cai Yuanpei returned from abroad again. In a letter to Wang Jingwei written a few days after assuming the post of [university] president, Cai Yuanpei wrote: "Based on my observation, if we make a solid start with education, it is possible to make our country a safer place".[34] After Cai Yuanpei arrived in Shanghai in November 1916, he and his KMT comrades again considered whether he should go to Beijing and become president of Peking University. Ma Junwu (1881–1940), an important member of the Revolutionary Alliance (Tongmeng Hui) who had also just returned from Germany and would soon become transport minister of the Constitution

[33] "The KMT Ministry of Transport Tea Party Chronicle" (continued), published in *Minli Bao*, 12 June 1913.

[34] From Zhang Xiaowei, *Cai Yuanpei Pingzhuan* (Critical Biography of Cai Yuanpei), Baihuazhou Wenyi Chubanshe, 1993, p. 72. See: Cai Yuanpei Quanji (Complete Works of Cai Yuanpei), vol. 3, p. 26.

Protection Army's warlord government, had no confidence in education's effectiveness when not directly part of political struggle in areas of turmoil controlled by warlords; Ma even advised Cai that corrupt Peking University would probably tarnish his revolutionary image. Sun Yat-sen's proposal to Cai Yuanpei was entirely strategic; in Sun's view the struggle for legitimacy in Beijing would undoubtedly play a role in the development of legitimate power for the KMT. Peking University was a gathering place for young people and intellectuals where it seemed entirely possible to develop progressive forces and expand the KMT's work.

Before Cai Yuanpei's appointment, the situation at Peking University which was transformed from the late Qing's Capital University, was not as simple as the Tongmeng Hui (Revolutionary Alliance) in Shanghai imagined. Peking University had historically benefited from Kang Youwei and Liang Qichao, the intellectuals behind the Reform of 1898, the year Capital University was established, and at that time the Reforms were in their heyday. Although Kang and Liang's reforming careers soon ended in the 1898 coup, the Dowager Empress Cixi never closed Capital University. After Zhang Baixi was appointed Minister of Education (Guanxue Dachen), W.A.P Martin, the head of foreign languages at Capital University, was replaced by Wu Rulun (1840–1903), a writer of the Tongcheng School who served Li Hongzhang, the powerful official behind the Foreign Affairs Movement. However, this did not affect the introduction of Western studies in any way. Wu set up the Book Translation Bureau (Yishu Ju) and hired Yan Fu as its Director (*zongzuan*). After the 1911 Revolution, Yuan Shikai appointed Yan Fu as governor (*zongdu*) of Capital University. Yan Fu's education and experience naturally led him to greatly appreciate Western knowledge. Yan Fu's reform of education would strengthen the influence of foreign language studies which brought the message home to xenophobic conservatives who attacked his measure of hiring a large number of foreign teachers as "blind worship of Western civilization". Then, in May 1912, Yan Fu applied to the education department to approve the name change from Capital University to Peking University, exemplifying how Yan Fu was tired of the old system of education, "Capital University" being a name created by the Qing government and so readily evoked the imperial examination system. In the spring of 1913, a number of Zhang Taiyan's students entered Peking University. Although this radical intellectual had changed his outlook on life since 1907, the influence of his reputation persisted. The entry of young teachers gradually ended the dreary calm of Peking University.

After becoming chancellor of Peking University, Cai Yuanpei wanted to promote the atmosphere of intellectual ferment he was accustomed to in Germany at Peking University, so he established a curricular policy that can be described as "inclusive". He maintained that freedom of thought was a prerequisite for a university to be "important". However, this educational and academic guiding ideology basically lacked the support conferred by a stable national political system. The condition that Cai Yuanpei could implement democratic activities within the relative independence of Peking University hinged upon temporary power vacuums created when power shifted from one state politician to another. The reason why Li Yuanhong agreed to Cai Yuanpei's appointment was the former's desire to establish his political image after he took over as president, and he did not care whether Cai Yuanpei became governor of Zhejiang or chancellor of Peking University. Therefore, intentionally or otherwise, Cai Yuanpei, under the academic banner of "inclusivity", quickly organized a group of important intellectuals who began to make a significant impact on history from different angles: in January, he appointed Chen Duxiu as the Dean of the Faculty of Arts; in April, Zhou Zuoren was invited to Peking University and in July became a professor in the Faculty of Arts; in July, Zhang Shizhao was also appointed a professor in the Faculty of Arts; in August, Hu Shi similarly joined the Faculty, as did Qian Xuantong and Liu Bannong in September; and in November, Li Dazhao was hired as director of the library.

In bringing Chen Duxiu to Peking University, Cai Yuanpei had a clear intention. As early as September 1915 in *New Youth*, Chen Duxiu had introduced Cai Yuanpei's advocacy of the Work-Study Movement, and Chen's explicit advocacy of "science and democracy" had left an "indelible impression" on Cai Yuanpei.[35] Chen had long been an activist, and during the Resist Russia Movement from 1902 to 1904, Chen shared the political stance of most Chinese intellectuals and students abroad, namely a lack of confidence in the Manchu government and a desire to participate in independent anti-Russian and anti-Qing activities. Chen had returned home from Japan with Zhang Ji, Zou Rong and others because of the incident sparked off by Yao Yu, a supervisor of the students in Japan

[35] Cai Yuanpei, "Wo zai Beijing Daxue de jingli" (My experience in Peking University), *Dongfang Zazhi*, 33:1; 1 January 1933.

from Jiangnan.[36] On his return to China, Chen became involved in the Resist Russia anti-Qing campaign, and established the *Anhui Vernacular News*, the earliest publication to effectively give voice to his own ideas. In this publication, Chen Duxiu published popular articles such as "The Partition of China", "Bad Customs", "A Discussion of the Nation", and "The Demise of the Nation". In the summer of 1905, Wu Yue (1878–1905), whom Chen had met in Shanghai in 1903, visited Chen in Wuhu to express his strong support for adopting the tactic of terrorist assassinations. Wu Yue was wary of the influence of newspapers as outlined by Chen Duxiu and expressed the hope that Chen Duxiu might participate in revamping the Tokyo Military National Education Council which in July 1903 had operated under the slogan "advocacy, assassination, rebellion". When Wu Yue was killed in September in his attempt to assassinate five Qing officials, Chen Duxiu decided to finally renounce participation in assassination missions.

Chen Duxiu did little in the period immediately after the 1911 Revolution, but a warrant for his arrest was issued after the failure of the Second Revolution. At the end of 1914, in the magazine *Jiayin* (The Tiger) edited by Zhang Shizhao (1881–1973), Chen published "Patriotism and Self-awareness" (Aiguoxin yu Zijuexin) in which he separated government from the nation, indicating that he had a new view of the social situation under the dictatorship acting in the name of the republican revolution, and began to emphasize that the nation should have a truly modern meaning. Chen began to shift his concerns from the minority ruling stratum to the general public. Chen Duxiu published this article just after Yuan Shikai dissolved the Kuomintang and was disbanding local assemblies at all levels, as well as strengthening authoritarian measures,

[36] Yao Yu had served as policy officer for the Chinese ambassador in Japan, Cai Jun, and he did not allow Chinese students to study at Japanese military schools, and he also resented the radical political attitudes of Chinese student in Japans. Chen Duxiu and Zou Rong accused Yao of seducing female students, taking the opportunity to vent the students' dissatisfaction with him. Xu Shouchang in *Impressions of my Deceased Friend Lu Xun* recorded this incident: "It is ridiculous that Yao Yu, who supervised the Jiangnan students, because he was having an affair with a woman surnamed Qian, was subsequently attacked by Zou Rong and four others who had broken into the women's dormitories and was attacked by having his queue cut off with scissors. They then rushed to the students' clubhouse to display Yao's removed braid, and I also excitedly ran to see". "Yao had to then sneak home". After the incident, Yao had the Japanese police arrest the perpetrators, and Chen and the others were repatriated to China.

such as newspaper censorship and postal supervision, and having plain-clothes police perpetuate terrorist functions.[37] At this time, in the eyes of intellectuals like Chen Duxiu, simply changing the relationships of power could not solve China's fundamental problems; ideological change might be the fundamental change required to promote the development of history—this was the basic starting point for Chen Duxiu when returned from Japan in the early summer of 1915 to start his publication.

New Youth (Xin Qingnian; masthead: *La Jeunesse*), the standard bearer of the New Culture Movement, was launched in 1915.[38] Chen Duxiu, in the article "Announcement to Youth" (*Jinggao qingnian*) in the magazine's inaugural issue, outlined "six principles" that were to serve as the basic characteristics of his envisaged youth of the new era: (1) Be independent, not servile; (2) be progressive, not conservative; (3) be aggressive, not retiring; (4) be cosmopolitan, not isolationist; (5) be utilitarian, not wishy-washy; and (6) be scientific, not imaginative. Intellectuals like Chen Duxiu were well aware that although Kang Youwei, Liang Qichao, and

[37] On 16 October 1913, Yuan Shikai proposed to Congress a revised covenant (constitution) in an attempt to concentrate as much power as possible in the hands of the President. The key points were: Without the consent of the Senate, the President may establish rules and regulations governing the appointment and conduct of officials, the President may appoint and remove civilian and military officials, declare war and conclude peace agreements, and have the power to issue emergency orders and financial emergency sanctions. Congress did not agree to Yuan's proposal. Some Kuomintang members were now determinedly drafting a new draft constitution for the Republic of China to limit the President's powers. On 14 November Yuan ordered the dissolution of the Kuomintang. On 26 January 1914, the "Covenant Conference", which was controlled by Yuan, was established. On 20 March, Yuan Shikai proposed an outline of the interim revised covenant (constitution). The essence of its seventh article was centralizing the power of the President which was now not subject to the legislature. Yuan changed the key word "*shuyu*" ("belongs to") in the original Provisional Covenant to "*benyu*" ("derives from" or "is invested in"), the meaning of which was ambiguous, in the new formulation "the sovereignty of the Republic of China is vested in the whole nation"; the legislative right of the Legislative Council was changed to the right of proposal so that the legislature became merely an advisory body. The Senate appeared to have been given greater authority because "the Constitution of the Republic of China is promulgated by the Senate", but it was brought under greater control by Yuan's lavish treatment. On 2 March 1914, Yuan published the Regulations on the Police, which made it clear that "secret associations are strictly prohibited" and "coalition strikes"; on 2 April, Yuan announced the implementation of the Newspaper Regulations, which gave the police the power to seize newspapers and arrest journalists and editors.

[38] Originally simply called *Qingnian* (Youth; La Jeunesse), the magazine changed its name with Vol. 2, no. 1, to *Xin Qingnian* (New Youth).

others achieved some results in their efforts to reform the political system, the revolutionists in the process of the Qing government's disintegration should have been able to seize the opportunity to advance the historical process. However, the opportunity to change the political system was lost because they were unable to get rid of the ideological value system that went with the *ancien regime*; the revolutionists were desperate to change the political system, and therefore the core of the problem was entrusted to a simple change of power. Such an outcome lacked effective constraints on the authoritarian inertia of old bureaucrats, who were now also included under the republican flag. Therefore, in order to solve the problem of realizing a true republic, it was necessary to make the republican democracy real—by introducing the ideological concepts of science and democracy, and abandoning the habits of Confucianism; this is the logic of enlightened intellectuals, namely through the replacement of the old culture with the new culture could fundamental social change be effected. In his "Letter in Defense against the Charges Leveled at *New Youth*", Chen Duxiu discussed this logical relationship from the perspective of supporting science and democracy:

> To support Mr. Democracy, we have to oppose Confucian teachings, the Confucian rites, chastity, the old morality, and the old politics; to support Mr. Science, we have to oppose the old arts and the old religions; to embrace Mr. Democracy and to embrace Mr. Science, we have to oppose the national quintessence and the old literature.[39]

In January 1917, Chen Duxiu published an article simply titled "Tentative Suggestions on Literary Reform" by Hu Shi, who was at that time in the United States, in *New Youth* (Volume 2, no. 5), and this article led directly to the rise and spread of the "literary revolution". Therefore, Chen Duxiu hoped that Hu Shi would return to Peking University to teach, and it seemed entirely conceivable that Cai Yuanpei would appoint him. While Chen Duxiu directed attacks on Confucianism and the traditional ethical system through the pages of *New Youth*, Hu Shi began echoing these sentiments in the field of literature. In his view, both in terms of strategy and personnel, the ideological and cultural reforms

[39] Ren Jianshu, Zhang Tongmo, Wu Xinzhong eds., *Chen Duxiu Zhuzuo Xuan* (Selection of Chen Duxiu's Writings), vol. 1, Shanghai: Shanghai Renmin Chubanshe, 1993, pp. 442–443.

propelled by criticism of the old morality and the old political system should all begin with the issue of language. However, Hu Shi's "Tentative Suggestions on Literary Reform" published in January 1917 was simple and academic in tone, and he clearly classified the problems that should be paid attention to in writing as eight points: (1) Write with substance. (2) Do not imitate the ancients. (3) Emphasize grammar. (4) Reject melancholy. (5) Eliminate old clichés. (6) Do not use allusions. (7) Do not use couplets and parallelisms. (8) Do not avoid popular expressions or popular forms of characters.

Hu Shi provided an interesting description of the origins of the "literary revolution" when he compared a colloquial comment by the character Shi Xiu in *The Water Margin* with its equivalent in the classical literary language and demonstrated that the vernacular language could be far more expressive, liberating the power of language. Regarding this as an academic revolution, Hu Shi, after his "Suggestions" were published, wrote to Chen Duxiu to say that these problems could not be solved overnight and that others should be allowed to express different opinions. However, Chen Duxiu identified the vernacular as an inevitable requirement of the new era, and argued that there was no need for discussion:

> I believe that condoning dissent and free discussion are undoubtedly principles for scholarly development, but when the aim is reforming Chinese literature, we should take the vernacular language as the literary orthodoxy, and it seems clear to me that opponents must not be allowed to discuss it, and the issue must be absolutely based on the ideas advocated by us, and these cannot be altered. Why is this? If in our nation's culture, the language has reached the stage where the vernacular can express ideas and describe things, then why on earth would there still be any doubts that this needs to be discussed? Those who want to reject Chinese vernacular literature and blatantly regard the classical language as authentic literature are like the calendrical experts of the early Qing dynasty who rejected the Western calendar and those in the Qianlong and Jiaqing periods who denied that the earth revolved around the sun so we do not have time to waste on this senseless discussion![40]

[40] Ren Jianshu, Zhang Tongmo, and Wu Xinzhong, *Chen Duxiu Zhuzuo Xuan* (Selection of Chen Duxiu's Writings), vol. 1, Shanghai: Shanghai Renmin Chubanshe, 1993, p. 302.

In his "Discussion of the Literary Revolution" published in *New Youth* (vol. 2, no. 6), Chen Duxiu completely linked the concept of literary revolution to the concept of political revolution, arguing that modern European civilization is "serious and splendid" and is "a gift of revolution". However, since the 1911 Revolution, there had been several political revolutions but the reality of China had not fundamentally changed, its internal rationale being spiritual. The purpose of opposing Confucianism was to eradicate the old morality that served the old political system, and the literary revolution sought to prevent access to Confucian and Mencian doctrine by means of language, the transformation from the classical language to the vernacular itself being the disintegration of vague Confucian dogma. Chen Duxiu believed that the tasks of the literary revolution were as follows: "Destroy the aristocratic literature, which is nothing but literary chiseling and flattery, and construct a simple, expressive national literature; destroy the outmoded, showy classical literature and construct a fresh and sincere literature of realism; destroy obscure and abstruse literature, and construct a clear and popular literature of society".[41] Chen Duxiu emphasized the content of literature, believing that as long as literature did not convey the teachings of Confucius and Mencius and did not "speak on behalf of the sages", but shifted the center of problems to the universe, life, and society, it could help achieve the goals of modern politics. The close link between literature and politics was very clearly stated at the end of the article: "In order to reform politics today, it is necessary to reform the literature that applies to the spiritual world of this politics".[42] Hu Shi later said that Chen Duxiu confused the content of literature with the form and pointed out that it was out of the question at that particular time to talk about reforming the content of literature. However, the focus of Chen Duxiu and of Hu Shi was not in fact the same: Chen's support for the vernacular was simply taking it as a tool to promote an ethical and ideological revolution, in other words, reforming politics through literary innovation in order to solve practical political problems. Yet Hu Shi believed that the text itself functioned according to its own logical procedures and that the important part of the literary revolution was the reform of the mode of language, maintaining grand illusions about the independence of literature.

[41] Ibid., pp. 260–261.
[42] Ibid., p. 263.

It is well known that even Western literature was first introduced to China through the medium of the classical language, not through vernacular *baihua* translations. The translations of Western literature by a contemporary of Yan Fu, Lin Shu (1852–1924), were extremely popular at the time, and because of the appeal of literature and fiction and the ability of Lin's prose to guide his readers' moods, his influence on young people far exceeded that of Yan Fu's translations. Lin Shu translated more than a hundred literary works, including novels, fables, biographies, and plays, including Dumas fils' *La Dame aux Camélias*, Dickens' *Oliver Twist* and *David Copperfield*, H. Rider Haggard's *King Solomon's Mines* and *Montezuma's Daughter*, and Sir Walter Scott's *Ivanhoe* and *The Talisman*. Most of the popular novels he translated included vivid delineation of characters and plotting and corresponding ethical values, and their powerful emotional impact young readers found difficult to resist. Lin Shu did not understand foreign languages, but by applying his own literary talents and style and his sensitivity, he translated cooperatively accepting his associates' advice; he so convincingly preserved the spirit of the original works that people were generally surprised and filled with admiration for his work. However, like Yan Fu, Lin Shu wrote in classical Chinese; he doggedly resisted and felt contempt for vernacular prose, and so Lin Shu came to be regarded as a target of the literary revolution.

Hu Shi later recalled in *Fifty Years of Chinese Literature*:

> Once *New Tide* opened the floodgates in 1919, many articles in the vernacular language appeared in response, not only in *New Youth*, *New Tide*, and *Weekly Review*, but even in Beijing's *National Gazette*. Since then, the response has gradually increased, but the greater the response, the greater the opposition. Opponents on campus produced the journals *National Cause* (Guogu) and *Citizen* (Guomin) in support of ancient literature. Off-campus opposition groups even vied to use the militaristic politicians of the Anfu Club to suppress the new movement.[43] In February and March

[43] Also known as the "Anfu Clique", this group of politicians was attached to the warlords during the Northern Warlord period and were specifically manipulated by Duan Qirui's crony Xu Shuzheng (1880–1925). They were known as the Anfu Club because their activities were based in Nei Anfu Hutong in the Xuanwumen district of Beijing. The group was founded in March 1918, and in August of that year it rigged the ballot for the new Parliament, which became known as the Anfu Congress, because of the more than 400 members of Parliament, more than 380 were members of the Anfu Cllque. In April 1926, the Government of Duan Qirui collapsed and the Anfu Clique was completely dissolved.

> 1919, rumors were flying about: some said that the Ministry of Education had intervened, and others reported that Chen Duxiu, Hu Shi, Qian Xuantong (1887-1939), and other literary reformers had been expelled from Beijing. Such rumors, though largely untrue, did reflect the psychological mood among opposition groups. At that time, the veteran fiction translator, Lin Shu, revered for his classical prose style, published several short stories in *Xin Shenbao* (The New Shanghai News) attacking figures in the New Culture movement at Peking University. One story, titled *Yao Meng* (Dream of Demons) was a *roman à clef* of sorts, in which the protagonists are thinly veiled caricatures of Peking University's President Cai Yuanpei (Yuan Xu), and of staff members Chen Duxiu (Chen Heng) and Hu Shi (Hu Hai). This novel is mawkish and not worth citing. In another short story titled *Jingsheng* (Master Jing), Lin Shu again used protagonists with thinly veiled names to attack prominent figures in the New Culture movement. He described an imaginary conversation between Tian Bimei (Chen Duxiu), Jin Xinyi (Qian Xuantong) and Di Mo (Hu Shi) in Beijing's Taoran Pavilion, in which Tian is railing against Confucius, and Di is advocating the use of vernacular language: Suddenly a "tough guy" enters the pavilion, by stepping over its collapsed broken wall. Pointing to the three men, he asks them, 'What's the meaning of your discussion? … You dare to utter the words of beasts to confound my pure vocation!' Tian wants to speak in their defense, but the tough guy places two fingers on Tian's head, causing an excruciating headache, and then extends a foot to trip up Di Mo, causing the latter excruciating back pain. Tian is myopic, so the guy rips off his spectacles. Fearing he might die, Tian hunches up like a porcupine. Laughing, the guy comments, 'Your madness is like that of Li Zhi, who was a social monster. Today, I will need to perfume my hands and feet, now that I've touched the bodies of you unnatural creatures. You should run away down the hill like rats, and not trouble me. …I will leave it to the ghosts to execute you.'"[44]

Whether or not soldiers and politicians directly interfered in academic debates at Peking University at that time, it is certain that Lin Shu and others did have powerful backers. This was not because Xu Shuzheng was a student of Lin Shu; crucially, Lin's thinking was consistent with that of the Beijing government. In an article titled "Rumors about Peking

[44] From Zheng Xuejia, *Chen Duxiu Zhuan* (Biography of Chen Duxiu), Shibao Wenhua Chuban Qiye Youxian Gongsi, 1989, (Taipei: The Times Cultural Publishing Enterprise Co., Ltd.,) pp. 244–245.

University" published in the 16 March 1919 issue (no. 13) of *The Weekly Review*, Chen Duxiu summed up Lin's actions as "relying on power".

After Chen Duxiu moved from his post as editor of *New Youth* in Shanghai to Peking University to take up his appointment as Dean of Humanities, Qian Xuantong joined the team at *New Youth.* Qian Xuantong had been a member of the National Quintessence group prior to the end of 1916, but in February of the following year he joined the enlightened progressives making almost slanderous accusations like they "studied archaic ghost stories and peddled the lies of the Tongcheng school of classical literature". Qian Xuantong was a phonologist and linguistic exegete by training, but as Qian saw it, the real purpose in "serving the ancients", "reviving the past", and "preserving ancient things" was to resolve the grim political problem of how to overthrow Manchu-Qing rule:

> I thought that the purpose of preserving the national quintessence was not simply wanting to restore ancient things; once the work of restoration was completed, the time would be ripe to reverse and overthrow every one of the measures introduced by the Manchu-Qing political system and restore the true Chinese past. We would not simply be restoring the Ming, but also the glories of the Han and Tang dynasties, and not only those glorious times but the even earlier Three Dynasties.[45]

Qian Xuantong had been a student of Zhang Taiyan for two years; Zhang's fierce anti-Manchu thinking, and his anger directed at utilitarianism, the former a racist issue and the latter a response to the bullying of the Chinese nation by the Western powers and to the crisis in the traditional system of ethics, would no doubt have made a great impact on Qian. His advocacy of traditional "writing, language, regalia, and garments" was not simply respect for cultural traditions and customs but encompassed ethnic nationalism which envisaged the restoration of ethnic Han rule and the maintenance of traditional moral structures to preserve the purity of the revolution. Qian Xuantong clearly thought that the political aims of Kang Youwei and his followers were, as his teacher Zhang Taiyan insisted, an attempt to effect reforms through the monarchy with the intention of achieving their own "greedy aims and political ambitions". Throughout Chinese history, all political parties had

[45] Qian Xuantong, "The changes in my attitude to the Manchu Qing over thirty years" (Sanshi nian lai wo duiyu Man-Qing de taidu di bianqian), *Yusi* (Thread of talk), no. 8.

been regarded merely as cliques who fought for power and wealth, and the roots of such cliques all lay in moral decline. Given that he was little influenced by or enthusiastic for the Confucian system and regarded utilitarian morality as an enemy, Zhang Taiyan pointed to the path of Buddhism. In March 1918, Qian Xuantong wrote in a letter to Chen Duxiu:

> My teacher has written a number of works in an effort to overthrow Confucian teachings and reform ethics, in the belief that if ethical issues are not fundamentally resolved, then this Republic would not be hanging out its sign for very long… I believe that this proposition of my teacher is the only way to save China today. However, this raises an issue: if we want to eliminate Confucian teachings, we have to eliminate the classical Chinese language; If we want to eliminate the childish, savage, and conservative ideas of ordinary people, we must first abandon the classical Chinese language.[46]

Qian's meaning was very clear: by abandoning the traditions of the literary language, and finding new modes of expression for daily life, new ideas will spread and people will be woken and enlightened more effectively. Qian stressed that only a change of language could effectively convey the ideas of such Western thinkers as Montesquieu, Feuerbach, Darwin, Nietzsche, Freud, Russell, Dewey, and Ibsen.[47] The problem here was far from being the difference between the classical language or vernacular language; the combination of new language and new content was changing people's thinking, which would naturally lead more and more people to think about patriarchal dictatorship, feudal oppression, and a series of related problems. Qian Xuantong's 180-degree turnabout in ideas in the May Fourth period surprised many people, such as Lin Yutang who wrote: "He completely abandoned the Confucian tradition, going to the opposite extreme in everything, so I think his personality

[46] Quoted from *Zhishifenzi yu Wusi Yichan: Zhongguo de Qimeng Yundong* (Intellectuals and the May Fourth Legacy: China's Enlightenment Movement), Taiyuan: Shanxi Renmin Chubanshe, 1989, pp. 97–98. Originally published in *Zhongguo Jindai Sixiang Shi Ziliao* (Historical Materials on Modern Chinese Thought), Beijing, 1957 (HK reprint), p. 19.

[47] In the inaugural issue of *Xinchao* (New Tide) published in January 1919, Fu Sinian introduced the thought of Feuerbach, Darwin and Nietzsche. In *New Youth*, vol. 7, no. 3, published in February 1920, Zhang Shenfu, in an article titled "Modern Psychology", introduced the psychology of Freud.

had become somewhat deranged".[48] But the urgency that imbued Qian's thinking is symptomatic of the sensitivity of the era to the decline of Confucianism.

There were precedents in Liang Qichao's writings for the proposal that language could change society and promote modern politics: "To renew a nation's people, one must first renew a nation's fiction. And so if one wishes to renew ethics, one must renew fiction; if one wants to renew religion, one must renew fiction; of one wants to renew politics, one must renew fiction; if one wants to renew customs, one must renew fiction; if one wants to renew scholarship and the arts, one must renew fiction: and if one wants to renew people's feelings and personality, one must renew fiction".[49] With the fall of the Qing government, the new language would serve for some time as a resource to legitimize power, and when warlords continued to be embroiled in the chaos of power struggles, new language played a role in expanding the influence of new ideas, and many intellectuals developed an unshakeable belief in the role played by language in indoctrinating or enlightening people. Luo Jialun (1897–1969), a student at Peking University, clearly enunciated the instrumental nature of literature in an "open letter" to Zhang Ji of the KMT which appeared in the second issue of volume 2 of *Xinchao*: "We are therefore very anxious to reform ideas. To be honest, the literary revolution is only our tool and an ideological revolution is our aim. But ideological revolution is never separable from the literary revolution".

Zhang Shenfu (1893–1986) was well aware of the role of language and writing before the outbreak of the May Fourth Movement: "Most people are aware that language and writing are instruments of ideology, and ideology should accord with one's own needs and convenience and be modified at any time. Everyone knows that people's thinking can be changed by language and writing".[50] The poet Zhu Ziqing (1898–1948), in an article titled "Integrity" (Qijie) published in the second issue of *Knowledge and Culture* on 1 May 1947, wrote:

[48] Lin Yutang, *Bashi Zixu* (Autobiography at Eighty), Zhongguo Xiju Chubanshe, 1992, pp. 56–57.

[49] Quoted from *Zhishifenzi yu Wusi Yichan: Zhongguo de Qimeng Yundong* (Intellectuals and the May Fourth Legacy: China's Enlightenment Movement), Taiyuan: Shanxi Renmin Chubanshe, 1989, p. 40.

[50] Quoted from *Zhang Shenfu Sanwen*, Zhongguo Guangbo Dianshi Chubanshe, 1993. This was quoted in turn from *Meizhou Pinglun* (Weekly Review), no. 6, 26 January 1919.

> The May Fourth Movement ushered in a new era. Liberalism was built on the basis of freedom in the social division of labor. Teachers are free entrepreneurs, not officials or officials-in-waiting. Students could also choose from a variety of careers and not simply remain as officials forever. They are thus independent from the ruling class and are no longer 'literati and officials' or 'scholar bureaucrat', but have instead become 'intellectuals', the collective being the 'knowledge class' (intelligentsia).[51]

The New Culture Movement had its opponents: apart from Hu Shi's classmates Mei Guangdi (1890–1945) and Wu Mi (1894–1976) who belonged to the group around *Critical Review* (Xueheng-pai) and disagreed with Hu Shi's claims, and Zhang Shizhao's group gathered around the journal *Jiayin* (The Tiger), there were others who questioned the Literary Revolution from different perspectives. In general, intellectuals argued that vernacular language was intended to provide the possibility for people who lacked a certain level of education to understand new ideas through a language they could understand, but Qu Qiubai (1899–1935), who later became a leader of the Communist Party, had such a view:

> The literature in the May Fourth classic style (the so-called vernacular), ... is simply a new delicacy served up at a banquet for Europeanized gentlemen ... the new classical language they have created ... is used to create so-called new works that the ordinary public cannot understand, like the ancient poetry of the past that commoners could not understand.[52]

Thus, it is easy to understand why, once a change in thought takes place, it is easy to direct it to a practical purpose: this was the rationale for the revolutionary literature that came later.

Li Dazhao (1889–1927) was recommended to Cai Yuanpei by Zhang Shizhao, who learned of Li Dazhao when the latter was in Japan and contributed articles to the journal *Jiayin* (The Tiger) founded by Zhang

[51] Quoted from *Zhishifenzi yu Wusi Yichan: Zhongguo de Qimeng Yundong* (Intellectuals and the May Fourth Legacy: China's Enlightenment Movement), Taiyuan: Shanxi Renmin Chubanshe, 1989, pp. 26–27.

[52] *Wusi: Wenhua de Chanshi yu Pingjia, Xifang Xuezhe Lun Wusi* (May Fourth: Cultural Explanation and Evaluation, Western Scholars Discuss May Fourth), Taiyuan: Shanxi Renmin Chubanshe, 1989, p. 194. Quoting from: *Qu Qiubai Wenji*, Beijing, 1954, pp. 885, 886.

Shizhao, Chen Duxiu, and others. When studying in Japan from 1913 to 1917, Li Dazhao maintained close ties and cooperation with the Kuomintang. Looking at Cai Yuanpei's overhaul of the teaching staff at Peking University, we can see his policy of magnanimous "inclusiveness" was confirmed by his continued retention of a number of conservative scholars such as Gu Hongming (1857–1928), Liu Shipei (1884–-1919), Huang Kan (1886–1935), Chen Hanzhang (1864–1938), and Cui Shi (1852–1924), yet the focus of Cai Yuanpei's interests was shifting to rapidly accumulate ideas and revolutionary power while the warlords were locked into an ugly struggle for power.[53] In any case, those seen as core founding members of the New Culture Movement formed an integral group that had been rapidly assembled by Cai Yuanpei. Cai Yuanpei told Wu Zhihui (1865–1953) that he wanted to transform Peking University into an "institution of pure scholarship", but he did not explain what he actually meant by "scholarship". Cai Yuanpei asked students to regard "research and scholarship as a calling, and not improperly regard the university as a ladder to power and wealth".[54] Cai also stressed that education and learning should avoid politics—but that statement was only accurate if limited to "gaining promotion as an official and making a fortune". Politics was unavoidable, and Chen Duxiu was clear from the start: the literary revolution triggered by Hu Shi was not a purely intellectual revolution, and Cai Yuanpei's policy of diverting education was soon confirmed by the actual political behavior of the students. Luo Jialun, a radical student at Peking University during the May Fourth Movement, recalled a remark Gu Hongming made to a class: "There are only two good people in China now; one is Mr. Cai Yuanpei and the other is me. Because after Mr. Cai was appointed to the Hanlin Academy, he refused to be an official, joined the revolution, and is still a revolutionary today. And me? Ever since I became a Qing official working for Zhang Zhidong, I too have never changed, and have remained a monarchist to the present day".[55] Gu's statement reflected his personality, but the ideological and political

[53] Cai Yuanpei at one point also invited Wu Zhihui and Wang Jingwei to Peking University, but possibly because these two men were determined to directly participate in politics, Cai was unsuccessful in this request.

[54] Quoted from Zhou Tiandu, *Cai Yuanpei Zhuan* (Biography of Cai Yuanpei), Renmin Chubanshe, 1984, p. 99.

[55] Zhu Weizheng, "Gu Hongming shengping ji qita fei kaozheng", *Dushu*, Beijing: Sanlian Shudian, 1994:4, p. 30.

orientation of Cai's understanding of "scholarship" is readily apparent. The same is true of this situation; the reason Cai Yuanpei retained Gu Hongming and others at Peking University was due to his respect for their learning, but that is not to say that they would be agreed to discuss academically such questions as whether the emperor could return to politics. In fact, Liu Shipei's analysis of such ancient texts as *San Li* (Three Classics of Ritual), *Shang Shu* (The Book of History), and *Xungu* (Hermeneutics) and Gu Hongming's elucidation of English poetry played no role in any of the actual attempts to restore the monarchy. Cai Yuanpei had a long political experience, so he was clear that those young people beginning to engage in subversive work had a positive effect on the real life of China's citizens.

In this atmosphere of "inclusivity" and "intellectual freedom", various study societies devoted to politics, economics, news, fine arts, music, sports, and other pursuits were rapidly emerging at Peking University. At first, students were relaxed in a small but free environment, and they had high hopes for their future after graduating, realizing their future lives would be completely different from those of previous generations of intellectuals. Fu Sinian (1896–1950), one of the editors of *New Tide* (*Xin Chao*), recalled the founding of that journal: As students of the new era, they needed to have their own organizations and to pursue their own interests. He and his classmates believed that graduating from school would never mean that "they leave the worlds of education and publishing", so "why not practice this when you are a student". However, the frequent gatherings simply became opportunities to gossip, and the hope of running a publication almost became a "pastime" for young people, until one day the dean of humanities, Chen Duxiu, offered them financial support on behalf of the school, which meant that the teachers could influence the ideas of the students in a practical way.[56] However, the prior training of the students had by no means been a game that was "purely academic", and they defined the revolutionary nature of the magazine from the outset. The students did not want their magazine to have a "classroom feel", nor did they want it to be a mish-mash of everything;

[56] Li Dazhao provided a room in the Peking University Library for the editorial board of *Xinchao*, and its printing and distribution were organized by Li Xinbai (1875–1951).

they wanted its basic elements to be very clearly spelled out, i.e., "(1) the critical spirit; (2) scientific ideas; and (3) innovative language".[57]

In fact, the students' political mood was quite evident from the start. In the inaugural issue of *New Tide*, Luo Jialun suggested that the time was coming when a Russian-style social revolution would replace the French-style political revolution. In this way, the publication subtly became a propaganda vehicle promoting a revolutionary atmosphere. Luo Jialun made this clear in a "Letter to Zhang Puquan" published in *New Tide* Volume 2, Number 2 (December 1919): "Our ideological revolution, needless to say, has as its main tenets: (i) transforming servile thinking into independent thinking; (ii) transforming autocratic thinking into democratic popular thinking; and (iii) transforming muddled thinking into logical thinking".[58]

However, Cai Yuanpei himself did not use Peking University as a short-term training base for political operations; rather he hoped that systematic education would lay the foundations for a revolution that was as truly effective. Cai Yuanpei first organized the Progressive Virtue Society (Jinde Hui) in 1918 to further separate the teachers and students of Peking University from the legacy of the former Capital College and to invigorate the intellectual atmosphere. Yet the relaxed intellectual environment, in turn, provided the conditions for new political ideas and activities. Among the teachers and students who joined the Society were some of the key figures who formed the backbone of the May Fourth movement, such as Li Dazhao, Luo Jialun, Fu Sinian, and Xu Deheng (1890–1990). Although the Society exhibited a connection with traditional moral education, it readily organized the new-style intellectuals of Peking University. Cai Yuanpei provided funding for Chen Duxiu's *New Youth*, exemplifying the "inclusivity" of his liberal political attitude. Later, when Cai Yuanpei read the critical letter from the Director-General of Education Fu Zengxiang (1872–1949) attacking the publication *New Tide*, he adopted a reasoned attitude in its defense. Cai informed Fu Zengxiang that Peking University not only had radical publications, but conservative publications such as *Guogu* as well. "The old and the new exist side by side, and they

[57] Zhongguo Shehui Kexue Yuan Jindai Shi Yanjiusuo ed., *Wusi Yundong Huiyi Lu (xu)*, Beijing: Zhongguo Shehui Kexue Chubanshe, 1979, pp. 171–172.

[58] Quoted from *Zhishifenzi yu Wusi Yichan: Zhongguo de Qimeng Yundong* (Intellectuals and the May Fourth Legacy: China's Enlightenment Movement), Taiyuan: Shanxi Renmin Chubanshe, 1989, p. 114.

complement each other", Cai commented. However, the problem was that the original intention of President Xu Shichang in asking Fu Zengxiang to investigate the radical tendencies of Peking University did not stem from concern for the balance of academic ideas or the lack thereof, but was driven by Xu's disgust and uneasiness with new ideas in general, as Cai Yuanpei was fully aware. On the other hand, from the commencement of publication of *New Tide*, its main editors were influenced by the Kuomintang. When students sent the magazine to the KMT's Shanghai offices, they were vindicating the fervent hopes and ideological encouragement of those intellectuals who had become KMT politicians. In his reply to the students, Zhang Ji not only described how the toxicity of the old customs, habits, and ideas persisted even after the people of the nation changed the political system in 1911, but he also called on young people to learn from their French teachers and participate in the political movement for ideological reform. "Where do republican politics come from?" he asked. "From the earnest struggle of all of you ...".[59] In such an atmosphere of "intellectual freedom", there was a natural outpouring of ideas and activity from the new-style intellectuals. This avoidance of official politics generated political ideas, and even action, demanding democracy. Cai Yuanpei's intellectual freedom was a fight to wrest political power from the autocrats and make use of it.

The political views of the "Citizens Society", in which Xu Deheng and Zhang Guotao (1897–1979) were prime movers, were simpler and clearer than those of the "New Tide Society". In Zhang Guotao's words, national salvation and survival were the prime tasks. Therefore, members of the "Citizens Society" believed that the focus on cultural revolution by members of the "New Tide Society" was not the main thing, otherwise the nation would cease to exist; changing cultural thinking could not play a major role at the present time. Because of this, when in May 1918 students studying in Japan protested against the *Sino-Japanese Joint Defense Agreement* signed at the Sino-Japanese Tokyo Conference which led to an uproar and more than a thousand Chinese students returned from Japan, members of the Citizens Society responded most clearly, with eight representatives of the students' petitioning team forming a Students National Salvation Association which included three Peking University students: Xu Deheng, Yi Keyi, and Duan Xipeng. With the support

59 "Tongxin", *Xinchao*, vol. 2, no. 2.

of Cai Yuanpei, Xu Deheng and other radical students began to make contact directly with radical students from all over the country and with key personnel of the KMT; from Tianjin, Jinan, Wuhan, and Jiujiang to Shanghai, students who began dabbling in politics met with activists including Zhang Tailei (1898–1927), Yun Daiying (1895–1931), Fang Zhimin (1899–1935), Cheng Tianfang (1899–1967), Zhang Wentian (1900–1976), Sun Yat-sen, Liao Zhongkai, Shao Lizi (1882–1967), Huang Yanpei, and others. Reporting in Shanghai on the student movement in Beijing, students also made a point of inviting members of the Extraordinary Congress of the National Assembly in Guangzhou, led by Sun Yat-sen, to Shanghai, to solicit the support of stronger political forces. Soon, a nationwide Students National Salvation Association was born. When the students returned to Beijing from Shanghai, Xu Deheng, Zhang Guotao, and others founded *Citizens Magazine* (Guomin Zazhi) on 20 October 1918, which was intended to "promote the national character, inculcate national knowledge, promote study and learning, and promote national products". Since the team producing *Citizens Magazine* were "all passionate patriots", to quote Zhang Guotao, this contrasted with the *New Tide* students who stressed that only through a cultural revolution could they awaken the national consciousness.

Although the board of *Citizens Magazine* differed in their views from the *New Tide* group, the concept of "national salvation" appealed to both groups. Within the teachers' ranks, Li Dazhao especially emphasized the importance of ethnic nationalism, and he worked to weld various student groups into a larger group rallying to the call in early 1919 for national awakening. Important members of the New Tide Society such as Luo Jialun and Kang Baiqing (1896–1959) joined up with members of the Citizens Society, and unaffiliated students such as Chen Gongbo (1892–1946) joined the Beijing Students Association. At the same time, the first issue of *Citizens Magazine* was published. In March, a Civilian Education Lecture Group was set up to promote the idea of national salvation through street speeches, and the main members of this body belonged to the New Tide Society and Citizens Magazine Society. The readiness of students to venture from their campuses into society was naturally triggered by their eagerness to save their country, but Cai Yuanpei had clearly emphasized the importance of civil education for Republicanism in the student movements contributing to political enlightenment, which undoubtedly became a catalyst for students unselfconsciously taking to the streets to dispel the depression that shrouded society. Two months previously he had told students that, in order to prevent the republic from wavering, citizens needed to be educated. The most effective method was through "public speaking", something he had long been advocating in his pedagogical activities. However, in the eyes of the authorities, this looked suspiciously like political incitement. In any case, from the time Cai Yuanpei became president of Peking University until 4 May 1919, the air of intellectual freedom at Peking University derived a generally high level of political enthusiasm. Even though later historians repeatedly recorded and studied the enlightening work carried out by the teachers and students during this stage, once the writings of students and teachers of this period are examined closely, we find that the practical meaning of "intellectual freedom" was to subvert traditional ideology and to establish a new ideology, with new ideas coming of course from the West. Thus, those who actively advocated Western ideas in the New Culture Movement can quite naturally be regarded "total Westernizers". However, the radical intellectuals of this period can even be regarded as an academic elite well-versed in traditional culture, who because they were very familiar with Western civilization and deeply understood the historical issues of traditional culture, for the sake of change in China, preferred to emphasize the importance of Western liberalism, pragmatism, and other doctrines. Hu Shi was very clear that the sole aim of the new trends of thinking was to "re-create civilization", and the Confucian package was of little use in the eyes of him and his colleagues.

In any case, the spirit of liberalism spread throughout Peking University because of Cai Yuanpei's ideas and promotion, and the formation and influence of the liberal atmosphere of Peking University can be regarded as intentional or inevitable. In this sense, the May Fourth Movement, which would soon break out, was simply the natural corollary of the liberal spirit of Peking University, and when news from the Paris Peace Conference came "like a thunderbolt on a sunny day" (Xu Deheng), the realistic orientation of the students stood in stark relief.

On 11 November 1918, as one of the victors in the First World War, China was given a great opportunity to shake off the oppressive and humiliating treaties earlier imposed on her. At the end of the War, China was encouraged by the "Fourteen Points" proposed by President Woodrow Wilson in his address to Congress, but Wilson's internationalism at the time was a strange mix of liberalism, imperialism, democracy, jurisprudence, and interventionism, which in itself concealed an inability to establish a genuine international order. In his speech, Wilson emphasized national self-determination and proposed the establishment of an international organization that ensured the political independence and territorial integrity of states. China was only permitted to have two representatives attend the Paris Peace Conference in Versailles, which opened on 18 January 1919. At the meeting, the representative of China, Gu Weijun (Wellington Koo, 1888–1985), ignored Japan's intimidation and published the previously secret Sino-Japanese Compact, declaring that China would reject Japan's claim to Shandong and repeal the Twenty-One Demands. However, the Chinese representative's request to resume the privileges of the defeated powers in China and reject Japan's Twenty-One Demands was debated at the meeting. Regarding Shandong, the government of Duan Qirui had signed a loan agreement with Japan in September 1918 to construct a railway from Gaomi to Xuzhou and another from Jinan to Shunde. In the contract Duan's government "willingly agreed" to cede to Japan all German rights in Shandong. The United States initially expressed support for China's interests, but in order to maintain the stability of the more self-interested international coalition, the United States finally agreed to Japan's request and German rights in Shandong were transferred to Japan. When news of China's failure at the Paris Peace Conference reached China, people were disappointed that Wilson's doctrine had not materialized. Chen Duxiu who had previously praised Wilson wrote in the *Weekly Review* (no. 20) published on the day the news reached China: "At the Paris Peace Conference, all nations stressed their own rights. Any principles and any permanent peace promised by President Wilson's Fourteen Points became worthless empty words".

One immediate upshot of China's rejection at the Conference was the May Fourth anti-Japanese demonstration by students from thirteen different educational institutions. The demonstrators protested the Nishihara Loans agreement signed previously by the Duan Qirui government with Japan, which enabled Duan to expand his military power and ceded to Japan the Northeast Railway construction rights. Angry students even burned down the home of Cao Rulin (1877–1966), who had negotiated the loan agreement, regarding Cao as a despicable traitor.[60] Peking University students went on strike and Cai Yuanpei resigned in anger over the arrest of students. A flood of telegrams was sent from all over the country to the Chinese delegation in Paris, urging or even threatening the delegation not to sign the pact. On 3 June, the Beijing government's arrest of students led to strikes by students, workers, and businessmen, and the situation was heating up rapidly. More than a dozen cities, including Shanghai, Nanjing, Xiamen, Zhenjiang, and Suzhou, participated in the show of solidarity. As a result, on the 10th, the Minister of Transport Cao Rulin, the Chinese Ambassador to Japan Zhang Zongxiang, and the President of the Mint Lu Zongyu were all removed from their posts. These three senior officials had all been students in Japan in their early years and so dealt with Japanese affairs and were considered to be a pro-Japanese grouping in the Beijing government of Duan Qirui. On the 11th, Xu Shichang proposed that he resign as President. On the 16th, the National Union of Students was established in Shanghai, and Peking University student Duan Xipeng (1896–1948) chaired the conference organized by the National Union. On the 28th, Chinese delegates at the Paris Peace Conference refused to sign the accord with Germany. As events came to a climax, Luo Jialun published an article titled "The Spirit of the May Fourth Movement" in the 23rd issue of *Weekly Review* on 26 May, and the expression "May Fourth Movement" immediately

[60] Cao Rulin (1877–1966) was the Chief Of the Bank of Communications when he was involved in negotiating loans with the personal representative of Japanese Prime Minister Masahiro Nishihara. In 1917, Japan loaned 25 million Japanese yen to the Duan Qirui government on two separate occasions. After April 1918, Duan Qirui borrowed six more loans from Japan through Nishihara, totaling 120 million yen. People's anger at Cao was based on this. On 13 July 1920, Wu Peifu even issued a scathing rebuke in a telegram to Duan Qirui:

Since ancient times China has strongly defended itself from foreign countries, and no sin is greater than selling out one's nation and no behavior is uglier than fawning on outsiders. The most vicious crime is being a Chinese traitor. Duan Qirui again controlled the country and regarded the thief as a father; he began to steal and sell the nation's rights and borrowed vast amounts of Japanese money to the detriment of his compatriots and went on to pretend to participate in the war but trained the army to assist the enemy. He finally encouraged foreigners to use foreign money to deliver foreign weapons to shed the blood of our people, the blood of the descendants of the Yellow Emperor, acting as a loyal servant of our enemy, and as a true Chinese traitor. From: Jin Chongji, *Ershi Shiji Zhongguo Shi Gang* (The Outline of Chinese History in the Twentieth Century), vol. I, Shehui Kexue Wenxian Chubanshe, 2009, p. 194.

became the term for this historical event. In an article summarizing the May Fourth Movement published in the following year and titled, "The Successes and Failures of Our Student Movement over the Past Year and the Policy to Be Adopted in the Future", this Peking University student confidently summarized the historical status of the May Fourth Movement:

> Whether we favor or oppose it, it is undeniable that the May Fourth Movement is the most significant event since the founding of the Republic of China. This event adds a new reform to China's political history and signifies a new era in China's social history and a new change in China's ideological history.[61]

For the Chinese, "the Twenty-One Demands that would destroy China" were utterly problematic, and even during the immediately preceding period from 1918 to 1920, the Japanese continued to behave recklessly in China. In August 1918, the Japanese clashed with the Chinese army at Manzhouli and then claimed the railway from Harbin to Changchun. In July 1919, the Japanese destroyed Chinese shops in Jinan; in September, Japan provoked Chinese troops in Changchun; in November, armed Japanese (called *rōnin* in Japanese) shot students and citizens in Fuzhou; and in the spring of 1920, students in Tianjin were arrested for protesting against the Japanese. In short, the Japanese frequently perpetrated violent acts in a number of cities (Jilin, Nantong, Suzhou, Vladivostok, Shanghai, etc.). However, with the stability of the European order at the end of World War I, the powers had the energy to rethink how to establish a new pattern in the Far East, based on the resolution of outstanding issues at the Paris Peace Conference (apart from the Shandong issue and the dispute between the major powers in the Pacific Ocean), Following the initiative of the United States, from 12 November 1921 to 6 February 1922, the United Kingdom, the United States, France, Italy, Japan, China, Belgium, the Netherlands, and Portugal held a meeting in Washington, D.C., at which China presented a nine-point proposal, which was consolidated as four general principles including respect for China's territorial integrity and political independence, desisting from concluding treaties among themselves to the detriment of China, respect for China's right to remain neutral in

[61] *Xinchao*, vol. 2, no. 4, p. 864. Quoted in Lin Yunhan, op. cit., p. 282.

wartime, and enjoying equal opportunities in business dealings At the same time in Washington, China and Japan signed a treaty and an annex resolving outstanding issues between the two countries regarding Shandong: China resumed Japanese sovereignty over the Shandong Peninsula, Japan only retaining some rights and interests, including land, consular buildings, public schools and cemeteries needed by Japanese communities. We cannot but say that this result derived in part from the pressure on the great powers stemming from the Chinese awareness revealed in the May Fourth Movement.

Lu Xun (1881–1936), a long-standing opponent of Confucianism who had published *A Madman's Diary* in *New Youth*,[62] wrote: "The various incidents that constituted the May Fourth movement brought renown to Peking University as its headquarters…".[63] This situation had come about as a result of Cai Yuanpei's efforts. This was also the conclusion of those who hated Cai because they also saw the student movement caused in part by Cai Yuanpei's reforms at Peking University, which of course was the reason why the Beijing government decided to replace Cai Yuanpei, a KMT member, with Ma Qichang (1855–1930), a conservative follower of the Tongcheng classical school, like Lin Shu. A champion of the humanitarian function of literature, Lu Xun's brother, Zhou Zuoren (1885–1967) commented many decades later in 1958, that Cai Yuanpei's achievements "should be regarded as among the greatest of Peking University".[64] Yet in the 1920s, Cai's achievements were mainly due to his liberal ideas in the field of thought that led to the inevitable student

[62] As early as 1900, when Lu Xun was a student of the Lukuang School attached to Jiangnan Lushi Xuetang, he commented that he had "lost all faith in Confucius and his disciples". It is easy to remember this acerbic passage from his *Diary of a Madman*:

> I opened the history book to look it up but found that this history did not refer to any particular period and on all its crooked pages the words 'benevolence and morality' appeared. I could not sleep, and carefully looked at the book again in the middle of the night, and found that between the characters on the page, two characters had been written again and again, spelling out the word 'cannibal'. (*New Youth*, vol. 4, no. 5, 15 May 1918).

[63] *Lu Xun Quanji*, vol. 6, Renmin Wenxue Chubanshe, 1963, p. 192.

[64] Zhou Zuoren, *Zhitang Xiaopin*, Xi'an: Shaanxi Renmin Chubanshe, 1991, p. 629.

movement, and later historians had difficulty separating the "New Culture Movement" from the May Fourth Movement.

Of course, for intellectuals who hoped to change society through cultural movements, there was another way of regarding the May Fourth Movement. Hu Shi, for example, initially expressed excitement regarding the May Fourth Movement, but expressed great regret concerning the movement several years later:

> From the point of view of the cultural movement we call "the Chinese Renaissance", the May Fourth Movement, which was launched by the students of Beijing and supported by the whole nation, was a historic political disturbance within the entirety of the cultural movement, one which transformed a cultural movement into a political movement.[65]

Hu Shi's teacher, John Dewey, lecturing at Peking University at the time of May Fourth, wrote in an article in the magazine *Asia* in 1921: "The movement is still, for the most part, a feeling rather than an idea. It is also accompanied by the extravagances and confusions, the undigested medley of wisdom and nonsense that inevitably mark so ambitious a movement in its early stages...".[66]

Cultural Trends and Political Implications

The May Fourth Movement appeared to be a continuation of the anti-Japanese patriotic movement of the Chinese students in Japan who in the previous year had staged a class boycott in the name of anti-Japanese national salvation. During the Paris Peace Conference, society in China was directly concerned with and followed the issues. For example, between 20 April and 2 May in Jinan, Shandong province, there were large meetings of students and workers calling for the return of Qingdao to the Chinese government in the name of "restoring national sovereignty and defending the country's territory". When students in Beijing finally took to the streets, the New Culture Movement was transformed into a broader social movement, expressing the aspirations and aims of the

[65] Tang Degang tr. and annot., *Hu Shi Koushu Zizhuan* (Hu Shi's Oral Autobiography), Shanghai: Huadong Shifan Daxue Chubanshe, 1993, p. 183.

[66] Quoted from *Zhongguo de Qimeng Yundong: Zhishifenzi yu Wusi Yichan*, Taiyuan: Shanxi Renmin Chubanshe, 1989, p. 10.

Kuomintang and those intellectuals who were soon involved in political affairs.[67] Indeed, although the war between the warlords brought turmoil and disruption to society, it left room for Chinese intellectuals to take advantage of the diversion and spread Western thought. During the period of the New Culture Movement, trends of thought and cultural ideas diversified.

The tragedy of the First World War in Europe and the outcome of the Paris Peace Conference disappointed many Chinese intellectuals. Given that science had not saved Europe from disaster, this also evoked a discussion in the intellectual community rethinking the relationship between science and traditional Chinese thought.

The China-related international situation for cultural traditionalists like Liang Qichao and Liang Shuming (1893–1988) seemed to underscore the failure of Western science, and so they thought that this might be the occasion for Eastern ideas to spread and provide a cure for Westerners. As the birthplace of science, why did the West face widespread decay and problems after the First World War? Liang Qichao, in *An Emotional Record of Europe*, a work he completed in Paris in that year, wrote mockingly of the West: "We who are accustomed to simple and uncomfortable lives can nevertheless still sense the hardships they endure. They lived for many years in an extremely rich and extremely convenient material civilization, yet the rich now have money but nothing to spend it on. The poor who in the past could buy something for a dollar can't buy anything now for four or five times that amount, so how are they to get by?".[68]

Liang Shuming, who had been invited to Peking University by Cai Yuanpei, was a scholar of Buddhism prior to 1921, after which he began his study of the Confucian classics. His *Eastern and Western Cultures and Their Philosophies*, published at the end of 1921, constituted the intellectual opposite of the scientism of Chen Duxiu and others. Holding an independent position, Liang Shuming boldly pointed out the impossibility of Liang Qichao using Oriental culture to provide a cure for Western maladies:

67 After the May Fourth Movement, many Peking University students joined the Kuomintang, such as Duan Xipeng, Luo Jialun, and Fang Hao (1894–1955), while a number of prominent students like Zhang Guotao, Luo Zhanglong (1896–1995), and Gao Shangde (1896–1925) joined the Communist Party.

68 Liang Qichao, *Ou You Xinying Lu: Xin Dalu Youji*, Dongfang Chubanshe, 2006, p. 11.

> They feel that each of the two cultures has its own shortcomings, so they are hoping to attain a perfection that they will use for a long time. They do not realize that a culture has its own basic attitude. Their fallacious belief in integration stems from this theoretical shortcoming. Yet the fact remains: how can we begin to integrate the fundamental spirit of one cultural group with the fundamental spirit of another cultural group?[69]

Liang's purpose was obviously not simple rejection of Western civilization, because he did not oppose science and democracy. He even devised a solution to the problem, that is, by eliminating the influence of the antisocial aspects of Hinduism and reviving the "resolute" aspects of Confucius, a philosophy that is enterprising could be recreated. After ridding of past absurdities, we can "fully receive" Western science and democracy, he argued, and then "look back and critically draw anew from China's original cultural attitudes". This was his three-step approach to intellectual idealism.[70] Liang Shuming even complained about the old-school figures who lacked wisdom but opposed new ideas. As he saw it, such conservatives "were simply disdainful but unconvincing, and there was no joy or positivity in their advocacy of old ideas. In particular, the content of their own thought was unusually empty, and they did not understand the

[69] Liang Shuming, *Dong-Xi Wenhua ji qi Zhexue.*

[70] Qian Mu (1895–1990) in his *Guoxue Gailun* (General Principles of Chinese Studies) completed around 1926 presented what is an obvious assessment of Liang Shuming's "three-step approach":

> He did not dare speak of harmonizing the cultures of the East and West, because he feared Chen Duxiu and his followers would scoff at his remarks, but he also refused to be silent and expressed his dissatisfaction with Confucius and Sakyamuni (565–486 BCE), ultimately dismissing his own research on Indian acculturation, in order to demonstrate the fairness of his attitude. When it came to Western civilization, we have to admit he argued for 'total acceptance' but premised on 'fundamental change'. He did not realize that 'fundamental change' meant that there could not be 'total acceptance'. Total acceptance naturally rules out fundamental change, so how could he say both things in the one breath? He also he was critical of Chinese attitudes. But his criticism was simply placating Chen Duxiu's arguments. Critically proposing Chinese culture but totally accepting Western culture was hardly a synthesis. Such confusion was tired and insincere, and insufficient to overturn Chen Duxiu's claims, let alone convince Chen Duxiu's followers. It was inferior to Liang Qichao's grey reconciliation theory, which was at least consistent. (Beijing: Shangwu Yinshuguan, 1997, p. 344).

fundamental spirit of antiquity. Therefore, how could they withstand Mr. Chen [Duxiu]'s clear mind and incisive writing enabled him to sweep and destroy everything and be Invincible".[71]

In February 1923, the journalist Zhang Junmai (Carsun Chang, 1887–1969) gave a lecture titled "The Outlook on Life" to science and engineering students at Tsinghua University. Unlike Liang Shuming, Zhang Junmai had studied extensively in Japan, Britain, and Germany, and was well informed and knowledgeable about Western society. He was well aware that even in the scientifically highly advanced Western society, attention was paid to the inner life of the human being, such as the "duration" theory of Henri Bergson (1859–1941), which demonstrated that Western thinkers did not renounce their understanding of the particularities of spiritual life simply because of the existence of science. Therefore, Zhang Junmai informed his confused college student audience:

> Science, however developed, does not have the power to provide solutions to problems regarding man's outlook on life; only human beings themselves can solve these problems. Many of the great ancient and modern thinkers have addressed the questions of human life and made their contributions, such as Yang Zhu's egoism, Mozi's (c.479BCE-c.381BCE) universal love, and Confucius and Mencius' spirit of compromise. From Confucius and Mencius down to the Song, Yuan and Ming dynasty Neo-Confucians, Confucian philosophy has focused on the cultivation of inner life, and the result was spiritual civilization. For the past three hundred years, Europe focused on the human domination of nature, so the result was material civilization.[72]

Zhang Junmai's statements were appealing to those who entertained no doubts about the intrinsic value of traditional culture. Zhang Junmai's willingness to divide the life of the spiritual and material worlds into two different spheres, as though such a method of analysis was established, subsequently provided the basis for a methodological discussion separating Western culture and traditional Chinese culture. For many traditionalists, the self-sufficiency of Chinese cultural traditions was not

[71] *Liang Shuming Quanji*, vol. 1, Jinan: Shandong Renmin Chubanshe, 1989, p. 344.

[72] Zhang Junmai, "Renshengguan" (The Outlook on Life), in ***Zhongguo Xiandai Sixiang zhong de Weikexuezhuyi*** (Scientism in Chinese Modern Thought), Nanjing: Jiangsu Renmin Chubanshe, 1989, pp. 117–118.

altered because of the influence of Western culture; as this was a utilitarian era—most people believed that "natural selection" was simply another expression for amoral utilitarianism, and maintaining the ideas of Confucius, Mencius, and the Neo-Confucians could ensure the "cultivation of the inner being". Zhang Junmai's methodological dichotomy was attacked by followers of scientism like Ding Wenjiang the focus of their attack asking how could the inner life be mere "metaphysics":

> Psychological content is the subject of science, and we know matter only as we psychologically perceive it through the senses, from its perception it is formulated as a concept, and as a concept it generates inference. Scientific research is no less than such concepts and inferences, so is there any difference between spiritual science and material science? How can we say that purely psychological phenomena are governed by the scientific method?[73]

Even sensory experiences, emotions, thoughts, and concepts are all related to science, so science can study any problem in the field of mind (spirit). Chinese intellectuals who returned from studying abroad were familiar with Chinese philosophical classics; in this respect they were the last retainers in the twentieth century of traditional Chinese writings, and so they undertook a very detailed scouring of the traditions of Confucius, Laozi, and Zhuangzi. However, the real world does not seem to have provided strong support for these traditionalists; on the contrary, the intellectuals who advocated Westernization used their victory in the 1911 Revolution to illustrate the incompetence of the Qing government, so that, now, if there was to be a foundation for rebuilding the nation, why would China retain its invalidated ideas to do so? Thus, as Hu Shi's friend Ding Wenjiang expressed it, ever since the Southern Song dynasty, the knowledge held by the literati has been impractical, leading eventually to the massacre and domination of the Chinese people by aliens. By the end of the Ming dynasty, reading had become "an indulgence in bereavement" and readers resembled "idiots". By the time the Opium War made its impact on the Chinese, who could even demonstrate what role those traditional classics once played? Ding Wenjiang asked directly: "What is

[73] Ding Wenjiang, "Xuanxue yu kexue" (Metaphysics and science), quoted in *Zhongguo Xiandai Sixiang zhong de Weikexuezhuyi* (Scientism in Chinese Modern Thought), Nanjing: Jiangsu Renmin Chubanshe, 1989, p. 119.

the value of this spiritual civilization?" In the understanding and application of cultural concepts, the expression "Chinese studies" was roughly equivalent to the totality of traditional culture which at that time was regarded as "metaphysics" as opposed to science. Ding Wenjiang had such an understanding of the term, as is clear from the following comment critical of him: "The psychology of these people is much like that of Zhang Zhidong in that they regard metaphysics as the corpus (*ti*) and science as its application (*yong*)". Ding Wenjiang mocked those traditionalists who acknowledged the need for and use of science, but also wanted to guard against science, attributing all Europe's political and social problems to "science", and extrapolating from Europe's problems proof of the value of "Chinese studies".

On the basis of the principles of empiricism espoused by his teacher John Dewey (1859–1952), Hu Shi believed that any cultural change must be verifiable and not deduced from general metaphysics. We also note that dialectics, which was then becoming an important ideological weapon for some intellectuals, was also beginning to attract criticism from Hu Shi because he found all metaphysics untenable, and he reminded people: If you insist on metaphysics, no matter what position or point of view you adopt, you will easily fall into the trap of all metaphysics, because dialectics can use subjectivity and arbitrary interpretations to confound "positive and negative issues" and such mistakes are almost the same as those derived from classical textual exegesis. Hu Shi showed an intrinsic sense of absolute skepticism, which was related to his empirical approach; everyone was free to examine anything in a particular situation and the theory of natural justice could also be questioned, but the authority and standards for such empirical examination were problematic. For example, on what can we judge the final result will be, and what is the true significance of sorting out the country's cultural heritage? In the end, Hu Shi reminded people that sorting out the country's cultural heritage may not make sense, as he explained:

> To acquire a little more knowledge and technology from the natural sciences is the way to life, while this old pile of paper is the road of death. For three hundred years the nation's first-class minds occupied themselves with this pile of paper, to no good end. We should change our ways. Once

you get good results in the science lab, then use whatever energies are spare to come back and sort out our country's cultural heritage.[74]

Hu Shi always adhered to the scientific standpoint, and he invariably regarded the spirit of doubt and the scientific method as weapons to change cultural and ideological realities so that the younger generation would always remain hopeful in their acceptance of everything from the West. Towards those who respectively attributed the material and the spiritual to Western science and Eastern culture, Hu Shi adopted a tone of mockery and ridicule. He described Liang Qichao and those who spoke of Western civilization as materialistic and Eastern civilization as spiritual as using "toxic words" to toxic effect, and he told people that it was impossible in discussion to separate the "material" from the "spiritual".

The revolutionaries were of course concerned with cultural and political trends in intellectual circles. During the student movement in 1919, Sun Yat-sen was still working hard to achieve success in the North–South peace talks. The political situation created by the student movement provided new political opportunities, encouraging Sun Yat-sen to re-examine the influence of ideas through publishing, and he instructed Dai Jitao and Shen Dingyi (1883–1928) to set up the *Weekly Review* (Xingqi Pinglun) as a southern response to Peking University's *Xinchao* and *Citizen's Journal*. At this time, Sun Yat-sen attached great importance to the student movement, and he wrote in a letter of the 18th: "How students have risen throughout the country over the past few months is surely a result of the effects of the new thought. Therefore, indoctrination of the whole country through knowledge expressing the fundamental propositions of our party will raise our people's general awareness so that when the time is ripe they will rise up united to eliminate the old and proclaim the new, and this will be the great achievement of our party's doctrines".[75] Sun Yat-sen saw with alacrity the source of new political forces, and in October of that year he reshuffled the Chinese Revolutionary Party as the Kuomintang, initiating political party politics that "consolidated the republic and implemented the Three Principles of the People as a general aim". Sun saw very clearly that the energy within

[74] Hu Shi, "Zhixue de fangfa yu cailiao", in *Zhongguo Xiandai Sixiang zhong de Weikexue-zhuyi*, Nanjing: Jiangsu Renmin Chubanshe, 1989, p. 78.

[75] Quoted in Wang Fumin, *Sun Zhongshan Xiangzhuan*, *xia* volume, Beijing: Zhongguo Guangbo Dianshi Chubanshe, 1993, p. 961.

the New Culture Movement and the resulting May Fourth Movement was both new and dynamic. As he said in January 1920: "Since the May Fourth Movement was unleashed by students at Peking University, patriotic youth have been generally preparing for the innovative enterprise of revolution with revolutionary ideas. So there is a fervor expressed in debate. Public opinion from every walk of life in China unanimously supports them. A variety of new publications founded by enthusiastic youths have flourished in response. This fresh and budding crop of solid publications exerts great influence in society. Despite the vicious and illegitimate government, none dare oppose them. This New Culture Movement, in our country today, has truly changed the world to an unprecedented extent. We can trace its origins back to its advocacy by several enlightened thinkers in the publishing world. As a result, public opinion has radically changed and a tide of learning has spread throughout the country so that all people are inspired and vow to die for the patriotic movement; if it can continue to grow, its future will be magnificent and long-lasting, without doubt. The success of our Party's revolution must depend on a change in thought. This is the military tactic of attacking the mind, which is why we call it renovation. Therefore, this New Culture Movement is of the greatest value".[76] Despite Sun Yat-sen's assessment of the New Culture Movement, in his view the new culture was only an auxiliary tool of the political revolution, and in terms of cultural tendencies Sun was still a defender of Confucian ethics.[77]

Hu Shi later complained: "After 1919, the leaders of the KMT and CPC, and even the research groups that broke away from the former Progressive Party (Jinbu Dang) led by Liang Qichao, all placed their hopes in the possibility of absorbing young students as a new political

[76] Quoted in Hu Sheng, *Cong Yapian Zhanzheng dao Wusi Yundong*, *xia* volume, Beijing: Renmin Chubanshe, 1984, pp. 964–965. Ref: Zhang Qiyun ed., *Guofu Quanshu*, Taipei: Guofang Yanjiuyuan, 1966, p. 779.

[77] Sun Yat-sen said in his sixth speech in *Sanmin-zhuyi*: "When it comes to China's inherent morality, Chinese people have not forgotten to the present day, first is loyalty and filial piety, second is benevolence, followed by faith, and then followed by peace. These are the old morality, still discussed by Chinese to the present day. But now, with oppression from foreign peoples and the invasion of the new culture, the forces of the new culture now cover China. People who are generally intoxicated with the new culture reject the old morality and think that with the new culture they cannot be the old morality. They do not realize that if what is inherent is good, then we should of course preserve it, and if it is bad then we should reject it".

force. After "May Fourth", the publications of all Chinese political parties, especially those of the KMT and the 'research departments' in Shanghai and Beijing, added vernacular literary supplements. The literary supplement of the *Republic of China Daily*, the organ of the KMT, was titled *Awareness*. The two major newspapers of Liang Qichao's group, *Beijing Morning Post* and the *National Gazette*, had many columns to which they invited university teachers and students to contribute. At that time, all political parties wanted to win the support of young intellectuals, and as a result every member of the intelligentsia was interested in politics".[78]

From May 1919 to October 1920, John Dewey and Bertrand Russell visited China in turn, which marked the beginning of the inclusion of the Chinese intellectual community as participants in the world of modern thought, and the Western thought that was introduced already encompassed a variety of schools of doctrine and thought. After the "May Fourth Movement", the seventh page of the supplement of Beijing's *Morning Post* and the "Study Lamp" supplement of Shanghai's *Times News* (Shishi Xinbao), two papers which belonged to Liang Qichao's research group, began to introduce Marxist theory, and *Morning Post Supplement* even published articles on Marxism in every issue from May 1919 onward. Soon, *New Youth*, *Republic of China Daily*, *Shishi Xinbao*, and *Republic of China Gazette* (*Minguo Gongbao*, published in Sichuan) all reprinted these supplements. Chen Puxian (1891–1957), who was a classmate of Li Dazhao at Waseda University, served as a reporter for the *Morning Post Supplement*, and he even went to Japan to study the workers' and other social movements there. It was Chen and his articles published in the *Morning Post Supplement* that first informed Li Dazhao about Marxist theory. In the second half of 1919 and in January of the following year, Li Dazhao wrote "My View of Marxism" and "The Economic Explanation of Changes in Modern Chinese Thought", which expressed Li Dazhao's earliest understanding of Marxist philosophy:

> Marx's theory of socialism can be divided into three parts. One part is his theory about the past, namely his theory of history which is also known as his theory of the evolution of social organization. The second is his theory about the present, which is his economic theory, also known as the economic theory of capitalism. The third is his theory about the future,

[78] Tang Degang, op. cit., p. 184.

that is his policy theory, also known as the theory of the socialist movement, which is social democracy. All three of his theories are inextricably related. But the competition between the classes is described as the golden thread that provides the fundamental link connecting these three sets of theoretical principles.[79]

Li Dazhao even joined the Japanese Socialist Alliance in December 1920, introduced by Maruyama Koichiro (1895–1924), which meant that his understanding of Marxism also benefited from the contemporary Japanese socialist movement and his study of Marxism was based on reading Japanese articles. By 1921 when he wrote "The Past and Present of the Russian Revolution", Li Dazhao had acquired a solid understanding of the Bolsheviks through the English-language books he came across at that time.[80] In fact, many of the active young Chinese students of Marxism were intellectuals who had studied in Japan, including Chen Duxiu, Li Hanjun, Chen Wangdao (1891–1977), Shi Cuntong (1899–1970), Zhou Fohai (1897–1948), and Li Da (1890–1966). Li Da introduced Lenin, Bukharin, and Plekhanov to Chinese readers. This shows that the ideas of Marxism first entered China from Japan rather than Russia and, later, the socialist movements in Europe and the United States continued to influence China.[81]

However, Hu Shi completely disagreed with the views expressed by Li Dazhao, Chen Duxiu, and others, and in the *Weekly Review* of 20

[79] Li Dazhao, "Wode Makesi-zhuyi guan", I, *Xin Qingnian*, vol. 6, no. 5, May 1919.

[80] In his *Eluosi Geming de Guoqu ji Xianzai* (The Past and Present of the Russian Revolution), he introduced a number of English books: Lenin and Trotsky, *The Proletarian Revolution in Russia,* New York: Communist Press, 1918; *The Soviets at Work. The international Position of the Russian Soviet Republic and the Fundamental Problems of the Socialist Revolution*, New York: Rand School of Social Science, 1918; L. Trotsky, *The Bolsheviks and World Peace*, New York: Boni and Liveright, 1918; *History of the Russian Revolution to Brest-Litovsk*, London: Leo and Unwin, 1919.

[81] Shao Lizi wrote: "When the Marxist Research Society began, it simply translated and wrote articles promoting Marxism". Li Hanjun, Li Da, and Chen Wangdao wrote a lot, and later Zhou Fuhai also wrote a bit. They were all students in Japan. At that time, Marxist books were mainly translated from Japanese. Li Da recalled: "At that time, Marx and Engels's writings were rarely translated, and we only read some works in Japanese.

China largely received Marxism with Japanese help, because no Chinese had translated Marxist works. Bourgeois scholars basically did not translate such works at all, and our people were unable to translate them". Ref: Ishikawa Yoshihiro, *Zhongguo Gongchandang Chengli Shi* (The History of the Founding of the Communist Party of China), Beijing: Zhongguo Shehui Kexue Chubanshe, 2006, pp. 35–36.

July 1919 he published an article that delineated the political differences within the elite of Peking University. Titled "More Study of Problems and Less Talk about Isms" (*Duo Yanjiu Xie Wenti, Shao Tan Xie Zhuyi*), Hu Shi made these comments on "delirious talk" about political doctrines:

> Civilization is not created as a totality, but bit by bit. Evolution is not achieved in a single night, but in tiny steps. People today love to talk about liberation and transformation, but we must realize that liberation and transformation cannot be achieved without specific analysis. The liberation that will liberate this or that political system, thinking, or person will be incremental; the transformation that will transform this or that political system, thinking, or person will also proceed with tiny steps. Re-creating civilization proceeds by examining this or that problem, and the re-creation of civilization proceeds through solving this or that problem.

Li Dazhao responded: If the overall direction is uncertain, how do we solve specific problems? As in Russia, "if the Romanov family had not been overthrown and the economic organization had not been transformed, nothing would have been solved, but now all is solved". Hu Shi countered with the argument that China's situation was complex and it could not be solved with a single "doctrine". Li Dazhao insisted on his interpretation of Marx's theories, saying that if economic problems were fundamentally resolved, other issues like those related to politics, law, the family, women's liberation, and workers' liberation would be solved. Chen Duxiu, on the other hand, emphasized the necessity and efficacy of political action and seemed to believe that if it was limited to research it would do little to change Chinese society. As for Hu Shi's empiricism, it was also largely an idealistic academic expectation, and if not limited to literary and evidential textual research, in the turmoil of civil war conducted by warlords how were people able to formulate any real plans, or have the peace of mind to conduct social experiments or realize social transformation?

In fact, when Hu Shi joined the editorial board of *New Youth* (early 1918), Duan Qirui was locked in a power struggle with Feng Guozhang, the war between North and South was complex and tense, and China's overall situation was one of utter chaos. Sun Yat-sen's southern political forces made little progress in their military efforts to restore the old parliament and faced the possibility of destruction. The question of how to eliminate the warlords left politicians scratching their heads. Sun Yat-sen, in order to achieve a partial victory, made contact with Duan Qirui, whose forces had been defeated in the major fighting between the Zhili and Anhui warlords, and with Zhang Zuolin (1875–1928) in the northeast. Even though this triangular alliance might not be seen by intellectuals like Hu Shi as criminal, they certainly regarded it as far from healthy. Hu Shi even joked that Sun Yat-sen was now the wife of three warlord cliques (Zhili, Fengtian, and Anhui). However, whether or not Li Dazhao or Hu Shi realized it, the ideological debate itself had no real impact on those in power. Intellectuals believed that the solutions to problems were based on a theoretical consensus, but in the view of the powerful, the nature and resolution of problems depended on achieving specific political objectives. In the same month that Duan Qirui wrested power from Feng Guozhang, Hu Shi published "More Study of Problems and Less Talk about Isms", which specifically targeted the praise of Wang Yitang's (1878–1948) "doctrine of people's livelihood" (*minsheng-zhuyi*) by the newspapers controlled by the Anhui Club—*Gongyan Bao*, *Xin Minguo Bao* (New Republican Daily), and *Xinmin Bao* (New People's Daily). Indeed, everyone was talking about the doctrine of people's livelihood, with Sun Yat-sen in the south also promoting the doctrine. Hu Shi found this situation both ridiculous and lamentable, prompting him to remark:

First, empty talk about any "ism" is facile; any person of little importance can do it, as can a parrot or a phonograph.

Second, empty talk about some imported "ism" is utterly pointless. Every single doctrine has been put forward at some time or in some place to provide a panacea for some society or other. If we do not study the needs of our actual society on the ground but mouth lofty and high-minded remarks about some doctrine, isn't this as useless as a doctor prescribing some medicine and reciting tips for a patient with no regard for the patient's actual symptoms?

Third, favoring a doctrine that only exists on paper is quite dangerous. Such a mantra can easily be used by shameless politicians to perpetrate all sorts of harm.

In fact, Hu Shi's article touched on the political divisions that called for a different approach. There were contradictions of different types within the Beiyang government (e.g., between Duan Qirui, Feng Guozhang, or Zhang Zuolin), the southern political group (e.g., Sun Yat-sen and Chen Jiongming), and the intelligentsia (e.g., Hu Shi, Chen Duxiu, or Li Dazhao) that could not be characterized as a single "problem" that could be addressed by a single "ism" or doctrine."Congress" (*guohui*), "Senate" (*canyiyuan*), and "Republic" (*gonghe*), terms that denoted the new political system, became tools in the unspoken game, the power struggle in which the main protagonists were the warlords, and they could be changed or explained at will. So even if no one was proclaiming a "doctrine", slogans could be randomly coined to resolve a "problem", so how could people identify among the numerous "problematic" slogans a real and agreed upon "problem"? Addressing the problems of the livelihood of a rickshaw driver was not just a matter of developing principles of social welfare or social equity; women's liberation or rectifying the family system was hardly a critical issue for a simple moral system; as for the question of "resolving North–South problems", this was not a theoretical issue but a question of real political operations. The man who proclaims anarchism and the man engaged in political manipulation are not one and the same at all, so it is necessary to distinguish between those who proclaim "isms". Recalling in his later years this period as deputy editor from mid-June 1919 to late August, Hu Shi said:

> My new attempt began in July when I wrote 'More Study of Problems and Less Talk about Isms'. My intention was to criticize those dangerous dogmas that are blindly accepted, whether anarchism, socialism or Bolshevism. In that column, which should have been titled 'Practical Issues and Abstract Doctrines", there were a number of articles that discussed the same topic. One was written by my colleague at Peking University, Professor Li Dazhao.[82]

People from the KMT group headed by Sun Yat-sen, such as Dai Jitao (1891–1949), Shen Xuanlu (1892–1928), Hu Hanmin (1879–1936), Shao Lizi (1882–1967), Zhu Zhixin (1885–1920), and Liao Zhongkai (1877–1925), were promoting socialism through newspapers like *Republic of China Daily*, *Weekly Review*, and *Construction*. Although their focus was on finding a theoretical basis for Sun Yat-sen's "people's livelihood", theorists such as Dai Jitao had a thorough understanding of Marxism and he had read the Japanese version of *Capital* in 1920. It was Dai Jitao and Li Hanjun, who with Chen Duxiu when he moved to Shanghai in early 1920 formed a small communist group to learn

[82] *Hu Shi Zhexue Sixiang Ziliao Xuan*, *xia* volume, Shanghai: Huadong Shifan Daxue Chubanshe, 1981, p. 201.

more about Marxism. In the same year, an associate of *New Youth*, Chen Wangdao translated *The Communist Manifesto* from the Japanese version, and it was published in August by the Shanghai Socialist Research Society after Chen Duxiu and Li Hanjun edited the text. This book later became essential reading for every member of the CPC.[83]

In summing up, a number of factors were influencing China: news of the success of the Bolshevik Revolution in Russia aroused general expectations regarding an idealized socialism; after the Paris Peace Conference, Western nations lost the trust of Chinese intellectuals; when Lenin told people that imperialism was the highest stage of capitalism and that now was the era when people all over the world would come together to achieve a new society, namely communism, and the socialist movement began to spread around the world, Marxist theory was rapidly welcomed as it encouraged people to liberate themselves from imperialism and the capitalist system. In July 1919, the Soviet government issued what came to be named for the Soviet foreign minister as the *Karakhan Declaration*, which announced to the Chinese people and the governments of North and South China the unconditional return of the historical rights and interests plundered by the Russian Empire from China, a policy completely different from that of the tsars and the imperialist powers of the past. When this information reached China in the following spring, many intellectuals and young people became extremely curious and interested in the Russian Revolution, and they had a completely idealistic vision of socialism, seeing it as the advent of a new era. In the second half of 1920, Shanghai's Marxist and communist activists continued to obtain information about the Russian Revolution from Bolshevik literature translated from English-language publications from Europe and the United States, which drew some intellectuals from Marxist academic research to Leninism with its characteristics as a violent movement. They began to learn that the constitutions and programs of the Communist parties of Europe and the United States emphasized the importance of revolutionary action, especially the dictatorship of the proletariat, which formed the basic context and raison d'être shaping the CPC.

[83] Marx was first introduced in a Chinese publication in 1899, and in 1906 a Chinese translation of *The Communist Manifesto* was published in a style half-way between the classical and vernacular languages.

The Political Propositions of the Intelligentsia

In the early 1920s, China's emerging intellectuals felt fully confident that they could change history, and they harbored few doubts regarding their own ideological and social influence. Hu Shi's "Our Political Proposition", published in *Nuli Zhoubao* (Endeavor Weekly) on 14 May 1922, was a manifesto written on behalf of Cai Yuanpei calling for "good government". During the period of warlord rule, the intellectuals who signed the manifesto were putting forward their political ideas:

1. The objective of political reform: We think that we will not discuss politics for now, and if we discuss politics, there should be a realistic and clear goal that everyone can understand. We think that the finest people in this country, regardless of whatever political organization they see as being ideal (whether populism, guild socialism, or anarchism), should now all regard "good government" as a commonly agreed upon goal and as a minimum requirement for reforming Chinese politics. We should work together for this common goal in combating the evil forces in our country.
2. "Good government", or at least what we call "good government" must have legitimate bodies that can supervise and prevent all abuses by illegitimate officials. On the positive side there must be two things: (1)The full use of political organs for the full benefit of all society. (2)Full accommodation of the freedom of the individual, and love and protection for the development of the individual.
3. The three basic principles of political reform and for our present and future political reform comprise three basic requirements: First, we demand "constitutional government" because this is the first step on the political track. Second, we demand an "open government" which encompasses open finances and open examinations for recruiting people; because we are convinced that "open-ness" (publicity) is the only weapon to dispel the darkness. Third, we demand "planned politics" because we are convinced that China's major failing is that she drifts without any plan, because we are convinced that planning is the source of efficiency, and because we are convinced that a mediocre plan is better than groping about without any plan.
4. Four, in the practice of political reform, we have a firm belief that China has become so corrupted for many reasons, but the only

important reason is "good people maintain a holier-than-thou attitude but do not act, while the wicked never stop acting". So, we are convinced that the first step in today's political reform is for good people to embody the spirit of struggle. All the best elements of society should strive to defend themselves and fight the evil forces on behalf of society and the nation.

Starting with the fifth item, intellectuals formulated a series of concrete political measures: on the question of North and South; on the convening of the parliament which was dissolved in the 6th year of the Republic (1917); on the abolition of the military; on the abolition of officials; and on direct elections. The list of proponents of these political ideas was as follows:

Proponent's name and position:

Cai Yuanpei, President of National Peking University
Wang Chonghui, Lecturer, National Peking University
Luo Wengan, Lecturer, National Peking University
Tang Erhe, Doctor of Medical Science
Tao Xingzhi, Director of Faculty of Education, National Southeastern University.
Wang Boqiu, Director, Faculty of Politics, Jurisprudence and Economics, National Southeastern University
Liang Shuming, Lecturer, National Peking University.
Li Dazhao, Director, Library, National Peking University
Tao Menghe, Dean, Department of Philosophy, National Peking University
Zhu Jingnong, Lecturer, National Peking University
Zhang Weici, Lecturer, National Peking University
Gao Yihan, Lecturer, National Peking University
Xu Baohuang, Lecturer, National Peking University
Wang Zheng, Secretary of the New Bank of the United States
Ding Wenjiang, Former Director of the Geological Survey
Hu Shi, Dean of Studies, National Peking University.[84]

[84] Cited by Peng Ming ed., *Zhongguo Xiandai Shi Ziliao Xuanji, 1919–1923* (Anthology of Materials on Modern Chinese History, 1919–1923), vol. 1, Beijing: Zhongguo Renmin Daxue Chubanshe, 1990, pp. 251–255.

As the representative of the intellectuals who advocated solving specific problems but did not agree to any comprehensive and fundamental solution to problems, Hu Shi's ideas were out of step with political reality. Regarding their three basic demands for present and future politics, namely "constitutional government", "open government", and "planned politics", Hu Shi's proposals naturally reflected the consensus of the signatories. However, in the view of intellectuals who advocate "isms" (doctrine), the goals put forward by this group of intellectuals actually necessitated resolving other matters first. The constitutional government was not proposed in 1922, because from the time of the late Qing reforms and especially the 1911 Revolution, "constitutionalism" had become a term that almost everyone used, so why had this problem never been solved? At this time, the Northern and Southern regimes had a completely different view of this issue. The Beiyang warlord governments did not value the political role of intellectuals such as Hu Shi, and their internal power struggles were almost overwhelming; Sun Yat-sen in the south was full of ideals, but he concluded in November 1923 that the revolution had not succeeded because of internal problems within the Party.[85] "The Communist Party's Proposals in the Current Situation", published on 15 June 1922 by the Communist Party of China (CPC) led by Chen Duxiu, pointed out before Sun Yat-sen the historical mistakes and problems of the KMT, while the Progressive Party of Liang Qichao and others was merely ridiculed in the CPC's writings.[86] At this point, the CPC made the central issue the overthrow of warlord politics: "Warlord politics is the source of China's internal and external woes, as well as the source of

[85] Sun Yat-sen wrote in "The Past Failure of the Kuomintang and Its Present Future Success": "In the twelve years since the 1911 Revolution, China's domestic struggles have increased, and the country has politically and economically regressed. What is the reason for this? In short, the struggle of our Party has not been successful. Before the 1911 Revolution, our Party members struggled, but since the Revolution, the ardor has dissipated, and the spirit of struggle has been gradually lost. Everyone thought that the 1911 Revolution's overthrow of the Manchu dynasty marked the success of the revolution, but the revolutionary cause failed to continue, and this is the main reason for the present situation". (Quoted from Peng Ming ed., op. cit., vol. 1, Beijing: Zhongguo Renmin Daxue Chubanshe, 1990, p. 491).

[86] "The Communist Party of China's Proposition in the Current Situation", in describing the KMT's first defeat in opposing Yuan Shikai, stated: "With the failure of the Kuomintang, Xiong and Liang on behalf of the non-revolutionary Democracy Party (Progressive Party) opportunistically organized a party cabinet, only to be played by Yuan Shikai, whereby they immediately failed ethically". (Quoted from Ibid., p. 132).

suffering of her people. If there is no new political organization - that is, democratic politics, to replace the current unsavory political organization, namely warlord politics, this situation will necessarily continue".[87] We are not quite sure why Li Dazhao, an important leader of the CPC, put his signature to "Our Political Propositions" drafted by Hu Shi, but it is clear that the views of Hu Shi and Chen Duxiu were very different at this time. Hu Shi believed that even in the face of warlord rule it was still possible for a good military leader to implement political reform. In April and May 1922, the warlord Wu Peifu won the approval of the North. His control of the Beijing government and the situation in the North were seen as the beginning of a sustained improvement in Chinese politics, especially in the eyes of progressive intellectuals like Hu Shi. Wu Peifu supported the student movement during the May Fourth period and after the battles between Zhili and Fengtian warlord cliques, Wu Peifu advocated "restoration of the rule of law and the reopening of Parliament", a political slogan that, though serving the interests of the warlords' political bloc, greatly appealed to intellectuals who lacked the skills of the political operator, and it even became evident to intellectuals that they could rely on Wu's political force to reform politics.[88] In Hu Shi's view, since Wu had unified the North, there was no need for the South to wage its war defending the Constitution.[89] So Hu Shi and Cai Yuanpei both signed a

[87] Idem.

[88] Wu Peifu advocated the restoration of the Republican Constitution of 1911 and the reconvening of the National Congress which had been dissolved by Duan Qirui in 1917. In fact, these moves had nothing to do with the intellectuals' yearning for democratic politics. Wu's main aim was to automatically remove political power from Sun Yat-sen's Constitutional Defence Army by restoring the Constitution of 1911 and reconvening the National Assembly, thereby gaining control over the whole of China. The whole matter of a new political system was then totally shunted aside.

[89] There are two important reasons for the defeat of the Fengtian Army in the Zhili-Fengtian battles. Firstly, Duan Qirui did not instruct his army to attack the Zhili armies, and secondly, Sun Yat-sen in the south was restrained by Chen Jiongming, and Sun at that time was linked in a political alliance with the Zhili and Anhui warlords. These allies for their own reasons did not form an overall force which could have defeated the Fengtian Army. It is worth noting that Hu Shi regarded Chen Jiongming expelling Sun Yat-sen from Guangzhou as the result of a mistake on the part of Sun. In his commentary in the "Weekly Column" of the June 25 issue of *Nuli Zhoubao*, Hu Shi wrote that "the conflict between Sun Wen and Chen Jiongming is a conflict of ideas" and that Sun was too insistent on his own position and so "could not avoid failure". Discussing the conflict between Sun Yat-sen and Chen Jiongming, Hu Shi emphasized that the former advocated unifying Chin and the latter stressed provincial autonomy.

telegram to Sun Yat-sen, hoping that Sun would end his Constitution Protection war. This move not only led to the KMT's dissatisfaction, but alarmingly showed the same in spirit as Cao Kun who asked Sun Chuanfang to telegram Sun Yat-sen.[90] For Hu Shi, the next task was to implement political reform with the support of the newly united powers. Therefore, it seemed that "constitutional government", "open government", and "planned politics" were all now possible. Criticism of the view that "good government" had prevailed came from all sides, and the CPC's ideas were naturally far removed from those of Hu Shi. The KMT was even angrier at Hu Shi's support for the KMT's removal from political power. Sun Yat-sen began to contact the CPC in order to strengthen his political power, while those who entrusted their hope to "good government" began to construct the "government for the good". In September, Wang Chonghui, Luo Wengan, and Tang Erhe, three of the signatories of "Our Political Propositions", entered the "good government", but in late November, the "good government" fell because of the differences between Wu Peifu and Cao Kun and their conflicting interests. In his biography of Ding Wenjiang, a geologist passionate about political reform, Hu Shi describes the feeling of total defeat at that time:

> At that time, we had a number of fairly specific ideas about current political issues, namely, the first to sixth paragraphs of the fifth item in the above document [i.e., "Our Political Proposition"- author], were, as we thought,

[90] Sun Chuanfang telegrammed: "Because President Sun in Guangzhou made Constitutional Protection his cause, when the constitution was restored, his responsibility ended. President Xu in Beijing selected a new parliament, but when the old national assembly was convened, the new parliament had no role to play. I hope that these two men now withdraw from politics in a timely fashion". (From Zhang Hongxiang, Xu Xingyun, and Qiu Qianhou eds., *Buyi Zongtong Cao Kun* (The Plainly Dressed President Cao Kun), Changchun: Jilin Wenshi Chubanshe, 1995, p. 131. Original book quoted from *Zhonghua Minguo Shiliao Conggao "Da Shiji"*, vol. 8, p. 65). In his letter to Hu Shi and Cai Yuanpei, the Kuomintang's Zhang Nanxian wrote with uncharacteristic anger: "The claims you make are biased, narrow, implausible, confused and contrary to genuine public opinion. They protect the militarists, will occasion war in future, and it is insulting for the most prominent intellects in our country to utter such comments. I'm very angry and very depressed, ... That you two can speak so carelessly on behalf of the intellectual community is a travesty of justice. The warlords are tyrannical, and it is up to politicians to correct them; if politicians are corrupt, then it is the duty of scholars to correct them. When today's scholars write like you, then our suffering people are doomed". *Hu Shi Wanglai Shuxin Xuan* (Selection of Hu Shi's Correspondence), vol.1, Beijing: Zhonghua Shuju, 1983, pp. 151–152.

all "modest" proposals. But later, as the situation evolved, we were forced to acknowledge that we had been far too optimistic! For example, there was not the slightest hope of implementing any curb on the "military"! We could only see how in 1922, after the defeat of the Fengtian army and its withdrawal beyond the Great Wall, the number of soldiers increased by the day, and after the change in military organization, there was an increase in new armaments and heavy artillery, and with every day there were preparations for revenge. There was a similar buildup of the Zhili armies, and there were daily preparations for the return of the Fengtian army from beyond the Great Wall. This situation he clearly saw and wrote several articles about the military situation in *Nuli* [*Zhoubao*] ... These studies were the starting point for his later work, *Minguo Junshi Jinji* (Recent Military Developments in the Republic of China), published by the Commercial Press in 1926. Because he often traveled to Fengtian in Jehol, he was fully aware of the preparations for war of the two northern warlords. So, in September, we wrote in *Nuli* [*Zhoubao*]: "Cut government expenditure, retire a thousand soldiers, yet this cut couldn't even afford one shot near Shanhaiguan. So, we recommended: (a) Provincial meetings should be convened by the Beijing government as soon as possible. (b) The Beijing government should openly mediate in the struggle between the Fengtian and Zhili forces and eliminate the scourge of war that is being forced on the people." Such a proposal was something that Li Yuanhong did not dare to make, nor did the cabinet of Yan Huiqing (1877–1950) and Wang Chonghui, or the newly convened former Congress even dare propose. The scourge of war in the North could not be eliminated, and the talk about disarmament became empty talk.

Take another example. We have advocated "an open North-South peace conference reflecting public opinion" and "North-South consultations to convene the National Assembly disbanded in 1917". Later, the Congress was convened, and sessions began on 1 August, but no "North-South consultations" were convened. Rather, on that day, the temporarily victorious Zhili army and its politicians made the clever move of establishing their own "orthodox" status, and so Li Yuanhong, whom they had originally supported, resumed his position and the old parliament was restored, in what was called "the rekindling of the law."

The "rekindling of the law" was in preparation for resolving the "greatest problem", namely the Presidential election. They explained that Li Yuanhong's term of office still had one year and four months left, and when he finished his term, the "law-and-order" Congress could elect Cao Kun president. We proposed an open North-South conference rather than reconvening the national assembly dissolved in 1917 through conference resolution, and regard this as a condition for the unification of the North and South, and as an organization to implement the "Tiantan (Temple of Heaven) Constitution" of 1917, but the warlords' lackeys had intended and prepared all along to bribe the old Congress to elect Cao Kun to succeed Li Yuanhong as president!

I cite these two examples to illustrate how Ding Wenjiang and we organized *Nuli Zhoubao* to criticize politics, and our enthusiasm to supervise politics can be said to have been a complete failure. In March 1923, I quoted some remarks made to me by Tang Erhe in the forty-seventh issue of *Nuli Zhoubao*:

"I advise you not to talk about politics. I read your critiques before, and I felt they made sense. But now that I am in the government, I can see that the situation is utterly different! It is not at all as you described. The world you talked about is quite unlike the world going on, so I advise you not to talk about politics."

Nuli Zhoubao lasted for a year and a half. At the end of November 1922, I was ill. On 17 January [1923],Mr. Cai Yuanpei tendered his resignation as President of Peking University because Peng Yunyi [1878-1943] was appointed the Minister of Education, stating in his resignation letter that he was "sad that there is no hope of political transparency and he cannot bear to be compromised, especially under education authorities like the present who uphold the decline of education, which will be seen by the nation's people and by ethics as criminal". He placed a notice in every newspaper, stating that "Yuanpei, in order to maintain his integrity, cannot have a relationship with educational authorities who advocate interference with the independence of the judiciary and trample on human rights". Cai's resignation was in fact in protest at the arrest of Finance Minister Luo Wengan (19 November 1922) and in protest at the "most important issue" of the day (namely, Cao Kun's blatant bribery of members of parliament in preparation for the presidential election). Regarding this issue, when I recovered from my illness I published an article defending Mr. Cai in *Nuli Zhoubao*, as well as a few articles on the Luo Wengan case and "the problem of bribing members of parliament". [*Hu Shi Wencun*, II, originally volume three, pp.226-249] After April, Ding Wenjiang strongly wished me recovery from my illness. The work at *Nuli Zhoubao* was taken over by him as well as his friends Gao Yihan, Zhang Weici, and Tao Menghe, and I was

> no longer required to write articles. By early October, the bribing of parliament to elect Cao Kun as president was a fait accompli. The publication of *Nuli Zhoubao* immediately ceased.[91]

Hu Shi and the others had no trust in the revolution, and they no doubt simply hoped that society would improve and progress. They seemed convinced that the government in power would not overturn the idea of reconstruction, so they never believed that the administrative and political problems the government faced would be solved after the revolution. On this point, Hu Shi at that time perhaps had a firm basis for his views, since the southern KMT not only lacked political strength but a consensus within the party was also lacking, while people were even less convinced by the political strength of the CPC led by his friend Chen Duxiu. As a result, for anything that warranted the name of social progress only the current government could be relied on. Hu Shi's criticism of the CPC was clear and, although he stated that he was not denigrating the Party's claims, he believed that because the Communist Party could not even meet its most minimal claims, it could never possibly attain any of its loftier propositions.[92] Therefore, the root of Hu's proposal of "good government" lay in his lack of trust in any basic progress being made by revolutionary politics. As he himself wrote in the 18 June issue of *Nuli Weekly*: "We should put aside our usual great expectations of politics for the time being, and only hope to progress an inch at a time. Only then will we be able to measure changes in real political governance". Hu Shi also realized that if the government had problems, then it needed to be supervised or amended, but if the government resisted supervision or amendment, then it simply needed to be changed. However, the violence or revolution required to effect that change would be events that Hu was reluctant to see. In fact, Hu Shi and his followers did not believe that social progress could be brought about by a one-off "fundamental solution", so he preferred to believe in the role of persistence and patience.

[91] Hu Shi, *Ding Wejiang Zhuan*, Haikou: Hainan Chubanshe, 1884, pp. 57–60.

[92] Zhou Enlai published an article titled "Reviewing Hu Shi's 'Efforts'" in *Shaonian* no. 6 (December 1922). He responded to Hu Shi's doctrine of moderation: "We highly despise your minimal claims, and especially reliance on your minimal efforts, which can never achieve anything. As for our doctrine that only by means of political struggle can the revolutionary means be achieved, we cannot be taken in by your non-revolutionary spirit". Quoted from Peng Ming ed., *Zhongguo Xiandai Shi Ziliao Xuanji, 1919–1923*, vol. 1, Zhongguo Renmin Daxue Chubanshe, 1990, p. 276.

The result was that a concrete solution was not supported by any group with power. In other words, he was not only ridiculed by experienced predecessors, but could not find accommodation with and was rebuked by all political forces. As soon as he expressed his views, Hu Shi offended the warlords he thought he could rely on.

Hu Shi should have realized that when he initiated a literary revolution, ideological liberation movement, educational reform, and the introduction of Western philosophy (Hu Shi being of course the main proponent of his teacher Dewey's pragmatism) among his compatriots when he came back to China, he was in fact calling for a comprehensive revolution. If the dream of "good government" was really feasible, then Hu Shi's step-by-step ideological and cultural construction project would have been welcomed. However, the political work that seemed to have concrete programs was never actually carried out. In the first comment on the contemporary situation issued by the CPC on 15 June 1922, it was stated that the only way of solving the real problem was to bring down the warlords and build democratic politics.[93] Thus, the term "good government" had come to be seen as a tool used by the warlords. Only when Wu Peifu and Cao Kun had defeated Zhang Zuolin and his Fengtian Army, and Cao Kun bribed the parliamentarians to secure the Presidency in October, did Hu Shi come to the realization: "We who talk about politics have reached the stage where we have encamped".[FN094][94] By 1926, Ding Wenjiang, the geologist and friend of Hu Shi who had advocated "good government" and maintained his delusional faith in the warlords, accepted at the beginning of May the post of head of the Shanghai Commercial Office conferred on him by Sun Chuanfang. He thus became involved in implementing Sun's "Greater Shanghai" plan, which actually did conform to Ding Wenjiang's concept of politics, namely administrative politics. While the hope of turning Shanghai into a "model city" was difficult to realize, according to Fu Sinian, Ding Wenjiang was provided with the opportunity to implement his idea of reforming politics—and he did not agree to wait for the opportune time to act. According to Hu Shi,

[93] *Zhonggong Dang Shi Jiaoxue Cankao Ziliao: Dang de Chuangli Qi*, Beijing: Zhongguo Renmin Daxue Chubanshe, 1979, p. 325.

[94] Geng Yunzhi ed., *Hu Shi Yucui*, Huaxia Chubanshe, 1993, p. 11. Quoting from "Yinianban de huigu", *Nuli Zhoubao*, p. 75.

Ding Wenjiang was able to achieve a degree of success during his eight-month term in the job.[95] Although many people censured Ding Wenjiang for working for Sun Chuanfang, the KMT was still not strong enough to govern the country, and so by relying on the power of the military to implement its ideals was regarded as opportunity by many intellectuals. The problem was however that relying on warlords was basically ineffectual. As Fu Sinian wrote in "Several Snapshots of Ding Wenjiang" published in *Independent Review* on 23 February 1936, Ding Wenjiang "was one of three men joining in the group of Sun Chuanfang, the other two being Chen Taoyi and Chen Yi. The three of them were testing the waters. However, once they were on the inside, they realized things were not so simple, and whenever Sun wanted to do something, he never consulted them".

Until the end of 1925, Hu Shi was still under the illusion that there was a place for public liberalism. In a letter to Chen Duxiu in response to the burning down of *Morning News* (Chenbao), he expressed confidence in his just liberal stance:

> The other day we were talking about how a mob in Beijing set fire to the offices of *Morning News*, and when I explained my position to you, you asked me, "So you think *Morning News* shouldn't have been burnt down?"
>
> For five or six days, I kept thinking about what you said. We've been friends for ten years, we've done a lot of things together, and we've often had differences of opinion, but nothing like this, so I have to say something to you.
>
> It is not surprising that dozens of rioters set fire to a newspaper. But you are the responsible leader of a political party and I am surprised that you take this matter for granted and think the mob "should" have burned the building down.
>
> Did we not both just publish a declaration calling for "freedom"? Didn't the rioters in Beijing that day declare that "the people have the freedoms of assembly, association, speech, and publishing"? Hasn't *Morning News*

95 Hu Shi in his *Ding Wenjiang Zhuan* introduced in some detail Ding's activities in working for the recovery of jurisdiction over the city's concession areas during his time in this job.

in recent years presented ideas? So, whether or not you and I agree with them, that hardly make them deserving of being burned to the ground by people proclaiming freedom, because the only principle of freedom is this: "Those who disagree with me are not necessarily wrong, nor are those who agree with me necessarily right; what the masses affirm today is not necessarily correct, nor is what they oppose necessarily wrong. There is the only reason why we call for freedom, namely, we expect dissenting opinions and beliefs to be tolerated. Those who do not recognize the freedom of dissidents are not worthy to fight for freedom, and they do not deserve the right to talk about freedom".

I also know that you who advocate dictatorship exercised by a particular class no longer believe in the word freedom. I also know that now I am talking to you today about freedom, you will probably laugh at me. But I want you to know that this is my fundamental belief. We are old friends, so although we have different political opinions and different careers, we still remain old friends, because you and I are both tolerant of dissent. At least I can say that my fundamental belief is to recognize that others have the freedom to experiment. If even this minimal point in common is swept away, not only can we not be friends, but we are even enemies. Don't you agree?

I remember that when in 1919 you were being detained in the police station, the signatures that secured your release include those of the old Tongcheng classicists Ma Tongbo and Yao Shujie. I remember that night when we dined at Taoli Yuan, I felt so happy because it seemed there was a ray of light in this dark society; at that time when there was intense opposition to vernacular literature, there were actually a few old classicists who were willing to risk their reputations to protect you. This society struggles to be 'human'.

But over the last few years, things have been very different. The nation is filled with intolerance. It is not the tolerance of the old forces, because they no longer have the ability to destroy dissidents. The most intolerant are a group of self-proclaimed modern figures. Personally, I have been subjected to a lot of attacks and slander over the years. During these two months while I have been out of Beijing, throughout my travels I have been reading your fellow youths whose remarks vilify me and it has really opened up my eyes. I am not afraid of such vilification, but I am somewhat saddened by it. I am afraid that this culture of intolerance will lead to a more cruel and miserable society, and that those of us who love freedom should be afraid that there will be no place left to stand.[96]

As Hu Shi notes, the background in which he wrote the letter was different from that of a few years previously. While working for "good government", Hu Shi had in *Nuli Zhoubao* in August called for a "federation of autonomous provinces", something that would have made Wu Peifu extremely unhappy. Initially, Hu Shi hoped that Wu Peifu would be able to unify China, stem the atmosphere of anarchy, establish stable political order, bring planning to politics, and promote the progress of all of society. Hu Shi's friend Chen Duxiu saw the idea of a "federation of autonomous provinces" quite differently. In Chen Duxiu's view, the focus of the question was not whether or not we advocate a "federation of autonomous provinces", but whether such a "federation" was simply a pretext for the warlords to dominate, providing a pretext for the legitimation of military control, leading to further social chaos. In his article titled "My View of China's Political Problems" published on 10 August 1922 in no. 15, volume 19 of *Eastern Miscellany*, Chen Duxiu clearly articulated his political views. After presenting what was almost a Marxist analysis of China's economic and political situation, he later put forward his strategic "targets" for solving China's political problems; among his four "targets", the first was "toppling the warlords and their parties that sell out the nation". Obviously other differences followed. Chen Duxiu wrote:

> How we achieve the above-mentioned targets is an important issue. The real targets of democratic politics are, of course, not maintenance of the status quo, and the use of enemy forces to achieve it, nor something small revolutionary forces could not achieve. Because all countries are

[96] From Zheng Xuejia, *Chen Duxiu Zhuan*, Shibao Wenhua Chuban Qiye Youxian Gongsi, 1989, pp. 1282–1284. *Chenbao*, published by the Research Department, played a role in supporting nationalist fervor and in reporting China's diplomatic failure at the Paris Peace Conference; on 2 May the newspaper also published the "diplomatic alert" of Lin Changmin, director of the National Association for Foreign Affairs, issued on behalf of the people. When Chen Duxiu was attacked by the Guogu (National Quintessence) faction, *Chenbao* gave him public support. Chen Duxiu himself quoted a passage from the newspaper's article "Rumors about Peking University", which wrote of the "sacrosanct" nature of freedom of thought and speech, as aspects of a "civilized country". (Ren Jianshu, Zhang Tongmo, Wu Xinzhong eds., op. cit., vol. 1, Shanghai: Shanghai Renmin Chubanshe, 1993, p. 504).

> built on power, feudal states are constructed on the power of warlords, democratic states are constructed on the power of the people, semi-feudal semi-democratic states are constructed on the power of both warlords and the people, and colonial states are constructed on the power of the home country. If there is no power there can be no country and no politics; only power can replace power, and the domination of this natural law is something we cannot avoid. Therefore, we should understand that if the power of the people cannot replace the power of warlords, warlord politics will not be overthrown, and democratic politics will not succeed. The power of the people must be concentrated in various popular organizations in order to manifest itself, and only political parties can directly participate in politics. The corruption of politics is the biggest key to people's solidarity, and political parties are the greatest means for the people to become engaged in politics. Therefore, it is delusional to advocate that people do not engage in politics, and if one advocates political involvement while not advocating the organization of political parties then this is surely the ultimate delusion.[97]

Although Hu Shi had the grace and equanimity to reprint Chen's article in the 3 September issue of *Nuli Zhoubao*, as an intellectual promoting a "federation of autonomous provinces" he was completely unimpressed by his friend's views. Hu Shi followed up on 10 September with an article talking issue with Chen Duxiu in *Nuli Zhoubao* titled "The Federation of Autonomous Provinces and Warlord Occupation". Hu Shi argued that his friend Chen Duxiu was looking at the problem superficially, and that he saw the origins of China's political turmoil in "feudal-style large and small warlords arrayed to one side who hold political, financial and military power, against whom the law and public opinion are ineffective, and business entrepreneurs and education are blocked". Hu thought, however, that Chen failed to see the psychological inertia implicit in "imposed unity", and was "dreaming". This "dream" of "imposed unity" was the key to the problem. After reviewing history, Hu Shi concluded: "The centralized form of political organization is a form imposed on China in which centralized politics is the least suitable, and this is one of the major reasons why China's warlords today fight each other. We can further say that, if we were to have a federal system of autonomous provinces, this would be an important weapon for

[97] Ren Jianshu, Zhang Tongmo, Wu Xinzhong, op. cit., p. 376.

bringing down the warlords of today". In his view, the central government did not have the capacity to sanction local warlords, so "today we cannot expect the central government to sanction warlords; an important weapon for sanctioning warlords and overthrowing warlords is increasing local authority, and a federal system of provincial autonomy". However, how the central government could or was willing to give more power to local authorities was a problematic premise, and in the era of warlord politics, the power of the central government was manipulated by warlords, and the scope of the power of local warlords revolved around transfers of power by the central government; the warlords controlled both central and local power, which meant that Hu Shi's theoretical federalism lacked a political basis. One of the foundations of federalism is that the military is a political tool, not the other way around, but now warlords controlled both central and local fiscal and political power.[98]

[98] As regards the financial aspects of the central government vis-a-vis local governments, statistics would suggest Hu Shi was not very clear. The basic condition for the control of government power is financial power, and in this regard, the financial situation of the central and local authorities in the warlord era can explain the problem. In view of Hu Shi's interest in local power, we can compare the proportion of local warlords' expenditures on war with local finances, and we can see that Hu Shi's expectations of federalism were slim:

Area year		*He Nan(Zhi Xi)*	*Zhe Jiang(Wan Xi)*	*Ji Lin(Feng Xi)*	*Si Chuan(internal war area)*
	military spending	45Million Yuan	25 Million Yuan	3 Million Yuan	6 Million Yuan
1919	Proportion in finance	60%	40%	60%	63%
1925	military spending	17 Million Yuan	10 Million Yuan	9 Million Yuan	26 Million Yuan
	Proportion in finance	85%	70%	60%	86%

In fact, all sources of local income were controlled by warlords. For example, from the 1910s to the 1920s, the likin tax was almost entirely controlled by the warlords. From 1916 to 1928, warlords obtained not less than 96 million yuan in likin tax. For example, in the first half of 1924 alone, Wu Peifu took 6 million yuan from the Ping-Han Railway, which is almost 50% of the railway's annual revenue, which in fact accounted for all revenue in Wu's accounts.

Fashionable political slogans became a tool for warlords seeking influence and political power, and the concept of "federalism" proposed by intellectuals naturally only benefited local warlords in their grab for power. On the other hand, however, the concept of "federalism" was in conflict with the desire of warlords to control central power, and such a term was an impediment to controlling the whole country by force. For any warlord who temporarily held central power, the concept of "unification" had political appeal because it accorded considerable legitimacy. However, Hu Shi cited the historical imperative of "long periods of division being followed by unity and long periods of unity being followed by division" to argue that a period of "division" was again imminent. In fact, Hu Shi's idea of "federalism" was difficult to implement; apart from the fact that local warlords who lacked central authority regarded "federalism" as a concept that could be used to justify controlling local authorities. For three political forces—the central warlords, the KMT, and the CPC, the concept of "federalism" was one that they could not recognize and accept. The purpose of federalism was to divide up political powers, but there was little difference between local tyrannies and the horrors of centrally concentrated power. Discussions of centralism vis-à-vis decentralization were null and void when warlords controlled both central and local political power.

Birth of the CPC and Its Early Political Strategies

New Youth, from its first issue until 15 April 1919 (no. 4 of Volume 5), functioned as the ideological voice of the Enlightenment Movement, and throughout this period, the magazine did not belong to any party or political group. However, after Chen Duxiu moved from Beijing to Shanghai in February 1920 and fully disclosed the magazine's political intentions in the magazine's "manifesto" in *New Youth*, vol. 7, no. 1 published on 1 December 1919, Chen clarified his anti-warlord and anti-imperialist (militarism) attitudes, and suggested that true democracy should confer political power to the people as a whole.[99] On 1 May 1920, *New Youth* (7:6) published its Labor Day commemorative

[99] "In Shanghai, Chen Duxiu met a group of political friends, a group who later became the founders of the Communist Party. Thus, after issue 7, *New Youth*, which had once promoted the principles of the 'literary renaissance' and the 'literary revolution',

Issue, which not only included Li Dazhao's "History of the May Day Movement" and "The Declaration of the Russian Soviet Federal Socialist Republic to the Chinese People and the Governments of North and South China", but also two articles on labor issues—Chen Duxiu's "The Consciousness of the Workers" and "The Question of Hunanese Female Workers in Shanghai's Cotton Mills". Chen Duxiu was editing the Labor Day commemorative Issue when a delegation led by Grigori Voitinsky, a member of the Russian Communist Party, entered China to study the Chinese revolution and help establish Communist organizations. In April, Voitinsky held talks with Li Dazhao in Beijing, at the end of April, he went to Shanghai and had discussions with Chen Duxiu, providing him with preliminary help forming the CPC. In May, the Marxist Research Society, the original organization of the CPC, was established in Shanghai, and in June, the Shanghai Communist Party, its prototype, with the editorial department of *New Youth* as its center of activities, was established. At the end of August, the Shanghai Socialist Youth League was established, and on 1 September Chen Duxiu published a "Russian studies" issue of *New Youth* (8:1), echoing Chinese interest in the Russian Revolution. Of course, this issue of *New Youth* also related to the impact and assistance of Voitinsky's work following his arrival in Shanghai. In this issue of *New Youth*, Chen Duxiu published "A Discussion of Politics" that resembled the manifesto of a political party. Chen Duxiu argued that the desire of Hu Shi and others to escape politics was completely impossible, and he even made clear that his own position was as a Communist. At the end of the article, Chen Duxiu fully revealed the spirit of the *Communist Manifesto*:

> I recognize that the use of revolutionary means to construct a nation of the working-class (i.e., the productive class) and the creation of politics and laws that will prohibit all internal and external plunder as the primary needs of modern society.[100]

Since the publication's political leanings were already evident and Chen Duxiu was fully engaged in forming a political party, there were clear differences of opinion between the Beijing and Shanghai elites, both from

gradually became the organ of the Communist Party of China." Ref: Tang Degang, op. cit., p. 186.

100 Ren Jianshu et al., op. cit., vol. 2, p. 164.

the perspective of the editorial policy of the publication and from the words and deeds of these individuals. In a letter to Hu Shi and Gao Yihan, Chen Duxiu not only defended his own views but expressed the hope they would cooperate with him. Hu Shi replied to Chen Duxiu: "If *New Youth* wishes to 'change its content', it will not be possible to restore our agreement to 'not discuss politics'".[101] Hu Shi even felt that "*New Youth* had almost become a Chinese translation of the publication, *Soviet Russia*".[102]

Although Chen Duxiu acquired some of his Marxist views through various Japanese publications or those translated from Japanese, even after *New Youth* published "What is the New Culture Movement?" in its 7:5 issue on 1 April 1920, there was still no sign of any great interest in Marxism, and in this speech Chen seemed to continue emphasizing the importance of art, music, and religion. Yet as far as Chen Duxiu's situation was concerned, it was impossible for him to return to Beijing and engage in a simple cultural revolution, and from different perspectives both the warlord government and his colleagues at Peking University restricted his words and actions. He needed to seek out new political opportunities. Simply editing *New Youth* could not completely satisfy Chen Duxiu's political ambitions, and the arrival of Voitinsky became the direct trigger for Chen Duxiu and his Shanghai counterparts setting up

[101] Ibid., p. 224.

[102] It is worth mentioning that Mao Zedong and Yun Daiying, two early CPC members were readers of *New Youth*. Mao Zedong in his early years wrote in *Xiangjiang Review* of Chen Duxiu: "Breaking through the net of all phenomena, he has developed an ideal world through his deeds and writings, to create a truth which is second to none. Previously there was Tan Sitong, and now there is Chen Duxiu. These men are bold and powerful and are quite unlike the usual scholars we find today". (From Zheng Xuejia, *Chen Duxiu Zhuan*, p. 147; the original book is quoted in "The Thoughts of Young Mao Zedong" in *Lishi Yanjiu*, 1979:3). Yun Daiying wrote in a letter to the editorial board of *New Youth* about the influence on him of Chen Duxiu and *New Youth*: "Our lives have always been subject to ignorance, but since reading *New Youth* I have gradually awakened, and it is like emerging from a dark place to see the dawn. ...... Since we gained this awareness, we see many of our friends still living in that dark hell, and I feel endless pity for them. So, we must not be confined by petty stupidity but must desire to fulfill the endeavor of aware people and be a 'new voice.'" (From Zheng Xuejia, op. cit., p. 148).

the CPC.[103] Subsequently, Beijing and Shanghai soon set up separate party branches.[104]

On 15 January 1921, Chen Duxiu had this to say in the closing remarks of a lecture he delivered at the Guangzhou Public School of Law and Politics titled "An Assessment of Socialism":

> I think that China's transformation and existence depend, for the most part, on the international socialist movement for help, and this cannot be concealed. As everyone knows, the domestic bourgeoisie is still naive and all know that foreign capitalism is oppressive, so the concept of class war is indeed something the Chinese should develop. When we open our eyes, we see how our capitalist politicians are too corrupt and incompetent to maintain the credit of representative system, and that democratic politics and parliamentary policies are more bankrupt in China than in Europe and America. And if China were to adopt the national socialism of Germany's

[103] It should be noted that although Li Dazhao introduced the theory of Marxism earlier, he did not quite agree with the actual Marxist party when he founded it. As he saw it, he and Chen Duxiu still lacked research on Marxism, and an understanding of the Russian Revolution was not enough; therefore, they needed to first devote themselves to the study of Marxism. To a certain extent, Li Dazhao's study of Marxist socialist theory has the elements of academic research, so he was very tolerant of anarchism and guild socialism. As for Chen Duxiu, his actual situation did not allow him to carry out academic research with ease. (See Zhang Guotao, *Wode Huiyi*, vol. 1, Dongfang Chubanshe, 1994, see vol. 1, Chapter 10 and vol. 2, Chapter 1).

[104] On 5–7 July 1920, W. Vilensky, the man who drafted the Karakhan Manifesto to China, convened a meeting in Beijing of Russian Bolsheviks in China, attended by G. N. Voitinsky, to discuss the topic of "the upcoming meeting of communist organizations in China and the establishment of a Communist Party of China", to clarify the directive for the founding a Communist Party of China, and promote the pace of founding a Communist Party of China. In the early days after Voitinsky's arrival in Shanghai, the original participants in creating this organization were Dai Jitao (the editor of *Xingqi Pinglun*), Shen Xuanlu [i.e., Shan Dingyi, 1883–1928], Li Hanjun, Shao Lizi (the editor-in-chief of *Minguo Ribao*), Zhang Dongsun [1886–1973] (who founded *Jiefang yu Gaizao* in Beijing in 1919), and Chen Wangdao (editor of *New Youth*). Dai Jitao, a member of the Chinese Nationalist Party of Sun Yat-sen, quickly withdrew from the formation of the Communist Party of China despite his participation in the writing of the Communist Party's platform, and Zhang Dongsun withdrew because he did not regard the formation of the Communist Party as an official political party organization; at the time, he was also an important member of the Research Department but wished to participate in some new academic organization. When he found that the Communist Party would be a radical political party, he quit.

Social Democratic Party, this would give corrupt bureaucrats a chance to do evil.[105]

On 23 July 1921, twelve members representing 53 Party members gathered at 106 Rue Wantz (Wangzhi Road) in Shanghai, at the home of Li Hanjun's older brother in Shanghai's French Concession and founded the Communist Party of China (CPC). Zhang Guotao, sent by Li Dazhao to represent the branch in Beijing, and Zhou Fohai, appointed to represent Chen Duxiu in Guangzhou, were the two delegates attending the meeting on behalf of Li and Chen who were unable to attend because of their work commitments. Nevertheless, Li and Chen were identified as founders of the Party, and ChenDuxiu was elected its General Secretary. Other delegates at the meeting were: Li Da and Li Hanjun from Shanghai; Dong Biwu (1886–1975) and Chen Tanqiu (1896–1943) from Wuhan; Mao Zedong (1893–1976) and He Shuheng (1876–1935) from Changsha; Wang Jinmei (1898–1925) and Deng Enming (1901–1931) from Jinan; Liu Renjing (1902–1987) from Beijing; and Chen Gongbo from Guangzhou. H. Maring (1883–1942, i.e., Henk Sneevliet) attended the meeting as the representative of the Communist International (Comintern) and Nikolskii (Vladimir Abramovich Neiman, 1889–1938) attended as the representative of the Red International of Trade Unions. On the 30th, the Concession police searched the venue of the meetings, so the meetings were moved to continue on a boat moored on Nanhu (South Lake) in Jiaxing, at which the Party's first platform and resolutions were issued. The main contents of the Party platform, recorded in Russian, were as follows:

1. The revolutionary army must, together with the proletariat, overthrow the capitalist class's regime and assist the working class until distinctions of social class are eliminated.
2. Until the end of the class struggle, that is, until the class divisions of society are eliminated, we recognize the dictatorship of the proletariat.
3. We will eliminate the capitalist system of private ownership and confiscate the means of production such as machinery, land, plant, and semi-finished products.

[105] Ren Jianshu et al., op. cit., p. 256.

4. We will unite with the Third International.

The newly formed Communist Party "recognized the Soviet system of management by organizing workers, peasants, and soldiers and using the social revolution as the main instrument of its policies". But in their organizational focus of power there were differences between Li Dazhao and Chen Duxiu: the former based his focus on the peasantry which made up the vast majority of the Chinese population and thus stressed the importance of the peasants, while the latter regarded the peasants as ideologically backward and so doubted their role in the revolutionary movement; the former followed the example of the Russian Narodnik movement which emphasized going to the countryside to mobilize farmers, and influenced Mao Zedong who worked as an assistant of Li Dazhao in the library of Peking University, while the latter emphasized the power of the urban working class, an emphasis which was thought to have led to the later failure of the early Chinese revolution led by the CPC.

The emergence of the Third International, the Communist International (Comintern) in March 1919, was largely motivated by the aim of consolidating the Russian Soviet regime and realizing the world revolution by calling for violent political revolution in Europe and the East.[106] In 1920, the Second World Congress of the Third International (better known as the Comintern) adopted *The Outline of Ethnic and Colonial Issues*, designating China a country in need of a "Communist makeover", in order to promote the international communist movement. G. N. Voitinsky, who had spent less than a year in China in 1920, had no specific objectives but interviewed such politically disparate figures as Chen Duxiu, Wu Peifu, and Sun Yat-sen, and surveyed the distribution

[106] On 24 January 1919, in response to the call issued by Lenin at an international conference in Moscow, the Comintern was set up for the following reason: "As the world revolution has advanced rapidly, raising new questions, as capitalist countries have banded together against the revolution under the hypocritical banner of the League of Nations, the revolution is in danger of being stifled. As the parties that betray socialism gather together to 'commiserate' and help their governments and bourgeoisie to deceive the working class again, and because of the accumulation of rich revolutionary experience and the internationalization of the entire revolutionary process, we must come forward with an initiative to place the issue of an international congress of the proletarian revolutionary political parties on the agenda". Ref: *Gongchan Guoji Youguan Zhongguo Geming de Wenxian Ziliao* (Documents of the Comintern on the Chinese Revolution), Series 1, Beijing: Zhongguo Shehui Kexue Chubanshe, 1981, p. 4.

and relevant promise of China's scattered revolutionary forces. His boss, the Soviet government's Far Eastern expert Vladimir Vilensky also gave Wu Peifu the epithet "bourgeois democrat" in *Isvestia* on 9 October 1920. Then, in the second issue of *New Orient*, published in 1922, Vilensky described Wu as "the best warlord" in China. He maintained, however, that the optimal political alliance for China was KMT–CPC cooperation. However, the strength of the CPC at this time could hardly compare with that of Sun Yat-sen's Kuomintang, a reality that made Maring, who arrived in China in June 1921 to guide the implementation of the Communist revolution, initially lack confidence in the CPC.

In August 1921, Zhang Tailei, who was sent to Russia by the Communist Youth League of China, brought back to China the strategy that won "the support of the majority of the masses" at the Third Congress of the Comintern, which led Maring to believe that conditions now made it possible to use the Kuomintang to oppose the imperialist powers and eliminate the warlords, so he quickly proposed a policy of KMT–CPC cooperation, which became in fact the first major political project of the CPC after its establishment.

The Third Congress of the Comintern, held in Moscow from 22 June to 12 July 1921, was a strategic study of the Leninist world revolution, tasked with examining why, after the Russian October Revolution, the revolutions in European countries, like Hungary, Italy, and Germany, had failed, and how to find a new revolutionary strategy. In his *Outline of Strategy*, Lenin stated: "The current priority of the Comintern is to fight for the majority of the working class under the influence of the Comintern, and to attract the most active part of the working class to participate in the direct struggle".[107] However, the representative from France, reminded participants of the complexity of social elements engaged in the confrontation between colonies and semi-colonies, on the one hand, and foreign imperialism and the feudal classes, on the other, with workers, small-scale self-employed craftsmen and tradesmen, farmers, and the bourgeoisie all participating. Making full use of all these forces is essential for realizing the revolution. As for the bourgeoisie, their democracy is completely different from communism, "but it should be recognized and affirmed that the struggle against imperialism should be a common struggle under the present circumstances". However, he

[107] Bela Kun ed., *Gongchan Guoji Wenjian Huibian*, vol. 1, Beijing: Sanlian Chubanshe, 1965, p. 261.

pointed out that the Communists should assume leadership over liberation movements by breaking with the nationalist classes, by exposing nationalists, and even by side-stepping and opposing bourgeois nationalist leaders if necessary.[108] Obviously, the Comintern was very clear: uniting with any class other than the proletariat could only be temporary and strategic, and the professional revolutionaries of the Comintern had no intention from the outset of entering into long-term cooperation in particular with the bourgeoisie. As early as June 1920, in *Draft Theses on National and Colonial Questions* for the Second Congress of the Comintern, Lenin presented the world conflict in clear and simple terms: "The world political situation has now placed the dictatorship of the proletariat as the order of the day. World political developments are of necessity concentrated on a single focus—the struggle of the world bourgeoisie against the Soviet Russian Republic".[109] At the Congress of Revolutionary Parties and Communist Parties of the Far East held in January 1922, Grigorii Zinoviev (1883–1926) in his opening speech as President of the Comintern called on participants: "The Communist parties of all countries and the workers of the whole world, especially the Far East, are uniting under the banner of the Comintern in order to finally defeat world capitalism".[110]Zhang Tailei, the representative of China to the Third Congress of the Comintern, was very sensitive to the political premise of the Comintern, and although his speech was only five minutes long, he made his views clear: "Once the bourgeoisie and the despotic rulers clash, for as long as it is necessary the bourgeoisie must be eliminated from the national revolutionary movement". He even said that although "the proletariat should help the bourgeoisie overthrow despotic rulers", they must seize power "before the bourgeois governments consolidate", and so the bourgeoisie must be subjected to the same fate as the despotic rulers they overthrew.

[108] Quoted from: Yang Yunruo and Yang Kuisong, *Gongchan Guoji yu Zhongguo Geming* (The Communist International and the Chinese Revolution), Shanghai: Shanghai Renmin Chubanshe, 1988, p. 36. Quoted from: *Notes and Records on the Third Communist International Meeting*, St. Petersburg, 1922, p. 479.

[109] *Liening Sidalin Lun Zhongguo*, Jiefangshe, 1950, p. 74.

[110] Yang Yunruo and Yang Kuisong, op. cit., p. 46. The First Congress of the Toilers of the Far East, held in Moscow, January 21–February 1 1922, Closing Session in Petrograd, February 2nd 1922, London: Hammersmith Bookshop Ltd., 1970.

Maring was undoubtedly aware of the political strategy of the Comintern, especially that of Lenin, and he understood that the aim of uniting with the KMT was only envisaged as an interim phase, because the purpose of the Comintern was not simply to help all ethnic groups achieve national independence, which was only a means or even a temporary strategy to contain hostile forces and protect the Soviet Union. The most fundamental goal was to eliminate the bourgeoisie from all over the world and realize the dictatorship of the proletariat, the result being to consolidate and expand the sphere of influence of the Soviet Union. It was for this purpose that Maring did not denigrate the existence of the CPC with its small numbers, because he and his comrades hoped they could effectively advance the democratic revolution quickly and facilitate the development of the CPC, so that it could eventually be the legitimate agent for the Comintern controlling state power in China.

As leader of the CPC, Chen Duxiu did not initially abandon the Party's principle of independence because the number of Party members was so few and he needed the support of the Soviet Union, but he was opposed to Maring's views outright. "In our contacts with Maring, we always feel he holds himself in the highest regard because of his position as the representative of the Comintern", Bao Huiseng recalled, "Moreover, at every meeting Zhang Guotao loved to be the chairman, and when we were arguing about some issue, Zhang Guotao would say for the record, let's wait for Maring to settle the matter, which made everyone very unhappy.[111] Chen Duxiu and Maring repeatedly discussed things three or four times, without coming to an agreement. Chen Duxiu as a result told everyone, we cannot rely on Maring, so we should rely on us Chinese to organize our own party and the Chinese revolution must be conducted by us, so we must do our own work at the same time as we conduct the revolution".[112] In any case, Maring's attitude shows that the Comintern saw the CPC Central Committee as a tool for exporting

[111] Bao Huiseng (1894–1979) was a native of Hubei native who chaired the first National Congress of the CPC. After August 1927, he broke away from the CPC. In December 1950, he was appointed as a researcher and counselor of the Ministry of Internal Affairs of the People's Republic of China. He wrote many historical materials recalling the early history of workers' movements and the CPC. In 1983, his memoirs were published.

[112] Zheng Xuejia, op. cit., p. 435. Chen Duxiu's view was based on two things: Maring sent Chen Bulei (1890–1948) to Japan to contact Japanese socialists without informing the Central Committee of the CPC. The work was in fact arranged by the Communist

revolution, and that the important thing was not to respect the CPC's organizational procedures but to carry out the orders of the Comintern. Linked to this was Maring's financial support for the Communist Party as the representative of the Comintern. Despite the arguments between Chen and Maring over funding, the harsh realities led Chen to quickly acquiesce in Maring's opinions.[113]Data show that the initial funding of the CPC basically came from the Comintern. Zhang Guotao recalls that after Maring helped Chen Duxiu get released from prison, Chen Duxiu began to report Maring's views to the CPC Central Committee after his meeting with Maring, and he "concretely specified how to use the grants from the Comintern; since then, accepting the economic support of the Comintern became common for the CPC".[114]

Before the second CPC Party Congress, Chen Duxiu published an article entitled "The First Proposition of the Current Situation" in the name of the CPC Central Committee. In this article, Chen Duxiu pointed out: "The CPC is the vanguard of the proletariat, but before the proletariat is able to gain power, in accordance with the current situation of China's political economy and the process of historical evolution, the proletariat in its current most important work should also unite with the democratic forces in the revolution against the feudal-style warlords, in order to bring about the collapse of the warlords so that democratic politics can be established". How to go about this was explained in this article: "The CPC's approach is to hold a joint conference with the KMT's revolutionary democrats and various revolutionary socialist

International, which Chen considered a show of contempt for the CPC, and he feared that if this continued the CPC might lose hands-on power.

[113] Zhou Fuhai recalled: "It was mid-September when Chen Duxiu returned to Shanghai, but Chen Duxiu and Maring were in disagreement. Chen refused to meet with Maring, because Maring had publicly said: 'Over the past year, the Third International has spent more than 200,000 in China, but the only result is a lack of effort by our Chinese comrades'. Chen Duxiu replied: 'How could we have spent so much, half of it goes on the good Western housing and food of the Third International's representative, so how can you falsely blame others?' In fact, how much was spent was confused. In the less than two months I spent as acting chairman, 12,000 yuan was spent, and the funds Zhang Guotao spent organizing the labor portfolio secretariat was paid directly to him and did not pass through my hands". Ref: Zheng Xuejia, op. cit., p. 439.

[114] Zhang Guotao, op. cit., p. 167. In a footnote on p. 169 explaining this, he wrote: "Prior to this, some money may have been receiving, like for setting up a foreign language school, to which Voitinsky would probably have made some contribution, but it would not have been a regular expenditure".

groups, and on the basis of the above principles jointly establish a democratic united front, to continue the war against feudal warlords".[115] On 10 July 1922, the Second Congress of the CPC was held. Among its resolutions was "Resolution on a National United Front" which also made the collective stance of the CPC very clear: "We are temporarily joining forces with the KMT to overthrow the enemy oppressors—the feudal warlords at home and foreign international imperialism. On the other hand, the proletariat's union with and assistance to the KMT is not a renunciation of its own party, because the KMT does not represent the proletariat, nor does it fight for the proletariat. Instead, it will unite with the proletariat, under the banner of the CPC, to fight independently for its own class interests".[116] Maring, who just returned from negotiations with Sun Yat-sen in Guangzhou, was critical of this position, pointing out that the Comintern's view was that members of the CPC should join the KMT rather than talk with the KMT on an equal footing. This idea, which allowed CPC members to dissolve into the KMT, might be seen as a political ploy, but it was actually the result of Maring having more confidence in the KMT in Guangzhou than he had hope for the Communist Party".[117]

When Maring first proposed that CPC members join the KMT in a personal capacity, Chen Duxiu flatly refused. In a letter (6 April 1922), he asked Voitinsky to convey to the Comintern the reasons for his refusal:

1. The revolutionary principles and foundations of the CPC and the KMT are utterly different.
2. The KMT's policies of alliances with the United States, Zhang Zuolin. and Duan Qirui are totally incompatible with communism.
3. The KMT has not published a party platform, and the people of provinces other than Guangdong regard the KMT as a party out for power and profit and, if the CPC joins the KMT, it will never have

[115] Zheng Xuejia, op. cit., pp. 459–460.

[116] Zheng Xuejia, op. cit., pp. 463–464.

[117] After arriving in Guangzhou from Guilin, Maring was impressed by the KMT's work, and in his report to the Comintern Executive Committee, he explained that the KMT were strong, because their armed forces had 12,000 sailors. Recalling his trip to Guangzhou, he later said: "I had a very good impression of the status and possibility of the Kuomintang: the seafarers' strike, the support for the strike, had a great impact on my views at the time". Ref: Yang Yunru and Yang Kuisong, op. cit., pp. 41–42.

the opportunity to develop and will lose all trust society has in it (especially among the youth).
4. Chen Jiongming, the powerful force in Guangdong, styles himself as a member of the KMT, but he is in fact opposed to Sun Yixian [i.e., Sun Yat-sen], so if we join the KMT, we will immediately arouse the hostility of Chen's faction, which means that we will not be able to operate in Guangdong.
5. The attitude to new party members of Sun Yat-sen's faction of the KMT has always been absolutely intolerant of their views and opposed to giving them power.
6. Comrades from districts of Guangdong, Beijing, Shanghai, Changsha, and Wuchang have in fact held meetings to express their absolute disapproval of the move to join the KMT, so in fact there is no possibility of joining.[118]

Soon after Maring returned to Moscow, in July he handed in a report to the Comintern Executive Committee in which he asserted: "As long as the CPC is unwilling to join forces with the KMT, the prospects for this small group carrying out propaganda will be bleak". Maring's proposal was formally approved by the Comintern, but Voitinsky subsequently presented Maring with an official document to the CPC on behalf of the Comintern's Far East Bureau and requested it to be implemented. The letter reflected an attitude that was not open to negotiations:

> The Executive Committee of the Comintern on 18 July decided that the Central Committee of the CPC must immediately move its address to Guangzhou upon receiving notification, and all work must be carried out in close contact with Comrade Philip.[119]

In fact, in the content of the manifesto issued by the Second Congress of the CPC, the political strategy which led to the subsequent accession of the Communists to the KMT served as a dangerous reminder to some leaders within the KMT, because the manifesto stated: "We the proletariat serve the interests of our own class and when the democratic revolution succeeds, the proletariat will only gain some of their freedoms and rights but cannot be completely liberated. With the success of democracy, the

[118] Yang Yunruo and Yang Kuisong, op. cit., pp. 43–44.
[119] Yang Yunruo and Yang Kuisong, op. cit., p. 55.

rudimentary bourgeoisie will develop rapidly and soon be in confrontation with the proletariat. Therefore, the proletariat will then have to deal with the bourgeoisie and carry out the second struggle which is 'the dictatorship of the proletariat united with the poor peasantry'".[120] In order to correct the views of Chen Duxiu and his followers as quickly as possible, Maring convened a special meeting at the West Lake in Hangzhou, from August 29 to 30 to study the question of CPC members joining the KMT as individuals. It was decided at the meeting that "CPC members could join the KMT in a personal capacity while simultaneously preserving the CPC, the latter directing its members' work within the KMT and leading the organization of the trade unions".[121] The CPC, led by Chen Duxiu, was founded with the help of the Comintern, and in its ideology and funding, Soviet Russia gave it decisive support. This wholly financial political input determined that the CPC had no possibility of making its own decisions freely. Chen Duxiu undoubtedly needed the support of the Soviet Union, and he knew that by relying on Soviet Russia the CPC could maintain independence from the KMT and other political parties and promote its own political operations. However, relying on the power of someone else and having ownership of power are two different things; reliance simply meant that the CPC was only the agent of the Soviet Russian world revolution in China, that the political and revolutionary strategy for the formulation of power was ultimately not in the hands of the CPC, that Chen Duxiu was merely executing Soviet Russian revolutionary instructions, and that the CPC was merely an implement executing Soviet Russian orders.

In fact, the implementation of the political strategy of the CPC's accession to the KMT was far more complicated than the leaders of the Comintern and the CPC thought, and no one had really calculated how to deal with the distribution of power and achieve respective goals in coalition with a political party of a different political nature. In order to achieve KMT–CPC cooperation, Maring criticized Chen Duxiu and sneered at Zhang Guotao's views. He did not believe in the political

[120] Wang Xueqin, *Chen Duxiu yu Zhongguo Gongchandang*, Dongnan Daxue Chubanshe, 1991, pp. 42–43.

[121] Maring: Notes on KMT Communist Cooperation (late November to early December 1922), Maring and the First KMT Communist Cooperation, page 91. This book is quoted from Yang Kuisong: "The Kuomintang's" Alliance with the Communist Party "and" "Anti Communist Party", Social Science Literature Press, 2008 edition, p. 7.

power of the CPC, yet demanded the CPC obey the KMT, while Chen Duxiu and Zhang Guotao were extremely sensitive regarding their loss of political power. The KMT also disagreed among themselves because of the instability of their own internal power structure and distribution of power. In November 1923, eleven KMT members including Deng Zeru of the Guangdong Provincial Party wrote to Sun Yat-sen warning him that Chen Duxiu, as the CPC's leading figure, might gradually replace KMT members to become leader of the KMT.

The Comintern's strategy of using the strength of the KMT to develop the CPC was clear,[122] and the members of the CPC in the KMT were fully committed to expanding their power. When the conflict between the two sides became apparent, in the arguments of the KMT official Zhang Ji and others, Mikhail Markovich Borodin insisted that the premise of Soviet Russian assistance to the KMT was to maintain the KMT. However, the reality was that the main leaders of the CPC like Chen Duxiu were clearly aware of the necessity of breaking with the KMT. The decision of the second plenary session of the KMT Central Committee in August to temporarily ease the conflict between the CPC and the KMT was largely due to Sun Yat-sen's death and the KMT leftists' efforts.

[122] In the report of Niloff, a Soviet Russian military adviser, this statement appears: "The Communist Party now realizes that its work in the KMT and the army was entirely mistaken and not strategic. When the Communists began doing this work, they thought they would simply make use of the Kuomintang, under whose wing they would increase their strength and the power of their own party. They did not realize that when engaging in the construction of the KMT, while watching out for the left wing of that party, they could openly seize the KMT's highest administrative organs, and the military's political organs, including the workers and peasants' movement. These actions resulted in widespread dissatisfaction within the KMT, and the two extremes in the party would split into the right wing and the Communists. They now convened a meeting of peasant groups and established an organizational committee, and to win a consensus they wanted to include a number of Kuomintang members, but this proved impossible, because among the farmers, there were no Kuomintang members. This was not simply among the extreme right KMT, but among the left, and the phenomenon was not confined to the peasants, but it was the same situation in the Central Committee of the Kuomintang. When the Communist Party of China grabs power, this is the practice. Chinese officials and generals hold high office and invariably take over all offices and install their friends (as Li Zhilong has done in the fleet). The former case is particularly true in the military. Political staff in the army occupy all important positions which are filled with the party, all over the party, who secretly take over while the officers do not realize it ..." Ref: Zheng Xuejia, op. cit., p. 615. Originally published in Guo Hualun, *Zhonggong Shi Lun* (History of the Communist Party of China), vol. 1, pp. 174–175.

KMT–CPC cooperation clearly encompassed the nationalistic anti-imperialist movement. Although the Nine-power Treaty signed on 6 February 1922 by all those attending the Washington Naval Conference addressed the feelings of the Chinese on paper, in fact the powers did not fully take into account the effective control of customs, salt industry, and post offices by foreigners, the continued control of the South Manchurian Railway by the Japanese, and the near ubiquitous problem of the treatment of labor and the foreign concessions in Chinese cities, so that the contradiction between the urban workers' movement and foreign business owners regarding the repossession of the concessions became regular political topics. However, in January 1925, the Fourth National Congress of the CPC decided to promote the peasants and workers movement. The "May Thirtieth Movement", which erupted on 30 May 1925, was one of the Communist Party's first efforts to influence the workers' movement and was considered to be a "high point of the Revolution". Henceforth, this radical workers' movement did not end until 1927, when the KMT purged the party. On 15 May Gu Zhenghong, a worker who joined the CPC in February, clashed with Japanese factory owners over wages and their treatment of labor. Gu was shot and killed, while several other workers were wounded, triggering a strike by more than 7,000 workers at several cotton mills the next day. Despite the declaration of martial law in the Shanghai Concession Area, on the following day and the 19th, the CPC issued two circulars calling for a major campaign showing solidarity with the Shanghai workers and opposing the Japanese. On the 24th, more than ten thousand Shanghai workers and representatives from all walks of life held a memorial service paying tribute to Gu Zhenghong, and they resolved to "bring together the workers' economic struggle and the burgeoning anti-imperialist struggle".[123] On the 30th, a demonstration and public lectures were organized with the participation of workers and students. Amid slogans calling for the overthrow of imperialism and reclaiming the foreign concessions, Cai Hesen (1895–1931), one of the leaders of the CPC, addressed the crowd, demanding the release of the arrested students. When the British military police who had arrested the students fired on the crowd, killing four students and more than a dozen people, as well as arresting more than a hundred people, then later shooting three more people and wounding more than a dozen

[123] Jin Chongji, op. cit., p. 229.

others, what came to be called the "May Thirtieth massacre", shifted the Chinese focus from opposition to Japan to anti-British imperialism. The leaders of the CPC, Qu Qiubai, Cai Hesen, LiLisan (1899–1967), LiuShaoqi (1898–1969), and Liu Hua, immediately formed an Action Committee, and on 1 June, the Shanghai General Trade Union was set up and headed by Li Lisan, and then the Shanghai Federation of Industry and Commerce was organized to expand the anti-imperialist united front led by the CPC, and to organize strikes by Shanghai residents, as well as workers' strikes and strikes by students and teachers, all protesting the imperialist slaughter. On the same day, the Central Executive Committee of the KMT issued a telegram in support of the strike by workers and students and called for an "economic break with Britain and Japan". The CPC Central Committee on 5 June issued "Letter of the CPC to the People of China Calling for Opposition to Imperialism's Cruel and Brutal Massacres" which made clear the party's political objective: "It has been decided that the abolition of all unequal treaties and the overthrow of all imperialist privileges in China are our main aims". The movement spread to 25 provinces, dozens of cities, and hundreds of counties across the country, with 17 million people participating in rallies, demonstrations, and strikes, triggering a nationwide wave of anti-imperialism. On 11 June the "Hankow incident", on 13 June the "Jiujiang massacre", and on 23 June the "Shaji (Shaki)-Shameen massacre" in Guangzhou saw British troops shoot and kill a total of 52 demonstrating Chinese. The Beijing government sent special envoys Cai Tinggan (1861–1935), Zheng Qian (1876–1929), and Zeng Zongjian (1882–1958) to Shanghai to investigate, and the "Shanghai Commission of Inquiry" composed of six nations (Britain, the United States, Japan, France, Italy, and Belgium) conducted a routine investigation. Finally, the Chinese side and the British and Japanese representatives in Shanghai discussed a "13-point" Resolution. The Resolution determined that the British inspector-general McCowan and his lieutenant in the Shanghai foreign concessions Iverson were removed from office and the Municipal Council paid an indemnity to the deceased and the wounded, and only when British and Japanese capitalists promised to compensate workers, subsidize their loss from strikes, increase wages, improve workers' lives, and recognize some of the trade union rights promulgated by the Chinese government did factories begin to resume work in mid-August. Even though a warrant for the arrest of Li Lisan was issued, the "May Thirtieth Movement" provided opportunities for the CPC to develop. At the CPC's third congress in June 1923, the Party had only 420 members, but following its accession to the KMT and leadership of the "May Thirtieth Movement", the CPC membership grew from 994 people at the beginning of the year to 10,000 people at the end of the year, while Yunnan, Guangxi, Anhui, and Fujian came to have their own Communist Party organizations.

In summer 1926, accompanying the Northern Expedition of Chiang Kai-shek's National Revolutionary Army and divisions within the KMT, CPC members working in the Wuhan government took advantage of the power of the KMT Left and adopted a number of radical measures, firmly taking control of the student and worker organizations. Without a doubt, the advance of the Northern Expedition seemed to provide conditions for peasant and workers' movements in Hunan and Hubei. In Wuhan, as soon as the call for a strike, directed by the provincial general trade union led by the CPC, was issued, a wave of increasingly bigger strikes targeting the businesses of British, Japanese, and even Chinese and calling for higher wages and improved living conditions was rolled out. There were sporadic street marches calling for the overthrow of capitalism and imperialism and pledging support for the world revolution. The tumultuous scenes on the streets attracted the participation of Hunan's youths and peasants with the encouragement of the Communist Party. The city was soon subject to "shop closures, factory shutdowns, and a market depression".[124] In turn, workers' pickets made "arbitrary arrests, organized courts and jails, inspected ships and trains, and cut off traffic at will", even enforcing sanctions against factory and shop owners, and confiscating their factories and shops. By January 1927, the radical revolution had spread to Hankou and Jiujiang and a movement to regain control of the foreign concession areas got underway. When the British relinquished their control of these concessions, this further fueled the popular radical movement, and the situation was similar in rural areas. The peasant movement in Hunan and Hubei was mainly led by the CPC, but the Left KMT was also inspired by the Comintern. When the seventh plenary conference of the Comintern Executive Committee greatly stimulated the CPC's activism in the peasant movement, the Left KMT also lent support to the overthrow of the rural gentry. After February 1927, inspired by the spirit of the Comintern's conference, Mao Zedong filled with romantic fervor predicted: "In the near future, tens of thousands of

[124] Ref: Yang Kuisong, *Guomindang de Liangong yu Fangong*, Beijing: Zhongguo Shehui Kexue Chubanshe, 2008, pp. 186–197.

peasants will rise up in the provinces of central and southern China, and like a violent storm, unlike anything ever seen, no power, however great, will be able to suppress them. They will rush through all the nets that bind them on the road to liberation". Qu Qiubai upheld the conclusion of Mao Zedong's *Report of an Investigation of the Peasant Movement in Hunan*: "China's peasants are on the move and Hunan is just the beginning". Deng Yanda (1895–1931) and Sun Ke (1891–1973) at this time fully supported the views of the CPC and promoted the peasant movement in Hunan and Hubei. However, the worker and peasant movement in Hunan and Hubei soon found itself in the midst of political anarchy and urban chaos, as the economic and financial situation deteriorated, and in May, the CPC held its fifth congress, further accepting the directive of the Comintern, boldly expressed in *Resolution on the Land Question*: "Confiscate all so-called public lands and the lands of shrines, schools, temples, foreign churches and agricultural companies".[125]

In summary, the sixth plenary conference of the Comintern Executive Committee, which concluded in March 1926, made Chen Duxiu's leadership of the CPC meaningless because it demanded that the CPC continue to establish a four-class alliance of workers, peasants, intellectuals, and urban petty bourgeoisie within the KMT. After the *Zhongshan* Incident, Chen Duxiu's efforts to unite with those "outside the party" were finally criticized by Moscow, which made Chen fully aware of the emptiness of his position. *Resolution on the Situation in China*, adopted by the seventh expanded plenary session of the Comintern Executive Committee held from 22 November to 16 December, once again emphasized that the CPC was unable to enact the strategy of separating from the KMT and conducting revolution "beyond the scope of bourgeois civil rights", even by confiscating foreign enterprises in China and nationalizing railways, transportation and land. The CPC was unwilling to acknowledge Chen Duxiu's idea that it should be independent of the KMT in the light of China's actual political situation. Whether because of personality reasons or the constraints of discipline and conviction as a member of the

[125] This is quoted from Yang Kuisong, op. cit., p. 205. The following is an observer's comment on the wave of destructive violence: "The infantile and bloodthirsty Communists reveled in the name of the proletariat and could not constrain their thinking to a strict concept of the proletariat". Ref: Pu An, "On the wings of imagination", Xin Tiandi, 1927:6. The book is quoted in Iechika Ryōko, *Jiang Jieshi yu Nanjing Guomin Zhengfu*, Beijing: Shehui Kexue Chubanshe, 2005, p. 62.

Comintern, Chen Duxiu lacked the effective political resources to change the situation, which condemned Chen to quickly become a victim of the escalating violence and political complexity.

After the KMT purged its ranks on 12 April 1927, Qu Qiubai attributed the ensuing crisis to Chen Duxiu. In mid-July, Borodin and Qu Qiubai held a discrete exchange of views at Lushan to decide on the election of a new leader of the CPC. After Dai Jitao's *National Revolution and the Chinese Nationalist Party* was published, Chen Duxiu said: "It was at the expanded meeting of the CPC Central Committee convened in Beijing in January this year that I proposed in the Political Resolution Committee that Dai Jitao's pamphlet was not a chance publication but an attempt by the bourgeoisie to consolidate its own forces to control the proletariat and move towards a reactionary stance, and we should be ready to withdraw from the KMT and become independent, to maintain our political stance, lead the masses, and not be controlled by the KMT. At that time, the representatives of the Communist International and the comrades in charge of the CPC Central Committee unanimously and strenuously opposed my proposal, saying that it implied that the overwhelming majority of CPC members were on the road to opposing the KMT. I was not resolute in my views and failed to stick to my proposal by respecting the International's discipline and the views of the majority in the Central Committee".[126] Historians are fully aware that China's political situation at that time was almost directly influenced by the power struggle between Trotsky and Stalin, and since Borodin implemented Stalin's strategy, the strategy of insisting that the CPC join the KMT could not be questioned in any way. In this way, the CPC accused Chen Duxiu of right-deviationist opportunism—exemplified by his negative attitude towards the Northern Expedition and suspicion of peasants' violent action—and this provided the basis for the CPC adjusting the power structure. The revolution had failed, and the responsibility for defeat needed to be apportioned skillfully. After Borodin was transferred back to the Soviet Union, the Comintern arranged for its representative, Vissarion Lominadze, to deal with the failure of the revolution. According to Zhang Guotao's memoirs, Lominadze almost entirely attributed the responsibility for the failure to the CPC:

[126] Zheng Xuejia, op. cit., p. 592.

> Lominadze introduced himself as the representative of the Comintern, ordered to correct the past mistakes in the Chinese revolution committed by Comintern personnel and the CPC, and to guide the work of the CPC. He did not enquire further about our current situation, but immediately declared that the CPC Central Committee had made serious right-opportunist mistakes and violated the instructions of the Comintern. Now the Comintern has decided to reshuffle the leadership of the CPC Central Committee. Chen Duxiu will no longer serve as secretary and will even be expelled from the party. If you two can get rid of opportunism, you can still participate in the leadership. Now, if you do not begin by first opposing opportunism, there is nothing more to discuss.
>
> When I asked him what mistakes the CPC Central Committee had made, he answered: The CPC Central Committee mainly gave up its efforts to win for the proletariat leadership in the Chinese revolution, for example, by rejecting the Comintern's directive on June 1st to arm workers and peasants, and automatically disarming the workers of Wuhan. The root cause of this error is that the Central Committee of the CPC has been under the control of petty bourgeois intellectuals, and lacks class consciousness and revolutionary resolve, so the correct instructions of the Comintern have long been misinterpreted by opportunism. Now the Comintern can no longer trust these wavering intellectuals and must boldly promote some staunch workers to assume the task of leading the CPC, and they must be given a majority in the CPC Central Committee.[FN127][127]

Recalling the "August 7" Conference at which Chen Duxiu was stripped of power, Zheng Chaolin (1901–1998) wrote:

> The significance of the August 7th Conference is clear today: Stalin's leadership of the Comintern wanted to take back the old line it had given to the CPC and change it to a new one. Lominadze, the International's representative, was ordered to come to China to complete the task. However, he could not change the Party's line as directed by the International's directives, because any change of line needed to be approved by a meeting at the highest levels of the CPC to determine as if the Chinese members agreed to abandoning the old line, and only a consensus could adopt a new line. The resolution of the Party's highest-level meeting was necessarily more authoritative than the Comintern's decrees for CPC members.[128]

[127] Zhang Guotao, op. cit., pp. 279–280.

[128] [FN128] Zheng Xuejia, op. cit., pp. 733–738.

Zhang Guotao wrote: "To sum up the historical lessons of the period of KMT-CPC cooperation, I would say that the national revolution is the urgent need of the Chinese revolution, as well as its central task. KMT-CPC cooperation is also necessary, because the KMT as a whole represents the general sentiments and demand for independence of the Chinese people, and the CPC is indeed the left wing of this revolutionary force biased towards embodying the interests of workers and peasants. However, the actual policy behind KMT-CPC cooperation was wrong; the CPC abandoned the decision of its second congress and was uneasy about the status of the minority bent on opportunism who blended with the KMT and tried to fish in muddied waters. Therefore, we can say that the policy of the CPC joining the KMT was basically simple opportunism".[129] In his view, the leaders of the CPC at any time who hold power do not agree. In the history textbooks of the CPC, Chen Duxiu was held responsible for failing to fight for the leadership of the Chinese revolution, and in the KMT textbooks, the main reason for the KMT's "purge of the KMT" was that the CPC violated the basic provisions of Sun Yat-sen's Canton Declaration and was eager to replace the KMT and implement communism, so neither party could provide political justification for Chen Duxiu. With the political situation serious, Chen Duxiu was expelled from the CPC on 15 November 1929; as early as the 1927 August 7 conference, Chen Duxiu's power as general secretary of the CPC was effectively assumed by Qu Qiubai. Just at the time of the Nanchang riots of 1927 (31 July), the CPC also implemented Stalin's policy and deludedly favored the KMT left, so the riots established the "KMT Revolutionary Committee". The August 7 conference also passed a bill proposing the revival of the Left KMT. By mid-December, however, the CPC availed itself of the opportunity provided by the fighting between Zhang Fakui (1896–1980) and the KMT's Guangdong and Guangxi armies to launch an uprising in Guangzhou and set up a Soviet, but it was soon quelled by Zhang Fakui. Stalin's strategy ultimately failed, and the responsibility this time naturally rested with Qu Qiubai, the leader of the CPC.

[129] [FN129] Zhang Guotao, op. cit., vol. 2, p. 290.

The Northern Expedition and the KMT Purge

When the CPC was founded, the revolutionary party led by Sun Yat-sen was riddled by internal strife, its military power was weak and it lacked Western support, while warlord turmoil exacerbated the difficulties of the situation. The victory of the Soviet Union revealed to Sun Yat-sen how if one succeeded in building a strong revolutionary force (political parties and army) one could achieve final victory in the revolution, and so the establishment of the CPC in 1921 clearly led Sun Yat-sen to pay attention to the Soviet Union.

At first, the Comintern did not know which forces in China could become their agents in China. In accordance with their habitual understanding, they contacted the warlords of the legitimate government, hoping to reach cooperation, and even pinned their hopes on Wu Peifu, but they soon discovered that only Sun Yat-sen could become an important force. In the spring of 1921, Maring and Sun Yat-sen began to talk and discuss the possibility of cooperation, and after July, Maring, who had evaded capture during the search conducted during the first meeting of the CPC, further realized that the KMT, led by Sun Yat-sen, had relatively greater power, and finally suggested that the weak CPC should join the KMT as individual members to strengthen the revolutionary forces and jointly conduct the war against the warlords.

In December 1921, accompanied by Zhang Tailei, Maring held political discussions with Sun Yat-sen in Guilin, and Ma proposed a coalition between the KMT and the CPC. Until then, Sun Yat-sen has been seeking the support of the United States, Britain, Germany, Japan, and other countries and, if he entered into an alliance with Soviet Russia, he calculated that this would attract intervention by the great powers. At that time, the Yangtze River basin was a British sphere of influence, and the Fengtian and Anhui warlord armies with whom Sun wanted to ally also had Japanese backing. At that time, the Soviet Union because of its economic difficulties had adopted its New Economic Policy and simultaneously faced joint intervention by the great powers, so in this situation an alliance with the Soviet Union was dangerous. As for communism, Sun did not think China could accept it.[130] In fact, given its weakness,

[130] On the issue of communism, Sun Yat-sen's remarks to Liao Zhongkai were quite similar to those of an orthodox Russian Marxist: "After the Soviet-Russian Revolution, Marx's communism was implemented, but I am very skeptical about this. While the

the CPC even seemed unqualified to join forces with the KMT, and until the time of second congress of the CPC in 1922 the CPC had fewer than 200 members. However, the 1922 Northern Expedition was extremely detrimental to Sun Yat-sen's KMT, and in mid-June, Chen's Jiongming's resistance forced him to go to Shanghai in mid-August to clean up his party's affairs. In fact, before that in May, when Sergei Dalin, as the representative of Youth Communist International, went to Guangzhou to hold discussions with Sun Yat-sen, he continued to suggest that the KMT and the CPC form a united front. In Shanghai, Sun had lost confidence in his domestic political and military power, and having received no commitment of support from the great powers, so in order to win the support of Soviet Russian strength, Sun finally agreed to an alliance with the Soviet Union, but insisted that an alliance between the KMT and CPC was not possible because the CPC had none of the power of the KMT. But he accepted Maring's suggestion that members of the CPC could only join the KMT as individuals in their own name, and Sun Yat-sen suggested the possibility of bipartisan cooperation between the KMT and CPC. This initially led to the Beijing government hoping that the Soviet Union would now shift the focus of their work to Sun Yat-sen's KMT. In January 1923, the Soviet Russian representative in diplomatic negotiations with the Beijing government, Adolf A. Joffe, left the banquet set up for him by Hu Shi and the intellectual community in Beijing filled with illusions, but he arrived in Guangzhou on the 16th, a day after Chen Jiongming's forces were defeated by the combined Yunnan and Guilin forces under the command of Sun Yat-sen. On 26 January, Sun Yat-sen's Sun Wen/Joffe Joint declaration, known in English as the Sun-Joffe Manifesto, was issued, and in March, the Soviet Union paid the Guangzhou Constitutional Protection government 2 million silver yuan as a political investment and sent a team of staff officers. In August, Sun Yat-sen ordered Chiang Kai-shek to go to the Soviet Union on a political and military visit. In October, Mikhail Borodin arrived in Guangzhou as

present world is in an era of capitalist prosperity, Russian industry and commerce were not very developed, communism could not have succeeded alone, so its implementation would have been far away". Later Sun agreed to cooperate with the Soviet Union, and his ideological basis was also related to this. He told Liao: "Now after listening to Maring, I realize that things were very difficult after the Soviet Union implemented, and so they changed to the New Economic Policy. This economic policy is spiritually similar to my doctrine of the people's livelihood, and so there is no need concern ourselves in cooperating with them". Ref: Wang Fumin, op. cit., *xia* volume, p. 1004.

the representative of the Soviet Union taking part in the planning and restructure of the KMT. In December, Sun Yat-sen dared to intervene in customs clearances and announced to Britain, the United States, France, and Japan that China was no longer dependent on the West and would ally with Russia.

Whatever the aims of the CPC, given its strong backing by the Soviet Union and the Comintern and the CPC's union of workers and peasants, Sun Yat-sen tried to use these forces to reorganize the KMT. Sun was of course aware that the political objectives of the two parties were inconsistent and he refused Maring's request to accommodate the CPC. Even in May 1922 he rejected Dalin's proposal of a two-party United Front with the CPC, but if CPC members joined the KMT in their own name, the possibility of using the opportunity to divide the Communist Party or reform the Communists might exist. Since rejecting the CPC would force it to develop independently, it would be better to absorb the CPC in order to digest it, while at the same time being able to gain the support of the Russian experience and the Comintern, which was of practical significance to Sun Yat-sen and some of the KMT leaders. In August 1922, not only did the Central Committee of the CPC formally decide that CPC members could join the KMT in their own name, but Sun Yat-sen also decided to implement a policy of "allying with Russia and accommodating the Communists". Subsequently, Sun Yat-sen continued to convene meetings to implement the work of transforming the KMT organization. At the end of the year, among the list of KMT cadres, Chen Duxiu, a CPC member, was appointed to the senate, Lin Boqu (1886–1960) was appointed vice-minister of the Ministry of General Affairs, and Zhang Tailei was appointed as an officer in the Propaganda Department. On 1 January 1923, the KMT published "Manifesto of the Chinese KMT Party" and the "Chinese KMT Party Platform" drafted by Hu Hanmin, which made it clear that the KMT was a revolutionary political party with the Three Principles of the People as its goal. The Sun-Joffe Manifesto began by declaring:

> Dr. Sun Yixian believes that Communist organization or even the Soviet system cannot be adopted for use in China, because China does not have the conditions that enable the Communist or Soviet system to be implemented successfully, and Joffe is in complete agreement with this view. Moreover, Dr. Sun believes that China's most important and urgent problem is achieving success in unifying the Republic of China, to achieve

the independence of the whole country. Regarding this great undertaking, Joffe has assured Dr. Sun that China has the warmest support of the Russian people and can rely on Russian assistance.[131]

Specific provisions may be summarized as follows: (1) China at present is not suited to implementing the Communist or Soviet system; (2) The Soviet Government reaffirmed its declaration of 27 September 1920 on the waiver of its privileges and interests in China; (3) We have reached a mutual understanding on the future management and reorganization of the China Eastern Railway, and have convened a Sino-Russian conference to resolve the settlement, which will be negotiated with Zhang Zuolin; and (4) the Soviet Union denies that it has any imperialist designs or policies in Outer Mongolia, or intends to separate it from China.

From the content of the Manifesto and its actual results, Sun Yat-sen took the initiative in "KMT–CPC cooperation". He refused to allow Communism or Marxism to replace his Three Principles of the People; he asked the leading cadres in his party to allow CPC members to join the KMT as individuals; he persuaded skeptical KMT comrades to accept his political strategy, telling them that this was to accrue more power against imperialism and the warlords, and that the Soviet Union would help the KMT effectively control the Communists in the party.

The Comintern issued a very clear order in its "Resolution on the Relationship between the CPC and the KMT" of 12 January 1923, and Chen Duxiu, under the direction of the Comintern, reported as follows to the Third Congress of the CPC in June:

Developments have shown that a united front alone is not enough, and we have received instructions from the Comintern on joining the KMT. Since the last party representative congress, we have been unable to hold another meeting of delegates soon enough to discuss the question. At first, most people were opposed to joining the KMT, but representatives of the Comintern Executive Committee persuaded our participants so we have decided to urge all members to join the KMT. From that time on, there was a major change in the political views of our Party. In the past, our party's propositions were idealistic and unrealistic, but later we came to

[131] First published in English, in Shanghai's *Yingwen Dalu Bao* on 26 January 1923, the Chinese translation was published in Shanghai's *Minxin Rikan* (28 January). Reproduced in Li Yunhan, *Zhongguo Jindai Shi*, Taipei: Sanmin Shuju, 2018, p. 324.

pay more attention to the current situation of Chinese society and began to participate in more realistic movements.[132]

In fact, Li Dazhao and Chen Duxiu joined the KMT soon after the Hangzhou congress, and later, Cai Hesen, Zhang Tailei, and Lin Zuhan consecutively joined the KMT. The Beijing-Hankou railway workers' general strike, which broke out on 7 February 1923, was suppressed by the warlord Wu Peifu, leading many in the party to realize that the CPC was still very weak. Some people were anxious that because the number of party members was very small, the CPC could not develop rapidly into a mass party. At Maring's urging, the conference decided to allow CPC members to join the KMT in a personal capacity, so more than 80 CPC members then joined the KMT, including the prominent CPC member Zhou Enlai.

Maring was so anxious that the CPC actively help the KMT, he and Chen Duxiu kept making suggestions and even criticizing Sun Yat-sen. For example, Chen Duxiu and Cai Hesen published articles in the CPC organ *The Guide* (Xiangdao), criticizing the KMT's erroneous decisions to limit itself to Guangzhou and rely on warlords to conduct the Northern Expedition. Maring was rewarded for this, however, with Sun Yat-sen's impatience and anger: "Criticism of the KMT by Chen Duxiu in his weekly newspaper must never happen again. If there is a hint of criticism through support for a third party said to be better than the KMT, then I will expel him from the party. If I were free to, I would expel the CPC from the KMT, for this I could refuse to receive any financial assistance".[133]

At variance with Maring's strategy, Mikhail Markovich Borodin, a representative of the Politburo of the Communist Party of Russia who arrived in Guangzhou on 6 October, reassured Sun Yat-sen that the efforts of the Russian Revolution were nothing more than nationalist goals, just like the task of the national revolution outlined in the Three Principles of the People. He strategically avoided mentioning Communism. He was accompanied to Guangzhou by almost forty experts who would assist Sun Yat-sen in restructuring the KMT, including the party's organizational structure and the construction of the army. Of course, Sun

[132] Jin Chongji, op. cit., p. 214.

[133] Yang Kuisong, op. cit., p. 22.

Yat-sen at this time also particularly wanted economic assistance from the Soviet Union. Borodin was hired by Sun as an organizational officer of the KMT. On 9 December, Sun Yat-sen announced the reshuffle of the KMT in Guangzhou.

From 20 to 30 January 1924, 165 delegates attended the First National Congress of the KMT, presided over by Sun Yat-sen, and the declaration reinterpreting the Three Principles of the People was drafted by Borodin and reviewed by Sun Yat-sen. Among the five members of the steering group was the CPC member Li Dazhao, and in the 29-member Central Executive Committee and Supervisory Committee there were three CPC members (Tan Pingshan, Li Shouchang [Li Dazhao], and Yu Shude [1894–1982]). The Communists also controlled the work of the Organizational, Worker, and Peasant Departments. In Beijing and Shanghai, the senior positions in the executive department were held by either CPC or KMT members who "accommodated the Communists", although there were still many KMT members who had serious doubts about CPC members joining the KMT. However, at the Congress Sun Yat-sen continued to stress the need to strengthen unity within the party, because the common goal was opposition to imperialism and the warlords. At the meeting, Li Dazhao issued a written pledge: "Our entry into the party is to contribute to the cause of the national revolution, and it is not to simply strike a bargain to further the communist movement in the name of the KMT".[134] Li Dazhao even made it clear that "if our members do not abide by the discipline of the party [i.e., KMT], It is reasonable that they be disciplined by them".[135] However, not all those within the KMT believed the CPC's commitment and, subsequently the KMT formed Left, Centre, and Right factions based on views or positions regarding the policy of "allying with Russia and accommodating the Communists".[136]

[134] Li Yunhan, op. cit., p. 325.

[135] Yang Kuisong, op. cit., p. 33.

[136] Most of the so-called Leftists were CPC members who had newly joined the KMT, the Centrists were those loyal to Sun Yat-sen like Liao Zhongkai, Wang Jingwei, and Hu Hanmin, and the Rightists were the old KMT members who were relied on to an increasingly small extent by Sun Yat-sen, such as Ju Zheng and Xie Chi. It is conceivable that those on the Right who have been committed to the Chinese revolution since the Tongmeng Hui (Revolutionary Alliance) did not approve of the CPC's theory of class struggle and had no trust in the CPC. Approval of KMT–CPC cooperation only stemmed from loyalty and obedience to Sun Yat-sen. In the CPC document titled "Resolution on

Despite the later constant conflict and mutual distrust within the cooperation, the adoption of the new party constitution by the Congress, the publication of the basic platform for the founding of the revolutionary state, and the establishment of an armed military force, namely the Army Officers Academy of the Chinese Nationalist Party (Whampoa Military Academy), laid the foundation for the KMT to promote national unification through the Northern Expedition, with Liao Zhongkai as party representative and Zhou Enlai as the director of the political department. The Soviet Union not only sent military instructors, but also paid one million rubles for the establishment of the military officers' academy and four million rubles for the newly organized KMT army. The era of the Great Revolution that would "overthrow the great powers and throw out the warlords" was regarded to have begun.

In any case, during the Northern Expedition period, with the support of the Comintern, the CPC from the beginning never intended to be limited to being assistants of the KMT, but hoped to expand their power and take the initiative in political action through the strength and influence of the KMT. Within the KMT there was serious unease with Borodin's participation in drafting the party platform and constitution and with the participation of CPC member Tan Pingshan in the provisional executive committee. Deng Zeru (1869–1934), head of the KMT's Guangdong branch, and others who during the Revolutionary Alliance period has made important contributions to Sun Yat-sen's revolutionary cause even thought that Chen Duxiu manipulated the formulation of the KMT's platform and had included the CPC's ideals in the KMT's documents, and In response to these political concerns, Sun Yat-sen arranged the interim executive committee and patiently stated on 3 January 1924: "When the Communist system was implemented at the beginning of the

the Work of the Communist Party within the Kuomintang" (May 1924), it was already very clear: "The battle between the so-called Left and Right of the KMT is in fact a battle between us and the KMT Right". (This book is quoted by Yang Kuisong, op. cit., p. 176.) Later, as Chiang Kai-shek concentrated power he began to openly 'limit the Communists', and he was considered to be the "new Right" of the KMT. The CPC also sought out and cultivated the Kuomintang Left among the young Kuomintang soldiers who agreed with the policies of "allying with Russia" and "supporting the workers and peasants". Those who agreed were revolutionaries, the opponents were counter-revolutionaries, and the waverers were centrists. In these complex political games, people's roles and factions could change or be seen to have changed. For example, in 1926 when the CPC wanted to effectively establish the power of Kuomintang's left wing, Wang Jingwei was seen as the leader of the Left.

Russian Revolution, it was utterly different from the Three Principles of the People of our party. The New Economic Policy now in place in Russia is state capitalism, which is similar to the Three Principles of the People of our party. Therefore, it is not our party that is learning from Russia, but Russia that is learning from our party".[137] In fact, if it was impossible for a member of the CPC to help the KMT formulate its platform without the intentional influence of the Comintern, it is a fact that Sun Yat-sen's Three Principles of the People as set out in the manifesto adopted by the party Congress were almost identical to the Comintern's views: for example, the interpretation of the concept of the principle of the people's livelihood clearly emphasized the need to rely on the workers and peasants. In a speech on the principle of the people's livelihood on the day after the Congress, Sun Yat-sen recalled:

> In Beijing a new class of young people worshipped new ideas, and when they heard of Russian communism, they sensed the doctrine of a brand new world and sent representatives to Russia, to plan joining forces with it, and on behalf of Russian propaganda, identified communism and the principle of the people's livelihood (one of the Three Principles of the People) as different doctrine. Our older comrades also decided that the principle of the people's livelihood and those of communism were absolutely different, so as a group they rejected it and the dark tide rose. However, the true meaning of the principle of the people's livelihood was misunderstood by both sides. ... There is no conflict between communism and the principle of people's livelihood, but the scope of each is vastly different..... Our Party not only subscribes to the principle of the people's livelihood, but what we call socialism, communism, and collectivism are encompassed by it.[138]

There is no doubt that Sun Yat-sen needed Soviet Russia at this time; the CPC was eager to develop its strength, and the Comintern needed to promote communist revolution through the CPC. The Russian Communist (Bolshevik) Party also needed to consider how to gain a foothold

[137] Li Yunhan, op. cit., p. 329.

[138] "The Prime Minister's Speech on People's Livelihood" (21 January 1924), Second Historical Archives of China ed., *Zhongguo Guomindang Diyi, Erci Quanguo Daibiao Dahui Huiyi Ziliao* (History of the First and Second National Congress Conferences of the Chinese Nationalist Party), *shang* volume, Nanjing: Jiangsu Guji Chubanshe, 1987, pp. 21–23. This book is quoted in Yang Kuisong, op. cit., p. 32.

when diplomatically isolated by the great powers. These were all factors in the KMT–CPC cooperation of this period. Nevertheless, members of the KMT had always been wary of the Comintern and the Communist Party of Russia.[139] To sum up, the guiding ideology of the CPC's participation in the KMT, whether or not there was internal agreement, contained the seeds of the future failure of KMT–CPC cooperation, but the instructions for sowing these seeds were issued by the Comintern.

No matter how the strategies of the parties changed and how they adapted to cooperation, their political differences were bound to result in conflict. On 31 May 1924, the Soviet Foreign Minister Lev Mikhail Karakhan (1889–1937) signed the "Outline China-Russia Settlement of Outstanding Issues" with the Beijing Government, which caused great dissatisfaction within the KMT. In the KMT's view, the Soviet Union's fence-sitting strategy, which sought to accommodate both the Beijing and Guangzhou governments, was intolerable, not to mention that the Soviet Union not only continued to station troops in Outer Mongolia, but also granted Mongolia self-government or self-determination, at a time when the CPC, though working with the KMT, did not raise objections to these Soviet policies. At the same time, members of the CPC in the KMT were also constantly arguing against KMT policies, such as Li Dazhao's public support for the initiatives of the Soviet and Beijing governments and, in May, *Resolutions and Manifesto of the Second Congress of the Chinese Socialist Youth League* was obtained by the KMT, revealing that the CPC was engaged in organizational activities within the KMT. This disproved Li Dazhao's earlier assertion that CPC members only joined the KMT as private individuals, as the following passage appeared in *Resolutions and Manifesto of the Second Congress of the Chinese Socialist Youth League:*

[139] This wariness quickly turned into clear confrontation. Shortly after the KMT's First Congress, Liu Chengyu, Feng Ziyou and others organized secret meetings and passed resolutions warning of Communists like Li Dazhao using cross-party opportunities to seize KMT power. In April, Sun Jingya told Sun Yat-sen that Li Dazhao had violated KMT party discipline by recognizing the legitimacy of the Beijing government because he acknowledged the Sino-Russian agreement between the Beijing government and Soviet Russia. Complicating matters is the fact that the agreement which was signed by the Soviet Union and the Beijing government in 1924 stipulated that communist ideas could not be disseminated in China (which was not stipulated in the treaty signed between the Soviet Union and the Guangdong government). Li Dazhao's arrest by the authorities in 1927 for spreading Soviet Russian communism in Beijing also shows that during this period the CPC was doing as much underground work as it could.

> Members of the League joined the KMT as ordered by the Executive Committees at all levels of the League, but these executive committees follow the orders of the CPC and its executive committees at all levels and the CPC instructs League members to follow their commands in all KMT matters.[140]

The KMT supervisory committee members Deng Zeru, Zhang Ji, Xie Chi, and others began preparing to impeach the CPC in June and submitted their case to the Central Executive Committee of the KMT in early July. They accused the CPC of endorsing the Sino-Soviet negotiations with complete disregard for the "justice of the [KMT] party", openly recognizing the Beijing government and attacking the KMT's National Revolution as an "incomplete revolution", of setting up a group within the KMT "to deceive the Prime Minister and national representatives of the party", and of publishing articles attacking the KMT in *New Youth* and *The Guide*. Sun Yat-sen agreed to convene a plenary meeting of the Central Executive Committee around August to discuss the impeachment case. On 23 August, at the second session of the first congress of the KMT, the arguing or contending parties agreed to communicate directly with the Comintern through the establishment of an international liaison committee for the Executive Committee and Political Committee. This solution provoked great concern in the CPC and was not unanimously accepted within the KMT, but at least Sun Yat-sen who was waiting for a shipment of Soviet arms to deal with the threat from the Guangzhou Chamber of Commerce was able to stifle opposition from within the KMT and agree to not break with the CPC. Although the Guangzhou Chamber of Commerce incident was settled with KMT–CPC cooperation there was no agreement with the CPC on whether the revolution would be achieved through cooperation with warlords or by mobilizing the people. On 23 October, the warlord Feng Yuxiang ousted Cao Kun and took control of Beijing, calling on Sun Yat-sen, Duan Qirui and Zhang Zuolin to come to Beijing to discuss state affairs. Sun certainly thought this was an excellent opportunity, but the CPC thought that there could not be any satisfactory outcome from engagement with the warlords.

Sun Yat-sen's death (12 March 1925) apparently opened up further controversy within the KMT about the question of "accommodating the Communists". Previously, many senior figures in the KMT like Zhang Ji,

[140] Yang Kuisong, op. cit., p. 44.

Wu Zhihui, Li Shizeng (1881–1973), and others had been anarchists in their early years, and they had had varying degrees of relationship with some of the later CPC leaders like Chen Duxiu. It was only because of subsequent changes in their political careers that they came to have insurmountable differences, which in the later period of the KMT–CPC cooperation made them even more vigilant and wary. In fact, the involvement of the Comintern and the CPC after joining the KMT in their work was obviously not limited to individual organizational activities. The CPC members in the KMT were mainly under the command of the Comintern and the CPC Central Committee, and this naturally attracted increasing attention from some members of the KMT. On 7 January 1925, Feng Ziyou (1882–1958), a veteran member of the KMT who had followed Sun Yat-sen since as an overseas Chinese merchant he had been a member of the Xingzhong Hui, now linked up with other like-minded KMT members and organized the "KMT Domestic and Foreign National Guards Alliance" in Beijing. They passed a resolution to expel the CPC from the KMT to ensure that the KMT's power did not fall into the hands of the CPC. Feng's actions further led to ideological confusion within the KMT. In short, with the death of Sun Yat-sen, the KMT lost its internal power and prestige, presenting the policy of "accommodating the Communists" with a serious crisis. In order to maintain the cohesion of the party, Dai Jitao stressed at the Third Plenary Session of the First Congress of the KMT in early 1925 that Sun Yat-sen's Three Principles of the People must be identified as the "ideological center" of the KMT. Even if at the beginning there was no opposition to the policy of "accommodating the Communists", in the later publication of his pamphlet titled *The National Revolution and the Chinese Nationalist Party* Dai Jitao also began to make it clear: "Any doctrine must have independence and exclusivity but must at the same time also be unified and authoritative; if these conditions are not met, then a doctrine will have no credibility or power". Dai Jitao made his own views clear: "In our organization, all senior cadres must not transcend the party".[141] Dai Jitao clearly disagreed with the Communist Party's theory of class struggle, saying that Mr. Sun Yat-sen's "regulated capital" and "equal land rights" were designed to avoid violent struggle between classes. Dai Jitao's pamphlet provoked a surge in the party's opposition to "accommodating the Communist Party" and an

[141] Yang Kuisong, op. cit., p. 82.

upsurge in passions. On 1 July 1925, Guangzhou established a Nationalist government, chaired by Wang Jingwei, from the Left wing of the KMT, and it entered into a conflict with the Beijing government regarding who had historical legitimacy. On 20 August 1925, Liao Zhongkai, a Nationalist who supported the KMT policy of accommodating the CPC, was assassinated, after which some members of the Executive Committee and the Supervisory Commission further strengthened their resolve to purge the CPC from the KMT, and on 30 August, Qu Qiubai, the leader of the CPC, simply stated: "Dai Jitao's proposition is essentially to eliminate the CPC, the political party of the proletariat".[142] In September, in view of the increasingly acute conflict between the KMT and the CPC, the Comintern issued the following instructions: "The leadership of the KMT should proceed with great care"; "The Party and the League should dictate instructions [to the CPC] to be implemented"; and "the Communist Party should not demand that its own members form the leadership of the state and army". However, in Guangzhou, Borodin did not heed these instructions, and continued to exclude the work of the KMT Right, such as Hu Hanmin and Xu Chongzhi (1887–1965), and a large group of KMT members were driven out of Guangzhou in various ways, as Borodin and the CPC effectively took over the Guangzhou KMT. On 16 November, some important KMT figures, including Lin Sen, Zou Lu (1885–1954), Shao Yuanchong (1890–1936), Ju Zheng (1876–1951), Dai Jitao, Ye Chucang, Zhang Ji, Xie Chi, and Wu Zhihui, as the Central Executive Committee in Beijing, jointly announced to various local supervisory committees: "It has been decided to hold the official plenary meeting of the Central Executive Committee presided over by the Prime Minister this month (on the 23rd)". On 22 November, Shao Yuanchong, Ye Chucang, Shen Dingyi, Zou Lu and Xie Chi decided on the topics on the agenda of the meeting and determined that there would be "separation from the communist faction". The next day, nine people—Lin Sen, Zou Lu, Shi Qingyang (1878–1935), Shi Ying, Qin Zhen (1885–1948), Shen Dingyi, Xie Chi, Mao Zuquan (1883–1950), and Fu Rulin (1895–1985), attended the meeting in the Western Hills of Beijing, called "The Fourth Meeting of the Central Executive Committee". The Conference issued the following Declaration:

[142] Yang Kuisong, op. cit., p. 84.

> Over the past two years, all speeches and work in our Party by those CPC members who joined our party have been subject to the resolutions and commands of the CPC's organs, and they entirely served the function of being the Communist Party's caucus. The departments and members of our party have repeatedly expressed their sincere intention to correct their advice and persuade them to fulfill the original intention in joining our party, but to no avail, and they continue to act to obstruct our party. Their intention in joining our party was to develop the Communist Party and to support the Soviet Union. This is not simply revealed by their actions, but the written evidence of this is there for all to see.
>
> The CPC members are loyal to communism, and although they have taken oaths to the contrary their obligations lie elsewhere. In our party they maintain their own doctrines and pursue their own work. Even though the imperial system has been overthrown and oppression has been eliminated, the CPC has its own agenda. Even though the history of the Soviet Union is different, and the social conditions are also different, the national revolution and class revolution are not one and the same. If the CPC members remain long hidden in our party, party members will belong to two different revolutionary groups, and internal divisions will effect a break in our ranks preventing our national revolution from progressing. If we do not separate, so that the two parties are clearly differentiated, then they will continue to struggle for their own doctrines; the revolutionary process provides an opportunity for cooperation, and we should negotiate with them so they actually serve our revolutionary organization.
>
> We should use this fourth plenary meeting of the Central Executive Committee of the Central Committee of our party to make a firm decision to ensure that all CPC members who joined our party cancel their membership of the party, otherwise the two revolutionary groups will, because of internal differences, lose their revolutionary power, needed to ensure the success of the national revolution.[143]

The "Western Hills Conference" revealed the main divisions in the KMT surrounding the issue of KMT–CPC cooperation. Although the Guangzhou group also held a "Fourth Meeting of the Central Executive Committee" in the absence of a quorum and issued a circular on 4 December declaring the resolutions of the Western Hills Conference illegal, given that it was acknowledged that many KMT elders attended

143 [FN143] Yang Kuisong, op. cit., p. 93.

the Western Hills Conference, that conference was in fact supported by many in the KMT. Thus, local KMT organizations also saw conflicts between the two factions to differing degrees.

In March 1926, the politically paranoid Chiang Kai-shek found it difficult to politically negotiate and make clear political judgments in his working communications with Kisanca, Borodin's successor, and Wang Jingwei. When Kisanca finally agreed to halt the advance of the Northern Expedition and Wang Jingwei showed contempt and impatience for his work, Chiang suspected he was subject to orchestrated attacks from different directions launched under the complex KMT–CPC cooperation. When the warship *Chung-shan* happened to put to sea on 18 March, Chiang Kai-shek concluded that Kisanca and Wang Jingwei were involved in a kidnapping plot targeting him, leading him to take drastic measures to "put down the *Chung-shan* plot", which led to the 20 March Zhongshan Incident: Chiang Kai-shek imposed martial law in parts of Guangzhou, the army occupied the *Chung-shan*, and arrested Li Zhilong (1897–1928) of the CPC who headed the Navy. He also detained the Communist representatives of the 2nd Division entrusted with defending Guangzhou, seized the weapons of the Soviet Advisory Guard, expelled 18 Soviet advisers including Borodin, and surrounded the provincial and port strike committees. Although after more than ten hours Chiang found that he had somewhat over-reacted and backed down to some extent, he later strengthened his resolve to rely on military power in dealing with Soviet advisers and CPC representatives. At the same time, regardless of whether his strategic policies were outflanked by the KMT Left or by the CPC and Comintern, he began to shift his focus from Kisanca and Wang Jingwei to restricting the CPC. In April, when Borodin again returned to Guangzhou, he found that Chiang Kai-shek's circle was beginning to grow increasingly distrustful of the CPC. On 15 May, the KMT convened the Second Plenary Session of its Second Central Committee to discuss a proposal jointly put forward by Lin Boqu, Tan Yankai (1880–1930), Chiang Kai-shek, and others to set up a bipartisan meeting to resolve the issue of disputes between the two political parties. Chiang Kai-shek tabled the *Party Rectification Work Bill*, its core provision being to limit the activities and power of the CPC within the KMT. It resulted in Tan Pingshan no longer serving as head of the KMT's Central Organization Department, and Mao Zedong, Lin Zuhan, and Liu Fen (1888–1928), no longer serving, respectively, as acting minister of the Ministry of Propaganda, as head of the Ministry of Farmers, and as head of the Secretariat.

At this time, Chiang Kai-shek had obviously accepted Dai Jitao's point of view, as he stressed in his speech on different occasions: a revolution can only have one doctrine and one political party, and it cannot have two centers and two doctrines. On 27 May, in his closing address to the second plenary session of the Second Central Executive Committee, Chiang Kai-shek used the following political logic to explain the relationship between the KMT, on the one hand, and the CPC and Comintern on the other:

> The world revolution must be unified, and so must the Chinese revolution. The world revolution has the unified command of the Third International, and China's national revolution should be under the unified command of the KMT.[144]

In a speech on 6 June, he made it clear to the Communists who had joined the KMT: "If I were a Communist Party member, in the current troubled environment, because of the demand for unity of the revolutionary forces and early success, I would necessarily quit the Communist Party and become a pure Nationalist party member in order to concentrate our revolutionary forces". "It will not be too late to rejoin the CPC once the National Revolution succeeds".[145]

Based on the adoption of the proposal of the Second Plenary Session of the Second Central Executive Committee to "rapidly launch the Northern Expedition", Chiang Kai-shek enjoyed a high degree of centralized power, and on 1 July, as commander-in-chief of the Northern Expedition, Chiang Kai-shek issued *General Mobilization Order of the Northern Expeditionary Forces*, and on 7 July, *Articles of the Organization Department of the General Command Of the National Revolutionary Army* which clearly defined the military and financial departments under the command of the Wartime National Government and accepted Chiang as the Commander-in-Chief. On the 9th, Chiang Kai-shek issued *Manifesto of the Northern Expedition*:

> The purpose of the Revolutionary War is to create a nation that is independent and free on the basis of the Three Principles of the People and to support the interests of the nation and the people. Therefore, the forces

[144] Yang Kuisong, op. cit., p. 142.
[145] Ibid., p. 141.

> of the revolution must be concentrated under the Three Principles of the People, in order to overthrow the warlords and imperialists on whom the warlords depend.[146]

On the 27th, Chiang Kai-shek successively pitted the military forces of the Northern Expedition against the warlords Wu Peifu, Sun Chuanfang, and Zhang Zuolin.

However, in July, an expanded meeting of the CPC formulated a strategy to divide the KMT. At that time, "'overthrowing Chiang Kai-shek' was a Leftist slogan, while 'supporting Chiang Kai-shek's dictatorship' was regarded as Rightist opportunism", Chen Duxiu told CPC comrades; even though we know that Chiang Kai-shek will be an enemy of the CPC in a year or three years' time, for now it is necessary to regard him as a "friendly force". The strategy of the conference was: "Expand close alliances with all those on the Left, work together with the Centrists, and openly oppose the Right", with the aim of securing leadership of the National Revolution.[147] Based on this goal, Chen Duxiu also published "On the Northern Expedition of the Kuomintang Government" on 7 July 1926 in *The Guide* (no. 161); in addition to expressing his own critical views, there is no shortage of praise in the article for Chiang Kai-shek's Northern Expedition. This attitude not only aroused the disgust of many students at the Whampoa Military Academy, but also played on Chiang Kai-shek's political nerves. He asked the Executive Committee of the CPC Central Committee to explain this article that undermined bipartisanship. At the same time, Chiang Kai-shek's attitude certainly turned the attention of Borodin and Chen Duxiu to making use of the KMT left. In September, the CPC Central Committee and the Comintern adjusted their strategy to maintaining Chiang Kai-shek's position as the central military leader and handing party power to Wang Jingwei, in order to implement "Wang-Chiang cooperation". In October, the Northern Expeditionary Army captured Wuhan, and in November and December Nanchang and Fuzhou, respectively, were captured. These results would

[146] Ref: Li Yunhan, op. cit., p. 346.

[147] Central Political Report; The Resolution on the Relationship between the CPC and the Kuomintang (July 1926), Selected Documents of the Central Committee of the Communist Party of China, vol. 2, Party School Press of the Central Committee of the Communist Party of China, 1989 edition, pages 169 and 176; Chen Duxiu: Report on the Plenary Session of the CPC Central Committee in July 1926 (July 21, 1926). These reports of Chen Duxiu are all quoted in Yang Kuisong, op. cit., p 148.

suggest that the Northern Expedition had not been significantly affected by the political struggle within the KMT.

In the political operations of the National Revolution, the biggest difference between Chiang Kai-shek and the CPC was how to view the workers' and peasants' movements. Chiang Kai-shek initially tried to defend Sun Yat-sen's policy of "supporting peasants and workers", but who led them? How to control the scope of the peasant and worker movement? For example, in his view, during the Northern Expedition, workers in Guangzhou were not able to strike, because this would not only affect rear production, but would make social order difficult to safeguard; workers' pickets might form a second government and the KMT would lose control. At this time in China, the peasant and workers' movement in various locations was not simply class struggle; China's class divisions then were far from being as pure and simplistic as the CPC leaders, let alone the Comintern, wanted. They had a complex social makeup, political intentions and personal motives, and the 22 February 1927 issue of Changsha's *Da Gong Bao* reminded readers that all peasant and worker movements have to rely on "revolutionary pioneers" who "wear worn-out shoes, carry torn umbrellas, idle about, wear green trousers, gamble on cards, and do nothing for a living". "These people behave badly, impose themselves on others, steal, and cause panic". At this time, Borodin also encouraged the use of gangsters and hooligans in the movement, as *Da Gong Bao* described: "The peasants have been oppressed too long, and steady elements do not readily emerge. If a gangster or hooligan is in charge, then the real peasants will rise up".[148] In the following month, Mao Zedong, in his *Investigation of the Peasant Movement in Hunan*, rebutted the KMT Right's claim that "the peasant movement is a movement of rogues", and he defended the "excessive" behavior of the peasants' associations as follows:

> A revolution is not a dinner party, nor is it writing an essay, painting a painting, or doing embroidery; it can never be so elegant, sedate, polite, gentle or restrained. A revolution is a riot, a violent act whereby one class overthrows another. ... In other words, every rural village must indulge in a brief period of terror....[149]

[148] Yang Kuisong, op. cit., p. 192.

[149] Mao Zedong, *Mao Zedong Xuanji*, vol. 1, Renmin Chubanshe, 1951, pp. 18–19.

This kind of worker and peasant movement led to predictable chaos in rural and urban areas, and it was simply that the dominant KMT and the CPC in its parasitic role within the KMT that saw things differently and followed different strategies. On the basis of the differences between the two parties, Chiang Kai-shek has become increasingly suspicious that the CPC had even launched a "movement to overthrow Chiang" within the wider social sphere, and in November 1926 anti-Chiang slogans began to appear in society and within the Whampoa Military Academy, leading Chiang to believe that "the CPC had a role in this".

When Hankou was occupied by the Northern Expeditionary Army on 10 October, this interim victory of the Northern Expedition led Chiang Kai-shek to consider whether he could move the party and government center to Wuhan. However, the "interim joint meeting" set up by Borodin in Wuhan on 13 December excluded Zhang Jingjiang (1877–1950), Chiang Kai-shek's key representative, from the "supreme authorities" (top leadership), which meant that Chiang Kai-shek's party and government power was completely stripped away. For this reason, Chiang strategically proposed to temporarily set up the highest organ of state power in Nanchang. The KMT in Wuchang was furious, and Borodin, backed by Moscow, decided to lead the Wuhan Nationalists in stripping Chiang Kai-shek of his political power in the party. In March, the Left of the Wuhan KMT held a second Third Plenary Session, and passed various resolutions intended to completely limit and weaken Chiang Kai-shek's power, including his position as commander-in-chief, the commander-in-chief previously being a member of the central committee. This meeting of the Wuhan government not only showed that the CPC was victorious in controlling the KMT, with the CPC members Tan Pingshan, Wu Yuzhang (1878–1966), and Lin Zuhan entering the core KMT and government leadership, but also completely revealed that the Left of the Wuhan KMT was ready to take back all power from Chiang Kai-shek. Given this situation, Chiang Kai-shek, who held military power, remarked: "I only know that I am a revolutionary, and if someone is going to hinder my revolution, and oppose my revolution, then I will take his life!"[150] On 21 March, Chiang Kai-shek's army entered Shanghai, prior to which Sun Chuanfang's army had already lost the propaganda battle within the Northern Expeditionary forces which it needed to win if it

[150] Chiang Kai-shek's speech is quoted in Yang Kuisong, op. cit., p. 164.

were to fight the National Revolutionary Army and so had fled Shanghai. On 23 March, the Northern Expeditionary Army occupied Nanjing. The "Nanjing Incident" took place on the same day.[151] The KMT urged Chiang Kai-shek to move to "protect the Party" as quickly as possible.

On 24 March 1927, Chiang Kai-shek's KMT representatives, Zhang Jingjiang, Shao Yuanchong, Cai Yuanpei, Jiang Menglin, and Ma Xulun, entered into discussions with Bai Chongxi (1893–1966), Pan Yizhi (1893–1945), Huang Fu (1880–1936), Wu Zhihui, and Li Shizeng in Shanghai regarding the separation of KMT party affairs from the CPC. On that day, the General Trade Union of Shanghai, under the control of the CPC, was preparing to carry out a general strike to reclaim the Concession area from the foreigners. Such a situation could easily lead to an incident in Shanghai like what happened in Nanjing. Shanghai's industrial, commercial, and financial communities no doubt hoped that the National Revolutionary Army would eliminate instability

[151] The Nanjing Incident on 24 March involved the harassment and looting by soldiers dressed in the uniforms of the National Revolution of the British, American, and Japanese consulates, as well as foreign shops, homes, schools, and hospitals, as well as the killing and beating of foreigners, including the American vice president of Jinling University and an American dean of Aurora University, as well as French and Italian nationals. This triggered British and American warships to shell the city, resulting in Chinese military and civilian casualties. This Incident became a reason why the imperialist powers questioned the Northern Expedition and intervened. A later investigation revealed that the soldiers of the National Revolutionary Army who perpetrated the Incident were officers and soldiers of the Sixth Army under its deputy party representative and Political Department director, Lin Zuhan, and soldiers and officers of Second Army under its deputy party representative and Political Department director, Li Fuchun. Both Lin Zuhan and Li Fuchun were members of the CPC. Earlier, the CPC had received secret instructions from Moscow issued by the Soviet Russian Embassy in Beijing: "All methods must be used to excite the population to exclude foreigners; in order to achieve such an objective, the various nations must be roused to use force against the masses and the end result must be provoking foreign interference. It can be done by any means, even by looting and many killings. In the event of conflict with European military forces, such an opportunity should be used to engage in radical action". (From Li Yunhan, op. cit., p. 360).

Li Zongren recalled: "This incident was deliberately created by the CPC. Because our army had swept through the southeast, the military was riding high. The southeast was a rich area, so when it came under our rule, we felt like a tiger with wings. Only at this time the rift with the CPC was becoming increasingly obvious, and the scene for purging the KMT of the Communists was being set. The CPC sought to preempt this with a murderous conspiracy that would drag our army in the east and south-east into a fight with foreigners, which would benefit the Communists. This was the reasoning behind the Nanjing Incident". Ref: Li Zongren, *Li Zongren Huiyi Lu* (Li Zongren's Memoirs), *shang* volume, Nanning: Guangxi Renmin Chubanshe, 1980, p. 456.

in this city and indeed throughout the country; they also understood that what the Communists in the Wuhan government wanted was clearly different from their expectations.[152] This was why Shanghai's capitalists wanted to support Chiang Kai-shek, in fact, the Communist Party-organized workforce had already launched mass rallies, demonstrations, and even armed operations to seize Shanghai. On the 25th, at the same time as restoring order and appeasing panicked foreigners in Shanghai, Bai Chongxi ordered Xue Yue (1896–1998) whose troops formed the garrison defending Zhabei, which was closely related to the Shanghai General Trade Union, to allow his troops to be relieved by Liu Zhi's (1892–1971) division. On that day, the Shanghai District Committee of the CPC responded to Bai's move by calling on party members to open their doors to take in party members, in preparation for "openly taking over politics" and "wrapping up the revolution".[153] On the 26th, the Shanghai District Committee of the CPC learned that the chairman of the General Trade Union of Ganzhou, Jiangxi Province, had been killed by the army and decided to "prepare for a general battles with armed and right-wing troops anytime, anywhere".[154] The strategies of the opposing sides constantly changed according to the situation, and on 28 March Cai Yuanpei, chairman of the KMT Central Supervisory Committee, chaired the Standing Committee meeting in Shanghai, at which Wu Zhihui proposed "investigating the CPC's attempt to usurp the KMT and the state". On 2 April, Wu Zhihui reminded another plenary meeting of the Central Supervisory Committee that the Communists who joined the KMT were plotting a "counter-attack"; later, Cai Yuanpei released evidence of the CPC's destructive activities within the

[152] John Benjamin Powell, the owner of *China Weekly Review*, an English language magazine in Shanghai, wrote that some Shanghai capitalists sent representatives to Hankou to learn about the Wuhan government's intentions and to Jiangxi and Hunan to check on the situation there. "As a result, these representatives were captured by the Communist Party, tied up and paraded through the streets in the countryside to show the public. On their shirts were written the words, 'imperialist running dog'. When these representatives fled back to Shanghai and reported the horrors of Hankou and its surrounding areas to Shanghai's financial and business communities, the latter immediately decided to take steps to prevent the Communist Party from coming to Shanghai". (John Benjamin Powell, *My Twenty-five Years in China* (Chinese language edition), Huangshan: Huangshan Book Society, 2008, p. 135).

[153] Yang Kuisong, op. cit., p. 169.

[154] Ibid.

KMT. The call to "purge" the KMT was about to be made. Wang Jingwei returned to Shanghai on 1 April. At this juncture, many people in the KMT still hoped that Wang Jingwei could restore unity within the party. For example, Li Zongren argued, "Today the only man with the prestige and ability to restore the unity of the party is Wang". Several members of the Central Executive Committee in Shanghai had meetings with him, hoping he would remain in Shanghai to lead the party. On 3 April, Chiang Kai-shek and Wang Jingwei held negotiations, and Chiang Kai-shek expressed hope that Wang would take charge of "party politics".[155] Following the meetings between Chiang and Wang, the two sides agreed to adopt a temporary emergency measure to limit as much as possible the radical behavior of the CPC and the KMT Left. After the meeting, Wang found that Chen Duxiu's newspaper on 5 April published a joint declaration that was unclear in its political meaning.[156] This unexpected development led Chiang Kai-shek to abandon completely any thought of negotiating with the Wuhan KMT and the CPC to resolve problems. He was ready to act, and on 9 April ordered the army to destroy the Party Departments of Jiangsu Province and of Nanjing City, which supported Wuhan Central, and seized the Shanghai General Political Department, which accepted the leadership of Deng Yanda in Wuhan. Chiang Kai-shek ordered Bai Chongxi and Zhou Fengqi (1879–1938), deputy commanders of the Shanghai martial law command, to disarm the armed men of the Shanghai workers' pickets.[157] On the 13th, Bai Chongxi's army openly shot and killed Shanghai workers and communists in the streets; on the 14th, Bai Chongxi was ordered to close the Shanghai special

155 "Jiang zongsiling tongdian shengming zhuanxin junlü" (Commander-in-chief Chiang's telegram announcing special forces), *Guomin Ribao* (Shanghai edition), 4 April 1927.

156 "Wang-Chen lianhe xuanyan: Guo-Gong hezuo daodi" (Wang and Chen's Joint Announcement: KMT-CPC Cooperation to the End), *Chenbao*, 6 April 1927.

157 Prior to the incident, the authorities were aware that the Communist Party was arming and training workers in Shanghai and so military preparations were made to meet the Communists. In view of the fact that the General Trade Union would hold a conference "welcoming President Wang's reinstatement" on the 12th, it seemed possible people were being organized to storm the Concessions again to trigger a second Nanjing Incident, which would lead to foreign protests and military intervention, so Chiang Kai-shek hoped to control the situation before the conference. In fact, a total of 7000–8000 concealed weapons were confiscated, and these were apparently prepared for use by the General Trade Union for an armed uprising.

municipal interim government acting under orders from the Wuhan government, and on the same night, Li Jishen (1885–1959) arranged for the army in Guangzhou to surround and attack the Guangzhou Workers' Representative Association, the Hong Kong Strike Committee, the All-China Federation of Trade Unions, organizations such as the Women's Liberation Association, the Copper and Iron Trades Union, and the Seafarers' Union, killing and wounding hundreds of workers and arresting thousands of people. On the 15th, Chiang Kai-shek issued "Proclamation of the Party Purge", and arrest warrants were issued for nearly 200 Communists, including Borodin and Chen Duxiu. On the 16th, Chiang Kai-shek approved the orders of the Whampoa Military Academy Education Minister Fang Dingying (1888–1976): "Completely purge the Party, and remove every single Communist from the Academy, to protect the party and the nation".[158] On the 18th, the Nanjing government was established, and with the statements, declarations, and wanted notices issued by the Nanjing government, Chiang Kai-shek provided the "purge of the Party" with the legitimacy of KMT procedure. Until August, there was a period during which there was a split between Nanjing and Wuhan, each having a KMT government and Party Central.

The Wuhan KMT government in April was in trouble caused by the Communist-led peasant-worker movement, and on 10 April, when Wang arrived in Wuhan, he maintained his position on the KMT Left and was furious with Chiang Kai-shek's actions. At the same time, since the workers and peasants of the Wuhan government were the responsibility of the Communists, they would surely carry out Stalin's destructive order of 3 March to mobilize the masses, arm the workers and peasants, and confront the KMT right, which resulted in social disruption, an economic crisis, and interference by the Great Powers. Even so, at the urging of Borodin, the Wuhan government decided to continue the Northern Expedition (known as the "Second Northern Expedition"), but the Wuhan government, because of its "Russian" coloring, did not win over the second group commander-in-chief Feng Yuxiang, nor especially did it win the cooperation of Yan Xishan. Until 1 June Stalin continued to send telegrams to the CPC, ordering them to organize workers' armed forces and use the political resources of the Wuhan

[158] Fang Dingying's Message to President Chiang and Chiang's Instructions (April 16, 1927), Yang Kuisong, op. cit., p. 243.

government to carry out violent revolution, an order that highly embarrassed Borodin and Chen Duxiu. Soon, the actions of the Comintern's representative M.N. Roy made Wang Jingwei realize that he had become a puppet of the Comintern's revolution in China, but Wang remained silent and with the help of Feng Yuxiang tried to come to an understanding with Chiang Kai-shek. On 21 June, Feng Yuxiang, who believed that "the communist doctrines … do not suit China's national conditions", met with Chiang Kai-shek (as well as Hu Hanmin, Cai Yuanpei, and Wu Zhihui) in Xuzhou. Feng's thinking was very clear: send away Borodin, and unite Nanjing and Wuhan. He returned to his camp, told his staff not to be used by the Comintern, and implemented a "purge of the Party". Although there was no use of force, the talks between Feng and Chiang and the subsequent "purge of the Party" further reinforced anti-communist sentiment within the army and presented the Wuhan government with a major crisis. In Wuhan, the general trade union, which was actually led by the CPC, was still exercising power, but by mid-July, again, the news of further workers' pickets of foreign factories and the resulting protests by the British consul worsened antipathy against the CPC within the KMT. Sun Ke angrily commented: "These tactics of the trade unions to undermine the national government simply show they do not recognize the national government".[159] The Wuhan government was now in even deeper trouble.

On 12 July, under the orders of the Comintern, the CPC Central Committee was reshuffled: Chen Duxiu was suspended and a five-member Central Standing Committee was set up comprising Zhang Guotao, Zhou Enlai, Li Weihan, Zhang Tailei, and Li Lisan. On 13 July, the Political Secretariat of the Comintern's Executive Committee adopted a draft resolution on China in accordance with the spirit of the meeting of the Soviet (Bolshevik) Politburo on the 8th, and published it in *Pravda*. At the same time, the CPC Central Committee issued an announcement on the political situation, making it known that the CPC would withdraw from the National Government, but people could at the same time see that the CPC was making follow-up arrangements: "The Communists must remain within the KMT and fight resolutely within all the KMT's organizations and among its masses to change the KMT's policies and restructure its leadership". At the same time, the CPC began to prepare

[159] Yang Kuisong, op. cit., p. 222.

underground organizations. When Wang Jingwei learned of this news on the following day, he made it clear: "The Communist comrades within our own party must be clear that there can be no conflicts of doctrine and policy within the one party, not to mention that there cannot be two leadership groups".[160] Thus, on 15 July, at the expanded meeting of the Standing Committee of the Central Executive Committee of the Wuhan Nationalist Party, Wang Jingwei announced that more than forty days previously the Comintern's Mr. Roy had given him a secret telegram from Stalin. Its core content was to implement agricultural and industrial policy and launch a land revolution, pointing out that the CPC had tried to turn the KMT into a Communist Party. Therefore, in order to end all actions and words "contrary to our party's doctrine and policies", I obtained the consent of the twelve members of the Central Executive Committee and on 16 July, the Wuhan Nationalist Party issued a decree restricting the CPC:

1. Any member of the Communist Party who is listed as a member of the KMT and who has served in any organs of the Party and government must immediately declare his separation from the CPC, otherwise he will be suspended; 2. All CPC members must not act against the National Revolution during the period of the National Revolution; and 3. No members of the KMT can join another political party, and those who break this rule will be regarded as anti-Party.[161]

On 18 July, the Central Committee of the Communist Youth League of China distributed its "Letter to the Hard-working Young People of the Country", which said that the Wuhan KMT in its massacres of the masses was already an enemy of youth. On the 25th, Wang Jingwei retorted at the 40th meeting of the Political Committee: "When have we killed people? Why are they so misinformed?" In its "Letter to the CPC" published in July, the Wuhan KMT stated the following reasons for their actions:

> We know that the Communist Party's methods cannot be adapted to China, and that the comrades of the Communist Party are determined not to be guided by our Party. We are planning for the future of China's entire revolution, in the interests of the poor people of the entire country, and we cannot fail to impose sanctions on our Communist comrades. However, we

160 Yang Kuisong, op. cit., pp. 224–225.

161 Jin Chongji, op. cit., p. 270.

> still recognize the Communist Party as a revolutionary friendly party, and do not hesitate to give the order to protect its physical freedom, to show that this party still recognizes that the Communist Party will stand with us in the revolution as a friend. Now that we have found that the Communist Party has published an attack on us, made up facts and vilified us, we are sincere in wanting just criticism from other parties, but we cannot tolerate vilification by other parties. If the Communist Party still acknowledges the necessity of the KMT revolution, and the Communist Party is still willing to work hard for it, then the Communist Party should, on its own, abandon its recent hostile attitude towards its own party. Otherwise, our Party is interested in the revolution and cannot fail to enforce harsh discipline on those who do not work towards that end.[162]

On 26 July, Wuhan began to purge Communist Party members from the government and the party, and on 27 July, Borodin left Wuhan to return home. While the Central Committee and Military Commission of the Wuhan Nationalist Party issued a decree to find out when Communists in the army had been urged to break away from the Communist Party, the CPC had organized the "81 Nanchang Uprising" under the banner of the Revolutionary Committee of the Chinese Nationalist Party.[163] In the "Manifesto of the Central Committee", those staging the "uprising" declared: "The so-called party governments of Wuhan and Nanjing have become the tools of the new warlords".[164] In response to this dramatic change, on 8 August, the Wuhan KMT Central Political Committee meeting resolved: "Tan Pingshan, Lin Zuhan, Wu Yuzhang, and Gao Yuhan (1887–1948), are all expelled from the party and from all current posts, and a general warrant for their arrest with Zhang Guotao and others will be issued". Dismissed from the party and stripped of their current posts were Mao Zedong, Deng Yingchao (1904–1992), Yu Shude, and several others.[165]Subsequently, the purges of the KMT in Wuhan and in Nanjing came together, so the CPC completely lost legitimacy and all its work was directed underground. On 13 August, at

[162] Yang Kuisong, op. cit., p. 227.

[163] Later, the CPC would designate the day of this uprising, as Foundation Day of the CPC Army.

[164] Yang Kuisong, op. cit., p. 228.

[165] Quick Records of the 44th Word Meeting of the Political Committee of the Central Executive Committee of the Kuomintang (August 8, 1927). Yang Kuisong, op. cit., p. 228.

the suggestion of Bai Chongxi, Chiang Kai-shek issued his Resignation Declaration, and on the 19th, the Wuhan government issued its *Declaration on Relocating the Capital to Nanjing*. In late August, the Nanjing and Wuhan factions (including the Western Hills faction) began to discuss cooperation in Jiujiang, in what was called "the coming together of the Nanjing and Wuhan factions". On 2 February 1928, the KMT held its Fourth Plenary Session in Nanjing and resolved, firstly, all resolutions relating to the policy of allying with Russia and accommodating the CPC will be canceled, and secondly, all those expelled from the party for opposing the Communists would be reinstated as members. On 2 June, Chiang Kai-shek, with the assistance of Feng Yuxiang and Yan Xishan, expelled the Fengtian warlord Zhang Zuolin from Beijing. He was killed by Japanese troops on 4 June and his son Zhang Xueliang (1901–2001) announced on the 20th he would support Chiang Kai-shek.

On July 14th, Sun Yat-sen's wife, Song Qingling (1893–1981), resigned from the Wuhan government. She agreed with the CPC's position that Chiang Kai-shek had betrayed the revolution, and she issued a statement protesting the violation of Sun Yat-sen's revolutionary principles and policies and rejected the implementation of the KMT's policies, saying:

> Sun Yat-sen's policy was clear. If the party leaders cannot carry out his policies, they are no longer true believers in Sun Yat-sen. The party is no longer a revolutionary party, but a tool of various warlords. Instead of becoming a dynamic force for the future happiness of Chinese, the Party will become a machine, a tool to oppress the people, a parasite that uses the present slavery to fatten itself.[166]

However, on 18 July, the Nanjing KMT Central Political Conference announced that the Nanjing National Government was established on that day.

In the spring of 1929, Nanjing, not Wuhan, was recognized as the sole seat of the National Government (Figs. 1, 2, 3, 4, 5, 6, 7, 8, and 9).

[166] *Song Qingling Anthology*, vol. 1, People's Publishing House, 1992 edition, 47 pages.

Fig. 1 Yuan Shikai (third from the left) worshiping at the Temple of Heaven after being proclaimed emperor, 11 December 1915

Fig. 2 Cai Yuanpei

Fig. 3 Chen Duxiu

Fig. 4 Hu Shi

Fig. 5 Foreign diplomats at the celebration in Beijing of victory in World War I, 1919

Fig. 6 Students rally before Tiananmen during the May Fourth Movement in 1918

Fig. 7 Cai Yuanpei (center) leading the Chinese educational delegation to the First Pan-Pacific Educational Conference, 1921

Fig. 8 1921, Three Chinese plenipotentiaries at the Washington Conference: (from left to right) Gu Weijun, Shi Zhaoji, Wang Huilong

Fig. 9 1926, Occupation of Hankou by the Northern Expeditionary Army, led by Huangpu officers

Chapter Three
1927–1937: The First Decade of the National Government

The training that people need is civil life under the Constitution. The training needed by the government and the party departments is the rule of law under the Constitution. Government chiefs with "foresight" must first thoroughly train themselves in the Constitution and keep themselves in check, before even hoping to be able to train their citizens on following the path of the Republic.

Hu Shi, "When Will We Have a Constitution?"

On 1 July 1925, the National Government, established in Guangzhou, was still in a stand-off with the northern warlord government. This chapter highlights the decade after the National Government's Northern Expedition leading to the reunification of the North and South. As a result of the Japanese invasion, the National Government moved from Nanjing to Chongqing on 30 October 1937, and the capital was only moved back to Nanjing on 5 May 1946, after the end of the Sino-Japanese War. On 21 April 1949, the civil war with the CPC led to a relocation to Guangzhou, on 1 August to Chongqing, and on 7 December 1949 to Taipei. The English name, officially used by the government, changed on 8 October 1928 from "the Nationalist Government" to "the National Government of the Republic of China".

L. Peng, *A History of China in the 20th Century*,
https://doi.org/10.1007/978-981-99-0734-2_5

If we do not eliminate the elements of corruption, bribery, perfunctory carelessness, and ignorance, and establish a clean and efficient administration, then, as with the revolution against the Manchu Qing dynasty, total opposition to our revolution will begin, and that day will come soon.

Chiang Kai-shek (1936)

"Tutelary Government" and Its Problems

After the purge of the KMT, the National Government, which made Nanjing its capital on 18 April, gave the KMT what seemed to be an opportunity to rebuild itself and society. But it is conceivable that the factional struggle within the party and the continued presence of local military generals left Chiang Kai-shek scratching his head. During the Northern Expedition, the need for the integration of forces and division of labor led the KMT to set up political branches in Guangzhou, Wuhan, Kaifeng, Taiyuan, and Beiping, under the respective control of Li Jishen (1885–1959), Li Zongren, Feng Yuxiang, Yan Xishan, and Li Yuying (1881–1973). The first four of these commanders had their own private armies, but their actual areas of interest and spheres of influence were different, as were their political views. At the conclusion of the Northern Expedition, the KMT naturally considered having a unified administration, with full control over local finances and taxation, and changing the private nature of these armies, thus reducing military spending across the board. At the Second Plenary Session of the Second Central Committee of the KMT, which began on 8 August 1928, Chiang Kai-shek tried to weaken these local military forces by decommissioning troops, and on 1 January 1929, the KMT convened a preparatory committee meeting to tackle reorganizing the army. In March, the KMT adopted a resolution stressing that "all military power and military orders belong to the highest military organ of the Central Government, in order to ensure absolute military unity", which of course meant that the power and influence of local military leaders would be restricted as much as possible; as a result, these generals (Li Zongren, Feng Yuxiang, Yan Xishan) would later be in armed conflict with Chiang Kai-shek. Within the KMT, the Right, led by Hu Hanmin and the Western Hills faction, and Wang Jingwei's so-called Left faction also competed for the right to speak and wield political power, with each of these factions locked in a political contest with Chiang. However, military power was in Chiang Kai-shek's hands, and he was relatively skilled at balancing the power of the Left and Right. At first, Chiang Kai-shek worked with Hu Hanmin and made Hu president of the Legislative Yuan, while Wang Jingwei's faction was pushed to the edge; when Chiang Kai-shek and Hu Hanmin disagreed on the issue of the Constitution during the tutelary period, Chiang drew closer to Wang Jingwei, as the strategic situation changed. In short, there were complex conflicts and links between central leaders and local forces, and in the first decade of the National Government, there were always factional struggles and power struggles, even though current events were so unstable. The decade from 1927 to 1937 is nevertheless regarded as one of construction for the National Government. On the one hand, the Japanese invasion of the Northeast presented China with a serious national crisis. During this period, the CPC seems to have been given the opportunity to recover from crisis and have some room for development.

From the beginning of the "purge of the KMT" to the Nanjing-Wuhan confluence, Chiang Kai-shek experienced a complex intra-Party political conflict. In order to promote unity within the KMT, Chiang Kai-shek heeded the advice of Bai Chongxi, and on 13 August issued his Resignation Declaration, resolving the conflict between Wuhan and Nanjing. However, before Chiang Kai-shek's return to the command of the National Revolutionary Army on 4 January 1928, the factional contradictions within the KMT, mainly between the factions of Nanjing, Wuhan, and Shanghai, were never resolved, leading Wang Jingwei and He Xiangning (1878–1972) to propose Chiang Kai-shek's reinstatement as President at the Second Preparatory Meeting for the Fourth National Congress. When Chiang Kai-shek returned to Nanjing from Shanghai, he began the institutional establishment of the National Government. He stressed that the construction of its political system should be based on Sun Yat-sen's Three Principles of the People and the *Outline for the Establishment of the National Government*. However, Sun Yat-sen's theories did not specifically touch on how to separate the Party and government, the implementational strategy for constructing the system, or the relationship between the central and local autonomy. As a result, Chiang Kai-shek followed his own interpretation and hastily published his agreed to *Amended Organization Law of the National Government of the Republic of China*, the provisions of which clearly defined the party's control over the government, through the government's subordination to the KMT Central Executive Committee. Various institutional arrangements exemplified the tendency to center the organization on Chiang

Kai-shek, which led on 3 June 1928 to Hu Hanmin and Sun Ke from Paris jointly telegraphing "The Outline of Tutelary Government", in a bid to stop Chiang in his tracks.

On 3 October 1928, an interim constitution, titled *Program of Political Tutelage*, was introduced by the KMT Central Executive Committee, which meant that the KMT was beginning to implement the legacy of the former premier, Sun Yat-sen; the government was moving from its period of military rule to a period of tutelary rule, in order to prepare for the constitutional period.

As early as 1906, when the *Revolutionary Alliance's Revolutionary Plan* was formulated, Sun Yat-sen told his comrades that the process of realizing the revolution should be divided into three phases, namely of "rule by military law", "rule by the Covenant", and "rule by the constitution". In 1914, Sun Yat-sen made a textual revision of revolutionary procedures in "General Outline of the Chinese Revolutionary Party":

> Our Party has advanced through three phases: first, the period of military politics, in which active military forces cleared all obstacles and laid the foundations of the Republic of China; second, the period of tutelary government, which is characterized by civilized governance, the supervision of the citizenry, and the construction of local autonomy, and third, the constitutional period, in which, with local self-government achieved and their national representatives elected, the Constitutional Council will be organized and the Constitution created. On the day the Constitution is promulgated, the revolution will have succeeded.[1]

During the KMT reshuffle in 1924, Sun Yat-sen emphasized his theory of revolutionary procedures. According to Sun's explanation, the role of "tutelary government" was to train the people in democracy so that the implementation of constitutional democracy could be carried out correctly and smoothly. Considering that the people are in fact "the last to be awakened" or even "not awakened" to democratic politics, the revolutionary party had the obligation to "force" the people to learn, which is why Sun Yat-sen wanted to set up a "period of political tutelage" in which "the Party rules the country".[2]

[1] Sun Yat-sen, *Sun Zhongshan Quanji*, vol. 3, Zhonghua Shuju, 1986, p. 97.

[2] In a speech on 6 March 1921 at the KMT's specially set up Guangdong Office, Sun Yat-sen for the first time used the expression "use the Party to rule the state".

In the *Program of Political Tutelage*, Hu Hanmin reminded comrades in the Party that the completion of the Northern Expedition should now entail the move from the "period of military rule" to the "period of tutelary rule". He stressed that "Party governance" meant that the Party was the core of political leadership ("rule by the Party, and with the Party's tutelary rule, deep foundations for constitutional government are laid") and the simultaneous establishment of a government "with a separation of five powers", means that a tutelary government with a system of five-power separation will "anticipate the final attainment of a constitutional government with a five-power arrangement". The six-article document meant that the regime was exercised by the KMT's highest authority, the National Congress of the KMT or the Central Executive Committee. According to Sun Yat-sen's "Outline of the Founding of the Republic of China", the establishment of the five chambers would take place in the constitutional period, but in order to check and balance the power of the chairman of the National Government, in the tutelary period the system of "five powers"—legislation, administration, justice, examination, and supervision, did not align with Sun Yat-sen's ideas.

From the 1911 Revolution to the period of the Beiyang warlord government, "Republican constitutionalism" and the construction of the legal system had the legitimacy of the state system, and the proposal of "tutelary government" meant that the constitutional governance of previous years had not in fact really been implemented. In addition, the "Second Revolution" against Yuan Shikai's restoration of the monarchy in the name of a constitutional monarchy and Cao Kun's bribery to install himself as President in 1923 left people utterly disappointed by earlier efforts to establish constitutional government. In May 1922, Cao Kun and Wu Peifu, the leaders of the Zhili faction in the wake of the war between the Zhili and Fengtian warlord cliques, temporarily took control of most of China, and the Zhili clique claimed to support the first National Congress and its Provisional Covenant Law and advocated the unification of the North and South. When a new cabinet was formed in September, Cao Kun and Wu Peifu began to push for the restoration of the first National Congress and Presidential elections, which seemed to meet Sun Yat-sen's demands. However, Cao Kun's election to the presidency was the result of wholesale bribery that rendered the National Congressional elections meaningless in people's minds and also shattered any faith people had in a representative system. The Republican jurist

Yan Shutang (1891–1984) later summed up the constitutionalism of the previous ten years:

> We in China mostly believed that the representative system could save the country and protect the people from the last years of the Qing dynasty to the second year of the Republic of China: the National Assembly was the central government, and the provinces had their representative assemblies. At every level the people elevated their representatives. But before long, elections and selections, open fraud, intimidation, and inducements were all-encompassing. The representatives of the people colluded with the staff of officials, and rather than being representatives for the benefit of the people they became the claws and fangs of officials. The central representatives of the people, the members of the National Congress, became increasingly divided and malign after 1912 and by 1922 Cao Kun bribed his way to become President, and most people regarded the representative system with utter contempt. The average person lost all faith in democratic governance.[3]

During the Beiyang period when military cliques controlled state power, the constitutional system[4] and procedures were still being used; "the non-Party judiciary" was also the mainstream and standard in officialdom, but its role and effectiveness needed to be recognized by the

[3] Yan Shutang, "First Draft of the Constitution of the Republic of China", *Duli Pinglun*, no. 60, July 1933. Quoted in Li Zaiquan, *Fazhi yu Dangzhi: Guomindang Zhengquan de Sifa Danghua 1923–1948* (Legal System and Party Rule: The Judicial Party Orientation of the KMT 1923–1948), Beijing: Shehui Kexue Wenxian Chubanshe, 2012, p. 18.

[4] The *Grand Presidential Decree* no. 1610 in the *Official Gazette* of 8 August 1920 reads:

> Judicial independence is the permanent regulation determining the nation is ruled by law, and it is intended to maintain its spirit of independence, one in which judges follow the rules and do not take account of party factions, and in which officials attend to their own portfolios and do not abrogate power or interfere. Our country's judicial reforms are rough in outline and are not refined, and so their foundations are flimsy. The Ministry of Justice shall be obliged to appoint judges from outside Beijing, and no person belonging a political party shall be listed from the date of the order, regardless of associations. Those party members already listed will be declared to be debarred, and if examination reveals they are openly or covertly selected they will be punished without fear or favor, otherwise the authority of the law cannot be consolidated. (Ref: Li Zaiquan, *Fazhi yu Dangzhi: Guomindang Zhengquan de Sifa Danghua 1923–1948* [The Legal System and Party Governance: The KMT Regime's Party Transformation of the Judiciary 1923–1948], Beijing: Shehui Kexue Wenxian Chubanshe, 2012, p. 10).

groups holding power. Otherwise, they could veto the results achieved through what appeared to be legitimate procedures. This meant that the system became merely decorative, and any change in politics depended on the military chiefs who wielded military power and controlled power in the system. In fact, during the Beiyang period, Yuan Shikai, Duan Qirui, Feng Guozhang, Cao Kun, and Wu Peifu who headed the military groups mostly exercised state power in this way. To sum up, before 1928, China's constitutional system was largely nominal and had not really been established. Warlords believed that absolute power was in their view military power and that soldiers were the only real voters, and that non-military political resources were only facades with no practical role. What troubled them was how to retain legislative, executive, and judicial power in the hands of their own factions so that they could do whatever they wanted.

Because the *Covenant Law of the Republic of China* was enacted by the KMT, Sun Yat-sen's early revolutionary efforts were intended "to protect the (Covenant) Law" (1917–1923), that is, to fight for the maintenance of the Law and the legitimacy of its interpretation, but the "bribed election of the President" meant that Sun Yat-sen could no longer trust the existing National Congress and the republican tinge of the constitution, and he believed that a new revolution was needed. With the end of World War I and the political crisis of the European parliamentary systems, as well as the effectiveness of Italian, German, and Soviet-Russian one-party rule in dealing with state affairs, and after the KMT's victory in the Northern Expedition, the KMT seemed confident that it could implement social transformation and development through the party system: the era of "party rule" began. KMT theorists argued that the "rule of law" had in the past not solved China's problems and that real constitutionalism required a number of "awakened" men of "foresight", though there was no one assessing those fulfilling this historical role, to implement effective educational and social organization for the entire population. At the 1924 KMT First Congress, the "Declaration" approved by Sun Yat-sen made it clear that the KMT's principle of "civil rights" (*minquan-zhuyi*) was different from Rousseau's "natural human rights", and that only citizens of the Republic were eligible to enjoy freedom and rights, which limited the rights of an individual within the scope of political positions so that only the KMT had the right to adjudicate. In July 1925, the National Government was established in Guangzhou, and the *Organizational Law of the National Government* stipulated: "The National Government handles the country's political affairs under the guidance and supervision of the KMT". In 1928, the KMT's *Program of Political Tutelage* stipulated: "The Republic of China, with the institution of tutelary rule, exercises political power under the leadership of the National Representative Assembly and National Congress of the KMT". This meant that the positions of the state and the governing political party had been reversed from the order in the constitutional provisions of Western republics. Previously, the platform of any political party could not be in conflict with the Constitution, and the law was superior to any party, but now the laws and policies enacted by the state or government could not be in conflict with the party's platform. In summary, the essence of "rule of the country by the Party" during the period of political tutelage placed the Party above the state and the Constitution, although Party departments at all levels under the central government could not directly lead all levels of government. For example, when the county-level party department was dissatisfied with the work of the county government, it could only submit opinions to the provincial-level party department which would transfer them to the provincial government; the reverse also applied, so that the county government could only submit opinions to the provincial government when it questioned a county-level party department, and the opinion was then transferred by the provincial government to the provincial-level party department. Thus, party departments could not exercise the right to intervene in government at the same level, but since the auditing power lay with the supervisory committees of the party at all levels, the party actually controlled the operation of different levels of government.

At this time, since the party's doctrine was the premier's Three Principles of the People, there was nothing more legitimate or genuine than this. However, according to Sun Yat-sen's three stages of logical political development, "party governance" was only a short-term strategy, the ultimate goal being to achieve constitutionalism as soon as possible. The *Program of Political Tutelage* also made it clear that although the four forms of "governance power" identified by Sun Yat-sen, namely election, dismissal, promulgation, and recall, were "used" by the KMT before the people had been trained in politics and "governance" was exercised by the five administrative divisions (executive, legislative, judicial, investigative, supervisory) entrusted to the National Government and implemented, these representative powers were temporary. At the same time, Sun Yat-sen stressed that the spread and inculcation of the Three Principles of the People were most important, and he warned comrades within the party:

> So-called Party rule does not permit party members to be officials, who can then govern China; In short, it allows the Party to implement its principles and when all the nation's people follow these principles, then China can be governed. Simply put, Party rule of the nation is not Party members governing the country, but the Party's doctrines governing the nation.

In any case, as the "legacy" of Premier Sun, "Party rule of the nation" became the general principle that KMT members must follow. In March 1929, the Third National Congress of the KMT adopted a document establishing the rules of the "tutelary governing system", and the "tutelary governing period" began. The Congress adopted the statement in *Strategic Legislation Determining the Exercise of Power by the Party, Government and People in the Period of Tutelary Political Administration* which said that the KMT had the right "to restrict the rights of popular assembly, association, speech, publication and so on within the scope of the law", which people found extremely alarming. Therefore, understanding and implementing "Party rule" was not as simple as Sun Yat-sen envisaged when he proposed it. In any case, Sun's theory, as interpreted by Party elders like Hu Hanmin, became aligned with the views of some members of the KMT who were at odds with those in the party who questioned "rule of the country by the party" and advocated constitutional and judicial independence.

This was a turning point in history, perhaps validating the existence of such a thing as the Zeitgeist. Hu Shi argued that in the past China's spiritual atmosphere "had been that of the Victorian era of thought, and from Liang Qichao to *New Youth*, so many events focused on personal liberation", which was followed by "an era of collectivism, and after 1923, whether the nationalist movement or the communist revolutionary movement, all belong to this anti-individualist trend".[5] Such an atmosphere was of course influenced by the Soviet revolution and the Marxist theory of class and liberation, and so theories emphasizing the importance of individual obedience to the collective became fashionable ideas. As Sun Yat-sen's legacy could not be questioned, the main bills adopted by the Third National Congress of the KMT included the *Supreme Law for the Period of Tutelary Government of the Republic of China on Affirming Premier Sun Yat-sen's Doctrinal Legacy*. The time of conforming to the

[5] Cao Boyan ed., *Hu Shi Riji Quanji* (The Complete Diaries of Hu Shi), vol. 6, Taipei: Lianjing Chuban Shiye Gufen Youxian Gongsi, 2004, p. 730.

unified will of the one-party system had come, and people no longer seemed to be interested in clinging to the logic of constitutionalism, but instead focused on how to implement strategies of leadership ideology and politics. In any case, "rule of the country by the Party" began to affect all aspects of political and social life, and, to be sure, also came to constitute China's resulting political system.

It is no surprise that "rule by the party" was opposed by liberal intellectuals. Hu Shi, Luo Longji (1896–1965), Liang Shiqiu, and others used their own publication, *Xinyue*, to publish articles critical of the KMT's "party-orientation" in everything and "party rule". In their view, so-called "party rule" was anti-constitutional "one-party dictatorship". In October 1928, the National Government adopted the *Communist Party Voluntary Surrender Law*, *Law on the Limitation of the Communist Party*, *Regulations on the Review of Propaganda* and *Interim Measures for the Treatment of Students Returned from Russia*. These regulations were all considered to be supra-legal (extra-legal). On 26 March 1929, *Republic of China Daily* reported that Chen Dezheng, Shanghai Special Municipal Minister of Education proposed a law calling for "the strict disposal of counter-revolutionary elements" at the Third Congress of the KMT, which stated that "whenever provincial and special municipal party departments have written proof that persons are counter-revolutionaries, the courts or other statutory receiving organs shall punish them for counter-revolutionary crimes". Such party-based law was regarded by those familiar with constitutional knowledge as extremely absurd. Hu Shi, who on 6 May 1929 in volume 2, no. 2 of *Xinyue* published "Human Rights and the Covenant Law (Constitution)", reminded readers that "if human rights are to be truly guaranteed today and if the basis for the rule of law is to be established, we should first promulgate a constitution of the Republic of China. At the very least, a covenant law for what is called the period of tutelary government should be enacted".[6] Hu Shi raised a clear question for the

[6] Chen initially refuted Hu Shi in *Republic of China Daily*: "In today's KMT-ruled China, to be honest, all the highest fundamental laws of the state are based on the premier's main legacy. A violation of the Premier's legacy is a violation of the law that can be penalized under national law. This is a certain truth, and it is nonsense for Dr. Hu Shuo ('Nonsense')". This book is quoted in Li Zaiquan, op. cit., p. 169.

National Government regarding its order to safeguard human rights, and he wanted to know what the specific provisions protecting human rights were. In response to the provisions' claim that individuals and groups should not infringe on the person, freedoms, and property of others, he wrote: "What most pains us today is that government organs or party departments acting in the name of government organs can infringe on the physical freedom and property of the people. Today, interference in the freedom of speech and publication, such as the confiscation of private property in various places, like the recent confiscation of electrical plants in various places, is carried out in the name of government organs".[7] Hu Shi even frankly cited examples of the KMT's actions at this time:

> Regardless of whom, the person only needs to be given a label like "reactionary element", "rotten member of the gentry", "counter-revolutionary", or "suspected Communist" for his human rights to have no protection. As a result, he can suffer physical harm, his freedom can be completely deprived, and his property arbitrarily confiscated, none of which is in any way "illegal". Any book or newspaper only needs to be labelled a "reactionary publication" for it to be banned, and this is not considered an infringement of freedoms. Any school, if set up by a foreigner only needs to be labelled as "cultural aggression", and if set up by a Chinese only needs to labelled as an "educational clique", a "reactionary forces", or some such and it can be shut down and its property confiscated, and none of this would be regarded as an illegal infringement.[8]

In response to Chen Dezheng's proposed law "to deal severely with counter-revolutionary cases", Hu Shi asked, given that it only required evidence supplied by the Party to establish guilt and determine punishment: "Isn't this a fundamental denial of the rule of law?" Hu Shi was completely opposed to "party rule of the nation" and to the party being above the law, and stated this frankly in his discussion of human rights and the Covenant Law (Constitution):

[7] Peng Mingzhu ed., *Zhongguo Xiandai Shi Ziliao Xuanji Disan Ce, 1927–1931*, Beijing: Zhongguo Renmin Daxue Chubanshe, 1988, p. 470.

[8] Ibid., p. 471.

> Not only is the authority of the government subject to sanctions of the Covenant Law, but the Party's authority is also subject to its sanctions. If the Party is not sanctioned by the Covenant Law, then there is still a special class in the country that remains above the law, so can we say that the "rule of law" still exists?[9]

Hu Shi even told the KMT that people should have the freedom to criticize the KMT and even Sun Yat-sen. Luo Longji, in his article "On Human Rights" (10 July 1929), also reminded the KMT that the people had no obligation to obey laws that had not been approved directly or indirectly by the whole people and thus had no authority over the people. He also told his readers that the KMT's ideology of Party rule actually came from the Soviet Bolsheviks; Hu Shi and many liberal intellectuals were also disgusted by the Communist Party's theory of class struggle. The human rights advocates who wrote in *Xinyue* were opposed to party power being superior to state power, party members being above the law, and the law being above all else; this led to the KMT arresting Luo Longji, who lost his teaching post at Guanghua University, but Hu Shi saved him. The KMT ignored the intellectuals, but the national government's problems in governing the country—inefficient institutions, corruption, and endless factional fighting, continued to lead to complaints and accusations from the general public, which in turn fueled a political crackdown by the authorities and inevitable violence to preserve the regime. There were regular arrests, kidnappings, and assassinations, especially of intellectuals, students, and journalists (including publishers and editors) who criticized the government, and those who sought to protect civil rights. Based on "party rule", the *Press Law*, introduced in September 1930, unequivocally stipulated that attacking the KMT and its doctrines meant breaking the law, which prosecutors had unlimited powers to interpret.

It is easy to see the party was placed above the law in the field of justice. Wang Chonghui, who had been justice minister since 1927, wrote in his

[9] "The Discussion of Human Rights and the Covenant Law" (Hu Shi Replies to Zhu Qinglai), *Xinyue*, 2:4. From Yi Zhuxian, Hu Shi Zhuan (Biography of Hu Shi), Changsha: Hubei Renmin Chubanshe, 1994, p. 311.

"Differences between the National Assembly and the National Congress" in late 1930:

> In the period of political tutelage, it is "rule by the Party", but this is not a dictatorship, and [the government] cannot act as it pleases. The mandate of "rule by the Party" means that the Premier entrusts us [in the party] with great responsibility, which like the "trust system" in British law confers a sense of duty (responsibility). For example, if I have a very important matter, which for some private reason, I cannot perform, I can entrust it to my own trusted friends to perform; or if someone has been entrusted in a will to carry out some action he can in turn entrust the task to a lawyer to execute, so this is entrusted because of the credibility of the trustee, which is not a right. Our responsibility is very great, and our great responsibility is entrusted to our party which represents the people to exercise this mandate, which is what we call "party rule".[10]

In the following year, Wang also made it clear that "the Republic of China has been governed by our party, namely by our party's doctrine and platform, wherein the spirit of nation-making resides, and it cannot be criticized or changed by anyone".[11] The KMT, through the distribution of various documents, articles, and publications to the staff of party, political, military, and police organs sought to promote the party's ideas, and through the organization of training courses, promoted the idea of "rule of the country by the Party", and even encouraged those in the judicial system to join the KMT. When the KMT elder Ju Zheng (1876–1951) was in charge of the judicial system (1932 1948), he stressed the importance of judicial "transformation by the party" (*danghua*), and he

[10] Wang Chonghui, "Guomin Huiyi yu Guomin Dahui de Qubie" (The Difference between the National Assembly and the National Assembly), *Zhongyang Zhoubao* (Central Weekly), No. 131, 8 December 1930. This publication is quoted in Li Zaiquan, *Fazhi yu Dangzhi: Guomindang Zhengquan de Sifa Danghua, 1923–1948* (The Rule of Law and Party Rule: Judicial Transformation by the Party of the KMT Regime 1923–1948), Beijing: Shehui Kexue Wenxian Chubanshe, 2012, p. 103.

[11] Wang Chonghui, "Minzhong duiyu Guomin Huiyi Yingyouzhi Renshi" (The Understanding of the National Congress Required of the People), *Zhongyang Zhoubao Xinnian Zengkan* (Central News Weekly's New Year Supplement), 1931. This publication is quoted in Li Zaiquan, *Fazhi yu Dangzhi: Guomindang Zhengquan de Sifa Danghua, 1923–1948* (The Rule of Law and Party Rule: Judicial Transformation by the Party of the KMT Regime 1923–1948), Beijing: Shehui Kexue Wenxian Chubanshe, 2012, pp. 103–104.

even issued specific proposals to promote "transformation by the party" throughout the judicial system:

1. Where the laws do not stipulate, they should be supplemented with the Party's ideas [Where the laws do not stipulate, these should be supplemented with the Party's meaning];
2. Where the laws and regulations are too abstract and cannot resolve specific concrete problems, the Party's ideas should be adopted to substantiate content, and with the limits of a law defined by the Party's ideas, the law is given concrete form [When the law is too abstract and empty to solve the actual specific problems, it should take the Party's ideas to enrich its content and install the specific form of the law within the boundaries set by the Party's ideas];
3. Where the law has become rigid, it should be brought to life with the party's ideas;
4. When the law manifests contradictions with actual social life and there is no other law to be invoked, the law may be declared null and void according to the party's ideas.[12]

Under the principle of "rule of the nation by the party", the government, army, education system and judicial system all implemented measures that embodied "transformation by the party".[13] The call for universal "transformation by the party" involved almost all major social players: "Artists, intellectuals, social organizations, and government writers were long involved in the later 'transformation by the party', and without the cooperation of these people, the 'transformation by

[12] Ju Zheng, "Danghua Sifa zhi Juti Fang'an ji Shishi Biaozhun Faze" (Specific Programs and Standard Rules for the Implementation of Party-based Justice). This publication is in Li Zaiquan, *Fazhi yu Dangzhi: Guomindang Zhengquan de Sifa Danghua, 1923–1948* (The Rule of Law and Party Rule: Judicial Transformation by the Party of the KMT Regime 1923–1948), Beijing: Shehui Kexue Wenxian Chubanshe, 2012, p. 215. Although the emphasis is on transformation by "party ideals" rather than by "party members", the KMT's political arrangement of promoting "party doctrine" through "party members" provided ample room for the CC system, which was the secret service organization that penetrated and controlled the party's organization system.

[13] As early as April 1924, Sun Yat-sen fired Zhao Shibei (1870–1944), head of the Supreme Court, who opposed the "party transformation" of the judiciary and he demanded that members of the judiciary join the KMT.

the party' of culture, society and government would have been almost impossible".[14]

Several articles by Chen Gongbo (1892–1946), such as "The Crisis of the National Revolution and Our Mistakes" and "My Attitude towards the Third Party", expressed extreme dissatisfaction with the high-level organizational system among those wanting to reorganize the KMT, a group that was emphatically anti-communist, and Chen's remarks led to the coming together of anti-Chiang forces within the party. This force was so influential that the CPC also noticed that "the bourgeoisie, inspired by Wang Jingwei and Chen Gongbo, are also developing a large reformist movement in places along the coasts and the Yangtze".[15] In fact, although Wang Jingwei was the major power in the KMT, the leadership of the faction calling for party reorganization, did not care, but became major players in the battle for effective power between Wang Jingwei and Chiang Kai-shek.

On 27 October 1930, Yan Xishan, Feng Yuxiang and the Guangxi warlord clique, together with the Reorganization and the Western Hills factions of the KMT, held an enlarged conference of all KMT members opposed to Chiang Kai-shek and issued *Draft Law on the Covenant of the Republic of China* (the "Taiyuan Covenant Law") in response to the Party's advocacy of "rule of the country by the Party", and this brought obvious pressure to bear on Chiang Kai-shek. After the end of the War of the Central Plains,[16] Chiang Kai-shek tried to adjust his political strategy to comply with this alignment. He even consulted Hu Shi and the liberals for their views and proposed the immediate convening of the National Assembly to enact the *Covenant Law*. However, on the

[14] John Fitzgerald, *Awakening China*: Politics, Culture and Class in the Nationalist Revolution, Sanlian Chinese edition, 2004, p. 31. This book is quoted in Li Zaiquan, *Fazhi yu Dangzhi: Guomindang Zhengquan de Sifa Danghua, 1923–1948* (The Rule of Law and Party Rule: Judicial Transformation by the Party of the KMT Regime 1923–1948), Beijing: Shehui Kexue Wenxian Chubanshe, 2012, p. 165.

[15] Mao Zedong, "Why China's Red Power Can Exist", Selected Writings of Mao Zedong (Vol. 1), 2nd edition, Beijing: Renmin Chubanshe, 1991, p. 48.

[16] This war (May–October 1930) saw Chiang Kai-shek pitched against the warlords Yan Xishan, Feng Yuxiang and Li Zongren, and the fighting took place mainly in Henan, Shandong and Anhui provinces. Wang Jingwei allied with the Western Hills faction and the warlords in order to challenge Chiang Kai-shek's Nanjing National Government, but with the help of Zhang Xueliang, who announced his support for the Nanjing government and took over Beiping on 18 September, Chiang Kai-shek won the final victory.

question of whether the Central Political Conference was the highest decision-making power in this matter, Chiang was very opposed to the then head of the Legislative Yuan, Hu Hanmin, and on 1 March 1931 Chiang simply placed the dissenting Hu Hanmin under house arrest. The National Conference, with the participation of farmers' associations, trade unions, chambers of commerce, educational associations, and other institutions, opened in Nanjing on 5 May 1931, and adopted the *Declaration of the National Assembly* at its eighth session on the 16th:

> On behalf of all the people, the Conference is respectful of Mr. Sun Yat-sen's entire legacy and will make every effort to promote its realization.

The "Covenant Law of the Republic of China for the Period of Political Tutelage" pushed through the National People's Congress by Chiang Kai-shek was interpreted by the KMT as a constitutional document, but its regulations included a provision that the Central Executive Committee of the Chinese Nationalist Party exercised central authority and that the power of interpretation also belonged to the KMT Central Executive Committee. As a result, party power came to replace the political power of the people as the basis of the law, even though the "Covenant Law" contained the phrase, "during the period of political tutelage in half of the provinces of the country ... the National Government should convene the National Assembly [National Assembly] and decide on the Constitution and promulgate it".

Chiang Kai-shek's house arrest of Hu Hanmin triggered sharp factional conflict within the KMT, and on 27 May 1931, the anti-Chiang United Front held an "Extraordinary Meeting of the Executive Committee of the Chinese Nationalist Party" (Wang Jingwei, Sun Ke, Deng Zeru, Li Wenfan, and Zou Lu being Standing Committee members) and the Guangzhou National Government, which confronted the Nanjing government, and they demanded that the national government democratize and oppose Chiang Kai-shek's military dictatorship, prompting another open split in the KMT. However, just as the armies of both sides were massing to prepare for the final battle, the unexpected September Eighteenth Incident prevented the unpredictable conflict.

On 18 September 1931, in what has come to be also called the Manchurian (or Mukden) Incident, the Japanese Kwantung Army blew up a section of the railway near Shenyang (Mukden), saying that it was the work of Chinese dissidents. The Japanese army responded by occupying Shenyang and capturing eighteen north-eastern cities, including Changchun, Anshan, Fushun, Yingkou, and Liaoyang. Japan had commenced its invasion of China. Despite the warning of the League of Nations, the Japanese army attacked and occupied other north-eastern cities until 6 February in the following year, when Harbin fell, and all three north-eastern provinces of China were finally occupied by the Japanese. The September Eighteenth Incident aroused the KMT's Nanjing and Guangzhou political factions to reconsider the situation; "the national interest now comes above all other interests", so Li Shizeng, Zhang Ji and others telegrammed Guangzhou, "to promote peace together". On 23 September, the Nanjing representatives Cai Yuanpei, Zhang Ji, and Chen Mingshu (1899–1965) traveled to Guangzhou with a personal letter from Chiang Kai-shek. While the Guangzhou side advocated overthrowing the dictatorship, they first proposed the slogan "Defeat the aggression of Japanese imperialism". On 14 October, Hu Hanmin was released. On 26 October, the Nanjing and Guangzhou parties held peace negotiations at Wu Chaoshu's residence in Gordon Road, Shanghai. The meeting discussed the diplomatic issues caused by the Japanese invasion and focused on the reform of the party and government system. Although the Shanghai peace negotiations contributed to the possibility of cooperation between Nanjing and Guangdong, the fourth national congress of the KMT held in accordance with a resolution of the peace conference was held in Nanjing and Guangzhou respectively, but because the Cantonese party held divided opinions Wang Jingwei and others were finally pressed to stage a further "Fourth National Congress" in Shanghai Big World (Shanghai DaShijie). On 15 December, given the pressure and strategic considerations of all parties, Chiang Kai-shek issued a telegram announcing that he was relinquishing power and calling on the main leaders of the National Government to begin dividing their labors to form a system of collective leadership covering the five powers (branches of government).[17] On 1 January 1932, the Sun Ke Government announced that it had assumed office, and it passed *Bill Guaranteeing Protection of the People's Freedoms* and other bills. However,

[17] Lin Sen served as the chairman of the National Government, Sun Ke (later Wang Jingwei) as President of the Executive Yuan, Zhang Ji (later Sun Ke) as President of the Legislative Yuan, Wu Chao-hui (later Wang Baohui) as the President of the Judicial Yuan, Dai Jitao as President of the Control Yuan, and Yu Youren as President of the Examination Yuan.

Sun Ke, who lacked the means of solving his financial and diplomatic difficulties, announced his resignation within less than a month after he became President of the Executive Yuan. On 17 and 19 January, Chiang Kai-shek and Wang Jingwei met in Hangzhou and completed the political arrangements for cooperation. On 28 January, Wang Jingwei presided over the interim meeting of the Central Political Conference as chairman of the KMT Central Executive Committee, and succeeded Sun Ke as President of the Executive Yuan. On the same day, the January 28 Incident (or Shanghai Incident) took place, in which the Japanese army launched an armed offensive against the Chinese garrison in Zhabei, Shanghai. In addition to resistance by the 19th Route Army, the National Government Police Guard also went to Shanghai to assist the 19th Route Army in fighting the Japanese armed forces. On 6 March, the KMT elected Chiang Kai-shek as chairman of the Military Commission at the second session of the Fourth Congress of the KMT, thus forming a political alliance within the KMT with Wang Jingwei serving as a political leader and Chiang Kai-shek as a military leader, in response to the crisis situation.

On the basis of the legacy of Sun Yat-sen's principles, the KMT factional struggle alone could not have prevented the political model from turning in the direction of democracy. However, on the basis of the authoritarian tradition supported by Confucian ideology, the political model of democracy was always a matter that was discussed rather than gradually implemented. When "tutelary government" was proclaimed in 1928, people were told that constitutionalism would be achieved in less than a decade (by 1935), yet that promise not only went completely unfulfilled, but the "one-party dictatorship" made it clear that China was in fact heading for a fascist dictatorship. In fact, after the Japanese occupied the three north-eastern provinces, people felt that the contradiction between the incompetence and corruption of the national government and its leaders was unbearable. At the Fourth National Congress of the KMT on 22 November 1931, Cai Yuanpei and others proposed to convene a meeting of the National Congress in order to unite more forces inside and outside the Party. However, the political structure of Chiang and Wang's joint rule prevented the KMT opposition from achieving the abolition of the dictatorship of a one-party government, but the conference once again highlighted the importance of democracy. Now that Wang Jingwei once again had power, he recognized constitutionalism in the abstract; at the same time, he reminded everyone not to repeat Cao Kun's bribery of Congress, making it clear that democracy would not be a mere formality; Sun Ke, who lost power, tried to weaken Chiang Kai-shek's power through the Constitution. Chiang Kai-shek agreed to revisit the constitutional proposal given that the political crisis at the time meant he needed more support,[18] but Sun Ke accepted the post of President of the Legislative Yuan. At this time, Sun Ke, who once thought the constitution was a waste of paper, told his party comrades that once the constitution was promulgated, the national government would have the broad support of the people. Sun Ke's legislature was sworn in on 16 January 1933 and began drafting the Constitution. Indeed, in order to show the national government's attitude to the rule of law at home and abroad, a number of books on the Constitution were published from the beginning of 1933. The work on the constitution took three years, during which time discussions and documents passed back and forth until 5 May 1936, when the draft constitution of the Republic of China (referred to as the "May Fifth Draft Constitution") was made public. However, the final text, which did not satisfy advocates of more democracy nor those who emphasized more centralization, was to be submitted to the National Assembly on 12 November for discussion, but finally, the full outbreak of the War of Resistance meant that it did not come into force and "tutelary government" continued.

In order to transition from "tutelary government" to constitutional government, the implementation of local self-government was an important task following *Outline of the Founding of the Nation*, which signaled: When every county of a province attains full self-government, the constitutional government begins; when more than half of the provinces of the country fulfill the criteria for the beginning of the constitutional government, a National Assembly can be convened to decide on and promulgate the Constitution. The National Government called for the completion of local self-government by 1935 thereby ending the period of "tutelary government" and entering the period of constitutional government. Yet the work of local self-government could not be implemented according to

[18] In fact, Chiang Kai-shek's political influence remained limited between 1930 and 1933. During this period, the KMT published a collection of speeches by Dai Jitao, Hu Hanmin, Wang Jingwei and other "party and state figures", but did not include Chiang Kai-shek. The Anti-Japanese War temporarily saw the government move from Shanghai to Luoyang, and the public called for immediate resistance to the Japanese invasion. Until 8 August 1932, when Wang Jingwei resigned as President of the Executive Yuan. Chiang Kai-shek faced general problems so at this point seeking Sun Ke's support was an effective political initiative.

a consistent timetable because of the particularities of different provinces and regions, and although elected municipal councils were established in Beijing by 1933, it was difficult for other provinces and cities to achieve self-government quickly. This was a huge system-changer, and although the Central Executive Committee established a Local Self-Government Planning Committee in January 1936, it is conceivable that the deepening of the national crisis and social chaos had seriously affected the advancement of local self-government.[19]

As a nation-building policy, the measures of "rule of the nation by the Party" did not produce effective results because of the KMT's national dominance. Organizations such as the Blue Shirts and the CC Department strengthened the "rule of the party".[20] On the other hand, from

[19] The Anti-Japanese War did not end until the 33rd year (1944) of the Republic, and the National Government was still promoting the propaganda and implementation of this system's construction. In that year, the teaching textbooks on "Local Self-Government" used in teacher training schools and senior secondary schools, which had been approved by the Ministry of Education, provided students with the following definition of local self-government:

In a particular area under state rule, with the permission of the law and under the supervision of the State, each local self-governing body will handle the public affairs of the local government in order to realize the Three Principles of the People. Following the interpretation of the Three Principles of the People of Sun Yat-sen, "the system of local autonomy in China is government of our own area locally by ourselves".

[20] The "Blue Shirts Society" started out as a group planned by the Whampoa graduate Teng Jie (1906–2004), who had studied in Japan. In July 1931, he returned from Japan and found that the KMT was in disarray, and that both the government and the people lacked preparedness to prosecute a war that seemed increasingly imminent. He drew up a plan to save the country and organized some Whampoa cadets to secretly organize a powerful group to attempt to save the nation. By September, this group numbered more than 40 people. Officially named the Three Principles of the People Enforcement Society, its aim was to punish the underground CPC, senior Japanese officials and those who served the Japanese army, as well as those who opposed the KMT's central government. Although kidnappings and assassinations were the hallmarks of the Blue Shirts, this organization's program shows that the fight against Japan remained the most important and sacred task. The organization had members in major cities and in the party, politics and military. On 21 January 1932, Chiang Kai-shek summoned Teng Jie and others (the other two main members being He Zhonghan [1900–1972] and Kang Ze [1904–1967]), and later the organization became a secret service organization that was only loyal to Chiang Kai-shek. The organization was described as the "Blue Shirts Society" because of the title of a book (*Zhongguo Guomindang Lanyi She*/China's KMT Blue Shirts Society) by another important member, Liu Jianqun (1903–1972), even though the book's title did not refer to the Enforcement Society, of which Liu would later become the secretary-general. Initially, Liu Jianqun was the secretary of He Yingqin (1890–1987).

when he began to hold power, Chiang Kai-shek did not think of the development of the party's ranks, and even thought that only in the period of revolution and turmoil was building party ranks effective and that in the period of nation-building, the development of party members should approach cautiously. Given that control of some areas was in the hands of local military generals, which also affected the KMT in the local development of its party organization, the practical coverage of the KMT organization developed slowly because of the lack of teamwork. Although the Nanjing Central Party Department proposed that "all citizens be KMT members", later in 1937 Chiang Kai-shek organized the Three Principles of the People Youth League to strengthen the purity of the political positions of party members.

The CPC Before and After the Five Encirclements and the Xi'an Incident

On 20 January 1928, the Central Committee of the CPC published its "Declaration of the Communist Party of China that the KMT is the Enemy of the People" in *Bolshevik* (volume 1, no. 15 issue). The declaration cited the arrest and killing of CPC members and workers and peasants following the April 12 Incident in 1927, saying that "the KMT is already an outright counter-revolutionary party of warlords, bureaucrats, and capitalists". Based on the KMT's various crimes, the CPC called on people under the leadership of the CPC to "create a Soviet China".

Earlier, his outrage over the decline of the KMT because of factionalism led him to write a report titled "A Modest Opinion on Reforming the KMT", which not only criticized the party's disengagement from the masses, the general lack of loyalty to the party and the lack of political and military achievements, but also suggested organizing a dedicated nationalistic and revolutionary team within the party. Organizationally speaking, under the Three Principles of the People Enforcement Society was the "Revolutionary Youth Comrades Society" (dissolved in 1938) and the lower level "Chinese Revival Society" (founded in 1939). In the 1930s, the most prominent Blue Shirts Society leader was Dai Li (1897–1946).

The CC faction (clique system), known as the Central Club (established in Shanghai in September 1927), was a political faction within the KMT, its personnel mainly distributed among the Organizational Department, the Central Administrative Bureau (Ministry of Justice Investigative Bureau), the local party departments at all levels, and the education system (particularly important in universities). The Chen brothers (Guofu, Lifu) were regarded as the leaders of the faction, although they have always denied the existence of the CC system. This is like saying that the CC system was less an organization, but a party faction.

From when Zhou Enlai, He Long (1896–1969), Ye Ting (1896–1946) and others launched the Nanchang Uprising, to the Autumn Harvest Uprising organized by Mao Zedong in Hunan and the Guangzhou Uprising launched by Zhang Tailei, Ye Jianying (1897–1986), and Ye Ting in Guangdong, as well as the armed uprisings organized by the CPC elsewhere, the CPC failed to score any military or political victory. But two years later, Li Lisan declared, "The Nanchang Uprising is of great significance in the history of the revolution. When the masses had no way out, the country acquired a new revolutionary center, and the Nanchang Uprising signaled a very important period".[21] On that day (1 August), the KMT and CPC members involved in or advocating the Nanchang Uprising also issued a "Central Committee Declaration" in the name of the Central Executive Committee of the KMT, which declared it "supports the Premier in achieving the Three Principles of the People (of the people, by the people, and for the people), and the Three Major Policies of allying with Russia, uniting with the CPC, and supporting the peasants and workers, and opposes all misinterpretation or betrayal of our principles".[22]

On 7 August, after the defeat of the Nanchang Uprising, the CPC Central Committee held an emergency meeting in Hankou, Hubei province, and published a "Letter to All Party Members". This document can be seen as a summary of the CPC's revolutionary work in the previous stage, focusing on a criticism of Chen Duxiu's "opportunism" and "policy of surrender" (capitulationism) and accusing Chen's CPC Central Committee of giving up its revolutionary leadership in the previous revolutionary struggle, especially on the issue of agrarian revolution. The Party's "Letter" concluded that previous party documents had sought to rectify the peasant movement for "excessive behavior", and then wanted to gradually solve the land issue through the erroneous policy of the extension of rural autonomy. In response to the proclamation of the Department of Rural Administration [of the CPC] requiring all rural villages to legally punish bad local gentry, the "Letter" stated that

[21] Li Lisan, "Report on Party History", Zhonggongdang Shi Baogao Xuanbian (Edited Collection of CPC History Reports), p. 267.

[22] Signatories were Sun-Song Qingling, Deng Yanda, Tan Pingshan, Peng Zemin, Lin Zuhan, Wu Yuzhang, Yu Shude, Yu Daiying, Mao Zedong, Deng Yingchao and 22 others. This document was published in Nanchang's *Republic Daily*.

"this proclamation and all actions of the Department of Rural Administration best showed our Party's counter-revolutionary approach at that time to land issues". In fact, all this was nothing more than a reflection within the CPC of the struggle between Stalin and Trotsky; Stalin wanted to promote armed revolution, and Trotsky thought the conditions for doing so were not yet ripe. Throughout the "Letter", the contradiction between Stalin and Trotsky was not mentioned, following the instructions of the Comintern, so that the "mistakes" in the Chinese revolution could only be borne by the CPC leader Chen Duxiu, whose failure was described as the result of his opportunism in selling out the revolution. The document fully expressed the determination to achieve success in the national revolution and the agrarian revolution by resolutely guiding the workers and peasants to carry out an armed revolution. The document also stressed that the anti-imperialist national liberation movement and class struggle were not opposed, condemning Chen's Central Committee: "Like the tide, the working class was advancing towards true civil rights for workers and peasants, but the central government did its best to prevent the workers' movement from embarking on this path of revolution". By conforming to Stalin's position, the "August 7" conference in Hankou made the decision to advance the armed struggle, and at this conference alternate Central Committee member Mao Zedong maintained his earlier passionate warning that political power was seized using the barrel of the gun. In its relationship with the KMT, the document reiterated the instructions of the eighth plenary session (18–30 May) of the Executive Committee of the Communist International (ECCI): "In the present situation the working class' political party, the CPC, does not have leadership within the KMT, so its plan to achieve leadership of the proletariat within China is impossible".[23] Chen Duxiu's Central Committee was condemned by the entire CPC for failing to carry out this directive, despite the fact that the Communist International did not realize that the conditions for the implementation of the directive simply did not exist.

[23] See "Zhonggong 'Baqi' Huiyi Gao Quandang Dangyuan Shu" (Letter of the "August 7" Conference of the Communist Party of China to All Party Members), quoted in Peng Ming ed., *Zhongguo Xiandai Shi Ziliao Xuanji Disansice Bupian, 1927–1937* (Documents of China's Modern History Supplement to the Third and Fourth Volumes: 1927–1937), Beijing: Zhongguo Renmin Daxue Chubanshe, 1992, pp. 36–66.

The earlier "violently" radical political goals inspired and supported by the spirit and documents of the "August 7th" conference were the direct reason why the CPC not only did not remain quiet and calm during the massacres carried out by the KMT in purging its ranks but also actively promoted armed uprisings. Based on the revolutionary momentum in the four provinces of Hunan, Hubei, Jiangxi, and Guangdong, which had experienced radical movements, the Politburo decided to stage uprisings at the autumn harvest and carry out its land revolution through armed struggle. It was arranged that Mao Zedong would travel to Hunan to organize what would be called the Autumn Harvest Uprising. Unlike the Nanchang Uprising, which was conducted in the name of the KMT, Mao Zedong stressed that "we should raise the flag of the Communist Party". On 18 August 1927, Mao Zedong was appointed by the Hunan Provincial Committee as Secretary of the Enemy Confrontation Committee.[24] In early September, the uprising rebels began to destroy the railway lines, to facilitate uprisings on the 11th in various counties and later an uprising in Changsha. However, the extent of damage to the railway was very limited, and the worker and peasant army in Anyuan, the peasant armies in Liuyang and Pingjiang, and the rural riots in Changsha all failed. On 19 September, the rebel forces gathered in Wenjiashi Town, Liuyang County, Hunan Province, and in view of the difficulties of the uprising, Mao Zedong decided to abandon his plan to attack Changsha and retreated instead further into the countryside. In his "Report on the Passage of the Autumn Harvest Riots in Hunan" (8 October 1927), the provincial party secretary Peng Gongda (1903–1928) presented this summary:

[24] In February 1926, Mao Zedong was reappointed a member of the KMT Peasant Movement Committee and also the director of the KMT Peasant Movement Lecture Institute. As the earliest region of the Northern Expedition, Hunan's KMT authorities accepted the instructions and financial assistance of the Soviet Union to establish the Agricultural Association (by June 1926, the Agricultural Association had spread throughout 17 provinces including Guangdong, Hunan, and Guizhou; more than 200 counties nationwide set up county associations, with more than 9.15 million members). The fierce initiatives of the Agricultural Association led different degrees of social unrest. On the basis of surveys conducted in Xiangtan, Xiangxiang, Hengshan, Liling and Changsha, Mao Zedong on 5 March 1927 published his *Report of an Investigation of the Peasant Movement in Hunan* in the 35th and 36th issues of the weekly *Warrior* (Zhanshi), the journal of the CPC's Hunan District Committee. Only the first two sections of *Report* were published in *Warrior*; later, on 28 March, *Zhongyang Fukan* (issue no. 7) published some other content.

> The Autumn Harvest Uprising in Hunan was intended to launch the peasants' land revolution. The main force in the uprising was the peasants, and the Party did the important work encouraging the peasants, with all Party members having gone out to mobilize them. The Communist Party of Hunan led this Uprising, but the peasant forces were not fully prepared. The Party did not pay fundamental attention to the peasant movement, and so wherever the riots broke out, simple military action suppressed them. Not only had they not set off any revolutionary frenzy among the peasants to seize land, but they even failed to win the interest of the peasants in this uprising, and this was the root cause of this Uprising's failure.[25]

On 29 September, uprisings occurred in Sanwan Village, Yongxin County, Jiangxi Province; fewer than 1000 men formed this regiment. At the same time, it set up a Party branch in each company, so that they could develop Party members among the soldiers and the Party representatives in each company could become the Red Army's political commissars, and each company's political committee would become political instructors so that this army could become a protective force for the Party. On 3 October, the uprising forces marched towards Jinggangshan, and on 27 October, the rebel forces camped at Ciping in Jinggangshan, and quickly absorbed the civilian forces there into their ranks. Later, the CPC cast the result of this move as the establishment of the first rural base to eliminate the "city-centered theory"; the dense forests and mountains of Jinggangshan would serve as hideaways in which the Red Army forces could survive and use guerrilla tactics to fight the regular army. Despite the failure of the Autumn Harvest Uprising, Mao Zedong had acquired China's earliest Communist army, largely comprising activists of the peasant movement, the unemployed miners of Anyuan, and some members of the KMT's Wuhan government.

The "August 7th Conference" also instigated a military uprising in Guangzhou on 11 December 1927 that became known as the Guangzhou Uprising. However, some of its main leaders had originally been important military personnel in the National Revolutionary Army (NRA): Ye Ting had been commander-in-chief of the Second Front Army of the NRA; Ye Jianying had been chief of staff of the NRA Fourth Army before the Nanchang Uprising; and the likes of Nie Rongzhen (1899–1992), Yun Daiying, and Peng Bai (1896–1929) had also been

[25] Peng Ming ed., op. cit., p. 79.

important figures in the Nanchang Uprising. However, the CPC regarded this uprising as an iconic historical victory following the Nanchang Uprising and the Autumn Harvest Uprising on the Hunan-Jiangxi border. Despite the failure of the Nanchang Uprising, the CPC tried to exploit the conflict between the KMT's Southern and Northern governments (led respectively by Li Jishenand Zhang Fakui [1896–1980]). On the basis of the active Guangdong trade unions and peasant associations,[26] they continued to search for a breakthrough in the armed revolution in Guangzhou to carry out the spirit of the "August 7 Conference". This was very bloody rioting.[27] But it enjoyed fleeting success; the rioters declared the establishment of the Guangzhou Soviet Government on the day of the uprising and even issued a Manifesto of the Guangzhou Soviet:

> On the night of 10 December and on the 11th, Guangzhou's proletariat seized political power. All the regime's power was now in the hands of the workers, peasants, and soldiers. The Red Guards and the Teaching Corps jointly seized the Public Security Bureau and all the government's

[26] At the time, the KMT's Wuhan government was fighting the Nanjing government, and Zhang Fakui's army, which belonged to the Wuhan government, was trying to compete with Li Jishen of the Guangxi clique for control of Guangdong when the Nanjing government's army attacked the Nanchang Uprising. The CPC took advantage of this contradiction (the CPC even secretly controlled the combative teaching and guard regiments of Zhang Fakui's army) to develop its own party organizations, trade unions, and peasant associations, organize workers' strikes in cities (the seamen's strike on 14 October) and launch anti-rent riots in the countryside (in September in Dongjiang and other areas). By 30 October, the remnant forces of the Nanchang Uprising launched a peasant uprising in Hailufeng and formed a Soviet government, led by Peng Pai, who founded a peasant movement workshop before Mao Zedong did so in 1924.

[27] Li Zongren, a powerful figure in the KMT's laurel system, wrote in his memoirs: "The whole city is on fire, and there are corpses everywhere. Members of the public were forced to wear red scarves around their necks to show their support for the Red Army, otherwise they would be killed. Zhang Fakui hurried to Zhaoqing, to urgently command Huang Qixiang to bring back his troops to quell the chaos. Huang then led his troops back to Guangzhou. Zhang and Huang regarded the Communist Party as being behind the chaos and destroying their joint plans in Guangdong and Guangxi, so filled with rage they launched a killing spree. People, regardless of whether they supported the Red Army or the Fourth Army, were killed for having worn a red scarf, or even if they hadn't. For a time, the whole city of Guangzhou was filled with the ghostly sounds of weeping and wailing, with untold numbers of innocent people slaughtered. The fires burned for several days and the best things in the city were destroyed by fire in one of the few apocalyptic events to take place after the founding of the Republic of China. (Li Zongren, *Li Zongren Huiyi Lu* [Memoirs of Li Zongren]).

> military and financial organs. Several minor places in the city were still in the middle of the purge. The Red Army used armor-plated vehicles, machine guns and cannons seized from the Public Security Bureau to quell counter-revolutionary revolts.[28]

But on the following day, Zhang Fakui's army and the Fifth Army stationed on the south bank of the Pearl River in Guangzhou, with the cooperation of British, American, Japanese, and French warships and marines, quickly defeated the uprising, and the leader of the uprising, Zhang Tailei, secretary of the Communist Party of Guangdong Province, died in the fighting. The Soviet embassy was involved in the Guangzhou Uprising; its diplomats were tortured to death and the consulate was closed. On the 13th, the remnants of the rebel army withdrew from Guangzhou, and some of the troops were formed into the Fourth Division of the Workers' and Peasants' Revolutionary Army in Huaxian (present-day Huadu), and a few people met up near Shaoguan with remnants of the Nanchang Uprising's army led by Zhu De (1886–1976) and Chen Yi (1901–1972). In May 1928, Zhu De and Chen Yi's troops went to Jinggangshan and rendezvoused with Mao Zedong's troops, and they merged their respective units into the Fourth Army of the Chinese Red Army of Workers and Peasants, with nearly 1000 men. In December, the Red Fifth Army, formed after the Pingjiang Uprising in Hunan Province and led by Peng Dehuai (1898–1974), also arrived in Jinggangshan. Henceforth, the CPC completely separated from the KMT.

On 18 June 1928, the Sixth National Congress of the CPC was held in Moscow. Guangzhou's violent revolution was fully affirmed, but the Autumn Harvest Uprising was not fully approved.[29] Qu Qiubai presented a political report on behalf of the Fifth Central Committee, but he also lost power because of his mistake of "Leftist [Left-deviationist] blind putschism", and the worker-born Xiang Zhongfa was elected general

[28] Peng Ming ed., op. cit., p. 126.

[29] *The Political Resolutions of the Sixth National Congress of the Communist Party of China* stated: "The mechanical application of the policy behind the Autumn Harvest Uprising in other places was playing with armed uprisings and military adventurism". However, it has been noted: "It is wrong to downplay the imperialist and reactionary forces, exaggerate the victory of the peasant movement, and underestimate the extent of the failure of the revolution. For example, the plan to stage an armed uprising in Hunan and Hubei without an assessment of the situation was wrong". (Peng Ming ed., op. cit., pp. 139–140).

secretary, the organizer of the "May Thirtieth Movement" Li Lisan was made propaganda minister, and Zhou Enlai served as military department chief. The core of the platform adopted at the meeting was the establishment of Soviet political power and the promotion of the agrarian revolution. At the same time, the focus of the Party's work was still on the city. On 15 December 1929, Chen Duxiu, who had been expelled from the CPC but who still cared about the fate of the Communist Party, and his comrades (who had been expelled with him from the Party as Trotskyites) wrote in *Letter Outlining Our Political Opinions*: "Recently, the Comintern further instructed the CPC to say that the revival of the Chinese revolution has matured. This is clearly the Comintern's description of the blind activism of the CPC since the 'August 7 Conference' until now".[30] Not surprisingly, Li Lisan was unsuccessful in carrying out the mission of the Comintern in the following year, and a series of workers' strikes and armed uprisings he organized in Hankou failed. The Comintern accused Li of being obsessed with staging uprisings, failing to organize workers effectively, and failing to allow the Communist Party to make steady progress in the ranks of the workers. Li Lisan became the leader of the CPC, succeeding Chen Duxiu who was held politically responsible for policy failures.[31] Li Lisan was criticized for his words and actions, which were condemned as "either the worst adventurism or the most shameful nonsense" in *Letter to the Central Committee of the CPC of 5 August 1930 from the Far Eastern Bureau of the CIEC (Executive Committee of the Comintern).*[32] The Party consensus was to blame Li Lisan for its failures.[33] At the end of September 1930 Qu Qiubai, who

[30] Peng Ming ed., op. cit., p. 241.

[31] In fact, Li Lisan also talked about the problem of "blind activism" in a report delivered to the Sixth Congress of the CPC on 23 June 1928, saying: "The revolution has suffered defeat, but some activists were impatient, and proceeded ahead of the masses, which was the source of blind activism and forced strikes". (Jin Chongji, *Ershi Shiji Zhongguo Shi Gang* [Outline History of China in the Twentieth Century], vol. I, Beijing: Shehui Kexue Wenxian Chubanshe, 2009, p. 315) In fact, this was a period of radicalism fueled by the Soviet-Russian revolution, and it was not just a few people in the CPC acting blindly. From 1929 to 1930, when the Communist International was criticizing Bukharin's "rightist deviation", the CPC following the Communist International's orders was forced to carry out violent revolution.

[32] Peng Ming ed., op. cit., p. 550.

[33] Xia Yan, who joined the Communist Party in 1927, had this to say at a conference of the Left League of Writers:

had returned from the Soviet Union, adopted a "conciliatory" attitude at the Plenary Session of the Third Congress of the CPC, making accusations of blind Leftist behavior and criticizing Rightist opportunism, so the urban uprisings were called off.[34] However, the Communist International did not endorse the views of Qu Qiubai and Zhou Enlai at this meeting, and in January 1931, at the Fourth Plenary Session of the Sixth Central Committee of the CPC held in Shanghai, Li Lisan and Qu Qiubai were marginalized, and the party's top leadership was in fact transferred from Xiang Zhongfa to Chen Shaoyu (Wang Ming, 1904–1974), by Pavel Mif, Stalin's representative, who served as Wang Ming's backer. At the meeting, Wang Ming became a member of the Politburo and Central Committee. Xiang Zhongfa was arrested by the KMT on 24 June, and although the mutiny was quelled, Wang Ming officially became general secretary of the CPC, which is generally regarded as the "beginning of the Bolshevikization of the CPC" with the "period of rule by the Wang Ming Leftist line". Three months later, Wang Ming returned to the Soviet Union with Pavel Mif to serve as the CPC's representative

"1930 was truly an unforgettable year because, under the leadership of the 'Cultural Committee', a number of left-wing cultural work organizations were set up. Under the ruthless white terror, when promoting Marxist-Leninist ideology and expanding the influence of the Communist Party, the CPC Central Committee under the auspices of Li Lisan, in April decided to prepare for 'Red May' operations, and on 5 (or 7) May, there was an unprecedentedly large flying rally on Nanjing Road, with a large loss of life. In early June, the Politburo adopted its resolution on the 'New Revolutionary High Tide and the First Victory in One or Several Provinces'. At the same time, it eliminated the formal organization of the Party, League and Trade Unions and set up 'Action Committees' at all levels.... After that, the erroneous Leftist line dominated the central leadership; as well as determining a national general riot plan centered on Wuhan, it concentrated the Red Army for an attack on the center of the city. I remember that at that time, the 'executive committee' in the Zhabei district of Shanghai issued a mimeographed publication emblazoned with the slogan, 'Our armies will meet in Wuhan, and our horses will drink from the Yangtze River'". (Xia Yan, *Lanxun Jiumeng Lu*, Beijing: Sanlian Shudian, 1992, p. 178)

In explaining why this happened, Xia Yan also stated that the Third International did not understand the reality of the Chinese revolution and implemented "blind commands".

[34] According to official statistics of the CPC, by September 1930, the number of Party members had grown to 229, and the number of Party members had grown from more than 40,000 at the time of the Sixth Congress to more than 100,000. The membership of the red trade unions exceeded 100,000. (Yang Zhonghu and Wang Ming eds., *Zhonggong Dangshi Jianming Duben* (A Concise Reader of the History of the Communist Party of China), Beijing: Renmin Ribao Chubanshe, 2019, p. 34)

to the Comintern.[35] Bo Gu then took over from Wang Ming. However, Mif's arbitrariness at the Fourth Plenary Session and his decision-making naturally aroused strong antipathy within the CPC.[36]

Mao Zedong was not at the heart of the Party's central decision-making; his actions in Hunan (Autumn Harvest Uprising) were not approved by the Comintern, and so he was expelled from the Politburo and the Hunan Provincial Committee on 14 November 1927. However, during the Sixth Congress of the CPC held in Moscow at the end of June in the following year, Stalin received a letter of request from Mao Zedong for Party authorization, and given that Mao's actions coincided with Stalin's strategy of forming a Red Army in China, Stalin urged the Comintern to support Mao Zedong and agree to re-establish the former committee of Mao and Zhu's army in Jinggangshan and formally establish the Red Army, with recognition by the CPC of Mao as secretary and Zhu De as commander of the army led by Mao Zedong. When KMT troops surrounded the Communists of Jinggangshan on 14 January 1929, Mao Zedong and Zhu De led the Red Fourth Army into southern Jiangxi, and then into western Fujian. During this period, the Gutian Conference suppressed the elements in the Red Army who favored brigandage and warlordism, and the redistribution of land ownership attracted peasants

[35] After the Fourth Plenary Session of the Sixth Central Committee, the CPC Central Committee sent a delegation to Moscow, the main members being Wang Ming, Kang Sheng (1898–1975), Chen Yun (1905–1995), Wu Yuzhang, Li Lisan, Rao Shushi (1903–1975), and Huang Yaomian (1903–1987). The main tasks of the delegation were to maintain the links between the Comintern and the CPC, to promote the Chinese Workers and Peasants Red Army, and to lead the work of CPC members in the Soviet Union.

[36] Luo Zhanglong (1896–1995), who was expelled from the party by Pavel Mif, later recalled:

"In order to discuss the sudden removal of the party's leadership by Mif and Wang Ming's clique and their rescinding of our party membership, we should have responded directly. In order to oppose Wang Ming's opportunistic line, and in order to keep the party's work from being locked in internal debate and not advancing the revolution, Shi Wenbin [1887–1942], He Mengxiong [1898–1931], Li Qiushi [1903–1931], Lin Yunan [1898–1931], myself, together with some other comrades then jointly prepared for an inner Party meeting at Shanghai Orient Hotel. … Taking part in that meeting, were representatives of the general trade union, the iron workers union, the seamen's union, the Shanghai general union, as well as reps from Shanghai, Jiangsu and other Soviets". (Luo Zhanglong, "Shanghai Dongfang Fandian Huiyi Qianhou" [Before and after the conference in the Shanghai Orient Hotel], *Xin Wenxue Shiliao*, 1981:1, quoted by Liu Xiaoqing, *Hongse Kuangbiao: Zuolian Shilu* [Red Rage: True Account of the Left-wing League of Writers], Beijing: Renmin Wenxue Chubanshe, 2004, pp. 177–178)

to support and even join the Red Army. By the first half of 1930, the CPC's Red Army had expanded to thirteen separate forces (with more than 60,000 soldiers). A few years later, Mao Zedong told Edgar Snow:

> On 7 February 1930, an important local party meeting was held in the south of Jiangxi to discuss the future Soviet program. Local party, military and political representatives attended the meeting. The issue of land policy was discussed in detail, and the struggle against "opportunism" waged by those opposed to the allocation of land was defeated. The meeting decided to allocate land and accelerate the establishment of the local Soviet; prior to this, the Red Army was only the organization of the local and township Soviet, but at this meeting, it was decided to establish a Soviet government in Jiangxi Province.[37]

"Those opposed to the allocation of land" mentioned here by Mao Zedong were some of those in charge of the Red Army and CPC groups in south-western Jiangxi at that time, who, in response to the land revolution, proposed to simply "confiscate the holdings of the landlords" rather than expand the scope of the land reform. Mao Zedong denounced them as the Trotskyite-Chen Duxiu line, which would lead to the elimination of the agrarian revolution. Mao launched a political struggle within the Party to "eliminate the landlords and rich peasants", after which the Party initiated the brutal political movement to "eliminate the Anti-Bolshevik League" in the Soviets of Jiangxi.[38] Clearly, there had always been different views and factions within the CPC, not

[37] Edgar Snow, Red Star Over China (Chinese language edition), Beijing: Waiyu Jiaoxue Yu Yanjiu Chubanshe, 2005, pp. 264–266.

[38] The AB League (Anti-Bolsheviks) was an organization founded by Chiang Kai-shek during the Communist Party's Nanchang Uprising, which was abolished after the 1927 "September 12" Incident. In order to purify the Red Army in the guerilla base areas and consolidate his leadership, Mao Zedong as early as September 1928 liquidated those in Jinggangshan designated as "opportunists" in the name of "cleansing the Party"; intellectuals, those born as rich farmers, and "all relatives of KMT reactionaries and soldiers" were purged as Party members. Between 1930 and 1931, Mao Zedong carried out a purge of the "AB Regiment", targeting the forces of Li Wenlin (1901–1932) in the local Red Army in south-western Jiangxi, and then extended the "liquidation" campaign to the Central Soviet area, where tens of thousands of Red Army officers and soldiers were tortured and killed as members of the KMT AB Regiment. (Ref: Gao Hua, *Hong Taiyang Shi Zenyang Shengqi de: Yan'an Zhengfeng Yundong de Lailongqumai* [How the Red Sun Rose: The History of the Yan'an Rectification Movement], Hong Kong: Chinese University Press, 2004)

unlike the factional struggles within the KMT. The main faction of this period tended to follow the instructions of the Comintern and this was Wang Ming's "international faction" who made their official appearance at the Fourth Plenary Session of the Sixth Central Committee and mostly comprised those who had gone to the Soviet Union and studied at Sun Yat-sen University in Moscow; this faction was also mockingly termed the "Twenty-eight and a Half Bolsheviks", comprising 29 persons, whose main representatives were Wang Ming, Bo Gu (Qin Bangxian, 1907–1946), Zhang Wentian (Luo Fu, 1900–1976), Shen Zemin (1900–1933), Wang Jiaxiang, and Yang Shangkun (1907–1998).[39] Although Mao's unorthodox behavior was always questioned and criticized by the Comintern-authorized Central Committee of the CPC, only Mao Zedong's forces survived in the mountains of Jiangxi and promoted the Chinese revolution, which kept the Comintern's evaluation of Mao basically positive. In fact, after the KMT purged its ranks, the CPC across the country subjected its members to large-scale purges and killings. In Shanghai, the CPC Central Committee, already in crisis, with the KMT's

[39] Sun Yat-sen University was established in September 1925 and was not open to the public. Its first group of 340 students were sent by both the Kuomintang and the Communist Party of China. Many of these students were later prominent leaders of the KMT and CPC, such as Deng Xiaoping (1904–1997), Chen Boda (1904–1989), Wu Yuzhang and Chiang Ching-kuo (Jiang Jingguo, 1910–1988). There were also important, well-connected figures like: Feng Yuxiang's children Feng Hongguo (1910–1973), Feng Funeng (?–1979), Feng Fufa (1913–?); Shao Lizi's son Shao Zhigang (?); Ye Chucang's son Ye Nan (?); and the daughter of Yu Youren (1879–1964), Yu Xiuzhi. On 26 July 1927, after the split between the KMT and CPC, the school changed its name to the Sun Yat-sen Communist University of the Toilers of China but was officially dissolved in 1930. The concept of "half" in "28 and a Half" emerged from the "ten-day conference" in the summer of 1929, at which one of the 29 attending the conference (Xu Yixin, 1911–1994) hesitated about whether to set up a Party branch. Within China, the mocking description of "28 and a half" men served to castigate the CPC members who failed to Sinicize Marxist theory. In fact, Wang Ming, Zhang Wentian and Wang Jiaxiang did not attend the "ten-day conference". In 1966, Kang Sheng, then an adviser to the Central Cultural Revolution Group and a member of the Standing Committee of the Politburo of the CPC Central Committee, said: "There was not a single good man among the twenty-eight and a half". Those members of the group who were still living on the mainland were all subject to political investigation, with some of them imprisoned or even persecuted to death (e.g., Chen Changhao [1906–1967], Ms. Zhang Qinqiu [1904–1968], Wang Shengrong [1907–2006]). Sheng Zhongliang (1907–2007), one of the "28 and a half" Party members, published (under the name Yueh Sheng, Sheng Chung-liang) *Sun Yat-sen University in Moscow and the Chinese Revolution: A Personal Account* (Lawrence, Kansas, 1971) which is a useful reference for this history.

destruction of the CPC's organization, many of the party's senior cadres were arrested, such as Gu Shunzhang (1904–1935) and Xiang Zhongfa who were successively arrested and betrayed by the party. The CPC lost a large number of party members, so by the autumn of 1931, those "international" members were also willing to submit and travel to Jiangxi to find safety in the territory of Zhu De and Mao Zedong. By this time, Mao had more self-confidence and political resources, so much so that even with Soviet-trained officials on his side, he dared to speak out and insist on his own ideas, not simply obeying the views of the rest of the party. On 7 November Mao became chairman of the people's committee of the "state" founded in Ruijin and designated the Chinese Soviet Republic. There was undoubtedly conflict. The "international" faction, based on their own orthodoxy and close relations with the Comintern, tried to get Mao to follow their rules, and the party's real power was still in the hands of the "international" faction, especially after the "Ningdu Conference" in October 1932, when Mao's power was significantly weakened. Until 15 January 1934, at the Fifth Plenary Session of the Sixth Central Committee of the CPC, Mao Zedong's guerrilla tactics against the KMT's regular army to protect the Red Army forces were still criticized, so that Mao Zedong was prevented from being elevated to the Politburo of the CPC Central Committee. By July, Mao Zedong could not even attend party meetings; he was chairman of the Central Executive Committee only in name and the international faction still controlled the CPC, despite differences of opinion between Moscow's Wang Ming and Bo Gu, the leader of the Soviet region. Indeed, in history is difficult to apply moral judgments because every historical figure has opponents and supporters; both outside attacks and internal accusations are the results of a specific context. The intra-party struggles and conflicts made use of terms—"leftist", "rightist", "blind", or whatever "isms"—which often expressed how the lines and strategies of different factions were applied in political practice and power struggles, but finally only the end results and their influence can serve as the basis for historical judgments. Mao Zedong was at this time not a powerful voice and would continue to experience frustrations and endure risks, having to rely on his own assessment of situations. He would use whatever methods he could to interact with those in the party with different opinions and even different positions in battling those at least who were inflexible communist believers; at the same time, within his own team, he might adopt complex political skills in order to consolidate his influence, but eventually he achieved victory over the international faction and other leaders and attained supreme leadership in the party. In fact, it was in 1934 that, given his endless differences with Bo Gu and others, Wang Ming began to reassess Mao Zedong. In that year, with his assistance, the Comintern published "The Second Congress of the Chinese Soviet", which included Mao Zedong's report delivered at the Second Congress of the Chinese Soviet, and in the 1930s within the CPC only Wang Ming and Mao were accorded such political treatment.

After the purge of its ranks, Chiang Kai-shek's KMT was busy with the Northern Expedition and the wars between the new warlords; Chiang Kai-shek initially seemed to ignore the strength of the CPC, which provided the latter with a breather. The development of the CPC's armed forces in various parts of the country was clearly a threat to the KMT government. After the end of the Central Plains War, in December 1930 Chiang Kai-shek arranged the first encirclement of the Communists in Jiangxi. In three battles over ten or so days, the KMT army lost more than 10,000 troops and the divisional commander Zhang Huizan (1884–1931) was killed; one of the reasons for the defeat of the KMT troops was that the Communist Party implemented Mao Zedong's guerrilla tactics that enticed the KMT to advance and were well suited to fighting the regular KMT army once they entered the mountains. As a result, the Communist Party of China extended the Soviet region in Jiangxi to Guangchang, Shicheng, and Ruijin, and as far as Shanghang and Changding in western Fujian. After the defeat of the KMT's second siege, which began on 1 April 1931 and ended on 31 May, the power and area of the CPC were further expanded. Aware of the seriousness of the problem, Chiang Kai-shek soon began to personally organize a third encirclement campaign on 21 June 1931. The siege began on 1 July, when the KMT deployed 130,000 troops to surround the Communist army numbering more than 50,000. When the KMT army first conquered Lichuan, Guangchang, Ningdu, and Xingguo, Wang Jingwei and Li Zongren announced the establishment of another government in Guangzhou, forcing Chiang Kai-shek to transfer some of his troops to the border with Hunan and Guangdong. On 18 September 1931, the Japanese occupied Shenyang, using as a pretext the detonation of dynamite found by the railway lines at Liutiaogou, near Shenyang. Chiang Kai-shek, on the one hand, urged Zhang Xueliang to avoid fighting, and at the same time, in order to cope with the September 18 Incident and mobilize the army to strengthen the defenses of North China, the encirclement of the Communists was ended without announcement, the

KMT's third siege of the CPC ending on 20 September. The complex factional struggle within the KMT and the Japanese army's approach consumed Chiang Kai-shek's energy and resources, and by November, the Japanese had occupied almost the entire Northeast, so that the campaign to encircle the CPC could not proceed. Chiang Kai-shek was in trouble, and on 30 November he announced the policy of "expelling the foreign threat by first pacifying the country internally" (*rangwai bi xian annei*):

> To expel the foreign threat, we must first pacify the country internally and with unity we can withstand humiliation; there has never been a disunited country able to defeat an external enemy. Therefore, today's external threat cannot be defeated either militarily or diplomatically if we do not first seek domestic unity, otherwise we cannot succeed.[40]

On 28 January 1932, the Japanese provocations in Shanghai led to the resistance of Chen Mingshu's 19th Route Army of the KMT, and the National Government and the Japanese army signed a ceasefire agreement, which temporarily made Shanghai an area in which troops could not be garrisoned. On 9 March, the Japanese-backed state of Manchukuo

[40] Peng Ming ed., op. cit., p. 412. "In fact, Chiang Kai-shek had adopted such a strategy of "*rangwai bi xian annei*" as early as 23 July 1931, when he issued 'Declaration to All Compatriots' at his Nanchang Headquarters, in which he stated: 'We must fight for the future of the country tenaciously, making every effort to pacify the nation domestically and drive out the foreign invaders'. At this time, Chiang's problems were many: (1) the rebellion of the Guangdong and Guangxi warlords; (2) the rebellion of the warlord Shi Yousan (1891–1940); (3) the marauding 'Red bandits'; and (4) 'the massacre of Korean nationals in China'. Chiang hoped that after he resolved these domestic problems, he could lead a united national attack on the Japanese 'imperialists'. If he was to effectively drive out the 'foreign' invaders, he had to solve his domestic problems before the necessary conditions were met, and the siege of the Communists was one of his major domestic tasks. When the September 18 Incident occurred, Chiang Kai-shek also adopted a policy of 'non-resistance' and did not 'declare war', because China's national defense capacity was weak; 'if I made no announcement, then China's land, sea and air forces would not have a chance to build up, and within three days the coast and the Yangtze River basin would be ravaged by the enemy, and the nation's political, military, infrastructural and financial veins would all be cut'". (The passage is from: Ichieko Ryōko, *Jiang Jieshi yu Nanjing Guomin Zhengfu* [Chiang Kai-shek and the Nanjing National Government], Beijing: Shehui Kexue Wenxian Chubanshe, 2005, p. 143) On 26 January 1932, the editorial of the *Republic of China Daily*, "The Concretization of the Policy of Domestic Pacification and Driving out the Foreign Invader" explains the policy as follows: "By seeking political, financial and military unity, he would establish the nation as a strong and important power, and a firm foreign policy direction would win over international public opinion". (The passage is requoted from Ichieko Ryōko, op. cit., p. 144)

was established, with Puyi as Emperor, and the KMT government faced another political challenge. At the same time, the CPC was expanding its armed forces and other activities. Based on his readiness to devote all his efforts to the Anti-Japanese War, Chiang Kai-shek decided to completely eliminate the CPC and deal impartially with the warlords, removing the domestic obstacles to the Nationalist government, and finally deciding on the policy of "first securing the peace domestically and then taking on the foreign threat to the country". In February 1932, the Nationalist Government launched its fourth encirclement of the Communists, with He Yingqin as "commander-in-chief of the forces seeking to eliminate the Communist bandits in Jiangxi, Guangdong, Fujian, and Hunan". This encirclement began in January 1933 and the siege lasted 121 days, with more than 150,000 KMT troops participating. The Communist army numbered little more than 60,000 troops. Most were under the command and leadership of Mao Zedong's factional commanders, like Zhu De, Zhou Enlai, Lin Biao (1907–1971), Peng Dehuai, Chen Yi, and He Long. The KMT, through the building of fortified emplacements, the use of armor, and the establishment of vigilantes to deal with the guerrilla tactics of the CPC, repelled the Communist attacks at Jinxi, Linchuan, Nanfeng, and Le'an. However, during the encirclement, the Japanese army had advanced to Yuguan and other passes through the Great Wall, posing a serious threat to north China, and the national crisis once again forced the National government to move its troops to the north. Wanting to eliminate the Communist Party forces as soon as possible while making final preparations for the Anti-Japanese War, and given local resistance failed to repel the Japanese offensive, the KMT signed the Tanggu Agreement with Japan on 31 May 1933. The agreement demarcated 22 counties in eastern Hebei as unarmed areas (stipulating that "all Chinese troops will quickly withdraw to the south and west of a line connecting Yanqing, Changping, Gaoliying, Shunyi, Tongzhou, Xianghe, Baodi, Lintingkou, Ninghe, and Lutai, a line which subsequently cannot be crossed") in an attempt to ease the Japanese military offensive. Hu Shi regarded this as "a last ditch resort".[41] For Chiang Kai-shek, anything that delayed all-out warfare with Japan and gave him the opportunity to strengthen his armed forces was utterly necessary. For almost a year from 17 October 1933 to 14 October 1934, Chiang Kai-shek accepted the

[41] Hu Shi, "The Importance of Protecting All of North China", *Duli Pinglun* (Independent Critique), joint no. 52–53 issue.

advice of Alexander von Falkenhausen, a German officer who proposed blockading the Chinese Soviet with a network of forts and roads, and so launched a fifth campaign of encirclement. Under Chiang Kai-shek's personal command was the 800,000-man strong KMT army, confronting the 150,000-strong Communist Army whose previously invincible guerrilla tactics were now unable to withstand the KMT encirclement. During the winter of 1933, the Communists now negotiated resisting Japan with Chen Mingshu whose 19th Route Army had earlier fought the Japanese in Shanghai before being transferred to Fujian to take part in encirclement of the Communists: the two sides ceased military operations and secretly signed a Preliminary Agreement to Resist Japan and Chiang Kai-shek on 26 October. The organization and activities of the Red Army in Fujian were protected by the Fujian Provincial Government and the 19th Route Army, and Chen Mingshu, Jiang Guangnai (1888–1967), Cai Tingkai (1892–1968), and Xu Qian (1871–1940) announced the establishment of the "Republic of China's People's Revolutionary Government" on 22 November, with the name of the army changed to the "People's Revolutionary Army" to confront Chiang Kai-shek's KMT Government. However, because the Chinese Communist Party doubted the revolutionary nature of Fujian, and finally based their decisions on the judgment of the Comintern, they ultimately did not provide military reinforcements to the Fujian People's Revolutionary Government as partners.[42] For example, at the Second National Congress of the Chinese

[42] In-depth study of the KMT political and military system in the 1920s and 1930s is a separate topic, but here we can simply note that the KMT's factional struggles continued throughout this period. The leading members of the 19th Route Army were formerly the 4th Regiment of the First Division of the Guangdong Army, which was established in 1921 during the period of cooperation between Sun Yat-sen and Chen Jiongming. Chen was the regimental commander, while Jiang Guangnai, Cai Tingkai, Dai Ji (1895–1973), and Chen Jitang (1890–1954) served as officers under him. The KMT's conservatism and weakness led to Chen's discontent after the 1930s, but within the party, Chen and Chiang Kai-shek drew closer, which is why he did not participate when Sun Ke and Wang Jingwei formed a rebel government in Guangzhou in May 1931. Prior to the "28 January Incident", Chen Mingshu was regarded as a political renegade, because of his links with the AB Regiment and his political views being close to those of the CPC Trotskyites. Although Chinese highly praise the 19th Route Army's bravery in Shanghai, the 19th Route Army did not receive the consent of the Nanjing government from the beginning to engage the Japanese army in Shanghai—but more than 40 million Chinese people donated money to support the 19th Route Army, which increased its forces to carry out a strong attack, but it was forced to withdraw after 33 days having received no reinforcements from the National Government. In May 1932, the 19th Route Army

Soviet Republic from 24 to 25 January 1934, Mao Zedong presented the government report which stated: "As for the so-called People's Revolutionary Government in Fujian, a comrade said that it was somewhat revolutionary in nature and not entirely reactionary, but that is incorrect. ... The People's Revolutionary Government was nothing more than a trick of the ruling class who used the false slogan of a 'third path between communism and reactionary politics to deceive the people".[43] On the other hand, on 22 November, Chiang Kai-shek published his *Letter to All Generals of the 19th Route Army*, which read:

> It is reported that fellows like Chen Mingshu and Li Jishen secretly occupied Fuzhou, and using the name of our 19th Route Army, together with the reactionaries of the third party, the Social Democracy Party, advocated uniting with the CPC, betrayed the KMT and resisted the National Government, organizing an incarnation of the CPC called the Production Party and establishing a so-called People's Revolutionary Government. They abandoned the Party's premier and the Party and state flags that had flown openly since the revolution, and flew instead their rebel flag with blue above, red below and five yellow stars. This was in the critical times of national difficulties, when the entire country stood together to encircle and eliminate the CPC, so their actions endangered the Party and State, which was truly a difficult situation to resolve.[44]

was transferred by Chiang Kai-shek to Jiangxi province to join the encirclement of the Communists, but Chen Mingshu and others did not seem to have much interest in besieging the CPC, given Chen's attempts to devote energy and resources to solving Fujian's social and economic problems. Finally, various grievances and conflicting views led to the eventual breakdown of cooperation between Chen Mingshu's group and Chiang Kai-shek, but Chen's agreement with the CPC was also never effectively implemented. Differences between them eventually became so great, each party went its own way. The CPC Central Committee on 25 December 1935, in its document "CPC Central Committee on the Current Political Situation and the Party's Mission" revealed: "In the past, the Red Army did not use its strength in a timely fashion to directly help the 19th Route Army (nor did 19th Route Army actively demand assistance) to break Chiang Kai-shek's attack on Fujian, which was wrong". (Peng Ming ed., op. cit., p. 467) Mao Zedong made a similar assessment to Edgar Snow, saying that one of the mistakes made during the Fujian events in 1933 was failing to join up with Cai Tingkai's forces. (Edgar Snow, *Red Star over China*, Chinese translation title: *Xixing Manji*, Beijing: Waiyu Jiaoxue yu Yanjiu Chubanshe, 2005, p. 284)

[43] 1 August 1934, in *Hongse Zhonghua* (Red China), quoted by Gao Hua, op. cit., p. 66.

[44] Peng Ming ed., op. cit., vol. 4, p. 63.

In January 1934, the 19th Route Army, which had won a reputation for its anti-Japanese resistance, was suppressed by Chiang Kai-shek's KMT forces, and the 19th Route Army became the Seventh Route Army of the National Army. Despite the increasingly serious situation in North China, Chiang Kai-shek still hoped to successfully complete his siege of the CPC and fully prepare for squarely taking on the Japanese army.[45] On the other hand, the strategy of deploying a "swift blitzkrieg" against the Communists, as proposed by his German adviser Li De (aka Otto Braun or Albert Chey, 1900–1974), was unsuccessful. Pushed back by the KMT's tactical use of intensive fortifications, on 28 April, the Communists were defeated in the Battle of Guangchang, and again on 6 October, in the Battle of Shicheng. On 18 October, the CPC officially abandoned its Jiangxi base and, in order to preserve its strength to minimize regular battles with the KMT army, moved its main force south. The 80,000-strong Chinese Red Army began the strategic retreat known as the "25,000 *li* Long March", and contact was lost between Moscow and the CPC. Although the KMT had established a tight military blockade line, Chiang Kai-shek possibly hesitated and allowed the main Communist force of 40,000 people to pass through, only to cut them off at the rear, his aim being to allow the main force to move into the southwest and pose a threat to local warlords, removing any friction and conflict surrounding the KMT army marching into the southwest—pursuing the CPC's armed forces could later also provide sufficient reason for the KMT Central Army successfully entering these remote areas. At the same time, Chiang Kai-shek's son, Chiang Ching-kuo, who had been studying in the Soviet Union since 1925, was still in Stalin's hands in the Soviet Union, and he did not want to lose his son by totally annihilating the Communists. On 10 November, Chiang Kai-shek's army entered Ruijin, and in the first half of

[45] Chiang Kai-shek wrote in his diary on April 5, 1934: "The Japanese bandits want to conquer and incorporate Hebei into the northeast and destroy our government before 1936 to solve their China problem. But it is the dream of a sick man, which we must now endure". (From Jin Chongji, op. cit., vol. 2, p. 351)

the following year, he announced the end of the KMT's fifth siege of the CPC's Jiangxi Soviet.[46]

In January 1935, the Chinese Communist Army occupied Zunyi, Guizhou. At the beginning of the Long March, the Communist Party's ranks were led and directed by the Comintern's early "three-man clique" comprising the military adviser Li De, together with Bo Gu and Zhou Enlai. However, the opposition, led by Mao Zedong, repeatedly questioned Li De's military command and its results. Although Wang Jiaxiang and Zhang Wentian were members of the Comintern faction, they were often in disagreement with Bo Gu's views. Mao Zedong took advantage of their differences to win their support, treating Wang Jiaxiang as the "Red professor". Yet Zhang Wentian was at this time taking over the role of "chairman" of the People's Committee formerly held by Mao Zedong. The three of them soon joined up as the party's alternate "three-man clique" and began to change the Party's power structure, attempting to topple Li De and Bo Gu from their positions, in order to change the dismal fate of the Party. They won the support of Zhu De, Zhou Enlai, and others, and resolved to convene an expanded meeting of the Politburo as soon as possible. At that meeting, Bo Gu, Zhou Enlai, and Li De were investigated and confessed their errors in the military line in leading the Long March. The town of Zunyi provided the conditions for the conference. An anxious Bo Gu agreed to the proposal of the new "three-man clique" to hold a conference in Zunyi which had been temporarily secured, in order to sum up the reasons why the Red base had been lost. The conference, held from 15 to 17 January, was attended by 20 people (18 full members and 2 non-voting participants),

[46] Fang Zhimin's northward anti-Japanese advance team was annihilated by the KMT in January 1935; the defensive forces of Xiang Ying and Chen Yi left behind were largely wiped out by the end of March, and their remnants were driven deep into the mountains; on 18 June, Qu Qiubai, who had been arrested in mid-March, was executed in Changding, Fujian province; and remnant Communist forces scattered in southwestern Fujian, the border areas of Hunan, Hubei and Jiangxi, in eastern and northern Fujian, and in the border areas of Anhui, Zhejiang and Jiangxi were all completely annihilated.

and after Bo Gu and Zhou Enlai separately presented political and military reports, Mao Zedong made a strong attack on Bo Gu's previous military decisions. This was, in fact, an attack on the previous Comintern line, after which Wang Jiaxiang, Zhang Wentian, Zhou Enlai, and Zhu De all presented critical comments. The atmosphere and effect of the meeting supported Mao Zedong: the responsibility for the party's earlier failure was ascribed to Li De, and especially to the party secretary, Bo Gu. The conference proceedings were finally drafted by Zhang Wentian, "The CPC Central Committee's Summary Resolution on Opposing the Enemy's Fifth 'Encirclement'", and condemned and criticized Bo Gu and his summary report. The "Resolution" denied Bo Gu's statement that the reasons the central Soviet base failed to crush the fifth encirclement should be "attributed to the superior strength of the imperialist and KMT reactionary forces". Its sharp repudiation of the previous "pure line of defense" resulted in Li De being no longer allowed to dabble in military leadership and command; Zhou Enlai remained the top military leader, Bo Gu continued to be party secretary, and Mao Zedong became a member of the Standing Committee of the Politburo. After the conference, Mao Zedong, through a decision of the Secretariat, became "the assistant to Comrade Enlai's military command"—quickly becoming one of the three members of the new military command team (March 1935); Wang Jiaxiang was for health reasons soon unable to work on the team, and Zhou Enlai, who had no qualifications to be the supreme leader but was a suitable assistant, deferred to Mao. In early February, though not through the party's strict organizational procedures, Bo Gu was replaced by Zhang Wentian. Because Zhang had been trained in Moscow, it was felt such a change would not make the Comintern uneasy. By this time Zhang followed Mao Zedong's practical advice, so with Zhang's support Mao became the actual supreme leader of the Communist Party. In any case, the Zunyi Conference was a defining moment for Mao Zedong, from which more and more people in the party decided that the Communist Party was beginning to move from defeat to victory.[47] However, after the Zunyi Conference, the Red Army's numbers were reduced by half.[48]

[47] There are no specific statistics which demonstrate that the Red Army suffered significant losses as a result of the fighting before the start of the Long March. By the time it arrived in Zunyi, the Red Army had shrunk from about 80,000 to less than 50,000, in large part because soldiers who had not joined the Red Army for a long time left the army midway through the march. However, in the available material, there is no evidence that Bo Gu's replacement by Zhang Wentian was formally voted on or was in line with the party's disciplinary procedures. Chen Yun's manuscript account records: "In the march from Zunyi to Weixin, the Standing Committee separately decided to replace Comrade Bo Gu with Comrade Luo Fu as the leader with overall responsibility". Yet, according to Zhou Enlai's memoirs, "The chairman sought me out to say that Luo Fu would now be taking over from him as leader" and "convinced everyone that at that time Luo Fu had taken over". In his account *Zhongguo Jishi* (China Chronicle), Li De wrote that after the Zunyi Conference, "Mao simply joined the Politburo Standing Committee, having already been a member of the Politburo. Bo Gu to begin with remained general secretary, but a month later, in February 1935, after a long hesitation, he agreed to cede his position to Luo Fu, but continued to serve as a member of the Politburo and secretary of the Central Committee". However, there is information that after the arrest of Xiang Zhongfa for treason, the Provisional/Interim CC Politburo decided not to have a general secretary. Bo Gu mentioned at a meeting of the Politburo on 13 November 1943 that the Interim Politburo "went to a meeting at a hotel (comprising four men: Ming, Zhou, Lu, Bo) and they decided not to have a general secretary. At that time, they decided that I would be secretary, though my real position was general secretary, but at the CC meeting there was no decision about my being general secretary". (See: *Hongse Juece: Zhongguo Gongchandang Zhongda Huiyi Shilu* [Red Decision-Making: A Record of Major Meetings of the CPC], Hunan Renmin Chubanshe, pp. 93–94; Peng Ming ed., op. cit., vol. 4, pp. 340–342)

[48] In September 1984, the Central Committee for the Collection of Party History Materials, together with the Central Archives, edited and published the "Zunyi Conference Documents" in order to highlight the importance of the Zunyi Conference for the leadership of Mao Zedong over the whole Party and the whole army as described in "Resolution on Several Historical Issues Since the Founding of the People's Republic of China". The "Counter-Report" by Zhang Wentian, criticizing the military line of the "Three-Man Regiment", was drafted and adopted at the Zunyi Meeting, but it was merely mentioned but dismissed as unimportant in "Resolution of the Enlarged Meeting of the Political Bureau of the Central Committee: Summary of the CPC Central Committee on Opposing the Enemy's Five Encirclements and Suppressions, Reviewing the Mistakes of the Military Line of Comrades Bo Gu, Zhou Enlai, and Li De". On 20 March 1943, the Central Committee of the Communist Party of China issued its "Decision on the Adjustment and Streamlining of the Central Organs", with Mao Zedong as the "Chairman of the Politburo", which was composed of Mao Zedong, Liu Shaoqi, and Ren Bishi, with Mao Zedong as the "Chairman of the Secretariat". Zhang Wentian's time as general secretary of the Communist Party of China from 1935 to 1943 was no longer mentioned in later Party history. (See: He Fang, *Dangshi Biji: Cong Zunyi Huiyi dao Yan'an Zhengfeng*

On 14 June 1935, Mao Zedong's troops (numbering more than 10,000) and Zhang Guotao's Red Fourth Army (more than 70,000) joined forces at Maogong in northwestern Sichuan Province; later the two armies marched northwards to Lianghekou on 24 June, where the two leaders disputed where to march next. Mao wanted to go to northern Shaanxi, but Zhang Guotao wanted to go southwards to the Sichuan-Xikang border to establish a base there. Finally, on 5 August, at a meeting in Maoergai, they decided to go to northern Shaanxi. In September, the Communist army was defeated in battle by the KMT army, and possibly in the absence of joint consultation, Mao Zedong and Peng Dehuai, Lin Biao and Ye Jianying separately led the First and Third regiments of more than 6000 soldiers in the name of the "Red Army's Shaanxi-Gansu Guerrilla Brigade" in flight to near Xigu in south-western Gansu, but due to a lack of understanding of the area's natural geography the troops suffered massive losses.[49] In response to Mao Zedong's decision, an angry Zhang Guotao rebuilt the CPC Central Committee in Zhuokeji together with Zhu De and Liu Bocheng. At this time, Wang Ming in Moscow had only just learned from Chen Yun and his team after their arrival there of the basic events at the Zunyi Conference.[50]

(Notes on Party History: From the Zunyi Conference to the Yan'an Rectification), Vols. 1 and 2, Hong Kong Lee Wen Publishing House, April 2005).

[49] Wang Ming recalled in his memoirs: "When the troops set out, they did not have adequate material security (first and foremost, they had inadequate reserves of food and winter clothing) nor had they been provided with required information about the climate, nature, and other conditions in these snowy mountains and marshes. As a result, the Red Army's First and Third regiments suffered much heavier losses than other forces. In September 1935, for example, the First and Third had respectively 17,000 and 8000 troops on the ground, but as a result of the mass deaths of soldiers, the army soon had only 5000 men left. Moreover, in October, after two small battles, the regiments gained reinforcements, but they still only totaled 5700 men. Ref: Wang Ming, *Zhonggong Wushi Nian* (50 Years of the Communist Party of China), Dongfang Chubanshe, 2004, pp. 24–25.

[50] Although Chen Yun's article "The Heroic Long March" (*The Communist International*, Chinese Edition, 1–2 joint issue, 1936) introduced the conditions of the Red Army during its twelve-day break in Zunyi, it made no mention of the Zunyi Conference. Chen Yun explained to Wang Ming: "This was neither a party congress nor a central plenary meeting, but at best only a regular meeting of the Politburo, so why mention it?" Chen Yun added details of what was discussed at the meeting: "Two of the leadership positions were changed; Mao Zedong had long wanted to succeed Zhou Enlai as a member of the General Political Committee, so he formed an alliance with Luo Fu on the condition that

On 19 October Mao's forces of just over 2000 troops arrived in Wuqi town, 50 kilometers from Yan'an, to meet up with Xu Donghai and Liu Zidan, leaders of the Red Fifteenth Army, which numbered less than 10,000. The reorganization of the Red Army and the revamped leadership of the CPC made it very clear Mao Zedong already held the power within the party: Zhang Wentian was general secretary of the Party, Liu Shaoqi was secretary of the Workers' Movement Committee, and Zhou Enlai was secretary of the Working Committee in White Districts (KMT-ruled districts); military leaders included Ye Jianying, Lin Biao, Nie Rongzhen and Peng Dehuai, while Mao Zedong was chairman of the Soviet's Central Executive Committee, and Qin Bangxian was chairman of the Soviet Central People's Committee. However, under the pressure from the KMT army, the territory of the Soviet in northern Shaanxi was reduced, and in July 1936, the Central Committee of the CPC moved from Wuqi to Bao'an. Despite internal contradictions, but based on the possibility of survival and development, the armies of Zhang Guotao and He Long hemmed in by the KMT army were finally able to rendezvous at Huining with the Red Army of Northern Shaanxi in late October. However, Zhang Guotao was not willing to submit to Mao Zedong's control, and proposed the establishment of a Western Route Army, which he would separately lead: Xu Xianqian's led army did not fight the KMT army and was driven back, which finally left him with only slightly more than 700 men when he arrived back in northern Shaanxi; Zhang Guotao and He Long led a force of 15,000 men, but in mid-November, these Red Army troops were surrounded by KMT troops at Tongxin town, and the Communist Party of Northern Shaanxi, located not too far from Tongxin was also under serious threat from the KMT army. Now, only political tactics could ease the threat to the party. On 1 December 1936, the Central Committee of the CPC wrote an open letter in the name of the leaders of the Chinese Workers and Peasants Red Army (with nineteen signatories including Mao Zedong, Zhu De, Zhang Guotao, Zhou Enlai, Peng Dehuai, He Long, and Lin Biao) expressing the hope that Chiang Kai-shek would end his siege of the Red Army and resist Japan together with them.

As early as May 1935, when the Japanese army entered eastern Hebei, the KMT went on to sign a compromise agreement with Japan, and

he would replace Bo Gu as secretary. Now that the problem was resolved, what need is there for further discussion?" (Wang Ming, *ibid*., pp. 29–30)

in October the Japanese foreign minister Hiroda issued three principles governing Sino-Japanese relations: 1, China would cease its anti-Japanese actions; 2, Japan and China would cooperate economically, with Japan having responsibility for industry, and China for agriculture; 3, on the basis of mutual defense against Communism, the Japanese army could station troops in China. This signaled that Chiang Kai-shek knew that the Anti-Japanese War was about to break out, but he did not have enough resources to deal with the various local Communist forces and those warlords who used the "anti-Japanese" banner to rival the KMT government. After the KMT purged its ranks and broke off diplomatic relations with the Soviet Union, the National Government once again hoped to achieve cooperation of the Soviet Union in order to acquire more resources and power to resist the advance of the Japanese army. At the same time, the Comintern also hoped through the establishment of a strategy of a "united front of anti-fascist peoples" to expand world-wide cooperation and, if the KMT continued the siege of the CPC, it would fail to win support from the Soviet Union, so the KMT could not but relax its siege of the CPC and adjust its political strategy. At this time, calls for a national people's anti-Japanese resistance were coming from every part of China, and in this time of national crisis the encirclement of the Red Army of fellow Chinese lost its appeal. At the 7th World Congress of the Communist International, from 25 July to 20 August, Chen Shaoyu (Wang Ming) on behalf of the Central Committee of the CPC and the Chinese Soviet government, issued the "Declaration to All Compatriots Calling for Resistance to Japan and the Salvation of the Nation" or the "August 1st Declaration", which stated: "As long as the KMT troops stop attacking the Soviet base and only use their forces against Japan, regardless of past and present feuds with the Red Army and regardless of any differences between them and the Red Army on internal issues, the Red Army will not only immediately cease hostilities, but will also willingly work hand in hand with them to save the country".[51] However, on 13 November of that year, the Communist Party of China issued domestically "Declaration of the Central Committee of the Communist Party of China that the Japanese Imperialists Are Annexing North China and Chiang Kai-shek Is Selling out North China" which contained the following call:

[51] Peng Ming ed., op. cit., p. 375.

> The masses of all China! All mobilize together! Arm, organize, support and participate in the war against the Japanese and Chiang Kai-shek led by the Communist Party of China! Only with the general mobilization of the entire nation and resolute armed struggle can we achieve final victory in the anti-Japanese anti-Chiang Kai-shek struggle. All anti-Japanese and anti-Chiang Chinese people and armed forces, regardless of party, creed, gender, occupation, and age, should unite to overthrow the Japanese imperialists and Chiang Kai-shek's KMT and win victory in this bloody battle! We should use all means of struggle---workers' strikes, peasant uprisings, soldier mutinies, businessmen's strikes, military and police strikes, mass demonstrations, guerrilla warfare, and any other military action against Chiang, to fight against Japanese imperialism and the national traitor Chiang Kai-shek. The Chinese Soviet government and the Workers and Peasants Red Army are willing to willing to join with any armed forces that oppose the Japanese and Chiang Kai-shek, and are willing to assist all anti-Japanese and anti-Chiang organizations in any way.[52]

On 25 December 1935, the main leaders of the CPC, Mao Zedong, Zhang Wentian, Zhou Enlai, Bo Gu, Liu Shaoqi, Deng Fa (1906–1946), and Zhang Hao (Lin Yuying, 1897–1942), who had returned from Moscow to convey the spirit of the "Seventh Congress" of the Comintern, met in Wayaopu. The meeting studied the current political situation and strategy, as well as the future military strategy. Zhang Wentian drafted the *Resolution* of the CPC Central Committee on the Current Political Situation and the Party's Task in accordance with the requirements of the Comintern to establish a united front against fascism. The *Resolution* proposed the establishment of a common national defense government and anti-Japanese coalition of all classes and groups under the leadership of the CPC, and stressed that it was a "union of all classes", so that all troops willing to resist Japan could become members of the anti-Japanese coalition. The CPC took advantage of the country's plight in the hope of expanding its power and sphere of influence, including its territory, so it announced the change of the Soviet Republic of Workers and People's into the Soviet People's Republic, which it hoped would become the legitimate political center for Chinese people from all walks of life. Although the *Resolution* stressed that the main danger within the party was a "closed-door policy" (*guanmen-zhuyi*), the CPC extended the anti-Japanese national salvation movement to cities across

[52] Peng Ming ed., op. cit., pp. 379–380.

the country and tried to establish a broad anti-Japanese national united front.[53] However, Chiang Kai-shek was still described in the *Resolution* as a "traitor" (*maiguozei*). In June 1936 the Guangxi&Guangdong Incident 'opposing to Chiang and resisting the Japanese' was started.[54] Mao Zedong saw this as an opportunity for the survival of the CPC, and he continued to stress the need to integrate forces against Chiang, but the CPC's proposal to establish an anti-Japanese coalition with the Southwest was rejected. Beginning in July, the situation changed dramatically, and Chiang Kai-shek finally reached a compromise with the leaders of Guangdong and Guangxi, Chen Jitang and Li Zongren. In view of this, in order to win more popular support and follow the Comintern's directive, the injunction to oppose Chiang finally disappeared from CPC documents. In fact, as early as the autumn of 1935, Pan Hannian (1906–1977), appointed by the CPC to lead its delegation to the Comintern, on his way through Hong Kong held negotiations with Zhang Chong (1904–1941) who had been appointed by Chen Guofu (1892–1951) to negotiate a ceasefire to resist Japan; subsequently, the CPC's search for a ceasefire and

[53] The first person in the Party to propose the "anti-Japanese national united front" was Wang Ming. In November 1934, Wang Ming put forward this slogan in "New Conditions and New Strategies", and in August 1935, after the Seventh Congress of the Comintern, Wang Ming drafted "Declaration to Compatriots for Resistance to Japan and National Salvation" (August First Declaration) (October), and in November, Wang Ming proposed "allying with Chiang against Japan" in a new article.

[54] In the 1930s, Chiang Kai-shek faced off against Guangdong and Guangxi in a struggle with all the local warlords and military generals. After the crackdown on the 19th Route Army and the removal of the Communist Red Army from Jiangxi, Chiang Kai-shek's army began to approach the provinces of Guangdong and Guangxi. This posed a huge threat to local forces in Guangxi led by Li Zongren and Bai Chongxi, and to Li Jitang in Guangdong. The two provinces' leaders sought to demonstrate the legitimacy of their forces by retaining Hu Hanmin, a KMT veteran who returned to Guangdong after Chiang Kai-shek released him, from custody, but Hu's death (9 May 1936) deprived them of the opportunity. On 1 June, the leaders of the two provinces urged the Nanjing government to promote anti-Japanese resistance and they renamed their troops the Revolutionary Army of Resistance to Japan and of National Salvation. This army's plan to leave for north China was blocked by the Nanjing government. The two sides had different considerations—the leaders of the two provinces knew that their forces were not hostile to Nanjing and Chiang Kai-shek did not want a civil war at this time, so the two sides finally reached a compromise: Guangxi would come under the command of Nanjing, with Li Zongren appointed director of the Guangxi Pacification Office and Bai Chongxi a member of the KMT Military Conference Executive Committee, while Guangdong's Chen Jitang fled to Hong Kong.

shared resistance to Japan did not stop.[55] On 5 May 1936, Mao Zedong and Zhu De jointly issued "Telegram Calling for Ceasefire and Consistent with Resistance to Japan", and the CPC quickly advanced the possibility of effecting a ceasefire with the KMT. On 25 August, the CPC issued an open letter calling for the establishment of a KMT-CPC united front, abandoning the slogans calling for opposition to Chiang Kai-shek. On 1 September, the Central Committee of the CPC resolved to "force Chiang to resist Japan". On 17 September the Politburo of the CPC Central Committee decided to replace their "Soviet Republic" with a "democratic republic".

After the Tanggu Agreement, Zhang Xueliang's Northeast Army was transferred from the Beiping-Tianjin region to Shaanxi to encircle the CPC; in accordance with Chiang Kai-shek's deployment, if the armies of Zhang Xueliang and Yang Hucheng had been added the KMT armies, the winter of 1936 would likely have seen the total collapse of the CPC.

Indeed, Chiang Kai-shek had difficulty making headway with his strategy of "prioritizing domestic stability and unity over national defense", and most people tended to agree that at present, given the problems facing the nation, priority should be given to the threat to the nation, which trapped Chiang Kai-shek in a dilemma in his political and military operations. Coupled with the complex international situation and political background, Chiang Kai-shek is unable to bring the Soviet Union completely around to the KMT side, and using only existing resources to fight a war of resistance poses a problem that call for effective action. At the same time, the CPC is clearly the weaker enemy of the KMT, and the CPC's own survival and the development of their own strength are

[55] In December 1935, the CPC's underground party in Shanghai arranged for Zhang Zihua (1914–1942) to go to Nanjing to negotiate with the head of the KMT in Hong Kong, Zeng Yangfu (1898–1969). In May 1936, Chen Lifu and Zeng's classmate Chen Xiaocen (1897–1992, a person considered "very pro-Communist" by Chen Lifu, and to have "friends in the CPC") asserted: 1, welcome the armed forces of the CPC to participate in the anti-Japanese war; 2, when the CPC's forces take part in fighting the Japanese, they will be regarded in the same way as the KMT's central army; 3, if the Communists have any grievances they can voice their views to an organ for handling democratic views yet to be established; 4, the Communists can select a region where they would be free to experiment with their political and economic ideals. On 31 August, Zhou Enlai wrote to Zeng Yangfu: "The national crisis is at a critical juncture, and without unity we cannot achieve anything". On 1 September, Zhou Enlai sent a letter to Chen Guofu, calling on the KMT and CPC to "cooperate once again so the country's fortunes can be turned around with such a move".

still the main tasks they face. In several rounds of negotiation at different levels, the questions of recognition of the KMT's leadership and whether or not the CPC army retained its independence were at the heart of the debate between the two parties. In October 1936, after several rounds of negotiations and exchanges of documents between the two sides, the *Draft Agreement between the KMT and CPC on Resistance to Japan and National Salvation* took shape in October 1936:

1. From the date of the signing of this Agreement, the two sides immediately cease their military hostilities.
2. The KMT side agrees that the National Government Military Commission will order the cessation of attacks on the Red Army and assaults on the Soviet region, and lift its economic blockade. It acknowledges that after separate consultations it will, on the one hand, redeploy forces used to attack the Red Army away from their present areas to take part in the Anti-Japanese War; on the other hand, a suitable base for the Red Army must be demarcated and, all necessary military materiel, food and personnel supplies provided, so that the Red Army has peace of mind in fighting the Japanese. The CPC side agrees that the Soviet Government's Revolutionary Military Commission will order the Red Army not to attack KMT forces, and that in the anti-Japanese war they will not change the organization and leadership of the Communist Party personnel in the Red Army. All the nation's armed forces, including the Red Army, will implement a unified organizational and command structure, with the Red Army responsible for defined lines of defense and battle lines.
3. The KMT side agrees to reform the current political system, abolish all laws restricting democratic rights, the freedom of speech, publication, assembly and association, to punish all Chinese traitors and pro-Japanese elements, release political prisoners, release arrested Communist Party members, and no longer undermine Communist Party organizations or arrest Communist Party personnel. For its part, the CPC agrees that it will stop statements calling for overthrowing the KMT regime and actions designed to overthrow it, and that when a democratic republic is established throughout the country and a national parliament calls for elections by universal suffrage, representatives of the Soviet regions will be elected as

representatives to the National Congress, and that the Soviet regions will implement the same democratic system as the whole country.

4. The KMT and CPC jointly acknowledge that, prior to the convening of the all-China National Congress and the establishment of democratic government, in order to carry out a real armed war against Japan, it is necessary to convene an Anti-Japanese National Salvation Congress or the National Defense Conference based on the election by all factions, walks of life and military forces in the country, and that such an anti-Japanese National Salvation Congress or National Defense Conference has the power to decide on all anti-Japanese and national salvation policies and programs.
5. The KMT and the CPC jointly acknowledge that, in order to carry out genuine armed resistance against Japan, there is a need to quickly establish a unified military command organ (military commission and general command) throughout the country, and through this military command organ take all practical military steps against Japan. The KMT acknowledges that the Red Army Military Commission and their General Command will need to send representatives to the National Military Commission and the General Command and ensure that their representatives carry out their work smoothly; the CPC acknowledges that KMT personnel will hold the leading positions in this organ.[56]

This "draft agreement" shows that the CPC made a clear compromise with the KMT on the question of leadership, by recognizing the KMT's dominant position in the country's military command and accepting the KMT's terms for the reorganization of the Red Army and the restructuring of the Soviet. Even so, the defeat of the Red Army in the Ningxia campaign in mid-to-late October led Chiang Kai-shek to change the terms of cooperation, and he even asked the Red Army to retain only 3000 soldiers, which led the CPC to believe that the KMT might have been hoping to eliminate the CPC through cooperation, so subsequently, there was no positive progress in negotiations between the two parties. On the other hand, in late November, during the Battle of Shanchengpu, the Red

[56] "Telegram of Luo Fu and Mao Zedong to Zhu De, Zhang Guoxuan, and Xu Qiangqian", 11 October 1936, see *Selected Documents of the Central Committee of the Communist Party of China regarding the Anti-Japanese National United Front Document*, vol. 2, Beijing: Archives Press, 1985, pp. 287–290.

Army under Peng Dehuai destroyed a whole brigade led by Hu Zongnan (1896–1962), and this military victory gave the CPC confidence that it could maintain its position and sue for peace through military confrontation. As a result, the negotiations on cooperation between the KMT and CPC reached a complete impasse, and the CPC was still fighting to wrest any possible advantage.

Zhang Xueliang and Yang Hucheng, influenced by the "anti-Japanese national united front" strategy of the CPC, on 12 December 1936 conspired and kidnapped Chiang Kai-shek in Xi'an (at the same time Zhang Xueliang organized a plane to fly to Yan'an and bring Zhou Enlai, Yan Jianying and Bo Gu to Xi'an), and on the 13th, Zhang and Yang issued a telegram "to the nation", putting forward eight propositions for national salvation, and informed the CPC of discussions on how to move forward. This was the "Xi'an Incident". Zhang Xueliang and Yang Hucheng's move had been anticipated at an early date.[57] and on 17 October, *Salvation Times* (Jiuguo Shibao), a Chinese newspaper in Paris, had reported[58]:

> According to a cable from Beiping of 12 October, the AAP journalist [Edgar] Snow, who after returning to Beiping from a trip to Shaanxi, reported that troops of Zhang Xuellang stationed in Shaanxi, who were mostly northeasterners, were particularly pained by the loss of their homeland, and many expressed opposition to the civil war "encirclements of the Communists" and called for resisting Japan, to "take us back to our

[57] In January 1936, Zhang Xueliang began secret negotiations with the CPC. From February to May, Zhang held secret meetings with Liu Ding (in Shanghai), Li Kenong (in Luochuan), and Zhou Enlai (in Yan'an) to discuss a KMT-CPC ceasefire and unified opposition to the Japanese. Zhang was told that the CPC's Red Army was willing to join forces with the Northeast Army to form a national defense government and anti-Japanese coalition force, and hinted at the support of the Soviet Union, with Zhang serving as the chief of the defense government and commander-in-chief of the anti-Japanese coalition forces. Zhang Xueliang even tried to get Stalin's support by arranging for Mao Zedong's son to be escorted to study in the Soviet Union. In June, Zhang and Yang signed a secret truce with the CPC.

[58] In May 1935, the CPC's delegation to the Comintern founded the Chinese newspaper, *National Salvation* (Jiuguo Bao). Its editorial department was in Moscow, but it was printed in Paris. The original editor-in-chief was Li Lisan, but after the Seventh Congress of the Comintern that position was held by Wu Yuzhang. In November 1935, the newspaper was closed by the French government but with the assistance of the French Communist Party resumed publication on 9 December, renamed *Salvation Times* (Jiuguo Shibao).

homes!" This was something you could hear at any time among the troops. On the fifth anniversary of "September 18th", a large-scale anti-Japanese conference was held in Xi'an, with more than 12,000 participants from all walks of life, and Zhang Xueliang gave a speech to the meeting and proposed anti-Japanese slogans. On 4 October the "Northeast Compatriots National Salvation Federation" was formally set up in Xi'an and, in addition to groups from all walks of life joining, many officers and soldiers under Zhang Xueliang as well as personnel from all levels of government in Shaanxi province, flocked to actively participate in the group.[59]

Not only did they respond to the anti-Japanese issue, but Zhang Xueliang and Yang Hucheng also allowed the CPC to express their dissatisfaction with the KMT Government in propaganda materials within the area under their jurisdiction. On 7 December, Chiang Kai-shek arrived in Xi'an, where he tried to arrange for Zhang Xueliang and Yang Hucheng to complete their final decisive siege of the CPC. However, previous work by the CPC had changed Zhang and Yang's view that the Japanese were pushing forward and they wanted Chiang to accept the idea of cooperating with the CPPC, but Chiang believes that such a view would expose the KMT army in its war with the Japanese to attacks from the rear by the Communists. With little knowledge of the CPC's background negotiations and cooperation with the National Government, Zhang Xueliang and Yang Hucheng shocked China and foreign countries by "kidnapping" Chiang Kai-shek in what was called the "Xi'an Incident", but the military officers who had previously been in conflict with Chiang Kai-shek did not stand by Zhang Xueliang. On the 13th, Feng Yuxiang telegrammed Zhang Xueliang, advising him to "first release Chiang back to Nanjing", expressing the hope that Zhang Xueliang would "discuss state matters with him". On the 14th, Yan Xishan asked Zhang and Yang whether "their 'peremptory act' would ultimately increase anti-Japanese forces or reduce anti-Japanese forces? Brothers, can you guarantee that this won't play out as a murderous domestic massacre?" Hu Zongnan in a telegram

[59] Chen Yimin, Jiang Pei eds., *Lao Xinwen, 1931–1939* (Old News: 1931–1939), Tianjin: Tianjin Renmin Chubanshe, 2003, p. 137. In fact, Edgar Snow in his *Red Star over China*, specifically introduced Zhang Xueliang's Northeastern Army and his relations with Yan'an. When an agreement was reached with the Communist Party, "the Red Army sent several representatives to Xi'an, put on uniforms of the Northeast Army, and joined Zhang Xueliang's staff, helping to restructure the political training methods of his army. …… This reform is carried out in extreme secrecy". (Edgar Snow, *Xixing Manji* (Red Star over China), Beijing: Waiyu Jiaoxue yu Yanjiu Chubanshe, 2005, p. 34)

on the 23rd expressed the hope that Zhang and Yang "premise their actions on mutual protection from foreign humiliation, and assume the revival of the nation to be their duty". Western media all reacted differently; some tended to regard the Incident as a Soviet "trick". The Xi'an Incident obviously disrupted the Soviet Union's plan to rely on Chiang Kai-shek leading an anti-Japanese war and preventing a possible Japanese attack on the Soviet Union. After the October Revolution, the Soviet Union had occupied Mongolia's undeveloped northern region, defined its boundaries with "Outer Mongolia" and established the People's Republic of Mongolia as a constituent member of the Soviet Federation. If the Japanese occupation of the northeast were to expand further from east to west, when they arrived and took control of the Suiyuan and Xinjiang areas of Inner Mongolia, the Soviet Union would face a direct threat from the Japanese. The Soviets were desperate to have the KMT army hold the Japanese down and shift the critical pressure onto the Kuomintang army, which was far more powerful than the armed forces of the CPC. In line with Soviet plans, on 13 December, Moscow contacted the CPC to remind them that the Xi'an Incident would trigger pro-Japanese efforts within the KMT to step up cooperation with Japan and thwart the "anti-Japanese national united front" advocated by the CPC.[60] There was of course a school of thought within the CPC that called for the assassination of Chiang.[61] On the 15th, fifteen Red Army officers, including Mao Zedong, Zhu De, Zhou Enlai, and Zhang Guotao, telegrammed the KMT and the National Government urging them: "Accept Zhang and Yang's demands, stop the civil war being re launched, remove Chiang, and deliver the verdict of the Chinese people". However, at Moscow's request, Zhou Enlai, who had arrived in Xi'an as the representative of the CPC, could only mediate in accordance with seeking a peaceful solution to the serious incident that sparked national concern. On the 16th and 20th, Moscow twice informed the CPC that it must pursue a peaceful solution to the matter, and in a telegram issued by Dimitrov on the 16th,

[60] Stalin wanted China to drag Japan into a war in order to protect the Soviet Union itself. As early as 15 August, Moscow told the CPC that the Red Army and Chiang Kai-shek's army must stop their hostilities and join forces in the war against Japan. In early September, the CPC began negotiations with the KMT. On 25 November, Germany and Japan signed an international treaty on anti-communism, forcing Stalin to demand that China draw up a joint government plan as soon as possible.

[61] The Communist Party even had a plan for Ye Jianying to go to Xi'an in August and November to discuss military cooperation and "seize Chiang" with Zhang Xueliang.

the Comintern Secretariat first clarified its position: "Zhang Xueliang's action, regardless of his intentions, will objectively only be harmful to the forces of the Chinese people to form a united front against Japan, and will only encourage Japan's aggression against China".[62] The CPC initiated a political arrangement that would "restore Chiang Kai-shek's freedom". Also on the 16th, the 30th meeting of the Political Committee of the KMT decided to promote He Yingqin as Commander-in-Chief of the "army to restore order" and assume responsibility for "sweeping away rebels"; the Nanjing government believed that by controlling Zhang and Yang it could save Chiang Kai-shek's life. William H. Donald, Zhang Xueliang's former adviser and a friend of Chiang Kai-shek, also went to Shaanxi on the 14th to help negotiate. Based on his special relationship with Zhang and Jiang, Donald played a significant role in the communication and coordination between Xi'an and Nanjing. Zhang Xueliang, on the other hand, soon found himself isolated because of his "reckless and rash" actions. He saw the bad military discipline displayed in Xi'an by Yang Hucheng's army after the Incident; he learned of Chiang's anti-Japanese strategy and of "the suffering he felt for being held responsible for national salvation" from Chiang's diary. Zhang gained new insight into the political strategy of the CPC. He also realized that he could not be the leader of a coalition government, given the nation's grave concern when it was learned from the Soviet newspapers *Pravda* and *Isvestia* that his actions had been publicly condemned by the Soviet Union.[63] Zhang decided to change his decision immediately and protect Chiang Kai-shek. Chiang maintained his position throughout and did not negotiate with Zhou Enlai after he arrived in Xi'an, which was of course a deliberate gesture. Chiang Kai-shek knew the importance of regaining

[62] From Yang Tianshi, *Jiang Jieshi yu Nanjing Guomin Zhengfu* (Chiang Kai-shek and the Nanjing National Government), Beijing: Zhongguo Renmin Daxue Chubanshe, 2007, p. 512.

[63] On 14 December an article in *Pravda* commented: "The Nanjing government is making headway, uniting all domestic forces in the anti-Japanese cause and, although the reactionaries tenaciously resist these moves, the reasons for the mutiny of Zhang Xueliang's troops are watered down by this development". "Zhang Xueliang had every opportunity to resist Japan, but if he now refuses to resist, he will simply be ceding the northeastern provinces to the Japanese without a fight. Now there are also those who opportunistically view the anti-Japanese movement and hold high the anti-Japanese flag in order to divide the country, so that China is sacrificed to foreign invaders".

his freedom, and through Nanjing he arranged for his wife Song Meiling and her brother Song Ziwen to come to Xi'an to demonstrate his willingness to negotiate. Moscow assisted the CPC to resolve the situation. Through Bo Gu, it made it known that Chiang Kai-shek's son, Chiang Ching-kuo, would be allowed to return from the Soviet Union to China to be with the beleaguered Chiang Kai-shek, and negotiations between Zhou Enlai and Chiang Kai-shek would finally happen. On 27 December, Xi'an's *Liberation Daily* reported under the headline "Sincere Undertaking: Chairman Chiang Accepts the Idea of National Salvation":

> Chairman Chiang issued the following decision to Director Yang before taking off at 4 p.m. of the 25th from Xi'an Airport:
>
> First, order the forces of the Central Government who have entered the Northeast to withdraw to Tongguan from the 25th onwards, and inform them: "If from today (25th) onwards, any troops are further engaging in civil war fighting, then I(Jiang)will have to be responsible for it";
>
> Second, stop the civil war and concentrate all national strength on national defense;
>
> Third, reshuffle the government, pool the talents of all parties, and support the anti-Japanese policy;
>
> Fourth, change foreign policy and unite with all countries sympathetic to China's national liberation;
>
> Fifth, Release all arrested leaders in Shanghai, and issue orders to that effect;
>
> Six, Full responsibility for all military and political matters in the northwestern provinces shall be given to Generals Zhang and Yang.[64]

After Chiang Kai-shek's return to Nanjing, the Communist International was still reminding the CPC not to persist with its previous mistakes: To eliminate Chiang Kai-shek and overthrow the Nanjing government they should exert themselves to establish a united battlefront, and not think that having an agreement with Chiang Kai-shek in

[64] Chen Yimin and Jiang Pei eds., op. cit., p. 149.

Nanjing was surrender, but they should at the same time to establish an alliance with Xi'an against Nanjing, because the present task is "opposing the common enemy" of Japanese imperialism.[65] On 10 February 1937, the Central Committee of the CPC contacted the Third Plenary Session of the Fifth Central Committee of the KMT and proposed five demands and four guarantees.

The five demands were:

1. Stop all civil war fighting, concentrate national strength, and be united towards the outside world;
2. Guarantee the freedom of expression, assembly, and association, and release all political prisoners;
3. Convene a meeting of representatives from all political groups, all walks of life, and all armed forces to pool national talent and jointly work for national salvation;
4. Quickly complete all preparations for the Japanese War of Resistance;
5. Improve people's lives.

Four guarantees:

1. We will stop the policy of the armed uprising against the National Government throughout the country;
2. We will change our name from Government of Workers and Peasants to the Chinese Republican Special Administration Government, and the name of the Red Army to the National Revolutionary Army, directly under the guidance of the Central Government and the Military Commission of Nanjing;
3. We will implement a democratic system of universal suffrage in the area of the Chinese Republican Special Administration Government;
4. We will stop the policy of confiscating land of landlords and resolutely implement the common platform of the anti-Japanese national united front.

[65] "Telegram from the Secretariat of the Communist International Executive Committee to the CPC Central Committee on the policy of the CPC leadership after the Xi'an Incident" (19 January 1937). See Peng Ming ed., op. cit., Beijing: Zhongguo Renmin Daxue Chubanshe, 1993, p. 571.

In the eyes of some in the KMT, the peaceful settlement concluding the Xi'an Incident did provide an important opportunity for renewed cooperation with the CPC, so that Song Qingling, He Xiangning, Feng Yuxiang, Sun Ke, Li Liejun, and others jointly proposed to the Third Plenary Session of the KMT on 15 February 1937, "taking this opportunity to restore the three major policies of Premier [Sun Yat-sen] [the alliance with Russia; unity with the CPC, and assistance to workers and peasants, ed.] to address the crisis facing the party and the nation". They based themselves on the fact that "over the past six months, the CPC has repeatedly written to our party's Central Executive Committee, proposing KMT-CPC cooperation and joint resistance to Japan, showing that unity has become the unanimous request of the people. The recent Xi'an Incident especially confirms this point".[66] The upshot was that the CPC accepted the advice of the KMT government: it stopped armed attacks on the KMT army; the Red Army changed its name to the National Revolutionary Army and accepted the command of the Military Commission of the central government in Nanjing; and the National Government accepted the "anti-Japanese national united front" proposed by the CPC. After returning to Nanjing, Chiang Kai-shek changed from being regarded as a "national traitor" to the leader of the anti-Japanese resistance, and military operations against the CPC were completely terminated. Now, although the Chinese Communist Army operated under the name of the National Government, this army was not under the control of the KMT, so the CPC acquired legitimacy without needing to accept the leadership of the KMT. Importantly, compared with the first KMT-CPC cooperation, the CPC now had control of its own base, and its political and military operations gained considerable autonomy. This provided sufficient conditions for the development of its own strength and sphere of influence. Before the Xi'an Incident, the Shaanxi loess plateau which lacked adequate food resources, population, weapons, and ammunition made conditions difficult for the CPC, and the KMT's constant sieges had deprived the CPC of the economic and military strength to continue resisting the encirclements.

[66] Peng Ming ed., op. cit., pp. 445–450.

The Beginning of Party Literature and Art

The KMT''s "purge of the party" and the accompanying massacres greatly changed the view of reality of some radical intellectuals. As an intellectual, novelist, and one of the earliest members of the CPC, Mao Dun (Shen Dehong, 1896–1981) described the mental state of some intellectuals in this period:

> The failure of the Great Revolution in 1927 saddened me and made me pessimistic, which forced me to stop and consider in what direction the revolution was moving. The principles of communism convinced me that the example of the Soviet Union was beyond reproach, but what path should the Chinese revolution follow? In the past I thought I knew, but in the summer of 1927, I found I had no idea! In the Great Revolution I saw the enemy's actions, from disguising itself as the far Left to conducting massacres of revolutionaries, and I saw all sorts of things in our own camp: on the Right from wavering and compromise to flight, and on the Left from the childish and fanatical belief to blind action. What I saw and heard at the heart of the revolution was the endless debate and the authority of the Comintern representatives; I admired their familiarity with the theories of Marxism-Leninism and their articulate volubility, but I doubted that they really understood a society as complex as China. I was shocked that the mass peasant movement in Hubei and Hunan was so easily destroyed by the White Terror and I was dismayed by the rapid failure of the Nanchang Uprising. After living such a life, I needed to stop and think alone.[67]

As early as the May Fourth and New Culture movements, intellectual circles began to divide, and during the warlord phase and the Northern Expedition the speed and complexity of these divisions characterized the special landscape of ideological and cultural circles in the 1920s, as intellectuals from different positions became deeply involved in the complexity of Chinese politics. Founded on 8 June 1921, the Creation Society was originally a literary group in Japan during the May Fourth New Culture Movement, comprising Chinese students there like Guo Moruo (1892–1978), Cheng Fangwu (1897–1984), Yu Dafu (1896–1945), Zhang Ziping (1893–1959), Tian Han (1898–1968), and Zheng

[67] Mao Dun, *Wo Zouguo de Daolu* (The Road I Travelled), vol. 2, Hong Kong: Joint Publishing Company, 1984, pp. 1–2.

Boqi (1895–1979). The early self-expression and personalities of Creation Society members thrilled young readers, although some of the members' works evoked a somewhat morbid romantic mood. With changes in the complicated political situation, the ideological tendency and position of this group changed from romantic reverie to the direction of revolutionary literature which paid attention to reality, and the debate about revolutionary literature was born.[68]

In 1927, Guo Moruo, one of the group's key members, initially wanted to bring Lu Xun into the Creation Society to signal a critical position, an idea that was soon opposed by people who returned from Japan like Cheng Fangwu who hoped "to propagate Marxism". The new members of the Creation Society who returned from Japan adopted the opposite strategy: they wanted to gain a reputation for criticizing Lu Xun. Feng Naichao (1901–1983) in the first issue of *Wenhua Pipan* (Cultural Critique) described Lu Xun as "an evasionist who views life with a drunken gaze and lacks revolutionary enthusiasm".[69] For a somewhat populist starting point, the second issue of *Cultural Critique* published "How to Build Revolutionary Literature". Its author, Li Chuli (1900–1994), asked in the article: "What class did Lu Xun belong to and for what class did he create literature? What class of person's suffering did he truly express?" The articles published by members of the Creation Society aroused Lu Xun's rebuke, which excited young readers, who launched into critique and attacks on Lu Xun. "Fascist" Among them, Guo Moruo, under the pseudonym "Du Quan", published in the first issue of the second volume of the *Creation Monthly* on 10 August 1928 "A Feudal Remnant on the Literary Front", in which he described Lu Xun simply as "a feudal proto-capitalist remnant", "a dual counterrevolutionary figure",

[68] Xia Yan (1900–1995) has described the historical background of how this period produced debates on revolutionary literature: "From the late 1920s to the early 1930s, not only China, but also the Soviet Union, Europe, and Japan saw the spread of extreme leftist ideas; Soviet literary and artistic circles had a group called "RAPP", Japanese literary and artistic circles had a group called "NAPP". Later, associates of the Creation Society and our people who had just returned from Japan were to varying extents were influenced of the left-leaning opportunism of Fukumoto Kazuo, while Chinese intellectuals were "strengthened by hatred of the KMT's murderous policies and anger over Chen Duxiu's capitulationism, which was also reflected within the CPC, so that the 'leftist' sentiment in the Party developed rapidly". (Xia Yan, op cit., p. 137)

[69] Feng Naichao, "Debates on revolutionary literature, Lu Xun, Left-wing League of Writers", *Xin Wenxue Shiliao*, 1986, no. 3.

and "an unfulfilled Fascist". This was a melee within the field of the new literature. The members of the Sun Society, founded in early 1928 in Shanghai, who included Jiang Guangci (1901–1931), Qian Xingcun (A Ying, 1900–1977), Meng Chao (1902–1976) and Yang Cunren (1901–1955), also participated in the war of criticism attacking Lu Xun; at the same time, there were also accusations and conflicts flying between the members of the Creation Society and the Sun Society and within the ranks of the Creation Society itself. However, the atmosphere was also steeped in the KMT purge of CPC members and radicals in 1927. In the eyes of radicals, reactionary and conservative forces would necessarily fight back against the forces of the revolution. At this time, Marx's theory not only provided a weapon for the CPC but also for young people with a strong rebellious spirit, not to mention that most members of the Creation and Sun societies were CPC members for whom revolution was the indispensable and fashionable doctrine of the era. Jiang Guangci in "Modern Chinese Literature and Social Life" described revolutionary literature as follows:

> The revolution moves so fast many people cannot keep up. Although literature is the expression of social life, our literature is slow to express our lives because our social life has been buffeted so forcefully by the waves of the revolution and changes have been so rapid. Although our writers use their pens keenly, no sooner has one thing been described than another has already happened, ... thus, our literature necessarily falls behind.[70]

Jiang Guangci's sense of urgency was shared by many activists, but the strife within new literature circles was soon halted by the Intervention of the CPC. Zhou Enlai, who returned from Moscow in October 1928 (having participated in the Sixth Congress of the CPC in Moscow in June and been elected a member of the Standing Committee of the Political Bureau of the CPC Central Committee, Secretary-General and Minister of Organization), decided to direct radical forces among intellectuals towards the clearer political line of the CPC. He not only directed Yang Hansheng (1902–1993), secretary of the Political Department and a CPC member at the Whampoa Military Academy, to join the Creation Society but also commissioned Li Fuchun (1900–1975), propaganda minister of the Jiangsu Provincial Committee of the CPC, to play a part

70 Liu Xiaoqing, op. cit., p. 24.

in Shanghai cultural circles. Before this, under Zhou's instructions, Yang Hansheng, Li Yimeng (1903–1990), who joined the Creation Society at the same time, and Pan Hannian (1906–1977), who was also a member of the CPC, formed a party group. Soon afterward, together with more than 20 CPC members in the Sun Society, including Jiang Guangci and A Ying, the three formed the Third Street Branch, of which Pan Hannian was branch secretary. When Li Fuchun met with Yang Hansheng to discuss measures to stop internal disputes, Yang who was already secretary of the Third Street Branch transferred to become secretary of the Cultural Branch, which brought together many intellectuals directly under the leadership of the Jiangsu Provincial Committee of the CPC. Under the organization of Pan Hannian, who was an officer of the Propaganda Department of the CPC and secretary of the newly established Cultural Work Committee, CPC members within the Creation and Sun societies reached a consensus through effective liaison meetings to stop attacking Lu Xun. Other participants included Rou Shi (1902–1931), Feng Xuefeng (1903–1976) and Xia Yan, who all had close relations with Lu Xun. In November 1929, Li Lisan, minister of propaganda of the CPC, instructed Wu Liping (1908–1986), an officer of the Central Propaganda Department who had returned from Moscow, to unite left-wing literary, artistic and cultural circles to engage in revolutionary struggle on the literary and artistic front while jointly confronting the enemy (imperialism and KMT) and ending the attack on Lu Xun. He also asked Wu to get in touch with Lu Xun. In fact, in October, eleven CPC members, including Pan Hannian, Feng Xuefeng, Xia Yan, and Yang Hansheng, participated in a meeting at the Gongfei coffee shop on the intersection of Sichuan and Darroch roads in Shanghai, to form a "Left-League" and discuss a program for a "League of Left-wing Chinese Writers" previously proposed by Li Lisan. All twelve foundational members of the Chinese Left-wing League of Writers Preparatory Committee, except Lu Xun and Zheng Boqi, were members of the CPC.[71]

[71] In his memoirs, Xia Yan reviewed in detail the situation before and after the establishment of the Chinese Left-wing League of Writers, describing the process of "the CPC Central Committee's intervention" in the debates and organization of the new Left-wing League. Xia also recalled that "at a Central Committee Work Conference in 1964, I asked Comrade Li Lisan, and he said that he asked Lu Xun to talk and but the decision to stop the debate as made by the CPC's Central Committee" …… (Xia Yan, *Lanxun Jiumeng Lu*, Beijing: Sanlian Shudian, 1992, p. 143.)

In March 1930, under the organization and coordination of the CPC, Lu Xun, Shen Duanxian (Xia Yan), Yang Hansheng, Yu Dafu, Feng Naichao, Feng Xuefeng, Zheng Boqi, and Guo Moruo (who was abroad) founded the Chinese Left-wing League of Writers at the Chinese University of the Arts in Shanghai.[72] The Left-wing League's platform made their political position clear:

> Our art is necessarily dedicated to the bloody struggle for "victory or death".
>
> If art takes as its content the sorrows and joy of mankind, then our art must take as its content the feelings felt by the proletariat in this dark class society's "medieval world". Therefore, our art is anti-feudal, anti-bourgeois, and against the "lost social status" of the petit bourgeoisie. We are unequivocally engaged in the creation of proletarian art.[73]

At the founding meeting of the Chinese Left-wing League of Writers, "Marxist Art Theory and Critical Theory" were clearly written into the resolution of the General Assembly, so that the political tendency of literature as a tool of ideological enlightenment was obvious. Given the clarity, relevance and urgency of the leadership and political tasks of the CPC, Lu Xun, as the spiritual leader of the Left-wing League, said in February 1931 after the execution of five League members (Rou Shi, Hu Yepin [1903–1931], Yin Fu [1909–1931], Ms. Feng Jian [1907–1931], and Li Weisen [1903–1931]), that the psychological atmosphere was even worse than during the KMT's white terror six years earlier.[74] Even more clearly,

[72] This was a university established in 1929 after the previous Shanghai Yida was shut down. Chen Wangdao was its President, and most of the lecturers were members of the Left-wing League, including Xia Yan, Xu Xingzhi (1904–1991), Peng Kang (1901–1968), Zhu Jingwo (1901–1941), Feng Naichao and Zheng Boqi.

[73] Quoted from Tang Tao, *Zhongguo Xiandai Wenxue Shi Jianbian*, Beijing: Renmin Wenxue Chubanshe, 1984, p. 23. Original source: *Mengya Yuekan*, 1:4, April 1930.

[74] After the May Thirtieth Incident in 1925, Lu Xun wrote in "The Rose without Flowers": "China only lets tigers and wolves enter and feed, no one cares. Only a few young students are in charge and they should have been quietly studying, but the current situation gives them no peace of mind. If the authorities had a modicum of conscience, wouldn't they ask themselves how they could evince a little goodness? …… But they finally [had the students] killed! …… The blood debt must be repaid in kind. The longer they default, the more interest they'll have to pay! All of the above is empty talk. What's the point of writing?" *Lu Xun Xuanji* (Selected Works of Lu Xun), vol. 2, pp. 259–260.

"proletarian revolutionary literature is still emerging, because it belongs to the vast revolutionary masses of hard-working people ... The blood of our comrades has proved that proletarian revolutionary literature and the revolutionary hard-working masses are subject to the same oppression, the same slaughter, the same fight, the same fate, and so this is the literature of the revolutionary hard-working masses".[75] Literature, with the support of "the hard-working masses", will not become a superfluous or useless thing, and literature will more clearly serve a weapon of class struggle.

The "Great Revolution", the Communists' and radicals' previous iteration of KMT-CPC cooperation and the Northern Expedition, and its failure inspired young people with ideals when contemplating the possibilities of the future. Among intellectual circles, the liberal, enlightened, and pluralistic ideological situation of the May Fourth Movement was replaced by radical revolutionary consciousness, and the two early ideological tendencies among intellectuals represented by Chen Duxiu and Hu Shi extended to become divergent political attitudes. The more radical thought of the Left-wing League was readily apparent in Mao Dun's article written during the early period of the League, "Review of the May Fourth Movement: Report of the Research Society of Marxist Literary and Art Theory":

> May Fourth was the inevitable struggle that broke out when feudal thought became an obstacle to the development of China's bourgeoisie. The development of this struggle, it is now apparent, has clear stages: Initially, the vernacular literary movement was the war of the vanguard, which was followed by the expansion of the front line to feudal ideology itself (opposition to the old Confucian ethics, etc.), and then extended to the actual political struggle, which was the "May Fourth" student movement. - However, the proletarian movement subsequently arose, and the age embarked on a new movement, and "May Fourth" was buried in the tomb of history.[76]

Mao Dun was obviously explaining that true proletarian literature began with the Left-wing League. The logic behind this thinking came,

[75] Lu Xun, "China's Proletarian Revolutionary Literature and the Blood Before It", *Lu Xun Xuanji* (Selected Works of Lu Xun), vol. 3, p. 120.

[76] Mao Dun茅盾, *Wo Zoushang de Daolu*, vol. 2, Hong Kong: Sanlian Chubanshe, 1984, p. 65.

of course, from the Soviet Union and from Marxist theory as articulated by the Soviet Union. At the founding meeting of the Left-wing League, Pan Hannian's speech, "The Significance and Mission of the Left-wing League of Writers", was based on the logic of Marx's basic ideology:

> The old economic foundation of society has been shaken and will inevitably collapse, and in this period of rapid change, the political culture, art and so on at the upper level of its society must change with it. The historical form of the development of Chinese literary movement is naturally based on the process of China's economic development..... Now the Chinese revolutionary crisis is deepening and the struggle of the proletariat is more acute, which has promoted leftist thought in the general cultural movement, and there has been further understanding and application of correct Marxist theory. The meaning of petty bourgeois individualism has been gradually criticized and overcome, so the literary movement has advanced to a new, second stage. The Chinese Left-wing League of Writers, launched by more than 50 left-wing writers in Shanghai, is powerful evidence of this.[77]

Although Lu Xun agreed to become a member of the Left-wing League, he had reservations about their radical attitude and warned at their founding meeting: "If you don't get in touch with the actual social struggle and simply concern yourself with writing essays and studying problems from behind a glass window, it is easy to be radical and 'leftist'". However, as soon as you encounter reality, you will immediately shatter. Locked in the house, it is easiest to discuss radical ideas, but it is also easiest to be 'rightist'". Lu Xun even pointed out: "The revolution will of course entail destruction, but what is more needed is construction. Destruction is joyful, but construction is troublesome. So, for those who harbor romantic illusions about revolution, the closer they are to, and the more involved they are in, the revolution, the more easily will they be disappointed ······".[78] The CPC controlled this mass organization,

[77] Quoted from Liu Xiaoqing, *Hongse Kuangbiao: Zuolian Shilu* (Red Hurricane: True Account of the Left-wing League of Writers), Beijing: Renmin Wenxue Chubanshe, 2004, p. 50.

[78] From Liu Xiaoqing, op. cit., pp. 51–52. In fact, Lu Xun did not participate in the specific preparations for the Left-wing League, nor did he participate in the revision of their program or assume any specific position in the League. After reading the League's documents, he agreed with their overall content, but also said: "I wouldn't have written articles of this nature in this way".

and the seven members of the League's Standing Committee were "nominated by the Cultural Commission, agreed to by the Central Committee, and submitted to the Congress for endorsement votes". The League set up an internal Party-Youth League [caucus] organization, and the Central Propaganda Department of the Cultural Work Committee directed the League's work. In fact, Leagues were established in Beiping, Tokyo, and other cities and regions, and even Malaya had a Left-wing League, all promoted and led by the CPC, which determined the de facto nature of the League as a "second CPC".[79]

In the first half of 1930, it was Li Lisan, a member of the Standing Committee of the Political Bureau of the CPC Central Committee and Minister of Propaganda, who advocated radical violent revolution, and in his view, the climax of a new round of revolution was coming. In addition to organizing military operations to stage armed uprisings and occupy the cities, it was necessary to activate the intellectual and cultural community to participate in urban demonstrations. Li Lisan, accompanied by Pan Hannian and Feng Xuefeng, visited Lu Xun, inviting him to participate in the upcoming large-scale demonstration in Shanghai, in the hope that he would be at the forefront of the procession as the flag bearer of the radical revolutionaries; Li even offered to give Lu Xun a pistol "in case of any accident". Li Lisan's invitation was rejected by Lu Xun, who politely said: "I have always advocated 'trench warfare', but not standing up to fight as a warrior. As for China's revolution, it seems it will be a 'protracted war', which will require we engage in 'tenacious fighting'".[80] Lu Xun also refused Li Lisan's request on taking leave that he should issue a declaration. However, Li Lisan did not take Lu Xun's doubts into account, and instructed the League to organize writers to participate in the "bloody May Day" activities: demonstrations, "flying rallies", posting slogans, and

[79] Zhou Yang later recalled: "We felt that the Left-wing League at that time had become a second Party. Why a second Party? This was because it was actually the same as the Party. Being basically a group of writers, it could be more extensive, be more open, and more discuss literature. But later it was devoted to politics and even demonstrations. In this way people grew afraid of it". (Zhao Haosheng, "Zhou Yang laughingly discusses historical achievements", *Mingren yu Yuan'an: Zhongguo Wentan Dang'an Shilu, Er* (Celebrities and Misjudgments: Chinese Literary Archives, II), Beijing: Qunzhong Chubanshe. Quoted in Liu Xiaoqing, op. cit., pp. 115–116) Mao Dun, op. cit., wrote "The Left-wing League said that it was a literary group, rather than say it was a political party".

[80] Liu Xiaoqing, op. cit., pp. 101–102.

distributing political leaflets. For a long time, the League's members who participated in these events popularized a revolutionary slogan: "A slogan and a flyer are almost a red grenade!" As can be imagined, such political activities often resulted in the arrest of many participants, and the writer's main job of fighting through writing was completely ignored. Mao Dun recalls this period clearly, noting that, based on political struggle, the CPC leaders were not interested in the writer's job, and he recalls Feng Naichao's speech at the May Day mobilization meeting: "On the eve of the climax of this revolution, revolutionary writers should not hesitate to join in this grueling action, and even if the status of the writer's work is tossed aside, this cannot be cause for regret".[81] A large number of memoirs document doubts and grievances about the adventurism of this period, but under the direction of the CPC, the literary artists involved in the League had to take on the risks of this adventurism in the knowledge that they were going to fail. Xia Yan recalls:

> For example, in one flying rally on Nanjing Road, the head of the Zhabei District Committee assigned one or two hundred people to "occupy" a "charitable" organization near Shandong Road (this was a soup kitchen run by the Chamber of Commerce), resulting in more than 20 people being arrested. After I got out of harm's way, I met Li [Lisan] on the Bund. He said to me angrily, "This is like waiting for comrades to take the initiative and take themselves off to the police station". I had some sympathy for him but I dared not to even say "I agree" to him. On another occasion, I was in a small group writing slogans like "Arm to Defend the Soviet Union" at a corner vegetable market. It was raining lightly and the road was slippery, and Kong Deyi (Mao Dun's wife) who was in our group accidentally slipped. She was covered with mud, and when we sent her home, she was grumbling. We criticized her when she said, "If we couldn't even protect ourselves, how could we defend the Soviet Union?"[82]

On 29 May, the League held its second general meeting of all members to prepare for the next day's demonstration to commemorate "May Thirtieth". The meeting apparently failed to learn from the lessons of the past and criticized some writers for not caring about political struggle. Lu Xun's speech at the meeting expressed his different views, stressing that

[81] Mao Dun, op. cit., p. 47.

[82] Xia Yan, op. cit., pp. 179–180.

being a writer required bravery to write, and that "writers should also dissect themselves from time to time. If they do not, I fear that some of us who are now on the left will in the future be on the right".

In August, the League's Executive Committee, in its "Formation of the New Situation of the Proletarian Literature Movement and Our Tasks", continued to use radical political language and slogans to encourage writers: "The whole world is on the eve of the revolution". "The proletarian literary movement should fight to the death for Soviet political power"; "The Soviet literary movement should begin with this bloody period". The CPC maintained that the literature of this period could be summed up as the workers and peasants leading the literary struggle, and that the "cultural level of political education of the workers and peasants made them rise up for the Soviet regime and struggle in a vast indoctrination movement".[83] The bourgeoisie and petty bourgeoisie were clearly excluded, and in October, the League's organization expelled Jiang Guangci, and the third page of *Red Flag Daily*, the newspaper of the CPC's Central Committee, published the news of Jiang's political fate under the heading, "The fallen member of the petty bourgeoisie Jiang Guangchi (sic.) expelled from the Communist Party":

> Because the revolutionary struggle sharpened, he wavered and retreated, seeking only personal enjoyment and avoiding the hard struggle. The Bolshevik Party must resolutely and unflinchingly wean out opportunistic and wavering elements and call on every comrade to work faithfully for the revolution, sacrifice everything for the revolution, and establish the leadership role of the Party.

Such a move, which followed criticism of Li's "left" opportunistic line at the Third Plenary Session of the Sixth CPC Central Committee, shows that extreme political tendencies continued to exist throughout the Party. In any case, Jiang Guangci was expelled from the Party and the League after he was seen as "drifting onto the path to counter-revolution", and "when the White Terror was most intense, he broke free of the organization and fled to Japan", and his novella, *Lisa's Grief* "gave readers the impression that he sympathized with the grievances of the descendants of the White Russian counter-revolution". In November, Lu Xun's valued writer Yu Dafu was also expelled from the League as a "reactionary

[83] Mao Dun, op. cit., p. 50.

opportunist"; earlier, Yu Dafu had told Agnes Smedley, "I'm just a writer, not a warrior", which roused a great deal of antipathy among members of the League.[84]

On 17 January 1931, a group of CPC members who opposed Wang Ming's line met at the Oriental Hotel, to convene a conference opposing Wang Ming and the Twenty-eight Bolsheviks. From that evening until the 19th, thirty-six people were believed to have been arrested as the informants against Tang Yu (also called Wang Juefu) who had returned from Moscow Oriental University.

Attempts by the intellectual community and some members of the CPC to save those arrested were unsuccessful, with 23 people, including Li Weisen (Li Qiushi), Rou Shi, Hu Yepin, Yin Fu, and Feng Jian (collectively known as the "Five Martyrs of the Left"), shot dead by the KMT on 7 February.[85] Lu Xun wrote his famous essay "Remembering the

[84] Mao Dun said: "The Resolution disdained writers from the petit bourgeoisie (and all members of the League happened to be writers with petit bourgeois origins) and wanted to shift the 'focus of the organization's foundation' to the workers and peasants, that is, to train worker and peasant writers. The cultivation of worker and peasant writers was of course beyond reproach, but it indeed showed 'the narrow concept of the organization' by ignoring the role of writers of petit bourgeois origins, not letting them create, asking them to sever their old social relations, and so on. In fact, during the decade of the League not one 'worker and peasant writer' was trained, but it did produce a group of excellent young writers of petty bourgeoisie origin; it was these new writers under the leadership of Lu Xun, who stormed into the battle, won a great victory, and became the backbone of the Chinese revolutionary literary movement". (Quoted from Mao Dun, op. cit., p. 51)

[85] Xia Yan explained: "In fact, although Comrades Li Chuli and Ke Zhongping(1902–1964) were sentenced, they were not involved in the incident in the Oriental Hostel, nor were they arrested at the same time". (Xia Yan, Lan Xun Jiumeng Lu, Beijing: Sanlian Shudian, 1992, p. 190).Among the 23 people shot dead were important cadres of the CPC, such as Cai Bozhen (1905–1931, Secretary of the Zhabei District Party Committee), Ouyang Li'an (1914–1931, Communist Youth League Jiangsu Provincial Committee and Shanghai General Trade Union Minister), and Long Dadao (1901–1931, Shanghai General Trade Union Secretary-General), but the leader of the CPC, Wang Ming did not show any sadness and surprise about the incident. He believed that among the arrested people there were anti-Party elements, and he even dismissed He Mengxiong (1898–1931) from the party. In fact, although Li Lisan's leadership ended at the party's September meeting, there was no new leadership replacement, leading to a leadership struggle within the party. As a laborer, He Mengxiong and Wang Ming, who joined the Communist Party in 1922, became leaders of both camps. Based on support for Wang Ming, who is likely to gain leadership, Kang Sheng managed to hand over the list of He Mengxiong's camp to the Kuomintang, which used their forces to wipe out Wang Ming's political opponents, including five left-wing writers such as Rou Shi, who is considered to

Forgotten", but the proliferation of raids, detentions, arrests, and terrorist shootings made even those who did not believe in communism so worried about the human rights situation that people with different political positions, both leftists and KMT figures, organized or joined the Chinese Civil Rights Protection League (Zhongguo Minquan Baozhang Tongmeng).[86] Indeed, this KMT-inflicted massacre, the assassination of Yang Xingfo, secretary of the Civil Rights Protection League, on 18 June 1933, and the increasing persecution of intellectuals and dissidents pushed more people to the side of the CPC politically.

It was also in 1931 that Qu Qiubai, who had been ostracized by Wang Ming's CPC, arrived in Shanghai. Qu Qiubai loved literature and took an active interest in the work of the Left-wing Writers League, and on the basis of his influence and previous status in the party, Qu Qiubai actually participated in the leadership of the League.[87] Xia Yan recalled:

have been a member of the He Mengxiong's Group. The material shows that Lu Xun was not aware of the struggle within the Party. This incident is described in KMT propaganda as the result of infighting within the CPC.

[86] On 29 December 1932, nine people, including Song Qingling and Cai Yuanpei (then a member of the Executive Committee of the KMT Central Committee), launched the China Civil Rights Protection League in Shanghai with the aim of providing legal aid to political prisoners, investigating prison conditions, publishing facts about civil rights in the country, and fighting for the freedom of speech, publication, opportunity, association and so on. In addition to Song and Cai, the executive committee members of the Shanghai branch of the China Civil Rights Protection League comprised Yang Xingfo (1893–1933), Lin Yutang (1895–1976), Yi Luosheng (Harold Isaacs, 1910–1986), Zou Taofen (1895–1944), Chen Binhe, Hu Yuzhi (1896–1986) and Lu Xun. Other important members of the League's committees were Wang Zaoshi (1903–1978, Propaganda), Zhou Jianren (1888–1984, Investigation), and Shen Junru (1875–1963, Law). Hu Shi, chairman of the executive committee of the Beiping branch of the China Civil Rights Protection League, was expelled in March for publicly disagreeing with League members such as Song Qingling and Cai Yuanpei on the factual issues stated in the "Appeal of the Beiping Military Commission's Review Institute". In March 1933, the League also launched a broader national rescue group, the National Humiliation Self-Defense Society, which further put forward the idea of arming the anti-Japanese people. The KMT's radical stance against the group and the CPC's use of the group soon ended its normal activities in June.

[87] Feng Xuefeng, secretary of the Left-wing League's caucus and secretary of the Cultural Committee, said: "Comrade [Qu] Qiubai came to work as a leader of the Left-wing League, but this was not the decision of the Party, and was only dictated by his personal enthusiasm". At the same time his relationship with the League became so close that his poor health was related to the white terror of the time". (From Liu Xiaoqing, op. cit., p. 160)

"Around the time of the founding of Left-wing Writers League its leaders were transferred or sacrificed ··· the leadership was weak and their work was difficult. At that time Pan [Hannian] said: 'Now I can tell you, the Central Committee has decided that cultural work in the Shanghai area will be led by Qu Qiubai. He is experienced and has very good relations with Lu Xun and Mao Dun. So, at present and future meetings of the 'cultural committee', he will participate' (soon after that Yang Hansheng also quietly told me this news). This was a pleasure for us at the time, because before that, we only knew that Qu Qiubai had been criticized but we did not know the specific details of his situation; secondly, he was himself also a writer and artist, so we thought things would improve in the future".[88] In Shanghai, Qu Qiubai urged the Left-wing League's Executive Committee to adopt a new resolution, "The New Mission of China's Proletarian Revolutionary Literature", in November. The document, drafted by Feng Xuefeng and revised by Qu Qiubai, emphasized the importance of literary creation, and the focus of the work shifted from street politics to writing, and thereafter, the Left-wing League of Writers stopped dangerous activities like staging flying rallies and leaflet drops. At the same time, Qu Qiubai and Lu Xun also spoke a common language in their translations of Russian literature and literary thought, and in this revolutionary period of red rage, Qu Qiubai and Lu Xun's cooperation more or less stifled the extremism in left-wing literary and artistic circles of the CPC instigated firstly by Li Lisan and then by Wang Ming. Until January 1934, when he left Shanghai for the Central Committee of the CPC in Jiangxi province, Qu Qiubai maintained a close personal friendship with Lu Xun.

Before the founding of the Left-wing League of Writers, there had been a debate between Lu Xun and Liang Shiqiu (1903–1987) about whether literature transcended social class, and Lu Xun used the expression "the tired flunkey of a family of deceased capitalists" to describe the position of Liang Shiqiu of the Crescent Society (Xinyue Pai). Later, Qu Qiubai, and Feng Xuefeng criticized Hu Qiuyuan's concept of "the free person", and the core of these disputes was whether literature and art had a class nature and political function. The debate in the Left-wing League regarding whether literature and art have a class position has initiated the proposal by Su Wen (1907–1964, originally known as Dai Kechong and

[88] Xia Yan, op. cit., p. 202.

aka Du Heng) of "the third type of person". In 1932, the third issue of the first volume of *Xiandai* (Modern Age), founded by Shi Zhecun (1905–2003), published "On the 'New Text' and Hu Qiuyuan's Literary Theory" by Su Wen, who had taken part in the founding meeting of the Left-wing League, in which Su described the "third type of person" that he maintained existed:

> When the "free member of the intellectual class" and the "unfree and partisan" class debate to establish hegemony in the literary world, it is the third type of person, not these two, who suffers most. These "third type of persons" are what are called writers.[89]

Shi Zhecun helped Su translate a bit: the so-called "third type of person" are those persons who stand between the bourgeois liberals and their literary theory and the proletariat and their literary theory, and are unwilling to accept the theoretical direction of either of these two groups.

Those who upheld the Left-wing League's position on literature and art believed that such a "third type of person" could not emerge, and one author with the penname "Yijia" retorted:

> Every writer, whether intentionally or unintentionally, whether writing or silent, is always the representative of the ideology of a certain class. In today's world of class society, there is no escaping this, and so it is impossible for this "third type of person" to emerge.[90]

After Su Wen published "On Literary Interventionism", an article arguing that Left-wing literature "has become the gramophone of particular political power", Lu Xun presented Su Wen's article "On the Third Type of Person" and asked that it be published:

> Writers who live in a class society but want to transcend class, who live in an age of conflict but want to be independent of struggle, or who live in the present but want to write works for the future are actually mentally

[89] Liu Xiaoqing, op. cit., p. 343.

[90] Liu Xiaoqing, op. cit., p. 345.

> and emotionally deluded that they do not exist in the real world. To be such a person is just like trying to pull the hair on one's head by hand, to fly away from the earth.[91]

The Left-wing League's critique of "the third type of person" related to the political attitude of the Comintern (expressed as "left-leaning") within the CPC; when this "left-leaning" atmosphere was questioned within the party, the party organization also reversed its earlier extremist work style, so that Zhang Wentian (using the penname "Goethe") wrote an article, "The Closed-door Doctrine on the Literary Front", which emphasized that "revolutionary bourgeois writers of literature are not our enemies, but our allies".[92]

The KMT was also aware of the importance of its own party's ideological propaganda tools in the field of culture and art. In the summer of 1930, the KMT launched a "nationalist literary and artistic movement", and although the promoters were people like Pan Gongzhan (1895–1975), director of the Shanghai Education Bureau, and Wang Pingling (1898–1964), their backers were Chen Lifu and Chen Guofu of the CC Clique. While banning the radical publications of the Left-wing League of Writers, the KMT also published critical articles on the ideas of Left-wing League through publications it controlled, like *Avant-garde Monthly* (Qianfeng Yuekan) and *Literary Monthly* (Wenyi Yuebao). However, the statement in its "manifesto" of the "nationalist literary and artistic movement" that "the highest meaning of literature and art is nationalism" was despised. In Lu Xun's view, nationalist writers were only "the corpses floating by Shanghai's Bund". As soon as the "nationalist literary movement" made its appearance, it attracted radical criticism.[93] In October

[91] Liu Xiaoqing, op. cit., p. 346.

[92] Xia Yan wrote in his memoirs that the abandonment of the "leftist" line by the League was signaled by the publication on 3 November 1932 "in the Party journal *Struggle* of 'The Closed-door Doctrine on the Literary Front'". Ref: Xia Yan, op. cit., p. 207.

[93] At this time, the Left-wing League members could already use Marxist theories of class struggle in theoretical debates. Mao Dun criticized the "nationalist movement" in his "The Present Phenomenon of 'Nationalist Literature'" as follows: "Generally speaking, in the revolutionary movements of oppressed peoples, national revolution-centered national literature also has a considerable revolutionary role to play, but there is no pure and simple social organization in the world, so the oppressed nationals themselves necessarily also encompass two struggling classes—the ruling class and the oppressed worker and

1931, the Executive Committee of the Left-wing League published an article entitled "An Announcement to Revolutionary Writers, Proletarian Writers and All Youths Who Love Literature", in which calls for attacks on the nationalist literary movement were equally startling:

> All proletarian writers and revolutionary writers of China: The tips of your pens should be the workers' guns and the Red Army's rifles, as you valiantly forge ahead! Sweep away and eliminate the madness and delusion of nationalist humanism and pacifism! Act immediately, there cannot be a moment's delay.[94]

In January 1935, "ten renowned professors" in the fourth issue of *Cultural Construction* published "Our Declaration on Cultural Construction from the Position of China" which won the support of the National government[95]:

> China has disappeared from the realm of culture, and China's political form, social organization and the content and forms of its thought have lost their characteristics. People nurtured by the politics, society and ideas lacking characteristics will also gradually not be reckoned to be Chinese. So we can say with certainty: surveying things from the field of culture, in the modern world there is of course no China and within China's territory there are almost no Chinese.

The ten carefully selected professors affirmed in a timely manner that the new China-based cultural construction would not be old fashioned or blindly copied, in taking China as their basis, they were "adopting a critical attitude, applying scientific methods to review the past, and grasping the present to create the future". However, they stressed that they would

peasant masses. In this situation, nationalist literature often becomes a means for the ruling class to deceive workers and peasants. This is a general observation. As for China, the ruling classes that are an alliance of feudal warlords, rural gentry landowners, bureaucrat compradors, and the bourgeoisie have long been in collusion with imperialism to step up the exploitation of workers and peasants, so the slogans of nationalist literature are completely reactionary". (Ref: Mao Dun, op. cit., p. 75)

[94] Liu Xiaoqing, op. cit., p. 221.

[95] The ten professors were Wang Xinming, He Bingsong (1890–1946), Wu Yugan (1898–1990), Sun Hanbing (1903–1940), Huang Wenshan (1898–1988), Tao Xisheng (1899–1988), Zhang Yi (1901–1986), Chen Gaoyong (1902–1976), Fan Zhongyun (1901–1989), and Sa Mengwu (1897–1984).

achieve the tasks announced in the declaration ("to allow China to raise its head high in the field of culture, and to endow China's politics, society and ideas with Chinese characteristics, we must devote ourselves to China-based cultural construction"), but they had no concrete constructive measures.

In fact, the discussion of "the construction of a China-based culture" in 1935 was directly related to the cultural policy of the KMT government, and developments from Sun Yat-sen's nationalist stance to the "nationalist literary and artistic movement" implemented by the KMT's CC Department, leading up to this final "China-based theory" were all the result of the KMT's political operations. The KMT's newspaper *Zhongyang Ribao* (Central Daily) enthusiastically evaluated the advocacy by the ten professors of "constructing a China-based culture, which reveals the new awakening of China's intellectual class and its firm agitation for the nationalist revolution".

Obviously, the appeal from intellectual circles and its official recognition by the KMT provided a legitimate ideological basis and support for traditionalists in the literary and artistic fields, who naturally combined artistic issues according to their own understanding and who did not understand that the well-planned and carefully coordinated articles were produced for an intellectual elite that had little understanding of the complexity of party politics. Whether intentionally or not, the traditionalist artistic views of this period in fact became part of the ideological propaganda of the KMT, just as Hu Shi's critical answer to the ten professors was not limited to science:

> We cannot fail to point out that the ten professors cannot give up their "China-based standard", but when they write that their declaration is "not old-fashioned", it is in fact their conservative psychology that is to blame. Their manifesto is also one of the most fashionable manifestations of today's general reactionary air. Fashionable people certainly refuse to be honest about their archaic tendencies, so their conservative psychology is concealed behind a smokescreen of eclecticism and compromise.[96]

[96] Hu Shi in "A Tentative Review of 'Our Declaration on Cultural Construction from China's Position'", *Da Gongbao* (31 March 1935). The discussion in intellectual circles arising from the conflict between traditional culture and Western culture in the late Qing dynasty and the early years of the Republic of China was still spontaneous, but the cultural debate in the 1930s is difficult to disentangle from the interference of political operations. If the reader is interested, the debate, politics and operational background

Whether it was the CPC or the KMT, the ideological debate in the field of culture and art began invariably as party propaganda tools in the 1930s, but given the KMT's conservative stance, people tend to think that the CPC's manipulation of the Left-wing League was more effective in the political game than the KMT.

In the winter of 1935, Agnes Smedley, who had returned to China from Moscow, brought a letter from the writer and translator Xiao San (1896–1983), written at Wang Ming's request, and handed it over to Lu Xun at the Uchiyama Bookstore in Shanghai, asking him in turn to pass it on to the head of the Left-wing League. Xiao San's letter addressed the entire leadership and important members of the Left-wing League. In it, Xiao San, after summing up the work of the League over the previous five years, questioned the League's "closed-door policy" (the CPC's term at the time for its policy excluding forces from outside the CPC, in contravention of the Comintern's position) and "sectarianism" (the expression used within the CPC to characterize factions with different views):

> Many influential writers are still standing outside the common front ... comrades, here we have to trace the origins of the League's closed-door policy. We believe that the League's doors closed with the advocacy of "proletarian literature", because as soon as that slogan was introduced, the League shut up shop. Because of that slogan and policy, we could not unite generally progressive writers (given writers could not proletarianize overnight) and liberal writers. At the beginning, especially, the attitude of proletarian writers to the non- proletarian writers was even more abusive, and there was a general attitude calling for "mass uprising to punish those who are not members of our race".
>
> ......
>
> Many manifestations of the internal work of the Left-wing League did not seem at all like that of a literary group, an organization of writers, or an organization to educate writersand attract scholars to an anti-imperialist

of 'the construction of China-based culture" are fully discussed in Zhao Libin, *Minzu Lichang yu Xiandai Zhuiqiu: 20 Shiji 20–40 Niandai de Quanpan Xihua Sichao* (Nationalist Position and Modernity's Pursuit: The Intellectual Trend of Total Westernization from the 1920s to the 1940s), Beijing: Sanlian Shudian, 2005.

> and anti-conservative united front; they are like a political party, specifically the CPC! It came to be generally believed that the League was the Communist Party. Joining the League was like making a decision to be decapitated but this is something that the literati cannot decide on immediately.

Xiao San's letter concluded: "Abolish the League, issue a declaration dissolving it, and alternately launch and organize a broad literary union".[97] After Zhou Yang received the letter, he made it clear to the Cultural Committee that this was the directive of the CPC's Delegation to the Comintern in accordance with the resolution of the Seventh Conference of the CPC and the spirit of the CPC's "August First" Declaration [of 1935], which aimed to expand the united front in literary and artistic circles. As a result, the earlier debates on topics like the class nature of literature and art and "the third type of person" no longer completely suited the new situation, and the present task was that as long as literary and artistic workers supported the anti-Japanese and national salvation causes they could be invited to participate in the soon-to-be-established Chinese Writers Association.

Lu Xun at first did not agree with dissolving the League and had previously had no good feelings about Zhou Yang, Xia Yan, and others. Finally, Lu Xun proposed that if the League was to be dissolved, a declaration also needed to be issued. This proposal initially met with Zhou Yang's consent, but finally did not. They would not comply with Lu Xun's requirement that a declaration be issued, so relations between Lu Xun and Zhou Yang and the others further deteriorated.[98]

97 Liu Xiaoqing, op. cit., p. 494, quoting *Sanshi Niandai Zuoyi Wenyi Ziliao Xuanbian*, Sichuan Renmin Chubanshe.

98 In his reminiscences of the early history of the League, Mao Dun wrote that although Lu Xun was the commander of the League, "he was after all not a Party member, but an 'object' of the united front, so while most Party members in the League paid him great respect, they did not obey him". Later, discussing the dissolution of the League, and summing up the League's sectarianism and closed-door policies, Lu Xun told Mao Dun, "They actually shut me out". When Lu Xun's proposed declaration was not published, he completely lost his trust in Zhou Yang and the others. Mao Dun recalled: "From then on, Lu Xun was even more distrustful of Zhou Yang and the others for their various initiatives, activities, and their more uncooperative attitude. Zhou Yang and the others organized their new literary and artistic united front organization (initially called the 'Writers' Association', later named the 'Writers and Artists Association'), which Lu Xun

In March 1936, the League was dissolved without a mention. In fact, Zhou Yang, as the Party leader in charge, initiated a new political strategy, and in February put forward a new slogan, as Xia Yan recalled:

> Around the beginning of February, Zhou Yang told me when I ran into him at the "Cultural Committee": Now we want to politically set up an anti-Japanese united front. There should also be a corresponding slogan that unites the majority of those in literature and the arts. Therefore, we plan to put forward the slogan of "National Defense Literature" in accordance with the spirit of the August First Declaration. I asked him if the "Cultural Committee" had studied the matter and he said that Zhang Hanfu and Hu Qiaomu had agreed to, so I also agreed. It seemed natural because the term "national defense literature" had been used as early as 1934 by Zhou Libo [1908-1979], and in the Soviet Union the term was also used. Hanfu and Qiaomu also had more experience in theory and Party work than me, so I headed off resolutely to relay the news to the theater and film industry.[99]

"National defense literature" was not a term accepted by all literary colleagues and, in the eyes of some, the slogan blurred the boundaries of literature and art. Previously, literary and artistic workers had worked to expose the darkness of KMT rule through literature and art, but this slogan could be used by any political party, so how was the new literary and artistic united front to deal with the class divisions of class positions between the proletarian masses and bourgeois interest groups? In joint consultations between Hu Feng (1902–1985], Feng Xuefeng and Lu Xun, Lu Xun confirmed the use of the slogan "popular literature of the national revolutionary war". However, in *Wenxue Congbao* Hu Feng published on 1 June, "What do the popular masses demand from literature?" This article caused widespread controversy in literary and artistic circles; Zhou Yang and the others were extremely dissatisfied with the use of new slogans other than "national defense literature". Zhou Yang's rebuttal was clearly based on the CPC's position:

> The core mistake of those opposed to national defense literature was not understanding the significance of the national revolutionary united front.

said he would not join. He told me, he had enough of a 'foreman's' suffering and did not want to be fooled again". (see Mao Dun, op. cit., vol. 2)

[99] Xia Yan, op. cit., p. 310.

> ... Here I would like to point out that Mr. Hu Feng in his "What do the masses demand of literature?" provides an inadequate assessment of the situation of the national revolution. He erased the iron-clad fact that a united front of salvation pervades the country, and made no mention of "the united front" or "national defense literature"; if the theorist Hu Feng did not deliberately fail to refer to these facts, then he seriously misunderstood the basic situation.[100]

Lu Xun also participated in the debate via Feng Xuefeng because he was seriously ill, but he did not mention that the new slogan was his. As with other debates, literary differences and party positions, personal views and sectarian prejudices filled the debate until 15 October, when the first issue of the second volume of *Zuojia* (The Writer) published an article attributed to Mo Wenhua titled "As I See the Significance of This Literary Debate" which concluded: "The significance of this debate is not about a slogan, but about overcoming the closed-door policy and sectarianism in the literary world". Mo Wenhua was in fact a penname used by one of the CPC's leaders, Liu Shaoqi, so the Party clearly thought it had to change its mode of argument, and in fact, the Party was concerned and directed the "two slogans" debate.

In the year or so after the Central Red Army began the "Long March", the CPC underground organization in Shanghai and the Party's center lost contact. However, the advance of the Japanese army led to a nationwide upsurge in the movement opposed to the civil war and calling for anti-Japanese national salvation; based on these beliefs and will, even though the KMT continued to report victories in the encirclement of the CPC in the news media, the left-wing cultural movement under the leadership of the CPC never ceased. It was not until late October 1935 that the lack of contact with the Central Government changed: the Shanghai underground party obtained the 1 October issue of the *National Salvation Times* from Agnes Smedley, and saw the "August First Declaration" and bought a copy of the Third International's official newspaper *International Newsletter* from a foreign bookshop, and read Dimitrov's long political report, delivered to the 7th Congress of the Communist International from 25 July to 20 August, in which, based on the international situation at that time, he proposed establishing a working class anti-fascist united front in capitalist countries, and in their colonies and semi-colonial

100 Liu Xiaoqing, op. cit., pp. 523–524.

countries to establish a national united front against policies of imperialist aggression"; Xia Yan saw this news as "welcome dew after the long drought". When Pan Hannian returned to Shanghai in 1937 and relayed Mao Zedong's speech, "On the Strategy against Japanese Imperialism", delivered at the meeting in Wayaopu in December of the previous year, to literary and artistic circles under the leadership of the CPC, the political strategy calling for the comprehensive establishment of the anti-Japanese national united front got underway.

Ten Years of Construction

He Lian (1895–1975), who received his Ph.D. in Economics from Yale University and was dean of the School of Economics at Nankai University in 1931, lamented the situation in China after the victory of the Northern Expedition: "We live in the north, but I truly support the government in Nanjing, as in 1928, when I went with Jiang Tingfu and several friends from Tianjin to Nanjing. How excited we were when we saw the new national flag in Nanjing—for us, it seemed like the symbol of a great new era".[101]

However, after the purge of the KMT, many of that party's initiatives did not make a good impression because they were mainly based on simply maintaining the regime. As leader of the KMT, Chiang Kai-shek felt that he had learned the lesson of working with the CPC, that he had his own political ideas and methods, and that he was almost instinctively cautious and careful. Revolutionaries not slaughtered for their suspected ideals fled to the CPC, while most opportunists or cautious conservatives remained in the KMT, where no one was willing to shoulder responsibility actively, which naturally weakened the revolutionary nature of the KMT. Given that many worker and peasant activists were massacred, it became very difficult to maintain normal contacts with workers and peasants, so the KMT quickly lost the understanding and sympathy of its own popular social base. On the one hand, at a time of military regression the entry of warlords and old bureaucrats into important positions in the KMT and national government at all levels weakened the spirit of the KMT, and on the other hand, facilitated the actions of terrorist organizations like

[101] Lloyd E. Eastman, *The Abortive Revolution: China under Nationalist Rule,1927–1937,* Harvard University, 1974. Chinese edition: *Guomindang Tongzhi xia de Zhongguo: Liuchan de Geming*, Beijing: Zhongguo Qingnian Chubanshe, 1992, p. 11.

the "Blue Shirts", but also seriously weakened the revolutionary color of Chiang Kai-shek's KMT. In many people's eyes, Chiang Kai-shek's role increasingly approximated that of a fascist dictatorship, because all who opposed him and other KMT leaders were seen as counterrevolutionaries, although Chiang's chosen position, to consolidate his power and that of the KMT regime, was to regard them as corrupt officials. In particular, the CPC revealed that the KMT did not represent the masses of workers and peasants, but rather the party represented the interests of the capitalists, even though China's capitalists (businessmen, bankers, industrial and general industrial investors) in the 1920s and 1930s were also squeezed by imperialism or foreign capital.[102] Such an image and the ongoing propaganda of the CPC easily roused the antipathy of the poor masses.[103] Everything affected the KMT's effective political system—although it kept telling its people that the ultimate goal of the country was constitutionalism.

[102] A Japanese observer commented: "China's present situation is described by some as a revolution, and by others as a reaction to revolution. I think it is revolution, a revolution in progress. However, the revolution is also varied, and the ongoing revolution in China is limited to domestic problems, in the same way as the French Revolution 150 years ago. Therefore, the main body of the revolution is the emerging capitalist class, which is now established in Shanghai in a distinctive form. Outside Shanghai little is happening". (Tachibana Shiraki, "Shanghai Magnates, Communist Party of China, Feng Yuxiang", *Xin Tiandi*, July 1927, the book is quoted by Iechika Ryōko, *Chiang Kai-shek and the Nanjing National Government*, Beijing: Shehui Kexue Wenxian Chubanshe, 2005, p. 101) This observer's view was that Shanghai's capitalist class was an emerging force, so it needed to combine with political forces to ensure that it could operate in peace rather than in chaos, so it supported the revision of customs duties and avoid the CPC-led workers' movement. This is why the bourgeoisie in Shanghai sought to establish an alliance with Chiang Kai-shek's KMT, which was clearly the financial source of the KMT's efforts to consolidate its power by removing its dependence on Russian finance.

[103] Edgar Snow, on entering the Soviet zone, asked some children why they wanted to converse with the Red Army:

> "How do you address the communists?" I asked.
> "The Communists were the ones who helped the Red Army fight the white bandits and the KMT", opined a 10-year-old child.
> "What else?"
> "They helped us beat the landlords and capitalists!"
> "So what is a capitalist?" The question might have troubled a child, but another replied, "A capitalist is someone who doesn't work for himself, but let's others work for him".

Despite the contradictions and problems, witnesses to history, such as Albert C. Wedemeyer, believe that the decade from 1927 to 1937 was the "Golden Decade" of the National Government, the first decade of which China began to become a modern state: The unification of north and south by the Northern Expedition led to the beginning of relatively effective rule by the National Government over more than 80% of China's territory. Moreover, Chiang Kai-shek's strategy of "pacifying the nation domestically and driving out the foreign invaders" gave the National Government about five years for construction (1932–1936). At the beginning of this period (in September 1931), the Nanjing National Government formally became a non-permanent member of the League of Nations, and in the face of a serious national crisis, the National Government took the Chinese issue to the international forum to discuss and solve the problem; modern architecture rose from the ground up; city streets, plumbing networks and the amenities of modern life were constantly improving—so that people often thought of the image and lifestyle of major cities such as Shanghai as though it were Europe; even decorative elements similar to those in European cities, such as architectural ornamentation and public sculpture, conveyed a new sense of urban life, which was why Chiang Kai-shek hoped to demonstrate the national government's approved path during the modernization drive by promoting the "New Life Movement". On 19 February 1934, Chiang Kai-shek gave a speech on "The Meaning of New Life" in Nanchang, where he advocated a New Life Movement influenced by the German post war order: first militarization, then a focus on production, and subsequent integration with cultural activities. The physical fitness of the nation and its individual citizens as the requirement of modern life was of course influenced by Germany, and the "Fifth National Games" held in 1933 already showed the government's efforts to improve the quality of the people, when "physical strength is national strength" became a resounding slogan, after which sports in schools were further popularized. However, it is difficult to assess the achievements of a movement that sought to evoke a new attitude to life, since the people's way of life was required to conform to standards of manners, propriety, integrity, and shame—words which people at the time associated with the English concepts of "courtesy", "justice", "honesty", and "self-esteem", invariably associating the elements of this New Life movement with the atmosphere of Confucian traditional thought, even though Chiang Kai-shek was a Christian. Chiang Kai-shek indeed called on people to study the *Four Books* and *Five Classics*, especially to read classics like *Great Learning* and *Doctrine of the Mean*. In May, the KMT even passed a resolution to mark 27 August as the anniversary of Confucius' birth and to restore sacrifices to Confucius throughout the country. This move, reminiscent of Yuan Shikai, provoked a backlash from intellectuals. Lao She (Shu Qingchun, 1899–1966), Cao Yu (1910–1996), Ye Shengtao (1894–1988), Zheng Zhenduo (1898–1958), Chen Wangdao and Yu Dafu jointly published "Our Opinions on the Cultural Movement", which sarcastically made the following critical comment:

> We believe this archaistic movement can have no future. Recruiting the classics to save the country makes the 1898 Reforms and the 1911 Revolution redundant. If using "Chinese studies as the corpus and Western studies as the application" could have saved the country, then Li Hongzhang and Zhang Zhidong would have achieved success. Though we realize that the reasons why at the current juncture we have moved to the point where we suddenly have such a reactionary phenomenon are not simple, we cannot fail to point out the crux of the problem and call for introspection.[104]

At this time, people still remembered "overthrowing the Confucian shop" during the enlightenment movement more than a decade previously, but at the same time as promoting traditional morality, the KMT also listened to the advice of German military advisers, hoping that such a move would promote the national spirit, and achieve the goal of becoming a strong country through struggle. Starting in Nanchang, with the involvement of the Blue Shirts, the New Life campaign spread across the country, and on every street one could see signs condemning spitting, urging public health to prevent disease, calling for the elimination of flies and rats to prevent disease spreading, and prohibiting drinking, whoring, and gambling, but the campaign ended in 1936.

From Chiang Kai-shek's second retreat from politics until he became president in 1935, the operators of the National Government were people centered on Sun Ke and Wang Jingwei, and the Nationalist Party's Fourth Plenary Session held in November 1931 adopted a basic policy of nation-building. Addressing the urgency of construction, the KMT proposed a policy stressing "talent" and widely recruited talented individuals from inside and outside the party to aid in national construction. "We must

104 *Chen Bao*, 26 August 1934, quoted from Jin Chongji, op. cit., p. 370.

attract talented individuals, implement direct democratic elections and realize democratic politics", Sun Ke announced at the conclusion of the KMT's Fourth Plenary Session. This atmosphere led to more professionals becoming involved in nation-building, in the legal, educational, economic, and financial sectors, as well as in transportation and communications, and even in the publishing industry. The famous magazine *Independent Critique* was founded on 22 May 1932—although the magazine's leading authors, Hu Shi, Fu Sinian, Jiang Tingfu, Ding Wenjiang, and others, maintained a clear distance from the CPC.

The domestic and external policies which had as their main purpose surrounding the CPC and resisting the increasingly serious incursions of the Japanese army required, first and foremost, that the KMT strengthen the armed forces and their power. Based on the severing of diplomatic relations with the Soviet Union, Chiang Kai-shek's KMT began to rely on German military advisers to achieve its military goals. The national government hired Max Bauer, Hermann Kniebel, Georg Wetzell, Hans Von Seeckt, and Alexander von Falkenhausen as military advisers through private contracts. In 1933, when the KMT surrounded the CPC, the number of German advisory experts in different types of work ran into the hundreds, and they trained 300,000 soldiers for the KMT's army. It was some of the suggestions made by German military advisers that provided tactics and methods that led to the final success in the KMT's siege of the CPC, and the army established mechanized units, increased their armory, and built army hospitals. In addition to developing the Navy, on which construction began in the late Qing, an air force was also fully launched; the National Government established an aviation school in Hangzhou in 1928, which was then transformed into a Central Aviation School in 1931, and the China Aviation Machinery School was established in Nanchang in 1936. By 1936, China had 855 aircraft of all kinds, and by May 1937, the country had six air force regional commands. In the area of military industry, in addition to the construction of factories, military enterprises were also jointly organized with Italy and Germany. These military undertakings, which were completed before 1936, provided the basis for the anti-Japanese war after 1937. But it was the hiring of German military advisers that made it easy for Chiang Kai-shek, who had been confined by factional fighting within his party, to accept the Fascist approach passed on to him by his advisers: Colonel Bauer, for example, was involved in the Nazi movement in Germany, and the advisers he had chosen for the advisory panel were consistent with his ideological tendencies; Hermann Kniebel himself was an avid Nazi, and he even took part in the Nazi demonstrations during the Munich beer hall putsch in May 1929 (his imprisoned cellmate was Hitler), At the suggestion of the German military advisers, many Chinese officers went to Germany to study, at a time when German fascism was flourishing. Thus, the fact that Chiang Kai-shek after his first fall from office began to think about organizing his own terrorist organization, the Blue Shirts, and making it completely loyal to himself, naturally reminds us of the influence the Nazi Brown Shirts and Black Shirts had on him, even though Chiang Kai-shek's aim was to replenish the weakened spirit and will of the KMT.

The promised diplomatic gains were not evident after the 1921 Washington Conference. After the May Thirtieth movement, calls for the abolition of unequal treaties again arose, and the Beijing government did little in that regard. On 26 October 1925, the representatives of China and the United Kingdom, the United States, Japan, France, and other countries met in Beijing to discuss tariff autonomy. On 12 January 1926, China discussed the issue of legal rights with the British, American, and Japanese powers, who had previously conducted a survey of Chinese justice, saying: China needs to improve the administration of justice, so that it can abolish extraterritoriality. In January 1927, Belgium declared the end of the old treaties and established a new treaty of equality. In January and February 1927, Chinese soldiers and civilians clashed with British sailors in Wuhan and Jiujiang, leading to the eventual recovery of the concession areas of Wuhan and Jiujiang by agreement between China and the United Kingdom. Subsequently, China recovered the British concessions in Zhenjiang (31 October 1929), Weihaiwei (18 April 1930), and Xiamen (17 September 1930). In 1928, after the National Government reiterated its announcement of tariff autonomy from the previous July, ten countries, including Britain, the United States, the Netherlands, Norway, and Belgium, signed new tariff agreements with China. By May 1930, Japan also signed a Sino-Japanese tariff agreement (so many unequal treaties had previously been signed with Western powers that it was not until 1943, when China was in a stalemate in its war with Japan, that the National Government finally completed rescinding all the unequal treaties bequeathed from history). In February 1930, the National Government began to set up courts in the shared concessions, and in July 1931 Chinese courts began to be established in the French concessions and Chinese nationals began to be protected by Chinese law.

This progress in the legal field was led by Wu Chaoshu and Wang Chonghui; Wu presided over the formulation of a number of legal documents including the *Household Registration Law*, *Railway Law*, *Budget Law*, *Primary School Law*, *Secondary School Law*, *Teachers' Training College Law* and the *Vocational Schools Law*. After the death of Wu Chaoshu (1934), experts in the legal profession, under the leadership of Wang Chonghui, a graduate of Yale University, drafted a series of basic laws necessary for the modern state, such as the *Savings Bank Law*, *Code of Criminal Procedure*, *Civil Procedure Law*, *Central Banking Law*, *Export Tariff Law*, *Insurance Industry Law*, *Fiscal Revenue and Expenditure System Law*, and the *Court Organization Act*.

Tariff autonomy was implemented on 1 February 1929, which quickly saw an increase in tariff revenues from an average annual of $121 million in 1928 to $244 million, though this was subsequently affected by the Japanese invasion. However, the annual income from tariffs exceeded 300 million, and the tariff amount increased significantly as a result of the increase in the tax rate. The salt tax, as the main tax, increased from $85 million in 1929 to $218 million in 1936. Income from other taxes was also a source of national government revenue (which in turn increased the tax burden on society to varying degrees). A large proportion of national government spending was military spending. For the purpose of dealing with warlords and the CPC, after the 18 September Incident, preparations began for the anti-Japanese war, and it seemed military expenditure would be difficult to reduce, and at the same time construction began on various undertakings. In this way, the increase in the fiscal deficit was inevitable. However, a portion of the deficit also included future gains, such as the increase in education funding from $13 million in 1934 to $42 million in 1937, all of which had potential social benefits. In terms of fiscal consolidation, even in such a difficult fiscal situation, the National Government was striving to establish a budgetary system that would provide the basis for rationalizing fiscal operations. The national government achieved a unified tax system, and changed the differences between the central government and local governments in financial benefits, and the unification of the country achieved such a goal, providing conditions for large-scale economic construction. However, natural disasters, local wars and grassroots mismanagement and official corruption always affected much of China's rural areas to varying degrees, so people had different responses to the tax system. At that time, a Japanese researcher,

Matsumura Yūji, left a record of the Republic's government in the countryside in the 1930s in his study, *The Social State of China's Economy* (1949):

> After the 1927 revolution, the fortunes of the Fei family, a landowning entrepreneur, declined rapidly. This was partly due to the increase in the independence of its tenants, but also partly because of the development plans introduced by the new National Government. It suddenly increased the tax burden on Fei's land, and the depression from 1931 onwards had exacerbated the situation. According to Zhang Zhongren's history of the Fei clan, the clan's 600 *mu* of ancestral land near Suzhou saw failed harvests over successive years, and the Fei clan even sold some of these fields to pay taxes, yet the situation remained dire. Fei Changsheng in desperation asked the government to confiscate all the family's land to settle their taxes, but his request was certainly refused. He could not pressure his poor tenants to pay their rent, and once again in 1935 he wrote a very moving letter to the government, but died of illness before it was sent.[105]

At the same time, in the specific implementation of the tax system there were too many complexities and problems; not only did farmers themselves have a very low standard of living, but landlords also could not avoid bullying from grassroots government officials and local rogues. There was of course some imbalance between the rich and poor in different cities and regions, but in any case, the tax burden left over from history continued in a disguised manner; even if the temporary taxes levied during the Northern Expedition did not end with the Northern Expedition, such as the "army surcharge" being renamed the "reconstruction surcharge", rural surcharges came one after the other and indirect taxes were endlessly rolled out everywhere.[106] To be sure, taxes and abuse

[105] Quoted from Lloyd E. Eastman, *The Abortive Revolution: China under Nationalist Rule, 1927–1937*, Beijing: Zhongguo Qingnian Chubanshe, 1992, p. 237.

[106] Even Chiang Kai-shek complained: "Government spending continues to rise. Any plan must start with a new tax, which is often a fixed tax on demand, and various miscellaneous taxes were created, sometimes at random by (local governments) to impose a nameless tax on each household, resulting in a huge amount of tax, and people suffer under this heavy tax burden". (From Lloyd E. Eastman, *The Abortive Revolution: China under Nationalist Rule, 1927–1937*, Beijing: Zhongguo Qingnian Chubanshe, 1992, p. 254).

of taxes—the expansion of bureaucracy and corruption—were an unaffordable burden for farmers and the general population, so that poverty remained widespread.

With the help of the United States and Britain, the National Government implemented reform of the currency system. On 8 March 1933, the National Government implemented a reform to "abolish the tael for silver dollars", standardize the differences and fluctuations in the value of silver resulting from regional differences, in weight and percentages. On 1 July, the new silver dollar began to circulate, although the financial reform was introduced when the surge in the price of silver on the international market led to a rapid flow of silver abroad, triggering inflation, high-interest rates and a series of economic crises. In November 1935, paper currency (notes issued by the Central Bank, Bank of China and Bank of Communications) began to circulate, and for the first time China's society and economy began to operate under a unified monetary system, and silver began to be concentrated in the central government. Although the 288,000,000 yuan stored in silver in that year was only one-third of that in April 1934, it was later recognized that the circulation of paper currency did provide an effective tool for the Nanjing government to unify the country. In that year, the United States not only sent a large "economic mission" to China but also extended 1 billion yuan in economic assistance.

In the modernization drive, unified units of measurement also provided conditions for the realization of mechanized development and daily economic life, and the introduction of foreign capital and technology was made possible with the publication of the Three-Year Plan for Heavy Industry in March 1936. This saw fundamental digital growth and structural changes in industry, minerals, agriculture, water conservancy, and other fields. In terms of sovereignty, the military and the economy, the construction of roads, railways, and aviation was of great significance, and during the years of "domestic peace and external resistance" the National Government completed the development of roads from the previous 1000 km to 16,000 km, and railways from the previous 8000 km to 13,000 km, as well as the establishment of eleven air routes and 47 airports. In some major cities, the basic network of communications (urban, long distance and international) was built, postal powers were fully assumed and developed, and by 1936 there were 14,000 post offices throughout the country. With the support of Cai Yuanpei, president of the Central Research Institute, free compulsory education, which Zhu

Jiahua (1893–1963) had suggested a modern China should have, was implemented. A balanced mix of higher education, universal primary and secondary school education, and vocational education was introduced, even at a time when the national crisis was increasingly pressing, and the number of schools and teachers continued to grow. In 1937, there were more than 2000 secondary schools, 1000 normal schools, and 300 vocational schools, as well as undertakings serving modern cities' social welfare such as health and medical institutions, in which institutions at different levels began to emerge, ranging from modern hospitals to clinics.

However, since it was the KMT that controlled the operations of the National Government, and military and political objectives were the basis of the KMT's "tutelary government", the national government in fact did not regard the industrial and commercial capitalists as playing a significant role in the market, but as a source of revenue for the National Government and the KMT. The KMT tightly restricted private ownership of factories, mines, and land resources, so that the national economy was not on a fully liberal economic track; only bankers could, through special relations and transactions, obtain solid influence, as long as they were willing to take the initiative and lend money to the National Government. As a result, the national economy, manipulated by the national government, remained state capitalism of the type that could be seen clearly in Sun Yat-sen's thinking: emphasizing the use of state power to build enterprises, avoiding large enterprises falling into the hands of private and foreign investors, and not permitting the emergence of private capitalism and a wealthy class. In this way, businesses and enterprises necessarily became state wealth, and the state even nationalized marketing companies, as the Nanjing government nationalized the Merchants Steamship Company (Lunchuan Zhaoshangju) in 1932. Such a guiding principle inevitably increased the burden on private capitalists and individual enterprises, necessitating private enterprises to borrow from banks at high interest rates (15–20 percent interest). On some domestic goods almost the same tariff had to be paid as on imported raw materials they would have had to import, which greatly hampered the development of private enterprise.

Despite the effects of the war, the government's economic construction plan was half realized in the ten years when the KMT declared in 1935 that "the red bandits had been eliminated". The prototype of a market began to emerge so China was described as the "world's largest market". On 23 January 1935, Japan's Foreign Minister Hiroda delivered a speech outlining a "non-threatening, non-aggression" China policy, provided that China completely ban the anti-Japanese boycott movement. On 13 February, Foreign Minister Hiroda and Japan's Commercial Attaché in Shanghai Yokosuka Heitarō published an outline of Sino-Japanese economic support, involving the exchange of private industrial inspection missions between the two countries, assistance to Chinese agriculture, increased imports of Chinese goods, and assistance to the Bank of Shanghai.[107] The KMT echoed such demands and expectations for peace between the two countries. Chiang Kai-shek, Wang Jingwei and Sun Ke all made positive statements about seeking cooperation with the Japanese. Chiang Kai-shek explicitly accepted and promoted an end to the "anti-Japanese boycott", his other aim being to eradicate the anti-Japanese strongholds of the CPC. However, the intellectual community had little trust in the Japanese side's statements: Fu Sinian, for example, regarding "Sino-Japanese economic support" as only a "shortcut to the demise of China"; Hu Shi also commented that "as long as 'Manchuria' exists, it will be difficult for China-Japan relations to really improve".[108] It is conceivable that the Japanese proposal and the National Government's obedient response disgusted Chinese intellectuals and nationalists; in fact, by year's end the suspicions of intellectuals seemed to be confirmed by the establishment of the Japanese-backed "Eastern Hebei Anti-Communist Autonomous Defense Committee" (25 November) and the "Hebei-Chahar Political Council" (18 December).[109] More and more people believed that Chiang Kai-shek's national government was following a

[107] "Japan's Commercial Attaché in Shanghai Arrives in Tokyo Yesterday for Meetings with Hiroda", *Zhongyang Ribao*, 12 February 1935.

[108] Hu Shi, "Zhong-Ri tixiu, da ke wen" (Sino-Japanese support, in reply to questions), *Duli Pinglun*, no. 143, 25 March 1935, pp. 2–3.

[109] The Eastern Hebei Anti-Communist Autonomous Defense Committee (25 November) was established by Yin Rugeng (1885–1947), Administrative Inspector-General of the Jimi and Luanyu Districts of Hebei Province, and others, under the direction of the Japanese, and on 25 December 1935, it was changed to the Eastern Hebei Anti-Communist Autonomous Government, and Yin simultaneously issued a declaration signaling that move and one detailing the new organization. The government was originally located in Tongzhou (but moved from Tongzhou to Tangshan in August 1937), administered an area of about 8200 square kilometers and a population of about 6 million. Fiscal revenue accounted for 22% of that of Hebei Province. On 1 February 1938, it was incorporated into the "Interim Government of the Republic of China" formed by Wang Kemin in Beiping. The main demands of the Eastern Hebei Anti-Communist Autonomous Government were "North China autonomy" and an "anti-Communist autonomous buffer

strategy of surrender and non-resistance. In the last month of 1935, the CPC's Hebei Provincial Committee used the nationalist passions of students to lead and organize a high-profile student movement that embarrassed the national government. On 9 December thousands of students from higher education institutions, including Beiping Northeastern University, China University, and Beiping Normal University, took to the streets to demand that the government oppose the establishment of autonomous government in North China, stop the civil war as soon as possible, and work together with foreign allies. In a petition to the government, students called for freedom of the press, speech, and assembly and bringing an end to political repression. On 16 December, more than 10,000 students and citizens from different schools held a demonstration under the organization of the underground CPC to prevent the establishment of the Hebei-Chahar Council of State Affairs. The influence of what was called the "December Ninth Student Movement" was so extensive that the famous words, "North China is so big, it can no longer provide space for a quiet desk", from "Letter to the Nation's People from the Tsinghua University National Salvation Society", were relayed throughout the country. Soon, the students' fury and passion extended to Tianjin, Guangzhou, Wuhan, Nanjing, Shanghai, and other cities. In this atmosphere, various national salvation groups and civil society organizations emerged. This period of national crisis has been

zone", which represented further encroachment on China by Japan. Based on cooperation with Japanese businessmen, the Yin Rugeng regime had an impact on the revenue of Tianjin Customs and the trade of the National Government, leading to the closure of many factories and shops, rising prices and the increase in unemployment.

In 1935, Japan proposed "the autonomy of the five provinces of North China", hoping to control more territory by making the "North China question special". Because the previous Ch'in-Doihara Homei Agreement (27 June) and He-Umezu Agreement (6 July) gave Japan control over Chahar and Hebei respectively, the Japanese asked He Yingqin to grant North China autonomy. Under pressure from Japan, the National Government changed the administrative system in North China and on 18 December established the Hebei-Chahar Council of State Affairs (which administered Hebei and Chahar and the two special cities of Beiping and Tianjin). The 29th Army Chief Song Zheyuan was appointed chairman of the committee, and Song had independent personnel, finance and tax powers. Japan regarded the local regime as an autonomous body of the Nanjing government. Japan's aim was to establish a buffer between Manchuria and the Republic of China, to strengthen the security of Manchuria, and to provide conditions for further incursions to follow. In the view of the National Government, their acquiescence was only a stopgap measure to avoid a head-on conflict. The Hebei-Chahar Council of State Affairs only lasted one year and seven months.

repeatedly blamed on the use by the government's military police of high-pressure hoses, beatings, and arrests to suppress patriotic action by the students on the streets. The national government, on the other hand, was indeed trying everything in its power and strategy to drag out positive resistance as much as possible and to buy time: "Wherever possible, the construction of military, economic, financial and educational undertakings continued". Chiang Kai-shek was widely questioned as early as May 1928 because of the Jinan Incident.[110] But as Chiang Kai-shek said in his speech to the KMT's Fifth Congress that year: "Our sacrifices have not yet reached their limit, and we never speak of sacrifices lightly".

Indeed, the first decade of the National Government came with a huge historical burden: most people were more familiar with Manchu Qing life than with the injunctions of the Republic, when people's modern consciousness depended on universal enlightenment; local military generals never had a sense of the overall situation and, although some used real problems to justify their words and deeds, "military responsibilities and obligations" obviously consumed vast resources of the national government; factions within the KMT could never be quashed, and the ongoing debates over how to understand Sun Yat-sen's legacy or whether power in the Party should be more concentrated or democratized influenced the decision-making and political arrangements of the central government. In the view of the KMT, the CPC, which had always been fomenting trouble, had been holding up flags that seemed more in line with people's ideals, so the National Government could not relax its vigilance, and its military sieges of the Communists consumed a great deal of the country's resources. Coupled with the blows and destruction delivered to China's finances, economy, and national psychology

[110] The Jinan incident is also known as the Jinan Massacre. In April 1928, Chiang Kai-shek's Northern Expeditionary Army advanced northwards, and in early May was blocked by the Japanese in Jinan, who were attempting to halt the Northern Expedition and again assume the privileges it had taken from the Germans in 1919. The Japanese massacred the staff of the National Government and the members of the National Revolutionary Army, as well as many Chinese civilians (more than 17,000 were massacred and thousands were wounded). In the end, these shameful acts were angrily criticized by Chiang Kai-shek's Foreign Minister, who signed an agreement with Japan to end the conflict, fearful that the Northern Expedition might be weakened or even totally derailed by a lack of military capability, as a result of the Japanese military action. This humiliating backdown was criticized and angrily condemned across China. But by the second half of the year, Chiang Kai-shek's Northern Expeditionary Army had wiped out the armies of Wu Peifu and Sun Chuanfang and forced Zhang Zuolin to flee from Beijing.

by Japan's invasion, any ruling party or leader facing such a chaotic and complex situation could only find their tasks nerve-wracking and inevitably flawed, leaving the people dissatisfied and the social situation permanently unstable. However, against this background, the National Government still insisted on "modernizing" the country as much as possible. Indeed, Chiang Kai-shek no longer believed in cooperation with the Communists, which is why Chiang, after driving out the Soviet-trained military officers, cooperated militarily, industrially and culturally with Germany in an effort that ended only when the War of Resistance was about to break out.

Though no one wanted it, the situation was this: given the objective historical conditions the National Government faced after the completion of the Northern Expedition, no person, political party, or organization who sought political integrity, social tranquility, harmony, and a cheerful political outcome for all could succeed in establishing order within chaos. The bureaucracy, corruption, inefficiency of administrative efficiency, the mediocrity of public officials, Party factionalism, persecution of dissidents outside the party, and serious violations of freedom of expression that characterized this period of KMT rule are also the same problems that persist in the mainland to this day.

It is clear that the achievements of the National Government in this decade made most people aware that the modernizing trend in Chinese society was irreversible; as the country faced a profound crisis, the strong atmosphere of nationalism tolerated the ills and problems endured under the KMT, once the KMT's attitude to the Japanese became increasingly clear. In fact, before and after the Xi'an Incident, Chiang Kai-shek was indeed a national leader who, in the eyes of most people in the country, was strongly dependent on the fate of the state and individual, and after the Marco Polo Bridge Incident on 7 July 1937, Chiang Kai-shek's image gained unprecedented recognition. In any case, Chiang Kai-shek did manage to keep factional conflicts within the KMT to a minimum during the decade, and despite military engagements of varying magnitude (whether with warlords or the Communists) he was able to lead the national government in its modernization drive. In summary, the ten years of construction were not only a precondition for victory in the all-out anti-Japanese war but was also the legacy of the Republic of China (Figs. 1, 2, 3, 4, 5, 6, 7, and 8).

Fig. 1 1930s, teachers, students and nude model of the 17th graduate class in Western painting at the Shanghai Art School

Fig. 2 1931, Pang Xunqin's *The Enigma of Life* (oil on canvas) exemplifies the artist's understanding of Western modernist art

Fig. 3 1932, Ceremony honoring the officers and soldiers of the Nineteenth Route Army who fought in the Songhu Battle resisting the Japanese

Fig. 4 1932, Gao Jianfu's *Flames on the Eastern Battlefield* (Chinese-style painting), 166 cm × 92 cm

Fig. 5 1934, Cai Yuanpei emerging to placate young students surrounding the KMT's Central Party HQ

Fig. 6 Li Hua, *Roar! China* (woodcut), 1935

Fig. 7 1936: Sha Fei's photograph of Lu Xun with young woodcut print artists: (from the left) Lin Fu, Cao Bai, Bai Wei, Chen Yanqiao

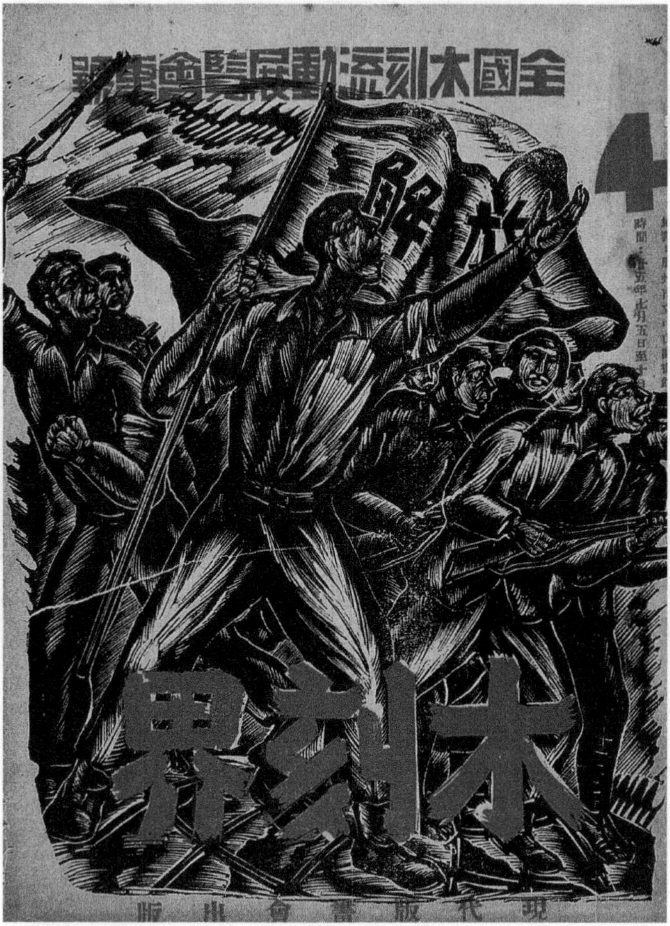

Fig. 8 Tang Yingwei, *Advance*, woodcut, 26.4 cm × 19.3 cm (cover of the fourth volume of *Woodcut World*)

Chapter Four
1937–1949: From the War of Resistance to Civil War

The reactionaries are one of the world's groups who most fear freedom of speech. They are afraid that the people will overturn them, they are afraid that the people will come to see the true face of these great times, and they are even more afraid that their ugliness will be exposed to the masses. They therefore use every despicable means to prevent people from seeing, hearing, or speaking out; they do not allow popular newspapers to exist and do not extend freedom to journalists of integrity.

Mao Zedong, *Xinhua Daily*, 1946

The classes who support the present regime are urban residents, government teachers, intellectuals, and business people. Yet this group of people now does not hold the Nanjing regime in high regard. The KMT's overbearing style made liberal thinkers abhor them; the harsh treatment of government teachers since the beginning of the Anti-Japanese War led to their complete loss of faith in the regime; the corruption and cheating of government officials created all sorts of difficulties that left businessmen angry; financial mismanagement and civil war resulted in constant price surges about which city residents complained.

Chu Anping, *Guancha*, 1947

L. Peng, *A History of China in the 20th Century*,
https://doi.org/10.1007/978-981-99-0734-2_6

The Course of the War of Resistance

The Marco Polo Bridge Incident of 7 July 1937 was the final outcome of the Japanese military forces' total disregard for the views of civil servants with whom they had been in constant dispute and conflict. The irrepressible warrior spirit of Japan's strong young soldiers, encouraged and instigated by politicians, was based on thinking of themselves as fulfilling a "sacred" mission and constantly striving to have the military dominate their nation's politics, so that the civil service of the government became simply expendable, and those who failed to obey were killed. Beginning in the spring of 1931, the militarists engineered several political assassinations and coups, and although they went on trial, their justified defense in court gained considerable support. On 15 May 1932, when a group of young soldiers stormed the home of prime minister Tsuyoshi Inukai (1855–1932) and assassinated him, they were judged to have shown "patriotic dedication".[1] In fact, some senior military leaders have long been fixated on China, and a number of politicians and oligarchs who shared their ultimate purpose, which doomed Japan to embark on an adventurist policy sooner or later.[2] In 1936, Hirota Kōki (1878–1948)

[1] There were twenty main members, namely five naval captains, including Tsukano Michio (DATES) and Mikami Taku (1905–1971), as well as eight naval reserve officers, and others.

[2] Japan's need for raw materials and markets due to industrial development after the Meiji Restoration was well known, and in the "Introduction" we already touched on Japan's annexation of Korea (1875) and the Russo-Japanese war fought on Chinese territory (1904–1905). Later Japan wanted to acquire German interests in Shandong (1914), and so on.

From 27 June to 7 July 1927, Prime Minister Tanaka Giichi (1864–1929), an army general, presided over the "Oriental Conference" at the Residence of the Foreign Minister of Tokyo, where he convened Japanese military and political officials to study and discuss the "continental policy" involving China. The conference focused on separating Manchuria from Chinese territory, placing it under Japanese control and granting Japan its sovereignty. After the meeting, Tanaka wrote up the conference document "Imperial Active Fundamental Policy towards Manchuria and Mongolia" and secretly presented what came to be known as the Tanaka Memorial to the Emperor. It stated:

Manchuria-Mongolia comprise Fengtian, Jilin, and Heilongjiang as well as Inner and Outer Mongolia, a vast area of 74,000 square kilometers and a population of 28 million people. It is more than three times larger than the territory of the Japanese Empire (excluding Korea and Taiwan), but has a population only one-third of our country's. Not only is the land highly sought after, but its farms, mines and forests produce great wealth that is unmatched ... the administrations of several cabinets have administered Manchuria-Mongolia, perfecting our new continental policy.

took over as prime minister, and from 1933 onwards, when he became foreign minister, he exhibited an extremist attitude and enlisted army radicals in the government cabinet. In 1936, Hirota issued a proposal to China, the fifth article of which ("Japan will provide advisers to every department of the Chinese government") was instantly reminiscent of the Twenty-one Demands, and it was rejected by the Chinese. China at this time had been engaged in several years of nation-building and

If we want to conquer China, we must first conquer Manchuria-Mongolia, and if you want to conquer the world, you must conquer China first.

If we can completely conquer China, then other nations such as Asia Minor, India, and Southeast Asia will fear us, respect us and surrender to us, so that the world will recognize East Asia as ours".

In 1931, a member of the Political Allies Council, Yōsuke Matsuoka (1880–1946, who would later be designated a Class A war criminal) told the Japanese House of Representatives: "I think the Manchuria-Mongolia issue is a matter of life and death for our country and is a lifeline for our people. This must be considered from the position of defense and economics".

Itagaki Seishirō (1885–1948), who took part in the planning of the September 18 Incident, wrote in his Manchuria and Mongolia from a Military Perspective: "In the war against Russia, Manchuria and Mongolia are the main battlefield; in the war against the United States, Manchuria and Mongolia are the source of supplies. Thus, in fact, Manchuria and Mongolia are vital in the fighting with the United States, the USSR and China".

At the end of 1930, the Japanese Minister of Intelligence, Tatekawa Yoshitsugu (1880–1945), convened a plan presented in his "1931 Annual Situation Report" which proposed three stages in resolving the Manchuria and Mongolia question: 1, breaking the status quo; 2, establishing a regime friendly to Japan, and 3, occupying all of the Northeast. In June 1931, Tatekawa convened a meeting in his capacity as Minister of Operations of the General Staff to draw up "An Outline Program for Settling the Manchurian Problem", which involved "immediate military action" if necessary.

On 1 May 1935, the Japanese government revised the Imperial Defense Policy and the Imperial Military Service Program, to read: "The initial goal of the war against China is to occupy key areas of North China and the area adjacent to Shanghai, protect the Empire's rights and interests and the Japanese diaspora".

On 3 June 1935, the Japanese Ministry of the Army formulated the "Shōwa 12 (1937) War Plan against China", which included specific arrangements for the war against China, and outlined its mission objective: "Within three months, to reduce to nil China's capacity for resistance, and achieve the goal of a rapidly concluded war".

In 1936, the construction and development of the Japanese army was completed, Japan advocated military expansion with zaibatsu and warlord power gradually assuming the upper hand.

In January 1937, the Japanese Kanto Army formulated its Outline Five-Year Plan for the Industrial Development of Manchuria, and on 29 May, the Japanese Ministry of the Army formulated its Outline Five-Year Plan for Important Industries, covering the northeast and north of China.

preparations for war with Japan, and so it dared to put forward proposals more in keeping with China's demands, such as requiring the withdrawal of Japanese troops from Hebei and Chahar and curbing the Japanese-inspired autonomy movement. In early 1937, Prime Minister Hirota's successor Hayashi Senjūrō (1876–1943), was prepared to negotiate with China in a conciliatory manner. Moreover, the situation in China after the Xi'an Incident gave the National Government more self-confidence and nationalist resources—the basic political pattern of the National Anti-Japanese National United Front constituted a force of resolute resistance. The Japanese militarists changed the Diet and the voices calling for military action against China were deafening; at a time when Tokyo was still considering its options, the Kanto Army decided to push ahead with outright military action.[3] On 7 July, under the pretext of looking for soldiers who disappeared near the Marco Polo Bridge, Japanese soldiers entered the nearby town of Wanping to conduct a search. Ji Xingwen (1907–1958), who headed the 219th regiment guarding Wanping, and the local county governor, Wang Lengzhai (1892–1960), jointly carried out a search and informed the Japanese they had not seen the missing soldiers. When the Chinese side refused the request of the Kanto Army, the latter began shelling Wanping and the Marco Polo Bridge early the next day and attacked the 219th Regiment's positions on the same day and occupying the town of Wanping which was garrisoned by the 29th Army of Song Zheyuan (1885–1940). On this occasion, the national government, which had a preparatory plan, no longer needed an expedient pretext to confront the Japanese invasion and attack.[4] Chiang Kai-shek, who was hosting a gathering of an officer training group and people from various walks of life in Lushan on 17 July, delivered a speech there, which is often quoted:

[3] In 1905, after the end of the Russo-Japanese War, Japan established the Kanto Army in order to protect the leases it acquired and the South Manchurian Railway. In 1928, in order to control Manchuria which Japan now occupied, the headquarters of the Kanto Army was moved from Dalian to Shenyang in an attempt to gain control of Manchuria, as well as to stem a possible drive south by the Soviet Union.

[4] In 1935, the National government was already considering turning Sichuan, Guizhou and Yunnan into anti-Japanese rear bases; in the winter, Chiang Kai-shek instructed Zhang Zhizhong to build field barricades in Shanghai and Nanjing; and in 1936, the national government completed setting up its headquarters and military deployment for fighting the Japanese.

> We have finally reached the moment, when we can only sacrifice everything and fight the anti-Japanese war to the end, and only if we have the determination to "sacrifice everything" will we be able to win the final victory. If we are uncertain or harbor illusions, we will trap our nation in a desperate place.
>
> As soon as the war begins, everyone, regardless of location or age, will have the responsibility of defending our soil and the determination to sacrifice all.

Chiang Kai-shek announced four conditions for resolving the dispute surrounding the Incident, the core of which was the inviolability of Chinese territory and sovereign independence. Although Chiang made it clear that the Chinese government's position was "to fight back, but not seek war", he called on "the nation to risk their lives in order for the country to survive". In fact, China's military power and war resources were still far inferior to those of Japan.

The presidents of Peking University, Jiang Menglin (1886–1964), Tsinghua University, Mei Yiqi (1889–1962), and Nankai University, Zhang Boling (1876–1951), all attended the talks in Lushan. The moods of these intellectuals differed of course, but two days before Chiang Kai-shek's speech (14 July), the diary of Wu Mi (1894–1978) captures how intellectuals were thinking:

> Reading the newspapers, we know that the war situation is highly volatile and that disaster is imminent. In the future we will either see (a) the fall of North China and our enslavement, or (ii) the ruination of war with massive destruction. In essence, our previous peaceful, comfortable, salubrious and dignified lives would no longer be possible. The best time of my life is now over. It did not last long, but the beginning did not bring joy and married love, but troubles, loneliness, despair and great pain. Looking back on life, is there anything I do not regret? Now or in the future I may commit suicide, become a monk, uphold one's principles, or sacrifice myself for a cause; whatever the outcome, I will be left with endless regret. ...

For the CPC, the full-scale outbreak of war was clearly an opportunity for the CPC to acquire legal status, and on 23 July Mao Zedong, on behalf of the CPC, issued a positive statement in swift response:

> We Communists with one heart and one mind will faithfully implement our declaration.[5] At the same time we firmly support Mr. Chiang Kai-shek's declaration, and are willing to work with the Kuomintang and compatriots across the country to defend the land to the last drop of blood, and will oppose all wavering, hesitation, compromise, and retreat, to resolutely fight the anti-Japanese war.[6]

On 26 July, the Japanese occupied Langfang, and the National Government voluntarily withdrew its troops from Beiping in order to protect the city's historical sites and to win time to devise a strategy. On 30 July, Tianjin fell. At the beginning of August, those military leaders who had previously opposed or disagreed with Chiang Kai-shek's arguments at the National Defense Joint Meeting that the critical moment for national survival had now arrived, decided to abandon their previous positions and rally around in the face of the national disaster, and even the CPC's military leaders participated in the meeting. On 9 August, the Chinese guards in charge of protecting the Hongqiao Airport in Shanghai shot and killed two Japanese soldiers, Lieutenant Ōyama Isao and Saito who were attempting to force their way into the airport. The Japanese immediately placed the navy, air force and army on combat readiness, and on 12 August, the Japanese military headquarters drew up plans to send in its army. The "Battle of Shanghai", which began on 13 August, marked the beginning of an all-out war between China and Japan: Zhang Zhizhong (1890–1969), commander of the Beijing-Shanghai police, who advocated "pre-emptive resistance against the enemy", delivered a speech the next day: "Yesterday (13th) at 4 pm, Japanese warships suddenly bombarded us north of Zhabei with heavy artillery. The sound of artillery continued all night, and resident losses were surprisingly heavy. At the same time, infantry emerged from the concession area and attacked our defense security team, but we remained calm and never returned a single shot. When the Japanese had earlier launched their large-scale land, sea and air attack, we were forced to respond to defend our territory and sovereignty. As of today, the peace has been completely shattered and our sacrifices have reached the limit, and in opposing the aggressors and saving the nation from being lost, honor does not allow us

[5] Referring to the July 8th Manifesto of the CPC calling for the War of Resistance against Japan.

[6] Mao Zedong, Mao Zedong Xuanji, vol. 2, Renmin Chubanshe, 1952, p. 302.

to look back".[7] Also on 14 August, the National Government issued "Letter on Self-Defense in the War of Resistance", and on the 15th, Japan began a national military mobilization and established a combat base. Three months after the Battle of Shanghai, unlike the Battle of Beiping and Tianjin, the Japanese front lines in Shanghai were effectively blocked by the 87th and 88th Divisions of the National Army, with Chen Cheng (1897–1965), Gu Zhutong (1893–1987), Zhang Zhizhong, and Zhang Fakui (1896–1980) serving as field commanders and Chiang Kai-shek (Jiang Jieshi) 蔣介石蔣中正 as commander. The Chinese side had 700,000 troops, while Japan's land, sea, and air forces total 270,000, with China and Japan giving no ground in battle. Li Zongren wrote that on the battlefield soldiers "in their thousands faced death and injury every hour". The tragic extent of the Battle of Shanghai war was described by General Wedemeyer (1896–1989) as "the bloodiest battle the world has seen since the Battle of Verdun". The National Army lost 250,000 men, with ten generals among the dead. In the end, the Chinese army could no longer oppose the Japanese army and withdraw on 9 November to Hangzhou and Nanjing, as Li Zongren described: "But at this time the front line of our armies collapsed, and we withdrew in haste, through the bombing of enemy aircraft day and night; men and horses were trampled in the complete chaos".[8] The Chinese armies thus suffered many casualties in the evacuation. The earlier annihilation of several hundred Japanese troops by Lin Biao's 115th Division on 24 September at Pingxing Pass in north-eastern Shanxi, came to be regarded as the first victory of the Eighth Route Army under the CPC's command, and that small battle was later repeatedly celebrated by the CPC. On 20 November, the National Government decided to move the capital to Chongqing, and on 13 December Japanese troops captured Nanjing, the capital of the National Government. Japanese troops carried out a large-scale massacre in Nanjing: in the arson, looting, rape, and shooting, nearly 300,000

[7] Zhang Zhizhong Huiyi Lu, vol. 1, Zhongguo Wenshi Chubanshe, 1985, p. 122.

[8] Li Zongren, *Li Zongren Huiyilu* (Memoirs of Li Zongren), Guilin: Guangxi Renmin Chubanshe, 1980, vol. 2, p. 696.

Chinese were killed in what came to be known as the internationally infamous "Nanjing Massacre".[9] On the 24th, Hangzhou fell, and the Battle to Defend Shanghai was declared lost:

> Shanghai and Nanjing were successively lost, as was the cream of China's land, sea, and air forces. The whole country was at a loss and in a state of unspeakable despair. As a result, Wang Jingwei and the faction calling for peace felt smug, as though they had foreseen this outcome. There was a clamor for compromise at this juncture, spurred by the logic that if national military and civilian resistance was not resolute, then it was really better not to engage in further fighting.[10]

After signing the Sino-Soviet Non-Aggression Treaty in August, the Soviet Union provided nearly $US300 million in low-interest loans, thousands of aircraft, 2000 pilots to man them, and hundreds of military advisers to help China fight its war of resistance against Japan. Stalin's aim was to prevent a Japanese invasion of the Soviet Union by supporting China's resistance to Japan and thus containing Japanese military forces.

Based on the daily maintenance and management of the occupied territories, Japan began to seek the establishment of puppet regimes in the occupied territories of Inner Mongolia, Beijing and Nanjing. On 22 November 1937, the Japanese army merged the "Southern Chahar Autonomous Government", "Northern Shanxi Autonomous

[9] The International Military Tribunal for the Far East stated in its judgment on the "Nanjing Massacre": "All resistance had ceased as the Japanese Army entered the city on the morning of 13 December 1937. The Japanese soldiers swarmed over the city and committed various atrocities. ... Organized and wholesale murder of male civilians was conducted with the apparent sanction of the commanders on the pretense that Chinese soldiers had removed their uniforms and were mingling with the population. Groups of Chinese civilians were formed, bound with their hands behind their backs, and marched outside the walls of the city where they were killed in groups by machine gun fire and with bayonets. ... Estimates made at a later date indicate that the total number of civilians and prisoners of war murdered in Nanking and its vicinity during the first six weeks of the Japanese occupation was over 200,000. That these estimates are not exaggerated...These figures do not take into account those persons whose bodies were destroyed by burning, or by throwing them into the Yangtze River, or otherwise disposed of by Japanese...Despite the denials of mass abuse by witnesses of Japanese origin, the contrary testimony of neutral witnesses of various nationalities, unquestionable and credible, is overwhelming. This covert crime began on December 13, 1937, when it occupied the city of Nanjing and did not stop until early February 1938".

[10] Li Zongren, op. cit., p. 700.

Government" and "Mongol League Autonomous Government" into the "Joint Committee of Mongolia and Territories". On 14 December 1937, "Beiping Security Maintenance Committee", "Tianjin Local Security Maintenance Committee", "Henan Autonomous Government" and "Shanxi Province Interim Government" were merged in Beiping into the "Interim Government of the Republic of China". In January 1938, when the National Government was very clear about long-term resistance to the Japanese, the Japanese Imperial Council began to formulate its "Fundamental Policy for Dealing with the Chinese Incident". Showing the Japanese military that war was its major premise, the Japanese government decided to "support China's newly emerging regime" to replace the national government—or merge it with the "newly emerging regime", and so adjust its diplomatic relations with China. On 18 March, the Japanese army merged the Shanghai Municipal Government (established on 5 December 1937), the Nanjing Autonomous Commission (established on 1 January 1938) and the Hangzhou Security Maintenance Council (established on 1 January 1938) in Nanjing as the "Chinese Republic Restoration Government" in preparation for "promoting the substantive collapse of Chiang Kai-shek's regime". After the National government moved to Chongqing, the well-trained administrative officials who remained in the fallen city either lost their roles or became officials and staff at all levels of the puppet regime.

In February 1938, the Japanese General Staff drafted the "Program for the Construction of the Shōwa Military System" and decided to implement an overall war system, "with unreservedly unified deployment of the entire forces of the country, to always guide and use it to carry out the purposes of the war". "The means used was separating military forces, the economy, politics, and ideology, so that they interrelate and influence each other, but the military is the decisive force".[11]

After the occupation of Nanjing, the Japanese army's next goal was to occupy Xuzhou, which was under the jurisdiction of China's fifth war zone, because it was the junction of the north–south Tianjin-Pukou (outside Nanjing) Railway and east–west Longhai (Lianyungang-Lanzhou) Railways. The occupation of Xuzhou would open up the north–south rail lines for the Japanese Army. In late March 1938, the 40,000 troops of the Tenth Division of the Japanese Army arrived near

[11] Li Qingshan, *Zhengmian Zhanchang Kangzhan Zhenxiang*, Huawen Chubanshe, 2017, p. 193.

Tai'erzhuang, 30 kilometers northeast of Xuzhou, and the Japanese army rushed aircraft and tanks to the area to cover their drive and three days later the Japanese army entered Tai'erzhuang. The Second Group Army under commander-in-chief Sun Lianzhong and the Japanese army fought to the death in the stony lanes of Tai'erzhuang. On 3 April, more than two-thirds of the town was occupied by the Japanese. When more than seventy per cent of the men under Sun Lianzhong and the commander of the 31st division Shi Fengcheng in the Second Army Group had sustained casualties but still manage to hold Tai'erzhuang stubbornly, they organized suicide squads to launch a counterattack against the enemy and succeeded in recapturing three-quarters of the town's streets. By dawn, the Tang Enbo's troops had broken out and were besieging the enemy from the rear, and in a general attack on the Fifth War Zone, the Japanese army sustained more than 20,000 casualties, and their main force was defeated. The news reports emanating from Tai'erzhuang gave the Chinese great encouragement and confidence and re-acquainted the international community that the Chinese army was fighting the anti-Japanese war. On 15 May, more than 300,000 troops from the Northern and Southern Japanese forces began a siege of Xuzhou, and the Fifth War Zone began what Li Zongren termed a "planned retreat". On May 19, the Japanese occupied an abandoned Xuzhou, but the withdrawal of the army from Xuzhou was not like the tragically hasty withdrawal after the Battle of Shanghai and the military forces were protected. On 4 June, the Japanese attacked Kaifeng, and two days later the defenders had to withdraw. On the 9th, in order to resist the rapid Japanese attack, Chiang Kai-shek ordered the destruction of the Yellow River embankments; the flood effectively halted the Japanese 14th and 16th Divisions, and the Japanese Cavalry Unit that had taken Xinzheng was totally annihilated by the National Army. The transportation of the Japanese army's military needs and ammunition supplies was greatly hampered, and the flooding also caused the Japanese mechanized forces to lose significant effectiveness. But at the same time, the breach of the Yellow River embankment caused a huge loss of life and property for ordinary people, and the subsequent disaster and displacement of victims obviously originated from this.

After the capture of Xuzhou, the Japanese army's next target was clearly Wuhan. Japanese headquarters hoped to force the National government to surrender by capturing Wuhan. The relocation of the capital to Chongqing would be a time-consuming process, but

Chongqing and the surrounding southwest region have a clear geographical advantage in wartime. The mountains, cliffs, rivers, and rugged roads recommended the area as a rear base for the anti-Japanese resistance. However, Wuhan, in the middle of the Yangtze River valley, still served as the capital until the military and political center could be relocated to Chongqing. Guo Moruo recalled this period: "Although Nanjing's National Government and Central Party Departments all moved to Chongqing, the KMT's key figures in the party and army were almost all concentrated in Wuhan. Leaders of opposition parties and prominent figures in cultural circles were almost all concentrated in Wuhan. Wuhan became the de facto capital of the Anti-Japanese War".[12] In any case, with the urgency of the war, universities, secondary schools, and factories across the country moved inland.[13] Universities such as Peking University, Tsinghua University, and Nankai University migrated inland, first to Changsha as the Changsha Temporary University, and then on the orders of the Ministry of Education to Kunming, where it changed its name to Southwest United University. Some tertiary institutions from Beiping and Tianjin moved to Xi'an, and institutions of higher learning in the southeast coastal areas such as Central University, Fudan University, and Jiaotong University moved to Chongqing. Eventually, Chongqing, Kunming, Chengdu, Xi'an, and Lanzhou, became the major cities where tertiary educational institutions and enterprises were relocated; Chongqing alone housed 25 institutions, a wartime educational

[12] [Guo Moruo, *Hongbo Qu* (Floodwaters), Beijing: People's Literature Press, 1979, p. 20.

[13] Hong Kong's *Gongshang Ribao* (Business Daily) on 10 June 1939 reported the following statistics:

It is estimated that more than 300 factories have been relocated to Sichuan, Yunnan, Hunan and other provinces. These factories can be divided into nine categories, namely mining plants, electric motor factories, radio manufacturers, chemical plants, canneries, ceramic kilns, glassworks, printed stationery factories, hardware manufacturers, textile mills, and leather tanneries and finishing plants. The distribution shows that about 44% went to Sichuan, 39% to Hunan, 6.9% to Guangxi, 6.5% to Shaanxi and 3.6% to Yunnan, Guizhou and other provinces. In addition to the considerable output of military industrial products, the production of all kinds of commodities and industrial products increased. The daily necessities required by the locals in Sichuan, Yunnan, Hunan, Guangxi, Jiangxi and Shaanxi provinces were supplied by domestic factories, and their quality also quite improved, and this was one good aspect of domestic industrial improvement after the Anti-Japanese War began.

migration that bequeathed a special historical and cultural landscape for China during the eight-year war.

It was in Wuhan that the national government's military committee was reshuffled and Zhou Enlai of the CPC was appointed deputy director of the political department, recalling the first period of KMT-CPC cooperation. During the second period of cooperation, the CPC adopted a strategy of only partially disclosing the CPC's organization and membership, while most of its hidden members continued to work underground in order to respond to any possible changes in the political situation. The KMT handed over the Third Office of the Political Department to members of the CPC to manage so that the Third Office became an effective base for the CPC to publicize its anti-Japanese message to the masses. On 29 March 1938, the KMT held an interim National Congress, which, in addition to passing the resolution making Chiang Kai-shek the first president of the Kuomintang, also established the Three Principles of the People Youth League and adopted the "War of Resistance Nation-building Program". It also established the National People's Political Council as the highest national public opinion institution in wartime as the focus of popular concern, and when people from different parties or dissidents, including the CPC, participated in the founding conference of the National Political Participation Conference held in Wuhan from 7 to 15, July people regarded it as a positive measure of the Anti-Japanese National United Front and thus were greatly encouraged. Regarding military arrangements, on 14 June, the national government formed the Ninth War Zone on the basis of the Wuhan Defense Command, and Chen Cheng was appointed commander of the war zone. On 25 July, under the cover provided by the navy and air force, the Japanese 11th Army under its commander, Okamura Yasuji (1884–1966), began a general assault on Jiujiang; on 29 September, the strategically located town of Tianjiazhen was captured by the Japanese. In early October, the 106th Division of the Japanese Army was nearly destroyed by the forces of General Xue Yue, commander of the 2nd Corps of the National Army, but finally, the Chinese army withdrew from Wuhan in mid-October. Previously, from June onwards, people, government agencies, and military agencies had already begun to withdraw from Wuhan, and all heavy and military-industrial plant that could not be withdrawn was destroyed. On 21 October, Japanese tanks had already entered the city of Guangzhou, which delivered supplies to Wuhan. On 26 October, Wuhan fell. The field for the Battle of Wuhan extended to include Jiangxi, Anhui, Henan, and

Hubei; the Chinese army has 120 divisions involved, and the Japanese army put in 12 divisions, plus an additional 400,000 soldiers. In the Battle of Wuhan, the Japanese killed and wounded came to more than 200,000. Although Wuhan fell and the situation was very serious, China having not yet received timely assistance from the international community, the Japanese army's front line had obviously been overextended, and the original plan of hoping to complete the war in China within three months had completely failed. By the end of the Battle of Wuhan, Japan had deployed 26 divisions to the Chinese mainland, leaving only one defense regiment in Japan. Chiang Kai-shek published "Letter to the Nation's Soldiers and Civilians Announcing the Retreat from Wuhan" on 31 October, in which he asked people to adhere to a "more sympathetic, compassionate, down-to-earth, tough, courageous, and progressive fighting" spirit to sustain a "protracted and comprehensive war of resistance".

In May 1938, Mao Zedong published "On Protracted Warfare" in Yan'an. This article foretold the Sino-Japanese war. Mao reminded people that Japan is "first in the East" in terms of military power, economic power, and political organization. However, due to the reactionary and barbarous nature of the war launched by Japan, and the consumption it entailed, China's War of Resistance against Japan was progressive and more widely supported internationally than the Fascist forces, and China's War of Resistance, though protracted, would eventually be won. Mao Zedong presented a realistic picture of China's situation: "China's military, economy, politics and culture today are not as strong as Japan's, but in China itself, there are more progressive factors than in any other historical period".[14] In fact, contrary to the original design to quickly end the war, Japan's occupation of Wuhan was only a superficial victory, because of the extension of the front line and the city's need for military and economic resources became increasingly difficult to meet; a long-running war was already something the Japanese had to calculate an estimate, and in preparation for future war Japanese generals were even using the term "one hundred-year war".

In "On Protracted Warfare", Mao Zedong accused the KMT of subscribing to arguments that "resistance meant national subjugation" or "continuance of the war meant national subjugation", and emphasized the progressiveness of the CPC and the army under the leadership of the

[14] Mao Zedong, *Mao Zedong Xuanji*, v. 2, Renmin Chubanshe, 1952, p. 411.

CPC. Indeed, the Eighth Route Army and New Fourth Army under the leadership of the CPC started out with no more than 30,000 troops, and their weapons were far fewer than those of the National army, but based on their power and strategy, the CPC placed its troops mainly in the mountains away from frontline battlefields and in areas occupied by the Japanese army, in order to establish bases behind enemy lines, try to avoid face-to-face fighting with the Japanese, and conduct guerrilla warfare.[15] In November 1937, these various bases jointly established the Shanxi-Chahar-Hebei Military Region, and on 10 January 1938, the Military and Political Congress of the Shanxi-Chahar-Hebei Border District was held in Fuping county, Hebei province, and a provisional administrative committee was established, although the KMT was not yet aware of it. However, this local regime played a role in holding back the Japanese, so it was approved by the National Government, and by the end of 1938, the border area covered more than 70 counties, with a population of nearly 12 million. In the following year, the Eighth Route Army and New Fourth Army began to enter northern and central China. By 1940, the Eighth Route Army had grown to 150 regiments, with a total of 400,000 troops, and the population of the controlled (liberated) areas had reached 40 million. In any case, the CPC had its own army which although it appeared to be at the mercy of the National government, provided the basis for land reform and, as long as a majority of people benefited from the reform measures, the CPC had the support to consolidate its territory. Of course, the development of the Party's organization and its own forces was an important task of the CPC, and all its work was carried out in accordance with the will of the CPC and was not affected by orders of the Kuomintang, although this was totally inconsistent with Chiang Kai-shek's initial offer that the CPC obey the decrees and military orders of the KMT. In 1939, the Japanese army did note that the CPC's army was an independent political and military organization, as described in a Japanese military document: "In the future, the cancer for security in North China will be the Communist Party of China, and how we

[15] Lin Biao's report to the Communist International delivered in 1941 while he was recuperating in the Soviet Union reveals the CPC avoided fighting the Japanese at the beginning of the war: "When the Japanese army went to war with the KMT army, I asked the Central Committee more than once to agree to attack the Japanese. But without receiving any reply, I had to make the decision to fight the Battle of Pingxingguan". (Quoted from Chang Jung and Jon Halliday, *Mao: The Unknown Story*, Chinese language edition, Hong Kong: Open Press, 2006, p. 175.)

defeat this opposition fighting organization which organically combines the army, government, Party and the people, will be fundamental to our current stage of public security and liquidation".[16]

After the Seventh July Incident, Chiang Kai-shek also wanted to coordinate with the British, American, German, and even French ambassadors. On 31 July, Hu Shi recorded in his diary how Chiang Kai-shek invited Mei Yiqi, Zhang Boling, Tao Xisheng (1899–1988), Chen Bulei (1890–1948) and himself to lunch to discuss the possibility of maintaining a diplomatic path with Japan. Since November, the Japanese side had entrusted the German Ambassador Oskar Trautmann to mediate Japan–China relations in view of the fact that it would "destroy China within three months". After Chiang Kai-shek rejected Trautmann's mediation at a meeting of senior generals in Nanjing on 2 December, on 16 January 1938 the Japanese Cabinet issued a statement to China declaring that "it would not negotiate with the National Government", which meant that Japan would not engage in any further negotiations with Chiang Kai-shek's government, and the war would continue until the collapse of the National Government. Two days later, the two sides recalled their respective ambassadors and diplomatic relations between the two countries were completely broken off. In late February 1938, Chiang Kai-shek arranged for Gao Zongwu (1905–1994), a young and capable diplomat who had studied Japanese political and economic issues, traveled to Hong Kong to liaise with Japan and gather intelligence to deal with any future possibilities—peace talks remained one of the paths that were never renounced. During that month, Gao Zongwu arranged for Dong Daoning, head of the first section of the Guizhou Division, to go to Japan to "spy on the true attitude of the highest authorities in the enemy stronghold". Dong brought back a letter from the Japanese chief of staff, Kagesa Sadaaki (1893–1948), to his former classmates in Japan, He Yingqin and Zhang Qun (1889–1990). In April, Gao sent a letter to Jiang. Subsequently, Chiang Kai-shek's negotiating terms were ignored by the Japanese military. At the beginning of June, Gao was inspired by Zhou Fohai, then vice-minister of propaganda, and flew back to Hong Kong via Hankou to negotiate with Aki Nishiyoshi, director of the Nanjing office of the

[16] Japanese Defence Department War History Department, *Dazhanqian zhi Huabei Zhi'an Zuozhan* (The North China Pacification War Prior to the Great War), Taipei: National Defence Ministry's History and Politics Editing and Translation Department, 1988, p. 352.

South Manchurian Railway, to negotiate with Wang Jingwei, who holds a position of influence with the Japanese.[17] In the same month, Gao Zongwu flew to Tokyo without telling Chiang Kai-shek, and in talks with Japanese army ministers, chiefs of staff and other powerful figures, Gao's information enabled the Japanese to reach a decision. Wang Jingwei's push for peace within the Kuomintang was thwarted and he had wanted to implement a peace movement from outside the government which would influence Japan's policy toward China. In the following month, a meeting of the Japanese cabinet, on the basis of the proposal of Military Headquarters, formulated a "Provisional Response in China Strategy", adopting the policy of "overthrowing Chiang Kai-shek" and "making use of elite persons in China". Although Wang Jingwei initially denied the possibility of a separate peace with Japan, on 21 October he told Reuters, "If Japan puts forward negotiations and conditions that do not hinder the survival of the Chinese state, our people will accept it as a basis for discussion, depending on the conditions put forward by the Japanese side".[18] At the end of October, Mei Siping (1896–1946) brought back the Japanese document which made It clear to Wang Jingwei what the Japanese government expected of him: he should leave Chongqing, set up a separate government, and clarify his basic negotiating terms. On 3 November, Japanese Prime Minister Prince Konoye issued a five-article declaration announcing the "establishment of a new order in Asia". However, more people tend to think of this as Japan's ambition to rule Asia, and although "united defense against the Communists" was tempting for the KMT, Chiang Kai-shek and Wang Jingwei discussed how to deal with the issue of Japan; the former insisted on resistance against to stop the CPC growing, the latter believed that only cooperation with Japan could truly counter the CPC. On 20 November, at Wang Jingwei's request, Gao Zongwu and Mei Siping went to Shanghai to conduct secret discussions with the Japanese representatives Imai Takeo (1898–1982), Itō Yoshio and Kagesa Sadaaki, and there they signed a memorandum on

[17] On 27 June, six men (Xi Yixian, Dong Daoning, Itō Yoshio, Gao Zongwu, Matsumoto Shigeharu and Kagesa Sadaaki) held a further meeting at the Repulse Bay Hotel in Hong Kong, hoping to broker a ceasefire and peace talks. Matsumoto lamented in his book: "This was a gathering of men from so-called hostile countries during wartime, as well as being a gathering of comrades that was quite emotional".

[18] Quoted from Gao Zongwu, *Gao Zongwu Huiyi Lu* (Memoirs of Gao Zongwu), Beijing: Zhongguo Baike Quanshu Chubanshe, 2016, p. 12.

a Japan–China agreement. When German radio broadcasted the news that Wang Jingwei on behalf of the Military Commission had left Chongqing on 18 December to discuss peace with Japan, Chiang Kai-shek also told the media on 27 December: "We are well aware that the tactics of the Japanese militarists are to threaten, entice and provoke divisions and there is nothing they will not do; Mr. Wang has a clear stance known to all. During the past few years, for the party and the nation he has made every effort and endured suffering in the war of resistance against the Japanese, as is especially known to our allies in the central government, and I am personally deeply moved".[19] However, on 29 December, Wang Jingwei issued a letter "to President Chiang and all comrades of the KMT Central Executive Supervisory Committee" advocating peace negotiations with Japan. The purpose of the letter was to clarify the fundamental change in the Japanese government's policy on Sino-Japanese diplomatic relations after 22 December.[20] For the sake of "friendly relations between good neighbors", "common defense against Communism" and "lifting

[19] *Shenbao* (Hong Kong), 28 December 1938.

[20] The media published the content of Wang Jingwei's "clarification":

Firstly. For friendly relations between good neighbors, we solemnly declare that Japan has no territorial claims on China and makes no demand for compensation for military expenses. Japan will not only respect China's sovereignty, and will copy the precedent of the Meiji Restoration, and, as conditions for allowing freedom of residence on the mainland, return the concessions and abolish her extraterritorial rights, so that China can be fully independent. The Japanese Government solemnly states that we will rely on peaceful methods; not only will we preserve the integrity of the northern provinces but will restore to China all territory acquired since the beginning of the Anti-Japanese War, so that China's independence and integrity of sovereignty and administrative power can also be maintained. In this way, we abide by our declaration and seek a reasonable solution to the question of the four northeastern provinces, which will conform to our due determination.

Second. We seek common defense against Communism. Over the past few years, the Japanese Government has repeatedly proposed that this should be based on non-interference in the military and internal affairs of our countries. Today, the Japanese Government has already stated that such concerns can be eliminated when a Sino-Japanese Anti-Communist Agreement, in the spirit of the Sino-Japanese-Italian Anti-Communist Agreement, is concluded. The purpose of our defense against Communism is to prevent the Communist International plotting disturbances and ensuring the Soviet Union cannot exert influence. The Chinese Communists must declare their willingness to strive for the realization of the Three Principles of the People and completely abandon their organization and propaganda, and abolish the special organizations of their border district governments and armed forces, and fully abide by the legal system of the Republic of China. The Three Principles of the People are the supreme principle of the founding of the Republic of China, and all organizations and propaganda that run counter to this

the economy", peace talks with Japan were proposed. Wang Jingwei was so keen to promote this "peace movement" that, in addition to the stated reason and purpose of establishing a peaceful regime based on Sun Yat-sen's Pan-Asianism, there may also have been an intention to engage in a political power game with Chiang Kai-shek, with Wang Jingwei counting on a new central government to eventually replace Chiang Kai-shek's national government. On 1 January 1939, the Kuomintang decided to expel Wang Jingwei from the Party; In May, Wang and Zhou Fohai and others discussed the establishment of power in Nanjing. At the beginning of June, Wang Jingwei, Zhou Fohai and Gao Zongwu went to Japan to discuss cooperation in establishing the Nanjing regime with the Japanese government, but Japan did not agree on continuing to use the design of a white sun on a blue sky as the national flag, so the two sides were negotiations for several months. On 19–20 September, Wang Jingwei held talks with Wang Kemin (1879–1945) and Liang Hongzhi (1882–1946), the leaders of the new "Reformed Government of the Republic of China" and the "Provisional Government of the Republic of China", which had been established with the support of Japan, to discuss their merger and the establishment of a new central government; On 30 December, Wang and Japan signed a secret compact in Shanghai.[21] To Wang and many other people's surprise, Gao Zongwu and Tao Xisheng, who had long

supreme principle we will automatically and actively sanction in order to fulfill our duty to safeguard the Republic of China.

Third. We must lift the economy. Over the past few years, the Japanese government has repeatedly suggested that if we do not resolve our political disputes then we cannot talk about lifting up the economy. The Japanese Government has solemnly stated that it respects China's sovereignty and the independence and integrity of its administration, and that it does not wish to impose economic independence in China, nor does it wish to require China to restrict its relations with third countries, but that in order to seek economic integration in accordance with the principle of equality between China and Japan, this proposition should be endorsed in principle and should be discussed in accordance with this principle in order to discuss specific options. *Shenbao* (Hong Kong), 31 December 1938.

[21] (1) The three countries, Japan, China and Manchukuo, reach an accord on the principles of being friendly neighbors, mutually defense against Communism, and economic cooperation. (2) Japan has sent advisers to the new central government to work together on new construction. (3) For Japanese and Chinese defense against Communism, the Japanese army will be stationed in key places in North China and Mongolia. (4) We recognize the fait accompli situation since the Incident and the continuation of this state of affairs as the situation progresses. (5) The new central government will compensate Japan for the loss of its rights and interests in China since the Incident.

been involved in the peace movement, revealed the specific details of "the secret agreement between Wang and the Japanese" to Hang Kong's *Ta Kung Pao* on 21 January 1940, before the establishment of Wang Jingwei's regime, creating a furor throughout China, where the Japanese were reviled by nationalists given that tens of millions of Chinese had died as a result of Japanese aggression. Few were willing to believe that there was still an opportunity for equitable peace talks with Japan, so the peace negotiations roused intense popular ire. On 30 March 1940, the Japanese-backed Wang Jingwei regime was also established in Nanjing as the "National Government", and Wang declared this was a ceremony marking the return of the National Government to the capital. At the center of the podium hung a portrait of Sun Yat-sen. Wang Jingwei continued to adhere to the principle of "five separate" offices (Yuan) of government with Wang serving as president of the Executive Yuan, which was reminiscent of the arrangements of the Wuhan National Government in the 1920s, an attempt to establish a new national government. At the end of the year, Wang also held the Third Plenary Session of the Sixth Congress of the Central Executive Committee of his Kuomintang, which he said aimed at achieving peace inwardly and "establishing a new order in East Asia" with foreign cooperation with Japan.[22] In the years that followed, it was clear that the regime was completely held hostage by Japan.

In 1939, Chiang Kai-shek's National government was still supported by the Soviet Union, with Soviet loans, weapons, and military advisers contributing to Chiang Kai-shek's strategy of actively attacking the Japanese. In the autumn, the Battle of Changsha forced the Japanese to withdraw to their original line of defense, encouraging Chiang Kai-shek to launch this offensive strategy into the winter; the winter fighting saw the Chinese army's offensive inflict tens of thousands of Japanese casualties. In December, in the Battle of the Kunlun Pass in southern Guangxi the Chinese army won the battle to take the pass and further remind the Japanese army that the war in China would be very long, but the end result of this battle was unsuccessful with the loss of Binyang. The winter

[22] In November 1944, Wang Jingwei died in Japan, and Chen Gongbo became President of the Executive Council and acting chairman of the Military Commission. In the following year, Japan unconditionally surrendered, and the regime was dissolved. Its main leaders Chen Gongbo, Zhou Fohai and Chen Bijun (1891–1959), Wang Jingwei's widow, were convicted of treason.

offensive did not achieve its original goals and the battlefields in 1940 were finally stalemated.

In 1940, in order to prevent international aid from reaching China, the Japanese bombed the railway from Vietnam and forced Britain to close the Burma Road. At the same time, the Japanese army, in an attempt to reach the Chinese capital Chongqing, launched an attack on Yichang, and on 14 June Yichang fell. With the Japanese military's sustained strategic bombing of Chongqing after 1938, the Japanese army attempted to deliver comprehensive spiritual shock and destruction to the rear of the resistance. However, the attack on the Shijiazhuang-Taiyuan Railway launched by the 8th Route Army under the command of Peng Dehuai and the subsequent Hundred Regiments Campaign that lasted more than 100 days (20 August–5 December) pinned down around 200,000 Japanese and 150,000 pseudo-Nationalist troops of Wang Jingwei troops and so was a great inspiration.[23] On the other hand, the Hundred Regiments Campaign concentrated all army units under the CPC, namely 105 regiments with a total strength of 200,000 troops, and the 8th Route Army lost tens of thousands of casualties; this depletion of military forces led to a long period of difficulties in countering the Japanese drive. Later, after the Chinese Communist army fought a few large-scale battles, the Japanese army came to appreciate the strength of the Communist Party and their strategy of relying on the people (militia and guerrillas), and so strengthened their security measures in North China. The Japanese army henceforth no longer distinguished between the people and the military, and so launched a sweeping drive against the Communist bases in North China. In the places where the Communist Party had previously established local power and organizations, the Japanese carried out total armed occupation, resulting in a marked reduction in the area of the bases. The protracted state of the war led to harsh social, economic, and psychological dilemmas, especially regarding people's livelihood and food for soldiers at the front, and the four-fold increase in the price of rice led to widespread panic.

[23] Although the campaign won widespread praise from the national government and the national media for easing the pressure on the frontal battlefield, Mao Zedong believed that too much of the Chinese Communist Party's military was consumed and directed the Japanese's attention to the Eighth Route Army, which was not conducive to the growth of the Chinese Communist Party.

In 1941, the relationship between the KMT and the CPC was strained by the "South Anhui Incident", which affected the stability of the anti-Japanese military forces. In order to avoid conflict with Japan as much as possible, the Soviet Union also signed the Treaty of Neutrality with Japan, and the Soviet Union even agreed to the Japanese occupation of the northeast, which meant that the Soviet Union stopped all aid to China, including arms, and renewed tension, confrontation and conflict between the KMT and CPC worsened. At the same time, when Hong Kong fell to the Japanese, the mainland's access to goods became scarcer; inflation increased dramatically, and China only received US aid nine months later as a result of the outbreak of war between Japan and the United States. In September, the Japanese launched the Battle of Changsha, in an attempt to eliminate the main force of the National army's Ninth War Zone, but the result was still a return to the pre-war situation of both the Japanese and National armies.

Soon, the international situation changed: in June 1941, the German army attacked the Soviet Union. On 8 December, Japan's naval and air forces attacked Pearl Harbor, the US naval base in the Pacific, pulling the previously neutral United States into the War and the Pacific War broke out, with which Japan initiated its system of total warfare.[24] China, which previously had fought alone for four years against the Japanese invasion, and the United States, which had previously supplied the Japanese with oil and steel, and Britain, which also had colonies in Asia, declared war on Japan and Italy, thereby forming the World Anti-Fascist United Front. Now, the Chinese battlefield became the "Chinese theater" of World War II, and Chiang Kai-shek was promoted to supreme commander of the Allied China theater, which included Vietnam and Thailand. In January 1942, China was ranked among the Big Four in the Declaration of the

[24] The Japanese historian Shinobu Seizaburō has described Japan's military strategy at that time:

The "Fifteen-Year War" covering the 15-year period from 1931 to 1945 comprised three stages: from the Manchurian Incident and the China Incident to the Greater East Asian War. The object of aggression extended from Manchuria and Mongolia via China Proper to Southeast Asia. The developments in Manchuria and Mongolia were the subject of war between Japan and Russia. Developments in China Proper were the subject from the 1911 Revolution onwards, and the developments in Southeast Asia were the subject from the First World War onwards. The Japanese Army learned from the lessons of World War I the need to form a total war system and began to develop the concept. Shinobu Seizaburō, *Riben Zhengzhi Shi* (History of Japanese Politics), v. 4, Shanghai: Shanghai Yiwen Chubanshe, 1988, p. 400.

Twenty-six United Nations against Aggression. Against this backdrop, the United States began to provide substantial assistance to China, arranging for military and diplomatic personnel to participate in the Chinese War of Resistance, and integrating Claire L. Chennault's Flying Tigers, who had volunteered to fight in China, into the US 14th Air Force to support China's air force on 4 July 1942. Beginning in 1942, the United States increased its financial and material assistance to China, and in October the United States and Britain informed China of their willingness to enter into a new equal agreement with China and abolish extraterritoriality in the old treaties. On 11 January 1943, China and the United States and Britain signed the New Treaty on Equality between China and the United States and the New Treaty on Equality between China and Britain.

In the early days of the Pacific War, the Japanese occupied or controlled Hong Kong, Malaysia, the Philippines, Singapore, and Indonesia within a few months, and the Allies suffered continuous defeat. But during the third Battle of Changsha in Hunan, China, the Japanese suffered heavy losses inflicted by the 300,000-man Chinese army, and General Xue Yue trapped the Japanese troops, completely surrounding and defeating them. When the Japanese army retreated across the Yangtze, they were effectively attacked by the Chinese army, and eventually retreated to their original garrison; it was officially acknowledged that 52,000 Japanese troops lost their lives in the fighting and the Chinese army demonstrated its tenacity and fighting power to the Allies. At this point, an American journalist had this to say: "China's third major victory, at Changsha, proves the point that if the Chinese army is as well-equipped as the Japanese it can easily defeat the Japanese". Now, the Chinese military was cooperating with the Allies and quickly formed an important part of the Allied expeditionary forces sent to Burma to fight in the War. In early 1942, the United States also sent Joseph Stilwell to serve as chief of staff of Chiang Kai-shek and as US commander in China. China's 100,000-strong expeditionary army, which was initially defeated after going into Burma to fight the Japanese, suffered further losses during the retreat, as well as hunger and disease, with casualties totally 61,000. However, the Chinese army's victory at Yenangyaung made a great impression on the American soldiers, English missionaries and journalists they saved. After retreating from Burma to India, the Chinese Expeditionary Force was trained by US military instructors until 1943, when the team was restructured into two armies. On 28 November, the Chinese army in India, under the cover of Allied air forces, attacked and conquered Yupong, and the situation was followed by an attack on northern Myanmar and western Yunnan. Despite the huge sacrifices suffered by the Chinese army in more than a year of arduous counter-offensives, Allied aid to China could be channeled to China's rear via the Sino-Indian highway as a result of the campaign. When the United States and China retook Burma in early 1945, Chiang Kai-shek saw it as a unique contribution of Stilwell and named the supply route the "Stilwell Highway". After the outbreak of the war in Europe, it was the United States, not the Soviet Union, which began to give China substantial sums of money (loans totaling more than $1.5 billion) and military aid.

It is conceivable that the sharp conflict between the KMT and CPC as a result of the South Anhui Incident placed the Eighth Route Army in its bases behind enemy lines in a precarious position. Throughout 1942, the Japanese army sought to severely damage or even eliminate the Eighth Route Army and initiated a broad campaign to eliminate the sweep of what the 8th Route Army controlled. In May, the Japanese attacked and surrounded Taihang Mountains Eighth Route Army headquarters and the CPC's Northern Bureau, and the Eighth Route Army's deputy chief of staff Zuo Quan (1905–1942) died in the attack. During this difficult period's large-scale sweeps by the Japanese, the only recourse of the Eighth Route Army was to use guerrilla tactics to evade the Japanese army's constant and powerful attacks and search for possible shelters from the Japanese warplanes. This situation only changed in 1943, when the bases that had been swept through were gradually restored. In October of that year, the National Army and the Japanese army fought at Changde in western Hunan. The purpose of the Japanese Changde campaign was to contain or even destroy the Chinese army, which was being redeployed southwards to western Yunnan and Burma; for the National government, the loss of Changde would place Chongqing in a precarious position. The battle for Changde lasted until the end of December, and by early January 1944, when the two sides had retreated to their pre-war strategic positions, there were more than 40,000 Japanese and 50,000 Chinese casualties.

On 30 October 1943, supposedly at the urging of the United States, Fu Bingchang (1895–1965), as the representative of China, signed the Declaration on Universal Security, together with the foreign ministers of the United States, Britain, and the Soviet Union. The "Four Nations Declaration" emphasized "joint action" by the four countries to establish an international organization of universal significance. In the following month, China and the heads of state of the United States and Britain held a summit in Cairo, in which the core issue was the situation in Asia. The summit explicitly demanded Japan's unconditional surrender, and Chiang Kai-shek stressed that China would take back all its lost territory. However, Chiang Kai-shek did not want to meet with Stalin, and so many of the military resolutions of the Cairo conference were revised or even vetoed at the meeting after Franklin D. Roosevelt and Churchill flew to Tehran to meet with Stalin.

After the Battle of Midway, the Japanese Navy and Air Force were weakened. With their near loss of naval power in the Pacific and the collapse of control over the Chinese mainland, the Japanese forces scattered across Southeast Asia lacked supplies and contact with the outside world. In January 1944, the Emperor of Japan approved a battle plan code-named "Operation Ichigo", according to which Japan attempted to establish a mainland transportation route running from Japan through Korea, North China, Central China, South China, Vietnam, and then Thailand to Singapore to replace the maritime route and to serve as a backup for the Japanese withdrawal from the war, while at the same time attempting to destroy Allied air bases in Hunan and Jiangxi. In summer and autumn, the National army lost Changsha and Hengyang. The United States believed that, in addition to continuing to assist China, it should try to reconcile the Chinese National government with the Chinese Communist Party in order to increase resistance. In the early autumn of 1943, Chiang Kai-shek and General Stilwell clashed over whether to arrange for the 18th Group Army of the CPC to join forces against Japan. Chiang Kai-shek totally distrusted the CPC, and he did not agree with lifting the military blockade against them, believing they would sooner or later work with the Soviet Union to overthrow his regime, and so he rejected Stilwell's proposal that Stilwell serve as commander of the National Army and the Eighth Route Army's joint operations against Japan. By 1944, the military arrangements cooperation between Stilwell and Chiang Kai-shek could no longer avoid political issues. The Japanese army drew closer to Chongqing, and the war presented the National government with an unprecedented crisis. At this time, the cooperation with Chiang Kai-shek had not been smooth and Stilwell, through the Joint Chiefs of Staff, asked Roosevelt to demand that Chiang Kai-shek hand him complete command over the Chinese armed forces, including those of the CPC. Chiang Kai-shek made what he thought was the necessary response, and eventually expressed his desire to President

Roosevelt to recall Stilwell, with whom he refused to cooperate.[25] His determination was such that he was even prepared to "return to fighting alone" without US aid. Patrick Hurley, who arrived in Chongqing on 7 September, was sent by the President to examine the conflict and issues between Chiang Kai-shek and Stilwell. Roosevelt heard Ambassador Clarence Gauss' assessment of Chiang Kai-shek that favored Stilwell; in Gauss's view, Chiang Kai-shek, like many KMT generals, saw the CPC as the major enemy and that his Japanese strategy was simply defensive. However, Hurley warned that if the United States lost Chiang Kai-shek it risked losing China so Roosevelt agreed to Chiang Kai-shek's request. The result led to an angry Stilwell arranged for a reporter to publish an article in *The New York Times* arguing that his dismissal "represents a political victory for a dying anti-democratic system that is more concerned with maintaining its political standing than driving the Japanese out of China". After October 1944, General Albert C. Wedemeyer succeeded Stilwell as commander-in-chief of US forces in China and chief of staff of the National government forces. However, to Chiang Kai-shek's embarrassment, by early December, the Japanese army had actually seized control of the Beiping-Hankou, Guangdong-Hankou, and Hunan-Guangxi railways, completing the China leg of Operation Ichigo, and controlled Luoyang, Changsha, Guilin, Zhengzhou, Xuchang, and several hundred other large cities and towns. Within eight months, the Japanese had taken control of 200,000 square kilometers of Chinese territory and destroyed 36 Allied air bases in Guilin and Liuzhou. After the fall of Guilin and Liuzhou, and the collapse on 2 December of Dushan in

[25] Chiang Kai-shek's agreement with Stilwell's ideas were mostly political. In July 1944, Xu Yongchang (1885–1959) recorded Chiang Kai-shek's deliberations on the issue: "Mr. Chiang advocated full acceptance for the following reasons: (1) The Eighth Route Army would under his [i.e. Stilwell's] command, and it [i.e. the CPC] could not make trouble as before and its various nefarious deeds and false propaganda would be clearly revealed; (2) In the future, when our army moves in and out of the Northeast, it will come into contact with the Soviet army, and if the US army is in the middle, there will at least be some justice". Ref: *Xu Yongchang Riji* (Diary of Xu Yongchang), entry for 23 July 1944, as cited by Deng Ye, *Lianhe Zhenghe yu Yidang Xunzheng* (Coalition Government and One-Party Tutelary Rule), Beijing: Shehui Kexue Wenxian Chubanshe, 2011, p. 26). Later, on 18 September, Roosevelt forced Chiang Kai-shek to hand over the role of general commander to Stilwell, and at the same time the CPC, by proposing a coalition government, were attempting to force him to cede political power. Agreeing to Roosevelt's plan made it difficult to resist the CPC's demands on the government, and pressure from both directions led Chiang Kai-shek to abandon implementing Roosevelt's order.

Guizhou, General Wedemeyer even proposed that the National government move from Chongqing to Kunming. On that day, Chiang Kai-shek wrote in his diary: "As the enemy continues to penetrate Guizhou, our strategy should be to give up Guiyang, and wait for our forces to concentrate before launching any counter-offensive. The overall situation might seem hopeless, but we should defend Chongqing to the end". Regardless, the situation for the KMT army seemed hopeless, and people trapped in the rear faced social disorder and economic decline and were increasingly losing trust in the KMT, as they found themselves unable to escape the ravages of war. At the same time, with his people facing inflation, official corruption, government incompetence and inefficiency, Chiang Kai-shek's reassurance to the nation on New Year's Day that "China's victory was within sight" sounded far from inspiring.

During the war, China was in ruins and problems persisted, and the Kuomintang lacked sufficient confidence to maintain its regime, so through a more rigorous and larger secret service organization to guard against possible problems, it imprisoned intellectuals and banned newspapers. This constantly aroused the anger of intellectuals who hoped for freedom and were filled with idealism, so conflicts and differences were inevitably exacerbated. Intellectuals who were sincere in their feelings and deeply disturbed by the fate of the nation were naturally moved to express their discontent, and under the organization of the CPC, increasing numbers of students and teachers were fighting the KMT dictatorship in various ways. At the same time, the CPC began to turn the Eighth Route Army that had been strengthened over the previous seven years into a regular army, and to switch its military strategy from guerrilla warfare to regular campaign warfare, in an effort to cooperate with the US military and enter cities. By the end of 1944, the Eighth Route Army and the New Fourth Army had grown to 780,000, serving a total population in the base areas of 90 million. The Japanese army in North China Army reported: "Of the three special municipalities and 400 counties occupied by the Army, only seven counties (1.4 per cent of the total) have good security, as do the three special municipalities. There are 139 counties (31.5 per cent) in which there is little deployment of troops and these are subject to the activities of the CPC. There are also 295 counties (66.9 per cent) that fall into an intermediate group, in which most administrative forces are not fully implemented and people tend to favor the Communist Party".[26] However, it was not until the end of 1944 that there was serious disharmony and de facto division between the KMT and CPC that weakened anti-Japanese military and social forces and greatly increased the speed at which the Japanese army advanced in China.

On 9 October 1944, China, the United States, Britain, and the Soviet Union simultaneously published the draft declaration of the United Nations Organization. From 4 to 11 February 1945, Roosevelt, Churchill, and Stalin met in Yalta, on the Black Sea coast, to study how to fight for the final blow to Japan after the Soviet Union defeated Germany, so that the war with Japan might end as soon as possible. At the same time, they decided to meet in San Francisco on 25 April to establish United Nations and issue its charter. On 5 April the Soviet Union informed Japan that the neutrality agreement signed by the two countries in 1941 was no longer in force, greatly encouraging the CPC, which had not received US support. On 1 May Hitler committed suicide, and after the Germans surrendered a week later, Soviet troops began to be redeployed from Europe to Asia. On 25 June, Gu Weijun, representing China, attended the signing of the Charter of the United Nations, which is attended by 50 countries.[27] On 6 July Japan began asking the Soviet Union to mediate a ceasefire between Japan and the Allies, meaning it was already aware of its future defeat. On 26 July the Potsdam Declaration, signed by Truman, Chiang Kai-shek and Churchill, called on Japan to surrender unconditionally. As a result of the refusal to surrender by Japan's Supreme Council for the Direction of the War chaired by Prime Minister Suzuki Kantarō, on 6 August the United States dropped the first atomic bomb on Hiroshima, and on 8 August the Soviet Union formally deployed troops to China's northeast. On 9 August the United States dropped a second atomic bomb on Nagasaki, and on 10 August the Japanese Government decided to surrender unconditionally to the Allies. On 14 August, Wang Shijie representing China and Molotov representing the Soviet Union signed the Treaty of Alliance and Friendship between the two countries, and on 2 September Japan and the Allies

[26] Li Jifeng, *Cong Chenlun dao Guangrong: Kangri Zhanzheng Quan Jilu 1931–1945* (From Collapse to Glory: Complete Record of the Anti-Japanese War 1931–1945), Hohhot: Yuanfang Chubanshe, 2008, p. 450.

[27] On 10 January 1946, the first inaugural meeting of the United Nation was held in London and the Republic of China became a permanent member of the Security Council.

signed the letter of surrender aboard the *USS Missouri*, docked in Tokyo Bay, bringing to an end China's bitter war of resistance and survival. Statistics that during the eight years of the all-out anti-Japanese War, 1.5 million Japanese troops were deployed on Asian battlefields and 22 large-scale battles in which there were more than 100,000 troops were fought between the Nationalist and Japanese armies and in them, 206 generals died. The Chinese Nationalist army lost 3.21 million men, the air force lost 4321, and the navy was wiped out. In the first four months of the Anti-Japanese War, 25,000 young officers from the Huangpu Military Academy fought in the war, and of them, more than 10,000 were killed. Civilian deaths numbered between 20 and 30 million.

KMT-CPC Relations During the War Against Japan

Although the Xi'an Incident changed the relationship between the KMT and the CPC, in January 1937, Yan'an proposed that the National Government pay the CPC half a million yuan for military spending per month. However, up until 13 August 1937, when the Japanese army launched a large-scale attack on Shanghai, negotiations on cooperation between the KMT and CPC were still continuing, and the focus remained on command of the army and the corresponding political arrangements. From the start, however, Stalin, who had been directing the Chinese Communist Revolution, had been inclined to rely almost exclusively on the KMT for controlling China's anti-Japanese situation, because, in terms of military power and legitimacy, the CPC could not match the KMT. On 21 August, the Soviet Union and the National Government issued the Sino-Soviet Non-Aggression Treaty, and the Soviet Union supported Chiang Kai-shek with deliveries of fighter bombers, artillery, and transport vehicles, increased loans to the National Government, and sent groups of military advisers and experts to China to cooperate with the KMT army. All this has nothing to do with the CPC, whose weapons came only from seizures from the Japanese army after battles. Stalin at this time knew that continued support for the CPC meant trouble for the KMT, and the Soviet Union did not now need to export revolution, but to allow China to at least resist and consume the Japanese troops, in order to prevent the Soviet Union from being attacked by Germany and Japan. Vasily Chuikov (1900–1982) came to China in December 1940 as the Soviet military attaché to China and general adviser to Chiang Kai-shek, and he made Stalin's ideas very clear:

> The Chinese Communist Party and the Chinese working class are too weak. It is difficult to say how long it will take for the masses to acquire the strength they need. Given the situation in Europe, Hitler's victories suggest Britain and the United States can only gradually increase aid to Chiang Kai-shek.
>
> It is hoped that, with our assistance and that of our British and American allies, Chiang Kai-shek, even if he cannot drive out the Japanese aggressors, he can at least hold them at bay for a long time.
>
> Only when the hands and feet of the Japanese invaders are tied can we avoid warfare on two fronts when the German invaders attack our country.[28]

However, Mao Zedong was aware that this was disadvantageous for the CPC, but over a long period he had stressed within the Party that during the Anti-Japanese War, the ethnic revolution had precedence over class struggle. But from the beginning, both Chiang Kai-shek and Mao Zedong knew that if they lost power to control their armies, they would lose control. In the course of KMT-CPC cooperation, the KMT worried about the possibility of the CPC regaining its independence and strength, and the CPC worried about any complete reorganization by the KMT which would end the independence of the CPC. Given the war was in full swing, Chiang Kai-shek had ordered the Red Army to participate in the fighting, and the two sides had no time to discuss political arrangements, given the overwhelming urgency of the war. As a result, on 22 August, the KMT Military Commission ordered the Red Army to be transformed into the Eighth Route Army (later becoming the 18th Group Army) of the National Revolutionary Army, with Zhu De as the commander-in-chief of the Eighth Route Army and Peng Dehuai as its deputy commander-in-chief. Although the army is still under the command of the Military Commission, specifically under the commander of the Second Military Zone, Yan Xishan, the CPC was obviously able to maintain the independence of its army. Its army could not only openly and legally carry out its own military activities, but it also obtained stable financial support from

[28] Li Qingshan, *Zhengmian Kangzhan Zhenxiang* (The Truth about the All-out War of Resistance), Beijing: Huawen Chubanshe, 2017, p. 94.

the KMT; previously the CPC had faced a major crisis in sourcing funds for maintaining its army.[29]

The adaptation of the armed forces was also intended to be a political rearrangement. But when Chiang Kai-shek tried to get KMT officials into the border base area government and serve as senior staff officers at the headquarters of the Eighth Route Army, he was rejected by the CPC. This shows that the mistrust between the KMT and the CPC always existed even when the survival of the country was at stake, and it affected the Anti-Japanese War. To politically force the KMT to agree to CPC demands, when Chiang Kai-shek ordered the CPC to send troops to the front line in North China (in September), Mao Zedong held back one division as a negotiating ploy to force Chiang Kai-shek to agree to the Party's plans. At this time, the CPC was most urgently pressing Chiang Kai-shek to issue the CPC declaration in order to legitimize the CPC, and this goal was rapidly achieved. On 22 September, the KMT agreed to issue the CPC's "Declaration of the CPC on Addressing the National Crisis":

1. Mr. Sun Yat-sen's Three Principles of the People are necessary for China today, and this Party will strive for their complete realization.
2. We will discontinue all policies to overthrow the Kuomintang regime and conduct a Red campaign and will end the policy of violently confiscating landlords' holdings.

[29] Chiang Kai-shek wrote in his *Jiao Fei Zhanshi* (A Military History of Suppressing the [Communist] Bandits): "After the government reorganized the bandit armies, their three armies comprised three divisions and five supplementary regiments, all of which were regularly paid funds in line with the treatment of the National Army, but the funds received by the Bandit Party [i.e. CPC] from the Government were not paid to their armed forces but used as local subsidies provided to their peripheral organizations and cultural institutions and used to destroy national unity, t as political combat funds for organizational, propaganda, infiltration and subversion work against the War of Resistance forces. Organizations such as Chongqing's *Xinhua Daily* and the various local 'Life Bookstores' (Shenghuo Shudian), as well as *Masses Magazine*, *Liberation Weekly*, Yan'an's 'Anti-Japanese University', 'Northern Shaanxi College' and so on, are all funded using this military expenditure, but they want to falsely accuse my government of discriminating against the 18th Group Army, and claim that they are not receiving the same treatment as the National army".

This passage is quoted from Endō Homare, *Mao Zedong Goujie Rijun Zhenxiang: Lai zi Ridie de Huiyi yu Dang'an* (The Truth About Mao Zedong's Collusion with the Japanese Army: Memoirs and Archives of Japanese Spies), Hong Kong: Mingjing Chubanshe, 2016, pp. 102–103.

3. We will abolish the current Soviet government and implement civil rights' politics with a view to the unification of political power throughout the country.
4. Cancel the name of the Red Army to the Citizens Revolutionary Army, under the control of the National Government's Military Commission, and stand ready to serve and fulfill our duties in the anti-Japanese front.[30]

Whatever speculation and understanding of Chiang Kai-shek's true intentions regarding the CPC or Mao Zedong personally, due to the limitations of the anti-Japanese situation and domestic political conditions, he delivered a statement on the day following the CPC's "Declaration", announcing that a second round of KMT-CPC cooperation was in force:

> I am of the view that in our revolution, the combatants are not driven by personal motives and private views, but strive to implement the Three Principles of the People. In this autumn of survival and crisis, we should not take into account everything in the past, but work for a new beginning for the nation and strive for unity, in order to protect the life and survival of the country.......As long as any party in the nation sincerely wants national salvation and is willing to work together under the banner of the national revolution against the enemy, the government will sincerely welcome them to unite and join in concerted efforts under the leadership of our party. The Chinese Communist Party has thrown aside its prejudices and affirmed the importance of national independence and national interests, and we only hope that they are sincere and consistent in implementing the points in their Declaration, and that they will, under the unified command of resisting humiliation and national salvation, contribute their abilities to the nation, and strive with our compatriots from all over the country to fulfill the mission of the revolution. In short, the foundational principles of China are the Three Principles of the People created by our first Prime Minister

[30] Ref: *Emancipation* (weekly), 18th issue, 2 October 1937. The "Declaration" was titled "Declaration of the CPC on Addressing the National Crisis", it bore the seal of the Central Committee of the CPC, and was dated 22 July 1937. On 7 July 2014, on the occasion of the 77th anniversary of the July 7th Incident, when KMT member Hao Bocun visited the Marco Polo Bridge Chinese People's Anti-Japanese War Memorial in Beijing, there was scant information about the KMT available. When Hao asked the curators in the museum whether they had a copy of "Declaration of the CPC on Addressing the National Crisis", the answer was: "No".

> and these are unshakable and unchanging. The Chinese nation has awakened in unison, is absolutely united, and must adhere to the policy of impartiality, gather the entire strength of our people, defend ourselves and help each other, in order to counter the violent enemy and save the nation from peril.[31]

The second KMT-CPC cooperation thus began, although the goals of both sides had not all been achieved. Later, there would also be constant suspicion, contradictions, and conflicts, but there were also some individual gains. For the KMT, cooperation was not only in line with the domestic situation and ethnic righteousness, but it did also actually increase the strength of the anti-Japanese resistance. For the CPC, their army acquired legitimacy and from their serious economic crisis they acquired access to the National government's financial security; from limited political activities they moved to openness in political activities, and especially in later cooperation, the CPC continued to maintain the independence and autonomy of its Party and the Red Army forces, which meant that this cooperation not only enabled the CPC to transform decisively from crisis to vitality, but also provided a legal basis for the future rapid development of the CPC. After its Luochuan meeting on 25 August the CPC decided to wage guerrilla warfare on its own and Mao Zedong informed the CPC's cadres.

The Sino-Japanese war is a great opportunity for the development of our Party, and we have decided that the policy is to devote 70% of our efforts to developing ourselves, 20% to seeking compromise, and 10% to fighting against Japan. In order to make our comrades aware of their work and to be able to work towards common goals even when contacts with headquarters are severed, I am happy to point out the following policies for comrades. These can be implemented in three stages:

1. The stage of compromise. During this stage, we should make sacrifices, ostensibly to obey the National government and pursue the Three Principles of the People, but in fact only to cover the survival and development of our Party.

[31] Cited from: ***Zhonggong Zhongyang Kangri Minzu Tongyi Zhanxian Wenjian Xuanbian*** (Selected Documents of the Anti-Japanese National United Front of the CPC Central Committee), vol. 2, Beijing: Beijing Dang'an Chubanshe, 1985, pp. 823–824.

2. In the competitive stage, with two or three years of work, the Party's political and military base will be established, and continue to develop until it can compete with the National government and destroy it, while at the same time trying to eliminate the KMT's power north of the Yellow River.
3. In this offensive phase, we will penetrate central China and establish bases, cutting off the Central army's traffic through the region it is isolated and cut off, until our counter-offensive forces are ready to mature, and then we can seize leadership from the Kuomintang.[32]

This secret policy was clearly different from the commitments made in the CPC's public "Declaration of the CPC on Addressing the National Crisis". In the eyes of some in the KMT, the CPC was using the National Revolutionary War to realize its own development and then seize power

[32] Mao Zedong's speech at the Luochuan conference was quoted in a number of history books, such as Xu Zhongyue, *Zhongguo Jindai Shi* (Modern History of China), Hong Kong, CUHK Press, 2000. Endō Homare's *Mao Zedong Goujie Rijun Zhenxiang: Lai zi Ridie de Huiyi yu Dang'an* (The Truth About Mao Zedong's Collusion with the Japanese Army: Memoirs and Archives of Japanese Spies) also cites Mao's Luochuan speech, and the author writes that: "These secret orders were revealed in 1940 by Li Faqing, branch Party secretary and member of the cavalry company under Yang Chengwu of the Eighth Route Army's 18th Group's Independent First Division". Endō Homare also described her sources of information as follows:

This information was published in 1977, in Mei Liangmei, *Dui Ri Kangzhan Qijian Zhonggong Tongzhan Celüe zhi Yanjiu* (Study of the Communist Party's United Front Strategy during the Anti-Japanese War), Taipei: Zheng Zhongwen Ku, 1977, Ch. 3, Sect. 4 ("Mao Zedong's Secret Instructions to the Eighth Route Army"), p. 41.

The information is cited in the following two volumes:

Jiaofei Zhanshi, v. 11, p. 1035.

ROC Ministry of Justice and Administration's Bureau of Investigation (Sifa Xingzheng Bu Diaocha Ju) ed., *Zhong Gongdang de Celüe Luxian* (The Strategic Line of the Communist Party of China), 1956. The appendix is the original text of a speech by Zhang Hao.

Li Faqing's testimony was recorded in the appendix on p. 68 of the book (but the book did not disclose his name, but only his position and army rank. This book is held in the National Library of Taipei. *Jiaofei Zhanshi* was written by Chiang Kai-shek, and edited in 1962. Another source documenting the debunking by Li Faqing, secretary of the Chinese division of the Eighth Route Army, of the total intrigue of the CPC during the Anti-Japanese War, is: "Diba Lujun Zhongguo/zhong Guo shuji Li Faqing jieshu Zhonggong zai Kangzhan zhong Zhengge Yinmou" in Qin Xiaoyi, ed., *Zhonghua Minguo Zhongyao Shiliao Chubian* (The First Collection of Important Historical Materials of the Republic of China), v. 5, pt. 1, Taipei: Party History Committee of the Central Committee of the Nationalist Party of China, 1985, pp. 357–358.

in the country. In fact, it was on this basis that Chiang Kai-shek never believed Mao Zedong's expressed anti-Japanese motives. At the same time, Mao Zedong sought opportunities to preserve Communist strength by contacting the Japanese either directly or through the Wang Jingwei regime in order to minimize fighting with the Japanese and even discuss a ceasefire. As Mao Zedong later commented in an off-hand remark to Japanese visitors, it was the Japanese who helped the CPC.[33]

[33] In 1939, Stalin and Hitler signed the Treaty of Friendship and Mutual Assistance (the Molotov-Ribbentrop pact). The Moscow Comintern Executive Bureau informed Yan'an and instructed the CPC to contact the Wang Jingwei regime in Nanjing recognized by the invading Japanese army, and if necessary, join forces with Wang against Chiang, which meant uniting with Japan against Chiang. It was with the utmost secrecy that Mao Zedong entrusted Pan Hannian with the task of liaising with the Wang regime. In his memoir, *Zhonggong Wushi Nian* (50 Years of the Communist Party of China), Wang Ming wrote: "Mao Zedong did not let the Politburo of the CPC Central Committee know in advance and, through the radio station of the Central Military Commission of the Communist Party of China, privately ordered Rao Shushi the New Fourth Army Military And Political Committee to send representatives in his name to negotiate with Japanese representatives and Wang Jingwei on the issue of opposing Chiang Kai-shek, while ordering the cessation of military operations against the Japanese army and Wang Jingwei". Ref: Wang Ming, *Zhonggong Wushi Nian* (50 Years of the Communist Party of China), Orient Press, 2004, p. 190. After receiving Mao's instructions, Rao Shushi handed over to Pan Hannian, the intelligence chief of the New Fourth Army, the task of discussing anti-Chiang cooperation with the Japanese and Wang and. In the autumn of 1939, Pan Hannian, using the pseudonym "Hu Yueming", joined the CPC in Shanghai through Yuan Shu [1911–1987]. Yuan had in 1933 served as a CPC spy in the Party Affairs Investigation Section of the KMT's Central Organization Department, which had been established by the CC Clique in 1927. After 1938, he investigated the Statistical Bureau of the Central Executive Committee of the KMT. While working in the KMT, Yuan Shu's identity was reporter for the "New Voice Communications Agency". In May 1935, his CPC identity was revealed and he was arrested by the KMT, but Iwai Eiichi (b.1899) helped secure his release, and later he served as the responsible person for Iwai's Japanese intelligence agency. He accompanied him to see Iwai Eiichi who was serving as deputy intelligence chief in the Japanese Consulate General in Shanghai, to seek the latter's help, and on the basis of the assessment of Pan Hannian as "a person who could provide information to the Japanese side", Iwai issued Pan with a "special pass" for work. At the same time, Pan at Iwai's offices received a monthly activity fee of HK$2,000 from the Japanese Ministry of Foreign Affairs (equivalent to a five-year salary of a Chinese police officer in Hong Kong in 1939). Available literature and original materials reveal that after Iwai and Pan met, Iwai commissioned Pan to "write a report on the internal situation of the Communist Party of China and future trends". At the end of the year, Pan Hannian submitted to him an 80-page document in Japanese titled "On the operational procedures and construction of the New Fourth Army". This report describes the activities and policy of the New Fourth Army in the Jiangnan region, especially in the southern region of Anhui, as well as the guerrilla warfare of the New Fourth Army and their reverence for the Kuomintang leader Chiang Kai-shek (in the Archive of Japanese Diplomatic History,

In October, the Military Commission ordered that the CPC's armed forces scattered in the Jiangnan region be transformed into the New Fourth Army under the National Revolutionary Army of Gu Zhutong,

this document designated "Confidential No. 795" was dated 23 March 1940). After the fall of Hong Kong on 25 December 1941, the CPC moved its intelligence agencies there to Shanghai, and Pan Hannian met with Iwai more often, so that Iwai arranged special liaison meetings. Iwai described the meeting in this way: "The meeting place is usually in a chocolate shop opened by foreigners on the left after entering Nanjing Road from the Bund". Iwai recalls in this book that after Pan wanted an introduction to meet with the Japanese military, he wrote:

"One day [after March 1940, ed.], Pan Hannian, through Yuan Shu, proposed to me that the CPC wanted a ceasefire with the Japanese army in North China, and requested I contact the Japanese side to help negotiate. Although I knew nothing about the military situation, in North China the Japanese and Communist army fronts were intertwined, so even if the armistice provided many specific details on how to achieve this, I thought it would have been very difficult to achieve. But when I am asked to do something, even if I feel it is impossible I will not refuse to drop the matter, but do my best to help. So with Pan Hannian's request, I decided to go first to ask Kagesa Sadaaki, to see if he felt it was feasible. After contacting him, I approved Yuan Shu taking Pan Hannian to Nanjing's top military advisory office to meet Kagesa Sadaaki. Eventually, as expected, there seemed to be no significant result, and at that time, after Pan had been introduced to Kagesa he also met with President Wang Jingwei. It is possible that they may have discussed a ceasefire with the armed forces of the Wang Jingwei government, but it seems that would have been fruitless.

Still, as stated previously: In Shanghai there were secret meetings with Zhang Xueliang, in order to have Chiang Kai-shek participate in the anti-Japanese national united front, so he went to enemy occupied Nanjing to meet with Chen Guofu. Coming into the Japanese control area then engaged in war, Yuan Shu and Chen Fuji [1897–1959, CPC intelligence] approached me through the auspices of Yuan's Pan-Asian Establishment Movement, and in the name of ceasefire negotiations in North China with the local Japanese army they met again with Iwai Eiichi, and even met with the new government's supreme leader Wang Jingwei…… From Pan Hannian's quiet appearance, one cannot imagine whence he derived his courage, but such an activist is really admirable". Original work, p. 165, cited in Endō Homare, op. cit., pp. 137–138.

In the autumn and summer of 1942, together with Li Shiqun, whom Pan Hannian had known since his early years as a CPC member though he later joined the KMT and was now chief of Wang Jingwei government's Number 76 Secret Service, Pan Hannian went to Nanjing to meet Zhou Fohai, in an attempt to negotiate a ceasefire between the CPC and Wang Jingwei armies.

In spring 1943, Pan Hannian, through Li Shiqun, met with the Japanese Army's Togō Daisuke, and continued to discuss a ceasefire between the Communist and Japanese armies. Zhou Fohai wrote in his diary on 2 March 1943:

"Xiao Yue (Zhou's ministry-style army) came to discuss the CPC's dissatisfaction with Chongqing, and wanted to cooperate with my government. Previously Pan Hannian had been sent to Shanghai to contact Li Shiqun, but because Li was politically powerless, he now sent Xiao Yue to meet me. As I was in ill health, I rescheduled discussions for later".

commander of the Third War Zone, and that the military cooperation between the KMT and CPC begins in a comprehensive way. However, while the KMT struggled to resist the advance of the Japanese advance

Ref: *Zhou Fohai Riji Quanbian* (Zhou Fohai's Complete Diaries), Beijing: Zhongguo Wenlian Chubanshe, 2003.

Vladimirov, a TASS correspondent and liaison officer assigned to Yan'an by the Comintern in May 1942, recorded in his diary on 18 August 1945, towards the end of the Anti-Japanese War:

"I unintentionally saw a telegram from the headquarters of the New Fourth Army, which fully confirmed that there was a long-standing relationship between the leadership of the Communist Party of China and the Supreme Command of the Japanese Army.

The cable also showed that relevant reports of contact with the Japanese military command were sent to Yan'an on a regular basis.

I later confirmed that the link between the Chinese Communist army and the Japanese staff had been maintained for a long time. The two ends of the connection are Yan'an and Nanjing".

On 21 August, Vladimirov also recorded:

"Ye Jianying told Mao Zedong that I already knew the contents of the telegram sent by the headquarters of the New Fourth Army. The Chairman of the Central Committee of the Communist Party of China [i.e. Mao Zedong] explained to me at length why the CPC leaders decided to establish contact with the Japanese occupation forces.

This was a shameful matter, so Mao wanted to make his explanation persuasive.

The conversation showed how unseemly all this is. Relations with the Japanese command had long been established under extreme secrecy, and only a few of the Party's leaders were aware of it. One of Mao's agents (or as Mao calls him "the contact man") can be described as affiliated with the headquarters of General Okamura Yasuji in Nanjing. Whenever needed, he can travel unimpeded between Nanjing and the headquarters of the New Fourth Army under the close protection of Japan's counter-espionage agencies.

The chairman of the Central Committee of the CPC sends essential information to the headquarters of the New Fourth Army, waiting for this agent (who was originally from Japan). The agent's intelligence, always translated into code at the headquarters of the New Fourth Army, is then sent to Yan'an". (Vladimirov, *Yan'an Diary*, Oriental Press, 2004, pp. 561–563.)

After the Communist Party took power, Rao Shushi, one of the "Gao-Rao Anti-Party Clique", was formally arrested on 1 April 1955. Later, on the basis of Mao Zedong's request that senior party cadres take the initiative in reporting historical problems or face severe punishment, Pan Hannian, implicated by his former work with Rao Shushi, submitted documents on involvement in 1943 with Wang Jingwei to Chen Yi, leader of the East China Organization Group. Chen Yi then also handed the materials written by Pan to Mao Zedong, who noted: "This person can never be trusted". On 3 April, Pan Hannian was arrested and imprisoned for life. The events are thought to have something to do with Mao's attempts to erase all evidence of these events from the historical record. Luo Qingchang, who was at that time the deputy director of the Office of the Premier of the State Council, secretary-general of the Central Investigation Department of the Communist Party of China and head of the Pan Hannian Review Group, wrote an article in March 1995 titled "The Historical Lessons of the Wrongful Case against Pan

on the battlefield, the Chinese Communist-led army adopted guerrilla warfare to expand its armed forces and bases behind enemy lines. This situation always disturbed Chiang Kai-shek, who again and again strongly feared that during such a difficult period of the Anti-Japanese War, the

Hannian", which confirmed all Pan Hannian's work was carried out under the leadership of the then-CPC Central Committee:

"The three of us [the other two team members were Xu Ming, secretary of the Prime Minister's Office, and Di Fei, director of the 12th Bureau of the Ministry of Public Security, ed.] examined the telegrams and related records between Pan Hannian from March 1939 to August 1948, arranged by month, how Pan Han's year was reported, and how the central government directed, for three months. According to the archives, the work done by Pan Hannian at that time, such as accessing the inner workings of the Japanese authorities in China and the use of Li Shiqun, were known to the Central Committee, as the archives record. And at that time, given the two-faced policy adopted for the revolution, the Central Committee also issued instructions that fully endorsed Pan Hannian's actions. The central government fully approved of his work". Ref: CPC Shanghai Municipal Party History Committee ed., *Pan Hannian zai Shanghai* (Pan Hannian in Shanghai), Shanghai: Shanghai Renmin Chubanshe, 1995, p. 365.

In 1956, Mao Zedong hosted a delegation led by former Japanese Army Lieutenant General Endō Saburō in Zhongnanhai, and told them:

"You [the Japanese Imperial Army] were also our teachers, and we want to thank you. It is true that you fought against, but you taught the Chinese people, who were like scattered sand, that we needed to unite, so we should thank you". Ref: Wu Xuewen, Wang Junyan, *Liao Chengzhi yu Riben* (Liao Chengzhi and Japan), Zhonggong Dangshi Chubanshe (Communist Party History Press), 2007.

On 24 January 1961, Mao Zedong to the Japanese Socialist Party congressman, Kuroda Hisao:

"When Japan's Nangō Sabur met me, he said: 'Japan invaded China. Apologies'. I said to him: 'We do not see it this way. By occupying most of China, the Japanese militarists educated the Chinese people, who would otherwise have been unaware that if we did not unite, we would still be in the mountains and unable to go to Beijing to see Beijing Opera.······ If 'thanks' are due, I would rather 'thank' the Japanese militarists". Ref: *Mao Zedong's Writings on Foreign Affairs*, pp. 460–461.)

"On 10 July 1964, Mao Zedong, in a meeting with the delegation led by the Japanese Socialist Party's Sasaki Kōzō and Kuroda Hisao came to China, spoke about the historical situation of the Chinese Soviet's escape to Yan'an, made the following remarks:

'How many troops were left? From 300,000 our armies had shrunk to 25,000. Why should we thank the Japanese Imperial Army? When the Japanese Imperial Army arrived, we fought the Japanese Imperial Army, and then cooperated with Chiang Kai-shek. Our twenty-five thousand troops fought for eight years, and over that time grew to 1.2 million troops, and our bases had a population of 100 million. Don't you think we should thank you?'" Ref: University of Tokyo Institute of Modern Chinese History tr., *Long Live Mao Zedong Thought*, (final volume), Tokyo: San-Ichi Publishing Company, 1975.

In 1972, when China and Japan established diplomatic relations, Mao Zedong expressed his views to Japanese Prime Minister Tanaka Kakuei's views on the opportunities the Japanese invasion of China provided for the development of the CPC:

CPC would be developed so vigorously it would pose a deadly threat to the KMT in the future. Indeed, the CPC, in different documents and propositions, acknowledged the political platform of the KMT's Three Principles of the People, and at one point even tried to show its support for the KMT by participating in the KMT's three youth groups. However, in the end, it was difficult to achieve real cooperation because of differences in their political beliefs. Based on the experience of the first CPC-KMT cooperation and his own political judgment, Chiang Kai-shek told the CPC's representatives Zhou Enlai and Wang Ming: "I would welcome the withdrawal of CPC members from the CPC to join the KMT, or that the CPC abolish its name and simply join the KMT. But if the CPC insists on maintaining its own party, I also acknowledge that any cross-party approach will be impossible".[34] Chiang Kai-shek gave more thought to the feasibility of political operations and the security of the Kuomintang, when in the following month the CPC responded to Chiang Kai-shek with a long-winded exposition its political position: "…The cooperation between the two parties in opposing the common enemy and the realization of a common platform is one matter, while the so-called merger of the two parties is entirely another matter. The former is necessary for China now, while the latter runs counter to fundamental principles. The CPC is sincerely willing to work with the KMT to struggle for a China that can achieve the Three Principles of the People, namely national independence, civil rights freedom, and people's livelihood and well-being. But the CPC cannot give up its Marxist beliefs, and must not merge the CPC's organization with that of any other political party".[35] It is clearly impossible to interpret belief in the Three Principles of the People as a Marxist belief, even if Chiang Kai-shek strategically (pointedly) told the Communists in negotiations that "Sun Yat-sen said

"You should acknowledge what you have achieved, and what was your achievement? If you hadn't waged the war of aggression against China, how would our Communist Party be strong? How would we have taken power? How would Chiang Kai-shek have been defeated? How can we thank you? We don't want your war reparations!".

[34] "Telegram of Chen, Zhou, Bo, Wu and Dong to the Secretariat of the CPC", 13 December 1938.

[35] "Zhonggong Zhongyang zhi Enlai Zhuan Zhongguo Guomindang zongzai Jiang xiansheng dian", 22 January 1939.

that the Three Principles of the People are not incompatible with communism".[36] The political position of the CPC was very different from that of the KMT from the outset, and the Three Principles of the People were the basic political bottom line of Chiang Kai-shek. On the basis of his experience of the first failed KMT-CPC cooperation, it is easy to understand that Chiang Kai-shek refused to participate in that type of KMT-CPC cooperation again. In fact, in the course of the negotiations on KMT-CPC cooperation, the two sides even discussed the possibility of jointly forming a "large party"; in the midst of these complexities, the KMT in early 1938 put forward propositions of "a single doctrine", "one leader", "one political party" and "one army", in order to emphasize the unity of command and deployment under the leadership of the KMT.[37] This idea is, of course, targeted the incongruity and conflict between the CPC and the KMT during their initial cooperation. The CPC at first disagreed, and Wang Ming criticized an article published on Mao Zedong's behalf (*Xinhua Daily*, 9 February 1938), but soon Mao attempted to ascertain whether or not forming a "big party" would enable cooperation and development. Later, the KMT proposed to strategically try out cooperation through a single organization of the two parties and other parties by forming a Three Principles of the People youth group. But when the CPC proposed concrete cooperation measures to once again clarify the political and organizational independence of the parties participating in the alliance, Chiang Kai-shek also re-emphasized the leadership of the KMT, and demanded that "not only should the CPC respect its own party and obey its leadership, but all existing parties in the country must be assimilated under the Three Principles of the People".[38]

On 5 November 1938, Mao Zedong frankly explained the independence of the CPC within the united front at the Sixth Plenary Session of the Sixth Central Committee. He completely disagreed with the slogans of "everything goes through the united front" and "obey the united

[36] From: Yang Kuisong, *Kangzhan Qianhou Guo-Gong Tanpan Shilu* (True Account of KMT-CPC Negotiations before and after the War of Resistance), Hong Kong: Xinxing Chubanshe, 2013, p. 111.

[37] In February 1938, when Zhu De was military commander of Second Military Region's Eastern Route, Yan Xishan and Wei Lihuang enlisted seven and a half regiments for Zhu De to direct.

[38] Qin Xiaoyi ed., *Jiang Zongtong Ji* (Anthology of President Chiang Kai-shek), Taipei: National Defense Institute, 1969, p. 1037.

front in everything", and he agreed with Liu Shaoqi's explanation that this meant "everything" would go through Chiang Kai-shek and Yan Xishan. However, he did not explain to the Party that since "Chiang Kai-shek and Yan Xishan" had been replaced by the "united front", how could the preceding sentence "everything goes through" could be explained?[39] Mao Zedong did not consider these written strategies, his core problem being that he could not leave major decisions completely to the Kuomintang, as he frankly outlined strategies to party comrades:

> At present, some first require the consent of the KMT, for example, expanding the three divisions to three armies, which can be described as a sentencing preceding a beheading. Some are presented as a fait accompli, such as developing an army of more than two hundred thousand troops, which can be described as a beheading preceding the sentencing. There are temporarily also beheadings with no sentencing at all, as there may be no agreement at present, such as us convening border district conferences. There are temporarily also no beheadings with no sentencing orders, because these would hinder the big picture.[40]

The KMT's comparison of such arrangements of the CPC with the CPC's "Declaration" reveals their extreme skepticism. In fact, by the beginning of the summer of 1939, the CPC's armies had grown by 30,000 or 40,000 men to 220,000 since the reorganization took place, and the areas under its control were far from confined to northern Shaanxi and northern Gansu, but extended to large areas behind enemy lines in Shanxi, Chahar, Hebei, and Shandong. At the same time, the national government's military orders and political decrees were often ineffective; the CPC's power developed rapidly, and by the end of 1939 or so, China had direct command over more than half a million troops. Such a state of affairs exacerbated Chiang Kai-shek's great unease. Thus, in 1939, the KMT began drafting *Measures for Handling the Problem of the CPC*, a

[39] In a conversation with Mao Zedong, Wang Ming countered Liu Shaoqi's statement: "According to Shaoqi, if 'everything will go through the anti-Japanese national united front' this is equivalent to everything 'going through Chiang Kai-shek and Yan Xishan' slogan, but this is not correct; at the same time, he says that the statement 'all must obey the anti-Japanese national united front' is, by his logic, equivalent to 'all must obey Chiang Kai-shek and Yan Xishan', which is correct. Is this at all logical?" Ref: Wang Ming, op. cit., p. 74.

[40] Mao Zedong, "The question of independence in the united front", Mao Zedong Xuanji, v. 2, Renmin Chubanshe, 1952, p. 504.

document that took six months to draft and which showed that the KMT was highly alert politically and militarily to restricting the development of the CPC. The document presented regulations addressing the political and military actions of the CPC. In military matters, "the Eighth Route and New Fourth armies had to comply with the unified provisions of the Ministry of Military Affairs, there was absolutely no free recruitment allowed, in particular they could not levy or confiscate civilian guns, and take any opportunity to privately expand their military forces". In terms of party affairs, "the CPC should immediately stop all absurd propaganda that opposed the policies of the KMT and stop disseminating communist ideology"; On the administrative front, "the central government absolutely refuses to recognize the CPC's so-called 'Shan-Gan-Ning Border Area' organization and regards this as a local issue and instructs the provincial governments to automatically restore their jurisdiction by all necessary means".[41] In fact, in order to strive for the broadest possible anti-Japanese cooperation, the "Shan-Gan-Ning Border Area" established in March 1939 and the subsequent Jin-Cha-Ji-Sui Border Area government were still allowed by the National Government, even though this document reveals that their existence was inconsistent with the rules publicly formulated by the two sides. At the same time, the national government allowed the CPC to set up offices in Chongqing, Chengdu, and Xi'an, publish *Xinhua Daily* in Chongqing and set up bookstores and distribution. But this was far from enough for the CPC, which continued to develop political power and build up military forces not recognized by the Nationalist government. The CPC's reasoning was that such developments were conducive to the growth of anti-Japanese forces and strength, while the KMT felt it was completely losing its command of, and initiative in, the Anti-Japanese War, and there would be a huge crisis if political and military power shifted away from the KMT to the CPC. In the autumn of 1939, Zhou Enlai went to Moscow, with one of his targets being to obtain weapons and military supplies from the Soviet Union in order to expand CPC military power; he also reaffirmed the long-known Soviet stance about China's resistance to Japan: the whole country should join forces to fight Japanese aggression, rather than rubbing shoulders with the Kuomintang which would weaken the anti-Japanese forces. Nevertheless, the KMT and CPC held negotiations and communicated on

[41] *Measures for Handling the Problem of the CPC*, 1939–1940.

the adjustment, demarcation, and command structure of the areas under control. However, the friction between the armies of the KMT and CPC was constantly increasing, and at the end of 1939 in KMT-CPC dual-controlled Ningxian and Zhenyuan, the military conflict reached a climax. Thereafter, military friction between the two sides spread from small areas to the whole country; by this, the CPC had now gained more room to maneuver and, unlike before, the CPC began to rely more on the military, rather than just political, rivalry to gain the advantage. On 4 May 1940, in response to the views of the New Fourth Army commander, Xiang Ying, who disagreed with the CPC Central Committee and was regarded as having serious right-wing views, Mao Zedong issued instructions to Xiang Ying, who was then secretary of the CPC Southeastern Bureau, on behalf of the Central Committee calling for the independent development of the CPC's military and political forces:

> This policy of development policy has been repeatedly pointed out to you by the Central Committee. What we term development is not subject to the restrictions of the KMT and goes beyond the scope of what the KMT can allow. We do not want others to appoint our officers and do not rely on their superiors, and we will independently and freely expand our army and resolutely establish bases. In these bases we will independently activate the masses and establish a CPC-led anti-Japanese united front regime that can develop into enemy occupied areas.[42]

Many historical documents show that the CPC made use of the biggest national crisis of the Anti-Japanese War to develop its own forces; the New Fourth Army which was originally set at 12,000 soldiers later developed to number more than 100,000 troops. In the constant negotiations and political games with the KMT, the CPC gradually gained political and military leverage. For example, in response to Chiang Kai-shek's dictatorship, the CPC used the means of a democratic society—"freedom of assembly, expression and publication"—to win moral and political support throughout the country, which left Chiang Kai-shek trapped in an extremely passive situation—the advance of the Japanese army and the severity of the international situation made Chiang Kai-shek unwilling to allow the CPC to develop but he was unable to besiege

[42] Mao Zedong, "Develop forces resisting the Japanese and resist the attacks of anti-Communist conservatives" Selected Works, vol. 2, Renmin Chubanshe, 1952, p. 727.

and successfully eliminate the CPC armies. In such a situation, the CPC did not regard its previous commitments to cooperate as an obstacle to independently developing its armed forces. In an order issued to the Southeastern Bureau, Mao Zedong's instructions to the New Fourth Army were very specific: Don't worry about the criticism, restrictions, and pressure coming from Gu Zhutong, the Nationalist Commander-in-Chief and others:

> From the west to Nanjing, east to the sea, south to Hangzhou, and north to Xuzhou, we should as quickly and systematically as possible take control of all areas we can. We should independently expand the army, establish political power, set up financial organs, collect anti-Japanese taxes, set up economic organs, develop agriculture, industry and commerce, open all types of schools, and train cadres in large numbers. The Central Committee wants you within a year to expand anti-Japanese armed forces to 100,000 people in areas behind enemy lines in Jiangsu and Zhejiang provinces, but I do not know what your specific measures will be?[43]

Xiang Ying was still hesitant to carry out the Central Committee's order, but Chen Yi, captain of the first detachment of the New Fourth Army had already begun to actually implement the order. At the same time, the CPC and KMT continued to discuss satisfying the requirements of each side, such as the Shaan-Gan-Ning border area becoming the Northern Shaanxi administrative region, the 18th Group and the New Fourth armies being expanded, and the CPC then calling for the area of military operations to be further expanded to include Shandong and Suiyuan provinces and military provisions increased. On the other hand, the Nationalist Military Commission from July ordered the 18th Group Army and the New Fourth Army to fight north of the Yellow River, with the Yangtze River basin going to the National Army; implementing this plan was delayed and the plan was revised by the leaders of the 8th Route and New Fourth armies. When Gu Zhutong discovered that the New Fourth Army had not moved north of the Yangtze River as required by the Nationalist Command and he thought they were launching an attack

[43] Mao Zedong, ibid., pp. 727–728.

on the 40th Division of the National Army,[44] according to Chiang Kai-shek's military orders, he decided to impose immediate sanctions in time. In seven days of military conflict (6–14 January), Gu Zhutong's KMT army annihilated nearly 10,000 New Fourth Army troops; army chief Ye Ting was court-martialed, while the senior generals Xiang Ying and Yuan Guoping were shot by their deputies when fleeing the battlefield. This event came to be called the "South Anhui Incident". The Incident embarrassed Chiang Kai-shek before the nation and the international community, though he had no regrets about taking action against the

[44] Considering which road to take in order to cross the Yangtze from Zhenjiang, the KMT's Han Deqin's group came into armed conflict with the New Fourth Army. In order to prevent Xiang Ying's group reinforcing the New Fourth Army„ Chiang Kai-shek demanded that Xiang Ying's troops cross the Yangtze from south to north in eastern Anhui. Mao Zedong did not comply with orders and demanded that Xiang Ying's "go to Southern Jiangsu". Mao did not inform the Nationalist Military Commission, and Xiang Ying followed Mao's instructions and moved south. On 3 January, Commander Ye Ting received a telegram from Chiang Kai-shek reiterating that he should take the road to Southern Anhui: "The (KMT) forces along that road have been ordered to provide you with cover". Xiang Ying sent a telegram to Chiang Kai-shek to verify the final route to be taken, but the telegram was seized by Mao Zedong (no CPC military commander was allowed to contact Chiang Kai-shek directly). In the absence of a reply, Xiang Ying continued to march as Mao Zedong had directed. On the 4th, Ye Ting and Xiang Ying entered the KMT garrison area, but because of a lack of prior communication, they were thought to be making a provocative attack on the National Army. On the 6th, Gu Zhutong ordered Xiang Ying's army to "conduct a complete clean up". On the 9th, Liu Shaoqi of the Jiangbei Command of the New Fourth Army informed Yan'an that they had run into Xiang Ying's troops, but Mao that he knew nothing about it. On the 10th, Xiang Ying again telegraphed Chiang Kai-shek, but Mao again concealed communications. On the 12th, Mao asked Zhou Enlai in Chongqing: "Make a serious representation to the KMT, that they immediately end the siege". On the 13th, Mao Zedong asked Zhou Enlai to "appeal to the whole country for help" and solicit the views of the Soviet Union as soon as possible, hoping for the Soviet Union's support for the CPC's military attack on the Kuomintang. On 15 January, Zhou met with Soviet Ambassador Alexander Panyushkin [1905–1974], to no avail. Mao then contacted Dimitrov and wanted to tell Stalin to "consider whether we could give us specific military assistance". On 23 February, Stalin approved Dimitrov's order to Mao: "We don't think a split is inevitable. You should not try to effect a break. On the contrary, you should make every effort to prevent civil war. Please reconsider your position on this issue". According to the CPC history documents on the violent liquidation of the AB Group, the "South Anhui Incident" is regarded as another of Mao Zedong's opportunities to destroy old enemy in the party, in this case Xiang Ying. (See Chang Jung and Halliday, Mao Zedong: The Unknown Story, Chinese edition: Hong Kong: Open Press, 2006 edition.)

New Fourth Army.[45] Just as the whole country was engaged in a deadly war with Japan, there was once again open infighting within the Chinese armies. The KMT and CPC had different interpretations of this incident; unlike the KMT which saw the CPC as not complying with orders, the CPC saw the incident as the result of cooperation between Japan and the KMT's pro-Japanese factions, and even refused to attend political discussions in protest. In any case, the tragic killing between allied forces made a very negative impression on the outside world and the international community. Later, although Chiang Kai-shek dissolved the New Fourth Army, the remaining 90,000 New Fourth troops continued to accept the leadership of the CPC, who appointed Chen Yi as its acting chief, the KMT-CPC cooperation was in a dire crisis. The following month, without Stalin's response to the plan to split with the KMT, Mao told Zhou Enlai that the CPC attitude to the KMT should be militarily defensive and politically offensive; not hindering Chiang Kai-shek's resistance to Japan while preserving the strength of the CPC was Mao's preferred strategy. As stated in a report of 1 October 1940, one year after the exchange of communications between the CPC and Japan, the Japanese Army's General Staff in North China stated in a report:

> The ultimate aim of the CPC is to bring down the Chongqing government and take over power in the country. But the CPC is currently still very weak, and cannot seize power from the KMT. So, the task of the CPC's army now is to ensure the Japanese and Chongqing governments are locked into a war for as long as possible, so the CPC can build up strength during this period. Therefore, military conflict between the KMT and CPC is not conducive to the expansion of their own armies; on the surface they obey the Chongqing government, but in private they try to ensure that the Chongqing government not negotiate with Japan and they work to prevent this. Because if the Japanese and Chongqing governments do not fight for a long enough period, the Communist armies will not have enough time to grow strong.[46]

[45] On 16 January 1941, Chiang Kai-shek wrote in his diary: "For the New Fourth Army, our research is earnest and our determination is very strong, so this matter should be completely resolved, in order to establish prestige and advance our program, even if the Russian armaments and aircraft are suspended".

[46] Japanese Defence Department War History Department, *Dazhanqian zhi Huabei Zhi'an Zuozhan* (The North China Pacification War Prior to the Great War), vol. 1,

Previously, the CPC had repeatedly propagandized the danger posed by the KMT's forces capitulating, even attempting to get Moscow to agree to support an attack on Chiang Kai-shek. However, the CPC never discovered any signs of a possible surrender to the Japanese army in Chiang Kai-shek's words and deeds—initially Mao warned that Chiang Kai-shek might defect to Japan, but found that the Japanese continued to attack the KMT's armies. The CPC constantly adjusted its strategy, so perhaps a compromise with the KMT compromise was also a way to take the overall situation into account and build up strength. So, in March, Mao Zedong instructed Zhou Enlai to go to Chongqing for negotiations and directed to secure only what would enable the CPC to "expand its army, defend its lands, establish Xinhua Daily and take fewer people on the road",[47] in order to maintain detente between the two sides. In a directive dated 18 March 1941, Mao warned the Party: "Throughout the country and in every base area, it is important to not erroneously estimate that the KMT and CPC have finally split or are about to split, otherwise many incorrect views may result".[48]

In fact, as Chiang Kai-shek saw the situation at that time, it would still not have been difficult to exterminate the Communist armies, but the trouble lay in the lack of political legitimacy, which neither the public nor the international community would agree to. The KMT and CPC wanted to appear to have cooperated and compromised, but this was not enough to keep the two parties together. After the South Anhui Incident, almost all CPC military forces were no longer commanded by the KMT and the National government no longer provided them with funding; the CPC began to issue its own decrees and regulations, establish banks, and issue currency.[49] In short, in the four or five years from the Xi'an Incident

Asagumo News Agency, 1968, p. 384. 2016, p. 142. This book quotes Endō Homare, op. cit., p. 142.

[47] "Mao Zedong's Telegram to [Zhou] Enlai", 12 March 1941, in *The South Anhui Incident* (Anthology of Documents), p. 232.

[48] Mao Zedong, Mao Zedong Selected Works, vol. 2, Beijing: Renmin Chubanshe, 1952, pp. 756–757.

[49] From 1941 to 1944, Yan'an also sought a significant income from opium cultivation to solve the CPC's economic crisis, as Soviet materials reveal: By 1943, a total of 44,760 kilograms of opium were sold, worth 2.4 billion in paper currency. During this time, the National government was struggling with drought- and locust-induced famine in northern China. The famine killed 3 million people and created millions of refugees.

to the South Anhui Incident, the CPC gained significant military and political influence, but its military strength was still weak.

After Japan's Konoe cabinet adopted the *Outline for Implementing Imperial State Policy* in September calling for the Japanese armies to move south, the Soviet army had the opportunity to move troops stationed in the Far East to Moscow, which naturally meant that the Soviets and the Soviet-backed CPC forces were less likely to be attacked by the Japanese. Regarding how to view the new international situation, Mao Zedong at this time even considered that if an alliance emerged between Germany, Italy and the Soviet Union, the CPC might form an alliance with Japan in China, because in Mao Zedong's view, the CPC's main enemy was Chiang Kai-shek. Even though the Soviet Union and Japan signed a treaty of neutrality on 13 April 1941 and it seemed the CPC could follow the Soviet Union and Japan, the idea was not likely to be put forward after the outbreak of the Pacific War.[50]

In December 1941, the international anti-fascist united front was formed, and the KMT and CPC put forward strategies and adjustments to meet the requirements and conditions of the new situation. In order to win the support of the international community, especially the United States and Britain, the KMT as far as possible used various means to demonstrate to the international community that China's anti-fascist struggle was based on a united front with all parties, especially the CPC, and that his country was not part of the international anti-fascist united front. The CPC, which was fighting hard against the Japanese behind enemy lines, was still in a precarious situation, and the shortage of resources made the leaders of the CPC aware of the need to scale down

[50] Wang Ming recorded a quarrel he had with Mao Zedong in October 1940: Mao commented, "What shouldn't be allying with Britain, the US, France and the Soviet Union, but with Germany, Italy, and the Soviet Union". When Wang Ming questioned his remark, Mao explained: "The Germans, Italians and Japanese are all poor farmers. What's the benefit of fighting them? Even if we win, there is no profit to be had. The British, Americans and French are rich, especially the British which you can see from how many large colonies they have! Defeating them would be very profitable when you divide up their colonies. You might say I'm taking the fascist line, but I'm not afraid of that. China should establish a united front with the Japanese and Wang Jingwei against Chiang Kai-shek, not the anti-Japanese national united front you are proposing". Ref: Wang Ming, op. cit., p. 187.

the conflict with the KMT and continue to gain more support. Moreover, after the South Anhui Incident, the KMT continued to restrict and combat the development of the CPC to varying degrees.

At the end of December 1941, Lin Biao, head of the 115th Division of the Eighth Route Army, returned home from the Soviet Union unsure of the difficulties the CPC might face as a result of the outbreak of war between the Soviet Union and Germany. Chiang Kai-shek, for strategic reasons, asked that Lin Biao be accorded facilitated passage, and arranged for Hu Zongnan to meet with Lin in Xi'an to see if it was possible to engineer a shift in direction from the CPC. On the basis of Mao Zedong's instructions, Lin Biao stressed the importance of winning victory in fighting against Japan, but told the KMT that the CPC already had the support of "700,000 fierce lions", that mature political and military experience had made the CPC stronger, and that the continuation of the civil war in the current situation with the enemy would have extremely serious consequences. Even so, Lin Biao made it clear that the CPC continued to believe in the Three Principles of the People and hope for a unified military command under the principle of fairness. In July 1942, the CPC and the KMT issued a declaration to commemorate the fifth anniversary of the outbreak of the "September 7th" Anti-Japanese War. The text was completely different from the political tone after the South Anhui Incident: "We are willing to do our best to discuss with the KMT authorities the resolution of the past disputes between the KMT and CPC, and to discuss with the KMT and other anti-Japanese parties all the relevant issues relating to achieving the final victory of the anti-Japanese war and the construction of a post-war New China".[51] In the subsequent KMT-CPC negotiations (11 July), Zhou Enlai and Dong Biwu even made the following promise to KMT representative Zhang Zhizhong: "At present, the CPC's army is temporary, but under a true democratic republic the CPC would not need to permanently retain its own army; the current interim regime organized by the CPC is based on the needs for the Anti-Japanese War, and the CPC has no intention of competing with the central regime under the leadership of the KMT". Although the new international context and political atmosphere led Chiang Kai-shek to express the idea of inviting Mao Zedong for negotiations, the terms of cooperation between the two parties in the negotiations never

[51] NNN in *Jiefang Ribao* (Liberation Daily), 7 July 1942.

met their respective basic objectives. The conditions for the CPC were pushed back to "the army not being expanded" and "the war zone not being adjusted after the war", but as the basis of the CPC regime rested on the insistence that "the border areas must be legitimized", the CPC's demand that "Communists must enjoy the rights and freedoms of citizens" was a question of principle that always concerned the KMT.[52] At its 10th Plenary Session of the KMT's 5th Central Council held from 12 to 27 November in that year, the KMT adopted "Results of its Investigation of Future Communist Party Policy" which stated: "Our policy of clemency towards the CPC simply requires that henceforth it does not violate the law, does not disturb the social order, does not organize the army to cut off [and control] regions, does not hinder the anti-Japanese war, does not undermine unity, and can fulfill the declaration to the nation of 22 September 1937 to address the national crisis, obey the orders of the government, faithfully realize the Three Principles of the People, and regard the army and people of the entire country with equanimity".[53] However, subsequent negotiations between the two sides still had little effect.

By the spring of 1943, the situation in which the KMT and CPC sometimes fought and sometimes negotiated was once again deadlocked. There were also different opinions within the KMT and the CPC on whether to cooperate and how to cooperate, but at every opportunity, the senior leaders of the KMT and CPC would promote the possibility of cooperation. But at different times, the two sides alternated, and in the end, the KMT's goal of restricting or even breaking up the CPC and its armies did not change. In the past few years, the fact that the Communist armies grew from tens of thousands to hundreds of thousands provided a sufficient basis for the KMT to criticize and even accuse the CPC of "organizing the army to cut off regions" and "undermining unity". In any case, the CPC always insisted in negotiations on the "legitimation" of the CPC and on the need for the expansion of its armed forces. This worried many members of the KMT—there was no evidence in previous years that the CPC would strictly abide by the unified military decrees

[52] Mao Zedong's "Mao Zedong's Telegram to Lin Biao via Zhou Enlai", 25 October 1942.

[53] Rong Mengyuan ed., *Documents on the Congresses and Plenary Session of the Central Council of the KMT*, *xia* volume, Beijing: Guangming Ribao Chubanshe, 1985, pp. 793–794.

of the National Government, and for Chiang Kai-shek, given the enemy China currently faced, this was not the time to discuss the establishment of a multi-party government. In June 1943, when the Communist International was dissolved, Chiang Kai-shek saw a marked decline in CPC's international power, making it even less concerned about the most basic provisions proposed by the CPC for negotiations, and he seemed to want to see how much weight the CPC, which was in an unusually difficult situation, placed on making an offer to the KMT.

Chiang Kai-shek's difficulty was that, given the main purpose of the international anti-fascist united front and its interrelationships, it was difficult for him to openly "defend against" or eliminate the CPC by military means. But he also tried to surround and eliminate the CPC's bases and forces, and through the propaganda machine inform the world that the CPC had worked constantly to deceive people while preserving its power, effectively "undermining the anti-Japanese war effort and harming the country". However, in the paralysis and intensity of the Anti-Japanese War, people and the international community were more in favor of cooperation with the CPC in order to concentrate forces on the fight against the Japanese army. On the CPC side, Mao Zedong's strategy remained as stated at the Luochuan meeting:

> We need to calm down and not go to the front line to act as anti-Japanese heroes, avoid head-on conflict with Japan and go behind Japanese lines and fight guerrilla warfare, find ways to expand the Eighth Route Army and establish anti-Japanese guerrilla bases, and do everything possible to save and strengthen our party's armed forces. As for the Government's orders urging us to go to the front line, we should use various pretexts to delay their implementation, and only after the Japanese army has killed and injured large numbers of National army troops can we sit back and seize power from the KMT.

Until June 1942, a Soviet journalist in Yan'an had this impression of the CPC's army: "The Eighth Route Army is not taking the initiative to launch military operations to stop the Japanese invasion but is limiting itself to half-heartedly fighting local defensive battles. As soon as the enemy launches an attack, the Eighth Route Army retreats into the mountains to avoid conflict. So, the Japanese face no opposition in actually preparing their rear command for war against the Soviet Union".[54] In late September of that year, Vladimirov also visited areas controlled by the Eighth Route Army and found that: The CPC hopes, through the confrontation between the Japanese and KMT forces, to establish its own bases and ultimately seize power from the KMT.

In November 1943, the international situation once again impacted China; in response to China being part of the united front against fascism, the leaders of the United States and Britain, at the landmark Cairo Conference, hoped that Chiang Kai-shek would further take into account the overall situation, continue to cooperate with the CPC in Yan'an, and propose the establishment of a "coalition government" as a change from the one-party government. To this end, Chiang Kai-shek once again relaxed the siege of the Shaan-Gan-Ning border area and attempted to discuss cooperation with the CPC. Mao Zedong, realizing that the War of Resistance against Japan might be coming to an end and that the political situation in China needed to be re-examined, argued that it was necessary to negotiate with the KMT for strategic reasons. Therefore, Mao Zedong told his comrades: "Our Party supports the two principles of supporting Chiang's Anti-Japanese War and Chiang's national construction, and this remains unchanged".[55] However, the political and military negotiations between the two parties subsequently had no real purpose at all, with neither party holding any hope for an outcome of the negotiations. Chiang Kai-shek clearly admonished his colleagues: "The CPC is

[54] Vladimirov, op. cit., p. 26. On 9 July, Vladimirov recorded:

The ranks of the Eighth Route Army (and, of course, of the New Fourth Army) have long since stopped taking the initiative in attacking and counter-attacking the aggressors. Despite a ferocious offensive by frenzied Japanese troops in south-eastern China and Japan's threaten to invade the Soviet Union, this situation continues without change. The Chinese Communist armies are not resisting the current Japanese sweep of the occupied territories, and they retreated to the mountains or crossed to the other side of the Yellow River. The leadership of the CPC regards the KMT as the main enemy and spares no effort to seize territory controlled by the central government and uses all means to achieve its objectives.

These obviously separatist activities jeopardize the liberation movement of Chinese opposition to the aggressors, aggravate the sacrifices of the Chinese people and lead to military conflict with the KMT. The KMT's power is, for the time being, something the CPC can only hope for (p. 36).

[55] "Telegraph from Mao Zedong, Zhou Enlai to Dong Biwu", 18 February 1944.

100 per cent committed to implementing communism, and their advocacy of the Three Principles of the People is mere camouflage".[56] The CPC also changed its political strategy at this time: Zhou Enlai's essay "On Constitutionalism and Unity" published then put forward the idea of "resolving the KMT-CPC relations in a democratic way", opposing party rule and implementing democracy.[57] At the same time as increasing numbers of young people were moving from KMT-controlled areas to Yan'an, the CPC was also penetrating KMT-controlled areas through underground CPC organizations and other ways to expand its influence through various channels.

In January 1944, given a frontal attack by the Japanese army and possible US intervention between the KMT and CPC, Mao Zedong informed the KMT Military Commission's Military Orders Department in Yan'an that the Communist Party wanted to resume negotiations with the KMT in order to adjust KMT–CPC relations. In April 1944, He Yingqin (1890–1987) prepared a document for the negotiations, titled "Draft political solution to the CPC problem", which discussed the "guideline policy" that "National military decrees must be unified". He included a note stating that "in the past, the CPC did not comply with the tasks ordered by the Centre and in fighting the enemy, they would mobilize in an unauthorized manner, their most important breaches being attacking friendly armies, expanding their own armies, and violating military orders". He also noted: "As for the seizing territory and harming local officials, the [CPC's] most important breach of political decrees being enacting laws and regulations that contravened Central decrees and issuing their own currency and postage stamps. Such sabotage of military and political decrees must completely cease, and they must strictly abide by the military and political decrees of the State, if a solution to the situation is to be found". Negotiations between the two sides began on 3 May with Wang Shijie (1891–1981) and Zhang Zhizhong representing the government and Lin Boqu representing the CPC, but as of

[56] President Jiang's instructions on preparations to be made by outside journalists going to Yan'an and for Lin Zuhan's [i.e. Lin Boqu] trip to [Chongqing], 15 March 1944.

[57] See Zhou Enlai: "On Constitutionalism and Unity", 12 March 1944, Zhonggong Zhongyang Wenxian Yanjiushi (Documentation Research Office of the Central Committee of the Communist Party of China) ed., *Zhou Enlai Nianpu* (Zhou Enlai Annales), Beijing: Renmin Chubanshe, 1998, pp. 572–573.

5 June, no agreement had been signed. The reason was that the negotiations coincided with the implementation of the Japanese Army's Ichigo Plan, the Nationalist army was losing on the battlefield and Mao Zedong was constantly changing tack in the process of negotiating. Previously, KMT–CPC negotiations were largely limited to arrangements regarding troop numbers, as with Lin Biao's proposal in the previous year to expand the Eighth Route and New Fourth armies to four armies with twelve divisions which saw both two sides weighing into the debate. After the Japanese advanced their Ichigo battle plan and Luoyang fell (25 May), Mao Zedong insisted conditions far exceeded previous demands and now involved nation-wide political demands, such as implementing democratic politics, relaxing bans on political parties and enacting local autonomy. On 5 June the CPC even held a meeting on urban work to study how future urban recovery operations would be carried out. In June 1944, when US Vice President Henry A. Wallace visited China, he hoped that Chiang Kai-shek would agree to the US arrangement for a U.S. military advisory mission to visit Yan'an, but Chiang Kai-shek was very opposed to this and told Wallace: "The CPC has already abandoned the task of fighting the Japanese, has launched a plot to seize power, and attempted to take advantage of the national disaster to fulfill its goals;...".[58]

The United States tried to gain a thorough understanding of Yan'an in order to formulate a policy more in line with US-China and even US-Soviet policy, and Roosevelt hoped the KMT would accept the US proposal that the United States send a mission to Yan'an. The proposal was rejected by Chiang Kai-shek, who feared that the United States would have the wool pulled over their eyes in Yan'an and provide support to the CPC, which would create huge trouble later. In any case, the increasingly influential Yan'an spurred Roosevelt's strong desire for support from Chiang Kai-shek, who in response to a request that was almost an ultimatum agreed to Washington's arrangement. On 22 July and 7 August, the first 18-member U.S. military observer mission (called the "Dixie mission"), led by David D. Barrett, a military attaché in China, arrived in Yan'an on two separate flights in a US Air Force C-47 cargo plane. What followed were uninterrupted flights between Chongqing and Yan'an transporting members of the US military observer mission. Indeed, this was an excellent opportunity for the CPC, who not only

[58] *Jiang Zongtong Milu*, v. 13, pp. 145–148.

wanted US assistance but also hoped to work with the United States in the future to eventually replace Chiang Kai-shek. Mao obviously wanted to make use of the members of the Dixie mission in Yan'an and he kept in close touch with the Americans through Zhou Enlai, who was well-spoken in English and familiar with Western habits. Mao even considered changing the name of the Communist Party in order to impress the American.[59] Yan'an's performance for the members of the Dixie Mission was so effective that Service and Davies were very hopeful about Yan'an's future and believed that if the KMT did not radically change the current political, economic, and social landscape, the CPC would eventually defeat Chiang Kai-shek. The problem here, of course, was that the United States wanted China to establish a regime that was in line with American values and interests. Some aspects of the political life in Yan'an might also have led the Americans to imagine it met the standards of a democratic society, such as "simple government by pure soldiers" and the "three-three system" of the border zone regime (the CPC holding one-third of seats with the others divided between moderate forces and elected representatives). Moreover, in Yan'an the members of the Dixie mission were able to see young people coming and going, looking enthusiastic and even laughing and paid little attention to the "rectification movement", in stark contrast to the emaciated refugees, lame beggars, and obviously suffering women and children often to be seen in KMT-ruled areas. The mission's members almost believed that supporting Yan'an was more likely to lead to the establishment of a democratic regime than supporting the KMT, which would naturally preempt the Soviet Union to exert excessive influence on the CPC. In short, the United States, by further participating in China affairs, came to see its historical mission as fostering liberal democratic values and corresponding free enterprises, and further promoting its business and strategic interests in China. However, the mission observed

[59] On 22 August 1944, during the visit of the US military delegation to Yan'an, Vladimirov wrote:

Today, Mao Zedong summoned me and told me: "We have been thinking about renaming our party, not calling it the 'Communist Party', but some other name. This would be more favorable to the situation in the special area. It would especially ensure good relations with the Americans". Ref: Vladimirov, op. cit., p. 267. In addition, the Soviet liaison officer Sun Ping recorded that on 12 August 1944, Mao Zedong told him: "We're thinking about changing the name of the party, rather than the 'Communist Party', something else. This situation will be better for us, especially in our relationship with the United States". Quoted by Chang Jung and Joe Halliday, op. cit., p. 256.

and analyzed few of the problems in Yan'an's ideological realm, using Western logic and balance to arrange what they saw as possible scenarios; these revealed obvious differences in American public opinion, like those between Hurley and other members of the mission.

In September of that year, the KMT decided to use its Congress to make public the issues surrounding negotiations between the KMT and the CPC, in an attempt to show people how the CPC's "words and actions are not one and the same" and how the KMT government is "open and transparent". Indeed, it was at this meeting that those attending learned that the Chinese Communist armies had grown to 477,500 troops, as well as 1.2 members of militias. At the same time, the CPC had established 15 bases and had its own government. However, the CPC's strategy at this time changed radically; on the 20th, the *Liberation Daily* published an article revised by Mao Zedong, which had a very different meaning from any political demands previously negotiated, telling people: The KMT "throughout the negotiations has operated with a spirit of arrogance and arbitrariness, attempting to place the interests of the KMT alone above national interests, forcing others to obey it". As a consequence, the CPC would not obey the KMT's "fascist political decrees" and "defeatist military orders". Thus, in the view of the CPC, it was no longer the CPC that jeopardized legitimacy, but the KMT. That the CPC at this time could dare to make such a statement was undoubtedly the result of the KMT regime's corruption and dictatorship caused by its failures in the political, military, social, and even cultural realm and its loss of popular support; the CPC through the previous seven years of anti-Japanese war had won sufficient political and military strength that it was able to effectively resist the KMT.

Washington has certainly noted that the conflict between the KMT and CPC has seriously affected China's war of resistance, but the other question was how could China be unified when the war ended? For the United States and Chiang Kai-shek, solving the CPC problem has been a top priority. General Hurley, who had previously handled the Stilwell crisis as presidential envoy, began to dig deep into the dispute between the Communists, with Chiang Kai-shek's consent.[60] From November 7 to 10, 1944, Hurley discussed with Yan'an the five conditions stressing the

[60] Chiang Kai-shek wrote in his diary on 5 November 1944: "If by allowing Hurley to mediate, he succeeds, it is in my interest, and if his mediation fails, it will not be no loss to me as it will expose the procrastinating scheming of the [Communist] bandits".

idea of a democratic state based on equality and stipulating that "China has only one central government and one army" with the KMT government as its core. His main purpose was not to build relations with the CPC on behalf of the United States, but how to resolve the dispute between the two major political groups, the KMT and CPC, after the victory of the World War. At the same time, he sought to eliminate the Soviet Union's ideological influence on the CPC as much as possible, so that Yan'an's military bases and political resources were also used by the United States. Hurley, who earned a law degree as a young man, was president of the Tulsa City Bar Association at the age of 28. As John P. Davies, also a member of theUS Military Observer Group in Yan'an, noted, "When Hurley arrived in Yan'an, he wanted to unite Chiang Kai-shek's KMT with the Communist Party, which was not much different from persuading Republicans and Democrats to accept bipartisanship in times of national crisis".[61] Before returning to Chongqing, Hurley thought his Yan'an trip had helped the two parties had reached an agreement that met the requirements of both parties, and after Mao signed the proposal of cooperation on behalf of the CPC Central Committee, Hurley signed on behalf of the United States.[62] As an American, Hurley could not see clearly how Chiang Kai-shek and Mao Zedong, as Chinese, were thinking. In a 24 December letter to Secretary of State Stettinius, he wrote optimistically: "Even if there are differences between the principles upheld by the Kuomintang and those held by the Communist Party of China, they are not very deep". By this time, the United States had said it could cooperate with the CPC.[63]

[61] Davies, *China Hand*, p. 136.

[62] The State Department later insisted that the signature did not represent the United States, but merely that of a witness.

[63] In early November 1944, John P. Davies, a member of the US Military Observer Group, a political adviser to Wedemeyer who had been the first to propose sending aUS military observer mission to Yan'an, visited Yan'an. The mission's analysis concluded: The United States should be concerned that if political and economic cooperation between Yan'an and the Soviet Union developed, it would affect US interests in China. As long as Yan'an's political and economic structures were not controlled by the Soviet Union and the Communist Party of China was fully independent, the United States could consider cooperating with Yan'an. The United States even drew up a cooperative plan for US troops to land in China and provide the Chinese Communist Party with 50,000 weapons and ammunition to cooperate with attacks on the Japanese, for the Chinese Communist Party to consider.

The document Hurley brought back to Chongqing from Yan'an showed that the CPC had revised the five conditions of the Nationalist government, the major change being to reconstitute the national government as a coalition government. Although the CPC stressed that the coalition government would follow Sun Yat-sen's Three Principles of the People and included principles of human rights to please the Americans like justice, freedom of belief, freedom of the press, freedom of expression, freedom of assembly, and freedom of association that the Communist Party needed at this time, the CPC's core problem was to have equal standing with the KMT in government. The KMT knew that the formation of a coalition government would mean that "tutelary government" would be rendered meaningless. In Chiang Kai-shek's view, a coalition government was merely a step in the CPC's attempt to seize state power. Chiang Kai-shek's was shocked by Hurley's lack of understanding of the CPC and lack of Chinese experience. Indeed, Hurley did not understand that the relationship between the KMT and CPC was completely unlike that of the Republicans and Democrats in the United States, and, in Hurley, like Stalin, believed the CPC were not communists in the true sense, whereas Chiang Kai-shek was well aware of their deep ideological ties to the Soviet Union. Zhou Enlai, who returned to Chongqing with Hurley, had further discussions with the KMT representative Wang Shijie, and in the meeting on 22 November, Zhou Enlai insisted on "coalition government", while Wang Shijie told him that tutelary politics was the legacy of Mr. Sun Yat-sen and that "Mr. Jiang also has no right to decide freely". Hurley did his best, telling Mao that Chiang Kai-shek agreed that the Communist Party would be a legitimate political party, but that the army must be handed over to the national government. The latter was key because Chiang Kai-shek wanted to retain power by force and Mao Zedong wanted to seize power by force. Hurley failed to mediate, but he was appointed ambassador to China on 29 November.

Democratic politics depended on rules and the trust that these rules would be enforced. In March 1945, when the Kuomintang hoped to achieve political consultation between parties through the path of convening a constitution of the National Congress, Zhou Enlai of the CPC proposed to convene a Communist Party meeting. The CPC did not agree with the composition of the National Assembly, believing that the congresses first formulated by the KMT in 1936 were no longer legitimate, and so did not believe it could produce anything resembling a constitution. By 2 April, at a press conference in Washington Wedemeyer insisted that the United States could still only work with the Nationalist government, not with the Communist Party. In May 1945, the US' interaction with the Communists ceased, and as a result, the more Chiang Kai-shek refused to cooperate, the more people expressed doubts about the KMT; the more Mao Zedong offered to cooperate, the more people felt good about the Communist Party. In any case, military defeats, economic crises, and widespread social antipathy towards the KMT led the CPC to see it as a good time to actively attack the KMT's politics. The overall decision-making of the Second World War entailed the formulation of strategies for the various war zones, so that, just as the world's anti-fascist united front had to cooperate with the Soviet Union, Washington shifted for a time from fully supporting Chiang Kai-shek to favoring the formation of a KMT-CPC coalition government in order to defeat Japanese imperialism as soon as possible.[64]

Indeed, in terms of the results of the War of Resistance, China had achieved great success: China's position in the international community had never been higher, and people noted China's important contribution to the anti-fascist war of the Second World War: On the battlefield, China held down more than 1.2 million Japanese troops, more than half of the number Japan deployed overseas. However, it was clear that the Soviet Union would demand payment acceptable to few Chinese from China for its support at the end of the war. When Song Ziwen went to Moscow to negotiate with Stalin, Stalin insisted on the basic elements of the Yalta secret agreement; clinging to the memory of Russia's loss to the Japanese in 1905, he hoped that Japan's colonial privileges and those trading ports opened to the European powers since the Opium War could now be part of the Soviet Union's sphere of influence. Although the Yalta Agreement, signed by three countries, made it clear that the Soviet Union would assist China by declaring war on Japan after Germany surrendered, it also provided that: (1) The status quo of the People's Republic of Mongolia would be preserved; (2) The rights of the Russian Empire in the past would be restored to the Soviet Union, and Dalian port would be

[64] In fact, John S. Service, a member of the US Military Observer Group, also floated the idea of a coalition government in China during a visit to Yan'an in September 1944. But in the end, the United States has no confidence in working with the Chinese Communist Party. At a press conference in Washington on April 2, 1945, Hurley corrected his previous strategy of de facto deepening the conflict between the two parties, declaring that the United States was only cooperating with the Kuomintang.

opened as an international port although the Soviet Union must be guaranteed special rights in that port; and, (3) The China Eastern Railway and the Southern Manchurian Railway to Dalian would be jointly operated by a Sino-Soviet Company to safeguard the special rights of the Soviet Union. In short, this compact is clearly at odds with the Nine-Nations Convention, the Atlantic Charter, and the Cairo Declaration. From the world landscape that emerged after the end of World War II, securing the Soviet Union's cooperation was simply allowing one dictator to fight another, and the result of the Yalta deal was that the United States and Britain forced China to pay the high price of selling out its democratic hopes, whatever Roosevelt's starting point.

The resolution of the Yalta conference ensuring the Soviet Union's participation in the war forced Chiang Kai-shek to think about how to deal with China's northeast and Xinjiang and how to deal with the CPC after the Soviets entered China. In particular, he believed that the relationship between the Soviet Union and the CPC could easily lead to future Soviet support for the CPC. Worried about the future, Hurley also explained to Wang Shijie the urgency of the KMT negotiating with the Communists: "The United States intends to prevent the Soviet Union from recognizing the Communist government as an adversary after it joins the War in the Far East".[65] However, negotiations between the KMT and the Soviet Union involved a number of sovereignty issues and the question of Outer Mongolia and, from the beginning of negotiations in Moscow on 30 June until the day Japan formally announced its unconditional surrender,[66] the two nations' only agreement was the Republic of China-Soviet Union Friendship Treaty, the content of which was based on the basic elements of the Yalta secret agreement.[67] On the day the second atomic bomb was dropped on Nagasaki, Stalin reminded Song: If the Sino-Soviet treaty of friendship is not signed in time, China's

[65] Academia Sinica Institute of Modern History, *Wang Shijie Riji* (The Diary of Wang Shijie), 21 November 1944 entry, Taipei: 1990.

[66] The document was signed at 6 a.m. on 15 August but dated 14 August. This was based on the fact that on the 14th Japan has not formally announced its surrender, but if dated on the 15th, the agreement declaring war against Japan would have been invalid.

[67] Due to subsequent political changes in China, with the CPC seizing political power on the Chinese mainland with the help of the Soviet Union, the Republic of China on Taiwan accused the Soviet Union of breach of contract, and the Treaty of Friendship between China and the Soviet Union, after the adoption of the Sixth Standing Committee of the United Nations, expired on 25 February 1953.

northeast will fall into the hands of Chiang Kai-shek's enemy, the CPC, which is a matter of great concern to Chiang Kai-shek. Earlier, on 9 July, Stalin clearly told Song: "China must have only one government and one army". Now, Stalin reiterated that the Soviet Union only recognized and supported the central government led by Chiang Kai-shek, respected China's sovereignty in the northeast, and the Soviets would withdraw from China within three months of Japan's surrender, with other conditions largely upholding the Yalta agreement. Chiang Kai-shek, of course, knew the seriousness of the costs, and he knew that if he rejected the Soviet terms, Stalin would likely support the ideologically similar CPC. Believing that Stalin did not support the CPC as the leading political player in future China, he agreed.

The Yan'an Rectification Movement and *Talks at the Yan'an Forum*

Given the fierce fighting between the KMT and Japanese armies, Yan'an enjoyed a measure of wartime security and relaxation compared to the KMT-ruled rear and frontal battlefields. In view of the need to further consolidate his leadership in the party, Mao Zedong decided to launch a final purge of the Party's political opponents, allowing Liu Shaoqi, Kang Sheng, Chen Yun, Peng Zhen, Gao Gang and Li Fuchun to organize a "central rectification movement committee" to assist the Party's rectification campaign in line with his requirements. On 2 February 1942, Yan'an's *Liberation Daily* reported: Mao Zedong gave a speech calling for the rectification of our "learning style", "Party style" and "literary style". This is considered to be the beginning of the Yan'an rectification movement, which was quite unlike the KMT's use of consultative or open means of conflict to resolve internal conflicts. Mao Zedong's "rectification" was a political movement carried out through the interpretation of the legitimacy within the Party through ideology, with the concept of Marxism as the center. The aim was to criticize the Comintern faction, mainly represented by Wang Ming, and the forces of "dogmatism" and "empiricism" represented by Zhou Enlai.[68] The battle for the right to

[68] Looking back at the rectification movement, Wang Ming wrote:

"Anyone who had studied in the Soviet Union, was an intellectual, or who worked in theory or politics was required to admit to being a 'dogmatist', while those of worker or peasant origin, as well as those who were actually employed in [Party] work, had to admit

control the CPC's ideological voice entailed complete acquisition of political and military leadership within the party. The movement did not end until the second half of 1944 when foreign journalists and the US Military Observer Group visited Yan'an.

Edgar Snow, the first journalist to inform Western countries about the CPC, made this basic judgment about the CPC before 1937:

> Finally, of course, the political thought, strategic line and theoretical leadership of the CPC are under the close guidance of the Communist International, if not under its active and concrete command, and the Communist International has actually become a branch of the Communist Party of Russia over the past 10 years. At the end of the day, this means that, for better or worse, the Communist Party, like the Communist Party of every other country, often must fill the broad strategic needs of the Soviet Union, which belongs to Stalin's dictatorship.
>
> Some of this is at least obvious enough. By sharing in the collective experience of the Russian Revolution, the CPC has undoubtedly benefited greatly from the leadership of the Communist International. But it is also true that the serious setbacks suffered by the Chinese Communist Party in their painful growth and development can also be attributed to the Communist International.[69]

Mao Zedong never had any interest in the internationalist school, with whom he was in continuous conflict, but at different times and in specific political contexts, Mao Zedong always carefully pursued his political strategy lest he face rejection. By the time war broke out between the Soviet Union and Germany, Mao dared to openly ignore the Communist International and even the Tass reporter sent to work in Yan'an, and even wondered whether the Soviet Union could defeat Germany.[70]

to being an 'empiricist'. As a result, the vast majority of Party leaders, cadres and ordinary Party members were accused of making mistakes of 'dogmatism' and 'empiricism'. At the same time, Mao Zedong applied the label of 'dogmatism's captives' and 'dogmatists' accomplices' to 'empiricists' and thus linked them with 'dogmatists' to prove that the main fight against 'dogmatists' was correct". Ref: Wang Ming, op. cit., p. 59.

69 Edgar Snow, op. cit., p. 608.

70 On 25 May 1942, Vladimirov, a Tass reporter working in Yan'an, wrote in his diary: "In the second half of 1941, as the Germans approached Moscow, the Chinese Communist leaders became more unfriendly towards the Soviet group, and by the end of November, that had developed into open hostility. Senior staff of the Communist Party of

The Yan'an rectification movement readily reminds people of the history of the CPC's intra-party struggles in the early 1930s that saw the purge of "reactionaries" and the "AB clique". In this somewhat murky history of the CPC, Mao Zedong had complex differences with Bo Gu, Zhang Wentian and others, and the Internationalist faction in the CPC explained orthodox Marxism–Leninism, promoted Soviet-Russian ideology and criticized Mao, suggesting that he needed to read Marxist–Leninist writings as soon as possible and realize the importance of mastering the ideological discourse.

For a long time, within the CPC, the interpretation of Marxism–Leninism was in the hands of the Internationalists and some elite intellectuals who have studied Marxism since the late 1920s. It was precisely because of this lack of interpretation and Mao's lack of legitimacy as a Comintern identity that Mao Zedong was often subject to criticism from Wang Ming and others. Indeed, in Mao Zedong's pre-1937 writings, we see no full discussion of Marxist philosophy. However, most of the political elites in the party who worked with Mao Zedong in the 1930s were educated in Moscow, which brought pressure to bear on Mao Zedong. He needed to familiarize himself with Marxist philosophy and integrate its systematic vocabulary into the interpretation of the Chinese revolution, while at the same time be theoretically prepared to exert the ideological and cultural authority of the Party and address the esoteric questions that the elites might raise so that he could always rebuke and guide them in philosophical theory and not just military strategy. Between 1936 and 1937, Mao Zedong read a large number of Soviet philosophical texts translated into Chinese, and his "On Practice" and "On Contradiction" are believed to have been written after such reading. Soon, he began to deliver lectures on dialectics. In 1938, in the midst of the Soviet Union's tumultuous purges, Wang Ming's important supporter Mif was shot, which caused Wang Ming to lose influence in the party, so in October 1938, at the sixth plenary session of the Communist Party of China, Mao Zedong could say this:

China would not meet us. Mao Zedong, busy with his work, never met a Soviet reporter once and Kang Sheng sent someone to shadow us". Ref: Vladimirov, op. cit., p. 20. In his memoirs, Wang Ming also documented Mao Zedong's remarks about the Soviet Union and Germany: "Stalin cannot defeat Hitler". See: Wang Ming, op. cit., Ch. 2.

> Departing from Chinese characteristics to discuss Marxism is only abstract and empty Marxism. Therefore, the Sinification of Marxism, so that it bears the characteristics of China in its every expression, is in other words to apply it according to the characteristics of China, and this has become the problem the whole Party must urgently understand and solve. The eight-legged foreign style of prose must be abolished, vacuous and abstract tunes must be sung less, dogmatism must be put to rest, and replaced by a fresh and lively Chinese style, a Chinese style which Chinese people like.

The idea of paying attention to the characteristics of China was very much in line with the trend of anti-Japanese nationalism at that time. Mao Zedong had begun to exercise the right to interpret Marxism within the Party. In his essay "The Current Situation of The Anti-Japanese War and How to Persist in the Enduring War for Final Victory" (20 October 1938), Wang Ming reminded his audience that in the Sinification of Marxism, attention should be taken to not allow materialist dialectics be replaced by Confucius' compromise theory and cumbersome philosophy, to allow the old Chinese culture to replace the new doctrine of Marxism, and to not ignore the international experience because of nationalization, but Wang Ming's reminders had no effect.

Strategically, Mao Zedong did not simply use Chinese experience to counter international Marxism. From 1939, Mao began to use Stalin's Marxist textbook, *The History of the Communist Party (Bolshevik) of the Soviet Union*, to promote the Sinification of Marxism China. Published during Stalin's purges, this work provided a model for "Resolutions on Certain Historical Issues of the Party" that set out the historical conclusions of the CPC in the later period of the Yan'an rectification movement. Obviously, in the Sinification of Marxism, Mao Zedong summed up what he thought was the essence of the theory of "class struggle" and "the dictatorship of the proletariat", popularly expressed as "power comes from the barrel of the gun".

In fact, the so-called Yan'an rectification movement began with a speech on "Transforming Our Learning" delivered by Mao Zedong at the Yan'an Cadre Conference on 19 May 1941. Mao Zedong hoped that the whole Party and the whole army would seriously study *The History of the Communist Party (Bolshevik) of the Soviet Union* rather than original classics of Marx and Engels as core materials. Because "*History* was the highest synthesis and summary of the world communist movement over the past hundred years and a model of the combination of theory and practice, it was the only complete model for the world", anyone with basic theoretical common sense can see that, Mao Zedong's aim was, as he explained, to legitimize completely the Sinification of Marxism perfectly legal, which could produce new and different interpretations when not needed to achieve its goals.[71]

Mao Zedong began by saying: "Twenty years of the Communist Party of China are the two decades in which the universal truths of Marxism-Leninism and the concrete practice of the Chinese revolution have been increasingly combined". It is precisely because of this combination that "the Chinese revolution is completely new".[72] Here, "the concrete practice of the Chinese revolution" becomes the reason for the particularity of the issue of reforming the original theory. Mao Zedong made this assessment of the familiarity of the International faction with the theory of Marxism–Leninism:

> Many comrades' study of Marxism-Leninism does not seem to be for the needs of revolutionary practice, but for simple learning. So, although they read, but they are unable to digest it. They are only to quote isolated statements by Marx, Engels, Lenin and Stalin, rather than using their positions, views and methods to study the current situation of China and the history of China in a concrete way, and to analyze the Chinese revolution and solve the problems of the Chinese revolution.[73]

What were the problems of the Chinese revolution? How should Marxism and the Chinese revolution be combined to produce a theory that guided the Chinese revolution? Mao Zedong wanted his audience to think for themselves and discerningly study Marxist theory. In this lecture, Mao Zedong apparently pointedly announced to the whole party that he did not like theorists, who he said were "not realistic and were intent on winning mass approval. They are flashy but unsubstantial, acerbic but unstable. They regard themselves as the emissaries of god, filling the heavens". He even compared them to:

[71] In fact, in late 1942 and early 1943, Mao Zedong told Soviet journalists: "The experience in *The History of the Communist Party (Bolshevik) of the Soviet Union* is not applicable to the CPC and is harmful". Vladimirov, op. cit., p. 102.

[72] Mao Zedong, "Transforming Our Learning", *Mao Zedong Xuanji*, v. 3, Beijing: Renmin Chubanshe, Feb., 1953, pp. 815–816.

[73] Ibid., p. 817.

Reeds on the wall, hanging heavily but providing no support,

Bamboo shoots between hills, with sharp tips and thick skin but empty inside.[74]

In order to speed up the compilation of Sinicized Marxist theory, Mao Zedong appointed Chen Boda and Hu Qiaomu as secretary of the Political Bureau of the CPC Central Committee and as his private secretary in 1939 and 1941 respectively, to assist his theoretical research.[75]

In February 1940, with the return of the Chinese representative to the Communist International, Ren Bishi, to Yan'an, the Chinese delegation to the Communist International ceased to exist. On 22 June 1941, when the Soviet-German War broke out, Stalin's energy for paying attention to and controlling CPC politics was further weakened. In September 1941, Mao Zedong presided over an expanded meeting of the Political Bureau of the CPC Central Committee and began to criticize Wang Ming's "leftist" opportunism for taking the International road. Mao even simply thought that Marxism, as interpreted by the International faction, was nothing more than false Marxism, and linked the ideological roots of his "subjectivism" to the influence of Bukharin, Zinoviev and others, regarded by Stalin as "enemies of the people". This conclusion completely deprived Wang Ming and others of their ideological and political legitimacy within the Party. At this time, the Communist International lost control over the Communist Party of China, which gave Mao Zedong greater freedom to completely Sinicize Marxism. On 1 February 1942, Mao Zedong presented a report titled *Rectifying the Party's Work Style*, calling for the mobilization of the whole Party in rectification, at the inaugural ceremony of the Yan'an Central Party School, and now Mao Zedong could calmly call on the whole Party to carry out an "ideological revolution". On the basis of "Reforming Our Learning", Mao Zedong continued to put forward the important tasks of the Communist Party of China at this time for the International faction:

[74] Ibid.

[75] Chen Boda was a thinker who had spent time in the Soviet Union and who used Marxist concepts to explain Chinese philosophy in the "Leftist" ideological circles of Shanghai in the 1930s, while Hu Qiaomu was a behind-the-scenes member of the "Leftist" movement led by the CPC. They played an important role in making Mao Zedong Thought a theoretical and systematic part of Chinese Marxism.

> Our important tasks are to oppose subjectivism in order to rectify our style of study, to oppose sectarianism in order to rectify the Party's style, and to rectify the style of writing by those writing in the eight-legged Party style.[76]

Throughout his speech, Mao Zedong regarded subjectivism as "anti-Marxist" and "unable to coexist with the Communist Party". Mao Zedong hoped to "raise rich reality to the theoretical heights it deserves" and examine "all problems, or major problems, of revolutionary practice and raise them to the theoretical level". Here, Mao Zedong talked about intellectuals in particular, and he regarded many people as confused about the concept of what an intellectual was. He made no distinctions when he stated:

> There are many intellectuals who think they have knowledge and display their knowledge, unaware that such a display is bad, harmful, and hinders their progress. They should realize that many so-called intellectuals are in fact the least knowledgeable, and that workers and peasants sometimes have a little more knowledge than they do.[77]

Mao Zedong defined the scope of "knowledge" as being of only two types, "knowledge of production and struggle" and of "class struggle"; the knowledge of natural science and of social science was the "crystallization" of these two types of knowledge. Thus, intellectuals in Yan'an discovered that they all lacked these two types of knowledge so even the title of "intellectual" appeared to have lost its value. As far as the knowledge of production and struggle was concerned, they should learn from workers and peasants, and in terms of the knowledge of class struggle, they should obey the Party's commands and become true intellectuals; "the only way to do so was to make them participate in practical work and become practical workers, and make those engaged in theoretical work study important practical problems".[78]

[76] Mao Zedong, *Rectify the Party's Style*, op. cit., p. 834.

[77] Ibid., pp. 837–838.

[78] Ibid., p. 839.

The issue of "style of study" mentioned in "Rectifying the Party's Work Style", the question of the Party eight-legged style of writing, was elaborated in a keynote speech by Mao Zedong on 8 February 1942, at the Yan'an Cadres' Conference. Mao Zedong believed that the concrete embodiment of subjectivism, sectarianism, and dogmatism within the Party was "the eight-legged Party essay" and that the "Party eight-legged style" was a place where dirt was hidden and must be cleaned out. The core issue of "Party eight-legged style" was considered to be another form of the "eight-legged style" of dogmatism, which is "the foreign eight-legged style". Mao Zedong suggested that the May Fourth Movement opposed the old eight-legged style of writing, as well as old dogmas, and advocated science and democracy. However, in his view, because the leaders of the May Fourth Movement had "no critical spirit of historical materialism", this led to the emergence of formalism; such formalism was bourgeois and when this formalism developed along "left-ist" lines, it evolved into the party's subjectivism, sectarianism, and the "Party eight-legged style".[79]

All these concepts were extremely serious for intellectuals in Yan'an, regardless of whether they were senior leaders within the Party or military, or idealistic intellectuals who came from KMT-ruled areas to the holy place of the revolution but who developed fresh doubts, because they were all running counter to the cause of the Party. These questions, then, could easily evolve into questions about the nature of revolution or counter-revolution, involving ideological methods, levels of thinking, and the scope of knowledge.[80]

In fact, Mao Zedong's purpose was simple: After politically and organizationally purging Wang Ming's International faction, it is necessary to fundamentally, that is ideologically, completely eliminate the influence of the Marxist classics often cited by dogmatists (Internationalists). He used

[79] Mao Zedong, "Oppose the Party's Eight-legged Essays", Selected Works of Mao Zedong, vol. 3, Beijing: Renmin Chubanshe, 1953.

[80] In mid-April 1942, after Mao Zedong listened to Kang Sheng and others' reports on rectification work, he pointed out: "In study and inspection work, we implement the examination of cadres, their ideas and organizational concepts in our supervisory work; through this examination work, we detect counter-revolutionary elements, to be eliminated, in order to consolidate the organization". (Wang Xiuxin: A Review of The 'Rescue Movement' in Yan'an, "Party Documents" No. 3 of 1990.)

a whole new vocabulary to explain—or what may be described as "re-create"—Marxism, to formulate a new theory he believed to be in line with the reality of the Chinese revolution, and to fill the vacuum left by the fall of "dogmatism" with this new theory. Mao Zedong believed that only in this way could he truly consolidate his leadership in the whole Party, the whole army, and the entire liberated region. Therefore, the rectification movement can be regarded as Mao Zedong's first planned and strategic effort to establish ideological foundations and system, and in future history Mao Zedong used the methods of the Yan'an rectification movement to carry out every ideological struggle in the political and cultural fields until the outbreak of the Cultural Revolution in the 1960s.

In January 1942, Zhang Wentian, minister of the Central Propaganda Department and president of the Central Research Institute, decided to leave the agency on his own initiative to conduct social research at the rural grassroots level. On the eve of his departure, he told scholars and researchers at the Institute: "Comrade Mao Zedong's attitude to learning and method of learning are always solid and down-to-earth, and in them theory is closely related to reality and is a model from which the whole Party can learn". As for himself, he said "I am just a gentleman who lacks reality". It is conceivable that in a period when the classical writings of Marxism–Leninism had not yet been popularized among the middle and lower classes of the leadership and masses, what was called "dogmatism" could only occur among some senior leading cadres. These cadres tended to be those who had been to the Soviet Union to study or work, and Mao Zedong's targeting of the International faction was self-evident. Therefore, *Liberation Daily* published a series of critical articles and editorials deriding the "red professors" which placed theoretical researchers in a very awkward position; leaders such as Wang Ming, Bo Gu, and Zhang Wentian were well aware that their political situation was not good. On 2 February 1942, the day after Mao Zedong's speech on "Rectifying the Party's Work Style", an editorial published in *Liberation Daily* stated: "A person who can cite warnings from Leninism cannot be called a theorist; only a person who can solve practical problems in the spirit of Leninism can be called a theorist".

Given that it was not expected that the review and understanding of the "red professors" would soon work, Mao Zedong began to take advantage of a wider range of forces. On 19 March, *Liberation Daily* published an editorial entitled "Promoting Democracy", demanding Party members "listen to different views". In an effort to mobilize a broader force to engage in the fight against "dogmatism" and "sectarianism", in March Mao Zedong also prepared a draft resolution on the relationship between Communists and non-party members, warning Party members:

> Any non-Party member who is willing to cooperate with our Party has the right to criticize our Party and its members and cadres. Except for malicious attacks by anti-war forces, all well-intentioned criticism, whether written, oral or otherwise, should be humbly listened to by Party members and organizations. Genuine criticism should be accepted, even if it is not true, and it can only be interpreted fairly and well after the criticism has been fully delivered and carefully considered. It is absolutely impossible to overstate, that rejecting criticism from non-Party personnel or misinterpreting well-intentioned criticism as an attack, will cause Party personnel to keep silent about the Party's mistakes. Non-Party personnel will have the right to file complaints about Party members and cadres who violate government decrees or Party policies and. except for the need to act in accordance with the law, have the right to file complaints with Party committees at all levels, up to the Central Committee of the Party.
>
> *Xinhua Daily*, *Liberation Daily* and the other newspapers and publications of the anti-Japanese bases should draw on statements made by the vast number of non-Party personnel, so that all those who oppose fascism and Japanese imperialism have the opportunity to speak out in our Party newspapers and, as far as possible, the latter should invite non-Party personnel to participate in editorial meetings, so that newspapers and publications can do a better job. Party newspaper workers must learn how to attract non-Party personnel to write articles in Party newspapers, and how to write and produce newsletters. The subjectivism and sectarian attitudes of some Party newspaper workers need to be criticized.[81]

It is quite normal for theoretical injunctions to be misinterpreted. When naive young people listened to Mao Zedong's mobilization report, they responded by exposing and criticizing what they saw as problems and failed to understand the real purpose of the rectification movement.

[81] *Mao Zedong Xinwen Gongzuo Wenxuan* (Mao Zedong's Selected Press Writings), Beijing: Xinhua Chubanshe, 1983, p. 94.

On 9 March 1942, *Liberation Daily*, headed by Bo Gu, published Ding Ling's "Feelings on March Eighth", and shortly after the newspaper's literary and artistic columns published Wang Shiwei's "Wild Lilies", Xiao Jun's "A Discussion of 'Love' and 'Tolerance' among Comrades", Ai Qing's "Understanding and Respecting Writers", and Luo Feng's "A New Age of the Feuilleton", essays which made political waves among Yan'an's population of more than 30,000.

The articles by Ding Ling, Xiao Jun, Ai Qing and others discussed how the status of intellectuals was not respected in Yan'an, where leaders prevailed and there was a brutish attitude to hierarchical leadership. There were simplistic working methods, a lack of democratic style, a lack of friendship and equality between comrades, and the status of women needed to be improved; these phenomena were at odds with what they imagined Yan'an to be like before arriving there.

Wang Shiwei (1906–1947) arrived in Yan'an in October 1937, first entered the Lu Xun Art Institute, and was then transferred by Zhang Wentian to the Compilation Department of the Marxism-Leninism Academy, where he translated a large number of Marxist–Leninist works over the years, and always maintained friendly relations with Zhang Wentian, Wang Xuewen, and Fan Wenlan. Because of its character and its May Fourth values developed in his early years, Wang Shiwei's "Wild Lilies", published in *Liberation Daily* (23 March 1942), presented a vivid and theoretical critique of the problems in Yan'an at this time. Through his discussion of the categories of food and clothing in Yan'an, Wang Shiwei analyzed the ideology and history of the hierarchical system prevailing there; given it was impossible to discuss Yan'an's absolute egalitarianism, Wang Shiwei was clearly suggesting that the old order might still prevail. In hinting at the "dark face" of Yan'an society, he hoped that people would pay attention to harmful influences on the revolutionary cause. Directly borrowing Mao Zedong's favored expression that "the sky has not fallen in", Wang Shiwei comprehensively theorized that such a borrowing simply reflected the habit of old-style urban intellectuals arguing with each other, not realizing that such a borrowing might violate the special authority behind the expression, even though Wang Shiwei did not explicitly mention Mao Zedong:

> After "theory" becomes "necessary", "theory" becomes a "national form" whereby "the sky does not fall in". Yes, the sky hasn't fallen, but will or won't our work and careers be lost if the "sky does not fall"?

Wang Shiwei hoped to "use the dynamism of the fighting Bolsheviks to dispel the darkness and prevent it spreading", and he even warned: If the darkness must come and cannot be prevented, then "on that day, the day of the revolution, the sky will 'necessarily' fall".

The essays by Wang Shiyi and the others addressing problems were multi-faceted, but was raising these issues harmful or forgivable? The opinions of Wang Shiyi and others resonated with Yan'an's literary and artistic intellectuals, especially those from big cities, and even aroused the response of figures such as Fan Wenlan (1893–1969), then vice president of the Central Research Institute, and of Xu Teli (1877–1968), president of the Academy of Natural Sciences.[82]

On 31 March 1942, Mao Zedong issued a warning at a symposium in a revised edition of *Liberation Daily*. On 3 April, the Ministry of Central Propaganda issued "Decision on the Yan'an Discussion of the Central Determination and Comrade Mao Zedong's Report on the Correction of the Three Styles" (the "April 3 Decision"), which emphasized that "the inspection committee for the leadership of the rectification shall not be organized by means of mass elections". On 5 April, *Liberation Daily* published an editorial drafted by Hu Qiaomu, titled "The Correction of the Three Styles Must Be Properly Conducted", which pointed out that Wang Shiwei's "erroneous views and approach not only do not help the rectification of the three styles, but are indeed harmful". On 13 April, the editorial board of the Central Youth Committee's Light Cavalry Team made a preliminary confession in *Liberation Daily*. After that, Wang Shiwei was accused of being "anti Party" and "anti leadership". After May, Fan Wenlan, Ai Qing, Zhou Yang and Ding Ling participated in the criticism of Wang Shiwei. In June, Wang Shiwei was labeled an "anti-Party activist", "a bandit", and a "KMT agent". This came at a difficult juncture and crisis point in the Anti-Japanese War, but the internal atmosphere in Yan'an seemed to be filled with gunpowder.[83]

[82] Fan Wenlan called on people to "take the arrow of democracy and shoot evil", while Xu Teli encouraged young people to "speak up and seriously criticize themselves". See Li Weihan, "Research work and wind-up movement at the Central Research Institute", *Chronicle of the Yan'an Rectification Movement*, 1982 edition.

[83] Vladimirov, the Tass correspondent in Yan'an, wrote in his diary on 18 May 1942, that he was puzzled: "In the context of a long war with Japan and a life-or-death situation in China, Mao Zedong talked at length specifically about the issue of 'rectifying the Party's style'. The Party's style might have needed to be overhauled, but it was certainly a secondary issue". Vladimirov in Yan'an documented a CPC meeting in February:

A large number of people were familiar with and agreed with Wang's point of view and ideological logic. People from cultural circles, intellectuals from literary and artistic circles, and young people who came from the city to Yan'an had undoubtedly originally led liberal cultural lives, and their incisive academic and even political views of the conflict informed the spontaneous and unbridled expression of their views. However, after they arrived in Yan'an, they gradually found that the environment there was different from the city; the free and ideal world they had imagined had been organized and disciplined by the needs of the revolution and their views were considered to be "liberal". In the field of literature, the "Lu Xun Academy faction" centered on Zhou Yang and the "Literary Resistance faction" represented by Ding Ling continue to champion respectively the debate between "eulogy" and "exposé" of the "Left-wing League" period, despite the fact that in the "Left-wing League" period the CPC had consciously guided and controlled literary artists. However, the nature of those literary and artistic groups and the scope of the participants determine the limits of indoctrination of any ideology. So, to a certain extent, although Yan'an literature and art before May 1942 generally reflected Yan'an life, the concept of freedom in intellectual circles was still regarded as reasonable. However, the expression of liberalism was seen as an expression of a lack of organization and discipline by the leaders and cadres of the Communist Party of China accustomed to military life and harsh political realities, and they considered it to be harmful to the revolution. The Wang Shiwei incident encouraged Mao Zedong's need to expand the scope of the movement and to rectify the ideas in the field of literature and art, that is carry out a comprehensive reorganization to Sinicize Marxist-Leninist ideology on the political front, in ideology, and in the field of literature and art.

In April 1942, Mao Zedong had a meeting with Ai Qing to sound him out about the ideological trends in Yan'an literature. Mao Zedong asked Ai Qing: "Now literary and artistic circles in Yan'an have many problems, we read many different opinions in many articles, some of these articles

Mao Zedong suddenly turned his attention to sectarianism, dogmatism, empiricism and subjectivity, describing them as the Communist Party's arch-enemies. In the scolding, no person's name was mentioned. Mao Zedong ended his report with a very messy and illogical speech. He warned certain people, and then criticized them, but he was spoke ambiguously, even though the whole tone of his speech was intimidating. Ref: Vladimirov, op. cit., p. 18.

are even distributed from Japanese plane, and some should be published in the KMT's publication *Words of Conscience* (Liangxin Hua). What do you think?" Mao Zedong then had three meetings with Liu Baiyu. During this period, Mao Zedong also invited lecturers from the Lu Xun Academy to Yangjialing for discussions, including He Qifang (1912–1977), Yan Wenjing (1915–2005), Zhou Libo (1908–1979), Cao Baohua (1906–1978), Chen Huangmei (1913–1996) and Yao Shixiao (1909–2002). According to Liu Baiyu, "It was the Party Central Committee that criticized the confusion and errors in literary and artistic thinking among us". Liu Baiyu obviously felt that Mao Zedong's invitations were usually for casual or relaxed conversations, but that "at this time the atmosphere felt a little different" and "his usual friendly conversation, as though with an old friend, was now absent". Opening the door and looking out at the mountains, Mao Zedong commented: "The Central Committee has almost put the economic problems in the border areas in order to make free up its hands to rectify the literary and artistic problems. Before the meeting, Chen Yun specifically put Ding Ling and I to the Central Organization Department, he is the organization minister, want us to stand firm".[84] During this period, Mao also met with Ding Ling, Xiao Jun, Li Bozhao, Ouyang Shan, Cao Ming, Shu Qun, and others. On 20 April 1942, the meeting of the Central Study Group addressed the necessity to conduct a rectification in Yan'an where there were as many opinions as people speaking out and "liberal thinking was strong". Mao spoke angrily about the need for rectification: "We must do it until people are crying out in pain and are beaten to a pulp".[85]

In fact, Mao's "Talks at the Yan'an Forum on Literature and Art" (later "Talks"), which had a lasting and decisive influence on Chinese literature and art from the spring of 1942 onwards, embodied Mao Zedong's ideas on literature and art and were part of the Yan'an rectification movement. The real purpose of the Yan'an rectification movement, which targeted subjectivism (dogmatism, empiricism), factionalism, and the "Party eight-legged essay", was to completely eliminate the power of the International

[84] Liu Baiyu, "Why Chairman Mao convened the Yan'an Forum on Literature and Art", *Shiji* (Century), no. 5, 2002.

[85] Mao Zedong, "Guanyu zhengdun san feng" (On the rectification of the three styles), *Dang de Wenxian*, no. 2, 1992.

faction within the CPC, represented by Wang Ming,[86] and the influence of "empiricism" within the Party, establish the absolute authority of the Party Central Committee with Mao Zedong as its core, and politically and ideologically establish Sinicized Marxism with "Mao Zedong Thought" as the guiding ideology for the entire Party.

The Yan'an Forum on Literature and Art held a total of three sessions. On 2 May 1942, Mao Zedong provided the introduction to the proceedings, expressing the hope that literary and artistic workers attending the conference would speak freely on their positions, attitudes, work objects, and work and study issues, but in fact Mao Zedong had clearly identified what he regarded as the problems of these intellectuals before the meeting.[87]

Until 2 May, writers like Xiao Jun and Ding Ling did not see the seriousness of the situation, and at the beginning of the Forum, Xiao Jun's remarks that were immediately refuted by Hu Qiaomu's denunciation of

[86] In fact, after the rectification movement, Wang Ming, who was ill, was very isolated in Yan'an. On 12 June 1943, Vladimirov wrote in his diary, "But physical pain is only part of the disaster. Wang Ming had had enough of Mao Zedong's crackdown on the Internationalists within the CPC. Mao regarded Wang Ming as the main 'dogmatist' and a 'follower of the opportunists Chen Duxiu and Li Lisan', and a 'the greatest heretic with no experience in revolutionary struggle'. This isolated Wang Ming. In these circumstances, few people dared to maintain even minimal contact with him". Ref: Vladimirov, op. cit., p. 131.

[87] Liu Baiyu recalled Mao Zedong's conversation with him in Liu Baiyu, ibid.:

"You have a lot of writers there, you bring them together, read them my speeches, and then let voice their opinions. There will be positive opinions, but what I need are negative views. Comrade Liu Baiyu, am I clear?" Chairman Mao said to me, "You are the branch secretary, and you have a lot of Party writers there". Chairman Mao read me the first half of his Speech and asked me for advice: "After you listen to my opinions, first tell me what you think. Secondly, tell me the truth, who said what and how they said it, basically what opinions they hold?" Liu Baiyu, "Why Chairman Mao convened the Yan'an Forum on Literature and Art", *Shiji* (Century), no. 5, 2002.

liberal speech.[88] Even though He Qifang criticized his own ideas,[89] Ding Ling, on the other hand, stuck to her views on "eulogy" and "exposé".[90]

Many of the first-hand accounts of those attending the Forum recorded Mao Zedong's expression during the meetings, it was not in fact until 23 May that Mao Zedong presented his "closing" speech and delivered direct criticism of many of the views expressed.

[88] Xiao Jun made a speech titled "My views on current literary and artistic issues", which was later also published in *Liberation Daily*. It reported:

Xiao Jun before the convening of the Forum took into account his own integrity and his propensity for talking very openly, so in order to avoid differences of opinion at the meeting and disputes with comrades, he planned to go about practical tasks and only return after the Forum concluded. It was Mao Zedong who wrote several letters asking him to attend. So, when he spoke first, he was outspoken and said everything on his mind. According to He Qifang's manuscript and Zhang Ding's recollections: Xiao Jun spoke about how the red lotus with its white roots and green leaves is the one plant; Confucianism, Taoism, and Buddhism are one family of teachings; Party members, non-Party members, and progressives are of the one mind; politics, military matters, literature and art can also be the one family. Being of one family, all are equal, and none can predominate. When we make revolution, we must, like Lu Xun, smash the old world to pieces and never write articles that celebrate virtue. For a Forum like today's, I could have written a hundred thousand words, but while I appreciate Romain Rolland's new heroism I want to be a Chinese writer and a world writer above all. Ref: Gao Jie, "Liudong de huoyan", *Chuanji Wenxue*, no. 5, 1997.

Liu Baiyu recalled:

"I remember that the first speaker at the Forum was Xiao Jun. He spoke to the effect that the writer is independent and free, saying that Lu Xun was not under the command of any party or organization in Guangzhou. He was very clear that writers do not need the leadership of the Party. Xiao Jun's voice did not falter. I heard someone in the opposite corner loudly say: 'I want to speak!' As soon as I looked up, it was Hu Qiaomu. Hu Qiaomu's speech was very sharp, and his fierce criticism of Xiao Jun was incisive. I can't remember exactly how, but I saw Hu Qiaomu wrote in his reminiscences of Mao Zedong that Chairman Mao was very pleased with my speech and, after the meeting, asked me to come to his place for dinner and said he was congratulating him on the contretemps". Ref: Liu Baiyu, idem.

[89] He Qifang said in his speech to the Forum, "I was inspired to hear the teachings in the Chairman's Introduction. The soul of the petty bourgeoisie is impure, self-interested, cowardly, fragile and vacillating. I felt that I was in desperate need of transformation". Ref: Gao Jie, ibid.

[90] Ding Ling said in her speech to the Forum: "In the end, should literature and art be mainly eulogy or exposé? Or is it something 'half and half'? One half, I think, should, of course, be a warm anthem of praise for the move to the light. But we must not lay down our arms and stand idly by, and so should mercilessly expose the darkness that impedes progress". Ref: Gao Jie, ibid.

Many intellectuals from cities still carry the liberal habits they had developed in the cities, whether praising or criticizing the surrounding environment and for a politician in desperate need of political goals, too much prevarication is not only disturbing, but it can also seriously affect the atmosphere of the "holy place of revolution". Those intellectuals who were still politically "naive" had already heard of the functional expression of literature and art in the cities. Now, Mao Zedong wanted them to be more aware of their tasks in this historical period:

> After the outbreak of the Anti-Japanese War, revolutionary literary and artistic workers came to Yan'an and various anti-Japanese bases, which is a good thing. But though they had reached the bases, this is not to say that they had been fully integrated with the people in the base. If we want to move our revolutionary work forward, we need to bring the two together completely. We are meeting today to make literature and art a wholesome part of the entire revolutionary machine, as a powerful weapon to unite and educate the people, fight and destroy the enemy, and help the people fight the enemy with one heart and one virtue.[91]

What follows is a basic account of the content of *Talks*.[92]

At the beginning of the "Introduction" of *Talks*, delivered on 2 May, Mao Zedong, on the one hand, regarded "May Fourth" culture as a revolutionary cultural army "formed in China and helping the Chinese revolution to gradually narrow the territory of China's feudal culture and culture adapted to imperialist aggression, so its strength gradually weakened". On the other hand, the movement "did not combine with practical work because the reactionaries at the time separated the two fraternal armies it contained". However, even if the revolutionary literary and artistic workers came to Yan'an, "this is not to say that they were fully integrated with the people of the base".

Mao Zedong reminded all people to "stand in the position of the proletariat and the broad masses of the people" and, as for Party

[91] Mao Zedong, Talks at the Yan'an Forum on Literature and Art, *Mao Zedong Xuanji*, v. 3, Beijing, Renmin Chubanshe, 1953, p. 870. Subsequent citations, if they do not indicate the source, are from this version and page numbers are omitted.

[92] The official text of *Talks* was written by Hu Qiaomu. Liu Baiyu recalled: "The manuscript was written by Hu Qiaomu, who took over from Ai Siqi (who worked for *Liberation Daily*) as secretary of the Culture Committee and was my immediate boss". Ref: Liu Baiyu, op. cit.

members, they "stand in the position of the Party". Such a reminder simply to let everyone know that, in the recent past, any words and deeds not formally authorized and agreed to by the Party organization might be erroneous, or even completely incorrect.

Mao Zedong had at this time already begun to partially answer questions from people like Ding Ling. By dividing people into three different kinds, he could suggest three kinds of attitude, thereby replacing concepts of literature and art with political views. In this way, "eulogy" or "exposé" became political attitudes that reflected political positions rather than differences in subject matter, methods and interest as Ding Ling and others previously understood them.

As for the objects of literature and art, Yan'an was completely different from the variegated scene of greater Shanghai and from the KMT-ruled areas. In Yan'an, the structure based on the masses was simple; "the audience of literary and artistic works in the base areas were the workers, peasants, soldiers and revolutionary Party cadres". "Since the object of literary and artistic work were the workers, peasants and soldiers and their cadres, the problem was understanding and becoming familiar with them". How were they to become familiar with them? Mao Zedong referred to "the rich and vivid language of the people". When it came to familiarizing themselves with the workers and peasants, Mao Zedong again had this to say:

> The cleanest people are the workers and peasants; even though their hands are black and their feet are covered with cow dung, they are cleaner than the bourgeois and petty bourgeois intellectuals. This is called emotional change, from one social class to another. We literary and artistic workers born as intellectuals must, in order to have their works welcomed by the masses, subject their own thoughts and feelings to change and transformation. Without effecting this change or without this transformation, nothing will succeed and they will make no impact.

In this, although Mao Zedong was "introducing" the Forum, he had, in fact, already come to a political conclusion about those who styled themselves intellectuals. He maintained that intellectuals who had not been reformed did not belong to the proletariat of the revolution. The influence and political role of the earlier quotation continued down to the 1970s, when this statement about intellectuals served as a classic quote for any subsequent revolutionary struggle and political movement critical of intellectuals.

Young people who had experienced Western thought in the 1920s and 30 s or read Western writings were familiar with the expression of human nature since the May Fourth enlightenment movement. In their lives and attitudes, they recognized a kind of "abstract humanity" that could not be simply divided into social classes, and the simple values ("the ideology of sharing one glass of water") that prevailed in Yan'an before 1939 was just one expression of the revolutionary passion of free love opposed to feudal marriage in the 1930s. Mao Zedong emphatically asked: Since literary and artistic workers wanted to become Marxist-Leninists, why were they unclear about the basic view of Marxism regarding class struggle? Even "love" between comrades must be analyzed, he warned:

> In class society, there is only class love, but these comrades want to pursue love that transcends classes, abstract love, as well as abstract freedom, abstract truth, abstract humanity, and so on. This is an indication that these comrades are deeply influenced by the bourgeoisie. This influence should be thoroughly eliminated and they should humbly study Marxism-Leninism. Literary and art workers should learn literary and artistic creation, which is correct, but Marxism-Leninism is the science that all revolutionaries should study, and literary and artistic workers cannot be an exception.

Mao Zedong's talk of "abstract humanity" made those at the Forum immediately think of Zhou Libo's explanation of the works of Western writers like Montaigne and Stendhal at the Lu Xun Academy, and Mao Zedong obviously disagreed with the Academy's view of the complexity of human nature.[93] Mao Zedong separated "literary creation" from the

[93] Although Zhou Libo wanted to fight on the front line, he expressed in his letter to Zhou Yang that he hoped to light the torch and "create a new world" in North China, but Zhou Libo's lectures at the Lu Xun Academy still touched on the works of foreign writers like Montaigne, Stendhal, Balzac, Moliere, Maupassant, Gogol, Tolstoy, and Lessing. His lecture notes discussed "deep observation of human nature", "existing and possible principles of human nature and aesthetics", and "complex human nature". These statements and humanitarian views were clearly incompatible with the view of "class nature". These revolutionary intellectuals who had come from "studio rooms" did not regard the cultural art and the struggles of reality as a contradiction, but simply saw themselves the custodians of a love of human knowledge and human qualities.

science of Marxism–Leninism, and did not think that "literary creation" itself had fundamental importance in the liberation base of Yan'an.

In the "Conclusion" delivered on 23 May, Mao Zedong further cautioned that it made no sense to look for a definition of literature and art in books already written. There are only two central issues: "One is [literature and art] for the masses and the other is how [to create literature and art] for the masses". This was more or less the core of *Talks*. Mao Zedong mentioned to people present at the Forum the characters with whom they were familiar, and he wanted to tell them that even Lu Xun agreed that there was no literature beyond class. The background logic of this was: Zhou Zuoren (Lu Xun's brother) was a Chinese traitor, and now all his writings must be regarded as treasonous Chinese literature. As for "the literary and artistic forms of the past", as long as "new content is added, they can become revolutionary and serve the people"; Mao Zedong saw form and content as different paper and wrapping.

Although Yan'an had almost no industry, according to the basic concepts of Marxism, Mao Zedong made what served the "popular masses" the ordering criterion:

> So, our literature and art are firstly for the workers, which is the class leading the revolution. They are secondly for the peasants, who in the revolution are the vast majority and its most resolute allies. They are thirdly for the armed workers and peasants, namely the Eighth Route Army, New Fourth Army and other people's armed forces, which are the main force in the Revolutionary War. They are fourthly for the urban petty bourgeois working people and intellectuals, allies of the revolution who can cooperate with us for a long time. These four kinds of people form the largest proportion of the Chinese nation and the vast majority of its people.

In view of Mao Zedong's subsequent criticism of the "kingdom of small bourgeois intellectuals", the fourth category of the person constituting his "popular masses" cannot in fact be included.

Mao Zedong criticized "many comrades": "On many occasions, there is complete sympathy for intellectuals from the small bourgeoisie, and even their shortcomings attract sympathy and even praise. The bourgeois intellectual lacks closeness, understanding, research, and friendly intimacy for the masses of workers, peasants and soldiers, and so they are not good at depicting them. If they describe them, they dress them in the clothing of working people, but their faces are those of petty bourgeois intellectuals. In some respects, they do love workers, peasants and soldiers, as well as cadres who were originally workers and peasants. But sometimes they do not love them, whether some aspects, their feelings, their stance, or their budding literary and artistic forms (wall newspapers, murals, folk songs, folk tales, etc.). They sometimes love these things in order to poach them to decorate their own works, and even love them in their pursuit of backward things. Sometimes they openly despise them, preferring the things of petty bourgeois intellectuals and even the bourgeoisie. These comrades have a stance that is that of petty bourgeois intellectuals, or, to put it more elegantly, their souls still sojourn in the kingdom of petty bourgeois intellectuals".

As a result, "why do people's problems remain unsolved, or not explicitly solved?" Moreover, "why is the human problem a fundamental problem and a question of principles?" Yet, "why is this fundamental problem not solved, so many other problems are not easily to solve".

The division of camps formed by the never-ending conflict of views in the field of literature and art was dubbed "sectarianism" by Mao Zedong. He argued: "To get rid of sectarianism, we can only achieve our goal by putting forward the slogans of workers and peasants, of the Eighth Route Army, and of the New Fourth Army, and implementing them effectively; otherwise, the problem of sectarianism cannot be solved". Mao's idea was that as long as every literary and artistic worker sang just the one theme, or even the same revolutionary theme, "sectarianism" would naturally not occur, and there would be no difference between similar things. In this way, the solution to political and ideological problems and the solution to literary and artistic problems could be combined.

In the second part of his written *Conclusion*, Mao Zedong dealt with the issues discussed by Yan'an's literary and artistic workers:

On the concepts of "popularization" and "elevation", Mao Zedong reminded them of the nature of "elevation": "What is the basis for the elevation of literature and art? Is it from the basis of feudal classes? From the basis of the bourgeoisie? From the basis of petty bourgeois intellectuals? No, it can only be elevated from the basis of the masses of workers, peasants and soldiers". In view of the fact that "the problem before the workers and peasants now is that they are fighting the enemy in a brutal and bloody struggle, and that they are illiterate and uncultured because of the long period of rule by the feudal classes and bourgeoisie", "the task of popularization is more urgent".

> In general, the raw materials of literature and art in the life of the people form, through the creative labor of revolutionary writers, the ideas for the people's literature and art. In this, there are both advanced literature and art developed from the primary literary and artistic foundation to elevate the needs of the masses and to first provide high-level literature and art needed by the cadres of the masses. In turn the guidance of this high-level literature and art is invariably the primary need of the vast majority of people today. Whether high-level or primary, our literature and art are for the people, firstly for the workers and peasants, for whom it is created and by whom it is consumed.

Clarifying the importance of popularization temporarily suspended the authority of the work of the expert. "Cadres might have a level of understanding that is advanced and complex, but the general public finds it difficult to understand", but "our specialists should not only serve our cadres, but should mainly serve the masses". In this way, the easy-to-understand "wall newspapers of the masses", "newsletter literature", "small drama troupes", "choral singing of the masses" and "art of the masses" became the focus of experts' attention. Mao Zedong warned experts not to be "nobles standing on the necks of the 'lower classes'". This not only encompassed the issues of the "elevation" or "popularization" of literature and art[94]; It targeted the attitudes of writers and artists.

When discussing the relationship between the Party and literature and art, Mao Zedong explicitly used the concept of class analysis and struggle. He concluded that literature and art must obey politics. Mao quickly linked the "politics" he discussed to classes and the masses, and directed the focus of attention of those attending the Forum, to a minority of politicians separated from Yan'an who needed to be understood by the Party's leaders with actual power according to different circumstances:

> What we call literature and art are subordinate to politics, which refers to class politics and mass politics, not the politics of a few politicians.

[94] Looking back at the "formalization" and "specialization" of teaching at the Lu Xun Academy in Yan'an at the time, Hu Qiaomu said: "In that environment, Chairman Mao was very opposed to devoting classes on literature at the Lu Xun Academy to Chekhov's novels, or perhaps Maupassant's novels. He was dissatisfied with this practice. But speaking about literature and writing, he felt there had to be typical works to educate students. Chairman Mao was attempting to find a way to solve the problem of popularization and elevation". Ref: Hu Qiaomu, ibid., p. 60.

> Politics, whether revolutionary or counter-revolutionary, is the struggle between classes, not the behavior of a few individuals. The ideological and artistic struggles of the revolution must be subordinated to political struggle, because only through politics can the needs of classes and the masses be expressed in a concentrated way.

Here, Mao was gratuitously making a critical comment about Wang Ming and others.[95]

In response to literary criticism, Mao Zedong proposed "political standards" and "artistic standards". "On this issue, Mao once again linked the differences in political stance to differences in artistic standards, to show that so-called "artistic standards" are meaningless. He wanted to judge the quality of a work by its political effects. Good or bad works are judged by whether they are "welcomed by the masses and good for the masses", but in the thinking of the masses, who is the spokesman providing the legitimate explanation of a work's nature? Mao Zedong even regarded "anti-national, anti-scientific, anti-masses", and "anti-communist" literary and artistic works as one and the same thing, thinking that it was important to "strictly criticize and refute" them because their common characteristic might be that their motives and effects sought to undermine the unity of resistance against Japan. But who were the arbiters distinguishing what was "anti-national", "anti-scientific", and "anti-communist"? Even with the special needs of the revolution and resistance against Japan, what kind of system could serve as a counterbalancing tool for literary bureaucrats, without allowing them to explain these concepts fully? Who was the judge who determined which works by literary and artistic workers in Yan'an have serious political problems and can advance correct principles of criticism?

Mao Zedong was very aware of the particularity of literature and art, and that the intellectuals beneath the podium valued the particularity of literature and art; he was even fully aware of the relative independence of artistic question. However, in his view, this was not an era in which to

[95] "Revolutionary politicians, political experts who know the political science or political arts of the revolution are simply the leaders of the thousands of politicians of the masses. Their task is to gather the opinions of these mass politicians, refine them, and then return them to the masses, for their acceptance. Their practice is not a workshop behind closed doors; they are smart and form a group unrelated to the aristocratic type of so-called 'politician'. This is what distinguishes the proletarian politician from the decadent bourgeois politician". Ref: Mao Zedong, *Talks*.

discuss the particularity of literature and art.[96] Therefore, he enjoined his audience to ponder this indeterminate realm through the expression of historical dialectics:

> But any class in any class society always places political standards first and artistic standards in second place. The bourgeoisie always disregards the literary and artistic works of the proletariat, no matter how high their artistic achievements. The proletariat must also first examine the way literary and art works of the past treated the people and adopted non-progressive and different attitudes historically. Some politically fundamentally reactionary things may also have some kind of artistic nature. The more reactionary the content of the work and the more artistic, the more it can poison the people and the more it should be rejected. The common characteristic of all exploitative class literature and art in the period of decline is the contradiction between its reactionary political content and its artistic form. We demand the unity of politics and art, the unity of content and form, the unity of revolutionary political content and the best possible art form. Art works lacking in artistry, no matter how politically progressive, are also powerless. Therefore, we oppose both art works that are politically erroneous, as well as the so-called "slogan-style" trend that only has a correct political view but has no artistic power. We should fight on two fronts on the issue of literature and art.

Finally, Mao Zedong directly addressed issues he had gathered before the symposium in a "research survey".

"The theory of human nature".—"In class society, there is only human nature that is class nature, and there is no human nature that transcends classes".

[96] Ding Ling many years later was still not hostile in her understanding:

"I thought Chairman Mao, with his literary genius, literary cultivation and character, would naturally appreciate those works with high artistic characteristics and would even appreciate works of artistic quality that were not political. Naturally, all artistic masterpieces that can be passed down will have some ideological content, but Chairman Mao being a great politician and revolutionary, responsible for leading the Communist Party and commanding the national revolution, would naturally want to include all matters and work in the political track of the revolution. In the course of the revolution, his sense of responsibility would he ensure he would promote something, even when what he promoted might not necessarily be something he personally liked, but he would feel obliged to promote it". Ref: Ai Ke'en ed., *Reminiscences about Yan'an Literature and Art*, Beijing: Zhongguo Shehui Kexue Chubanshe, May 1992, p. 56.

"The basic starting point of literature and art is love, love of mankind". To which he countered: "In the world there is no love that is baseless, or hatred that is baseless". As for the "love of mankind", there has been no such unified love since human beings divided into social classes. This issue is mentioned in his Introduction, in which Mao Zedong attributes "abstract love" to "loving the enemy" and "loving the ugly phenomena of society". If a literary or art worker's political stance is considered wrong, then his "love" is likely to be reactionary.

"All literary and artistic works describe what is light and what is dark, in equal proportions". Regarding this view, he wrote: "The literature of the Soviet Union in the period of socialist construction mostly writes about the light. It also describes shortcomings in work and does include negative characters, but these descriptions can only be sidelined by the overall light and cannot exist in equal proportions. The bourgeois writers of the reactionary period depicted the revolutionary masses as thugs and depicted themselves as holy, thereby inverting the light and darkness. Only true revolutionary writers can correctly solve the problem of eulogy and exposé. All dark forces that endanger the masses must be exposed and all the people's revolutionary struggles must be celebrated, which is the basic task of the revolutionary literary artist".

"The task of literature and art has always been exposure". "It is the era of the critical essay and we still need Lu Xun's writing", and "I'm not singing praises, works of a eulogist are not necessarily great, and works of those portraying the darkness are not necessarily insignificant". These concepts are all associated with the previous issue. Mao Zedong's response meant that "exposure" and "criticism" were selective and must be based on a correct class position. "Lu Xun lived in a period of dark rule in which there was no freedom of speech, and so he used the satire in his essays to fight, and in this Lu Xun was completely correct. But while the revolutionary artist enjoys full democratic freedom in the Shaan-Gan-Ning border area and in the anti-Japanese bases behind enemy lines, where we only cannot give counter-revolutionaries democratic freedom, the form of our essays should not simply be the same as those of Lu Xun". At the same time, Mao Zedong regarded essays as a satirical style that "the people cannot easily understand", and because of this case, critical essays are problematic. At this time, those familiar with Lu Xun's style of writing discovered that, although Lu Xun was acknowledged, writing essays in Yan'an like those of Lu Xun would be making a political mistake. Given that articles that raised questions about Yan'an were aimed at phenomena in the Communist Party's region, Mao Zedong was very sensitive to the mention of "darkness":

> Literary works that praise the bourgeoisie are not necessarily great, while works that depict their dark aspects are not necessarily minor; works that praise the proletariat are necessarily great, while those that depict their dark aspects are necessarily minor. Shouldn't this be the reality of literary history? As for the people, they are the creators of human history, so why are they not praised? Why do we not praise the proletariat, the Communist Party, New Democracy, and socialism?

Mao Zedong consciously avoided those whose opinions were not proletarian, but were phenomena that occurred in Yan'an under the rule of the proletariat's political party. Although Mao Zedong had supported the publication of Xiao Jun's essays in *Literary Monthly* and Zhou Yang's discussion of "black spots in the sun", he ultimately regarded those who "exposed" "darkness" as "the canker in the revolutionary ranks".

"It's not a question of stance; if the stance is correct, the heart is good, and the meaning can be understood, but if it's expressed badly, the effect is bad". Is the question of effect a question of stance? Mao Zedong simply demanded that writers who did not meet the standards "must be fully sincere about the mistakes of their work and be determined to correct them". Because the "effect" is a reflection of "stance".

Mao Zedong said after indicating what he considered problematic in the literature and art of Yan'an:

> Our job is to give them a round of applause and say: "Comrades", your approach is not ok. The proletariat cannot move towards you or rely on you, because in fact you rely on the big landlords and big bourgeoisie, who endanger the life of the Party and nation. Who alone can be depended on? Only by relying on the proletarian vanguard can the face of the Party be transformed and the world be transformed. We hope that the comrades in literary and artistic circles will recognize the seriousness of this great debate and actively participate in this struggle so that every comrade can be perfected and our entire team will be truly unified and consolidated ideologically and organizationally.

Now, Mao calls those who make comments "comrades" in inverted commas, and they are almost classified as reactionary "big landlords and big bourgeoisie", and their opinions are regarded as "endangering the life of the Party and nation". Now, it is easy to see how many intellectuals and cultural figures became victims of political struggle in the rectification movement.

Mao Zedong reminded those who came from Shanghai's "studio rooms" in the final part of his conclusion of *Talks*[97]: "From the studio room to the revolutionary base, one not only passes through two worlds, but also experiences two historical eras". The revolutionary base represents "an era in which the people and masses who have not held power throughout millennia of Chinese history now hold power", so there is nothing familiar about this age, the people and their lives inhabiting it, so already completed literary and artistic works have no meaning. The cartoonist Hua Junwu has vivid memories of the incongruity he experienced after coming from his studio room to Yan'an:

> Yan'an is a world of farmers. My cartoons used to be influenced by foreigners and had a "foreign feel", but after I came to Yan'an, they were no longer foreign. How can one's own art be understood by the masses? I experimented. I ran a cartoon wall newspaper at the Lu Xun Art Academy, and outside the school I also ran a wall newspaper in the Catholic church. I found that among the intellectuals at the Lu Xun Art Academy, my cartoons had some traction, but when I displayed them on the street outside the Academy, farmers would pull them down and were not interested in them. Seeing this, I was distressed. It wasn't just the cartoon, but singing was also a problem. Comrade Chen Yun said that our singing sounded malarial, and that if we sounded foreign, people would not accept it.[98]

Talks not only marked the establishment of Mao Zedong's literary thought but also the beginning of the CPC's "Party literature and art". Thereafter, the audience, stance, opinions, and methods served by literature and art had to be examined and verified by the Party's literary and artistic officials at different levels. In such a system, "serving the workers, peasants and soldiers" became obligatory, because once a work was considered to have a problem of stance or an erroneous attitude,

[97] The "studio room" or "cubbyhole" (*tingzijian*) was a cramped and dark room located at the back of traditional Western-style storied houses in Shanghai and enclosed by the staircase, so the rent was relatively low. Until 1949, poor writers, artists, intellectuals and low-level staff in institutions mostly rented such rooms.

[98] *Renmin Ribao*, 23 May 2002, p. 12.

then not only was the literary and artistic creation itself criticized but the literary and artistic worker himself might also be destroyed. Politics became paramount, but it was up to the leadership to decide the kind of politics literary and artistic workers must obey.

On 2 June 1942, the Central General Study Committee, headed by Mao Zedong, was inaugurated. In view of the fact that the Central General Study Committee was empowered to arrange and inspect the rectification notes of senior cadres, set up subordinate study groups, and demand any opinions from the leadership to the masses from the organs to the schools, the Committee, which became the earliest model for the Central Cultural Revolution Leadership Group during the later Cultural Revolution, had in fact already taken over the Politburo. With the establishment of the branch Study Committees Zhou Yang, who played a failed role in the internal conflicts of the Leftist movement of the 1930s, took charge of the Central Cultural Committee system. Zhou Yang provided Mao Zedong with the ideological and sectarian background of the urban intellectuals, and now, as a literary thinker, he very clearly represented the Party, rather than an academic opponent, as he set to work supervising and managing literature and art.

In fact, the purpose of strengthening the Party's leadership and rectifying the ideological style from every aspect was to thoroughly establish Mao Zedong's absolute dominance within the Party. The end of the rectification marked the emergence of the concept of "Mao Zedong Thought", and at the 7th National Congress of the CPC in 1945, Mao Zedong Thought was formally made the Party's guiding ideology and course of action.[99] His ideological theory of literature and art also became

[99] In February 1941, Zhang Ruxin, a teacher at the Marxism-Leninism Institute, whose dean was Zhang Wentian, began to use the concept of "Mao Zedong's Thought" in his article "The Educator of the Bolsheviks". On 18 February, he began to explain the concept of "Mao Zedongism" in "How to Learn from Mao Zedong" published in *Liberation Daily*. On 1 July 1942, Deng Tuo published an editorial in the *Jin-Cha-Ji Daily* published by the local branch of the Central Committee of the CPC, titled "In Commemorating July 1st, the Whole Party Learns to Master Mao Zedongism". In July 1943, Wang Jiaxiang put forward the concept of "Mao Zedong Thought" in his *The Road to Liberation of the Communist Party of China and the Chinese Nation*. In 1944, Zhou Yang, as editor-in-chief of *Marxism and Literature* (published by the North China Bookstore), presented the literary theories of Marx, Engels, Plekhanov, Lenin, Stalin, Gorky, Lu Xun and Mao Zedong in five sections: "ideological literature and art", "the nature of literature and art", "literature and art and class", "proletarian literature and art" and "writers and critics". In his Preamble, Zhou Yang explained Mao Zedong's *Talks* as

the basic theoretical basis for the whole Party and for literary and artistic circles led by the Party. This literary thought, which takes the political leader's literary thought as the only ideological principle to be followed, became the dogma that was in force until 1976, and became the instrument of political propaganda and struggle of the leaders and authorities who controlled literature and art at different times.[100]

After May's *Talks*, the words "the unity of the Party's leadership" already appeared in *Decision on the Unified Leadership of the Party in the Anti-Japanese Bases and the Adjustment of Relations between Organizations* adopted by the Politburo of the CPC Central Committee on 1 September 1942. In 1943, in Mao Zedong's "Decision of the CPC Central Committee on The Method of Leadership" (draft), we see the expression of "a unified and single approach in the division of labor" for any task, (which explicitly stated that this included rectification study and propaganda work). Anyone who sees these words in political work as unrelated to literary and artistic work is naive and lacks an understanding of literature and art under the leadership of the CPC, because Mao Zedong reminded everyone very clearly of Lenin's ideas in *Talks*:

> In the present world, all culture or literature and art belongs to a particular class and political line. Art for art's sake, art transcending classes, and politically parallel or independent art do not in fact, exist. Proletarian literature

the Sinicization of Marxist literary and artistic thought: Comrade Mao Zedong's Talks at the Yan'an Forum on Literature and Art gave a new direction to revolutionary literature and art and are a landmark document in the history of Chinese revolutionary literature and thought. They are the most popular and concrete generalization of Marxist literature, art and science and literary policy, and therefore the best textbook of Marxist literature and art science and literary policy. In 1945, Liu Shaoqi made it clear in his Report on the Amendment of the Party's Constitution that the ideological theoretical basis of the CPC was "Mao Zedong Thought, the product of the combination of Marxism-Leninism and the reality of the Chinese revolution".

[100] Zhou Yang said in 1952: "Every achievement we made in literary and artistic work is the result of the correct implementation of Mao Zedong's literary and artistic line". When he said that "the achievements in literary and artistic work are still too small compared to the great struggle of the Chinese people and their achievements in various fields", he attributed the crux of the problem to "one of the most important reasons being we insufficiently implemented Mao Zedong's literary and artistic line". See: Zhou Yang, "Resolutely Implementing Mao Zedong's Literary Line", in Beijing Normal University Literary Theory Group ed., *Wenyi Lilun Xuexi Cankao Ziliao* (Study References in Literary Theory), internal issue, Beijing: Gaodeng Jiaoyu Chubanshe, 1956, p. 152.

and art are part of the whole revolutionary cause of the proletariat and, as Lenin put it, are "the cog and the screw" in the whole revolutionary machine.[101]

In July 1942, the rectification movement reached its climax, and the Lu Xun Academy held a four-day seminar from the 28th to the 31st. In the fine art department's conference hall, teachers and students could hear the confessions of how their own "new lives and the subjects of their new works were isolated", and how "we sometimes adopted an anemic and decadent intellectual attitude to painting for the working people". "I used to despise popularization", Hua Junwu said in his confession. "I had lived in the city for a long time and was subject to bad influences, so I am still nostalgic for the emotions Matisse imparts: a school of goldfish, French windows, a sidewalk and a drinking fountain. In the end these are things that delight me and psychologically I have long had an aversion to rural life".[102]

In April 1943, the rectification campaign entered the stage of organizational review. A large number of young people with ideals and enthusiasm who went from KMT-ruled areas to Yan'an were subjected to political persecution through "forced confessions". According to Kang Sheng, Mao Zedong's chief assistant in the rectification campaign, who

[101] Lenin in his "Party Organization and Party Literature" wrote:

"Overthrow the non-Party writers! Overthrow the superman writers! The literary cause should be part of the overall cause of the proletariat and the 'cog and screw' in a unified, great socialist democratic machine driven by the vanguard of the whole working class' consciousness". Ibid., p. 136.

By 1949, Mao Zedong could speak with great confidence on behalf of what he called the "people" to imperialist America:

"Dear gentlemen, you're right, that's what we are. All the experience that the people of Chinese have accumulated in the decades can simply be called the people's democratic authority or dictatorship we implemented; in short, we deprived the reactionaries of their right to speak and only let the people have a voice.

But after 1949, did the CPC not explain who the people are? And whose voice will be taken away? In fact, in different political movements, the concept of "the people" is determined by those who provide the ideological voice of Marxism-Leninism or Mao Zedong Thought - if their power has not been removed by the Party. It will soon be seen that, while they can see healthy smiles and scenes of socialist construction in these colorful literary works, they will also find that artists and their artistic work are always only a part of the political tools used in the endless process of removal and being removed.

[102] Huang Gang, "The peace is long gone! The debate on the rectification at the Lu Xun Academy in Yan'an", *Liberation Daily*, 4 August 1942.

was responsible for the arrest, interrogation, and execution of agents in Yan'an, in a speech at a meeting of the Political Bureau of the Communist Party of China (CPC) Central Committee on 2 August, announced that more than 1400 KMT agents had been uncovered in the Yan'an region in just a dozen days.

On 1 July 1943, Kang Sheng, representing the Rectification Committee, published an article titled "Rescuing the Lost"; with the rectification campaign entering the "rescue" stage, those deemed to be "lost" were required to write confessions, often facing arrest, interrogation, beatings, and even execution. Many Party members, Youth League members, and intellectuals who came to join the revolution from KMT-ruled areas were asked to state in their confessions that they were "counter-revolutionaries", "enemy elements", "national traitors", or even "agents of the Soviet Union". Wang Ming, who was in Yan'an during the rectification campaign, wrote:

> To that end, they do whatever it takes to arrest people, torture them and make them "confess". They terrorized these people, betrayed them, vilified them at "mass meetings", "rectified" them at small meetings, and psychologically and physically abused them until they were driven insane. They used non-stop interrogation methods to elicit "confessions". They were particularly brutal to provincial and county committee cadres who had come from KMT-ruled areas. These cadres were specifically called on to participate in the "rectification". They asked these cadres to "confess" to their alleged "crimes".[103]

Even in the art field, the "rescue" movement led to brutal political struggles among the Lu Xun Academy's teachers and students. The screening for "spies" created a situation in which everyone was at risk. According to Li Qun's "Reminiscences of Life at the Lu Xun Academy" about 80% of people were designated as "spies". The art teacher Shi Bofu (1907–1982) was detained after being accused of being a "spy" and his wife, in grief, suffocated herself at home with her four daughters. Chen Tiegeng, a former revolutionary youth and printmaker, experienced repeated political persecution until he was psychologically destroyed, and

[103] Wang Ming, op. cit., p. 126. Wang Ming's comment on "non-stop interrogation methods" is: "Some people are interrogated around the clock. This causes people to lose consciousness, and when they regain consciousness, they continue to be interrogated, which can force them to 'confess' their 'guilt' in a state of confusion".

Yan Han recalled in his "Thanks for the Suffering" that he could hear the voices of people running to the cliff to shout about the injustice at night. During the "rescue campaign", people often heard of a person "hanging himself", "jumping off a cliff", and "throwing himself into a well". In these dangerous struggles, the phenomena of comrades accusing each other, of brothers beating each other up, and of couples denouncing each other were very common, and this phenomenon only again became as common during the Cultural Revolution.

Of course, the main goal of the rectification campaign was to completely break the "International faction" represented by Wang Ming and establish the authority of Marxism and Mao Zedong Thought in China. As Mao Zedong repeatedly told his comrades in the Party during the rectification campaign:

> The struggle between me and Wang Ming is not a personal struggle, but a battle of principles. Wang Ming is the main representative of Russian Marxism in the Communist Party of China, and I am the main representative of Chinese Marxism. Therefore, the struggle between us is between two ideologies, two theories, and two lines, and the two methods of the Chinese revolution. If we did not struggle with Wang Ming, we could not have ended the Russian Marxism in our Party leadership; if we had not ended the rule of Russian Marxism in the Communist Party of China, we could not have established Chinese Marxism in the leading position in the Communist Party of China.[104]

No matter how political propaganda and theoretical interpretation are invoked, no one doubts that this was the decisive power struggle between Mao Zedong and Wang Ming. In April 1944, Mao Zedong had a private conversation with Wang Ming, who he hoped would accept his position and views on the rectification. Soon after, the CPC Central Committee received a letter from Dimitrov to Wang Ming, in which Dimitrov endorsed Wang Ming's disagreement on the rectification campaign, but Stalin supported Mao Zedong based on his power in the CPC at the time, but wanted him to maintain "unity" with Wang Ming. At a time of widespread discontent in Yan'an, Mao Zedong also began to instruct Kang Sheng to ease contradictions within the Party and let the rectification campaign enter the stage of "overturning verdicts and restoring his

[104] Cited by Wang Ming, op. cit., pp. 127–128.

reputation". Many people's labels of "counter-revolutionary elements", "national traitors", or "enemy agents" were removed. Vladimirov, a Soviet journalist in Yan'an, wrote about the rectification campaign:

> Mao is convinced that no one knows what is happening here! The rectification campaign has seen 30,000 cadres rectified. No one can escape the eyes of the secret service, and every word people say, he knows. As a result, most people accept "ideological transformation".[105]

"Ideological transformation" was so thorough that by June 1944, the *New People's Daily* reporter Zhao Chaogou who had earlier come to Yan'an observed: "Asking the same question of twenty or thirty people, I find that from intellectuals to workers, their answers are almost identical". Regardless of whether you're asking them about Hitler, Tojo, life, or political issues, they invariably answer, "more or less".[106]

When Zhao interviewed Wang Shiwei at this time, the latter kept talking about his mistakes. Emotional and sounding angry, he told the reporter that he had given up literary criticism and was now "interested in politics". Zhao noted that Wang Shiwei after his experience with "Wild Lilies" was left with serious psychological trauma. Three years later, Wang was hacked to death with a knife by a young man said to have been a model cadre.

From 23 April to 11 June 1945, the Seventh National Congress of the CPC Central Committee was held, at which the newly adopted Party Constitution clearly endorsed Mao Zedong Thought as unifying Marxism–Leninism and Chinese revolutionary practice as the guide to all work of the entire Party.

The CPC's Strategy of Democracy

The call for democracy and freedom was revived by the Communist Party of China as early as the beginning of the War of Resistance. After the September 18 Incident, there has been no more influential slogan

[105] Vladimirov, Yan'an Diaries (Chinese language edition), Beijing: Dongfang Chubanshe, 2004, p. 575.

[106] Cited by Jung Chang and Jon Halliday, Mao Zedong: The Unknown Story, 2006 edition, p. 216.

than "common resistance to the Japanese", but this became increasingly unpopular when it was linked with Chiang Kai-shek's policy of "domestic pacification preceding opposition to the external enemy". The CPC took advantage of this background to promote the anti-Japanese war and launch a nationwide student and social movement, which gained widespread sympathy and support. The intellectual community participated in urging the National government to actively fight against the Japanese. In 1935, prior to the Beiping student movement in May, Shen Junru (1875–1963), Zhang Naiqi (1897–1977) and others organized the "United National Salvation Federation" and issued the "Preliminary Political Program for Anti-Japanese National Salvation", which called for the release of political prisoners, all political parties immediately arranging for representatives to formulate a common national salvation program, and the establishment of a unified anti-Japanese regime, propositions which was naturally not to Chiang Kai-shek's liking. In July, Shen Junru, Zhang Naiqi, Zou Taofen (1895–1944), and Tao Xingzhi (1891–1946) jointly published "The Basic Conditions and Minimum Requirements for Solidarity against Humiliation", which demand that the KMT stop "besieging the Communists". On 23 November, the National Government, on the orders of the Japanese Consul General in Shanghai, arrested Shen Junru, Zhang Naiqi, Zou Taofen, Shi Liang (1900–1985), Li Gongpu (1902–1946), Wang Zaoshi (1903–1978) and Sha Qianli (1901–1982), the seven leaders of the National Salvation Society for "endangering the Republic of China", in what was referred to as the "Seven Gentlemen Incident". Prominent Chinese like Song Qingling, He Xiangning, Zhang Xueliang, and Yang Hucheng and international friends like Bertrand Russell, John Dewey, and Albert Einstein called for the release of Shen Junru and the others. The Communist Party of China was also involved in the rescue campaign. After the July 7 Incident, the seven gentlemen were released on bail, but the indictment was not dropped until February 1939.[107] The "Seven Gentlemen" incident involved the issue of how to deal with freedom of expression and political prisoners at that time. The KMT adherence to the logic of "one-party discipline" on this issue meant that KMT directives were supreme orders above the law, and this authoritarian approach generated antipathy towards the KMT and the government. However, by echoing the intellectual community's demand for democratic freedom, the Communist Party of China increased its allies. On 25 February, *Xinhua Daily* also tentatively published an editorial stressing democracy, titled "The Question of Democratic Politics":

> Our future policy is: Firstly, strengthening the development of public opinion bodies, and preparing the current National People's Political Council and the provincial assemblies to function as a Senate, and gradually become truly representative popular bodies; Secondly, effectively implementing the anti-Japanese war and national establishment, stipulating that "during the Anti-Japanese War, there will be no violation of the highest principles of the Three Principles of the People and the scope of the law, and that the rights of speech, publication, assembly, and association will be fully guaranteed".

In fact, when the Anti-Japanese War fully broke out, the CPC knew that the national war could, through the concepts of democracy and freedom recognized by the UK and USA, provide the Communist Party with legitimacy and the opportunity to participate in state administration and even seize power. A few days after Chiang Kai-shek's speech at Lushan, Mao Zedong proposed the CPC's eight-point anti-Japanese defense program outlined in "The Policy, Approach and Future Opposition to Japanese Aggression" (23 July 1937), in which "reforming the political institutions" already mentioned "accommodating all parties and people's leaders to jointly manage state affairs". On 25 August, Mao Zedong, in his article "The Struggle to Mobilize All Forces for the

[107] Although the Communist Party of China and people from all walks of life actively worked to rescue the "Seven Gentlemen" who advocated anti-Japanese resistance, and stopping the siege of the Communist bases, they did not fare well later. In addition to Zou Taofen, Shen Junru, and Sha Qianli dying of ill health, Li Gongpu was shot dead by Kuomintang agents in Kunming on 11 July 1946, and Wang Zaoshi was classified as a rightist, who eventually died in prison on 14 January 1969. Zhang Naiqi was also classified as a rightist, and was brutally beaten during the Cultural Revolution. He died on 13 May 1977. Shi Liang's house was ransacked during the Cultural Revolution.

Victory of Resistance Against Japan", developed the eight major platforms into "Ten-Point National Salvation Program" for the Anti-Japanese War, which more explicitly laid out the intention to reform government institutions and participate in state administration: "The National Assembly will bring together the true representatives of the people, adopts a truly democratic constitution, decide on the anti-Japanese national salvation policy and elect a national defense government". Even though the all-out Anti-Japanese War had only just begun, Mao Zedong was able to write the following hopeful slogan at the end of the article: "Long live the New China of independence, freedom and happiness!".

In January 1940, Mao Zedong published "On New Democracy" in the first issue of Yan'an's *Chinese Culture*. Mao suggested that "the Chinese Democratic Republic to be established can now only be a democratic republic in which all the anti-imperialist and anti-feudal people unite under the leadership of the proletariat, and this will be the New Democratic Republic". Mao said such a state system was the same thing as the anti-Japanese united front proposed by the Chinese Communist Party, which clearly shows the CPC wanted a major share of state power. During this period, Chiang Kai-shek also adhered to the arrangements of the period of political tutelage, and he continued to emphasize "party rule of the nation" and "party nation-building" in his speech "The System of The Three Principles of the People and the Procedure for their Implementation" (7 May 1939), while Mao Zedong emphasized "the national body - the revolutionary classes of the united dictatorship and the political body - democratic centralism", his goal being to negate the Kuomintang's one-party dictatorship.

National governance in wartime faced a number of problems. People in the political, economic, and cultural spheres were seriously dissatisfied with the KMT's rule, the most unbearable aspect of daily social life being the soaring prices caused by inflation, while a minority of tycoons were able to accumulate wealth through abuse of power in those chaotic times (based on wartime conditions, people used the phrase "making money from the national troubles"). A plethora of heavy taxes made the majority of people's lives unbearable, while poverty, disease, and war-induced fear and despair, conditions almost synonymous with Chinese society. In 1941, when Japan attacked Pearl Harbor, Mary Clabaugh, a student of John Fairbank, described her Chinese experience, along with that of her young sinologist husband Arthur Wright (1913–1976), in a letter from Beijing:

> The stark brutality of life here, which so overwhelmed me at first, is gradually getting into proportion with other factors, although it is still terribly depressing. Horses fall dead as they are whipped to pull impossible loads. Mere children are pull ing rickshas and everyone knows they will die from it in a few years. Children fall into the lakes and are drowned while no notice is taken. Then their mothers slit their own throats with a sickle in grief. A young policeman falls asleep at his post, wakes up, and hangs himself on the spot, knowing that his job is lost and that he will starve, whereupon his aged parents poison themselves with opium, as their support is lost. The struggle to survive is simply terrific, and life can obviously mean nothing.[108]

An American journalist traveling in China in the 1940s was overwhelmed by what she observed:

> No worse luck could befall a human being than to be born and live there, unless by some golden chance you happened to be born one of the .00000099% who had power, money, privilege (and even then, even then). I pitied them all, I saw no tolerable future for them, and I longed to escape away from what I had escaped into: the age-old misery, filth, hopelessness and my own claustrophobia inside that enormous country.[109]

On 20 October 1940, Ma Yinchu, dean of Chongqing University's Business School, published "The fiscal solution for China's financial situation: Imposing temporary property tax on those who are making a fortune in these times of war" in a special issue of *Current Affairs* (Shishi Leibian), in which he wrote: "Now at the front in the anti-Japanese war millions of soldiers are sacrificing their lives, tens of millions of people are displaced by the upheaval and are homeless, while in the rear are the officials cum capitalists; they not only make no contribution to the government but take advantage of the conflagration and make a fortune; the injustice and irrationality of it are too much to bear". He was, of course referring to collusion between officials and businessmen: "China's current national troublemakers, in addition to businessmen, are those

[108] This letter was written on August 2, 1941. *Chinese Roundabout* by Jonathan D.Spence, W. W. Norton & Company Inc., 1992, p. 322.

[109] Martha Gellhorn, *The Face of War* (New York: Atlantic Monthly Press,1988), p. 70. (quoted from *CHINA1945 Mao's Revolution and America's Fateful Choice* by Richard Bernstein (Alfred A. Knopf, 2014), p. 107.

who use political power to make a fortune. Such conduct is not what officials should perpetrate. Therefore, implementing a tax on capital must begin with the powerful officials who are profiting from the national disaster. The financial difficulties of the country created by officials should above all focus on confiscating their entire wealth, in order to provide an example for the people".[110] The cartoon "Illustrated Phenomena" by the painter Ding Cong in 1944 vividly depicts the chaotic social situation of this period. This period of chaos could only be sustained by the police and agents; constant arrests and killings created panic, leading to the growing view of Chiang Kai-shek's Kuomintang government as a dictatorship.

The conflict with the Kuomintang made the CPC use possible opportunities and conditions to strive for political attitudes and positions that would win influence over the majority of the population, and during the Anti-Japanese War, because the national crisis transcended class conflicts, the CPC's strategy changed to establishing a united front for fighting all forces. Through the call for democracy and freedom, the CPC won the sympathy of moderates in different professional organizations from all walks of life. For example, the Chinese Democratic Political League, which was established after the South Anhui Incident was for a time sympathetic towards and allied with CPC, and this organization included many community members holding different positions at that time but all actively advocating resistance to the Japanese. Given that members were joining the group as individuals, the alliance was renamed the Chinese Democratic League. The "Platform for the Present Situation" initially issued by the League was at odds with Chiang Kai-shek's principle "Party rule of the nation": "Practice the spirit of democracy, end the party rule, and set up organs of state in agreement with all parties and factions before the implementing the constitution".[111] *Liberation Daily*, the media outlet of the CPC in Yan'an immediately echoed the positions of these centrists, saying: "For 30 years, all political movements in the country have revolved

[110] Ma Yinchu, *Ma Yinchu Chu Xuanji* (First Collection of Selected Works by Ma Yinchu), Tianjin: Tianjin Renmin Chubanshe, 1988, pp. 198–199.

[111] Zhongguo Minzhu Tongmeng Zhongyang Wenshi Ziliao Weiyuanhui ed., *Zhongguo Minzhu Tongmeng Lishi Wenxian: 1941–1949*, Beijing: Wenshi Ziliao Chubanshe, 1983, p. 8.

around two centers, one is national independence and the other is democratic politics".[112] However, Chiang Kai-shek did not see anything wrong with his political arrangement of following Sun Yat-sen's principles of "military politics", "tutelary rule", and "constitutionalism", especially at a time when the Anti-Japanese War required a high degree of unified command. Yet the centrists often expressed their positions on the basis of purpose, and the CPC's call for democracy was readily accepted by centrists, resulting in Chiang Kai-shek's obvious failure to win over fewer centrists than Mao Zedong.

Following the death of Lin Sen, Chairman of the National Government, in August 1943, Chiang Kai-shek took over as Chairman and President of the Executive Council in the following month. While Chiang now controlled all power of the state, party, and army. Dong Biwu, on returning from Chongqing to Yan'an, wrote a report titled "General Overview of the Great Rear Area" that described Chiang Kai-shek in this way:

> After Lin Sen's death, Chiang became President (Chairman), and the form of dictatorship became more complete. Under the Nationalist Government's original "National Government Organization [Organic] Law", power was only vested in the Head of State to receive guests; in fact, only the National Government's supervisory seal was stamped on appointments and orders. When Jiang became president, he amended the Organic Law, and the Chairman could supreme as Supreme Commander of China's Sea, Land and Air Forces. He could at the same time hold any post - President of the Executive and all other functions. In the past, the President of the five divisions (Yuan) of the National People's Government was proposed and adopted by the Kuomintang Central Committee, and now the post of Chairman was appointed through the KMT Central Committee; in the past the president of the previous five Yuan was accountable to the Kuomintang Central Committee but was now accountable to the Chairman. It can thus be seen that when others served as Chairman they had no power, but when Chiang became Chairman he held all power and others could not hold any office as he held all functions.[113]

[112] "Zhongguo Minzhu Yundong de Shenglijun", editorial, *Jiefang Ribao*, 28 October 1941.

[113] Zhongguo Xiandai Shi Ziliao Bianji Weiyuanhui (China Modern History Materials Editing Committee) ed., *Kangri Zhanzheng Shiqi Guomindang Tongzhiqu Qingkuang*

The CPC did not have to wait for the end of the war to begin its challenge to the KMT. Given the defeats of the Kuomintang army on the battlefield and the general popular grievances, the CPC repeatedly reminded the Chinese people that the KMT had implemented a dictatorship, and without democracy, today's problems could not be solved. On 12 March 1944, Zhou Enlai addressed representatives of various sectors in Yan'an at a ceremony commemorating the 19th anniversary of the death of Sun Yat-sen:

> This constitutional issue is being discussed on all fronts, and we very much agree with many of their views; we want to implement constitutional government, for which there are a number of prerequisites. We believe that the most important prerequisites are three: first, to guarantee the democratic freedoms of the people; second, to end the ban on political parties, and third, to implement local self-government. There are many freedoms and rights of the people, but the most urgently needed freedoms of the people are the freedoms of residence, assembly and association, and of speech and publication. People's homes can be illegally searched at any time, people can be illegally arrested, be secretly tortured or executed, or be forced to assemble for military training, people's freedoms of assembly and association can be prohibited, and peoples' rights of speech and publication can be subject to extreme restrictions and censorship. Under such conditions, how can people be guaranteed the freedom to discuss constitutional issues? Mr. Sun Yat-sen once said: "Now China is called the Republic of China, but to be worthy of the name requires that the country is really a republic of its citizens and for them to be able to speak out, there must be free speech. In such a situation, it would be a true Republic of China. Otherwise, it is only an ersatz Republic". Ending the ban on political parties recognizes the legitimacy the various anti-Japanese political parties in the country, and legitimacy is not seeing these parties as "traitors, and "dissidents"; not restricting and prohibiting all their activities that do not go beyond the scope of anti-Japanese democracy does not mean always trying to destroy them. When democracy meets these two prerequisites, local self-government can genuinely be implemented.[114]

Ziliao (Documents on the Situation in Kuomintang Controlled Areas during the Anti-Japanese War), June 1957, pp. 136–137. This book is quoted in Jin Chongji, op. cit., v. 2, p. 502.

[114] *Lishi de Xiansheng: Bange Shiji qian de Zhuangyan Chengnuo*, Shantou University Press, 1999, pp. 7–8.

The political struggle of the CPC against the KMT was based on the military and political situation, and with the relentless advance of the Japanese Army's Ichigo combat plan and the KMT army's series of defeats, the CPC made use of the situation to change its political strategy. On 6 June 1944, the beginning of the Normandy Landing opened up a second battlefront in Europe, but this did not diminish the continuation of the Japanese Ichigo Plan. While Wallace and Chiang Kai-shek discussed in Chongqing how to deal with the CPC, Yan'an carried out a large-scale propaganda publicizing American values, the CPC through different articles emphasizing the importance of democracy as a core American value. "Welcome to Mr. Wallace" was published by *Liberation Daily* on 23 June 1944. In the article, the CPC not only praised Roosevelt's four freedoms (freedom of speech, freedom of worship, freedom from want, and freedom from fear), but also claimed that the four freedoms could be "seen in practice" in areas controlled by the CPC. In the KMT-ruled areas, on the other hand, "public opinion is restrained and ideology controlled", so today's China must "immediately abolish dictatorship and implement democracy". In an editorial in *Xinhua Daily* on June 24th, the CPC lavishly praised the United States and its democracy:

> Why were General Eisenhower's Allied forces able to win in the north of France? Why was Admiral Nimitz's navy recently win major land, sea and air victories in Saipan, the Marianas and the Philippines? Why General MacArthur's forces able to advance daily in the South-West Pacific?
>
> Why were General Stilwell in northern Myanmar and General Chennault in China able to exert such great land and air power? Why did the United States become the munitions factory for democratic nations? The only answer is democracy and the expansion of democracy.[115]

On July 4th, *Liberation Daily* published an editorial written by Mao Zedong's secretary, Hu Qiaomu, saying: "The work we Communists are doing now is what Washington, Jefferson, Lincoln, and others have already done in the United States". On 10 August 10, Wang Shijie and Zhang Zhizhong formally replied to the twelve negotiating proposals put forward by Lin Boqu on behalf of the CPC, and in response to

[115] *Lishi de Xiansheng: Bange Shiji qian de Zhuangyan Chengnuo*, Shantou University Press, 1999, p. 126.

the requirement of democratic politics in the proposal, the views of the National Government were: "Within one year after the end of the Anti-Japanese War, constitutional government will be introduced and all political parties will be given equal status".[116]

However, in the political and military negotiations, the CPC took the KMT's defeat on the battlefield fighting the Japanese resistance as the basis for negotiations. Thus, after the defeat of the National army in the Battle of Hengyang (8 August), Mao Zedong demanded that the National government not be limited to the previously negotiated establishment of "five armies and sixteen, divisions", but that "our army of 470,000 demands full recognition from the Government". On 30 August Lin Boqu wrote in reply on behalf of the CPC: "All issues depend on whether the KMT is prepared to implement determinedly and sincerely democratic politics. If that is the case, constitutional government should be implemented immediately during, not after, the Anti-Japanese War".[117]

In September 1944, after the Japanese launched their Ichigo battle plan and besieged Guilin, Ye Shengtao wrote: "On this occasion the enemy entering Guangxi from Hunan is almost invincible, and they are advancing as rapidly as they did in the fighting in Henan. It appears that our soldiers can no longer be used. Even the elite soldiers have not yet been used and where more troops will come from is not even considered; all have become paper tigers that have been thwarted. Now and in the future, it is difficult to predict how the enemy's onslaught will be stopped". Ye Shengtao concluded: "As for our country's dispirited condition, it cannot be imputed to historical weakness; that bad politics is the main cause is something of which I am convinced".[118]

On September 15th, at the third meeting of the Third Session of the National People's Political Consultative Conference, Lin Boqu, on behalf of the CPC, reported on negotiations between the KMT and CPC, and

[116] *Wang Shijie Riji* (The Diary of Wang Shijie), 4 August 1944, in Deng Ye, *Lianhe Zhengfu yu Yidang Xunzheng* (Coalition Government and One-Party Tutelary Rule), Beijing: Shehui Kexue Wenxian Chubanshe, 2011, p. 31.

[117] *Lin Boqu Wenji*, Huayi Chubanshe, 1996, p. 406.

[118] Ye Shengtao, "Xixing Riji" (II), *Ye Shengtao Ji*, v. 20, Jiangsu Education Publishing House, 1994, pp. 295, 338.

stressed "in passing"[119]: "It is hoped that the KMT will immediately bring to an end one-party rule and that the National Government will convene representatives of all parties, factions, anti-Japanese forces, local governments and people's groups for a national conference and form a coalition government of all anti-Japanese parties". On 10 October, the Chinese Democratic Alliance published the "Political Proposal of the Chinese Democratic Alliance for the Final Stage of the Anti-Japanese War" which clearly indicated "an immediate end to the one-party dictatorship, the establishment of a coalition of parties, and the implementation of democratic politics", and demanded "convening a meeting of all parties to produce a government of unity in the war".[120] During September, the CPC not only began preparations for the second government's Coalition Committee of Chinese Liberated Areas. At the same time, it also began to revise the names of the new regime's military organizations, and so on 22 September, Liu Shaoqi proposed the concept of the "People's Liberation Army" at the Chairman's Group Meeting of the Seventh Plenary Session of the Sixth Central Committee's.

After Dushan was conquered by the Japanese, the CPC further believed that the KMT would be defeated. On 8 December, Mao Zedong and Zhou Enlai met with Hurley's translator, David D. Barrett (1892–1977) to express the latest attitude of the CPC to the previous negotiations with the Kuomintang, the essence of which was to prepare

[119] In fact, the concept of a "coalition government" emerged in a 4 September message from the Central Committee of the Communist Party of China to Lin Boqu, Dong Biwu and Wang Ruofei (1896–1946): "At present, the time is ripe for our party to propose to the Kuomintang and at home and abroad to restructure the government, and the plan is to require the National Government to immediately convene representatives of all parties, factions, forces, local governments and various popular groups, and to convene a conference, restructure the central government, and abolish one-party rule". Ref: *Zhonggong Zhongyang Wenjian Xuanji* (Anthology of Documents of the Central Committee of the Communist Party of China), v. 14, p. 323. This book is quoted in Deng Ye, ibid., 2011, p. 34. When Lin Boqu and the others asked the central government at the political conference how it envisaged forming a coalition government, Yan'an's response was that they propose it in the name of the CPC's Central Committee at the meeting. However, in private discussions with other democrats, Lin Boqu was not in favor of the idea, because it would not be accepted and would prompt a responsive stance. Lin's proposal was therefore appeared in the conference report, that is, informally.

[120] *Zhongguo Minzhu Tongmeng Lishi Wenxian (1941–1949)*, Beijing: Wenshi Ziliao Chubanshe, 1983, p. 32.

for a separate independent government, and Barrett recorded Mao and Zhou's statement:

> Since Chiang Kai-shek has refused to form a coalition government, we are determined not to give in and are determined to take a decisive step. We are proposing to the National Political Council that the regions under our control form a "joint committee" representing all these regions which would be the first step towards the formation of an independent government.
>
> We have closed the door, but the window is still open. The "five-point proposal" [the plan brought by Hurley from Yan'an to Chongqing, ed.] is the window. We are willing to return to the coalition government today, tomorrow or even the day after tomorrow. However, after that, we will wait until Chongqing, Kunming, Guiyang, Chengdu, and Xi'an have all been lost, and then we will not participate in accordance with our earlier terms.[121]

Barrett did not support Mao's intentions and believed that if the CPC set up a Joint Committee of the Liberated Areas such a move would make outsiders regard the CPC as trouble-making rebels. Moreover, it was not yet known whether the KMT army would be victorious or defeated, and if the KMT was victorious, the CPC's position would be untenable. Mao soon went back to the idea of "coalition government" and argued that if the KMT failed militarily, the CPC could take a "big share" (Zhou Enlai and Mao Zedong's term) of the coalition government and temporarily put the idea of setting up a Joint Committee of the Liberated Areas on hold.

In response to the "coalition government" proposed by the CPC, Chiang Kai-shek decided that the 11th Plenary Session of the Fifth Central Committee of the Kuomintang decided to convene the National Convention within one year after the end of the Anti-Japanese War, which would see constitutional government implemented ahead of schedule. The decision came very quickly, because on the day after Lin Boqu on behalf of the CPC put forward the proposal of coalition government at the Political Conference, Chiang Kai-shek told the meeting: "This session is considering a proposal to convene a Sixth National Congress

[121] David D. Barrett, *Dixie Mission: The United States Army Observer Group in Yenan, 1944*, Chinese translation, pp. 91–98. Quoted in Deng Ye, op. cit., p. 77.

of the Kuomintang next year and, if by that time the situation of the anti-Japanese war improves, there may be a need for an early implementation of constitutional government".[122] On 8 December Chiang Kai-shek further told the Legislative Council (Yuan) President Sun Ke: "There is no need to agree to a coalition government, but we can verbally agree to allowing the CPC to participate in the government and we can be bring forward constitutional government".[123] On 4 January 1945, as a strategy of preparing for the National Congress and implementing the constitution, Chiang Kai-shek also arranged a temporary measure: a "Wartime Executive Council", known as the Interim Cabinet, was set up in the Executive Yuan, "comprising seven to nine members. The CPC and other non-KMT party members could attend meetings of this Council. [Chiang Kai-shek] ordered the drafting of regulations governing the Council (this plan is intended to accommodate the CPC's demand for 'coalition government' and find a solution to the problem of the CPC)".[124]

At the 7th National Congress of the CPC in April, Mao Zedong directly reminded people that in China, the benefits of "political tutelage" or "one-party dictatorship" were no longer mentioned, and that it was time to abolish the one-party dictatorship of the KMT. Chiang Kai-shek also said at the opening ceremony on 5 May of the KMT's Sixth National Congress: "When I was at the National People's Political Consultative Conference last year and again on New Year's Day this year, I announced our determination to end the tutelary rule and implement constitutional government, and on 1 March, I addressed the Constitutional Implementation Council, and specifically stated that on 12 November this year, on the occasion of the Prime Minister's [Sun Yat-sen's] 80th birthday, we would convene the National Assembly to implement constitutional government". On 18 May, the Sixth National Conference called for the

[122] Qin Xiaoyi ed., *Xian Zongtong Jiang Gong Sixiang Yanlun Zongji* (Anthology of Thinking and Speeches of Former President Chiang), v. 20, Taipei: Guomindang Zhongyang Dangshihui (Kuomintang Central History Committee), 1984, p. 507. This is quoted in Deng Ye, op. cit., p. 82.

[123] *Tang Zong Riji*, 8 December 1944, Ministry of Public Security Archives' note: *Zai Jiang Jieshi Shenbian Banian: Shicongshi Gaoji Muliao Tang Zong Riji* (Eight Years beside Chiang Kai-shek: The Diary of Tang Zong, Senior Attendant Staff Officer), 1991, p. 476. This book is quoted by Deng Ye, op. cit., p. 82.

[124] *Wang Shijie Riji*, 4 January 1945.

abolition of the army's Party headquarters within three months, for no schools at any level to set Party branches, and for the three Youth Leagues to be under the leadership of the government. Chiang Kai-shek asked the whole Party to reflect deeply, otherwise, "we will really have nowhere to live and nowhere to bury the dead".[125] Chiang Kai-shek's "constitutional government" and Mao Zedong's "coalition government" look very similar, which was why Hurley who did not understand Chinese did not understand the difference between "coalition government" and "participatory government" when he intervened. However, Chiang and Mao's respective starting points were completely different, the former trying to consolidate the national government through "constitutional government", the latter wanting to overthrow Chiang Kai-shek's rule through "coalition government". In response to Yan'an's proposal to set up a Council of the Liberated Areas, Chiang Kai-shek pointed out that this was to "subvert the government and harm the nation", so the two sides had difficulty reaching a consensus. At the beginning of July, six representatives of the Democratic League including Huang Yanpei (1878–1965), Fu Sinian, Zuo Shunsheng (1983–1969), and Zhang Bojun (1895–1969) went to Yan'an to mediate, even though the Democratic League was a party outside the KMT and CPC debate. However, it didn't play a fundamental role, but the Democratic League's proposal to convene a political conference on how to solve the country's big problems was endorsed by the CPC, who told the mediators who had come to Yan'an: The purpose of the political conference is to discuss how to end the one-party dictatorship and establish a coalition government. By this time, Mao no longer regarded the national government as an absolutely legitimate government, and on April 1st he told John Stewart, the US ambassador to China: "Chongqing has a population of 190 million, but 160 million people live in the areas occupied by the Japanese and 100 million people live in the CPC areas".[126] He wanted to tell the Americans who were leaning toward Chiang Kai-shek that these statistics undermine the legitimacy of the Kuomintang regime, which was the reason why Yan'an was planning a joint Congress of the Liberated Areas. On 13 July, a few days

[125] Summary of Historical Events of the Republic of China, May 7, 1945. Quoted in Deng Ye, op. cit., p. 97.

[126] *Zai Zhongguo Shidiao de Jihui: Meiguo Qian Zhu Hua Waijiaoguan Yuehan S. Xieweisi Di'er Ci Shijie Dazhan Shiqi de Baogao*, Guoji Wenhua Chuban Gongsi, 1989, p. 338.

after the Democratic League representatives left Yan'an, the Communist Party of China set up the Preparatory Committee for the People's Representative Conference of China's Liberated Areas, with 25 members including Zhou Enlai, which meant that the Party would openly and independently launch the coalition government.[127] Now, the CPC could boldly demand on behalf of the people that the KMT extend rights to the people, *Xinhua Daily* publishing an editorial on 27 September, stating:

> The right track of democracy is the people having rights and being in charge. This is something that the people of the whole country know. During the eight years of the War of Resistance, the people have been demanding that they are accorded the rights they deserve. More than one hundred million people in the border regions and liberated areas have already been given their democratic rights that should be maintained; if not maintained, democracy is abolished. The people of the rear and the enemy-occupied areas still do not have democracy. Now they should have it, and if they are not given it, this is obstructing democracy. The world is a democratic world, and China too should be a democratic China. In a democratic China, the abolition and obstruction of democracy will not succeed.
>
> How to achieve democracy? Please travel the correct path of democracy: give the people their right to it![128]

Indeed, in 1945, at the 7th Congress of the CPC, Mao Zedong announced: The Communist Party now has 1.21 million members, 910,000 troops, 2.2 million militiamen, and 95.5 million people in the areas under its control. Although our armies' numbers and equipment still far short of those of the KMT's armies, in any case, in the eight years of the Anti-Japanese War, the CPC has developed into the only political and military force that can compete with the KMT, to the point where in the political and military contest with the KMT, the CPC has resources to spare. However, before the end of the War of Resistance

[127] Zuo Shunsheng, in his *Jin Sanshi Nian Jianwen Zaji* (p. 94), recorded what Mao Zedong said to him when he travelled with the Democratic League mediation delegation to Yan'an: "Chiang [Kai-shek] thinks that there cannot be two suns in the sky and the people cannot have two kings. I am not a heretic, but I want to show him there can be two suns". Quoted in Li Yunhan, op. cit., p. 485.

[128] *Lishi de Xiansheng: Bange Shiji qian de Zhuangyan Chengnuo*, Shantou University Press, 1999, p. 315.

against Japanese Aggression, much was in play, and the CPC did not limit itself to a single or fixed political strategy. Whenever possible, the party was also willing to access resources (political, military and popular) from any direction and via any means or channels in order to make itself safer and more confident. In March 1945, for example, the U.S. Military Observer Group had clearly discovered that the CPC would not listen to U.S. advisers in future. In January, Yan'an also tried to arrange a visit to the US President through US diplomats but was also eager for the United States to bypass the National Government in providing weapons and supplies directly to the CPC. But at this point Mao Zedong received information from Moscow in a briefing to Yan'an, once the Yalta meetings ended in early February, that the Soviet Union would participate in the war against Japan and support the CPC. Yan'an was heartened that a Soviet newspaper published a telegram from Mao Zedong and Zhu De to Stalin and agreed to a Yan'an newspaper publishing Stalin's reply. The CPC now felt it did not have to worry too much about hoping for Soviet support or enlisting U.S. help. By April and May, the pattern of U.S. policy toward China was basically defined: supporting Chiang's anti-Communism. When the CPC became clear about the American position, it completely changed its previous tone and political strategy. Although the United States airlifted about 14,000 pounds of radio and spare parts to Yan'an in April, Mao Zedong, at the 7th Communist Party Congress which began later that month, no longer took into account his previous friendly attitude and unkindly described the US government as "reactionary": "The anti Communist policy of the US Government illustrates the viciousness of the reactionaries of the United States, but all attempts by Chinese and foreign reactionaries to prevent the victory of the Chinese people are doomed to failure".[129] In his report to the meeting titled *On Coalition Government*, Mao Zedong made it very clear: he wanted to seriously highlight that the establishment of a democratic coalition government was "an issue of absolute concern to the Chinese people and allied democratic public opinion". Almost simultaneously (5–21 May), the Kuomintang held its sixth National Congress, which adopted its *Resolution on the Question of the Communist Party of China*. After the

[129] *Mao Zedong Xuanji*, v. 3, p. 1103.

meeting, Chiang Kai-shek told his army followers that must always be aware of the CPC's "conspiracy to seize power and turn China red".[130]

The CPC's loud propaganda for "democracy", mainly aimed at the KMT's one-party dictatorship, sought legitimacy for the CPC as a prelude to seizing state power. Mao Zedong effectively maintained the rhythm of promoting democracy and denouncing Chiang Kai-shek's dictatorship, but after the civil war broke out in 1947, the discussion of democracy in the CPC media, *Liberation Daily* and *Xinhua Daily*, ceased.

The Political Contest

At the end of the Anti-Japanese War, people cheered the victory! But new questions were coming thick and fast, and in his 15 August radio broadcast announcing victory over Japan, Chiang Kai-shek said with obvious concern:

> The fighting has not truly ended and the ensuing peace will surely show us that our tasks are difficult, and we must endure similar pain to wartime, and use even more force than in wartime to reform and to build. Perhaps at some point, encountering a problem will make us feel things are more difficult than in wartime, and increased difficulties will dog us at every step.[131]

These were not the words a national leader would use, and Chiang Kai-shek was indeed aware that the nation faced a new and even more complex crisis. The Soviet Union's occupation of the Northeast exceeded what was stipulated in the agreement with the Chinese government, while there was postwar support for the national economy, the establishment of social order, and concern over the approaching CPC's bid for state power. At the end of the Anti-Japanese War, national economic problems brought about by the war quickly came to the fore; the impact of the war on the scale and stability of production left little income, and tariffs were also greatly reduced because of the loss of coastal areas. The government obviously wanted to shoulder responsibility, but corruption,

[130] *Zongtong Jiang Gong Sixiang Yanlun Zongji* (Anthology of President Chiang's Ideas and Words), v. 21, p. 138.

[131] Zhang Qiyun, *Xian Zongtong Jiang Gong Quanji* (Complete Works of First President Chiang Kai-shek), v. 3, 1984, p. 3272. Quoted in Li Yunhan, op. cit., p. 481.

administrative inefficiency, and incompetence of officials strongly influenced the image of the Kuomintang and gradually shook the legitimacy of the regime. Therefore, during and after the Anti-Japanese War, the CPC's relentless attack on the KMT through propaganda had an increasingly obvious political effect with each passing year.

The fact that the United States dropped the atomic bomb on Japan which led to Japan's rapid surrender was unexpected by both the KMT and CPC, and after receiving news that Japan would surrender, both sides began adjusting their previous political, military, and diplomatic strategies and policies. Based on the ultimate goal of seizing power, the CPC, on the basis of its city working meeting of the previous June, made political and military arrangements for the postwar aftermath, and in August Mao Zedong made it clear to Wang Zhen: "Next year we are going to fight back; we will take over big cities, and rapidly establish and develop bases in southern China".[132] So, on August 10th, the day news came that Japan would surrender, the CPC's Central Committee telegrammed its Central China Bureau calling for taking over Japanese-occupied areas: "the first and sixth divisions will be responsible for seizing the line from Nanjing to Shanghai in southern and central Jiangsu", and "the fifth division will concentrate on occupying the line from Xinyang to Wuhan". At the same time, the CPC Central Committee demanded that "today, the chairmen of Jiangsu, Anhui, and Zhejiang provinces and the mayors of Shanghai and Nanjing two mayors would be announced; and that the fifth division would on that day draw up the list of candidates for selection for the positions of Wuhan Mayor and Hubei Provincial Chairman".[133] Over the next two days, several provincial presidents and dozens of municipal and county chiefs were appointed within the Communist Party of China. Through such an arrangement, the CPC was attempting to secure the legitimacy for its regime by having de facto proof that it controlled and occupied these provinces and municipalities.

[132] *Wang Enmao Riji*, 8 August 1944 entry, when Wang Zhen was deputy political commissar of the 359th Brigade, Zhongyang Wenxian Chubanshe, 1995. This book is quoted in Deng Ye, op. cit., p. 47.

[133] The Central Committee's Directive to the Central China Bureau on Taking Major Cities and Transportation Routes (10 August 1945), *Zhonggong Zhongyang Wenjian Xuanji* (Anthology of CPC Central Committee Documents), v. 15, pp. 213, 214. This book is quoted in Deng Ye, op. cit., p. 164.

On 11 August 1945, after consultation with the governments of China, Great Britain and the Soviet Union, the United States informed Japan, on behalf of the Allies, through specific documents that the Allies accepted Japan's offer yesterday to surrender unconditionally to the Allies. Chiang Kai-shek held a joint meeting of the Supreme National Defense Council and the Central Standing Committee on the same day to arrange the procedure for accepting the surrender. In a telegram to the Chinese army, including the 18th Group Army, on the same day, it was made clear that the various forces were on standby and that all provisions of the surrender would be implemented in accordance with the Allied Agreement. However, on that day, Zhu De, commander-in-chief of the 18th Group Army, in the name of the CPC's Yan'an General Headquarters, issued seven orders to the CPC forces in different regions: The CPC armies in the "liberated zones" will directly accept the surrender or elimination, if there is any resistance, of the Japanese puppet forces in the Japanese-occupied areas; cooperate in fighting with the Soviet army entering northeast China; cooperate with the Outer Mongolian army entering Inner Mongolia and the Suiyuan, Chahar, and Jehol fighting areas; enter Shanxi via the Tongpu Road and Fen River valley; enter and occupy all important transport routes and accept the surrender of the enemy and puppet troops; cooperate with the Soviets entering Korea to fight, taking control of strategic towns and forts occupied by the enemy and puppet troops, and implement emergency military control. The CPC's intention was clear: to seize the weapons and areas that the Japanese surrendered in order to strengthen the CPC.

On 12 August, Truman gave McArthur an order: "Senior Japanese generals in China (except in Manchuria), Taiwan, and French Vietnam north of the 16th parallel, and all land, sea, air and ancillary forces shall surrender to Chairman Chiang".[134]

On 13 August the CPC renamed the Shandong Wartime Administrative Committee the Shandong Provincial Government and appointed Li Yu as chairman of Shandong Province. They also ordered that in the Shandong Military Region, Jinan, Qingdao, and other cities and traffic routes be occupied as soon as possible. On the same day, an editorial in Yan'an's *Liberation Daily* began trial use of the term "People's Liberation Army".

[134] *Zhonghua Minguo Shishi Jiyao* (Chronicle of the History of the Republic of China), 13 August 1945.

On the 15th, Chiang Kai-shek, in his capacity as the supreme commander of the China theater of war, issued instructions in six clauses to the supreme commander of the Japanese army, Okamura Yasuji, and on the same day, Zhu De, in his capacity as commander-in-chief of the Anti-Japanese Army in the Liberated Areas of China, sent a message to the ambassadors of the United States, Britain and the Soviet Union, informing them: "The Government of the Nationalist Party of China and its Commanding Department cannot represent any of the Liberated Areas of China and any of the previously Japanese controlled areas of China when accepting the surrender of the Japanese and puppet forces and conclude any agreements and treaties for after the surrender".[135] At the same time, he telegrammed Okamura Yasuji demanding that the latter surrender to the CPC in an attempt to bring the previously Japanese controlled areas and their 160 million population under the control of the CPC. But Okamura followed the Allied instructions and ordered the Japanese forces in China to surrender directly to the National government.

On the 16th, Zhu De also telegrammed six demands to the National Government, insisting that the anti-Japanese people's militias in the liberated areas be allowed to participate in the accepting the surrender, including the collection of weapons and materiel. Chiang Kai-shek reacted to these orders and demands of the CPC as follows:

> Zhu De's seven "orders" and six demands are very obviously intended to undermine national unity and the military command system, and to allow the CPC to act freely, seize weapons from the Japanese and their allies, occupy and destroy traffic routes, expand bandit-occupied territory and, by especially relying on the Russian and Mongolian armies, cut off our north-east, Jehol, Chahar and Suiyuan, divide up our country and, under the slogan of "coalition government", waging political struggle and subversive activities against the National Government.[136]

[135] In a reply to Chiang Kai-shek's invitation on the 16th to Mao Zedong to come to Chongqing for negotiations, Zhu De defined the Communist Party's identity in similar terms: "On behalf of all anti-Japanese armed forces and 260 million people in the liberated areas of China, and of all the anti-Japanese forces in the conquered areas of China, I hereby make the following announcements and requests ...". The CPC's intention was clearly to show the Chongqing government that it was not the only legitimate regime.

[136] Chiang Kai-shek, *Su E zai Zhongguo* (Soviet Russia in China), p. 135. This book is quoted in Li Yunhan, op. cit., p. 478.

Despite this, by the time the Japanese surrendered, the CPC armies had 18 liberated areas in north, south, and central China, with a population of more than 100 million, more than 1 million regular troops, and 2 million militia. These figures may have been exaggerated—Mao wanted the Party's development and growth to be known at home and abroad, but the Party's military might have indeed been able to compete with the central army. For at least the first two weeks, the Central Army and the Chinese Communist army competed to retake the areas occupied by the Japanese. The National Government did not allow the Chinese Communist Party to accept the surrender of the Japanese forces without authorization, on the basis of the provisions of the Potsdam Declaration and its own laws, and the surrender rules of the Allies and the "peace treaty" with the Soviet Union had all been by the National government. This legally overturned the reality and legitimacy of the CPC's previous belief that legitimacy was conferred by the size of its liberated areas and it could establish CPC rule in the areas the Japanese had occupied. In the battle for wresting victory over Japan, the United States supported the National government; the United States sent 50,000 marines to occupy important ports and transportation routes and flew Central Army troops to Beiping, Tianjin, Shanghai and Nanjing, while Chiang Kai-shek's 500,000 troops quickly spread out to various regions. As a result, the Central Army took control again of important cities and transport routes in central, eastern, and southern China.

Until at least 23 August, the CPC was not aware of the contents of the Sino-Soviet Treaty of Friendship signed by the Soviet Union and the National Government, which contained the following statement:

> The government of the Soviet Union agrees to fully provide moral and military support as well as other materiel to China to the central government of China, the National government.[137]

The agreement obviously acknowledged that various matters in the Northeast, that is all issues involving the Northeast between China and the Soviet Union, were to be referred to the Chongqing government as the main body of the agreement; the Soviet Union's temporary obscuring of the CPC led to Yan'an to misjudge the current situation. On the other

[137] Treaty of Friendship between the USSR and the Republic of China, 14 August 1945. See: *Zhonghua Minguo Zhongyao Shiliao Chubian*, Part III (II), p. 655.

hand, the Soviets did not cease military operations after Japan's surrender on August 8th when they entered the Northeast. The 1.5 million strong military forces of Rodin Y. Molinovsky, commander of the Soviet Far East Army, covered the entire Northeast and parts of North China, and the National Government arranged as officers receiving them, Xiong Shihui (1893–1974), Zhang Jia'ao (1889–1979), and Jiang Jingguo, who served respectively as the chairman of the Military Committee Chairman for the Northeast Battalion, the Director of the Economic Commission and the Foreign Ministry's special envoy to the Northeast. Chiang Kai-shek, who concentrated used large resources to help Japanese soldiers and civilians return to Japan, was widely praised by the international community, and he said in his August 15th speech: "We have always said that we recognize only the Japanese militarists, not the Japanese people, as enemies. Today the enemy forces have been defeated by our Allies, and we must of course strictly oblige them by faithfully enforcing all the terms of the surrender, but we must not retaliate, let alone insult the innocent people humiliated by the enemy's armies. We can only show compassion for those duped by their Nazi warlords, so that they can extricate themselves from their mistakes and sins. We must remain aware that if you respond to the enemy's past atrocities with atrocities ... and respond by enslaving those who committed errors in good faith, then the cycle of revenge will never end".[138] However, the process of the KMT government's acceptance of surrender still attracted widespread complaints as problems arose, such as the shortage of receiving personnel and "systemic disorder, unclear accountability, the scramble for benefits and shirking of responsibilities". Chiang Kai-shek's inaction also led to obstacles to the reception process and occasioned popular discontent. Chiang Kai-shek ordered the Japanese army and the puppet military forces to cooperate when his army could not reach the Northeast in time. By the end of November, there were still 100,000 Japanese troops stationed in Shanxi, Chahar, and Hebei, which naturally offered the possibility of conflict between the Japanese puppet forces and the Chinese Communist army. In

[138] Chiang Kai-shek's policy on Japanese prisoners and nationals was expressed in his August 15th national address as "relying on virtue rather than vengeance", and this made a good impression internationally. From the first repatriation ships in November to the return of the last captives and expats in August of the following year, China helped repatriate 1,255,000 Japanese prisoners and nearly 800,000 Japanese expatriates. Added to those who subsequently returned home, a total of 3.1 million Japanese were repatriated.

punishing Chinese traitors, some puppet regime officials relied on KMT policy loopholes and pretended to have been working for Chongqing's institutions, changing the names on their signboards to those of government agencies. When people were reminded that it was important to not severely punish traitors, the policy of leniency towards those who had helped in anti-Japanese efforts during the war saw some traitors turned into patriots overnight, and some people even claimed that they had even engaged in secret underground patriotic work, thus naturally avoiding punishment, prompting some newspapers at the time to ask: Why did the government not punish officials of the former Manchukuo regime in a timely manner, even allowing them to become members of the new institutions of the National Government in the North-East? As corruption was widespread throughout the entire process of surrender and reconciliation, in the chaos, anyone with a sign announcing they had authority could confiscate property that had belonged to the Japanese puppet regime and make it their own. Chiang Kai-shek touched on this issue in a telegram to the new mayor of Shanghai, Qian Dajun (1893–1982): "I have learned through reliable channels that military and political officers in the Nanjing-Shanghai and Beiping-Tianjin regions have been living luxuriously and indulging in whoring and gambling and, under the guise of party and military organs have occupied huge mansion complexes as offices; they indulge in criminal activities with impunity, and practice deception and extortion. The rumors emanating Shanghai and Beiping are the worst. I did not know whether such officials can consciously cease this behavior. On receiving this telegram, can you issue orders to strictly prohibit whoring and gambling, and close all offices illegally set up under the name of government departments. All cases of extortion or illegal appropriation of residential homes must be strictly prosecuted by the municipal authorities and also reported to me. There must be no favoritism shown to these criminals".[139] These various examples of incompetence and corruption caused the Kuomintang to lose popularity rapidly after the end of the Anti-Japanese War. The US State Department's "U.S. Relations with China" (White Paper) (1949) revealed the results of US observations. In a report to Washington on 20 November 1945, Wedemeyer wrote he "believed that the KMT's inaction had caused resentment among the local people in the takeover area, and even after

[139] *Chongqing Xinmin Bao*, 2 November 1945.

the end of the war against Japan, the National Government lost most of its support".[140]

The Allied entrustment to Chiang Kai-shek of acceptance of Japan's surrender and the signing of the Sino-Soviet Agreement between the Kuomintang and the Soviet Union gave the Kuomintang a political advantage. At the same time, given the Soviet Union's war against Japan, there would necessarily be new problems. Unlike Mao Zedong who was excited by the Soviet entry into the war against Japan, Chiang Kai-shek was "worried" by the Soviet handling of relations with Outer Mongolia "and the rise and fall of Eastern nations". Now, Chiang Kai-shek decided to immediately restart negotiations to resolve the CPC problem. Chiang issued three public invitations to Mao Zedong (14, 20, and 23 August) to negotiate in Chongqing, and in response to the first invitation, Mao asked Zhu De to inform Chiang that on the issue of the surrender handover, "you and your government did not satisfy the people and could not represent the vast numbers of people in the liberated areas of China, the conquered areas of China and all the anti-Japanese people's armed forces". Mao himself ignored Chiang. At this time, the CPC was still planning to seize major cities, on 20 August, Mao Zedong also telegrammed the Central China Bureau: "Your policy of launching the Shanghai Uprising is completely correct, and in the hope this policy is resolutely and thoroughly implemented policy, we are sending our army's strong forces into the city to assist. In other cities, if there are conditions for an uprising, you should follow suit".[141] This would suggest that, until then, Mao seemed to be uninterested in Chiang Kai-shek's invitation to negotiate.

Also on the 20th, Chiang Kai-shek extended a second invitation to Mao Zedong: "These surrender measures were stipulated by Allied headquarters for each war zone, as they were for the Chinese war zone, and so it was not appropriate for Zhu De, as one of the commanders-in-chief, to break with our shared commitment to the Allied forces.······ The battle is over, and there should be no longer an internal battle. We should profoundly remember our country's difficulties and the sufferings of our people, and make joint efforts to engage in construction. How we build

[140] *Zhongmei Guanxi Ziliao Huibian* (Compilation of Documents on China-U.S. Relations), Series 1, Beijing: Shijie Zhishi Chubanshe, 1957, p. 192.

[141] Zhonggong Zhongyang Wenxian Yanjiushi ed., *Mao Zedong Nianpu*, xia volume, Beijing: Renmin Chubanshe and Zhongyang Wenxian Chubanshe, 1993, p. 9.

our nation and enjoy the fruits of victory in the anti-Japanese war very much depends on your consistent fairness in formulating common plans that can benefit all and not just one party! This telegram of invitation should warrant your kind and favorable consideration".[142]

People were hoping that KMT–CPC negotiations would quickly bring peace throughout the country, and so a reply from Yan'an to the National Government's invitation to negotiate was eagerly awaited. On the 20th, the anxious historian Gu Jiegang (1893–1980) wrote:

> The Communist Party's arrogant expansionism sees it intentionally tearing the nation apart, wanting Japan to surrender to the CPC, wanting to elect its own representatives to the United Nations, and wanting the United States to stop Lend Lease to the Kuomintang government, all simply intended to split China immediately. The people's fresh victories have ended the killing, but civil war is imminent, even though all people of conscience hate the Communist Party as the true scourge of China. The people are disgruntled with the KMT, but today's China cannot be divided.[143]

On 24 August, the day after Chiang Kai-shek extended his third invitation to Mao Zedong, Hu Shi sent a message to Wang Shijie to telegraph to Mao Zedong, which was clearly related to the Chongqing negotiations:

> The night before last I spoke until late with Dong Biwu, and he expressed his belief that the leadership of the Communist Party of China today should examine the world situation, cherish China's path ahead, strive to forget the past, and look to the future, in the determination to renounce force and prepare to build a new Chinese political party that does not rely on military force. If you can have this determination, then our domestic eighteen-year long dispute might be immediately resolved, and your efforts for more than two years will not be completely destroyed by civil war.[144]

[142] *Zhongyang Ribao*, 21 August 1945, p. 2.

[143] *Gu Jiegang Riji*, v. 5, entry for 20 August 1945, Taipei: Lianjing Chuban Gongsi, 2007, p. 513.

[144] Zhongguo Shehui Kexueyuan Jindai Shi Yanjiusuo Zhonghua Minguo Shi Yanjiushi ed., *Hu Shi Laiwang Shuxin Xuan* (Selected Correspondence of Hu Shi), Hong Kong: Zhonghua Shuju, 1983, p. 26.

Indeed, the whole country paid great attention to the peace talks after the war, generally approving of Chiang Kai-shek's invitations, welcomed and anticipated in the newspapers and media. *Central Daily News* (Zhongyang Ribao) in an editorial titled "No More Civil Strife" on 21 August 1945 commented: "We would like to ask Mr. Mao to come to Chongqing, to demonstrate by this action that he has no intention of civil war and reassure the people of the whole country who yearn for peace and happiness!" *Dagong Bao* (21 August 1945) expressed the hope that Yan'an would respect the provisions of Allied headquarters and "look forward to Mr. Mao and be generous in this trip". In an editorial published on August 22nd, *Liberation Daily* in Yan'an refuted Chiang Kai-shek's invitation letter explaining its opposition to the handover arrangements, without regard for the KMT-CPC declarations and agreements at the beginning of the Anti-Japanese War. It divided the Chinese armies divided into those of the KMT and CPC, and rebuked Chiang Kai-shek's orders for the Japanese surrender and handover stating, "they clearly do not understand what kind of regulations or provisions a country's army can 'actively promote', given that a division must be 'on garrison standby'". The editorial did not carefully explain the essence of the provisions of Allied headquarters to hand over power to the National Government's Chairman Chiang, and the surrender of the Japanese Army was to proceed in accordance with the provisions of the Allied headquarters to follow the orders of Chairman Chiang. Chiang Kai-shek's second invitation and public opinion reminded Mao Zedong that he had changed his political strategy of treating the Kuomintang on an equal footing, and his tone and language changed markedly in his second reply. He wanted Zhou Enlai to go to Chongqing immediately, and used a suppliant term in referring to the meeting; the use of the term "People's Liberation Army" was also immediately stopped. This meant that Mao Zedong temporarily still regarded the Eighth Route Army and New Fourth Army as part of the Kuomintang's army, at least on the surface, and the only legitimate government to be that in Chongqing; he also shifted the focus of negotiations from coalition government to the arrangements regarding the liberated zones and armies.

On 23 August, Chiang Kai-shek extended the third invitation to Mao Zedong, who expressed his views on the future at a meeting of the Politburo of the Communist Party of China (CPC) Central Committee: "We are now largely travelling throughout the country on French roads, a country whose government is led by the bourgeoisie but in which the proletariat participate".[145] This should be seen as the basic bottom line of the Communist Party's trip to Chongqing, meaning that it is now inconvenient to mention "coalition government" and we must prepare to "participate in government". In fact, before and after the meeting on the 23rd, the Soviet Union also telegrammed the Communist Party of China to urge Mao to negotiate with the National government.[146] Stalin demanded that the Chinese Communist Party stop its armed operations. Mao was clearly aware that conditions were not yet ripe for the CPC's all-out confrontation with the KMT, and that the Soviet Union's views were an understandable tactic, the Soviet Union having already helped the Polish Communist "Party strategically take over the regime. Accompanied by Hurley, Mao and Zhou Enlai flew to Chongqing together on 28 August. Mao told reporters at Chongqing airport: "The pressing domestic political and military problems should be reasonably resolved on the basis of peace, democracy, and unity with a view to achieving national unity and building an independent, free and prosperous New China".[147]

Public opinion in Chinese society was generally concerned about the progress of the negotiations, and following Japan's surrender ending the war, maintaining peace was what most Chinese wanted at this time, a mood described vividly in an article by Zheng Zhenduo:

> Since Mr. Mao Zedong came to Chongqing and began negotiations; a day does not pass without our inquiring about the situation of the talks and feeling concerned about whether the talks are going smoothly. A rumor

[145] *Hu Qiaomu Huiyi Mao Zedong*, p. 404.

[146] Wang Shijie wrote in his diary: "Mao's surprise acceptance of the invitation to Chongqing may have been facilitated in part by the declaration of the Sino-Soviet Treaty on 14 August 1945, which guaranteed Soviet aid to the only government in China (in fact the Soviet Union secretly also the CPC to negotiate with the central government)". Ref: *Wang Shijie Riji*, 27 August 1945 entry.

In a 1949 White Paper issued by the State Department of the United States, it was stated that:

[147] "Mao's unexpected acceptance of the invitation to Chongqing may have been facilitated in part by the declaration of the Sino-Soviet Treaty on August 14, 1945, which guaranteed Soviet aid to the only government in China". Ref: *Zhongmei Guanxi Ziliao Huibian*, v. 1, p. 169.

Sichuan Daxue Malie-zhuyi Jiaoyanshi, Zhonggong Dangshi Keyanzu eds., *Chongqing Tanpan Ziliao Xuanbian* (An Anthology of Documents on the Chongqing Negotiations), 1979, pp. 4–5.

of the slightest dispute is enough to frighten us. A small act of provocation is enough to make us grit our teeth. We remain hopeful and open, as we anticipate and look forward to the success of these talks. The publication of the proceedings of the meetings gives us momentary relief, but we cannot put aside our serious concerns. How the relationship between the KMT and CPC can be satisfactorily resolved remains central to those concerns.[148]

While in Chongqing, Mao Zedong as a political strategy changed his attitude of refusing to negotiate with and cursing Chiang Kai-shek, as Chongqing's media noted: "Mao Zedong now describes Chiang Kai-shek as the chairman or as a gentleman, not a reactionary 'fascist dictator', and he also now speaks of the National government rather than 'Chiang Kai-shek's regime'".

On the first day of Mao's trip to Chongqing, *Liberation Daily* published the "Declaration of the CPC Central Committee on the Current Situation" to clarify the basic tone of the negotiations between the CPC and the Kuomintang, stating:

> The Communist Party of China believes that in this new historical period, the great tasks before our people are: consolidating domestic unity, ensuring domestic peace, realizing democracy and improving people's livelihoods to achieve national unity on the basis of peaceful democracy and unity, building an independent, free and prosperous new China, and cooperating with Britain, the United States, the Soviet Union and all their allies to consolidate lasting international peace.[149]

The Declaration regarded that it was now necessary to require the National Government to implement a number of measures immediately, the main provision being "recognition of the democratically elected government and anti-Japanese forces in the liberated areas of China, and the withdrawal of the armed forces that surround and attack the liberated areas". This meant that the army led and developed by the Chinese Communist Party during the Anti-Japanese War must have complete

[148] Zheng Zhenduo, "Record of the KMT-CPC Talks", *Minzhu* (Democracy), No. 2, 20 October 1945.

[149] Sichuan Daxue Malie-zhuyi Jiaoyanshi, Zhonggong Dangshi Keyanzu eds., *Chongqing Tanpan Ziliao Xuanbian* (An Anthology of Documents on the Chongqing Negotiations), 1979, p. 1.

legitimacy. Other claims included the designation of areas where the Eighth Route Army and the New Fourth Army could accept the surrender of the Japanese, recognition of the legal status of other political parties, the freedom of assembly, association, and publication, and the release of patriotic political prisoners, a total of six articles. In Chongqing, a Reuters reporter asked Mao: What kind of compromises or concessions does the central government have to make in order to meet the demands of the Chinese Communist Party? Mao's answer was in line with what was already indicated in the Declaration, but once again he made it clear that a democratic coalition government would eventually be formed. Mao promised: "In any case, the CPC will adhere to the policy of avoiding civil war".[150] On the 29th before the formal negotiations began, Chiang Kai-shek decided on three basic principles:

> (i) The restructuring of the Government outside the current legal system is not up for discussion, i.e., convening meetings of political parties to discuss the nature of the state, or organizing a coalition government. (ii) Negotiated issues cannot be resolved in stages or in part, and all issues must be resolved on the present occasion. (iii) Given all political decrees and military orders are unified, all issues must take as the center.[151]

The negotiations between the CPC, represented by Zhou Enlai and Wang Ruofei, and the KMT, represented by Zhang Qun, Zhang Zhizhong, Wang Shijie and Shao Lizi, went on for 43 days. On the face of it, the KMT and CPC on 10 October signed *Record of the Double Ten Talks*, and this taken together with the conversations between Chiang Kai-shek and Mao Zedong, was limited to the principles and demands of both sides, and the basic principles of peaceful nation-building, expressed as follows: It is unanimously agreed that "on the basis of peace, democracy, unity, and agreement, and under the leadership of Chairman Chiang, there will be long-term cooperation to resolutely avoid civil war, build an independent free and prosperous new China, and thoroughly implement the Three Principles of the People. The two sides also recognized that the political democratization, nationalization of the armed forces, and

[150] Sichuan Daxue Malie-zhuyi Jiaoyanshi, Zhonggong Dangshi Keyanzu eds., *Chongqing Tanpan Ziliao Xuanbian* (An Anthology of Documents on the Chongqing Negotiations), 1979, p. 8.

[151] *Jiang Jieshi Riji*, entry for 29 August 1945.

the equality and legitimacy of political parties advocated by Chairman Chiang represent the necessary path to achieving a peaceful nation". On the issue of political democratization: "It is agreed that as soon as possible the period of political tutelage will be concluded and constitutional government implemented, with necessary preliminary steps taken by the National Government to convene the political consultative conference to which representatives of all political parties and prominent members of society will be invited to negotiate the national situation, discuss the peaceful nation-building program, and convene the National Congress to address all issues". *Record of the Double Ten Talks* clearly outlined the National Congress, people's freedoms, the legitimacy of different political parties, the secret services, the release of political prisoners, local self-government, the nationalization of the armed forces, local governments in the liberated areas, the issues of national traitors and Japanese sympathizers, and the protocol of the surrender. For example, it stated: "On the issue of the surrender, the CPC has proposed to rezone the surrendered areas and participate in the work of the handover. The Government has indicated that it will take part in the handover and will give every consideration to the work after receiving orders from the center".[152] The negotiations involved complex historical factors (such as the realities of "legal unity" and "party rule" insisted on by the KMT) and changes in the organizational structure of the regime (e.g., the nationalization of the armed forces), while the CPC focused on the future administrative affiliation of the liberated areas and whether their army overlapped with their liberated areas. The KMT suspected that the CPC was staking out future fiefs. Zhang Qun said, "we can only have one national army, not provincial armies". Given that the CPC felt that based on the KMT's one-party rule it was difficult for the KMT to represent the country, the CPC was unable to entrust its military and its regime to a one-party government. As a result, both sides adopted an ambiguous attitude towards the liberated areas, in what was seen as a "temporary status quo" (Zhou Enlai) or a "temporary approach" (Zhang Qun). In any case, the signing of the Double Ten Agreement meant that the Kuomintang further recognized the legitimacy of the Communist Party, which laid a broad foundation for the Communist Party's subsequent political advancement.

[152] *Record of the Double Ten Talks* was signed by Wang Shijie, Zhang Qun, Zhang Zhizhong, Shao Lizi, Zhou Enlai, and Wang Ruofei. It was also published in *Liberation Daily* on 12 October 1945. Ref: *Chongqing Tanpan Ziliao Xuanbian*, pp. 11–15.

Mao Zedong's words and actions in Chongqing showed flexibility; he spoke to the Chinese and foreign media, and his language at a government reception was clear and precise: "Recalling the anti-Japanese War, it was an extremely difficult time, but because of the concerted efforts of the whole country, this has now been safely passed, and Chairman Chiang's invitation to the CPC to come to Chongqing to discuss the national situation is greatly appreciated. The future will be a new era of peaceful development and nation-building, and it is necessary to unite and resolutely avoid civil war. Any other approach would be wrong. As a result, all parties should, under the above-mentioned principles, unite and thoroughly implement the Three Principles of the People in order to build a modern New China".[153] Mao Zedong even enthusiastically shouted out at a reception for him hosted by Zhang Zhizhong: "Long live Chairman Chiang!".

In fact, the Democratic League felt there was something untoward about the discussions between the two sides on the regime and the army, and on 18 September Zhang Lan (1872–1955) published an open letter to Chiang Kai-shek and Mao Zedong, criticizing both the CPC and the KMT:

> If democracy is something decided on by the people, isn't there something frightening about saying that "democracy must first be guaranteed by force"? If "unity must depend for its maintenance on military force", then is that not a short-sighted view of unity?[154]

On 19 October, the Democratic League issued a declaration at the National Interim Assembly, stressing that "a democratic coalition government is the only path to peace and unity in the country at present". Indeed, the Chongqing negotiations did not give too much joy to the centrists, and in the eyes of some democrats the Chongqing negotiations were limited to the interests of the two parties, the KMT and CPC, and provided nothing for other parties; because there was no real discussion of the issue of the coalition government, the negotiations were seen as a failure. Jiang Yuntian (1903–1994) of the Democratic Socialist Party told Mao Zedong, "The issues you discussed all failed, and I regret it! But from the people's point of view, even if the talks were successful, they

[153] Ref: *Chongqing Tanpan Ziliao Xuanbian*, 1979, pp. 6–7.
[154] Ref: *Chongqing Tanpan Ziliao Xuanbian*, 1983, p. 167.

would have been a real failure". In response to the between the KMT and CPC on the relative sizes of their military forces, he said this could evolve into "a domestic arms race".[155] In any case, the KMT ultimately refused to allow the CPC to legally unify the liberated areas under the political decrees and military orders of the National Government. The two sides in the negotiations had completely different starting points, and their back-and-forth language was simply a political contest, as Mao Zedong instructed on his return to Yan'an on 12 October: "It is an unshakeable principle that our armies in the liberated areas must hang onto every single gun and bullet".[156] For Chiang Kai-shek, the paramount problem to resolve was the military problem.[157] Later history proved that, on the surface, the two parties were divided on the question of whether the military should be nationalized or whether political democracy should come first, but in fact this was a struggle between both sides for absolute control of state power.

Although the Chongqing talks still left hope for peace, it was clear that the conflict between the KMT and CPC would not stop. When Mao Zedong returned to Yan'an, he told comrades in the CPC that the agreement we reached is "just words on paper". On the following day, the name of the Eighth Route Army was changed to the Northeast Volunteer Army. Hurley left Chongqing on September 22nd to report to Truman with satisfaction that the two-party negotiations had gone well, and in fact, Chiang Kai-shek and Mao Zedong, who had a political relationship of more than two decades, had no hope of the negotiations reaching a final outcome, because the latter's real goal was seizing power. On the day Mao Zedong and Zhou Enlai flew to Chongqing, Zhu De told a team in Yan'an preparing to travel to the Northeast that Chiang Kai-shek's troops were mostly in the south, and it would take them half a year to

155 However, Mao Zedong told the other side: "Honestly, without our hundreds of thousands of broken guns, we certainly could not survive, but none of you paid any attention". Ref: Jiang Yuntian, *Zhongguo Jindaishi Zhuanzhedian* (The Turning Point in China's Modern History), Hong Kong: Xianggang Youlian Chuban Gongsi, 1976, quoted in Deng Ye, op. cit., p. 208.

156 *Mao Zedong Nianpu* (*xia* volume), entry for 12 October 1945.

157 Chiang Kai-shek's bottom line was included in his diary entry of August 28th: "Mao Zedong's remained true to his original policy after coming to Chongqing. Political and military matters should be resolved as a whole; I am extremely tolerant of his political demands, but when they are strictly united with his military plans, they leave little room for maneuver".

reach Northeast China, so the Chinese Communist army should occupy the Northeast as soon as possible. On the following day, Liu Shaoqi also confidently issued instructions, urging CPC cadres and troops to leave as soon as possible for the three Northeastern provinces, assuring them "the Soviet Union will adopt a laissez-faire attitude and show us great sympathy".[158] In August, when the Chongqing talks had begun, the Central Committee of the CPC issued a "notice" to its forces to continue their offensive:

> In North China, we must also strive, strive to take all that we possibly can. Over the past two weeks, our army has regained fifty-nine cities or towns and villages of various size, and together with what we previously held, we now have a total of 175 cities and towns, which represents a great victory. In North China, we have recovered Weihaiwei, Yantai, Longkou, Yidu, Zichuan, Yangliuqing, Bikeqi, Bo'ai, Zhangjiakou, Jining, Fengzhen, and other places, and our armies are victorious in North China. Together with the Soviet and Mongolian armies that have arrived at the Great Wall, our Party will be in an advantageous position. In the immediate future we should continue our offensive, with a view to capturing as many of these routes as possible: the Beiping-Baotou railroad, the northern section of the Datong-Huayin railroad, as well as the Taiyuan-Shijiazhuang, Dezhou-Shijiazhuang, Baigui-Jincheng, and Dao-Qing routes, as well as cutting the Beiping-Shenyang, Beiping-Hankou, Tianjin-Nanjing, Qingdao-Jinan, Longhai (Lianyungang to Lanzhou), and Shanghai-Nanjing rail routes.We will take control of all we can, disregarding whether this is only temporary. At the same time, we must use all necessary forces to occupy as many villages, towns and cities as possible.

On 11 September, the Central Committee of the CPC telegrammed the Shandong Branch: "In order to take advantage of this time when the Kuomintang and its army have not yet reached the Northeast (estimated to not be a short period of time), to develop our strength rapidly, and strive to consolidate our position in the Northeast, the Central Committee has resolved to draw four divisions and twelve regiments from Shandong totaling 25,000 to 30,000 people and ship them across to the Northeast where they will be distributed for action, and to send Xiao Hua

158 *Zhonggong Dangshi Ziliao* (Documents on the History of the Communist Party of China), no. 16, p. 134.

to command them".[159] This should be seen in light of the agreement reached between Malinovsky and the CPC in Yan'an that month, whereby the Soviet troops would hand over Shenyang, Changchun, Harbin, and other large northeastern cities to the KMT government, while helping the Communists infiltrate other areas and regions of the Northeast. Such military actions were in sharp contrast to the role of the 8th Route Army described by the CPC negotiators in Chongqing.[160] In fact, on 14 September Yan'an decided to focus its strategy on the Northeast in order to "create a connective strategic base" (as suggested by Huang Kecheng [1902–1986]). On the 17th, Liu Shaoqi called Mao Zedong in Chongqing to suggest that the Communist Party of China implement the strategic policy of "developing northwards and defending southwards". On 3 October, the Soviet general told the Northeast Bureau of the CPC that its strategic approach of trying to control the entire Northeast was correct. Considering that this approach conflicted with the Sino-Soviet Treaty, Mao Zedong told the Party: "What we are doing in the Northeast we cannot discuss".[161] On 11 October, Mao flew back to Yan'an from Chongqing, and on the 13th gave the order for a full-scale offensive. On the 15th, Liu Shaoqi telegrammed the Central Bureau: "The focus of our operations in the liberated areas of central China should be on the railway lines, and the main purpose of the operation should be to eliminate and stop the northern advance of the [KMT] army".[162] On the 19th, Mao Zedong asked Chen Yi and Li Yu (1906–1986) of Shandong

[159] Liao-Shen Battle Memorial Museum ed., *Liao-Shen Juezhan* (The Decisive Liao-Shen Battle), v. 1, Renmin Chubanshe, 1992, p. 207.

[160] The following record appears in an interview by an Associated Press reporter: "Mao and Zhou insisted that the Communist Party was at present trying to avoid clashes with the Kuomintang forces. He also said that the Communist Party had retreated from many regions to avoid the danger of conflict. The Communists continued to fight the troops of the Japanese sympathizers, who 'still attack us' and have retaken many cities". Ref: Sichuan Daxue Malie-zhuyi Jiaoyanshi, Zhonggong Dangshi Keyanzu eds., *Chongqing Tanpan Ziliao Xuanbian* (An Anthology of Documents on the Chongqing Negotiations), 1979, p. 6. In fact, in some places the Japanese and puppet troops resisted surrendering to the Chinese Communist armies in accordance with Chiang Kai-shek's orders for the handover, and would only surrender to the Kuomintang army.

[161] Mao Zedong, "Kangzhan shengli sange yue lai de jushi he jinhou ruogan gongzuo fangzhen" (The situation in the three months since the victory of the War of Resistance and several future work principles), 12 November 1945, *Mao Zedong Wenji*, v. 4, Beijing: Renmin Chubanshe, 1996, p. 74.

[162] *Liu Shaoqi Nianpu*, v. 1, p. 514.

to "occupy a section of the railway in appropriate areas between Xuzhou and Jinan and expand the area we occupy to the north and south, and then choose a time to destroy one or two divisions of Chiang's army and let the good battle begin".[163] As a result of the Battle of Jin-Pu Line (Zouxian and Tengxian), the CPC won control of more than 200 kilometers of railways, eliminated more than 28,000 national troops, and cut off the northward passage of KMT troops to take over the northeast. On the 24th, the Chinese Communist Army in Zixian and Handan blocked the KMT's 40th Army, 30th Army and New Eighth Army, and on the 30th, the New 8th Army's commander Gao Shuxun (1897–1972) surrendered to the Communists, while on 2 November, the 40th Army's commander Ma Fawu (1894–1992) was captured. On the 24th, Fu Zuoyi (1895–1974), commander of the 12th War Zone of the National Army, wrote: "We continued to retreat for hundreds of *li*, from Fengzhen, Jining, Liangcheng, Wuchuan, Helin, and Taolin, all the way back to Sui-Bao line, and the Communist Army raced ahead, and even had the isolated cities of Zhangjiakou and Baotou surrounded by regiments, where they launched fierce attacks. This marked the country's unanimous opposition to the 'civil war'". In an open telegram to Mao Zedong, Fu Zuoyi appealed to Mao Zedong: "I dare to state categorically that I absolutely never complied with any order from Chairman Chiang to attack your army", and "if your army subsequently presses in on us, leaving us no alternative but to fight, then full responsibility for the civil war should be yours, so I hope that you are cautious".[164] Although Fu Zuoyi stopped the CPC's attack on the Ping-Sui railroad, by this time the CPC largely controlled most of the provinces of Chahar, Jehol, Hebei, Shandong and Shanxi in northern China, and the KMT could only take a small number of large and medium-sized cities. The fighting between the Communists and the KMT caused great anxiety, and Chu Anping (1909–1966), who observed and criticized both the Kuomintang and the Communist Party, wrote in issue no. 2 of his widely read *Keguan* (Objectivity), dated 17 November 1945:

[163] *Mao Zedong Junshi Wenji*, v. 3, Beijing: Junshi Kexue Chubanshe and Zhongyang Wenxian Chubanshe, 1993, p. 65.

[164] *Central Daily*, 26 October 1945, p. 2. *Kangzhan Shiliao Chugao* (First Draft of Documents of the Anti-Japanese War), v. 7, "Zhanhou Zhongguo, II" (Post-War China, II), p. 294. This book is quoted in Li Yunhan, op. cit., p. 508, and in Deng Ye, op. cit., p. 232.

> The main hope of ending the civil war now depends on the sense of responsibility of the two parties towards the people. It is obvious that the people are opposed to civil war, and today's China can no longer afford civil war, nor do international trends allow us to conduct another civil war. The CPC cannot indulge in such actions to win future political power, disregarding public opinion and ignoring the future of the country. The KMT, which has been in power for 20 years, is more responsible than others in the chaos the country now faces.[165]

Informed voices in the media had little effect on the CPC, and for the KMT, relations with the Soviet Union were in a quandary.

As stipulated in the Sino-Soviet treaty, the Soviet army would begin to withdraw from the northeast in November, so the seriousness and intensity of the situation in the Northeast was heightened. On 23 October, Mao Zedong instructed the Northeast Bureau to make every effort to occupy the entire Northeast. On the 25th, the Northeast Bureau called Yan'an and informed them that the Soviet army wanted the Chinese Communist army to "remain as masters", and that "until the 15th of the following month, if the KMT army attacks us, the Soviet army will cooperate with us in fighting back", adding that "apart from one-fifth of factories that [the Soviets] will requisition, the rest will be handed over to us".

On the 28th, Mao Zedong telegrammed the Northeast Bureau again: "The key to all the problems in the Northeast is to stop Chiang from successfully transporting his troops there and coming the handover in the coming two months, and we cannot be successful in this without the assistance of the Soviets".[166]

As of 31 October, the KMT forces had taken over four important cities in northern China: Beiping, Tianjin, Qingdao, and Jinan. However, the National Government faced difficulties in the Northeast handover. Given that the Ping-Han, Jin-Pu and Bei-Ning railways had all been cut by the Communists, the KMT troops had to enter the Northeast by sea. Although the United States agreed to support with transport ships, the Soviet Union, fearing that if the U.S. successfully helped the government

165 Zhang Xinying ed., *Chu Anping Wenji*, *xia* volume, Dongfang Chuban Zhongxin, 1998, p. 14.

166 On the 29th, Peng Zhen of the Northeast Bureau replied to Mao: "Your opinion has been formally relayed to the friendly party [i.e. Soviet army]". *Peng Zhen Nianpu*, vol. 1, p. 304.

forces take over the Northeast it would then go on to stymie Soviet interests in the Northeast, invoking the stipulation in the Sino-Soviet Treaty that the port of Dalian was a commercial, not a military, port, refused to allow government forces to land in Dalian. It was eventually agreed that the government forces could land at Huludao and Yingkou, but the Soviets did not provide any security guarantee that the Chinese Communist army could attack the Kuomintang forces. Indeed, on the verge of landing, the government forces were told by the Chinese Communist army not to land, landing fruitless. The United States contingent carrying the government troops was by regulation not allowed to participate in China's internal affairs and so it could not use military force to press the matter. It was delayed until mid-November, when government forces finally landed from Qinhuangdao, significantly delaying the handover. In fact, the Soviets in the Northeast were effective in helping the Communist Party seize local power. Soviet control of Lüda (Dalian) allowed the Communist Party to establish its own regime and gain the protection of the Soviet army so that the National Government never regained control and established administrative power in the city after the Anti-Japanese War, while the Japanese weapons and materials were handed over to the CPC to strengthen its armed forces. By the end of 1945, the Soviets had handed over to the Communist Party of China batches of weapons amounting to more than a quarter of the equipment needed to arm their 800,000 troops. Khrushchev later recalled: "We made an agreement with the allies first that we had no right to hand them over to any of the belligerent groups in China. Therefore, in handing over these weapons to Mao, we did not want to create the impression that we were violating our commitments. So, we transported the weapons to a certain place, and the Maoists 'stole' them to arm their troops".[167]

In view of the Soviet army's lack of cooperation with the National Government's takeover of the Northeast, Chiang Kai-shek adjusted his strategy and proposed a policy "first pacifying China within the Great Wall, then planning beyond it". On 15 November, Chongqing's Ministry of Foreign Affairs sent a note to the Soviet Embassy in China informing them that China had decided to withdraw its Changchun Northeast camp and shelve the Northeast issue, thereby internationalizing the Northeast

[167] Khrushchev: Khrushchev's Memoirs (Volume III) Social Science Literature Press, 2007 edition, p. 2244.

handover issue.[168] On the 17th, the Soviet Union sent a note to China stating that the Soviet Command strictly abided by the Sino-Soviet Treaty, and was not providing the Chinese Communist Army with help. The note also proposed: "If the Chinese government now wants the Soviet withdrawal from the three eastern provinces to be delayed for a certain period of time, then the Soviet government can delay its troops for a month".[169] On the 18th, Chiang Kai-shek convened a meeting to determine the extension of the stay Soviet army until 3 January 1946, before withdrawing from Northeast China, and in early December, the Soviet army proposed to extend the time to February 1st. At the same time, the Soviet army temporarily maintained its distance from the Chinese Communist Army.[170] It also instructed the Chinese Communist Army to withdraw from Shenyang, Changchun, and Harbin. In short, Stalin did not want to provoke a strong American intervention because of the deep dissatisfaction of China's government. The CPC Central Committee also informed the Northeast Bureau to adjust its strategy: "Our attempt to monopolize the Northeast, especially all the big cities in the region, is now impossible. Because the Soviet Union wants to take care of relations with the United States, it cannot completely deny Chiang's entry into the Northeast and takeover of the big cities".[171]

[168] Zhang Jia'ao wrote in his diary: "It is assumed that Chairman Chiang intended to withdraw the camp as a counter-offensive against the Soviet strategy of obstructing the handover and secretly assisting the 8th Route Army, and to test their true attitude". Ref: Yao Songling ed., *Zhang Gongquan Xiansheng Nianpu*, v. 1, Taipei: Chuanji Wenxue Chubanshe, 1982, p. 554.

[169] Zhu Huiqi, *Zhonghua Minguo Shishi Jiyao*, 17 November 1945.

[170] On 11 November, the Northeast Bureau of the Communist Party of China telegrammed Yan'an: "Yesterday, our friends suddenly informed Chen Yun that the Soviet side had allowed the KMT airlift troops to the major cities five days before the Soviet withdrawal, and did not allow us to clash with the KMT air forces during those five days... If we clash with the KMT airlift forces within those five days, then the Soviet side can only disarm us. Our friends have repeatedly argued that Moscow's interests should be the highest priority of Communists around the world". Ref: *Peng Zhen Nianpu*, v. 1, p. 315.

[171] "Zhonggong Zhongyang guanyu Dongbei gongzuo fangzhen yu renwu gei Dongbei-ju de zhishi" (Instructions of the CPC Central Committee on the Work Guidelines and Tasks in the Northeast To the Northeast Bureau), 9 December 1945, in Zhonggong Zhongyang Dang'anguan (Archives of the CPC Central Committee) ed., Zhonggong Wenjian Xuanji (Anthology of Documents of the CPC), v. 15, Beijing: Zhonggong Zhongyang Dangxiao Chubanshe (Central Party School Of the CPC Central Committee Press), 1991, pp. 465–466.

After the return of the Government's Northeast camp (office) to Changchun on 4 December, Malinowski, who was regarded as "lacking any trace of tenderness and compassion" by US diplomats in Chongqing, urged establishing economic cooperation in the Northeast, specifically establishing economic cooperation with the Chinese side in confiscating Japanese enterprises described as "war trophies".[172] On the 7th, Zhang Jia'ao told Slatkovski to wait until the handover of the Northeast has been completed before discussing economic cooperation, and that the proposal had already been passed on to Malinovsky. After rejecting it, the Soviet army told the KMT army commanded by Du Yuming that until the economic cooperation agreement was signed it was not permitted to travel to Heishan and Fuxin, as well as to Shenyang, Zhangwu, Chifeng or Duolun. By the end of December, when discussions between the two sides had proved fruitless, Chiang Kai-shek arranged for his son Chiang Ching-kuo to travel to Moscow to discuss with Stalin the issues of ownership of Japanese corporate assets and economic cooperation. However, Stalin, apart from providing an abstract expression of cooperation between China, the United States, and the Soviet Union, did not want the US military to enter the Northeast and stated that the Soviet Union was entitled to "war trophies" in the Northeast, so he did not meet the aspirations of the National government, Although Changchun, Shenyang, and Harbin, as well as cities in the Liaobei, Songjiang, and Nenjiang areas were taken over by the KMT, by the end of January of the following year, Liaoyang, Benxi, Anshan, Haicheng, Changwu, Tonghua, and other cities had been handed by the Soviet army to the Chinese Communist armies. On 1 February, Malinovsky threatened Zhang Jia'ao, saying that if an agreement on economic cooperation could not be reached, industries would shut down and continue to be destroyed, and

[172] On 27 October, Zhang Jia'ao made his first contact with Slatkov, an economic adviser to the Soviet Army. Slatkov asked Zhang about the KMT government's economic policy in the Northeast. But on the 24th, the Soviet Army has already negotiated with the former Manchuria Heavy Industries Co. Ltd. President Takasaki Tatsunosuke (1885–1964) and former Manchuria Electric Power Co., Ltd. Chairman Tairajima Toshio for the transfer of Japanese assets to the Soviet Union and signed an agreement on the 29th and 30th without the knowledge of the Chinese side. On 13 November, Zhang Jia'ao, upon learning of the agreement, wrote: "One of the important reasons for the Soviets' attention to and involvement in Manchuria's industrial and mining industry was to exclude the invasion of American forces and block the transport of our military". Ref: Yao Songling ed., op. cit., v. 1, p. 551.

order in the Northeast would never be restored. The subsequent situation was chaotic and complex: on 11 February the US government sent a note, refusing to recognize Japanese companies in the Northeast as "trophies" and affirming that the United States would also be involved in economic cooperation in the Northeast. Reiterating the policy of opening up to China and having secured its interests, the Soviet army retreated amid popular protests by Chinese students and international pressure, and the fighting between the KMT and CPC became increasingly intense, and economic cooperation was no longer an issue. But the Soviet army nevertheless succeeded in taking $2 billion worth of industrial wealth from the Northeast.[173]

Frank Hurley left Chongqing on 22 September after receiving a personal guarantee from Chiang Kai-shek that Mao Zedong's security would be protected. At the end of November, he resigned as ambassador to China; Yan'an broadcasted the news, saying the resignation of "the instigator of China's civil war" was a victory for the American people. By this time, Truman's basic policy was clear: to support Chiang Kai-shek, but not to become involved in the Chinese civil war and fight for Chiang Kai-shek. On 18 December 1945, when George C. Marshall, the President's special envoy to China, was appointed by Truman, he saw no objection in principle to the previous bipartisan views, such as an immediate end to the civil war, and the agreement to convene a political consultative meeting and nationalize the military. The core issue for the moment was a ceasefire under fair conditions, so Marshall drew up a draft armistice that would call for a ceasefire, which necessitated that Chiang Kai-shek alter his strategy of first focusing on securing territory within the Great Wall before turning his attention to the Northeast. In fact, the United States wanted him to intervene in the Northeast. The US, the KMT and the CPC have formed a three-man group, with the National Government represented by Zheng Jiemin, the CPC by Ye

[173] According to *Report on the Investigation of Northeast Industrial Losses during the Occupation by the Soviet Army*, issued in February 1947 by the Northeast Industrial Association and the Northeast Immigrant Japanese Liaison Office, Northeast industry lost US$1,236 million, together with incalculable amounts that would yield an overall total of not less than US$2 billion. Of this total, $220 million was lost in electricity, $204 million in steel, $194 million on railways and $159 million in machinery. "Northeast industry suffered losses of about $2 billion during the Soviet occupation", a US State Department report said.

Jianying, and the United States by Henry A Byroade overseeing the ceasefire. On 10 January Chiang Kai-shek and Mao Zedong issued separate ceasefire orders, raising a glimmer of hope for peace. During the ceasefire, the political consultations agreed to by the two sides in advance did take place.

As early as 15 September 1944, while proposing the concept of a coalition government, Lin Boqu (1886–1960) suggested convening a conference of political parties. During the negotiations between the KMT and CPC in February 1945, Wang Shijie proposed to change its name to the "Political Advisory Conference" in order to increase the number of non-party participants. During the Chongqing negotiations, Zhang Zhizhong proposed to convene a "political consultative meeting" recognized by both the KMT and CPC. According to the minutes of the Chongqing talks, the Political Consultative Conference would discuss the peaceful establishment of the country, the National Assembly, and the liberated areas. Given that the Political Consultative Conference meeting would be convened after the National Congress and the convening of the National Congress will signify the move from "tutelary rule" to "constitutional government", for the KMT, the form of a one-party dictatorship would completely disappear, and for the CPC, it meant that the liberated region regimes and the army would lose the basis for their continued existence. For third-party forces such as the Democratic Alliance, there will be an opportunity to participate in politics, and the Democratic League was so eager to meet that it urged "the government to formally convene a political consultative meeting within ten days".[174] Given that the KMT's sixth national congress had already announced the convening of the National Congress on 12 November, the CPC was trying to drag the Political Consultative Conference as far as possible to the time of the National Congress, so that the National Congress could not be held as scheduled. Yan'an instructed Zhou Enlai in Chongqing: "Avoid political meetings held under government coercion before November 12 and dragging them out (without revealing one is doing so) is fine".[175]

However, Truman's statement on China on 15 December appears to have inspired the CPC's strategy of using the Political Consultative

174 。*Zhongguo Minzhu Tongmeng Lishi Wenxian* (Historical Documents of the Chinese Democratic League), p. 101.

175 *Cong Yan'an dao Beijing* (From Yan'an to Beijing), Zhongyang Wenxian Chubanshe, 1993, p. 33.

COnference to launch a political offensive against the KMT. Truman's statement contained the following passage of relevance to the KMT and CPC:

> The United States and other United Nations countries recognize the current National Government of the Republic of China as the only legitimate government of China.
>
> The United States is well aware that the current National Government is a one-party government and believes that if the foundation of this government is expanded to accommodate other political parties in the country, it will push forward China's reform of peace, unity and democracy. The United States therefore strongly advocates that representatives of the major political parties in China hold national meetings to agree on ways to give them fair and effective representation within the National Government of China. The United States Government believes that this would require a revision of the one-party system of discipline established by Dr. Sun Yixian, the father of the Republic of China, as a temporary means of progressing towards democracy.
>
> The existence of autonomous armies, such as the Communist army, is incompatible with China's political unity and in fact prevents it from being achieved.[176]

The CPC's understanding of Truman's statement was that the United States would not directly participate in China's civil war and would not assist Chiang Kai-shek in reunifying China by force. "We demand that the upcoming political consultative meeting to be convened in Chongqing carry out the mandate of the meeting of representatives of all parties to end one-party dictatorship and restructure the national government".[177]

The meeting which ran for more than 20 days (10–31 January) decided that the National Government Council was the highest body of the state and that the National Government Council would be composed of 40 members, half of whom were to be nominated by the Kuomintang and the other half by the CPC and the other parties.[178] Five main topics

[176] *Liberation Daily*, 18 December 1945, p. 1.

[177] Idem.

[178] There were 38 participants: 8 KMT members, 7 from the CPC, 9 from the Democratic League, 5 from the Youth Party, and 9 prominent community members.

were discussed at the meeting: the restructuring of the Government, questions of executive rules, military questions, the National Convention, and the draft constitution, which were discussed in five corresponding groups. Because of the wide range of issues involved, there were too many issues on the agenda for discussion, ranging from the government, the army, legislative restructuring, the ruling party not being able to use state budget finances, schools abolishing KMT party education, trade monopolies and even the discussion of Sun Yat-sen's Three Principles of the People. In fact, all the issues ultimately called for the abolition of the KMT's one-party system of tutelary politics, an issue that intellectuals had been discussing ever since the 1920s. Once again, the Democratic League expressed a third-party stance, as Shi Fuliang (1898–1970) wrote:

> Now although the KMT army is called the nation's army and the CPC army is called the people's army, as we see it, both are the party armies, that is party-controlled armies. The army of the CPC cannot be handed over to the KMT, just as the KMT army cannot be handed over to the CPC.…… For nationalization of the army to occur, the KMT and CPC must simultaneously hand over to their armies to the state, and the country must become the people's state, not a country run by a single party or individual.[179]

Chiang Kai-shek set the tone for the meeting at the opening, saying the government was ready to implement popular freedoms (freedom of the individual, belief, expression, publishing, assembly, and association). He said that the existing laws should be repealed or amended in accordance with this principle, that political parties be allowed to operate legitimately within the scope of the law, that local self-government be implemented, and political prisoners released, except those who are national traitors and or present a danger to the republic. These issues had been previously raised, called for, and demanded to be addressed by the CPC and other political parties.

On the issue of restructuring the government, Chen Lifu defended the one-party system, saying that "the KMT's party rule emulates the Soviet Union", to which Lu Dingyi (1906–1996) retorted: "In the Soviet Union not everything was organized by the party, but by the people led by the party. In China, a one-party dictatorship is not possible, and

[179] Shi Fuliang, "Wode Da'an" (My Reply), *Xinhua Ribao*, 1 January 1946, p. 5.

China should only implement multi-party politics".[180] On the issue of the platform for peaceful national construction, the KMT representative Wu Tiecheng (1888–1953) stressed that the platform should be based on the original founding platform of the Republic of China, the policy platform adopted by the KMT's sixth plenary session, and the policy adopted by the National People's Political Assembly in 1946, but especially the platform for the anti-Japanese war. In its draft platform for the establishment of a nation at peace, the Communist Party of China makes it clear that: "The foundation of the current national government must be expanded immediately and reconstituted to accommodate anti-Japanese democrats and non-partisan democrats throughout the country and unite the nation with an interim united national government". Truman's statement was clearly a benchmark for Marshall, who submitted a hand-crafted draft law on the organization of the interim government of the Republic of China, replacing the Supreme Council of Defense with a Provisional State Council, comprising nine members of the Kuomintang, six members of the Communist Party, one member from the Democratic Alliance, one from the Youth Party, and three with non-partisan members. Chiang appointed the presidents of the various divisions of government (Yuan) and heads of ministries, 50% being Kuomintang, 30% Communist Party, and the other parties and independents making up the rest. Chiang Kai-shek was angry and worried, fearing that the plan was a proposal that the Chinese Communist Party would be afraid to come up with: "At the political consultative conference, the Communist Party was outspoken and forceful, and Marshall was alienated from the national conditions of our country. John K. Fairbank (Fei Zhengqing), the press director of the U.S. Embassy, is a left-winger in favor of the Communist Party, and there is a possibility of a repeat of the unfortunate events of the previous year".[181]

The discussions in the Military Group were intense and repetitive. The Youth Party's proposal called for "the separation of the military and the political party [i.e. KMT] so as not to turn political disputes into military disputes"; The Democratic Alliance's proposal called for "active-duty military personnel to be removed from the party [i.e. KMT]"; Zhou

[180] *Zhengzhi Xieshang Huiyi Jishi*, v. 1, pp. 413–415.

[181] Qin Xiaoyi ed., *Zongtong Jiang Gong Dashi Changbian*, v. 6-I, Taipei: Zongzheng Wenjiao Jijinhuii, 2003, pp. 24–26.

speaking on behalf of the CPC said, "China's military system today should be modelled on the reforms of democratic countries, especially the U.S".[182] However, both the CPC and KMT were vague about the issue of soldiers leaving their political parties, and although the small working group adopted the view that active-duty soldiers leave their political parties, on the following day Zhou Enlai and Shao Lizi both overthrew the decision.[183] On the question of the composition of the National Convention, the KMT used the 1936 National Assembly election as its basis, but the CPC, Democratic League and Youth Party did not agree, after which Wang Yunwu (1898–1979) proposed a compromise. As for the constitution, the core issue was whether there would be a presidential system or cabinet system, and in the discussions, Zhang Junmai (1887–1969) proposed allowing the Executive Yuan (Cabinet) take responsibility for the Legislative Yuan (Congress), the legislature could overthrow the cabinet, and if the Executive Yuan was not satisfied with the Legislative Yuan, the President could be asked to dissolve the Legislative Yuan, and through a general election produce a new Legislative Yuan. Such a design is also conducive to the establishment of local government and the confirmation of power, and Zhang's views were accepted by the majority. As a result, the Political Consultative Conference passed five panel motions to "close on an exciting note of extreme harmony" (Chiang Kai-shek's

[182] "Zhou Enlai's views on the nationalization of the armed forces", *Xinhua Daily*, 17 January 1946, p. 2.

[183] Liang Shuming records:

At the military panel meeting, I asked active-duty military personnel to abandon their party affiliations the party, regardless of whether any party should have members in the military. I put a lot of effort into explaining why it was necessary to do so, and my motion was actually passed that at the panel meeting on 21 January. At the time of passage, Mr. Shao Lizi said, "Mr. Liang means very well but, in fact, it can't be done". I banged the table and said, "Maybe it can't be done but I'm going to do it". I didn't realize that the next day, 22 January, it was overturned. When this decision was adopted on the 21st, it was because the representative of the CPC Lu Dingyi was present, and he did not oppose the meeting. On that day, the government also released Liao Chengzhi from prison, and Zhou Enlai on behalf of the CPC went to pick him up, so Zhou was also temporarily not present. The next day, Zhou Enlai entered the meeting and said: "Yesterday what passed does not count. We cannot allow our soldiers to leave the party, so yesterday's decision cannot count". Lu Ding was at this time red with embarrassment and could not utter a word. Shao Lizi said to me, "What do you think, or was I right?" Zhou and Shao were in agreement, so I could see it was pointless to argue. I had to agree with them and as a result my motion was overturned". Ref: *Liang Shuming Quanji*, v. 6, p. 918.

closing remarks). Zhou Enlai said at the closing ceremony that the political consultative conference "opened up a path for democracy-building in Chinese politics".[184]

However, some members of the Kuomintang and representatives of the old National Congress were very dissatisfied with the political consultative conference, and on 22 January Chen Guofu (1892–1951), the director of the third chamber, wrote to Chiang Kai-shek: "The political consultative conference will not have a good outcome. In any case, the CPC has benefited, and our Party has suffered.…… If China implements multi-party politics, it is quite possible to make mistakes at a time when the party, the government and the military are not sound. Please note we are at a dangerous juncture and we should follow a different course".[185] On 24 January, during the meetings, Chen Cheng (1897–1965) presented Chiang Kai-shek with six points of view, which included: "The Communist Party will never give up military force under any conditions", and "the present situation today shows the only way to achieve peace and unity is by military force".[186] Under Chiang Kai-shek's amendment to the draft constitution, article 1 was based on the peaceful national construction agenda adopted by the political consultative conference: respecting the Three Principles of the People as the supreme guiding principle of nation-building, the Kuomintang proposes that direct elections (the invisible National Congress) should be changed to indirect elections through a permanent body (the visible National Congress), with the National

[184] On the second day of the meeting, the Central Committee of the CPC issued internal instructions to the heads of central bureaus, district party committees and army committees: "The main form of struggle of the Chinese revolution has now shifted from armed struggle to the struggle of the unarmed masses with the parliamentary struggle, and domestic problems have been resolved by political means. All the work of the Party must adapt to this new situation". Ref: *Zhonggong Zhongyang Wenjian Xuanji* (Anthology of Documents of the CPC Central Committee), v. 16, Central Party School of the CPC Press, 1992, p. 63. By the second half of the year, the civil war was in full swing, and on 21 November, Liu Shaoqi summed up his work; The two months of the beginning of the year were "a bit of a mess". Ref: The transcript of Liu Shaoqi's speech at the meeting of the Political Bureau of the CPC Central Committee is quoted from Jin Chongji, op. cit., p. 572.

[185] *Chen Guofu Zhuan*, Taipei: Zhengzhong Shuju, 1980, p. 935. This book is quoted in Deng Ye, op. cit., p. 354.

[186] *Chen Cheng Xiansheng Huiyi Lu: Guo-Gong Zhanzheng*, p. 158. Quoted in Deng Ye, op. cit., p. 353.

Assembly exercising four powers, the cabinet system changed to a presidential system, and the abolition of the provincial constitutions in favor of provincial rules of self-government.

At the end of the political consultative meetings, the KMT and CPC began negotiations on the Marshall-led proposal for reorganization, with a three-member panel composed of Zhang Zhizhong, Zhou Enlai, and Marshall working on the proposal. Marshall repeatedly stressed the need for a truly non-interventionist national army that could not be used as a tool by any party to compete for power. The KMT and Communist Party of China discussed this back and forth, and finally accepted the following plan: the reorganization of the army would allocate 90 divisions in the first phase to the KMT's army, and 18 divisions to the CPC's. In the second phase, the national army would have 60 divisions, 50 belonging to the KMT and ten to the CPC. Both sides, KMT and CPC, were most concerned about the "co-formation and separated deployment", that is, the mixed reorganization of the two parties' armed forces and their divided stationing, designed to prevent the political parties controlling the army. In the course of the three-man panel discussion reports were, of course, constantly presented, and on 8 February, Liu Shaoqi according to a Chongqing report said: "The reorganization envisages the interpenetration of the KMT and Communist armies, with the aim of attempting to destroy or control the Communist army, and therefore we must not agree to it". Mao Zedong said at a Politburo meeting on the 12th, "The United States and Chiang Kai-shek want eliminate us through the unification of the national army, so we must unite without being eliminated. The separation of the military and the party is not our most dangerous threat; the joint reorganization of the armies is the greatest danger".[187] On the 22nd, the two sides accepted a compromise plan of Marshall, and on the 25th, the three-man group jointly signed the *Basic Plan on Army Integration and Incorporation of the Army of the Communist Party of China within the National Army*. The integration program reveals the significant extent to which the Communist Party's regional control of the army has narrowed, and how the Western region had been taken over by KMT forces, which significantly weakened the CPC's possible ties with the Soviet Union. The United States thought these results on paper could be implemented, so on the same day the establishment of

[187] *Mao Zedong Nianpu*, *xia* volume, p. 57.

the United States Military Mission in China was announced, and it was responsible for the training of the national forces of the national government, which now included the Chinese Communist armies. However, the CPC retained a two-handed policy in its strategy of integrating its army, concealing military and political cadres in well-placed positions in the liberated areas, thus ensuring the flexibility of the CCP army, but as Marshall announced that the CPC armies would be well-equipped in the integrated national Chinese Army, Zhou Enlai warned his comrades: If we are not supplied with gasoline and ammunition, then all this fine equipment is nothing more than scrap iron. Neither the KMT nor CPC trusted each other at all, so Marshall serious efforts in the meantime were useless, and as a result the entire military program quickly proved to be only a scrap of paper.

With the Soviet army's insistence on conditions of economic cooperation in the Northeast, the CPC's obstruction of the KMT army's takeover of the Northeast gradually became public knowledge throughout the country. On 16 January 1946, Zhang Xinfu (1898–1946), sent by the National Government to take charge of the Northeast handover for the Ministry of Economy met with the Soviets overseeing the takeover of the Fushun coal mines, but on his return, that evening from Fushun to Shenyang via Lishizhai railway station, Zhang and his entourage were killed by Soviet and CPC troops.[188] In this matter, the KMT believes that this was obvious collusion between the Soviet Army and the CPC; the

[188] Wu Liangping, then secretary of the CPC's Fushun Military District Political Committee, revealed in a document written during the Cultural Revolution:

> The KMT sent Zhang Shenfu and others to oversee the handover of the Fushun Mining Bureau and Fushun Coal Mine. At that time, our policy was to oppose the handover, and they were unable to show they had the right to do so. Within a few days, they left, and we dispatched people to send them off. On the way, a telephone call informed them that Soviet Red Army officers wanted them. We heard the phone call but couldn't figure out what was going on. At that time, the Soviet Red Army troops stationed in Fushun exerted military control over the Red Army, and we had no power to exert control. (I) listened to the conversation, allowed them to proceed and raised no objections, which was a major policy mistake. The Soviet Red Army told our troops that these were bad people and ordered us to kill them. This incident provided the KMT with material to use as anti-communist propaganda, and so the political influence of the CPC suffered a loss, which is something I sadly regret to this day. The major responsibility for this incident was mine, as secretary of the local Party committee. For this major policy mistake, I was removed from the work of the Northeast Bureau; I confessed to my crimes

CPC in an internal directive of 25 February provided the unified explanation that the KMT "colluded with the Japanese to carry out the Zhang Shenfu assassination, as an excuse to make anti-Soviet and anti-communist propaganda". The Soviet Ambassador Petrov replied to Chongqing's Ministry of Foreign Affairs on February 27th: "Zhang Shenfu was killed by thugs".[189] After the Zhang Shenfu massacre was revealed at the end of the month, large-scale anti-Soviet and anti-Communist demonstrations broke out in major cities across the country from 22 February to early March, starting in Chongqing. People felt the withdrawal of the Soviet army was long overdue. The article in the Yalta Agreement that maintained the rights of the former Russian Empire on be restored to the Soviet Union, the economic cooperation proposed by the Soviet army in the Northeast which exceeded the provisions of the Sino-Soviet Treaty, the Soviet army's demolition and removal of equipment from the Northeast, the Soviet army's support for the ethnic uprising in Xinjiang, the CPC's obstruction of the KMT army's entry to the Northeast to oversee the handover, and the four demands regarding the Northeast presented by the Communist Party of China on 13 February were all aspects of widespread dissatisfaction triggered by the Zhang Shenfu killing.[190] On 16 February, an anti-Soviet march was held in some northeastern parts of Chongqing, which was followed by an anti-Soviet march by more than 20,000 students from more than 20 universities and colleges in Chongqing, including Central University and Chongqing University. The students chanted slogans calling for a thorough investigation into the Zhang Shenfu massacre, the immediate withdrawal of the Soviet army from the Northeast, and demanding the CPC should immediately 'love the motherland'. On the 23rd, students from 72 major colleges and schools, including St. John's College in Shanghai, took to the streets and chanted slogans outside the Soviet Consulate in Shanghai. They called

and left work in Fushun at the end of January. Ref: Yong Guiliang et al., *Wu Liangping Zhuan*, Zhongyang Wenxian Chubanshe, 2009, p. 120.

[189] *Zhang Gongquan Xiansheng Nianpu Chubian*, v. 1, p. 673.

[190] On 13 February 1946, the CPC made four demands on the Northeast: 1. Reorganize the Northeast office [headquarters]; 2, recognize the CPC's army in the Northeast; 3, recognize the democratic autonomous regimes in the Northeast's counties; 4, the National government should limit the number of its troops in the Northeast.

for the immediate withdrawal of the Soviet Army from the Northeast, demanded the complete restoration of the Northeast, and called for the overthrow of any political party that betrays the motherland and of Red traitors. Demonstrations subsequently broke out in Beiping, Nanjing, Kunming, and Zhengzhou. A large number of prominent persons and intellectuals joined In the processions and in various declarations. They included 110 academics from Southwest United University who issued a Declaration on the Northeast, and among whom were leaders in their fields like the linguist Wang Li (1900–1986), the aesthetician Zong Baihua, the ethnographer and writer Shen Congwen, the physicist Wu Dayou (1907–2000), the sociologist Chen Xujing (1903–1967), the philosopher Feng Youlan (1895–1990), and philosopher Tang Yongtong (1893–1964). Twenty prominent intellectuals also signed a document protesting the Yalta secret agreements, who included Fu Sinian, Wang Yunwu, Zong Baihua, and Chu Anping. On 23 February, the Democratic League's Huang Yanpei, Shen Junru, Zhang Junmai and Peng Yihu (1887–1958) jointly issued four points in Shanghai:

> (1) We strenuously advocate the protection of our nation's full sovereignty, which cannot exceed the provisions of the Sino-Soviet Friendship Agreement, damaging our rights and interests. (2) We argue that the Soviet Union should continue to be asked to withdraw its troops in accordance with the agreement. (3) We advocate that all internal disputes in the Northeast should be resolved through political consultation. (4) We are opposed to Chinese fighting Chinese on any issue.[191]

On March 7, more than 40 cultural celebrities, including Chen Daisun (1900–1997), Gu Jiegang, and Qi Sihe (1907–1980), issued a letter expressing their opinions: "We cannot tolerate the presence in the North east, Chahar, Jehol or anywhere else in China of any special regime apart from the Chinese National Government, nor can we tolerate any further humiliating concessions by the Chinese government in implementing the Sino-Soviet Treaty". The media of the KMT and CPC presented different interpretations of these events, and on 24 February Chiang Kai-shek wrote in his diary: "Student demonstrations on the Northeast issue have been a lesson that Russia has not had in the past twenty-five

[191] Zhongguo Shehui Kexueyuan Jindai Shi Yanjiusuo ed., *Huang Yanpei Riji*, entry for 23 February 1946, Huawen Chubanshe, 2008.

years, and henceforth should halt their actions and not expand them".[192] On 26 February Mao Zedong described the street marches as "counter-revolutionary demonstrations" in an article written for the Xinhua news agency.[193]

From 1 to 17 March, the KMT held the Second Plenary Session of the 6th National Congress in Chongqing, where many topics were discussed, the key issues being the review of the Political Consultative meeting documents, the analysis of the implementation of the Sino-Soviet treaty, and the Northeast issue. The continuous quarrels exposed serious differences of opinion within the KMT, Chiang Kai-shek hoping to unify ideas through the party meeting, in order to implement the Political Consultative meeting's call to reorganize the government. Chiang Kai-shek agreed when someone in the party seriously suggested that the constitution must be amended. Sun Ke explained the amendment: "All amendments to the *May Fifth Draft Constitution* of 1936 shall be formulated in accordance with the Outline of National Establishment of 1924 and the basic principles of the Constitution of the Five Powers, and a decision shall be made on the basis of discussions by the National Assembly". At the outset, Zhou Enlai, as CPC negotiator, agreed to the three-point amendments to the constitutional draft rule decided on in a joint meeting of the Constitutional Drafting Review Committee and the political consultative conference's Integrated Group, but Yan'an vetoed Zhou's amendments. Hu Qiaomu in the 19 March issue of Liberation Daily published an article on the Second Plenary Session of the Kuomintang, stating that the KMT proposed that "the constitution should be based on the Outline of National Establishment, but this provision itself reeked of one-party dictatorship. The various parties at the political consultative conference have never and will never agree that the constitution of the country should be based on some particular party's documents". As a result, the CPC subverted the basis of the constitution put forward by the Kuomintang and as for the political consultative conference formulating the constitution, this political process and logic clearly touched on the basis of the legitimacy of the existing National Government, which the KMT clearly could not agree to. In April, the Second Congress of the Fourth National

[192] *Chiang Kai-shek's Diary*, 24 February 1946.

[193] Ref: *Mao Zedong Wenji*, v. 4, pp. 90–91. This source is quoted in Deng Ye, op. cit., p. 377.

Political Consultative Conference decided: "The special organization of the liberated areas of the CPC should be abolished in order to achieve unity". The CPC was equally opposed to this, arguing that it undermined the spirit of the political consultative conference. On 12 March, the Chongqing government was not informed of the sudden withdrawal of the Soviet army from Shenyang, but on the following day, the National army entered and occupied the city. Now, only the KMT and CPC were left to discuss the handover of the Northeast and this serious conflict became the main issue discussed at the second plenary session. Within the KMT there were recriminations and accusations regarding diplomatic relations with the Soviet Union and political issues with the CPC, about which there was no consensus. As a result, the two focus issues that the Second Plenary Session hoped to solve—the draft constitution and the Northeast issue—were not been resolved.

At the same time, the discussion of "bureaucratic capital" at the meeting showed the economic and institutional dilemmas facing the national government. The term "bureaucratic capital" was not a specific economic term but involved many forms of state capital at the time: bureaucratic equity or investment (e.g., the Soong family's enterprises), state-owned capital used or capital used by bureaucrats (really state-owned enterprises that could be power-seeking) and other forms of private capital directed or controlled by bureaucrats.[194] It is conceivable that a one-party system of governing the country could easily give bureaucrats, powerful men, and powerful family groups opportunities for personal gain, turning state-owned enterprises into private property or opportunities for individuals and special groups seeking illegal benefits. In the latter part of the Anti-Japanese War, people began to point to the pernicious effects of bureaucratic capital, and the Japanese puppet industries confiscated after the war not only caused the rapid growth of the national capital but also provided the opportunity for those bureaucrat groups illegally controlling and seizing it, arousing the general opprobrium of public opinion. For example, *Central Daily*, controlled by the CC Department, repeatedly published articles attacking the phenomenon: "Bureaucratic capital manipulates the entire economic lifeline, and bureaucratic capital can use its special powers to monopolize everything in order to hinder

[194] The term "bureaucratic capital" is thought to have first appeared in Qu Qiubai's "The Development of the Bourgeoisie in China" (1932) and became popular in the early 1940s. The economics world did not use the term casually.

the progress of start-ups. Therefore, bureaucratic capital, representing the interests of bureaucrats, if not subsequently liquidated, will not only damage the interests of the people, but will suppress the future of industrialization and have seriously deleterious effects".[195] At the Second Plenary Session of the Sixth Congress, many participants were extremely worried about the current economic problems, and were extremely dissatisfied with the failure of Executive Yuan President Song Ziwen to mention the issue of bureaucratic capital in his political report. They linked the phenomenon of official corruption to the process of taking over the Northeast at this time. In the *Party Reform Program*, compiled by Wu Tiecheng, secretary-general of the Kuomintang Central Office, and Chen Lifu, bureaucratic capital was been elevated to the political heights of "being hated by the entire country, and hated by the whole party". Historian Fu Sinian argued that China's national capital at this time was "a lot worse, and more pernicious than can be described. The reason for this is that various malign forces (naturally not limited to Kong and Soong) and powerful families control it, so there is general disorder, irrationality, paralysis, and corruption. Evil forces dominate, nourishing more evil forces, and with powerful cliques in control, those cliques simply continue to develop".[196]

From March 21 to 23, 1947, the Third Plenary Session of the Sixth Central Committee of the Kuomintang was held, and economic issues became the focus. One month before, there had been a dramatic increase in the price of gold and the US dollar in Shanghai, triggering a serious economic crisis, Song Ziwen stepped down and at the meeting, many participants demanded that public debt fraud must be held accountable, that the officials and businessmen responsible for bureaucratic capital be punished and have their property confiscated, and that corruption be punished, otherwise "the Kuomintang is doomed" (Gu Zhenggang). The policies of financial opening policy and the opening of the gold foreign exchange market were among the financial measures implemented by

[195] Political Department of the 208 Division of the Youth Expeditionary Force, "Second Plenary Session of the Sixth Central Office of the Chinese Nationalist Party", 1946, p. 114.

[196] Fu Sinian, "Lun Haomen Ziben zhi Bixue Chanchu" (On the Need to Eliminate the Capital of the Mighty Clans), in Chen Zhaotong ed., *Zhongguo Caizheng Lishi Ziliao Xuanbian* (Anthology of Documents of China's Financial History), v. 12, xia section, Beijing: Zhongguo Caizheng Jingji Chubanshe, 1990, p. 123.

Song Ziwen at that time, the most basic thing to maintain their effectiveness being to maintain the stability of market expectations and political and social stability. Inflation, civil war with the CPC, declining credibility of government governance, and the lack of social stability needed after the war itself eventually led to the run on gold. At that time, there was a comment: "Fundamentally speaking, the root of the problem of prices lies in currency, and the root of currency problems lies in the civil war. If the civil war does not stop, production cannot progress, issuing currency cannot be stopped, and prices cannot be reined in. The gold policy, even if it is used more smoothly, can only reduce the fluctuation of prices, but cannot fundamentally solve the problem of runaway prices". (Yan Rengeng, "An Investigation of the Gold Policy", *Century Review* [Shiji Pinglun], No. 8) The real cause of the financial collapse in the second half of 1948 was the result of the total failure of the Kuomintang's political and economic governance and its loss of credibility.

Although the CPC continued to follow a strategy of "fighting on the one hand and negotiating on the other", the CPC maintained a cautious attitude towards the United States in the course of the negotiations, and the CPC was aware of American values. Therefore, in exchanges of views with the United States, the CPC continued to use words like "Three Principles of the People", "democracy", and "freedom", as in a strategic statement Zhou Enlai made in his letter to Marshall on 31 January 1946:

> At present, the conditions necessary to adopt socialism do not exist in China. In theory the CPC is firmly based on socialism as its ultimate goal, but in the immediate future we have no intention of putting it into practice, nor do we think that there is a possibility of actually implementing it. We call for following the path of the United States, referring to the United States-style democracy and science, which will enable China to reform agriculture, industrialize, develop free enterprises and individuality, while also building an independent, free and prosperous China. We want to tell a story that will also please Your Excellency! It was recently rumored that Chairman Mao would travel to Moscow. Chairman Mao laughed when he heard this and jokingly remarked that he would prefer to go to the United States if he does go abroad for a holiday (that being more beneficial for his

current health). Because we believe much can be learned from the United States to benefit China.[197]

Although Marshall received Mao Zedong's plan to implement the armistice and begin political consultations and the army -reorganization program during his visit to Yan'an in early March, he was well aware of the anxiety and uneasiness Truman felt about Chiang Kai-shek and Mao Zedong. In fact, Chiang Kai-shek only needed American weapons and military equipment, and did not want the United States to be too interfering politically, which would be tantamount to interference in his government's internal affairs and delay him; for Mao Zedong, discussions under peaceful conditions could be delayed as much as possible, and if there were benefits for the Communist Party, of course, this was not a bad thing. But the CPC was simply using time as a delaying tactic so they would have as much time as possible to take over the Northeast. The conflict never stopped at all, and after Marshall returned to the United States on 11 March to prepare a $500 million loan for the National Government, the KMT and CPC greatly escalated the fighting. On April 14th, the Soviets withdrew from Changchun, and on the 18th, the CPC took it over. On the day Marshall arrived in the United States from Chongqing, he learned the news: "The CPC's attack and occupation of Changchun is a major violation of the armistice order".[198] In fact, before Marshall returned to China, Zhou promised him to stop the conflict, but now Zhou's explanation was that the KMT had occupied "seven of our cities" despite the armistice agreement, so the CPC had to occupy Changchun. Marshall was very impressed by the extraordinary diplomacy of Zhou Enlai's handling of negotiations and business. The CPC had no plans to stop the occupation, Liu Shaoqi told the Chongqing negotiating delegation. The Soviet army retreated from Harbin on the 24th, so "our army can occupy the city on the day after its withdrawal".[199] At this time, the nation's people hated and were angered by the war, and on 22 May, the Democratic League's Zhang Junmai, Huang Yanpei, Shen Junru, Zhang Bojun, and Liang Shuming jointly telegrammed Chiang Kai-shek and Mao Zedong, telling them the civil war in the Northeast has already "cost us our allies and the loss of the nation's hearts and minds", while proposing that the

[197] *Kangzhan Shiliao Chugao* (First Draft of the History of the Anti-Japanese War), vol. 7, "Post-War China, II", pp. 249–250, with English documents appended. This book is quoted in Li Yunhan, op. cit., pp. 497–498.

].

[198] *Maxie'er Shi Hua*, p. 114. Quoting p. 436.

[199] *Liu Shaoqi Nianpu*, *xia* volume, p. 37.

KMT and CPC agree to the three-point plan to send in no more troops and withdraw from Changchun. Finally, the months-long Battle of Siping ended, the government forces recaptured Siping. Given the CPC's military failure, Mao Zedong finally decided to withdraw from Changchun, and on the 23rd, the KMT forces occupied the city the CPC had presumed would be its capital. In that month, the National government moved the capital back to Nanjing. After the Battle of Siping, Marshall lost faith in the value of the CPC, and the CPC, in order to get full time to prepare, still used Marshall's mediation to continue negotiations with the seemingly strong KMT. Zhou Enlai used the delay to postpone the full outbreak of the civil war. At the same time, the CPC through its propaganda, emphasized that the KMT exercised dictatorship and sold out the country, while the CPC was the nation's genuine force for a peaceful and independent democracy. In July, the CPC even publicly accused the United States' military assistance to China as nothing but armed interference in China's internal affairs. In mid-June, Chiang Kai-shek told his military generals that the Kuomintang's ultimate enemy was "the Communist Party". On 2 July, Chiang Kai-shek and Zhou Enlai had a final meeting, but to no avail. On the 9th, Zhou Enlai continued to use what seemed generally acceptable to the Chinese people rather than the party position when he told an American professor: "The bad U.S.-Soviet relations often affect China's internal affairs, which is true. But from China's point of view, there is no way to get ourselves from it. If the KMT government were clever, it should automatically act as a bridge and not be willing to be a pawn of the country [i.e., the US]. If China's National government formed a coalition government (as was suggested at the political consultative meeting) and maintain friendly relations with all its allies, China would not be completely influenced by one country and could in turn positively influence international cooperation".[200] Zhou Enlai certainly could not publicly discuss the Soviet Union's promises to, and support for, the CPC. Chiang Kai-shek knew this leader of the CPC who was his former subordinate very well, and he no longer held out the slightest hope for the CPC. On 7 July, the CPC clearly attacked the United States and the National Government in its *Declaration on the 9th Anniversary of the September 7th Incident*, without taking into account the reaction of Marshall who had not yet left, signaling he had lost his role in recommending John Stuart Leighton as ambassador to

[200] "Zhongguo Buyao Chengwei Yiguo de Gongju" (China Does Not Want to Become the Tool of a Nation), 9 July 1946, in Central Documentation Research Office of the Communist Party of China and Nanjing Municipal Committee of the Communist Party of China eds., *Zhou Enlai Yijiusiliu-nian Tanpan Wenxuan*, Beijing: Zhongyang Wenxian Chubanshe, 1996, p. 535.

> China. On 14 July, Chiang Kai-shek and Soong Mei-ling went to Lushan to retreat for the "summer" and to command the war against the Communist Party, with the war in northern Jiangsu having begun on the previous day.

Following Li Gongpu's murder on July 12th, Wen Yiduo was also killed by the Kuomintang on the 15th. The assassination in Kunming strengthened the general dissatisfaction of Chinese intellectuals with the KMT, to the point of no return. The killings of Li and Wen also led many people in the United States to oppose continued assistance to the KMT's Chiang Kai-shek. During Chiang Kai-shek's stay in Lushan, Marshall there on eight occasions to discuss an armistice with Chiang, but in the course of the back-and-forth mediation, Marshall's patience came to an end.

The Civil War

On 3 July 1946, in order to provide a legal basis for the subsequent "CPC encirclement" campaign and avoid the social impression of heading a one-party dictatorship, Chiang Kai-shek, without informing the other parties, proposed to the Supreme National Defense Council that on November 12th the National Congress be convened to give its approval. From July to September, the KMT army won many battlefield victories from its attacks on the Communist-liberated areas to its move on Zhangjiakou, the military center of the liberated areas of North China. On 30 September, Zhou Enlai wrote in a memo to Marshall:

> I have been instructed to convey to you that, if the Kuomintang does not immediately cease all military action against Zhangjiakou and its surroundings, the Chinese Communist Party cannot but be convinced that the Government has declared a total end to the armistice and has finally abandoned any plan for a political settlement. The serious consequences of this should, of course, be borne by the Government.[201]

Chiang Kai-shek was determined to eliminate the Communist Party, and on 11 October, government forces seized Zhangjiakou, cutting the

201 *Zhou Enlai Yijiusiliu-nian Tanpan Wenxuan*, Zhongyang Wenxian Chubanshe, 1996, p. 654.

CPC off from the Northeast and depriving the CPC army of the possibility of receiving ammunition and food. In his diary on 12 October, Chiang wrote: "The recovery of Zhangjiakou is vital for cutting North China off from the Northeast. Success or failure for the Government and the Communist bandits is one and the same". On that day, the centrist intellectual Liang Shuming, learning from the morning newspaper that Zhangjiakou had been captured, blurted out: "I wake up and find peace is dead". There was widespread confusion and disappointment with the beginning of all-out military conflict between the KMT and CPC. The CCP then began to adjust the focus of its propaganda, leading to the perception that it was the United States and the Kuomintang that were obstructing peace and fomenting the civil war. Zhou Enlai received instructions from the CPC Central Committee to expose the United States and Chiang Kai-shek:

> Under the conditions of the national fight, all negotiations are intended to completely expose the reactionary side of the United States and Chiang, to educate the masses. As long as the United States and Chiang do not proactively abandon political negotiations in order to deceive the masses, then we should not take the initiative in declaring the final breakdown of negotiations with the United States and Chiang, so that we behave passively.[202]

The KMT and CPC finally tried to use the power of third parties to attempt to effect a ceasefire. Those prominent academics and intellectuals like Huang Yanpei, Shen Junru, Liang Shuming, Zhang Bojun, Zhang Shenfu (1893–1986), Luo Longji (1898–1985), and Jiang Yuntian simply wanted peace and found it difficult to understand the peculiar position of the two parties, given the fact that attempting to mediate between the KMT and CPC proved completely ineffective. However, Chiang Kai-shek announced a ceasefire for the third time on 8 November; given the upcoming Constitutional National Convention on the 12th, Chiang Kai-shek seemed confident that the ceasefire would give the CPC a little more time to change its position. On the 13th, after meeting with Zhou Enlai, Marshall decided that the CPC was not convinced of any of the KMT's proposals and initiatives. On the 15th, the Kuomintang and Chiang Kai-shek no longer waited for the CPC and the Democratic League and the

[202] *Zhou Enlai Nianpu*, 13 October 1946, p. 697.

National Convention in Nanjing was convened. In this situation, Zhou Enlai remained in Nanjing until 19 November before flying back to Yan'an; from his last meeting for negotiations with Chiang Kai-shek to the time of his departure, he insisted to the outside world that it was the KMT, not the CPC, that closed the door to peace. On the 21st, Mao Zedong, Liu Shaoqi and Zhou Enlai met to discuss more than a year of previous negotiations and proposed to get ready to overthrow Chiang Kai-shek.

On 25 December, after its third reading the National Convention adopted the *Constitution of the Republic of China*, and on 1 January 1947, the National Government issued an order: "The National Assembly has enacted the *Constitution of the Republic of China*, which is scheduled to be promulgated by the Republic of China on 1 January 1947, and will come into effect on 25 December of that year".[203]

Given the KMT's hardline stance and the negotiating terms insisted on by the CPC (Marshall described it as "an unwillingness to make reasonable concessions"), Marshall was eventually recalled to the United States by Truman in January 1947, when it became very clear to Marshall that there was deep mistrust and a lack of genuine cooperation between the two parties.[204] Both sides negotiating but preparing for the final military battle, with Chiang Kai-shek trying to make peace by force while the CPC was preparing for war throughout the peace talks, was the root cause of

[203] In his report to the Secretary of State on the following day, the U.S. Ambassador John Leighton Stuart wrote:

> The very day of the fall of Zhangjiakou coincided with the announcement of the order convening the National Congress. The former provoked a strong emotional reaction, while the latter led to debate over whether the president had the power to decide on the dates of the Congress without consulting the leaders of the other parties. Chiang's unilateral actions reflected his authoritarian tendencies. The Communist Party used this antipathy to him to pull the smaller parties into its own camp.

Ref: *Bei Yiwang de Dashi Situ Leideng Zhu Hua Baogao*, p. 24. This book is quoted in Jin Chongji, op. cit., p. 584.

[204] Marshall once commented to Gu Weijun: "I hear that the Communists can't be trusted, but the other side is no more trustworthy than the Communists". Ref: Gu Weijun Huiyi Lu, v. 5, p. 705.

Marshall's failure in mediation.[205] Truman began with a clear attitude: China, as a country which had not yet achieved national unity, was not entitled to substantial aid. Moreover, in U.S. policy analysis, large-scale military and economic aid to support any side in China's civil war is not in line with the U.S. postwar strategy for East Asia, at least in terms of possible benefits, and distant communist China, even with further Soviet support or even control, did not pose a direct security problem for the United States. In fact, while the KMT was not satisfied with the US move, the CPC once again launched nationwide anti-American propaganda, accusing the US's China policy of helping the KMT provoke civil war. At the same time, the United States also lost confidence in Chiang Kai-shek's KMT.[206] Although KMT Central held the Third Plenary Session of its Sixth National Congress on 15 March, Chiang Kai-shek said the KMT would "end its tutelary rule and return government to the people", and China will enter a period of constitutionalism. But this time people were most concerned about the deterioration of Chinese politics and the escalation of civil war.

On 18 March 1947, Hu Zongnan's forces occupied Yan'an, but three months later, his forces were annihilated by the CPC. Also in March, the CPC's army was officially renamed the Chinese People's Liberation Army, which meant the CPC has decided to launch a full-scale counter-attack against the KMT and move towards the goal of seizing power. On 22 May, the CPC signed the Harbin Agreement with the Soviet Union, and the Soviet Union began to fully support the CPC. A general arrest warrant for Mao Zedong was issued by the National Government's Supreme Court Prosecutor's Office on 25 June, but at a time when Mao's army and the political clout of the CPC were strong enough to counter Chiang

[205] Not only was the U.S. mediation ineffective, but the mediation of the centrist forces was also a failure. On 26 July 1946, Chen Lifu told the mediator, Huang Yanpei: "(1) The KMT cannot allow the Communist Party to coexist; (2) Third parties, in relation to the KMT and CPC, ignore the fact that the KMT is the orthodox party, and in mediating conflicts simply delay the resolution of the KMT-CPC problem". This book is quoted in Jin Chongji, op. cit., p. 581.

[206] Truman later wrote in his memoirs:

"Chiang Kai-shek was eventually defeated by the loss of popular support and American aid, because many of his generals had defected to the enemy with their troops armed with our weapons. It was only when these defections began to occur in large numbers that I decided to stop shipping supplies to China". Ref: *Truman Memoirs*, volume 2, pp. 103–104. This book is quoted from Jin Chongji, op. cit., p. 675.

Kai-shek's KMT, Mao Zedong had a clear view of the immediate future of the CPC he led. On 30 May Mao Zedong wrote a confident article for Xinhua News Agency, in which he provided an overview of the current political situation in the country. In his view, not only was the CPC on the front line militarily, but the CPC in KMT-ruled areas had opened up a second front to competing with Chiang Kai-shek's government through student and popular movements:

> Chiang Kai-shek's government, which is an enemy of the whole people, has now found itself under siege by the whole people. Whether on the military or political front, Chiang Kai-shek's government has lost ground and is been surrounded by the forces of its declared enemies. And I don't think it has any means of escape.
>
> There are already two fronts in China. The war between Chiang Kai-shek's army and the People's Liberation Army is the first front. Now there is a second front, which is the bitter struggle between the glorious and just student movement and Chiang Kai-shek's reactionary government. The slogans of the student movement are 'we want to eat, we want peace, and we want freedom'; in other words, they are opposed to hunger, civil war, and persecution.
>
> The student movement is part of the movement of all the people, and the upsurge of the student movement inevitably promotes the entire popular movement.[207]

In fact, the anti-American student movement, which took place in Beiping at the end of December 1946, then expanded to major cities across the country in the first quarter of 1947, and the "Anti-Hunger, Anti-Civil War, Anti-Persecution" national movement that first broke out in Nanjing in May.[208] This was a part of the CPC's political struggle with

[207] Mao Zedong Xuanji, volume 4.

[208] On the afternoon of 26 December 1946, a notice on the west wall of the Red House of Peking University reported: On the 24th, two U.S. Marines in Beiping raped a new first-year student of French at Peking University named Shen Chong (her great-grandfather was the late-Qing official Shen Baozhen, and a United States military court finally heard the case). On the 30th, thousands of students from Tsinghua, Yanjing, Peking University, Furen, and Shida held a march to protest the actions of the American marines, with slogans such as "Expel U.S. Troops from China". In January 1947, student strikes and marches spread to dozens of large and medium-sized cities across the country,

the KMT, through the political medium of a social campaign. The CPC played an effective role in the fight against the image and influence of the ruling Kuomintang, which after the Anti-Japanese War lost the ability to deal with a series of political and economic conflicts, naturally having to bear all the resulting social problems. The CPC obviously used the

with a total of 500,000 people participating. On 2 January, *Xinhua Daily* published an editorial stating that the student movement was "essentially the struggle between the united front that reflects the patriotism of the Chinese people and the dictatorial policy of the Kuomintang ruling group". A general an anti-government and anti-American movement subsequently began. The CPC Central Committee met on 1 February and named the student and popular movements "the second battleground", and on 8 March the National Union of Students Against Violence was established in Shanghai, marking the high point of the campaign. The student movement also led to responses from organizations in all walks of life, such as the Chinese Democratic League. After the Anti-Japanese War, the resources of the National government were exhausted, and its financial difficulties and handling of difficulties widely concerned society and sparked criticism and censure. In May, when inflation triggered a surge in prices that eventually led to a social crisis, more than 3000 students from Nanjing Central University, the Drama School and the Conservatory of Music staged a Friday march to the Education Department to demand better food in the schools' canteens and increased living expenses, which eventually turned into a massive anti-KMT social movement of "opposition to hunger and civil war". The CPC took full advantage of popular discontent with the government by organizing demonstrations against the rule of the KMT and its government. For example, a message from the Secretary of the Shanghai Bureau of the CPC Central Committee on 28 April read:

This upsurge is not some sudden riot, but a sustained and diffused ongoing struggle for life; the interaction of this struggle for life and politics will at a certain point converge into a comprehensive political struggle, In our ideological and organizational strategy, we are preparing to organize and lead this new high point, in order to advance the democratic movement in the areas controlled by Chiang. Ref: *Jiefang Zhanzheng Shiqi de Zhonggong Zhongyang Shanghai-ju* (The Shanghai Bureau of the CPC Center during the War of Liberation), Xuelin Chubanshe, 1989, p. 365.

On 20 May, student representatives from Shanghai, Hangzhou and Suzhou and more than 5,000 students from Nanjing Central University marched to the National People's Political Assembly. On that day, the KMT military and police used violence to suppress the students, after which the campaign added "oppose persecution" to its slogans as the anti-hunger and anti-civil war campaign reached its climax. Students in several cities across the country responded to this organized social movement and it won the support of 585 well-known academics and intellectuals (including anthropologist Fei Xiaotong [1910–2005], historian Wu Han [1909–1969], philosopher Jin Yuelin [1895–1984], literary scholar Yu Pingbo [1900–1990], Chen Xujing, and poet Bian Zhilin [1910–2000]). "We and others are well aware of today's chaos, the root cause of the economic crisis, and the economic crisis that is the result of a long civil war. All the worker and student movements are the inevitable product of the current situation". Ref: *Dagong Bao*, 29 May 1947.

KMT's incompetence and governance failure to justify its own just position and political legitimacy—the CPC's political achievements in turn made people lose confidence in the KMT.

On 30 June 1947, Chiang Kai-shek said at a joint meeting of the Standing Committee of the Kuomintang Central Office and the Central Political Conference: "In fact, the military has not failed and the economic foundation has not wavered, but we are completely shaken by the propaganda of the CPC and also by our own party members who do not listen to orders, do not act positively, and do not exert themselves; in other words, we have not failed, but we have been shaken up by ourselves".[209] Chiang Kai-shek decided to mobilize the entire country, put the nation on a wartime footing, and eliminate the Communist Party as soon as possible, to change the situation. On 3 July, the National Government adopted the measure with the lengthy title, "Proposal to implement constitutionalism on schedule and implement the plan for peaceful nation construction, in order to save the people in bandit areas, safeguard the survival of the nation, consolidate national unity, and generally mobilize the entire country to suppress the rebellion of the Communist bandits and remove obstacles to democracy". On 18 July, the National Government announced its Outline for the Implementation of the Constitutional Order of Mobilization to Suppress the Insurgency. On 20 August, the Standing Committee of the KMT adopted its "Plan to Suppress the Insurgency and Build the Nation". On 5 September, the Executive Council (Yuan) announced "Measures for Dealing with the Communist Party in Rear Areas". On 25 December, the National Government published "Regulations on Emergency Measures to Combat Crimes Endangering the State during the Suppression of the Insurgency", and the Government quickly introduced tight strict restrictions on processions, petitions, workers strikes and student strikes, in order to show that "suppressing the insurgency" only targeted the CPC. In April 1948, the National Government promulgated the *Special Crimes Court Organization Regulations*, in order to maintain the political atmosphere that had previously emphasized democracy and freedom. However, pressure from the provisions greatly intensified the confrontation between the government and the people, while activities of the underground organizations of the CPC exacerbated society's dissatisfaction and resistance

[209] *Xu Yongchang Riji*, 5 July 1947 entry, Taipei: Institute of Modern History of the Academia Sinica, 1991.

to the government and KMT, and the CPC's propaganda and agitation had the effect of casting the government's policy of "suppressing the insurgency and building the nation" as a fascist dictatorship. During this period, the centrist forces who had formerly spoken out freely also lost the opportunity to speak up. When the Chinese Youth Party and Democratic Socialist Party drew closer to the KMT because of their participation in the Constitutional Congress and the meetings restructuring the Government, the Democratic League, which like the CPC had been prevented from participating in the Congress, also lost its influence. On 7 October, Du Bincheng (1888–1947), a member of the Standing Committee of the Democratic League's Central Committee, was executed by the Martial Law General Command of Shaanxi Province on charges of "colluding with the Communist Army, plotting riots, and selling opium". On 5 November, the main leaders of the Democratic League met to decide on a course of action and announced the resignation of their colleagues, the dissolution of their headquarters, and the suspension of activities of their other organizations, such as the Peasants and Workers Democratic Party, the Democratic National Construction Council, the Democracy Promotion Association and the Jiusan Society. There is no doubt that Chiang Kai-shek had exhausted all means and the decline of the KMT reduced people to feeling that nothing could remedy the situation. On 13 October 1947, Life magazine published the reporter Theodore White's article, *A Report to the American People on China,* which stated: "Unless we reach out, the vulnerable Chinese army, along with their country, will be lost to the Russians".

On 4 May 1946, Liu Shaoqi presided over a meeting of the Central Committee of the CPC to examine the question of land reform in the liberated areas. Previously, during the Anti-Japanese War, the CPC had in 1942 waged a campaign calling for modest "rent reduction and interest reduction". Now, in order to consolidate its control of the liberated areas, in particular in preparation for the imminent outbreak of civil war, the resources required for the army and the war need to be addressed on the ground. Based on the rent reduction policy during the Anti-Japanese War, Hu Qiaomu drafted "Instructions of the Central Committee of the Communist Party of China on Land Issues" (simply called the "May 4th Instructions"), and quickly pushed land reform in the areas under the control of the CPC, through methods of struggle that included liquidating, confiscating, requisitioning, and offering equal parcels of land, so that farmers could in Sun Yat-sen's words "cultivate their own fields".

By the spring of 1947, two-thirds of the liberated areas controlled by the Communist Party of China had implemented land reforms, with the exception of war-torn areas, which led to a sharp increase in the number of troops. In August, September, and October alone, the number of people who joined the army in the liberated areas of the Communist Party of China reached 300,000, and between 3 and 4 million joined the militias and served as guerrillas. It is difficult to count precisely the increase in the number of civilian and logistical teams. The summer and autumn of 1947 saw the climax of the "basic levelling and uprooting campaign" of the land reform.[210] Liu Shaoqi held a land work conference in Xibeipo, and on the basis of the previous land reform, formulated the "Outline of China's Land Law". Liu Shaoqi stressed at the meeting that the land problem was the basic link connecting all problems in the liberated areas. The next step was to force the distribution of land in the hands of landowners to the majority of the peasants and the poor using political and military force, so there would no longer be divisions of class and all land would be evenly distributed, provided that they had support of the peasants and the poor who make up the majority of the population. The Outline called for "the abolition of all landowners' rights" and "the abolition of land ownership by all monasteries, temples, schools, institutions and organizations". Here, "abolition" had no basis for written laws, but the provisional regime of the Communist Party of China effected the judgment history, especially real political tasks and the need for temporary decrees. The principle of the "people's livelihood" among the Three Principles of the People advocated by the Kuomintang related to the land

[210] *Northeast Daily* on 14 June 1947 carried an article titled "Combined production to dig up pernicious roots; solving summer harvest difficulties raises the consciousness of the masses: "The people of Liuqu Huayuancun [in Shuangcheng], after acquiring the rights to their land in February [1947], enjoyed divided land but still did not enjoy real benefits as grain was not yet shared, so during the spring planting, there were problems arising from the lack of food, so the rural task force had to meet the urgent requirements of the masses, In addition to the proposed division and distribution of land and grain, they also called on the masses to dig up bad roots and unearth storage cellars. First, at the home of the Yan Chao, the former district leader of Huayuancun under the Japanese puppet government, they unearthed two grain hoards, and under some sorghum straw they discovered a large number of clothing and cloth. Then in six villages they uncovered eight underground hoards of grain hidden by landlords, totaling 95 *dan* of grain, as well as 533 items of clothing, 621 feet of cloth 621, as well as 154 *dan* of grain paid as rent, which solves the problem of food and clothing for the masses during the winter, and greatly improved the mood supporting mass production".

issue, but even though the Kuomintang promulgated a Land Law in 1930 and amended it in 1937, and in 1946, the political consultative conference included rent reduction, interest reduction and "farmers having their own fields" in the national reconstruction outline, these measures had not been implemented because of the War of Resistance and the outbreak of civil war, so the national government obviously never addressed the needs of the majority of farmers in the area of land reform. *Millard's Review* (aka *The China Weekly Review*), an English-language newspaper in Shanghai, made this assessment: "The real dividing line between the battlefields of the civil war is between two different regions: in one farmers farm their own land and in the others farmers farm the land for landowners", and this "this not only determines the future for the Nationalist and Communist parties, but also the fate of this country".[211] In fact, in the liberated areas controlled by the CPC, many places have carried out a number of land reforms, the earlier rent and interest reductions and the struggle and liquidation sessions changed the land ownership relations in some areas, and in many areas, there were now very few landlords with large holdings. Thus, in order to achieve equal distribution of the land, the land of rich and middle peasants was also redistributed, and in order to distribute the work smoothly, it was very common to beat up the landlord gentry at struggle sessions. In some places, it was even common to simply kill rich farmers and landlords, even though some of them had in fact helped and supported the CPC to meet the needs of the campaign to distribute land equally. But in any case, the result of more people gaining access to land won support, and this clearly contributed to the development of the Chinese Communist Army, which grew rapidly during the civil war mainly from land reform. At the same time, because the elites in the countryside were always the owners of more land, through the struggle against this class, the original political and economic structure of the countryside was completely destroyed, which would provide the foundation for the establishment of the new regime that would come soon. Mao Zedong said at a meeting at the end of December that both the Kuomintang and the liberated areas faced economic difficulties, but that "we engaged in land reform and Chiang Kai-shek did not", with the result that the CPC gained in the transition from defense to attack in terms of economic and human resources. One American observer wrote: "Mao Zedong's Land Law led

[211] This book is quoted in Jin Chongji, op. cit., p. 619.

to the confiscation of $US20 billion worth of land without compensation, leaving no chance of reconciliation between the Communist Party and the Kuomintang, shifting the main objective of the war from the protection of liberated areas to the defeat of landlords and compradors across the country, prompting large numbers of Chiang's troops to surrender to the People's Liberation Army, provoking farmers' riots in the Chinese mainland and inspiring demonstrations by workers, students, businessmen and clerks in the urban areas under the Kuomintang".[212]

On 10 October 1947. Mao Zedong drafted *Declaration of the Chinese People's Liberation Army* and put forward the slogan: "Down with Chiang Kai-shek's authoritarian government and form the democratic coalition government!" At the same time, the CPC had begun to fight to win over the vast middle ground. On 5 January 1948, in his opening speech at the Third Plenary Session of the First Central Committee of the Democratic League in Hong Kong, Shen Junru said:

> In today's domestic situation, the lines between democracy and opposition to democracy have been clearly defined, so everyone is clear what they are. In the past, the Kuomintang launched a civil war, adding to the suffering of the people, and in turn the Communist Party of China implemented land reform in the liberated areas, improving the people's lives, which shows the stark contrast between democracy and the opposition to democracy. Despite the collusion between the United States and Chiang, playing with any political conspiracy cannot deceive the people. The Democratic League firmly stands on the side of the people and resolutely fights on the side of the people's side, and this belief cannot be defeated.[213]

Soon, those groups that stopped operating during the suppression of unrest, including the China Zhi Gong Party and the Taiwan Democratic Self-Government League, all claimed to be close to the stance of the new democratic revolution. At the same time as the KMT's "Constitutional Congress" was held, the CPC issued its "May Day" slogan: "All democratic parties, people's organizations, and prominent social spokesmen must quickly convene a political consultative conference to discuss and

[212] William Hinton, *Fanshen: Documentary of a Revolution in a Chinese Village*, Beijing Chubanshe, 1980, p. 7.

[213] *Shen Junru Wenji*, Renmin Chubanshe, 1994, p. 557.

realize the convening of the People's Congress and the formation of a democratic coalition government".

On 29 March 1948, the First National Assembly of the Constitutional Congress was held in Nanjing, and although the National Assembly did not have the participation of the Communist Party of China and the Democratic League, the Constitution of the Republic of China came into effect and the period of tutelary rule officially gave way to the period of constitutional government. On 19 April, the National Assembly announced that Chiang Kai-shek had been elected the first president of the Republic of China during its constitutional term. After the National Assembly convened, Weng Wenhao (1889–1971) was appointed President of the Executive Yuan, Tong Guanxian (1894–1981) was appointed President of the Legislative Yuan, Wang Chonghui was appointed President of the Judicial Yuan, Zhang Boling was appointed made President of the Examination Yuan, and Yu Youren was appointed President of the Procuratorial Yuan. By this time, however, Chiang Kai-shek's government was in danger. From 8 to 13th September, the CPC held its first Politburo meeting at Xibeipo after its withdrawal from Yan'an, and Mao Zedong, in addition to deciding not to compromise with Chiang Kai-shek's regime, proposed the slogan, "Carry the revolution through to the end". He made it clear that the future regime "must not engage in a bourgeois parliamentary system and have a tripartite division of powers". At this time, Mao Zedong advised his comrades in the CPC that the future New China would be a state-run economy, socialist in nature. When writing *On New Democracy*, he wrote, "the difference between national capital and bureaucratic capital was not clear in our minds. Big industries, big banks, big businesses, whether bureaucratic capital or not, will be confiscated for a certain period of time after the national victory, in accordance with the principles of the new democratic economy. As soon as they are confiscated, they will be part of socialism".[214]

The rapid collapse of the KMT's military rivalry with the CPC showed clearly in October 1948: on 14 October, Lin Biao's forces occupied Jinzhou and on 18 October, Changchun fell after a long siege by the CPC in which no less than 100,000 people starved to death.[215] On 2

[214] *Mao Zedong Xuanji*, v. 5, p. 139.

[215] On 15 March 1948, the Northeast People's Liberation Army under Lin Biao initiated a siege of Changchun, and on 19 October, the Kuomintang defenders surrendered. There were no fierce battles during this period, but in addition to the Kuomintang soldiers

November 2, the PLA occupied Shenyang, and in the Battle of Liaoshen, the KMT army lost nearly half a million troops. In the Huaihai campaign that began in October (ending in January 1949), 400,000 KMT troops were killed. On 25 November 1948, Chiang Kai-shek wrote:

> After the military defeat, the social, political, economic, and diplomatic phenomena and people's loss of faith were unimaginable. Together with the refugees from the battlefield and young people fleeing to behind the lines difficult to resettle, the injured and wounded officers and soldiers along the way could not handle the chaotic situation, which was all the more distressing.[216]

The KMT's defeat was also clear to liberal intellectuals, who had tried to avoid politics. Earlier on 13 December 1948, Hu Shi, who two years earlier had chaired the National Assembly and accepted the draft constitution of the Republic of China for discussion, had not stopped his intellectual activities. However, there is a sad passage at the end of his letter that evening to the President of Furen University Chen Yuan (1880–1971) regarding academic issues surrounding Yang Xingwu's Chronological Biography: "Tonight as I write this brief note, I have been interrupted more than half a dozen times by phone calls, and I do not in the future whether I will ever find the peace and quiet again

who perished, no less than 120,000 (according to the CPC) to 150,000 (according to the National Government) citizens died of hunger and disease. Lin Biao reported to Mao Zedong on 9 September 1948: "… we did not allow starving people to leave the city and blocked those who had already come out, but it was very difficult to explain this to those who were starving and to the soldiers in our army. Those who were starving expressed their dissatisfaction with me, and constantly complained that the Eighth Route Army sees people dying and doesn't save them. They knelt in front of our sentries in groups begging to be allowed to leave, some abandoned their infants and children and ran, and others used rope to hang themselves in front of our sentries. Seeing this tragic situation unfold, our soldiers were heartbroken, and some knelt down with the starving people and cried together with them saying that they couldn't carry out their superiors' orders, and some even smuggled out refugees. After they were punished, another bias was identified, namely the insulting and shooting of bound refugees that resulted in their deaths (statistics on those killed and injured are not yet available)". (Quoted from Cai Xiaobin, *Da Bianju zhong de Zhuanzhedian* (Turning Point in the Great Change), Jincheng Publishing House, 2012, p. 201.)

216 *Dashi Changbian*, v. 7a, p. 158.

to pursue scholarship".[217] On 30 December 1948, Vice President Li Zongren of the National Government also proposed on five occasions to conduct peace talks with the CPC, but on that same day, Xinhua published Mao Zedong's article "Carry the Revolution through to the End". On January 15th and 23rd, the KMT's army defending Tianjin and Beiping surrendered to the CPC, in what was known as the Battle of Pingjin. By January, the KMT army had already lost a total of 1.5 million men. In the fight against the Kuomintang army, the Communist Party of China, by mobilizing the vast number of peasants, reforming the Kuomintang prisoners of war, using the human and material resources left behind by the Japanese and its puppet regime's military forces, together with the large number of unemployed workers, and the support of the Soviet Union, complemented and increased deployments, military equipment and logistics for the newly opened battlefields. At the same time, the KMT's army is unable to expand its strength because it was scattered and remained in urban and rural areas or in handover area, so it found it difficult to counter the flexible tactics of the Communist Party's concentrated forces. Even though the KMT under Chiang Kai-shek could satisfy general demands from inside and outside the party, Li Zongren, exercising the power of the acting president, could not save the KMT from total defeat.

At the end of March 1949, the Central Committee of the Communist Party of China and the headquarters of the People's Liberation Army moved to Beiping, where Mao Zedong and Zhu De arrived on the 25th. On that day, among the parties, cultural figures and intellectuals who welcomed the leaders of the Communist Party to Beiping were Li Jishen, Shen Junru, Huang Yanpei, Guo Moruo, Ma Xulun, Tan Pingshan, Zhang Bojun, Liu Yazi, Chen Shutong, Ma Yinchu, Peng Zemin, Mao Dun, Cai Tingkai, Ye Shengtao, Zhang Dongsun, Xu Deheng, Zhu Xuefan, Cai Chang, and dozens of others. In April 1949, the continued negotiations between the KMT and CPC in Beiping were almost at an end, and the terms put forward by the Communist Party in Zhou Enlai's domestic peace agreement (13 April) were simply unacceptable to the Kuomintang. The ensuing battles saw dramatic defeats for the Kuomintang. Unlike other intellectuals, Hu Shi was "re-commissioned" by Chiang Kai-shek to fly to the United States on the 6th of that month,

[217] Chen Zhichao ed., *Chen Yuan Laiwang Shuxin Ji* (Collection of Correspondence of Chen Yuan), Shanghai Guji Chubanshe, 1990, p. 191.

but as Fu Sinian had written in his 1947 letter to Hu Shi: "We rebuke the government but cannot forget the atrocities of the Communist Party, we rebuke the Communist Party but cannot forget the failure of the government. Will this contradictory method of argument save either hapless party from extinction?" This was the position of some liberal intellectuals, whether in Taiwan or on the mainland.[218] On 21 April, the Chinese Communist Army crossed the Yangtze River, and three days later, the flag of the Kuomintang above Nanjing's Presidential Palace was replaced by the red flag of the Communist Party of China. At the same time, the Communist army quickly advanced across the country in every direction. On August 18th, Mao Zedong published "Farewell, John Leighton Stuart", in which he described this recently departed successor of Marshall as US ambassador to China as "a symbol of the complete failure of the US policy of aggression". Yet Mao was well aware that John Leighton Stuart had been a devout missionary who founded a church school that became Yanjing University and had spent time in a Japanese prison. However, Mao Zedong wrote that "for most of his life his home had been China" but he was an American "who simply pretended to love the United States and love China".[219] Mao used the departure of John Leighton Stuart to formally "farewell" the United States in a contemptuous and even sarcastic tone, an attitude very different from the smiles he lavished on American diplomats, generals, and presidential envoys and servicemen who wanted to work together with him to reach an agreement in Yan'an only a few years previously (Figs. 1, 2, 3, 4, 5, 6, 7, 8, 9, 10, 11, 12, 13, 14, and 15).

[218] Fu Sinian, 20 February 1947, *Hu Shi Laiwang Shuxin Xuan*, xia volume, Hong Kong: Zhonghua Shuju, p. 177.

[219] Not long ago, Zhou Enlai rejected Mr. Strydom's visit to Beijing in June, portraying the U.S. ambassador as "a man who habitually hides his hypocrisy and deception in the face of amiability". Zhou Enlai has always shown himself to be a diplomatic expert with understanding and flexibility, but Zhou was well aware that in the end, he had to act from Mao Zedong's stance.

Fig. 1 Mao Zedong, Zhou Enlai and Bo Gu in Yan'an, 1937

Fig. 2 Helen Foster Snow during the period of KMT-CPC cooperation, 1938

Fig. 3 Photograph taken on 29 March 1938 depicting prominent cultural figures. In the front row (from the left) are Mao Dun, Xia Yan, and Liao Chengzhi, and in the back row (from left) are Pan Hannian, Wang Fuquan, Yu Feng, Ye Wenjin, and Situ Huimin

Fig. 4 Sixth Plenum of the Sixth Central Committee of the CPC at Qiaoergou, 1938. In the front row (from the left) are Kang Sheng, Mao Zedong, Wang Jiaxiang, Zhu De, Xiang Ying, and Wang Ming, and in the back row are Chen Yun, Bo Gu, Peng Dehuai, Liu Shaoqi, Zhou Enlai, and Zhang Wentian

Fig. 5 Group photograph of participants at the Yan'an Forum on Literature and Art, 1942

Fig. 6 1943: Gu Yuan, *Rent Reduction Meeting*, woodcut, 13.5 cm x 20 cm

Fig. 7 1943: Meeting of the Allied leaders of the USA, China, and the UK in Cairo. Chiang Kai-shek represented China

Fig. 8 1943: Wang Jingwei and Japanese PM Tojo Hideki entering the Japanese Prime Minister's residence

Fig. 9 1945: Cai Dizhi, *Evacuating Guilin under Attack*, woodcut, 23 cm x 32.2 cm

Fig. 10 Parade in Chongqing celebrating victory in the War of Resistance against the Japanese, 1945

Fig. 11 Mao Zedong, Patrick Hurley, and Chiang Kai-shek taking part in KMT-CPC negotiations in Chongqing, 1945

Fig. 12 1947: Gu Yuan, *Burning Land Deeds*, woodcut, 28 cm x 18.5 cm. The work records the struggle between the CPC and the KMT to formulate policies which would win over the peasants

Fig. 13 1947: John Leighton Stuart, President of Yenching University, with teachers and students

Fig. 14 1947: Yang Nawei, Silence is the Highest Form of Resistance, woodcut, 21 cm x 29 cm

Fig. 15 Henri Cartier-Bresson's photograph, *Gold Rush*, Shanghai, 1948

Chapter Five
1949–1953: A Confrontation between Two Regimes

You are right, I can live on, and for you, I must struggle to the end! But outside the storms must come and we really have no shelter. Until what time can I struggle without my nerves collapsing, God only knows! Can I struggle with fate? (Shen Congwen, "Letter to Zhang Zhaohe", 1949).

Since the mouth of the imperialist pig's snout reached China, there have been two very different views on the "China problem". One is the "China problem" viewed by imperialism, traitors, running dogs, landlords, and bureaucrats. In their minds, the so-called "China problem" is how to oppress and enslave the Chinese people and turn China into a semi-colonial or even a colonial problem. What Chinese people insist on is the problem of how to smash imperialism and its running dogs. Therefore, on this "China problem" is imposed the "problem" of the life-and-death struggle between the revolutionary people and the imperialist reactionaries. (Zhang Zige, writing in *Guangming Daily*, 1951)

L. Peng, *A History of China in the 20th Century*,
https://doi.org/10.1007/978-981-99-0734-2_7

The Establishment of the People's Republic of China

Four years after leaving China in August 1949, John Leighton Stuart wrote in his memoirs:

> It is also ironic. It was through the revolution for freedom that the United States was born and established the world's first truly republican system, which has shown its vitality, evolved and been perfected through countless trials. The history of the American people's struggle for liberal democracy and the American aid to China are both known to the whole world; they both encouraged China to embark on the path of reform. Sun Yat-sen's "Three Principles of the People" are the perfect application of Lincoln's immortal description of democracy to the land of China. The Communist ideal has been revised by the Soviet Union and has also deviated from its original ideal. But in China, we are accused of being imperialists, aiding the oppression of a reactionary and corrupt regime, and those who accuse us are winning the revolution under the slogans of democracy and freedom.[1]

On 10 January 1949, given that the Communist Party's seizure of power had been decided, Mao Zedong put forward eight conditions to the Kuomintang, which was seeking peace negotiations, and if the KMT did not accept them, "their talk of peace is nothing more than a hoax". The KMT apparently rejected the eight conditions that essentially spelled out the overthrow of the KMT regime. It was noted, however, that the CPC had proposed convening a political consultative conference to form a coalition government. In the second half of the year, Mao Zedong still remembered the political consultative conference held by the Kuomintang in 1946 and he had not forgotten to use the concepts of "democracy" and "freedom" to win cooperation and support of the majority of pro-peace intellectuals and partisans, not to mention that the KMT government has not yet left the mainland, hoping that people would in time regard the soon-to-be-born "New China" as the kind of democracy the people wanted. In order to give legitimacy to the soon-to-be-established Communist regime, the CPC decided to call for the participation of different parties and non-partisans in the "Political Consultative Conference" they now reorganized. From 21 to

[1] John Stuart Leighton, *Zai Hua Wushi Nian* (Fifty Years in China), Haikou: Hainan Chubanshe, 2010, p. 207.

30 September 1949, the First Chinese People's Political Consultative Conference (CPPCC) of the Communist Party of China was held in Beiping.

On 1 May 1948, when the CPC proposed convening the CPPCC, Mao Zedong described it as the "new political consultative conference" (the "New CPPCC"), to underscore the differences with the previous Political Consultative Conference convened by the Kuomintang, and its aim as forming a democratic coalition government. Those democrats and non-partisans who were invited to Yan'an to discuss China's future were enthusiastic about this development. Mao Zedong described the democratic coalition government as "the People's Republic of China", although the name was only finalized at the subsequent CPPCC meeting. At the preparatory meeting of the New Chinese People's Political Consultative Conference (11–19 June), Mao Zedong said that over the previous three years, "the People's Liberation Army had eliminated a total of 5.59 million reactionary Kuomintang troops" and that "this is a victory for all Chinese people and a victory for people all over the world". Mao Zedong clearly did not agree that both the KMT and the CPC have responsibility for the Civil War, and just as the "New Political Consultative Conference" was about to convene, Mao Zedong pointedly attributed the reasons for the Civil War to the United States. In "The Bankruptcy of the Micro-Historical View" (16 September), he wrote: "The Chinese people should be grateful to Dean Acheson as the spokesman for the American bourgeoisie, not only because Acheson explicitly confessed that the United States paid for the guns and Chiang Kai shek supplied the people who killed Chinese people in battle for the United States, so China's progressives have evidence to convince the country's backward elements. As you see, Acheson himself confessed that this bloody war, which had cost millions of Chinese lives in recent years, had been planned and successfully organized by American imperialism".[2] Indeed, during the Civil War, all those who cared about China's future and destiny did not want war, no matter who was fighting whom, and it was those third-party forces who expended enormous efforts mediating between the KMT and CPC who wanted it. The CPC was finally victorious in the civil war, but regardless, peace was generally welcomed.

[2] Mao Zedong, *Mao Zedong Xuanji* (Selected Writings of Mao Zedong), vol. 4, Beijing: Renmin Chubanshe, 1960, p. 1513.

However, concerns continued to exist about what kind of regime the forthcoming democratic coalition government would be. By September, Mao Zedong, who was victorious and in power, stopped referring to expedient concepts like "coalition government" and had no intention of reconsidering with Chiang Kai-shek the creation of a truly multi-party democratic state, which the CPC had repeatedly called for throughout most of the late 1930s and 1940s. On 30 June 1949, Mao Zedong laid down the basic principles of the future Chinese political system by publishing "On the People's Democratic Dictatorship" to commemorate the 28th anniversary of the CPC. He wrote to tell people that the so-called people's democratic dictatorship was a "people's democratic dictatorship based on the alliance of workers and peasants led by the proletariat (through the Communist Party)". No matter how backward China's industry may have been at this time and how very limited the number of workers in the country was, Mao Zedong described workers and peasants together accounting for 80–90% of the country, he said the alliance—in which peasants were in fact the majority—was the basis of the new dictatorship, and that the Communist Party of China was the vanguard of the working class because of its mastery of Marxism–Leninism.[3] Therefore, the "people's democratic dictatorship" needed to be led "through" the Communist Party. In the Party's executive arrangements, the CPC exercised power through the Politburo during the periods when the Central Committee was not meeting, and the Politburo comprised only seven members (the other six being Liu Shaoqi, Zhou Enlai, Zhu De, Chen Yun, Lin Biao and Deng Xiaoping), and the core of power was concentrated in the hands of the supreme leader. This was the basic power structure and political system of the People's Republic of China. At this time, Mao Zedong was undoubtedly familiar with British Prime Minister Winston Churchill's Iron Curtain speech on the Soviet Union and its Communism at Westminster College in Fulton, United States, on 5 March 1946, in which Churchill divided the world into two camps, US-led imperialism and Soviet-led socialism, but Mao did not use

[3] These sentences in Mao Zedong's "On the People's Democratic Dictatorship" could be recited by one or two later generations: "The cannon fire of the October Revolution sent us Marxism-Leninism. The October Revolution helped the world and China's progressive elements, using the proletariat's view of the universe as a tool to observe the fate of our country and reconsider our own problems. We would take the Russian path—that was the conclusion".

Cold War vocabulary at this time, and he was mainly focused on Chiang Kai-shek and the United States. Rebuking accusations of "dictatorship" by the Communist Party, Mao Zedong said: "'You are dictatorial.' Lovely gentlemen, you're right, we are. All the experiences the Chinese people have accumulated over decades have called for us to exercise the people's democratic dictatorship or the people's democratic authoritarianism, in short, to deprive the reactionaries of their voice and to give the people a voice".[4] He used the words of the Song Dynasty philosopher Zhu Xi, "deal with a man as he deals with you" to express his inverted political position: "The foreign reactionaries insult us for implementing 'dictatorship' or 'totalitarian rule', but they are the ones who practice dictatorship or totalitarianism. They impose a class dictatorship of the bourgeoisie over the proletariat and other people, class totalitarianism. Sun Yat-sen's description of the bourgeoisie who in modern times oppress ordinary people in various countries refers to these people. Chiang Kai-shek's counter-revolutionary dictatorship was learned from these reactionary guys".[5] Mao Zedong was now in Beijing the symbolic center of China's political culture and was no longer simply in Yan'an beginning to address the world as one of the "people". In "On the People's Democratic Dictatorship", Mao Zedong mentioned that the experience of the Communist Party of China is the popular masses contacted by the Party, the army led by the Party, and the united front led by the Party and that the Party occupies a leading position in all aspects. Those who participated in the 1946 political consultative conference would not have forgotten that opinion on the nationalization of the army was divided between the Communist Party of China and third-party forces and that the CPC believed that the army could not be handed over to the KMT, but only to the popularly elected coalition government. But now, Mao unabashedly emphasized the Communist Party's leadership of the army, so that the basic conditions needed for a democratic constitution, previously emphasized by most centrist forces, need not be discussed. Since the main leaders in the government were all cadres of the CPC, the main leaders of the Party and the government overlapped, and the Party (through its

[4] Mao Zedong, *Mao Zedong Xuanji* (Selected Writings of Mao Zedong), vol. 4, Beijing: Renmin Chubanshe, 1960, p. 1480.

[5] Ibid., p. 1483.

secretary, representative, person in charge, or first-in-command, according to the context) was the final decision-maker at all levels of government.

In the general outline of the *Organization Law of the Central People's Government of the People's Republic of China*, adopted on 27 September, the leadership of the CPC was omitted from the text:

1. The People's Republic of China is a country led by the working class and based on the union of workers and peasants, which unites the democratic classes and the people of all ethnic groups in the country.
2. The government of the People's Republic of China is governed by the People's Congress based on the principle of democratic centralization.
3. Before the National People's Congress is convened by universal election, the plenary session of the Chinese People's Political Consultative Conference shall exercise the functions and powers of the National People's Congress, formulate the Organization Law of the Central People's Government of the People's Republic of China, elect the Central People's Government Committee of the People's Republic of China, and exercise the powers of the State.
4. The Central People's Government Committee, on behalf of the People's Republic of China, exercises domestic state power.
5. The Central People's Government Committee organizes the Council of State Affairs as the highest executive organ of state affairs, the People's Revolutionary Military Commission as the supreme administrative organ of the state military, and the Supreme People's Court and the Supreme People's Procuratorate as the highest judicial and procuratorial organs of the state.

However, the Central People's Government Committee exercised its functions and powers on the basis of the "Common Program formulated by a plenary session of the Chinese People's Political Consultative Conference". The Common Program of the Chinese People's Political Consultative Conference, adopted on 29 September and regarded as an interim constitution, made it very clear that "the Chinese People's Political Consultative Conference unanimously agreed to take New Democracy, or People's Democracy, as the political basis for the founding of the People's Republic of China". Indeed, Mao Zedong had already written about this "political foundation" as early as 1940, and in "New Democracy", Mao Zedong used the October Revolution of the Soviet Union as the demarcation line placing the leadership of the Chinese revolution, and even the bourgeois revolution, in the hands of the proletariat, that is in the hands of the Communist Party, as Mao said in his speech:

> There are two kinds of world revolutions, the first is the world revolution which belongs to the bourgeoisie and capitalism. The period of this world revolution is long gone, and it came to an end when the first imperialist world war broke out in 1914, and especially when the Russian Revolution of October 1917 concluded. From then on, a second world revolution, the proletarian socialist world revolution, began. This revolution has the proletariat of capitalist countries as its main force, and the colonial and semi-colonial oppressed peoples as allies. Regardless of the class, party or individual among the oppressed peoples participating in the revolution and whether or not they are conscious of or subjectively understand this or not, as long as they oppose imperialism, their revolution will become part of the proletarian socialist world revolution and of the forces of the proletarian socialist world revolution alliance.

This view clearly came from Stalin, but the emphasis on party leadership is at the heart of Mao Zedong's view. In writing "On the People's Democratic Dictatorship", Mao's emphasis on the nature of the Party's proletarian vanguard provided the basis for the later state and political system to be set up. The words "workers and peasants", "the people", "the state", "democracy" and "the Party" are woven into different documents, so that the power structure of the new regime was no different from that of the Kuomintang period, except that the CPPCC was run by the Communist Party of China. By this time, people are already familiar with the principle of "democratic centralism"—the masses obey the Party, the lower level (organization) obeys the superiors (organization), and the whole Party obeys the Central Committee. As soon as it is understood that this concentration is not based on the count of votes, but on the personal will of the person in charge of the Party's organizations from the local to the central level.

The various democratic parties participating in the new CPPCC (Revolutionary Committee of the Chinese Nationalist Party, Chinese Democratic League, Chinese Democratic National Construction Association, Chinese Association for Promoting Democracy, Chinese Peasants and Workers Democratic Party, Communist Party of China, Jiusan Society and Taiwan Democratic Self-Government League) and a total of 45 units (of which the liberated areas had six units and the army had six units) participated in the meeting, which brought together a total of 662 full and supplementary representatives. It might have appeared like a meeting with wide representation, but in most units, there were different numbers of CPC members, and the list of participants was reviewed by the CPC before the meeting. The existence of these parties demonstrates what the CPC claimed to be a multi-party cooperative political system and it implements a policy of "long-term coexistence and mutual supervision". However, no political party or individual, apart from the CPC, had been the issue most heatedly debated at the KMT's political consultative conference in 1946. In the new CPPCC, no one proposed the nationalization of the military, which confirmed the decorative roles all democratic parties played in future cooperation with the CPC: the democratic parties could offer up opinions but whether or not they were accepted was decided by the CPC, which can also be interpreted as "democratic centralism".

The conference adopted the Common Program of the Chinese People's Political Consultative Conference which was constitutional in nature, as well as the "Organization Law of the Chinese People's Political Consultative Conference" and the "Organization Law of the Central People's Government of the People's Republic of China". Mao Zedong was elected Chairman of the Central People's Government of the PRC, while Zhu De, Liu Shaoqi, Song Qingling, Li Jishen, Zhang Lan and Gao Gang were Vice Chairmen. Zhou Enlai, Chen Yi and other 56 people were members of the Central People's Government Committee. The KMT's flag can only be raised in Taiwan, while the five-star red flag becomes the flag of the People's Republic of China on the mainland, with the Party as the leader with the largest of the five stars, while the remaining four small stars represented the workers, peasants, the small bourgeoisie, and national bourgeoisie (understood to be the 400 million Chinese people). The capital was changed from Nanjing to Beiping, but in 1928 the city's name had been changed from Beijing to Beiping; now it was renamed Beijing. Most importantly, Mao Zedong was not only chairman of the Central Committee of the Communist Party of China, chairman of the Politburo and secretary of the Secretariat of the CPC Central Committee, but also chairman of the People's Republic of China and chairman of the Military Commission. Henceforth, at future CPPCC meetings at all levels, no one could talk about the policies and initiatives of the ruling party as they did under the Kuomintang, and the qualifications of delegates depended first and foremost on agreeing to the basic principle of the leadership of the CPC.

Chiang Kai-shek's KMT was obviously excluded from the new CPPCC and the outside Youth Party had gone to Taiwan. Compared with the 1946 political consultative conference, no one discussed whether the army was truly nationalized or the number of votes the different parties had under the new authority. Of course, no one cared about the relationship between the various authorities of the government, and the leaders of all parties participated in the work of the government (democratic) in different forms, but the final opinions and decisions were made by the party central or by provincial and municipal local government party leaders (centralism). Delegates certainly could discuss and deliberate on the documents of Congress, such as the Common Program. For example, the 83-year-old Zhang Yuanji opined that the text of the Common Program was "very untidy and inconsistent throughout", and so on. He even made an untimely objection to the adoption of the Western calendar: We should begin a new cycle, but If adopt the Gregorian calendar to conform to international usage, this would be difficult at present. At the present time, we still regard our Republic as a Republic and democracy as democracy, so it is best to continue using the Republic of China era, so this year is the 38th year of the Republic". In any case, compared with the political consultative conference of the Kuomintang, the "New CPPCC" apparently took place and ended in a warm and harmonious atmosphere, and the convening of the new CPPCC provided the conditions for real izing the legitimacy of the new regime established by the CPC. People could look at the new government agencies: 11 of the 24 ministers were not CPC members, an aspect of the new regime's democratic image, and indeed a serious reason for the Party's eagerness to manage the country's experienced urbanites for the moment. In any case, there was widespread hope for the future of New China.

Some liberal intellectuals remained on the mainland. Liang Shuming, who discussed national liberation and social transformation with Mao Zedong in Yan'an in 1938, wrote to Mao Zedong and Zhou Enlai on January 6th to say that he would not participate in the "New CPPCC" convened by the Communist Party of China and that although he had in the past worked for democracy on all sides of the political spectrum as secretary-general of the Democratic League, he made it clear in a letter to Zhang Lan that month that he was "only speaking, not acting; just a man, no longer an organization". On 20 January, in Chongqing's *Dagong Bao*, Liang Shuming also published "A Difficult Problem in Peace Talks, and a Notice to High-Ranking People in the KMT" and "Notice to the Communist Party of China"; as a centrist, Liang warned both the KMT and CPC that his core concern was peace and unity. By this time the Kuomintang had lost its influence and the Communist Party was actively "pursuing impoverished bandits", when Liang Shuming told the Communist Party that the real solution to any problem could only be political means, not force. He admonished the Chinese Communist Party to "accommodate dissent", and even spoke somewhat uneasily about a conjectural future: "Today, the Chinese Communist Party has not only won the power to lead China but also proclaims that it leads China, and at the same time only when it always calls for 'unity' and 'democracy' (and does not promote one-party dictatorship) will I be its friend. If I say 'stop the war, I should not be committing the crime of 'counter-revolution'". In fact, when third-party forces in the north had previously promoted a centrist line or emphasized peace as the priority, the CPC regarded them as helping the KMT, depicting them as conspiratorial and "anti-people". Liang said he "had always disapproved of the excessive use of force by the Chinese Communist Party". As the situation changed he said, "I am firmly opposed to the civil war to the end! 我I cannot agree to the fighting because that side [i.e. the KMT] uses the expression 'suppressing the insurgency'; similarly, I can't agree to the others fighting because this side uses the term 'revolution'. If one gives way to a revolution, this does not mean that revolution is the same thing as the removal of evil". Just as the right wing of the Kuomintang and later the left often accused Liang Shuming of being a stubborn and obstinate intellectual, he was not liked by the CPC; in 1946 Liang Shuming, as an important third-party figure (being both secretary-general of the Democratic League and its representative at the political consultative conference organized by the Kuomintang), argued for peace. Worried about the deteriorating situation, he and other representatives submitted a proposal for a truce to Chiang Kai-shek, Zhou Enlai and Marshall at the same time in order to prevent the continuation of the civil war. Zhou Enlai was outraged when he saw their proposal because they had forgotten to inform Zhou Enlai in advance. In fact, the contents of his third-party proposal were seen by the CPC as being for the good of the KMT. Zhou not only disagreed with the proposal, but he also called Liang "a hypocrite". Liang Shuming, who thereafter resolved not to engage in politics, saw Zhou's anger as his own failure to act on national event, and he later wrote "One aspect of my guilt regarding the earlier peace talks" (May 1949), as an apology to the CPC. On 10 March, Liang Shuming published "Reply to Hong Kong Friends' Insults" in Chongqing's *Dagong Bao*:

> I know that the Communist Party is exclusive. Although you reject me, I do not have you as an enemy in my heart. I am not hostile to any party. In the past the KMT opposed me, and when I couldn't get tough with the coalition, I just had to look the other way—I knew he wouldn't last long. Today I know the Communist Party is coming, and I can only "coexist but not agree" with them. In the communist world, I will have to be careful. So, I decided that for the next three years, I would only speak but not act; I would simply be an individual and not part of any organization. So, before the publication of my most recent articles, on January 6th I wrote to Mao Zedong and Zhou Enlai.

As an invited member of the first session of the National Committee of the Chinese People's Political Consultative Conference (CPPCC) and a prominent member of the Standing Committee of the CPPCC, unlike Chen Yuan with the unsullied reputation, Liang Shuming, who refused Chiang Kai-shek's plane to Nanjing and stayed in Beijing because he saw "light", wrote an open letter to Hu Shi on April 29, 1949.[6] In the letter, he told people that Hu Shi had a deep distrust of the Communist Party, and that Hu had told Chen: "The Communist Party is coming, so there will be no freedom". To the surprise of the intellectual world, historians like Chen Yuan, who did not concern themselves much with politics, had already been able to make their point: "This false perception has only recently been dispelled. Now I know that 'all culture is subordinate to politics and guided by politics'".[7]

On October 1st, at 2 p.m., the first meeting of the Central People's Government Committee was held in the Qinzheng Hall in Zhongnanhai. The meeting was presided over by Mao Zedong, and when the Chairman, Vice Chairman and members of the Central People's Government were all announced, the Central People's Government under the leadership of the CPC was inaugurated. The meeting declared that this government

[6] This letter was published in *Renmin Ribao* (People's Daily) on 11 May 1949 and subsequently on 17 May in *Jinbu Ribao* (Progress Daily).

[7] Quoted from Chen Zhichao ed., *Chen Yuan Laiwang Shixin Ji* (Anthology of Correspondence with Chen Yuan), Shanghai: Shanghai Guji Chubanshe, 1990, p. 194.

was the only legitimate government in China. Lin Boqu was [s]elected Secretary-General of the Central People's Government Committee, Zhou Enlai was appointed Prime Minister and Minister for Foreign Affairs of the Political Council, Mao Zedong Chairman of the People's Revolutionary Military Commission, Zhu De commander-in-chief of the Chinese People's Liberation Army, Shen Junru President of the Supreme People's Court, and Luo Ronghuan (1902–1963) as Procurator-General of the Supreme People's Procuratorate. At 3 p.m., on the rostrum of Tiananmen Gate, Lin Boqu announced the beginning of the founding ceremony of the People's Republic of China. Mao Zedong and his comrades and allies ascended the historic symbol of power that is Tiananmen Gate and Mao Zedong announced to the world:"The Central People's Government of the People's Republic of China is established today!" China subsequently had two governments and two national days—in Taiwan, the Republic of China and on the mainland, the People's Republic of China.[8]

On that day, Tiananmen Square resounded with calls of "Long live Chairman Mao!" Zhang Yuanji, who had been asleep at night, wrote: "I could hear the cheers coming from the parade outside until well into the night". Soon, Hu Feng, who watched the ceremonial parade and the people marching, described the historical scene in his poem "Time Begins":

> The sea!
> The sea of cheering!
> The sea of singing!
> The sea of dancing!
> The gleaming sea!
> The sea coming from all directions!
> The sea flowing in all directions!

[8] On 8 November, Lin Boqu, secretary-general of the Central People's Government of the CPC, told a Xinhua News Agency reporter: "The People's Republic of China must set a new National Day, as recently stipulated by the Central People's Government. We commemorated October 10 because we wanted to arouse the people of the whole country, inherit the legacy of Mr. Sun Yat-sen and other revolutionary martyrs, overthrow the internal and external oppressors, and establish a true People's Republic of China. Now that the struggle of the people of the whole country has been successful, the old China is dead and New China has been born, there should be a new National Day. Citizens and overseas Chinese who hold memorial meetings on October 10 shall be allowed to do so, but it cannot be celebrated as National Day". Ref: *Renmin Ribao* (People's Daily), 9 October 1949.

Laboring, struggling, creating,
The sea flowing from the past
Laboring, struggling, creating,
The sea flowing to the future
In Hu Feng's view at this time, this was an historical new beginning.

The ceremony, the "ceremony of the national founding", was the first announcement that Mao had won political power, but he was still carefully arranging the final annihilation of the Kuomintang's army on the mainland. He certainly wanted to end the war as soon as possible, but he took a long-range approach to achieve final military victory, so that Bai Chongxi and Hu Zongnan were little aware of the movements of the Chinese Communist army gradually encircling them. The CPC had an outright advantage over the KMT's army, tightening the noose and quickly mopping up; there were sporadic revolts in Zhejiang, northern Anhui, Sichuan, Guangxi, Yunnan, south-west Shaanxi, and Tibet, so the Party needed time to clean up. Soon, however, on 23 May 1951, the representatives of China and the representative of Tibet, Ngapo Ngawang Jigme, signed the agreement regarding measures for the peaceful liberation of Tibet in Beijing. With that, the CPC had taken full control of all Chinese mainland territory.

Stabilizing prices and unifying finance as soon as possible became important measures in taking charge of the newly liberated areas. On 15 January 1949, the Central Committee of the CPC issued "instructions on the acceptance of bureaucratic capitalist enterprises" by central bureaus and began to dismantle the bureaucratic capital-controlled financial and transportation systems. However, due to the huge expenditure on war, but also the need for a large amount of additional currency, which of course led to rising prices, people felt very uncertain. As the CPC's economic expert and director at that time of the Central Committee for Finance and Economic Affairs, Chen Yun explained:"The present currency issuance plan should first guarantee the provision for military spending, followed by price stability. The reason for the rise in prices is the huge fiscal deficit, forcing us to issue more money, and to narrow or even eliminate the fiscal deficit, the key to military designation (spending) being early victory in the war of liberation across the country. The faster victory comes, the more likely it will be that we will reduce and even eliminate the fiscal deficit and control the issuance of money, thereby gradually stabilizing prices".[9] In sum, for the CPC at this time, the destruction of the Kuomintang and complete consolidation of power were prerequisites for solving economic problems until April 1950, when the country's fiscal balance began to close. In September, China People's Bank's total deposits were more than 12 times those of December 1949, and the new fiscal situation reflected the recovery of the economy from the turmoil of the war.

In "On the People's Democratic Dictatorship", Mao Zedong made clear the position of the CPC:

> "You lean to one side". That's exactly what happened. Leaning to one side is what Sun Yat-sen's 40 years of experience and the Communist Party's 28 years of experience taught us; to achieve and consolidate victory we had to lean to one side. Having accumulated 40 years and 28 years of experience, the Chinese people must either lean to the imperialist side or to the socialist side, without exception.[10]

The CPC's decision to "lean to one side", namely the Soviet Union, was the result of a number of factors, and now, based on the consolidation of the new regime and the current state of international political resources, Mao Zedong preferred to regard the Soviet Union as the most important resource favoring the future of the new regime. Mao Zedong knew that Stalin had said several years previously that the CPC was a "margarine"-style Communist Party, lacking the purity of the Communist cause, and that Mao was still weighing up and making use of the Soviet Union and the United States during the later period of the Anti-Japanese War and during the Civil War, suggesting that Mao could put ideological issues aside for the sake of the Party's survival and development. In fact, it was in the Northeast that the Soviet Union worked with the CPC to safeguard its interests and security in the Far East and the northern Pacific, and after the Chinese Communists gained the advantage in the Civil War, Stalin began to adjust his policy towards China, especially reassessing the CPC,[11] When the general momentum of the CPC assuming

[9] Jin Chongji, op. cit., p. 704.

[10] Mao Zedong, *Mao Zedong Xuanji* (Selected Writings of Mao Zedong), vol. 4, Beijing: Renmin Chubanshe, 1960, pp. 1477–1478.

[11] Even in January 1949, Stalin told Mao Zedong that the Nationalist government wanted the Soviet Union to mediate between the CPC and the KMT, and that the Soviet

power had been established, Stalin was undoubtedly reassured that guarantees regarding Soviet Interests as stipulated in the China-Soviet Treaty signed with the National Government would be upheld by the CPC. Given Soviet interests in the Northeast and the need to prevent the US troops from getting close to the CPC, from January 30 to February 7, 1949, Anastas Mikoyan (1895–1978), a member of the Soviet Politburo, was sent by Stalin to Xibeipo in China to hold discussions with Mao Zedong and Liu Shaoqi. Mao clearly told Mikoyan: China must move closer to the Soviet Union and we hope that the Soviet Union will help the CPC economically as soon as possible. On 26 June, Liu Shaoqi led a CPC delegation on a secret visit to Moscow to get word from the Soviets on terms of loans, sending experts and providing military assistance. In talks with the CPC delegation, Stalin even sent a message of handing over power to lead the Asian revolution to Mao, which indicated Stalin's further endorsement of Mao. All this allowed Mao Zedong to finally, and publicly, say "farewell" to John Stuart Leighton—and the United States, in the media.

During his visit to Moscow, Liu Shaoqi submitted a report on the handling of the China-Soviet treaty. The report stated:

> The Treaty of Friendship and Alliance between the Soviet Union and China in the past provided great help to the Chinese people, and in the future, with the continued recognition of this treaty by the government of New China it will make greater contributions to the Soviet and Chinese peoples, especially to the Chinese people. We are fully willing to continue to recognize this treaty, which, when the Soviet Union establishes diplomatic relations with New China, needs to be perpetuated and handled in three ways, as follows:
>
> 1. The new Chinese government will announce full recognition of the Treaty's continuing validity without calling for any modification.
> 2. In accordance with the spirit of the original treaty, the Sino-Soviet Treaty of Friendship and Alliance will be re-signed by representatives of the two Governments in order to add or remove passages or content in the light of new circumstances.

Union was willing to accept the proposal for peace talks between the two parties. Mao, however, rejected the idea.

3. An exchange of texts between representatives of the two Governments will maintain the status of the Treaty for now, but we will prepare to sign a new treaty at an appropriate time.

Of these three approaches, which one should we follow?

Stalin commented on the report: "Wait until Mao Zedong comes to Moscow before deciding on this issue".[12]

On 16 December 1949, Mao Zedong arrived in Moscow in the hope of signing a new Sino-Soviet treaty. On the same day that Mao Zedong arrived in Moscow, Zhou Enlai said at the 11th government meeting: Mao Zedong's mission during his visit to the Soviet Union was to repeal a treaty signed by the KMT government in 1945 that harmed China's interests and to sign a new treaty. At first, Stalin insisted that the Soviet-Chinese treaty previously signed with the National Government was based on the Yalta Agreement, which meant that a principled amendment was not possible. Stalin's considerations were complicated, namely whether Soviet interests in the Far East could be assured, and he feared that re-signing the agreement could lead to a re-examination of old and new treaties by the United States and Britain, and that the system established by the Yalta Agreement would be subverted. On 20 January 1950, Zhou Enlai led a Chinese delegation to Moscow for the third official meeting between Stalin and Mao Zedong. On the issue of sovereignty and national interests, the two sides revised the draft agreement several times, and finally, the Soviet Union abandoned the original agreement on the lease of Lüshun port as a naval base but also abandoned all rights and interests in Dalian and the Chinese Eastern Railway. However, Stalin abandoned these rights, about which he had always been very concerned, not, as the media maintained, as a result of the Soviet Union's friendship with New China, but based on Stalin's view that if the CCP's demands were not partially met, the latter could revert to the United States, which Stalin needed to prevent at all costs. In fact, from the second half of 1948 to the first half of 1949, when the United States was studying international issues, especially Sino-Soviet relations, it attempted to develop measures to exacerbate relations between China and the Soviet Union in order to prevent the two Communist regimes from drawing closer. Indeed,

[12] Quoted from Shen Zhihua, *Mao Zedong, Sidalin yu Chaoxian Zhanzheng* (Mao Zedong, Stalin and the Korean War), Guangzhou: Guangdong Renmin Chubanshe, 2016, p. 129.

on 5 January, during the Sino-Soviet negotiations, Truman announced at a press conference: The United States would not get involved in China's civil war and would not provide military assistance to Taiwan. On the 12th, Secretary of State Dean Acheson issued a reminder that it was Russia, not the United States, that had historically violated China's sovereignty and interests. On the 17th, the Soviet Embassy in China reported: "Now the US imperialists attach great importance to the issue of Sino-Soviet relations in their policy towards China. The US pins its hopes on trade to make China economically dependent if it recognizes the people's government, and would then exert political influence on China. The United States is afraid of China's participation in the Soviet-led socialist system".[13] All indications suggest that Stalin thought he needed to draw the CPC, which has already gained power, to himself so that the Soviet-led socialist camp could strengthen its confrontation with the Western camp because of China's accession. Mao eventually sidestepped discussions on Mongolia, the so-called sovereignty issue, and in order to obtain concrete, timely, and adequate economic and military assistance from the Soviet Union, he agreed to sign the Sino-Soviet Treaty of Friendship and Mutual Assistance and related documents. Mao Zedong told his people that China needed the Soviet Union as "a reliable ally, so that we can get on with our domestic construction work and jointly deal with possible imperialist aggression and strive for world peace".[14] On 14 February, after news of the signing of the treaty was announced, Liu Shaoqi said at a celebratory banquet that the signing of the treaty marked a "new era" in friendly relations between the two countries, even though this time Stalin promised Mao only a $300 m loan to China.

Consolidation of the New Regime

In June 1950, Mao Zedong was already thinking about China's entry into the Korean War, which would entail drawing on China's financial and economic capacity. In that month, the CPC held its Third Plenary Session of the 7th Central Committee, at which Mao Zedong presented a report stressing that the first of three conditions to be met for achieving basic improvement in the country's fiscal and economic situation was

[13] Ibid., p. 155.

[14] *Renmin Ribao* (People's Daily), 13 April 1950.

completing the land reform (the other two being adjusting industry and commerce and introducing requirements for frugality in state institutions). He argued that it was imperative to address the nation's financial and economic problems by confiscating the property of landlords. The Common Program, previously adopted by the CPPCC, states: "Where land reform has not yet been implemented, the peasant masses must be mobilized and peasants' groups set up; through such measures as eliminating local bandits and bullies, reducing rent and redistributing land, peasants will effectively have their own fields". Also in June, the CPC organized the second session of the CPPCC to consider "Draft Land Reform Law of the People's Republic of China" proposed by the CPC Central Committee, and Liu Shaoqi on behalf of the CPC Central Committee presented "Report on Issues Related to Land Reform". The "Land Reform Law" proclaimed that the purpose of land reform was "to abolish the feudal exploitation of land ownership by the landlord class and implement land ownership by the peasants in order to liberate rural productivity, develop agricultural production and open the way for the industrialization of New China". The land reform impacted the "newly liberated areas" with a population of more than 300 million, and the experience of the early liberated areas began to be introduced to the new areas as a means of fulfilling the promise of the New Democratic Revolution.

The land revolution had always been the goal of the Chinese Communist revolution, but at different times, because of different political and military objectives, different means and strategies were adopted. When the CPC controlled most regions and cities with the exception of Xinjiang, Tibet, and Taiwan, the purpose of land reform was not only to raise funds and mobilize manpower for the war, but also to liberate productive forces, develop economic construction, and fundamentally overturn the traditional system by eliminating local entrenched elites protected by the Kuomintang regime. The measures and policies of this time, compared with those of the past, were relatively careful and meticulous, reducing the revolutionary violence and fierce conflicts of the past. Farmers' concerns about the problems the land reform might bring, if for example the KMT staged a counterattack and confiscated the land that had been shared out, not to mention the threat to their lives, largely abated. Mao Zedong guided the entire Party to take flexible measures in this period to achieve its goals, and at the Third Plenary Session of the Seventh Central Committee Mao warned all Party members: There are still many enemies, but we should not attack them on all sides; the united front and incremental strategies are extremely important for the work of the Party. At this time the CPC needs more support and the scope of the united front needs to be readjusted, so Mao Zedong called on the working class, the urban bourgeoisie, and the national bourgeoisie, as well as the various democratic parties, to support land reform in order to eliminate the landlord class.

In the process of land reform how to deal with rich farmers became an important part of the strategy. Rich farmers made up 6% of the country's rural population, but their land produced almost half of the country's total agricultural output. Different Party leaders, depending on the region, had doubts about policies guaranteeing the rich peasants' economy, but Mao Zedong and Liu Shaoqi controlled the strategy of advancing land reform. On 12 March 1950, Mao Zedong issued a notice to the CPC Central Committee's Central-Southern Bureau and its various regional bureaus to "consult on the strategic issue of the rich peasants". Mao Zedong proposed that the land reform campaign being carried out in the winter should not only not touch the capitalist rich peasants, but also the semi-feudal rich peasants. Mao's reasoning based on the previous experience of the agrarian revolution was: the scale of the land reform was unprecedentedly large, and "excessive leftism" could easily occur and this could even result in "indiscriminate violence and killing"; the war had already ended, the social shock of the land reform was great, and the Party needed to prevent the landlords speaking out which might lead to resistance to the Party; and, the national bourgeoisie was closely involved in the land issue and needed to be stabilized, because "the united front between us and the national bourgeoisie has now been formed politically, economically and organizationally". In preparation for the new phase of land reform, Liu Shaoqi also responded:

> The policy we have adopted to preserve the rich peasant economy is certainly not a temporary policy, but a long-term policy. That is to say, throughout the New Democratic phase, it is all about preserving the rich peasant economy.

> Only when conditions are ripe, can the countryside be widely mechanized, collective farms be organized, and socialist transformation of the countryside be implemented. The existence of the rich farmers' economy would then no longer be necessary. All this can be achieved in the distant future.[15]

This meant that the rich peasant economy was protected compared with that in the previous land reform campaign, and this approach was also enthusiastically received by the group defined as "middle peasants". In short, the general line to be followed now was to rely on poor farmers and farm laborers, uniting with "middle" peasants and "neutral" rich farmers.

The new Land Reform Law was slightly different from the earlier China Land Law Outline, for example, the clothing, cash, and other property of landlords were no longer confiscated, and landlords were also allocated a parcel of land. The policy of "not touching the national bourgeoisie" meant that "the industrial and commercial enterprises run by landlords and the land and property directly used in the operation of industries and businesses would not be confiscated". No encroachment on industries or businesses could result from the confiscation of feudal land and property" (Land Reform Law of the People's Republic of China). In any event, however, the land reform campaign was a class struggle for the redistribution of wealth, as article 2 of the Land Reform Law makes very clear: The confiscation of landlords' land, farm animals, farm tools, surplus food, and surplus houses in rural areas. In order to avoid as much conflict as possible and to ensure the continuity of the campaign, the State Council has adopted documents such as the "Decision on the Demarcation of Social Classes in the Countryside" to divide the land as accurately as possible. The procedure for delineating social classes comprises "discussing class", "assessing class", "processing class", and "permitting class". Despite the specific criteria for the delineation, the work of those who relied solely on policies and their implementation was completely different from the principles of the rule of law. Personal interests, historical grievances, and agitational propaganda all played a part in the emotional "struggle meetings", ultimately resulting in the confiscation, appropriation, and redistribution of property and land in

[15] *Liu Shaoqi Xuanji* (Seletober 1951, when Maocted Writings of Liu Shaoqi), xia volume, Beijing: Renmin Chubanshe, 1985, pp. 40–41.

which errors and conflicts were difficult to avoid. However, the Land Reform Commission set up a "land reform review" procedure to reduce the problems that might emerge in the land reform process.

On the other hand, the policy in the "new liberated areas" was different from that in the "early liberated areas", and the rich peasants at that time did not receive the protection of their interests in the land reform campaign. After the Korean War broke out, with Chiang Kai-shek on Taiwan calling for a "counter-attack against the mainland", some local landlords and rich farmers also tried to use the new land reform policy to launch a "liquidation counter-offensive", demanding the return of property, and dozens of counties in several provinces saw incidents in which houses were seized to settle debts. A new coercive policy was immediately introduced, and on 20 December, for example, the North China Bureau issued a Directive on Suppressing the Counter-Offensive by Rich Peasants and Landlords, and armed repression remained a guarantee of the land reform. Indeed, as An Ziwen, head of the Organization Department of the CPC Central Committee, made clear on 10 October 1951, when he gave a report on ideological mobilization of the CPPCC National Committee's land reform working group:"Land reform is a class struggle... peaceful land reform is impossible".[16] Indeed, coercion, propaganda, mobilization, policy adjustment, trials, executions, and other forms of violent conflict occurred throughout the land reform campaign, and Liang Shuming mentioned rural problems he had witnessed to Mao Zedong after four months inspecting land reform work in eastern Sichuan Province's Yunmen Township in Hechuan County: He saw beatings of landlords during struggle sessions, and a landlord and his wife who could not endure the harsh corporal punishment meted out to them even suicided by throwing themselves into the river. Once ethics and social order were eliminated, clan relations, clan temples and shrines, and gentry organizations all ceased to exist; all resistance was crushed by the Communist army and the militias armed by the CPC. The Party had drawn clear class boundaries for the countryside and supported the actions of poor peasant laborers to "turn their lives around and become owners" (*fanshen zuozhu*), for example by encouraging and supporting peasants in various forms of struggle against landlords, so that people not only established

[16] Shao Yanxiang, "1951 nian dao Gansu" (Journey to Gansu in 1951), in Liu Ruilin ed., *Wengu* (Reviewing the Past), Nanning: Guangxi Shifan Daxue Chubanshe, 2007, p. 4.

clear opponents and objects of hatred, but also strengthened the sense of class struggle and vigilance so that they then formed the habit of accepting the Party organization or the Party's specific person taking charge as the sole referee. By September 1952, the land reform campaign had largely achieved its objectives, with 300 million agricultural areas participating in land reform, and the early liberated areas accounting for more than 90% of the country's total agricultural population. In any case, the CPC's historical experience in land reform provided the basis for the redistribution of land and property in the land reform campaign in the "New Liberated Areas", through which about 43% of the cultivated land was redistributed to 60% of the rural population At least by the end of 1952, the CPC had won the support and trust of most Chinese farmers through the land reform campaign, and political power in the countryside was concentrated in the hands of the Party and the government organizations controlled by the Party, providing the political and legal basis for the new regime to destroy private ownership, conduct large-scale social transformation, transfer resource to the state, and industrialize.

As early as March 1949, in view of the fact that rural grassroots political power had not yet been established in the newly liberated areas, which had a wide range of ramifications and covered a large area, the CPC did not have enough cadres to carry out land reform work, and Mao Zedong arranged a way in which the work of the newly liberated areas was carried out in view of local security and the lack of understanding of land reform among farmers: "In the countryside, the first step in the measured suppression of bandits and opposition to bullies, specifically the struggle against the empowered landlord class, is to complete the preparatory work in reducing rent and interest, so that when the People's Liberation Army arrives in that area after about a year or two it will be able to complete the task of reducing rent and interest, thereby providing the preconditions for the reallocation of land;...".[17] The land reform in the newly liberated areas was based at the outset on military action eliminating bandits and suppressing opposition. On 6 August 1949, Xinhua News Agency published an editorial, "Eliminating Spies and Bandits, Consolidating the Revolutionary Order", which stated: "Even in many cities and villages liberated by the People's Liberation Army, many places are controlled by spies, bandits and reactionary forces, so government

[17] Mao Zedong, *Mao Zedong Xuanji* (Selected Writings of Mao Zedong), vol. 4, Beijing: Renmin Chubanshe, 1960, p. 1430.

decrees cannot be implemented and the old regime cannot be reformed. Therefore, we have sent out a large number of cadres and revolutionary workers and students to the countryside to cooperate with the armed forces of the People's Liberation Army, mobilizing the vast number of peasants, eliminating bandits and spies, overthrowing the rule of counter-revolutionary bullies, stabilizing order, developing production, and then systematically carrying out various social reforms. These actions have necessarily become the central task of this period".[18] On 18 March 1950, the Central Committee of the CPC issued "Directive on the Suppression of Counter-Revolutionary Activities": "All bandit groups engaged in organizing armed mass riots, attacks on our public organs and cadres, and looting of warehouse materials must be resolutely suppressed and annihilated, without a moment's hesitation".[19] Between May 1949 and May 1950, the Communist Party of China eliminated not less than 1 million bandits and armed forces.

In addition to redistributing property, an important objective of the land reform campaign was to eliminate the landlord class and the hidden "counter-revolution" by those holding the same stance. Mao Zedong spoke of three major campaigns being waged simultaneously: the "suppression of counter-revolution", the "land reform campaign" and the campaign to "oppose America and aid Korea". The "counter-revolutionary suppression campaign", which ran from December 1950 to the end of 1951, was a nationwide political campaign conducted by the Communist Party of China through the national army and police (including the military's public security departments), to investigate and suppress counter-revolutionaries, which extended to all sectors and parts of the country.

In the past, the KMT had described the CPC as "bandits", meaning illegal and socially harmful armed groups, and now the KMT government and party members were described as "counter-revolutionaries" in a complete reversal: All forces opposed to the Communist Party could be designated as "counter-revolutionary", and those armed groups of

[18] Zhongyang Dang'anguan (Central Archives), *Zhonggong Zhongyang Wenjian Xuanji* (Selected Works of CPC Central Committee), vol. 18, Beijing: Zhonggong Zhongyang Dangxiao Chubanshe, 1992, p. 547.

[19] Zhonggong Zhongyang Wenxian Yanjiushi, *Jianguo yilai Zhongyao Wenxian Xuanbian* (Selection of Important Documents since the Founding of the Nation), vol. 1, Beijing: Zhongyang Wenxian Chubanshe, 1992, p. 141.

counter-revolutionary forces, now called bandits, included previous armed forces still remaining in some areas and any armed groups and individuals not approved by the Communist Party were all deemed to fall within the scope of those to be eliminated and suppressed. Before the KMT retreated to hole up in Taiwan, many troops and officers remained behind. For example, Bai Chongxi broke up his force of more than 30,000 regular troops and dispersed them to different places to establish armed units who could serve as undercover forces or agents for the KMT in Taiwan. They were officially classified as counter-revolutionary elements like spies, bandits, local bullies, stalwarts of the reactionary party, or leaders of religious sects and secret societies. Eliminating these KMT forces (including individuals designated as "imperialist spies") and all bandit forces associated with the KMT was clearly conducive to the consolidation of the new regime. This helped with effectively fighting the Korean War of "opposition to the USA and aid for Korea" and destroying the old rural system in the land reform campaign. Indeed, when the Korean War broke out, Chiang Kai-shek attempted to participate in the war, and the protection and support extended to Taiwan by the United States contributed to Chiang Kai-shek making military arrangements to launch a "counter-attack against the mainland". At the same time, there was a widely held view among the general public that "World War Three was about to break out", and hidden forces were indeed in line with Taiwan's preparations, as assassination and sabotage operations increased dramatically. In response to any possible "counter-offensive" or military conflict, on 12 February 1951, the Central People's Government promulgated "Regulations of the People's Republic of China on the Punishment of Counter-Revolution", which were considered to be legal weapons and sentencing standards, but in fact the standards were understood and implemented in accordance with the specific understanding of the Party and the Party's army implementing them". Mao Zedong first stressed in May that "the Party's mass line must be implemented to suppress the counter-revolution", and that the "Party committee leaders mobilize the entire Party and the masses". Mao Zedong stipulated that the death penalty should be strictly and prudently controlled in accordance with definite ratios, but Mao Zedong's statements had no legal basis. From December 1950 to September 1951, Mao Zedong issued a number of instructions relating to the suppression of counter-revolution; "as long as we do not kill in error, although the bourgeoisie complain, we should not be afraid of their complaints" (17 January 1951). We must suppress all counter-revolutionaries, but we must not kill in error" (30 March 1951), "The whole process of suppressing counter-revolutionaries must be under the unified leadership of Party committees at all levels, and all public security organs and responsible comrades in charge of organs concerned with repressing counter-revolutionaries must accept the leadership of the Party committee as resolutely as in the past" (10 September 1951). There is no doubt that all this did not follow any legal standards, and the entire counter-revolutionary suppression campaign took the views of party leaders or leaders at all levels as a standard, and in the campaign's specific implementation, the emergence of widespread violence and terror was entirely conceivable. The number of killings, incarcerations, and punishments in various places far exceeded the original plan, and most cases were not subject to strict judicial oversight, being based on political requirements. Sentencing standards in the course of implementation greatly exceeded the provisions of the "Regulations of the People's Republic of China on the Punishment of Counter-Revolution", just as in the early years of the KMT's indiscriminate killings of Communist Party members. When the suppression of the KMT counter-revolution was not carefully supervised, some KMT officials who participated in the 1911 Revolution, the Anti-Japanese War or had surrendered to the CPC in the Civil War were also shot as "active" counter-revolutionary elements. The campaign to suppress the counter-revolution was so fierce and terrifying that even Communist underground organizations in former KMT-rules areas were treated as counter revolutionary. No one could accurately clarify the criteria for terms like "local tyrants" (*eba*) or "popular indignation" (*minfen*), and the words were simply used by most Party cadres at all levels to make personal judgments on which to specifically act. According to indicators provided by the previous Party organizations, the tasks of suppressing counter-revolution readily led to arbitrary actions; in some places even if there was no evidence of any specific "crime" evidence, the mere fact of having been identified as counter-revolutionary was sufficient reason for being executed as "counter-revolutionaries". The campaign concluded at the end of 1951.[20] According to figures provided

[20] In fact, the end of the counter-revolutionary suppression campaign was different in every city and region. In Shanghai, for example, as recently as October 1951, the Shanghai Municipal Committee of the CPC supervised the campaign in accordance with "Resolution on Continuing the Suppression of Counter-Revolution" adopted by the Fourth

by Mao Zedong at the Lushan Conference in 1959, 1 million people were suppressed and executed. The incalculable numbers included: generals of the 1911 Revolution (e.g., Deng Yulin [1881–1951], Xia Zhishi [1887–1950], He Haiqing [1875–1950], Song Hegeng [1883–1952]); generals of the Northern Expedition of the National Revolution (e.g., Zhou Zhi [1890–1953], Sun Tianfang [1899–1974]); generals of the anti-Japanese War (e.g., Song Shitai [1893–1953], Chen Yinglong [1987–1951], Lin Bomin [1886–1952]); heads of CPC underground groups (more than 200 people such as Liu Bolu of Hengyang); intellectuals (e.g., the son of Zhu Ziqing [1898–1948], Zhu Meixian [1918–1951]; the cousin of Luo Guangbin [1924–1967], Luo Guangying [?-1951]); KMT generals and officers who defected to the CPC (e.g., Chen Chunlin [1900–1951], Xu Jingji [1900–1951], Yin Zuogan [1905–1954], Gan Qingchi [1900–1951], Ye Ganwu [1901–1950], Zeng Xiancheng [1912–1951], He Jiyuan [1908–1950], Tang Boyin [1897–1952], Liu Qingchu [1894–1951], Pan Fengming [1899–1950], Fang Dixia [1904–1951], Wang Yucheng [1912–1951], Xiang Liyuan [1912–1952], Yang Jianmin [1900–1951], Zhou Boying [1909–1952], Lin Zhiyun [1901–1952], Mei Ouchi [1897–1951], Zhao Juntu [1911–1952], Zhao Honghou [1904–1952], Tang Xianyao [1899–1951], Cao Sen [1906–1952], Liang Shunde [1909–1951], Peng Yongnian [1899–1951), Qin Shouyi [1910–1952], Jiao Dati [1903–1952], Xie Lingshi [1902–1952], Deng Shifu [1903–1952], Lie Yingjia [1903–1952], Guan Zhongzhi [1909–1952], Li Jianping [1900–1951]). Indeed, in the absence of transparency in the

National Public Security Conference. Of the five categories of counter-revolutionary elements, the reactionary heads of superstitious sects and secret societies remained basically untouched, nor had the order to attack counter-revolutionaries from other parts of China who had fled to Shanghai been issued. Suburban areas bringing together remote shantytowns, boat-dwellers, and concentrations of residents from outside the city had not yet set up anti-corruption committee mass organizations in the streets and factories, so the counter-revolutionary suppression campaign was still far from thorough. The Shanghai Municipal Committee of the CPC decided to combine the factory enterprise democratic reform, rural land reform, and the organs implementing the "Three Anti" and "Five Anti" campaigns, by mobilizing the masses, to combat hidden counter-revolutionary elements. The public security organs drew on more than 150 cadres and formed 16 working groups in 141 state-owned and public–private joint factory enterprises, arresting 127 counter-revolutionaries and handing over 62 people for "mass control". Assisting units in the establishing security organizations were 118 security committees. From November 1951 to November 1952, more than 3000 counter-revolutionaries were arrested throughout the city, and Shanghai public security authorities assisted public security organs in other localities in arresting more than 10,000 counter-revolutionaries who had fled to Shanghai.

archives, it is difficult to assess clearly the number of deaths and detentions at that time, and from the beginning of the land reform campaign in 1950 to the end of 1952, no fewer than 2 million people were shot, imprisoned, or consigned to hard labor ("reform through labor").No matter how many mistakes were made in its implementation, the land reform, based on widespread and open repression, greatly increased the deterrent power of the state machinery of the new society under the CPC. As for Mao Zedong, who demanded that the entire Party "must strike steadily, accurately and ruthlessly" in its repression of the counter-revolution, this was simply the concrete manifestation of the people's democratic dictatorship, the people's democracy, over the enemy's (counter-revolutionary) dictatorship, and there was no basis for leveling any blame at it. In fact, there were no fixed criteria for who was a member of the "people", and the Party or Party cadres (those in power) determined this according to the needs of different times, different politics, and even different strategies, and those who disagreed with the Party, or with the Party's current policies and other political arrangements, might be re-designated from being one of the people to being an enemy of the people. Historically, the role of the campaign to repress counter-revolution in consolidating the Communist regime was self-evident.

On 23 October 1951, when Mao Zedong opened the third session of the First National Committee of the Chinese People's Political Consultative Conference, he had already summed up the "great victory of the three major campaigns":

> In the past year, three large-scale campaigns—resisting America and aiding the DPRK, land reform, and suppressing counter-revolution, have been launched in our country, with great success. The remnants of the counter-revolution on the mainland will soon be largely eliminated. Land reform, with the exception of some areas inhabited by ethnic minorities, will be completed by 1952. The Chinese people are unprecedentedly united in resisting America and aiding Korea and are resolutely struggling against the aggressive forces of the US imperialists.[21]

Given that the regime had only recently been established, increasing fiscal revenue was hampered; large-scale economic construction required

[21] Mao Zedong, *Mao Zedong Xuanji* (Selected Writings of Mao Zedong), vol. 5, Beijing: Renmin Chubanshe, 1977, p. 48.

funds and the duration of the Korean War had significantly extended beyond the time originally planned for, resulting in huge military spending, not to mention that in October 1951 at the meeting of the Politburo of the CPC Central Committee it had been proposed to "use all methods to squeeze out money to build heavy industry and defense industries", so increasing financial resources was a major problem facing the CPC. At the third session of the CPPCC (23 October), Mao Zedong hoped to support the Chinese people's volunteer army by increasing production and boosting the Chinese economy. Taking stock of resources and controlling fiscal expenditure become important tasks at all levels of government. Corruption and waste are minimized and prohibited by any regime, but the system and methods of dealing with them are different. When the work of increasing production and controlling expenditure found corruption and waste were extremely widespread, Mao Zedong on 20 November approvingly endorsed Gao Gang's "Report on the Implementation of the Campaign to Increase Production and Savings, and Further the In-Depth Struggle against Corruption, Waste, and Bureaucratism": "In this nationwide campaign to increase production and make savings we must carry out a resolute struggle against corruption, waste, and bureaucratism".[22] On 30 November Mao Zedong further emphasized the seriousness of the problem in a telegram to Deng Xiaoping, the first secretary of the Southwest Bureau, and to the central bureaus: "The fight against corruption and waste is a major matter for the whole Party, and we have told you to pay serious attention to it. We need a major clean-up of the entire Party …".[23] On 8 December, Mao told his Party comrades that the struggle of the "Three Anti" should be seen as important as the suppression of the counter-revolution. Mao Zedong at this time saw the "Three Anti" as a violent political campaign to consolidate power. Although Mao had long warned the entire Party to be honest and honest, and not to learn from the armies of Li Zicheng's uprising against the Ming Dynasty who once they entered the city of Beijing began to search for people's wealth and enjoy the fruits of corruption. The issues at stake in the "Three Anti" campaign initially seemed to target the Party's leading cadres. However, according to an editorial in the *People's Daily* on

[22] *Jianguo yilai Mao Zedong Wengao* (Manuscript Writings of Mao Zedong after 1949). Beijing: Zhongyang Wenxian Chubanshe, 1988, p. 513.

[23] Mao Zedong, *Mao Zedong Xuanji* (Selected Writings of Mao Zedong), vol. 5, Beijing: Renmin Chubanshe, 1977, p. 53.

23 November, the problem of corruption mainly occurred among those who "inherited the corrupt habits of the Kuomintang reactionaries". This meant that Mao Zedong, who had worked on the editorial, did not focus on the Communist Party cadres who had just entered the city, but on the "99% of the total number of corrupt people" left behind by the KMT, and that the main opponents in the struggle were the remnant forces of the KMT, about whom Mao at this time said, "the whole country may have to shoot 10,000 to tens of thousands of corrupt people to solve the problem".[24]

On 5 January 1952, the Beijing Municipal Committee submitted to Mao Zedong its "Report of Opinions on the Development and Continuation of the 'Three Anti' Campaign", on which Mao wrote the following comment:

> It is important that all private businessmen who have had a relationship with organizations and engaged in corruption, bribery, tax evasion, theft, and other illegal acts confess or inform on all illegal actions. We paid special attention to Tianjin, Qingdao, Shanghai, Nanjing, Guangzhou, Wuhan, Chongqing, Shenyang and other provinces and cities in our strong efforts to launch this struggle. We have given the bourgeoisie three years, but on this issue they have launched an outrageous offensive (an offensive more dangerous and serious than a military offensive) against our Party, which we must counter with a resolute attack and heavy blows, so that within two to three months we can basically complete this task. We request Party committees at all levels to deploy their forces tightly and treat the struggle as a large-scale class struggle.[25]

From this announcement, it may be seen that the "Three Anti" campaign was reaching a climax, Mao Zedong will focus the struggle on the inner city bourgeoisie whom he had long singled out. Over the previous year or so, the CPC gradually gained a foothold, and Mao Zedong believed that the composition of the united front can be adjusted, that is, from a full-scale attack to a crackdown on the industrial and commercial bourgeoisie. In fact, the real reason that the "Three

[24] *Jianguo yilai Mao Zedong Wengao* (Manuscript Writings of Mao Zedong after 1949). Beijing: Zhongyang Wenxian Chubanshe, 1988, p. 549.

[25] Bo Yibo, *Ruogan Zhongda Juece yu Shijian de Huigu* (Recalling a Number of Important Policy Decisions and Events), Beijing: Zhonggong Dangshi Chubanshe, 2008, p. 116.

Anti" campaign quickly ushered in the "Five Anti" campaign was Mao Zedong's early assertion and belief that class struggle was necessary for the revolution. In the "Three Anti" campaign, people only regarded the completion of the Party's outlined tasks as important and did concern themselves at all with inaccuracies and mistakes in the whistleblowing, even fabricating data to vilify business owners.[26] In the subsequent "Five Anti" campaign, enforcement, forced confessions, and violence became increasingly frequent and horrific, and Mao Zedong began to move towards using the machinery of state to nationalize private industrial and commercial property.

On 26 January 1952, Mao Zedong issued the following directive: "In all cities of the country, first and foremost in large and medium-sized cities, rely on the working class, and unite with the law-abiding bourgeoisie and other city residents to wage a large-scale, resolute and thorough struggle against bribery, tax evasion, the theft of state property, stinting on labor and materials, and stealing economic intelligence, in order to cooperate with the fight against corruption, waste, and bureaucratism within the Party, government, army and people, which is now extremely necessary and timely".[27] At this time, according to Mao Zedong's logic, because the campaign targeted the bourgeoisie, he simply demanded that all "evil reactionary capitalists" could be arrested, imprisoned, executed by firing squad, have their property confiscated, or be fined, and to target the national bourgeoisie (*minzu zichanjieji*), the Party formulated policies "making use" (*liyong*) of them, "restricting" them, and "reforming" them. Soon, Mao Zedong outlined specific measures for carrying out the "Five Anti" campaign, demarcating targets according to levels of legality and illegality, and focusing the struggle on large and medium-sized cities, where there are many rich capitalists and industrial

[26] The "Three Anti" movement extended to all parts of the country and cities, and the number of people involved is difficult to calculate. According to Bo Yibo's recollections, the total number of Party and government organs participating in the "Three Anti" campaign above the county level numbered more than 3.83 million (excluding the army). It has been verified that more than 100,000 people embezzled more than 10 million yuan in old currency; of those 9942 were sentenced to fixed-term imprisonment, 67 were sentenced to life imprisonment, 42 were executed, and 9 given suspended death sentences. See: Bo Yibo, ibid., p. 102.

[27] Mao Zedong, *Mao Zedong Xuanji* (Selected Writings of Mao Zedong), vol. 5, Beijing: Renmin Chubanshe, 1977, p. 54.

and commercial enterprises; even small industrial and commercial households had to be assessed to determine whether they were law-abiding or not. He even assessed people according to fixed allocated percentages: only 10% of targeted households were law-abiding, whereas those committing serious or outright violations of the law accounted for 5% of targeted households. Most industrial and commercial households behaved with a mixture of legality and illegality, and so the vast majority of them need to be strictly investigated and punished—mainly by paying compensation, reimbursements, and fines, thereby providing the government with substantial income. Throughout the struggles of the "Five Anti" campaign, hundreds of thousands of businesses were investigated by the government; some capitalists were jailed, but most attempted to avoid a terrifying fate by paying taxes and fines. Those capitalists who could not pay in cash had to sign an agreement guaranteeing they would pay within a certain period. At the same time, the Party controls the numbers and proportions of people put to death in each locality.[28] In the "Three Anti" and "Five Anti" campaigns, the CPC also reorganized the trade associations and industrial and commercial federations, placing leadership control in its hands, and even helping reorganize a democratic national congress in which capitalists were concentrated. In accordance with the Party's need to change the person in charge, they required someone "who could represent the bourgeoisie, but above all the legitimate interests of the industrial bourgeoisie, and head a political group which could educate the bourgeoisie in the principles of the Common Program and of the 'Five Anti' campaign"; at the same time, the Party began to establish Party organizations in private enterprises. As in previous campaigns, many industrial and commercial businessmen endured accusations and suicides continued to occur; "physical torture" was widely employed in the campaign.[29] Mao Zedong warned against

[28] A CPC central document records: "At the end of the Five-Year Plan period, every locality can propose the number of people it is prepared to kill. This should be reported by units to the central government in large cities and provinces, but this should not be implemented or publicly announced until the central government co-ordinates the overall situation and then proposes proportionate controls". There is no evidence that these killings were planned in accordance with legal and law enforcement criteria. Ref: Yang Kuisong, *Zhonghua Renmin Gongheguo Jianguo Shi Yanjiu* (Research on the History of the Founding of the PRC), vol. 1, Nanchang: Jiangxi Renmin Chubanshe, 2009, p. 349.

[29] In Shanghai, in the first month of the campaign, more than 200 people were arrested of whom 48 capitalists attempted suicide, 34 of whom successfully (Bo Yibo, op. cit.,

such phenomena as much as possible, but by agreeing to execute by firing squad such senior Communist Party cadres as Liu Qingshan (1916–1952) and Zhang Zishan (1914–1952) he showed that he did not show favoritism. However, his main goal was to the bourgeoisie and strengthen control over industry and commerce. The "Three Anti" and "Five Anti" campaigns not only provided financial resources for the new regime but also stripped the bourgeoisie of its property; the elimination of the industrial and commercial bourgeoisie laid the foundations for the socialist transformation soon to be carried out. The "Five Anti" campaign led to the shutdown of industry and commerce and economic decline, affecting the national economy. Mao Zedong also adjusted his strategy to narrow the scope of the attack, through such formulations as "lenience in the past, strictness in the future" and "lenience for industry, strictness for business", policies that did not belong to any legal system. Mao Zedong also divided up the bourgeoisie, targeting capitalists who paid varying degrees of tax to the state to confirm the extent of their compliance with the law through the size of their contributions. Even though regarded as still breaking the law, Mao Zedong generously decided to designate the "basically law-abiding" household of capitalist Rong Yiren (1916–2005) as "totally law-abiding". Mao wanted this "pace-setter" to make an impact on the campaign in Shanghai, where the bourgeoisie was concentrated, and in other major cities across the country. Like the rural class of landlords eliminated in the class struggle, the bourgeoisie in the city was completely overthrown by the machinery of state established by the new regime. Subsequently, those "unpleasant and stinking" bourgeoisie could only survive in "public–private partnerships" arranged by the Communist Party.

Intellectuals held to be "nagging and querulous" were not welcomed by the authorities during the KMT era, but the leaders of the new regime knew the importance of intellectuals and technical personnel, and the new urban management and economic construction required their support. The question was: how could intellectuals be induced to agree to the Party's demands? Intellectuals could not be treated as a social class like landlords or even capitalists, and the new regime sought an effective and legitimate path to transform intellectuals and use their knowledge and

p. 120). Throughout February, 73 people committed suicide. In the first half of March, 53 suicided, and between 2 and 8 April, 67 suicided (Ref: Yang Kuisong, ibid., pp. 321, 329, 345).

technology. As early as May 1949, through the "Common Program" adopted by the CPPCC Plenary Session, the Party arranged its later work on reforming intellectuals and formulated a policy of "revolutionary political education for young and old intellectuals". On 6 June 1950, at the Third Plenary Session of the Seventh Central Committee of the Communist Party of China, Mao Zedong began to use the tone of the Yan'an rectification period to describe the transformation of intellectuals:"We should set up various training courses, universities for military studies and politics, and revolutionary universities for intellectuals, which can at the same time reform them. They can study social developmental history, historical materialism, and several other courses. We should create the means for preventing these idealists from opposing us. They talk about God creating people, but we talk about people apes evolving into people. Some intellectuals are old, in their seventies, but we must look after them as long as they support the Party and the people's government".

At its outset, the new regime was seen in contrast with what preceded it: the Kuomintang's "old society" and the Communist Party's "New China". At the very least, in the final two years of the civil war, as the Communists began to take over the cities, the KMT's collapse was in stark contrast to the Communist Party's aspirations; people were eager for change and saw the possibility of change, thus pinning their hopes on the Communist Party, which had previously been fighting for democracy and freedom. The newly established People's Republic seemed to be dynamic and thriving for those who had suffered greatly from the corruption and inability of the Kuomintang. Otherwise, it would be difficult to explain why the economist Ma Yinchu, who had previously dared to attack Chiang Kai-shek's regime, denounced the K'ung and Soong families for corruption, and finally went to prison, took the initiative when he became vice chancellor of Peking University on 1 June 1951 to set up "summer study meetings" at the university, and cheerfully told teachers and staff: "In building the New China, Peking University should play an exemplary role in this, and if we do not, we should apologize to the nation. Peking University is the university of the nation's capital and has a glorious revolutionary tradition ". Ma Yinchu then organized other department heads and professors at Peking University to respond to Zhou Enlai's suggestion and launch a political study campaign for Peking University teachers. He even invited Communist Party leaders, including Mao Zedong, to lecture at the school. Under Mao's direction, Zhou Enlai, on the 29th of September, delivered a report entitled "On the Reform of Intellectuals" to more than 3000 teachers from 20 universities in Beijing and Tianjin at Huairen Hall in Zhongnanhai. He admonished the intellectuals to their faces, telling them that, through reform, intellectuals need to "advance from the national position to the people's position and then to the working class's position". The national campaign to reform intellectuals' thinking began.

In *People's Daily* on 20 May, pro-Communist intellectuals read criticism of the historical figure Wu Xun (1838–1896) who was seen as "passionately promoting feudal culture".[30] On 23 July *People's Daily* published Mao Zedong's revised "Notes on the Historical Examination of Wu Xun", who was identified as a "big hooligan, big usurer and big landlord". Mao Zedong's view was that the recognition or tolerance of the praise of the "Biography of Wu Xun" was "recognition or tolerance of the revolutionary struggle that vilified peasants". Mao's move was aimed not at the landlords, but at the intellectuals who extolled the landlord class. Mao, it seems, was beginning to think about how to solve the problems of intellectuals who were unsure about the new regime and the Communist Party. In an editorial titled "We Should Pay Attention to the Discussion about the film *Biography of Wu Xun*", is a statement: "Bourgeois reactionary ideology is invading the fighting Communist Party". The film's director Sun Yu (1900–1990) was attacked as an "extreme rightist" and was subjected to physical persecution in 1957. At the same time that attacks were made on the biography of Wu Xun, the pedagogist Tao Xingzhi (1891–1946) who advocated setting up schools like those pioneered in the nineteenth century by Wu Xun, was also denounced and criticized. Previously the CPC had argued that Tao's educational thought

[30] In early 1951, the film "Biography of Wu Xun" was screened. The film depicts the story of Wu Xun (1838–1896) from Tangxian County in Shandong Province, at the end of the Qing. Wu Xun, from a poor background and illiterate, was repeatedly deceived. He decided to practice begging to save money so that children of the poor could be educated and protected from bullying. Thirty years of begging enabled him to set up three charity schools in the county. His deeds were welcomed by society, at the end of the Qing Dynasty, the Shandong governor Zhang Yao memorialized the Guangxu Emperor to honor him, after which he was given the epithets "righteous beggar" and "begging sage". In 1944, the educator Tao Xingzhi suggested that Wu Xun's life be made into a story. The screenplay was first written by the film's director, Sun Yu, and was shot in part in 1947. It was re-shot in 1950. *Masses Cinema* (Dazhong Dianying) hailed *Biography of Wu Xun* as one of the ten best domestic films of 1950. The film was well received by the educational sector. Before Mao watched the film, CPC leaders Zhu De, Zhou Enlai, and Hu Qiaomu had all seen the film and voiced their approval.

served the people, but now it is classified as "erroneous thought like that of Wu Xun" that needed to be purged.[31]

While political criticism replaced academic debate from the beginning, intellectuals felt the crisis surrounding their own "old ideas", which was strengthened after Zhou Enlai's report on the reform of intellectuals. On 23 October 1951, in his article titled "The Great Victory of the Three Campaigns", Mao Zedong wrote:

> Ideological reform is, firstly, the ideological transformation of every intellectual, which is one of the important conditions for China to realize all aspects of democratic reform and gradual industrialization. We therefore wish this movement for self-education and self-reform even greater success in its steady progress.[32]

The words, which read constructively, were translated into coercive demands in the internal document issued by the Central Committee of the CPC on 30 November, "Instructions on the Ideological Reform and Organizational Cleanup in Schools", which required school teachers to organize "the faithful and honest presentation of history" in order to discover "counter-revolutionary elements", to remove ideologically, politically, and organizationally "reactionary relics" from schools, and to establish Party leadership over schools and intellectuals. Institutions with a concentration of intellectuals began to be dragged into the campaign: on 18 December, the Chinese Academy of Sciences held a mobilization conference on ideological reform and study, and on 7 January 1952, the CPPCC issued its "Decision on extending the ideological reform and study campaign to people from all walks of life".

Most intellectuals' knowledge was derived from Europe and the United States, and during the war to "resist America and aid Korea", in accordance with the Party's demands, they were required to purge themselves of ideas that "support, fear or venerate the United States", and obviously, they should learn to "hate, despise, and denigrate American imperialism". Qian Junrui (1908–1985), a veteran leftist economist

[31] Ref: Li Yimang, "Get Rid of Erroneous Thinking like Biography of Wu Xun", *Renmin Ribao*, 2 June 1951.

[32] Mao Zedong, *Mao Zedong Xuanji* (Selected Writings of Mao Zedong), vol. 5, Beijing: Renmin Chubanshe, 1977, p. 49.

who in 1954 became Party secretary of the Ministry of Culture, stigmatized intellectuals for their "stubborn veneration for the Anglo-American bourgeois lifestyle, especially the so-called 'American way of life', their envy of America's 'wealth' (unable to see the poverty of the working people of the United States) and 'civilization' (yearning for the depravity of the Anglo-American bourgeoisie, yet ignoring the tragic cultureless status of the working masses in Britain and the United States), and their admiration, bordering on superstitious belief, for British and American science and technology".[33] Intellectuals in the field of the humanities had never had scruples about the free expression of ideas, and when discussing China's future industrial construction, the philosopher Zhang Dongsun (1886–1973) said without thinking that China's future industrialization must rely more on the United States than on the Soviet Union. Technology was supposed to not be a class issue, but at this time, the United States could not be considered more powerful than the Soviet Union, being imperialism that must be overthrown. As a result, Mao Zedong regarded Zhang Dongsun as a "dangerous enemy agent". Liang Shuming naively tried to explain Zhang Dongsun's position, but Mao ignored him. In this way, Yanjing University judged Zhang to be "consistently anti-communist" and a "Chinese traitor" who "served imperialism", and who must be severely criticized. But Zhou Peiyuan (1902–1993), the theoretical physicist, faced the same problem as intellectuals in the humanities: he was ordered to express his indignation and rebuke of American imperialism. He was educated at the California Institute of Technology and was inevitably asked to "self-criticize":

> In my first four years living in the United States, I saw only skyscrapers, cars, and the profligate lifestyle of the exploitative classes, but I didn't see monopoly capitalists brutally exploiting ordinary people.... I mistakenly thought that American "democracy" was good, people had free speech,... I didn't realize that the president of the United States and so-called government officials were the slaves of the monopoly capitalists, and the political debates reported in the newspapers were nothing more than partisan attacks between the various ruling parties. I went to America for the second time in 1943, and this was the most shameful chapter of my life. I came to the United States as a scientist and founded myself in a democracy that

[33] Quoted from: Li Honglin, *Zhongguo Sixiang Yundong Shi, 1949–1989* (History of Chinese Ideological Campaigns, 1949–1989), Hong Kong: Tiandi Chuban Youxian Gongsi (Cosmos Books), 2010, p. 63.

> touted itself as anti-fascist. But in fact, in early 1945, the Soviet Union's brilliant victories in Eastern Europe had shown the ultimate fate of fascist Germany. ... I became a tool of US imperialism but felt that I had earned a "reputation".[34]

Throughout the period of ideological transformation, famous intellectuals and artists who wrote confessions and self-criticisms included: film director Cai Chusheng (1906–1968), playwright Cao Yu (1910–1996), historian Chen Yuan (1880–1971), anthropologist Fei Xiaotong (1910–2005), philosopher Feng Youlan (1895–1990), painter Feng Zikai (1898–1975), musician He Lüding (1903–1999), literary figure Huang Yaomian (1903–1987), philosopher Jin Yuelin (1895–1984), architect Liang Sicheng (1901–1972), Liang Shuming, Mao Yisheng (1896–1989), sociologist Pan Guangdan (1899–1967), literary historian Tang Tao (1913–1992), literary historian Wu Mi (1894–1978), dramatist Zheng Junli (1911–1969), Zhou Peiyuan, and aesthetician Zhu Guangqian (1897–1986), as well as countless others.

Most people with access to higher education, especially abroad, were born into rich families, which were classified as the bourgeoisies, the exploitative class, or as feudalism, and their thinking was always inextricably linked to the feudalism of the "old society" or the ideas of Western imperialism and capitalism, and it was only through education in Marxism–Leninism that it was possible for them to shift their position to the side of the Communist Party and the people. Everyone's ideological change was different, and the authenticity of the change and their inner state of mind were difficult to identify. However, intellectuals were also classified according to the title and treatment of the school to which they were attached, as well as to their status, reputation, and dignity.The Party's takeover of the education system meant that the free employment and mobility of the past were much less possible. This was the period of institutional construction and ideological transformation of the CPC designed to consolidate the political, economic, military, and ideological fields as needed. The land reform, "Three Anti", "Five Anti", and counter-revolutionary suppression campaigns sought to eliminate hostile forces and establish communist ideology. A teacher who was considered to not meet the requirements of the Party and the people during this reform

[34] Chinese translation of Andrew G. Walder, *China Under Mao: A Revolution Derailed*, Hong Kong: Chinese University Press, 2015, p. 77.

period would find their titles and treatment denigrated. For acutely face-conscious and respected intellectuals, the language they were required to use in confessions and self-denigration in different settings was obviously anathema, regardless of whether or not they underwent any genuine ideological shift. More than two million intellectuals underwent an ideological transformation in the campaign. It was demanded that they embrace the new regime, accept the study of Marxist ideas and methods, and accept the leadership of the Party in future research and academic work. They were told and seemed to approve that the Party represented the interests of the people, given the concept of "the people" was always readily accepted by intellectuals who embraced socialist ideas and even utopian idealism. The demand that intellectuals change their ideology was so strong that those who were highly educated were at a loss at this time. The historian Gu Jiegang, for example, said: "I took in all this year's three campaigns—the Three Anti, Five Anti, and ideological transformation campaigns, but I never really understood any of them. But with every campaign I grew increasingly nervous and no longer had any space in which I could think calmly. When I had earlier written my preface to *Analyses of Ancient History* (Gushi Bian), while serving at Peking University as a teaching assistant for six years, I could read slowly before coming to any conclusions and these affected me for more than twenty years. Today, Marxism–Leninism is profound and all-encompassing going well beyond the limits of my work on *Analyses of Ancient History*, and my working comrades want me to go through it all again, but I now feel stupid and really do not know whether I am up to the task".

In any case, after two years of ideological reform, universities and other higher education institutions were required to offer courses in Marxism–Leninism and Mao Zedong Thought, and work on political thought became the top priority of every educational institution, even though "politics" and "tasks" were always arbitrarily adjusted and recalibrated during different periods of political campaigns.

Indeed, intellectual opinions at no given time became the basis for decision-making by political leaders, who were invited to open meetings and speak to motivate those they needed, repeatedly telling that now "the people" are the masters of this country. New China was in urgent need of consolidation and construction, and only those who contributed to society through actual labor were the object of respect. So, while Liang Shuming continued to articulate "China problems" he considered to be unrelated to the "revolution", the party and government showed concern for "model workers" such as Hao Jianxiu (b. 1935) and Zhao Guilan (b. 1945), and heroes unafraid to sacrifice themselves on Korean battlefields, "the most adorable people", as the title of a novel written in 1951 by the writer Wei Wei (1920–2008) described them.

Literary and artistic circles were obviously an important target for ideological transformation. In 1952, as a concrete interpreter of the Party's literary and artistic thought, Zhou Yang called on literary artists to "resolutely carry out Mao Zedong's literary and artistic line". He said that compared with Chinese struggle of the Chinese people and their achievements in various fields, the achievements of literary and artistic work were too few. The reason was that there was insufficient implementation of Mao Zedong's literary and artistic line: "Mao Zedong's literary and artistic line is the class line in literature and art, the mass line. If literature and art are to serve the people, they must first serve workers, peasants and soldiers. Literary and artistic workers must be combined with the masses of workers, and without this combination, literary and artistic creation will be cut off its source, and the ideological transformation of literary and artistic workers themselves will lose its basis".[35] Zhou Yang reminded people that literary and artistic thought must be proletarian, not bourgeois or even petit-bourgeois: "Because only with the ideology and stance of the proletariat can the workers, peasants and all other classes be correctly understood; only by using the art methods of the proletariat (revolutionary realism) can the workers, peasants and all other classes be correctly reflected; only in this way can it be guaranteed that literature and art are always in line with the needs of the masses and the needs of the actual struggle. Therefore, our primary task at present is to implement Mao Zedong's literary and artistic line in all literary and artistic work, and to fight against all tendencies to diverge from this line".[36] A *People's Daily* editorial published that year, titled "Continue the Struggle in Literature and Art in the Direction Indicated by Comrade Mao Zedong", informed people that after the victory of the revolution, "a large number of unreconstructed bourgeois and petty bourgeois artists joined the ranks of revolutionary literature and art, bringing with them ideological remnants

[35] Zhou Yang, "Jianjue Guanche Mao Zedong Wenyi Luxian" (Resolutely Implement Mao Zedong's Line on Literature and Art), in Beijing Shifan Daxue Wenyi Lilun Zu ed., *Wenxue Lilun Xuexi Cankao Ziliao* (Reference Materials on Studying Literary Theory), internal release, Beijing: Gaodeng Jiaoyu Chubanshe, 1956, p. 152.

[36] Ibid., p. 154.

of the old society and non-proletarian literary and artistic ideas. Some literary and artistic workers from the early liberated areas, after entering the city, were eroded and influenced by bourgeois thought, lost their original direction, and many leading comrades in literary and artistic circles gave up or neglected the work of ideological leadership and descended into the mire of routinism (routine behavior)". Based on *Mao Zedong's Talks at the Yan'an Forum on Literature and Art*, the editorial called on literary and artistic workers to "draw a line between proletarian and bourgeois literary and artistic thought". The editorial also suggested: "This problem was raised in the criticism of "Biography of Wu Xun" and in the literary and artistic rectification campaign, but its serious resolution requires greater efforts". In fact, Mao Zedong's aim was to complete the transformation of intellectuals in the entire ideological field, and to ensure that such transformation would achieve its purpose through the system. Indeed, as early as 2 July 1949, organized by the Party's literary and artistic leaders, the All-China Congress of Literary and Artistic Workers (later changed to the Chinese Federation of Literary Artists, referred to as the "Literary Union") was established. Zhou Yang, who delivered a report titled "The New People's Literature and Art" at the inaugural meeting, told the 824 participants (including writers, artists, musicians, dramatists, and others in various artistic categories):

> Mao Zedong's *Talks at the Yan'an Forum on Literature and Art* stipulates the direction of New China's literature and art; literary and artistic workers in the liberated areas consciously and resolutely implemented this direction, and through their experience proved this direction to be completely correct; they were convinced that there was no alternative direction, and if one existed it was an erroneous direction.[37]

The establishment of this system was so systematic, extending deeply into fields like "painting and embroidery",[38] which Mao Zedong once considered to be unrelated to the revolution, and embodied in the Artists

[37] Quoted from Hong Zicheng, *Zhongguo Dangdai Wenxue Shi* (History of Contemporary Chinese Literature), Beijing: Beijing Daxue Chubanshe, 2008, p. 15.

[38] Ref. CH2.

Association.[39] The ideological transformation campaign showed that in just three years Mao Zedong had completed his overall leadership of the country's political, economic, military, organizational (government, including people's organizations), and ideological fields.

During the Republican period, Academia Sinica, the central research institute, had 81 academicians in 14 divisions, and with the exception of 22 academicians who left the mainland to go to Taiwan, the United States, or other countries, most remained on the mainland for different reasons. Chiang Kai-shek in December 1948 arranged a special flight to "rescue the scholars" and a three-man group comprising Fu Sinian, Chen Xueping (1901–1999), and Chiang Ching-kuo attempted to get prominent scholars to leave the mainland as soon as possible. At that time, however, most scientists and intellectuals, including those abroad, held

[39] On July 21, 1949, the All-China Artists Association was established, and in 1953, the All-China Artists Association was renamed the "Chinese Artists Association" (the associations of artists of various provinces, cities and counties were established).

The "General Rules" of the Association's Constitution stipulate that the Association is a "voluntary organization of Chinese artists who actively participate in the revolutionary struggle and construction of the people Chinese with their own artistic creations" and that its task is to organize artists to "create works of a highly ideological and artistic nature in order to inspire the people's enthusiasm for labor and fighting". Among them, the constitution stipulates that the association will "organize artists to learn the art theory of Marxism-Leninism and socialist realism, to study the policies of the Party and the government, to study social life, and to adopt the method of criticism and self-criticism, and constantly reform and improve the artist's thinking". Although the charter covers the organization of exhibitions, publications and research into traditional cultural heritage, including the help of young artists, who have been called "young artists", and the promotion of the development of the cultural life of the masses, the direction of art, the basis of artistic thought and even international artistic exchanges, confined to the former Soviet Union and socialist countries, have been strictly regulated, and from the outset, artistic creation in New China must be carried out under the leadership of the Party.

The Federation and various associations (e.g., writers' associations, artists' associations, dramatists' associations, musicians' associations, etc.) are known as "mass organizations". In this system, local artists' associations accept the leadership of the local cultural associations, and the cultural associations establish Party committees or party groups to accept the leadership of the propaganda and organizational departments of the Party at the next higher level. The principal cadres of the Federation and various associations, such as the Secretary-General, set standards of treatment according to the corresponding levels of government agencies and are appointed by the Ministry of Propaganda and the Organizational Department of the Party. Like professors and managers in tertiary institutions, the salaries and benefits of the staff of the Federation and the associations are allocated by the State. The Federation and the associations are chaired by eminent persons or famous artists, but have no financial, personnel or administrative decisions.

illusions and hopes for the new government and decided that if they did not remain for now on the mainland they would return to their homeland from abroad after the founding of the New China. In the years that followed, however, most intellectuals experienced harsh political campaigns and unprovoked accusations, were tortured and abused or driven to suicide, even intellectuals like physicist Rao Yutai (1891–1968), and geologist and educator Xie Jiarong (1898–1966), who were not intellectuals working in the humanities but in pure natural sciences. Thus, the ideological transformation of intellectuals from 1951 to 1953 was in fact a prelude to a number of political campaigns involving intellectuals.

The Korean War

The CPC's hope to gain Soviet support in its campaign against Taiwan began with a desire that the USSR send troops, which Moscow rejected, but the latter agreed to provide military support by selling aircraft, artillery, and machine guns and sending military instructors to China. Just as the CPC was preparing to attack Taiwan in anticipation of the Soviet Union's timely military assistance, US policy on China, including Taiwan, began to change as a result of the signing of a new treaty between the CPC and the CPSU. Previously, the Truman administration's policy towards China or Taiwan was a "selective and focused" strategy of containment. Considering that, with the assistance and support of the Soviet Union, the Chinese Communist attack on Taiwan would put the KMT government under great threat, and that Taiwan could become part of the Soviet strategy for the Far East, containing the CPC was about containing the Soviet Union and the entire socialist camp. On 20 May General Douglas MacArthur, the commander-in-chief of America's Far East war zone, warned the Joint Chiefs of Staff that if Taiwan were controlled by the Communists, it would mean it falling into the hands of the Soviet Union and that America's defenses across the Pacific would collapse. He repeatedly stressed that Taiwan is "an unsinkable aircraft carrier and submarine tender, ideally located to accomplish Soviet strategy as well as to checkmate the offensive capabilities of the central and southern positions of the Far East Command's front line", and on 14 June MacArthur submitted a memorandum to the Joint Chiefs of Staff, calling for defending Formosa (Taiwan), which was brought back to Washington from Tokyo on the 24th. The day after the Korean War broke out, on 27 June, Truman issued a statement ordering the US Seventh

Fleet to enter the Taiwan Strait to "stop any attack on Formosa" and sent a US military mission to Taiwan to ascertain its military defense needs.

At the end of the Anti-Japanese War, the Soviet Union and the United States took over the north and south of the Korean Peninsula, respectively, to either side of the 38th parallel (38 degrees north latitude). Designed to maintain the postwar order, this was a temporary measure as stipulated by the Yalta Agreement. After 1910, Korea became a Japanese colony, and after World War II, Kim Il-sung in the North, who was supported by the Soviet Union and the CPC, and Syngman Rhee, who was supported by the United States in the South, worked hard to complete the cause of national reunification, but in May 1948, South Korea established the ROK government, and in September, Kim Il-sung established the DPRK government. The emergence of the Cold War led to a deterioration in relations between the Soviet Union and the United States. The nature of the 38th Parallel underwent change as ideological conflict between the two camps and the contest in Europe made the parallel a political and military demarcation line between the USSR and the USA. The rapid decline in people-to-people exchanges on both sides of the 38th Parallel and the fact that police and troops from the South crossed this sensitive border from time to time naturally led to new arrangements between the North and the South, and military adjustments by the USSR and USA who stood respectively behind them, as tensions increased. The US military had planned to withdraw from South Korea on 30 June 1949, in order to enable future Korea to acquire self-rule with US long range control. The US occupation forces, and the US government had consistently promoted "helping the North Korean people and the legitimate government of South Korea to establish a free and unified Korea". On the basis of his intelligence department's investigation and assessment of South Korea's military forces and North Korea's worrying military situation, Stalin arranged for Terenty Shtykov (1907–1964) to serve as general military adviser to North Korea and discuss with Kim Il-sung (1912–1994) the strengthening of North Korea's military power and complete the new weapons and ammunition configuration in June. At the same time, Kim Il-sung arranged for Kim Il (1910–1984), head of the political department of the Korean People's Army, to travel to China in secret to discuss with CPC leaders Mao Zedong, Zhu De and Zhou Enlai the situation and related North Korean issues, such as the transfer of three North Korean divisions formerly in the Chinese Communist Army to the North Korean government. Kim Il mentioned that the withdrawal of US troops may cause the South to use Japanese help to attack North Korea. In this situation, he asked, should North Korea launch an attack on the South? In response, Mao replied: "We believe that actions such as North Korea attacking the South can only be taken if the international situation is conducive to this in early 1950. If the Japanese invade North Korea, we will be able to quickly send our own elite troops to eliminate the Japanese".[40] Kim Il-sung knew that "our Chinese friends are busy with their own domestic affairs" and could not take part in serious discussions about North Korea. However, the South's Syngman Rhee continued to proclaim that he would attack the north, provoking Kim Il-sung to attempt to attack the South on his own initiative. On 12 August 1949, Kim Il-sung first proposed to the Soviet ambassador that he was "ready to attack the South" under the condition that the Soviet Union provided modern military weapons and equipped them with military advisers, and the CPC provided trained combat troops (from its Korean Division). On 12 August 1949, Kim Il-sung for the first time mentioned to the Soviet ambassador that North Korea was "preparing to launch an invasion of the South". Back in March, Stalin gave Kim Il-sung a pre-condition: military action could only be taken if the South first launched an offensive against the North. Various judgments, analyses, recommendations, and even military plans between China, the Soviets, and North Korea went back and forth until the end of January 1950, when Stalin and Mao both expressed caution about North Korea's plan to initiate an attack on the South. Just that month, however, Dean Acheson, the US secretary of state, gave a speech on North Korea. "Taiwan and the Korean Peninsula are not part of the US' Pacific line of defense", Mr. Acheson said.

On 30 January, even though Mao was still in Moscow, Stalin made a new assessment of the situation in the face of changes in the international situation and more complex factors, such as his view that the United States would not protect South Korea. Stalin, and he ruled out any concerns about the outbreak of the Korean War. Stalin decided to inform Shytkov to respond to Kim Il-sung's request and meet with him to discuss the war. In April, Kim Il-sung and Park Hong-yon (1900–1956) met in Moscow with Stalin, who told them that military action could be taken and that the United States would not be involved in a small war like in Korea. He told Kim who was eager to advance military

[40] Quoted from Shen Zhihua, op. cit., p. 198.

action, that the Soviet Union could support him by providing weapons and equipment, but: "If you encounter strong resistance, I can't help you at all; you must ask Mao for all help".[41] On 13 May, Kim arrived in Beijing for an evening meeting with Mao Zedong. Kim's haste prompted Mao to immediately verify the latest information with Moscow. Stalin called back and said,"Comrade Mao Zedong! In talks with North Korean comrades, Filippov [i.e., codename used by Stalin] and his friends suggest that they agree with the North Koreans' proposal for reunification, given that the international situation has changed. At the same time, they add, this issue must ultimately be resolved jointly by Chinese and North Korean comrades, and if Chinese comrades do not agree, the solution of this question must be discussed again and resolved. Details of the talks can be told to you by our North Korean comrades".[42] Whatever the strategic considerations, Mao did endorse in principle North Korea's use of Communism to re-unite Korea, which would undoubtedly furthered Kim Il-sung's support from China. On 29 May, Kim Informed the Soviet Union that the promised weapons and ammunition had arrived. On 19 June the Standing Committee of the Supreme People's Assembly of the DPRK issued a proposal for the joint establishment of a single all-Korean legislature and the formulation of a constitution, elections, and the formation of a government, whereby Kim Il-sung politically foreshadowed his military advance. Soviet military advisers assisted Kim Il-sung's military action plan, which was documented in "Preparations for and Progress of Military Operations of the Korean People's Army": "On 26 June, Kim Il-sung, on behalf of the Government of the Democratic People's Republic of Korea, issued a letter to the Korean people, describing the current domestic situation and proposing the task of defeating the enemy and re-establishing a unified Korea".[43] As the Korean People's Army advanced south with Soviet weapons and equipment, the China-Soviet Treaty signed between the Soviet Union and China began to have a practical effect: it was on the basis of the provisions of the draft agreement signed in February regarding the ports of Lüshun and Dalian and the Chinese Eastern Railway, that "in the event of war by Japan or any other country in collusion with Japan" at the proposal of the government of the

[41] Ibid., p. 217.

[42] Ibid., pp. 221–222.

[43] Ibid., p. 228.

People's Republic of China and with the consent of the Government of the Soviet Union, the PRC and USSR could jointly use the Lüshun naval base to help them fight together". This prompted China in the Korean War also to request proactively that the Soviets remain at the base during the Korean War and they accepted the Soviet Union's request to open to it fully the China Eastern Railway and the Northeast Air Corridor to facilitate the needs of the People's Army on Korean battlefields.

On 27 June, the UN Security Council adopted a resolution to send United Nations troops to repel North Korea's armed offensive against the South and restore peace and security in the region. The outbreak of war brought into effect NSC-68, which changed US policy towards the Soviet Union and China and, for the US, Korea was no longer simply an area temporarily occupied after the end of the War of Resistance, but an "interdependent" part of the entire Far East defense line including Japan, the Ryukyus, Taiwan, the Philippines, and Southeast Asia. Ideologically, the concerns raised by the signing of the Treaty of Friendship between China and the Soviet Union and the expansion of communism in Asia were strengthened by the Soviet Union and China's joint support for Kim's military campaign. On the same day that North Korea launched its offensive, the United States mobilized its air force and ground troops in Japan to bomb and attack Kaesong, Seoul, and Pyongyang, and the North Korean People's Army was blocked by South Korean and US forces as it advanced south. In early July, when the Korean People's Army was hit hard by US and South Korean forces, who destroyed 36 aircraft and five ships, Stalin was slow in responding to Kim Il-sung's request for the Soviet Air Force to protect North Korea and agree to the Chinese government sending troops into the country, which deeply disturbed Kim. However, on 5 July, Stalin sent a message to Zhou Enlai: "We believe that it is the right to concentrate immediately nine Chinese divisions on the China-North Korea border so that volunteers can enter North Korea to fight when the enemy crosses the 38th Parallel. We will do our utmost to provide air cover for these forces".[44] On 7 July, the first national defense conference of the CPC's new regime decided to draw a total of 255,000 troops from four armies and three artillery divisions to form the Northeast Border Guard and ordered the troops to be assembled by 5 August. On 12 July, Zhou asked North Korea to provide 500

[44] Ibid., p. 262.

maps of North Korea of different scales, inform him of the situation on the front lines, and "send samples of Korean People's Army uniforms as soon as possible". In late July, the CPC began providing North Korea with rifles, hand-held machine guns, heavy machine guns, and mortars. Mao Zedong told Kim Il-sung's representatives that China would send troops to North Korea and that "the Chinese side has prepared four armies for this purpose, a total of 320,000 men". On 5 August, Mao Zedong asked Gao Gang to complete all preparations for the Northeast Border Guard within August and "prepare for combat in early September". By 24 August, the Korean People's Army's air force had lost most of its planes, leaving only 36 fighter jets and 23 pilots. In response to Kim's frustration and deep unease, Stalin on August 28th told him: "Don't be upset by the failure to win back-to-back victories in the struggle against foreign interventionists, which can sometimes be accompanied by setbacks or even partial defeats. There are no consecutive victories in a war like this". Stalin promised: "We can provide the North Korean Air Force with strong and hard-hitting aircraft". In mid-September, the US military concentrated 150 ships and landed 70,000 troops at Incheon, and on the 17th occupied Seoul. On 27 September, Stalin was told that the Korean People's Army had been surrounded by coalition forces and that its tanks and artillery had been completely destroyed. Until this point, the fighters Stalin had promised as reinforcements had not yet appeared. Kim Il-sung began pleading with Stalin for direct military assistance and for the Chinese army and other people's democracies to set up volunteer forces to fight with North Korea.

On October 1st, Stalin sent a telegram to Mao Zedong and Zhou Enlai, giving a brief unfavorable assessment of Kim's forces on the Korean battlefield, saying: "I consider that, according to the current situation, if you can provide reinforcements for the North Koreans, even if five or six divisions would be good. You should immediately advance to the 38th parallel, so that our North Korean comrades can, under the cover of your troops, organize reserve forces north of the 38th parallel. Chinese troops can appear as volunteers and will, of course, be led by Chinese commanders".[45] On the same day, the Chinese ambassador to the DPRK received a joint letter from Kim Il-sung and Pak Hon-yong addressed to Mao Zedong: "At present the enemy is taking advantage of our serious

[45] Ibid., p. 276.

immediate crisis, not giving us time. If they continue to attack the area north of the 38th parallel, it is difficult to overcome this crisis relying on our strength alone. Therefore, we have to ask you to give us special help, that is, in the case of enemy attacks on the area north of the 38th parallel, and we very much hope the Chinese People's Liberation Army can directly assist our army in the fighting!"[46] Now seemed to be the time for Mao Zedong to draw a close to the previous episode in the war. In a message to Stalin on 2 October, Mao wrote: "Back in April this year, when Comrade Kim Il-sung arrived in Beijing, we told him to pay serious attention to the possibility of foreign reactionary forces invading North Korea. In mid-July, late July, and early September, we told our North Korean comrades on three more occasions that they were in danger of having the People's Army cut off by the enemy advancing from the sea towards Incheon and Seoul, and that the People's Army should make full preparations to retreat north in due course, preserve its main force, and aim to be victorious after a long protracted war".[47] Over 1–2 October, the Secretariat of the Central Committee of the CPC held a meeting to discuss whether China would eventually send troops. At the meeting, "many comrades of the CPC Central Committee" expressed concern about sending troops to North Korea given that China is still in the midst of a severe economic crisis, natural disasters, social instability, ongoing land reform, and continued widespread destruction by the remnants of the Kuomintang. On the 4th, Mao Zedong asked Zhou Enlai to recall Peng Dehuai to Beijing for a meeting to discuss the issue of sending troops, and the next morning, Mao and Peng together discussed the issue. Peng understood Mao's basic intention to send troops, so at the afternoon meeting of the Politburo, Peng Dehuai expressed the position that "an early fight is better than a late fight". Mao Zedong's view was: "Now that the Americans are forcing us to fight this war, hesitantly backing down or being fearful will get us nowhere. These psychological reactions are exactly what the enemy hopes for. Now we have only one path of action, which is that prior to the enemy occupying Pyongyang, we must immediately send troops to North Korea, however risky or difficult

[46] Ibid., p. 277.

[47] Ibid., p. 267.

it might be".[48] On 8 October Mao Zedong officially issued an order to organize the Chinese People's Volunteer Army, appointing Peng Dehuai as Commander and Political Commissar. At the same time, Mao Zedong arranged for Zhou Enlai and Lin Biao to travel to Moscow to secure Stalin's assurances of arms and air support. On 7 October, the United Nations General Assembly had already approved the occupation of the entire territory of North Korea by United Nations forces, and a multinational coalition led by the United States crossed the 38th parallel. This news left Stalin hesitant about providing air support to China's volunteer army. At this time, Stalin also needed to finally think about another question: Could Mao Zedong be a "Chinese Tito?" In the summer of 1948, Stalin finally found that the Yugoslav president Tito was not willing to heed Moscow's commands; to maintain the independence of his country and to preserve his hold on power, Tito decided to break with Stalin, as a result of which Stalin took powerful measures to purge the Communists of some socialist countries like the Soviet Union's elimination of counter-revolutionaries, causing no small shock in the socialist camp. Stalin was well aware of Mao Zedong's history of refusing to give in to the CPC's Comintern faction, and that perhaps eventually the socialist camp will have a second leadership center. Basically, he was concerned that Mao would do an about-face and not acknowledge Moscow['s leadership], so he needed to maintain vigilance. On the evening of the 13th, Mao Zedong, after organizing an emergency meeting of the Politburo, called Zhou Enlai, who was still in Moscow:

> After discussing the results with comrades in the Politburo, we agreed that it would be in the interest of our army to send troops to North Korea. The troops of the entire north-eastern defence forces were drawn in, as was control of all energy output from South Manchurian Power. We adopted the above-mentioned positive policy, as it is extremely beneficial for China, for North Korea, for the East, and for the world; we will not send troops until the enemy exerts pressure on the Yalu River, and the reactionary flames burn more intensely domestically and internationally. Then it will not be beneficial for various parties; firstly, the Northeast will be more unfavorable them, and if the entire Northeast Border Guard is drawn in, we will lose control of Southern Manchurian Power.

[48] Wang Binglin et al., *Jueze: Gongheguo Zhongda Sixiang Juece Lunzheng Jishi* (Decisive Choices: Documentary Record of Major Ideological Decisions in Debates during the Republic), Beijing: Renmin Chubanshe, 2010, p. 86.

> In short, we believe that we should go to war and must go to war; the advantages of war are great, but not to fight would be extremely damaging.[49]

On the 14th, Stalin telephoned Molotov to tell Zhou Enlai that the Soviet Air Force could only be stationed in China, and that in two months or even two and a half months, the Soviet Air Force was not prepared to participate in the Korean War. This message did not affect Mao Zedong's decision to go to war, in his heart, the nature of China's participation in the war far exceeds military objectives: the Chinese Communist Party participated in the socialist camp, and thus based on ideological positions on the "American imperialism" a positive challenge, while making the international community realize that the newly seized power of the Communist Party of China has dared to face the military power duel, which evokes great nationalist patriotic passion at home, consolidate the cohesion of the Communist Party of China, As for whether the Soviet air force will enter North Korea in two months' time, it is only natural that this threatening bet on Stalin, the head of the socialist camp, should also be seen as the result of Mao Zedong's character. On 19 October, United Nations forces attacked and occupied Pyongyang; on the same night, a total of 260,000 troops from the four armies and three artillery divisions of the Chinese People's Volunteer Army crossed the Yalu River into the Korean War without the cover of the Soviet Air Force; and on 25 October, the first battle of the Chinese People's Volunteer Army entering North Korea began. The CPC defined the Korean War as "resisting America and aiding the DPRK, to protect the home and defend the country". The CPC told its people that the Chinese People's Volunteer Army is participating in the war to defend the motherland and defend the newly born People's Republic of China—even though the Chinese people were not very clear that the Chinese People's Volunteer Army was fighting the army of the United Nations. After the first and second campaigns, the United Nations forces retreated to the 38th parallel. During the third campaign (31 December 1950–8 January 1951), Chinese and North Korean forces occupied Seoul. Mao Zedong's bold decision quickly won the large-scale assistance of the Soviet Union, which guaranteed the first

[49] *Mao Zedong Junshi Wenji* (Anthology of Mao Zedong's Military Writings), vol. 6, p. 117.

annual Chinese civil volunteer army ammunition, a large number of military equipment, weapons (torpedo speedboats, armored ships, submarine hunting ships, shore guns, cars, aircraft, etc.) are constantly being delivered to the hands of the Chinese army. When Zhou Enlai wanted the Soviet Union to supply 500 military vehicles, Stalin did not delay for a moment, replying to Zhou the same day: "In order to hand over the vehicles to you as soon as possible—I mean to give you new vehicles, and have instructed our military command they are not to be old vehicle transfers from Lüshun, but to deliver the new vehicles to Manzhouli". 140 vehicles would be handed over to Chinese representatives on November 20 and 355 vehicles would be handed over on November 25–26. The remaining vehicles will be issued as soon as possible, by 5 December this year. Another 1,000 vehicles will be delivered at Manzhouli Station".[50] Stalin was full of trust in Mao Zedong at this time, and in his view, the socialist camp was made stronger by the entry of Chinese troops to oppose the American troops, while at the same time providing practical support for the Soviet Union's Far East strategy and interests.

In 1953, the Korean War had to end. Mao's initial motives were limited to returning UN troops to the 38th parallel so that negotiations could be made to end the war. But with the gains of the previous three campaigns, Mao changed his strategy and goals, hoping to "drive the Americans into the sea" and achieve a full-scale occupation of North and South Korea. However, due to the lack of accurate judgment of China-U.S. military strength and lack of knowledge and strategy in international foreign policy, Mao Zedong lost the 13-nation proposal adopted by the United Nations on December 14, 1950, and the five principled proposals of the United Nations that gave China the opportunity to negotiate a truce in favor of negotiations. The Chinese Communist failure to adopt the proposals of those nations that opposed the American position disappointed many nations regarding China, and as a result, China lost a justification for being regarded seriously by international society. On January 30, 1951, the United Nations Political Committee voted 44 to 7 to approve the United States' proposal to declare China an "aggressor", which put the issue of China's seat in the United Nations on hold for a long time. The war that followed was tragic, and the Chinese and North Korean armies were severely damaged in the fourth and fifth campaigns

[50] Quoted from Shen Zhihua, op. cit., p. 341.

because of the miscalculations of Mao Zedong and Stalin. In late May, Peng Dehuai told Mao Zedong about the plight of the Chinese and North Korean forces in not being able to continue the war. On June 3rd Kim Il-sung was invited to Beijing to meet Mao Zedong, who wanted him to accept China's truce, while Stalin in Moscow insisted that the Chinese and North Korean armies should give a heavy blow to the UN. On June 10, Gao Gang and Kim Il-sung went to Moscow for discussions with Stalin, and after Gao and Kim told Stalin to his face that they wanted a truce, Stalin sent a telegram on the 13th: "Agree to the armistice".[51]

After lengthy negotiations and duels, on 27 July 1953, the United States and North Korea, and China finally signed a ceasefire agreement in Panmunjom, ending the Korean War. On the Korean battlefield, the total number of US troops killed and wounded in the Korean War was 142,000, of which 33,600 were killed; The volunteer army suffered 366,146 combat casualties and 382,741 non-combat casualties, resulting in a total loss of 748,886, seven times more after the third campaign. Nevertheless, at this time Chinese mainland, the propaganda of the heroes of the volunteer army and the propaganda of The Justice and Comprehensive Victory of China's participation in the war were on the rise, and in October 1953, the officers and soldiers of the Chinese Civil Volunteer Army Headquarters, who had not yet left North Korea to return home, enjoyed the wonderful performances of China's most outstanding performers, Chen Yanqiu, Shen Jinbo, Zhou Xinfang, Qi Yingcai, Ma Lianliang, and Mei Lanfang, in Korea, and the patriotism of the mainland people was at an all-time high. Mao Zedong told his people that the Korean War had enabled the Chinese army to "gain military experience, raise the political awareness of the people of the whole country, postpone the new imperialist war of aggression against China, and postpone the Third World War".[52] Of course, Mao Zedong also had another angle of judgment and conclusion. On 5 July 1957 Mao Zedong met in

[51] On September 12, 1953, when Mao Zedong summarized the Korean War at the twenty-fourth meeting of the Central People's Government Committee, he described the final armistice as forcing the United States to "cannot go down with peace", the main reasons for which were: "On the military side, the American invaders are at a disadvantage and beaten. If it does not, its entire front line will be broken, and Seoul could fall into the hands of the North Korean people".

[52] Mao Zedong, *Mao Zedong Xuanji* (Selected Writings of Mao Zedong), vol. 5, Beijing: Renmin Chubanshe, 1977, p. 103.

Hangzhou with Mikoyan, who had come to inform him that the "anti-party group" of Georgy Malenkov, who briefly succeeded Stalin, had been overthrown, and on the Korean War, Mao complained: "Stalin and Kim Il-sung deliberately concealed the timing and war plans of the war, but in the end China was implicated in the war, which was wrong and absolutely wrong".[53] Many years later, China's state media also publicly acknowledged the losses inflicted on China by the war. *People's Daily* of 1 June 2019 wrote:

> If it were not for Kim Il Sung's desire to unify the peninsula, how could war have broken out on the peninsula? China's involvement cost hundreds of thousands of lives, triggering a 20-year-long confrontation between China and the United States and even shelving the cross-Strait issue to this day. China bore most of the cost of North Korea's "willfulness" and recklessness.[54]

The Retreat of the Nationalist Government to Taiwan

On 1 October 1949 when Sun Yat-sen's wife, Song Qingling, and Kuomintang generals Fu Zuoyi, and Cheng Qian stood on the rostrum of Tiananmen Gate to witness the founding of the People's Republic of China, Chiang Kai-shek would have been in Guangzhou, where he was still discussing the next steps of the National Government with Li Zongren and Bai Chongxi. Chiang flew back to Taiwan on the 2nd, and on the 3rd, the National Government announced that it had severed relations with the Soviet Union. On October 10, Chiang Kai-shek issued the Double Tenth National Day Notice in Taiwan: he condemned the Soviet Union and said he would "fight to the end" against the Communist Party. On November 20th, Li Zongren entrusted his affairs to Yan Xishan and went to Hong Kong alone to fly to the United States for surgery, after he had written earlier to Chiang Kai-shek who was then in

[53] He Fang, in *Yanhuang Chunqiu*, 2013: 12.

[54] The headline of the *People's Daily* article was "Korean Central News Agency, Your Criticism of China Is Very Unreasonable". This was an article published in response to an article of 3 May published by KCNA (Korean Central News Agency) titled "No More Reckless Words and Deeds that Shake the Foundations of DPRK-PRC Relations", which attacked China's policy toward North Korea.

Chongqing. On December 5th, despite the advice of a four-member delegation appointed by Chiang Kai-shek, Li Zongren flew to Washington as "acting president" to seek US assistance. Chiang Kai-shek's last hope was to win the support of Liu Wenhui (1895–1976) in Sichuan and Lu Han (1895–1974) in Yunnan, but the Communist Party had already done its work by this time, and these two local warlords decided to cooperate with the Communist Party after receiving a commitment that they could retain their respective armies. On 10 December, Chiang Kai-shek flew from Chengdu to Taiwan, leaving the mainland for the last time. At this juncture, Chiang Kai-shek had nearly a million troops and irregular armed forces, close to 1000 tanks and armored vehicles, hundreds of aircraft, and 70 warships, as well as bases in Hainan Island, Zhoushan Island, Jinmen Island, Mazu Island, and the Penghu Islands. In April 1950, KMT troops led by General Xue Yue (1896–1998) withdrew from Hainan Island, and in May, 150,000 KMT troops withdrew from Zhoushan Island. After that, Chiang Kai-shek held only Jinmen Island, Mazu Island, Penghu Islands, and Taiwan Island as bases for counter-attack against the mainland; Taiwan's population at the time was about 11 million, of which the mainlanders were close to 15–20%.

Before 1945, Taiwan had gone through a period of Japanese occupation, which was a legacy of the defeat of the Qing government in the Sino-Japanese War. During World War II, the Cairo Declaration (1943) and the Potsdam Proclamation (1945) promised to return Taiwan to the Republic of China, along with the Penghu Islands (Pescadores) and the Northeast, after the end of the war. In 1944, the National Government established the "Taiwan Commission of Inquiry", which was followed by the promulgation of the *Draft Outline of Taiwan's Takeover Plan* and the holding of training courses for Taiwan's Party and government cadres. In the subsequent period, a spate of documents was released to facilitate Taiwan's management once it was regained after the War. On 1 September 1945, the Government of the Republic of China established the "Office of the Chief Executive of Taiwan Province" in Chongqing, and Chen Yi (1883–1950), as chief executive, established the garrison named the General Command of the Taiwan Provincial Police, in readiness to accept the surrender of the Japanese forces in Taiwan. On 25 October, after the surrender signing ceremony, Chen Yi declared: "From today, Taiwan and the Penghu Islands have officially re-entered Chinese territory, and all land, people and political affairs have been placed under the sovereignty of the National Government of the Republic of China.

This is an historically significant event, and I am proclaiming this to all Chinese compatriots and to the entire world".[55]

Between 1945 and 1949, Taiwan's society and politics were affected by the situation on the mainland. The postwar KMT corruption and enervation and the civil war led to social disorder, and the CPC used this background to establish underground organizations and induce radical students to stage "anti-American" rallies and activities, which reached a climax after the "Shen Chong Incident" in Beijing, and led to more than 10,000 students from Taipei and other provinces gathering in New Park (Xin Gongyuan) to demand that the US military "roll back". On the other hand, after the National government took over Taiwan, the group in power from the mainland became a new class that looked down on the indigenous inhabitants and, like the Japanese, did not give the locals full economic and political rights from the beginning, sowing the seeds of a long-standing conflict between Taiwanese and mainlanders. On 27 February 1947, the Monopoly Bureau in the course of conducting anti-opium operations injured a female opium dealer called Lin Jiangmai, which caused a public outcry resulting in an altercation in which a staff member of the Monopoly Bureau's Investigation Unit Fu Xuetong brandished a gun and issued a warning, not intending to shoot nearby residents watching the fight. This triggered more public participation and a full-scale fight with the gendarmerie ensued. On the following day (28 February), the conflict and violence spread rapidly, leading to the outbreak of what is called Taiwan's "28 February" Incident. Suppressed by the 21st Division of the Kuomintang army, many young students and civilians were killed and injured in Keelung and Kaohsiung. The incident triggered a widespread crackdown by the Kuomintang in Taiwan, including arrests and executions of members of social elites and local gentry. This social revolt, which was considered to have been triggered by the Kuomintang after the war in the face of crises and imbalances in various political, economic, and socio-cultural fields, constituted a complex nub of contention between the people of Taiwan and the government and ethnic groups—the historical, cultural, customary, and psychological differences between the residents and immigrants were clearly exposed during this period, the official verdict of the Incident only being reversed in 1988.

[55] Qin Feng, *Suiyue Taiwan, 1900–2000*, Nanning: Guangxi Shifan Daxue Chubanshe, 2005, p. 23.

After the "28 February" Incident, Chen Yi was replaced. The National Government abolished the Office of the Chief Executive of Taiwan Province and on 15 May established the Provincial Government of Taiwan, with Wei Tao-ming (1899–1978) as Chairman of the Province. In December 1948, Chiang Kai-shek decided to make Taiwan the last stronghold for his withdrawal, and his goal in "resigning" (*xiaye*) and making Li Zongren "acting president" was to devote his energies to building Taiwan as a "strong anti-Communist and anti-Russian bastion" as soon as possible. At that time, he asked Ch'en Ch'eng to be the provincial chairman. Based on the lessons of the "28 February" Incident, Chiang Kai-shek asked Ch'en Ch'eng to "firstly, rely more on Taiwan's superior education and encourage trustworthy people to participate in the government; second, especially cultivate Taiwanese youth and provide them with group training; and third, win over people's hearts and provide stability, in order to eliminate social fissures created by the '28 February' Incident". On 15 December 1949, the provincial government of Taiwan was restructured, with Chairman Ch'en Ch'eng re-elected as Southeast Governor and Wu Kuo-chen (K. C. Wu, 1903–1984) as Chairman of the Province. Thereafter, Taiwanese locals gradually entered government institutions and become involved in politics. The Government of the Republic of Taiwan continued to implement a five-division (Yuan) system, but the power of the legislature increased, as it decided on the appointment of the President of the Executive Council and had the power of inquiry. The actual implementation of Taiwan's management and construction was through the Taiwan provincial government's various institutions—internal affairs, finance, education, agriculture, forestry, transportation, public health, public security, and so on. It may seem that two large sets of government institutions do not match the tiny island of Taiwan, but the main functions of the central government were final decision-making power, national defense, foreign affairs, and possible "counter-attack against the mainland", the central government of the Republic of China corresponding to the central government of the People's Republic of China on the mainland.

No matter how Chiang Kai-shek reflected on the past and changed politics, there was a long time when anti-communist goals caused Taiwan's publishing and speech controls to remain harsh and terrifying. The elite intellectuals like Hu Shi, Luo Jialun (1897–1969), and Fu Sinian continued their academic work with limited freedom. US-style "free world" culture also to Taiwan spread. In fact, US support for Taiwan in all its aspects might look to its own interests but did not mean condoning the existence of an absolute authoritarian and totalitarian ideology. From the point of view of political values, the basic reason for Cold War conflict was ideological opposition, and the values of centralism obviously affected the control of Taiwan by the United States; the West unequivocally expressed its disapproval of the use of martial law to control Taiwan, but the Kuomintang understood this and justified it on the grounds of national security. In any case, Taiwan wanted the support of the United States, which also hoped to achieve its Cold War strategy through Taiwan, and as a result, Western culture gradually penetrated to the general public, in contrast to the total rejection and thorough criticism of Western culture on the mainland at this time. Although the Kuomintang had a high degree of control over the field of culture, the arts, and ideology, the publication of private newspapers and the popularity of various Western ideas, culture, and art did not follow the same unified model as on the mainland. For example, writers and artists were not forced by the government to conform to the same style, unlike on the mainland where writers and artists had to create according to the requirements specified by Mao Zedong in his *Talks at the Yan'an Forum on Literature and Art*.

Among a number of military and political measures, Ch'en Ch'eng's land reform changed the political, economic, and social structure of Taiwan, in contrast to the land reform methods enforced simultaneously on the mainland. On the mainland, the specific organization of land reform varied from place to place, but generally followed the following pattern of development: "A large number of land reform work teams have been organized in various places to go to the countryside, and these number more than 300,000 people a year. After the land reform work teams go to the countryside, they generally adopt the method of first visiting the poor and ascertaining what they feel bitter about, facilitating their linking up to hold grievance meetings. They then convene a meeting of peasant representatives. They organize brief training courses for peasant activists who unite then gradually penetrate the countryside to organize the peasants. From small groups of poor peasants and farm laborers, these develop into mass peasants' associations which include 'middle peasants' [peasants between rich and poor peasants, who generally own land, are self-supporting, and neither exploit nor sell labor-tr.]. Through many meetings of peasant masses and peasant representatives, the technique of having them articulate their bitterness at public grievance sessions is used to have the peasant masses to educate other peasants through recounting bitter personal experiences and to inspire the peasants' class consciousness. They also explain policies to the peasants to improve the peasants' political awareness and policy level. Then the peasant masses act consciously to confront the landlord class in a bitter face-to-face struggle, forcing the landlord class to bow their heads before the power of the masses".[56] This violent approach was part of the political strategy of the Communist Party's class struggle. However, in Taiwan, the aim of land reform was mobilizing farmers' enthusiasm for production through the redistribution of exchanged social resources without harming the landowners physically or harming their interests. Ch'en Ch'eng designed a three-stage Land Reform for Taiwan, starting with the implementation on 25 May 1951, through provisions issued by the Legislative Yuan, of the "375 Rent Reduction, whereby the rent paid by tenant farmers to landlords calculated on the annual harvest of the main crop grown would be calculated on average over two years and reduced to 37.5 per cent of the yearly harvest profit, compared with 56.8 per cent in the past and as high as 70 per cent in some places". The "375 Rent Reduction" obviously reduced land rent, thus easing the burden on tenant farmers, mobilizing their enthusiasm for production, while lowering land prices, in preparation for the later stage of the reform which would enable tenant farmers to purchase land. Taking into account the interests of both parties, tenant farmers were guaranteed that their leases of arable land could not be for less than six years and landlords could not terminate leases mid-term; when a lease expired, the original tenant farmer would have priority to renew the lease. At the same time, the tenant farmer had the priority right to purchase the land he worked on when the landlord sold land, and the landlord had the right to terminate a lease if the tenant did not pay the land rent due within two years. Once the "375 Rent Reduction Ordinance" was issued, more than 300,000 farmers obtained lease contracts, and in the first year of the scheme Taiwan's grain production increased by 30% and the average income of tenant farmers increased by 45%, leaving cash available after the harvest to purchase agricultural tools; cattle and bicycles came to be called "375 cattle" and "375 bicycles", and

[56] Liao Luyan, "Sannian lai Tudi Gaige Yundong de Weida Shengli" (The Glorious Victory of the Land Reform of the Last Three Years), *Renmin Ribao*, 28 September 1952. Lin Yunhui et al. ed., *Renmin Gongheguo Chunqiu Shilu* (Annales of the People's Republic), Beijing: Zhongguo Renmin Daxue Chubanshe, 1992, p. 28.

the money for a bride's dowry led to brides being referred to as "375 brides".

Beginning in 1951, the second stage of Taiwan's land reform, the "Public Land Release", was carried out. The commons and privately owned land from the era of Japanese occupation needed to be fully cultivated and used, and the original farmers, tenant farmers, independent farmers, and semi-independent farmers had the opportunity to acquire this land. This land was bought and sold in a unique way, whereby the purchase price was calculated as 2.5 times the profit from the annual harvest of normal crops (rice and sweet potatoes) and could be paid interest-free over a period of ten years. This approach provided an opportunity for farmers who did not have the money to purchase land, because they could make the initial payment for the land in the form of their harvested crops for the current year, while also being guaranteed revenue from the government. In all of Taiwan, 130,000 hectares of such land was sold to more than 236,000 households.

By 1953, the government announced a reform that would allow farmers to "cultivate their own fields" and each tenant farmer could acquire his own land. The reform enabled landlords to retain the amount of land specified by the government based on the landlord's livelihood and progressive strategy, the remainder then being resumed by the government and made available to tenant farmers. The levy also included the farmhouses, farm buildings, areas for sun-drying, ponds, and fruit trees used by tenant farmers, which could then be purchased by those buying land. Seventy percent of the cost of compensating landowners for the transfer of land was in the form of government bonds issued for crops and land which paid annual interest of 4% and were to be fully repaid over an average ten-year period. A further 30% of the payment was in the form of shares for public enterprises like cement plants, paper mills, mines, and forest plantations. The government would sell the requisitioned land at low-cost loans to farmers and land resources were rationally allocated for appropriately scaled economic development. This policy of requisition resulted in the take-up of 139,249 hectares of arable land, of which 55% was privately leased out by 166,000 landlord households, accounting for 60% of all registered landowners, while 194,823 households of tenant farmers took up land, accounting for 65% of tenant farmers who rented private arable land, so the number of tenant farmers was greatly reduced.

The basic results of the three-year land reform were: agricultural production increased by 21.63%, land productivity increased by 21.52%, and labor productivity increased by 15.22%; at the same time, the old leasing relationship between the tenant farmers and landlords in Taiwan disappeared, and farmers gained real independent status in politics, society, and law. Landlords invested the money they earned from land in industry and commerce, investing in publicly owned cement plants, paper mills, mines, and agricultural and forestry companies so that these became private enterprises, thereby contributing to the rapid development of industry and the urban economy. Many landlords become capitalists. This provided the conditions for the implementation of the first four-year economic development plan from 1953 to 1956.

Prior to the "Restoration" (Guangfu) marking the end of Japanese rule in 1945, there were farmers' associations in Taiwan that had coordinated interests and operated agriculture. The land reform began with the establishment of the New Farmers' Association, and the main heads of the Agricultural Councils, such as the Chairman and the Director-General, were the original local elites, rather than uncultured farmers, with the result that the Agricultural Council played an effective role: the rights and interests of farmers were protected, agricultural knowledge was disseminated, and the increase in agricultural production was assisted without any ideology or corresponding violent oppression. In fact, whether in Taiwan or the mainland, the relationship between landlords and tenant farmers was never as oppositional and irreconcilable as the CPC proclaimed, and China's traditional morality and rural culture determined the complexity of interpersonal relationships and emotional affinity. When Taiwan's landowners realized great economic benefits in the fields of stocks and industry and commerce, they began to participate in the election of local self-government, with the result that those elected to politics often represented the interests of local farmers in political governance, and the original rural culture and interpersonal order were preserved; on the mainland the class struggle nature of the landlord eliminated these possibilities.

Both the mainland land reform and Taiwan's simultaneous land reform were government-led, but the former sought to fight for the interests of peasants by confiscating the land of landowners, the latter used the exchange to redistribute wealth; the former exacerbated class conflicts, the latter eased class conflicts; the former left the landlords deprived of their land and without the means to engage in business, the latter provided the landlords who ceded land with the future opportunity to invest in industry and commerce. The root cause of this disparity was that the

CPC's land reform was aimed at eliminating the landlord class and private ownership and concentrating wealth in the hands of the Communist-controlled state, while Taiwan's land reform was aimed at freeing up productivity and developing society and economy with private ownership. From the standpoint of economic common sense, the consequences of Taiwan's land reform for the island's economy could be readily imagined, and with the reform, the KMT truly implemented Sun Yat-sen's early proposal that "farmers till their own fields".

During negotiations with Li Zongren, the CPC decided to attack Taiwan, and on 15 March 1949, *People's Daily* published a Xinhua commentary titled, "The Chinese People Will Definitely Liberate Taiwan":

> Those engaged in the struggle to liberate the Chinese people will not stop until Taiwan, Hainan Island and every last inch of land of the whole of China is liberated.

On 31 December, the CPC announced: "The glorious fighting mission of 1950 is to liberate Taiwan, Hainan Island and Tibet". The CPC was fully prepared to launch a military attack on Taiwan. At this time, the United States was not fully concerned about the fate of Taiwan, and on 5 January 1950, Truman announced a policy of non-intervention in Taiwan:

> The United States has no intention of encroaching on Taiwan or any other Chinese territory. The United States does not want special interests or rights in Taiwan at this time, nor does it want to establish military bases there. Nor has the United States used its armed forces to intervene in the current situation. The US government will not implement an approach that would lead to involvement in China's civil war. Similarly, the US government will not provide military assistance or advice to Taiwan's Chinese military.[57]

On 24 February 1950, the Legislative Yuan of the National Government formally decided to request Chiang Kai-shek's reinstatement, and the next day the Supervisory Yuan submitted the impeachment case

[57] Joseph W. Ballantine, *Formosa: A Problem for United States Policy (Washington, D.C., 1952)*, p. 120. This book quoted in Xu Zhongyue, *Zhongguo Jindai Shi*, volume 2, Hong Kong: Chinese University Press, 2000, p. 771.

against Acting President Li. On 1 March, Chiang Kai-shek officially returned to the presidency, and on 3 March he announced four policy guidelines:

1. Militarily, We Must First Consolidate Taiwan as a Base and Advance Our Plan of Regaining the Mainland.
2. In national defense, we first must completely rely on ourselves and our own efforts; at the same time, we must unite with the world's democracies, in a common and concerted struggle against Communism.
3. Economically, we must make labor a priority, promote thrift, and reward production.
4. Politically, we must respect the people's will and act in accordance with the law.[58]

On 22 July, the KMT's Central Standing Committee adopted the "Proposal for the Reform of the Nationalist Party of China", which clearly defined the Kuomintang as a "revolutionary democratic party" with clear objectives: national independence, people's freedom, political democracy, economic equality, and world peace. Chiang Kai-shek called for a cleanup of KMT organizations and institutions, and party members to re-register, affirming that Fu Zuoyi, Song Qingling and others were removed from the party. At the same time, just as the CPC on the mainland was executing KMT remnants, Chiang Kai-shek in Taiwan ordered the dismantling of communist underground organizations and the arrest and execution of Communists.

At first, for Chiang Kai-shek, retreating from Taiwan was only a temporary move, and he would reorganize the Kuomintang and its armed forces to launch a "counter-attack on the mainland", as he said at an expanded meeting of the Central Executive Standing Committee on 22 July:

> We must use Taiwan as our base for our counter-attacked against the mainland, as a vanguard of the Asian peoples' struggle for freedom, and as a heroic fighter for world peace. To that end, we must completely restructure our party in order to reorganize our revolutionary machinery and

[58] Chiang Kai-shek, "Zhaodai Guomin Dahui zai Tai daibiao chahui zhici" (Speech at the reception welcoming the representatives of the Citizens Congress in Taiwan), 3 March 1950, this book quotes in Li Yunhan, op. cit., p. 548.

> re-invigorate our revolutionary spirit. On the negative side, we must insist on the elimination of conflicts between factions and between individuals within our party. We can no longer tolerate the existence of individualistic acts and ideas that led to the demise of our thinking on the mainland, and if we do not resolutely prevent this, it will lead to our demise in Taiwan.

At the same time, US policy on Taiwan changed between May and June. On 17 May the US agency in Taiwan reported to Washington that "Taiwan's fate is decided, and the CPC may launch an attack between June 15 and the end of July". On 26 May at least, the State Department's message was to get the US agency in Taiwan to take steps "as soon and systematically as possible" to prepare for the evacuation. But after the signing of the Sino-Soviet Mutual Assistance Treaty, the US military's position became increasingly and obviously tougher. Initially, Truman hesitated to increase the defense budget substantially in response to the contents of Document No. 68 (NSC68), submitted by the National Security Council in April, which suggested that the Soviet Union might initiate war in 1954. But the outbreak of the Korean War caused the United States to re-examine the significance of Taiwan's position in the Asia–Pacific region. The United States now believed that the use of armed invasion and war by Communist forces directly threatened the security of the Pacific region and its military might in the region. America's previous "selective and focused" containment strategy gave way to one of "comprehensive containment". The establishment of the People's Republic of China on the mainland by the CPC did not affect the continued international recognition of Chiang Kai-shek's Nationalist government. With the Soviet Union's recognition of the People's Republic of China, some countries in the socialist camp in Eastern Europe, like Poland, Czechoslovakia, and so on, also recognized the PRC, which posed a serious challenge for Chiang Kai-shek. For Taiwan and the United States, it would be difficult for the Kuomintang government to successfully defend itself against a Soviet-backed Chinese attack. By mid-June, there had been a fundamental change in US policy towards Taiwan. Given that containing China effectively also contained the Soviet Union, and since some believed that "the Soviet Union had safely taken over Communist China", the United States regarded it as imperative to help sustain Taiwan's resistance and never allow the Communist Party to acquire Taiwan. At the end of July, the UN Army Commander-in-Chief General Douglas MacArthur visited Taipei to discuss with Chiang Kai-shek how to deal with the new situation in the Far East, which was followed by the establishment of a permanent US presence in Taipei. Chiang Kai-shek also proposed that Kuomintang troops participate in the Korean War, but the United States delayed any decision and replied finally did not agree to this, but the United States did send military advisers, weapons and ships to Taiwan—after the outbreak of the Korean War, the Seventh Fleet entered the Taiwan Strait to prevent the Chinese Communists from liberating Taiwan. From June 1950 to the end of June of the following year, US aid to Taiwan amounted to $98 million, and in the years that followed, US aid to Taiwan continued to flow. When the Korean War broke out, the CPC's military strength and resources were sunk into it, and the United States changed its policy towards Taiwan in favor of military protection, and so the CPC shelved its attack on Taiwan. In contrast, Taiwan continued to deploy "guerrillas", whom the CPC described as "remnants of the Kuomintang", "American-Chiang Kai-shek agents" or simply "gangsters", to engage in military or sabotage activities on the mainland, and this was actively continued until the 1970s, when the CPC's slogan, "We must liberate Taiwan", had gradually become less shrill.

On 28 April 1952, Taiwan and Japan signed the Sino-Japanese Agreement in Taipei, and on 5 August, the same year, the exchange of ratifications came into effect, and the two sides exchanged ambassadors. On 1 February 1953, the Sixth General Assembly of the United Nations voted to find that the Soviet Union had failed to comply with the Treaty of Friendship and Alliance between China and the Soviet Union signed on 14 August 1945, and on 15 February the Government of Taiwan annulled that Treaty. What satisfied Chiang Kai-shek now was that, in the eyes of the world (as articulated by the United Nations), the Republic of China remained the only legitimate government of the Chinese people.

In February 1953, President Dwight D. Eisenhower announced the end of the US' imposed neutrality on Taiwan, which allowed Taiwan's military to take military action against the mainland; in March, Karl L. Rankin, of the US representative office in Taiwan, was appointed full ambassador to the Republic of China, and on 2 December 1954, Taiwan signed the Sino-US Mutual Defense Treaty, and Foreign Minister George Kung-chao Yeh (Ye Gongchao, 1904–1981) informed the US that Taiwan's military operations were subject to US arrangements and Taiwan would not attack the mainland without the latter's consent.

However, on the mainland side, in January 1955, the Chinese Communist army bombarded the Tachen (Dachen) Islands, off the mainland coast near Taizhou, killing all the KMT troops defending them; attacks on Kinmen (Jinmen) and Matsu (Mazu) islands in 1954 and 1958, respectively, ended defeat for the Communists. As the United States continued to strengthen the defenses of Taiwan and made a commitment to ensure its security, the CPC judged that conditions no longer permitted it realizing the "liberation of Taiwan". Apart from the PRC's intermittent shelling of Kinmen (Jinmen) Island, mainland China, and Taiwan entered into a confrontational stand-off; both sides had governments and neither side denied that Taiwan was part of China (a province), but until October 1971, the Taiwan government represented China among members of the United Nations, even though the Chinese Communist Party controlled most of China 's territory (Figs. 1, 2, 3, 4, and 5).

Fig. 1 Photography by Henri Cartier-Bresson, Shanghai, 1949

Fig. 2 1949: Ceremony in Beijing's Tiananmen Square celebrating the establishment of the People's Republic of China

Fig. 3 1950: Zhongnanhai, the CPC Center discusses sending troops to aid North Korea

Fig. 4 1951: Struggle against landlords, Minhe County, Qinghai. Photograph by Ru Suichu

Fig. 5 1952: International merchant capitalists handing in "confessions" to the Five-Anti Committee of Shanghai's Huangpu District

Printed by Printforce, the Netherlands